ORGANIZATIONAL BEHAVIOR

A Management Challenge
Third Edition

ORGANIZATIONAL BEHAVIOR

A Management Challenge
Third Edition

Linda K. Stroh,
Loyola University Chicago

Gregory B. Northcraft,
University of Illinois

Margaret A. Neale
**Graduate School of Business,
Stanford University**

LAWRENCE ERLBAUM ASSOCIATES, PUBLISHERS

Mahwah, New Jersey   London

President/CEO:	Lawrence Erlbaum
Executive Vice-President, Marketing:	Joseph Petrowski
Senior Vice-President, Book Production:	Art Lizza
Director, Editorial:	Lane Akers
Director, Sales and Marketing:	Robert Sidor
Director, Customer Relations:	Nancy Seitz
Senior Acquisitions Editor:	Anne Duffy
Textbook Marketing Manager:	Marisol Kozlovski
Editorial Assistant:	Karin Wittig
Cover Design:	Kathryn Houghtaling Lacey
Interior Design:	Cheryl Asherman
Textbook Production Manager:	Paul Smolenski
Full-Service & Composition:	UG / GGS Information Services, Inc.
Text and Cover Printer:	Edwards Brothers, Incorporated

Lawrence Erlbaum Associates, Inc., Publishers
10 Industrial Avenue
Mahwah, New Jersey 07430

Library of Congress Cataloging-in-Publication Data

Stroh, Linda K.
   Organizational behavior: a management challenge / by Linda K. Stroh,
Gregory Northcraft & Margaret A. Neale.—3rd ed.
      p. cm.
   Previously published: Fort Worth: Dryden Press, © 1994
   Includes bibliographical references and index.
   ISBN 0-8058-3829-5
      1. Organizational behavior. 2. Management. I. Northcraft,
Gregory B. II. Neale, Margaret Ann. III. Title.

HD58.7.N68 2001
658—dc21   00-054360

Dedication

This book is dedicated to Greg, Angie, Joe, Brad, Brandy, Mulligan, Al, Dolphin, and Riley

BRIEF CONTENTS

CONTENTS

PREFACE

A book, like a large corporation, cannot be thrown together haphazardly; it must have a focus. And as with the focus of a large corporation, the focus of a book says a great deal about the people who created it, including the events that occurred as they wrote it.

As we prepared this edition of *Organization Behavior: A Management Challenge*, the world had just celebrated the dawning of a new millennium. Although there was much in the first and second editions that we wanted to continue to emphasize, profound changes had occurred in organizations across the United States and elsewhere around the globe that were transforming organizations and, consequently, the field of organizational behavior. The most profound changes have been in the area of technology and in the shift in organizations from a domestic to an international or global focus. Included in this edition are numerous examples of the effects of technological changes on organizations as well as ways that organizations are likely to face technological challenges in the future.

Not everything in the way organizations operate has changed, however. As always, to be effective, one must understand what goes on in the minds of managers and employees when they interact in organizations. And the real challenge of organizational behavior still lies in managing the uncertainty, conflict, and complexities of organizational life. However, unlike yesterday's managers, today's face uncertainty in an increasingly global marketplace. Without an understanding of how globalization affects the behaviors of organizations, a company cannot stay competitive. This third edition brings together the challenges managers face as they learn to adapt to a more globalized and ever-more-technologically sophisticated world.

In preparing this edition, we also saw a need to link even more closely research in organizational behavior with organizational life. Our goal was to make the wisdom and insights of organizational behavior research not just *available* to students but *accessible*—easy to learn and easy to apply. Accessibility makes education both rewarding for students and manageable for instructors. But like quality, accessibility cannot be added on; it must be built in. In an effort to make this edition even more accessible while also increasing the emphasis on research, we added many special features that help both the student and the instructor assimilate research and understand its practical organizational applications. Alone, neither research nor practical application is particularly useful. We have strategically merged these tasks by continually interweaving the presentation of concepts and theory with both formal and informal examples. Continued emphasis on scholarly research in the field has made this third edition of *Organizational Behavior* a strong learning tool for scholars and students alike.

ORGANIZATION OF THE TEXT

The five parts of this book have been designed to effectively present an overview of the challenges that managers and employees face in today's competitive organizations. Part One focuses on the core of the field of organizational behavior and introduces the challenges of managing behavior in organizations. Starting with the concept of the "knowing–doing gap," Part One creates a framework to help students answer the question "Does organizational behavior matter?"

Parts Two and Three provide foundation knowledge for meeting the challenges of organizational behavior. Most employees consider the individuals and small groups they interact with each day to *be* their organization, so the foundation of knowledge of organizational behavior is presented in Part Two, "Individual Behavior," and in Part Three, "Behavior in Groups."

Part Four applies this foundation knowledge to three primary issues in managing behavior in organizations: acquiring and integrating employees (Chapter 10, "Organizational Entry and Socialization"), developing jobs in which these employees will excel (Chapter 11, "Job Design"), and helping employees succeed within the organization (Chapter 12, "Managing for Performance").

Finally, Part Five examines the larger context of organizational behavior. Organizational behavior is not just the product of simple internal day-to-day interactions. Larger forces, including the environment, the structure of organizations, and the changes that organizations must endure, have profound effects on the success and survival of those day-to-day interactions. Also included in Part Five is a discussion of the topical issue of what constitutes inclusionary behavior in organizations. Chapter 16, discusses the evolution of the diversity concept; rather than focus on what divides employees in an organization, this chapter's emphasis is on inclusion and what brings employees together.

SPECIAL FEATURES

To aid the reader in more easily grasping the wisdom and insights of organizational behavior, photos and artwork are provided throughout the text. The captions that accompany both the photos and the figures create a parallel text—a second chance for the book to teach and the student to learn. The photos and figures also provide vivid and concrete examples of the major concepts presented in the text.

A number of other special features are included in *Organizational Behavior*, as part of our effort to make learning about organizational behavior more interesting and comprehensive. These features are summarized in the following sections.

FOCUS ON BOXED ITEMS AND VIGNETTES

Real-life examples of organizational behavior are presented in Focus On boxed features throughout the text and in vignettes at the beginning of each chapter. These examples are drawn from a broad spectrum of international and U.S. firms, the private and public sectors, and large and small organizations. The variety of examples promotes the understanding that organizational behavior has applications in every aspect of organizational life.

In addition to general Focus On features, each chapter contains an International Focus On feature as well as a Technology Focus On feature. Today's students will be working in an increasingly global and technical marketplace. These short features discuss critical issues that challenge managers today.

RESEARCH IN ACTION BOXED ITEMS

As part of our goal of highlighting the connection between high-quality research and effective application, this edition introduces boxed items that focus on research on organizational behavior. These features demonstrate ways that organizational research has changed organizational practice or a policy in significant ways. Each RESEARCH IN ACTION box is written by a leading expert in the field of organizational behavior. One of the hopes in developing this feature was that students would learn by gaining insights into the organizations of which they are a part, including their schools, families, and social clubs.

END-OF-CHAPTER LEARNING AIDS

Each chapter includes ON YOUR OWN experiential exercises, to be completed individually by students or used as a basis for classroom discussion. The exercises enable students to gain a working knowledge of organizational behavior while reflecting on their own aptitudes and abilities.

THE MANAGER'S MEMO is a unique slant on the typical end-of-the-chapter case. Each memo focuses on a real-life management problem and is followed by a series of questions. After students have read the memos, they may respond to the memo in writing or discuss the questions in class.

The discussion questions at the end of each chapter can be used as a basis for class discussion or as a chance for instructors to test students' learning. Again, in keeping with the explicit focus of this book, each part ends with a group exercise and/or comprehensive case. The part-closing exercises have been chosen for their appropriateness, regardless of class size. They encourage students to further integrate their understanding and application of material discussed in the book.

SUPPLEMENTAL PACKAGE

A comprehensive set of ancillary materials has been prepared for both students and instructors to accompany this edition of *Organizational Behavior*.

WEB PAGE

In keeping with the focus on technology throughout this book, a Web page has been developed as a supplementary resource. The Web page *www.organizationalbehavior.ws* provides information about the authors as well as PowerPoint slides for each chapter. By referring to the Web page, students can review lecture material before each class.

FOR THE INSTRUCTOR

The following items are available for adopters:

- *Instructor's Manual*—The *Instructor's Manual*, written by Mary C. Kern, Christine L. Langlands, Linda K. Stroh, Gregory B. Northcraft, and Margaret A. Neale, contains detailed chapter outlines, suggested answers to the discussion questions and THE MANAGER'S MEMO questions, and instructions for using the ON YOUR OWN exercises. The manual also includes case and group exercises related to each part of the book. Featured in the *Instructor's Manual* are all the PowerPoint slides as well as lecture notes and teaching tips. The *Instructor's Manual* provides a good overview of each chapter, and instructors should find it very useful as they prepare for class.

■ *PowerPoint Presentations*—This edition of *Organizational Behavior* includes a CD with a PowerPoint presentation for each chapter. Approximately 20 colored slides for each chapter are intended to help invoke students' interest. Included in the notes section of the PowerPoint presentation is the lecture material for each slide as well as helpful teaching tips.

ALSO FROM LAWRENCE ERLBAUM ASSOCIATES

Greenberg: *Organizational Behavior*, Reader, 0-8058-1215-6p, 1994
Ashforth: *Role Transitions in Organizational Life: An Identity-Based Perspective*, 0-8058-2892-3c/2893-1p, 2001
Cropenzano: *Justice in the Workplace*, Volume 2, 0-8058-2694-7c/2695-5p, 2001
Darley/Messick/Levine: *Social Influences on Ethical Behavior in Organizations*, 0-8058-3330-7 (cloth only), 2001
Denison: *Managing Organizational Change in Transition Economies*, 0-8058-3618-7c/3619-5p, 2001
Earley/Gibson: *Multinational Work Teams: A New Perspective*, 0-8058-3464-8c/3465-6p, 2002
Margolis/Walsh: *People and Profits? The Search for a Link Between a Company's Social and Financial Performance*, 0-8058-4011-7p (paper only), 2001
Pearce: *Organization and Management in the Embrace of Government*, 0-8058-3769-8c/4101-6p. 2001
Riggio/Murphy/Pirozzolo: *Multiple Intelligences and Leadership*, 0-8058-3466-4 (cloth only), 2001

ACKNOWLEDGMENTS

We have been reminded many times in the past years that a major undertaking such as this book requires the coordination and cooperation of a great many people. We would like to acknowledge their efforts and thank them for their contributions. We owe a great debt to Anne Duffy, the Lawrence Erlbaum Associates editor of this text, and to our project team—Molly Kern, Christine Langlands, Joanna Maciaszkiewicz, and Erica Fox—for their hard work on this third edition. We are also indebted to our colleagues, students, and administrators at Loyola University of Chicago, the University of Illinois, and Stanford University.

We are also indebted to the following active participants in this project whose thoughtful feedback provided through focus groups and manuscript reviews helped raise our understanding of organizational behavior to new heights:

John Austin
University of Washington

Max Bazerman
Harvard University

Stewart Black
University of Michigan

Stacey Blake-Beard
Harvard University

Jeanne Brett
Northwestern University

Denny L. Brown
Linden Inc.

Wayne Cascio
University of Colorado, Denver

Fran Daly
Loyola University Chicago

Gerard Farias
Loyola University Chicago

Daniel Feldman
University of South Carolina

Suzy Fox
Loyola University Chicago

Martin Greller
University of Wyoming

Terri Griffith
University of California—Berkeley

Maddy Janssens
Katholieke Univeriteit Leuven

Homer Johnson
Loyola University Chicago

Timothy Judge
University of Iowa

Ed Lawler
University of Southern California

Belle Rose Ragins
University of Wisconsin—Milwaukee

Randall Schuler
Rutgers University

K. Dow Scott
Loyola University Chicago

Patricia Simpson
Loyola University Chicago

Lamont Stallworth
Loyola University Chicago

Brad Stroh
Stanford University

Rosalie Tung
Simon Fraser University

Arup Varma
Loyola University Chicago

LIST OF REVIEWERS

We would also like to thank:

Talya Bauer
Portland State University
TalyaB@sba.pdx.edu

Stacy Blake-Beard
Harvard University
stacy_blake-beard@harvard.edu
blakest@gse.harvard.edu

Joan Brett
Arizona State University
jbrett@asu.edu

Catherine Cramton
George Mason University
ccramton@som.gmu.edu

Steven C. Currall
Rice University
scc@rice.edu

Peter Horn
Arizona State University
Peter.Horn@asu.edu

Timothy Judge
University of Iowa
tim-judge@uiowa.edu

Elizabeth Morrison
Stern School of Business (NYU)
emorriso@stern.nyu.edu

Organizational Behavior is subtitled *A Management Challenge* to reflect our belief that uncertainty, conflict, and complexity make managing behavior in organizations a difficult enterprise. The same could be said for writing a book on this topic. But, as is so often true of difficult assignments, writing this text has also been a marvelous learning experience for us all. We hope that exploring organizational behavior will be as rewarding for you.

Linda K. Stroh
Gregory B. Northcraft
Margaret A. Neale
2002

ABOUT THE AUTHORS

Linda K. Stroh is a Loyola University Chicago Faculty Scholar and Professor at the Institute of Human Resources and Industrial Relations. Linda received her bachelor's degree in Industrial Sociology from McGill University and her Ph.D. in human development and social policy from Northwestern University. Linda also has a post-doc from the Kellogg Graduate School of Management at Northwestern University. Linda is co-author of the book, *Globalizing People Through International Assignments*, and has written over 60 articles related to organizational behavior issues. Linda's research interests include international management, older workers and organizational effectiveness and efficiency. Linda is the academic advisor to the International Personnel Association.

Gregory B. Northcraft is the Harry J. Gray Professor of Executive Leadership at the University of Illinois, where he holds faculty appointments in both the Department of Business Administration and the Institute for Labor and Industrial Relations. He received his bachelor's degrees in psychology, and Russian language, and literature from Dartmouth, and psychology and philosophy from Oxford University. He received a master's degree and Ph.D. from Stanford in social psychology. His major areas of interest are negotiation and conflict management, managerial decision making, and the role of high-technology in job design and management. Professor Northcraft has won a variety of teaching awards, is currently Editor of the *Academy of Management Journal*, and is also co-author (with Robin L. Pinkley) of the recently published book, *Get Paid What You're Worth*.

Margaret A. Neale is the John G. McCoy–Banc One Professor of Dispute Resolution and Organizations at the Graduate School of Business at Stanford University. Prior to that, she was the J. L. and Helen Kellogg Distinguished Professor of Dispute Resolution and Organizations at the Kellogg Graduate School of Management at Northwestern University. She began her academic career at the Eller School of Business at the University of Arizona. She received her bachelor's degree in Pharmacy from Northeast Louisiana University, her master's degree in Hospital Pharmacy Administration from the Medical College of Virginia, and her Ph.D. in Business Administration from the University of Texas, Austin. Her major research areas include bargaining and negotiation, team composition and learning, and decision making. Her two books on negotiation with Max H. Bazerman (Harvard Business School), *Negotiating Rationally* and *Cognition and Rationality in Negotiation*, are widely read. She is the co-editor with Elizabeth A. Mannix (Cornell University) of an annual research series entitled *Research in Managing Groups and Teams*.

ORGANIZATIONAL BEHAVIOR

A Management Challenge
Third Edition

PART

1

Introduction

CHAPTER

1

Organizational Behavior: A Management Challenge

THE KNOWING–DOING GAP

Research, experience, and common sense all suggest that to maintain a competitive advantage, organizations must act on what they know—including what they know about treating people as assets.[1] Yet, even in the midst of today's brutally competitive environment, many organizations' actions still don't acknowledge the value and potential of their employees. Organizations often look to the latest management fad or quick fix to solve their problems—merging, acquiring, downsizing, outsourcing, reengineering—all the while ignoring basic people-management issues they know to be fundamental to business success.

In a survey of a restaurant chain, Jeffrey Pfeffer and Robert Sutton found that the restaurant's managers recognized the importance of sharing information with their people, providing them feedback, and involving them in initiatives to improve operations. However, there were big differences between what the restaurant managers believed produced success and what they reported actually practicing in their restaurants.

Pfeffer and Sutton believe this represents an example of the "knowing–doing gap." They suggest eight guidelines for closing this gap[2]:

1 Understand why before how. If you do not understand why something is happening, the how will be ignored.
2 Knowing comes from doing and teaching others how. Awareness comes before true knowledge.
3 Action counts more than elegant plans and concepts. We learn by doing.
4 There is no doing without mistakes. Reasonable failure should never be received with anger.

---

1. Pfeffer, J., & Veiga, J. F. (1999, May). Putting people first for organizational success. *Academy of Management Executive, 13*(2), 37–48.
2. Pfeffer, J., & Sutton, R. I. (2000) *The knowing–doing gap: How smart companies turn knowledge into action.* Harvard Business School Press: Boston, MA, pp. 246–262.

5 Fear fosters knowing–doing gaps; therefore, drive out fear.
6 Fight the competition, not each other.
7 Measure what matters and what turns knowledge into action.
8 What leaders do, how they spend their time, and how they allocate resources matters.

The Men's Wearhouse provides an excellent example of a company whose management acts on what it knows about managing people. Not only does The Men's Wearhouse management recognize employees' untapped human potential, but management also takes the responsibility for helping employees realize it. George Zimmer, the company's founder, has even stated that his business is the *people* business, not the suit business.[3] Zimmer's insight about the business he is in, combined with targeted action, have enabled The Men's Wearhouse to become a phenomenal success both financially and organizationally.

INTRODUCTION

This book is about **organizational behavior**—the description and explanation of how people behave in organizations. As a broad-based field, organizational behavior encompasses the study of leadership, power and politics, performance management, organizational design, and much more. Thus, any book about organizational behavior is necessarily about people and about closing the gap between what is known about how and why people behave in organizations and what we do about managing those people successfully.

Before we can begin discussing organizational behavior, we must first agree on what we mean by the word **organization**. J. D. Mooney provides a good working definition of the word in his book *The Principles of Organization:*

> Organization is the form of every human association for the attainment of a common purpose . . . the framework of every group moving toward a common objective. . . . It refers to the complete body, with all its correlated functions. . . . It refers to the coordination of all these [functions] as they cooperate for the common purpose.[4]

Mooney emphasized that organizations are "pure process"—not buildings, machines, or other tangible objects. Organizations are practices, procedures, and relationships entered into to coordinate human talents and efforts toward common goals. They are formed when people come together to combine their talents and efforts.

A quick look at the daily news reveals both the latest discoveries and breakthroughs achieved by organizations *and* the latest fiascoes and bankruptcies. Clearly, some organizations succeed in combining the talents and efforts of their members, and the results are major accomplishments. Other organizations never produce much of anything.

Why are some organizations successful, while others fail? Why are some workers fiercely loyal to and proud of the organizations to which they belong, while other organizations are plagued by absenteeism, turnover, and even sabotage from within? Why do 40% of new technological "wonders"

---

3. Pfeffer, J., & Sutton, R. I., p. 248.
4. Mooney, J. D. (1939). *The principles of organization.* New York: Harper and Brothers, p. 3.

fail to accomplish their stated objectives?[5] Why are 70% of mergers and acquisitions considered failures or only minimally successful?[6] We suspect that after you read this book, you will realize that many of these failures occur because managers don't make the most of what we know about how and why people in organizations behave the way they do.

Most managers recognize that buying a new technological innovation for an organization is fairly easy. Managing the creative, talented employees who must make the most of that innovation is not so easy. We live in an age of unprecedented wealth and abundance of business opportunity, but an organization's success—or failure—is still largely determined by how well the organization manages its people. Organizational behavior does matter. According to Rayport, an associate professor at Harvard University, "The success of e-commerce business will hinge largely on the art of management even as it is enabled by the science of technology."[7]

Before discussing the specifics of how and why people in organizations behave the way they do, it is important to have a basic understanding of what constitutes behavior in organizations. In this chapter we will contrast two approaches to understanding such behavior: a prescriptive and a descriptive view.

MANAGEMENT: A PRESCRIPTIVE VIEW

For an organization to accomplish its objectives, its managers must understand how and why people behave the way they do. Thus, an understanding of organizational behavior provides the foundation for good management and, as demonstrated by The Men's Wearhouse, organizational success.

From the point of view of someone joining an organization for the first time, perhaps a recent graduate of a business program, the importance of organizations probably seems obvious. Everyone knows that people come together and form organizations because organizations can accomplish things that individuals can't. Therefore, when discussing behavior in organizations, we are really talking about taking advantage of the performance benefits of groups over individuals. Jeff Bezos, the chief executive officer of Amazon.com, epitomizes someone who has acted on his understanding of this concept. You can read more about how Bezos acted on his prescription for management in "Focus On: Organizational Behavior."

Amazon.com is one of the great success stories of the latest generation of U.S. business organizations. Of course, whether Amazon.com can continue to succeed when faced with new challenges from the business environment is yet to be determined. Although Jeff Bezos is unquestionably important to this success story, Amazon.com could not have succeeded the way it has without the effort and commitment of thousands of people working together.

---

5. See, for example, Griffith, T. L., & Northcraft, G. B. (1996, March). Cognitive elements in the implementation of new technology: Can less information provide more benefits? *MIS Quarterly, 20,* 99–110; Griffith, T. L., & Northcraft, G. B. (1993, Winter). Promises, pitfalls, and paradox: Cognitive elements in the implementation of new technology. *Journal of Managerial Issues, 5*(4), 465–482.

6. Overman, S. (1999, August). Learning your M&ABC's. *HR Focus, 76*(8), 7.

7. Rayport, J. F. (1999, Third Quarter). The truth about Internet business models. *Strategy & Business, 16,* 5–7.

FOCUS ON ORGANIZATIONAL BEHAVIOR

JEFF BEZOS—A TWENTY-FIRST-CENTURY PROPHET?   Once a Wall Street whiz, Jeff Bezos is now the head of the biggest store on the Web, Amazon.com. The billionaire, who wears rumpled chinos to work, is considered by many, including *Time* magazine, to be "the leading prophet of the age of electronic commerce." The weekly news magazine named him the most important person shaping technology in 1999.

Amazon.com got its start as a tiny online bookseller in 1995, and later became the most powerful merchant in cyberspace, selling more than $3 million worth of merchandise, from books to music to toys, each day. Much of the company's success has been due to its development of a giant customer base and "its one-click ordering system, Amway-like affiliate network and here-everyone-knows-your-name customer service—to expand Microsoft-like into nearly everyone's business." What remains to be seen, however, is whether Bezos's strategic vision is remarkably accurate or terribly misguided.

In the late 1990s, Jeff Bezos turned the retail world upside-down. He has been a leader in identifying business trends that are likely to grow in importance. Three such trends are especially noteworthy:

1 Whether a company's base of operations is strictly in its home country or across the globe, connecting people is the key to building the synergies necessary for success.
2 Consumers are not a homogenous group; to market a product effectively, a company must target customers based on their multiple characteristics, including their race, age, and ethnicity.
3 Technology will continue to have an enormous impact on business. These three key trends—globalization, inclusion, and technology—are referred to and discussed throughout this book. As Amazon.com has found, understanding these three trends is critical to successfully managing behavior in organizations.

Source: Adapted from Anders, G. (1999, July 12). The view from the top: The past, present and future of the Internet economy, as seen by Amazon.com's Jeff Bezos. *Wall Street Journal,* p. R52; Buechner, M. M., Grossman, L., Hamilton, A., Syken, B., Thomas, O., Wice, N., & Winters, R. (1999, October 4). Digital 50—The most important people shaping technology today. *Time,* p. 25; Buechner, M. M., et al.

There are two reasons people come together in organizations: to enhance their **effectiveness** and to boost their **efficiency.** These terms are defined in Figure 1-1.

MANAGEMENT FUNCTIONS

Researchers have identified several primary **managerial functions** that managers must accomplish for organizations to outperform individuals and achieve effectiveness and efficiency. Henri Fayol is credited with first identifying these

Two Reasons for Organizing	■ FIGURE 1-1

Effectiveness: The ability of an organization to accomplish an important goal, purpose, or mission. Organizations combine the efforts and talents of many individuals, thereby bringing into reach objectives that would be out of reach for individuals.

Efficiency: The ability of an organization to maximize productivity per unit of resources (labor and capital). Organizations enable individuals to accomplish tasks more quickly and with fewer mistakes than if any individual were working alone.

■ FIGURE 1-2	Fayol's Management Functions

Fayol's five management functions represent a prescription for managing behavior in organizations:

Planning: Thinking before taking action

Organizing: Arranging for material and personnel resources

Coordinating: Setting up the policies and procedures that govern worker behavior

Commanding: Motivating and directing the efforts of the workforce in pursuit of the organization's plans

Controlling: Monitoring and correcting progress toward the organization's goals

---

functions in 1916, which, as shown in Figure 1-2, are planning, organizing, coordinating, commanding, and controlling.[8]

PLANNING. **Planning** is the thinking that precedes action in an organization. Planning is concerned with how the organization will produce or provide the goods or services that define the purpose of the organization. The focus is on identifying the strategies and tactics that will enable the organization to attain its goals and fulfill its mission efficiently. What resources (including people) are necessary to produce or provide the goods or services that are central to the organization's mission? How will these resources be obtained?

ORGANIZING. Once the organization has an action plan in hand, **organizing** must take place. Organizing occurs when the organization arranges for the material and personnel resources needed to accomplish its plan. Staffing, for example, is the process of supplying a workforce (people) to fill the organization's designed structures.

COORDINATING. **Coordinating** is the process by which a structure is created through which the members of the organization can produce its central goods or services. This structure has several distinct components. First is the structuring of individual job responsibilities and duties. Who will do what, and how will they do it? Next is the structuring of relationships among individual jobs. What will be the reporting relationships?

Who will be supervising whom? What departments will be necessary? How will these departments interact? Finally, there is the physical structuring of the facility. Given the nature of individual jobs and the desired departmental structures and reporting relationships, what is the best way to arrange everyone physically? Should there be walls between desks to provide privacy, or should supervision be "line of sight"? If the organization has production machinery, where and how should it fit into the physical layout? Creating these three organizing structures—the individual, group, and physical structures—represents the first concrete stage of implementing the organization's action plan.

COMMANDING. After operating structures have been put in place and a workforce has been hired, a manager must control the workforce's execution of the work. **Commanding** includes directing and motivating the workforce, often by generating direction and enthusiasm for the work through leader-

---

8. Fayol, H. (1961). *General and industrial management.* London: Pitman.

RESEARCH IN ACTION
A STRIKE OVER A PAIR OF BOOTS?

Jeanne Brett, PhD, Kellogg Graduate School of Management, Northwestern University; *jmbrett@nwu.edu*

In 1977 I spent a good part of the summer driving the hills and hollows of West Virginia, talking to coal miners and mine managers about the causes of wildcat strikes. Wildcat strikes are illegal because they occur when the labor–management relationship is supposed to be controlled by a contract. Illegal or not, these strikes were occurring regularly in the coal industry. At one mine with a low rate of strikes, I asked the mine superintendent about the one strike that had occurred the previous year. "That strike should never have happened," he said. When I asked why, he proceeded to tell me a fascinating story.

Miners usually leave their work clothes in baskets that they hoist to the ceiling of the bathhouse between work shifts. One night a miner discovered that his boots were gone. He couldn't work without boots. Angry, he went to the shift boss and complained: "Someone stole my boots! It ain't fair! Why should I lose a shift's pay and the price of a pair of boots because the company can't protect the property?"

"Hard luck!" the shift boss responded. "The company isn't responsible for personal property left on company premises. Read the mine regulations!"

The miner convinced a few buddies to walk out with him and, in union solidarity, the other workers followed.

"How could this strike have been avoided?" I asked. The superintendent replied, "I've bought boots for miners before, and the shift boss knows

that. The frustrated miner probably would not have started a strike if the shift boss had offered to buy new boots and had not read the mine regulations."

Three years later we were asked to consult at Caney Creek mine, where there had been 27 wildcat strikes in the previous 2 years. In one case, a federal judge had jailed 115 miners overnight for striking. Thinking back on the mine manager in the boot strike, we decided to set up a series of procedures and incentives for resolving disputes. The mine was strike-free for the year following the intervention and continued to have a low incidence of strikes until it was closed in the late 1980s.

Our work at Caney Creek led us to develop a general model for intervening in conflicts. The core of our model comes directly out of the boots story: Resolve disputes by focusing on underlying interests and by recognizing the rights and power of both sides. In the boots strike, the miner wanted boots; the mine superintendent wanted to avoid a shutdown. Although the mine superintendent had the right to say the boots weren't his problem, the miners had the power to make it his problem. The usefulness of our model is not limited to miners and wildcat strikes. This model (called *dispute systems design*) is widely used by consultants and researchers in dispute prevention today. Most recently, eBay has hired an Internet dispute resolution company to design and support the resolution of disagreements among participants in its auctions.

ship. Incentive systems or rewards and discipline or punishment procedures may also be used both to motivate and to direct workers' behaviors.

CONTROLLING. Controlling is the process of monitoring the progress of the organization in reaching its stated goals and mission. Controlling involves measuring the organization's performance, comparing its performance against standards, and taking corrective action when performance is substandard. As illustrated in this chapter's "RESEARCH IN ACTION: A Strike over a Pair of Boots?," corrective actions may be directed at getting the workforce back on track. Implementing changes in leadership or incentive systems often has this effect. Corrective actions also may be directed toward revising the organization's action plan, thereby giving rise to consequent changes at the organizing level.

ORGANIZATIONAL BEHAVIOR: A DESCRIPTIVE VIEW

Defining organizational life in terms of effectiveness, efficiency, and the five managerial functions—planning, organizing, coordinating, commanding, and controlling—paints a picture of the organization as a production system. This picture suggests that managers consider all the relevant inputs; formulate plans; design and put in place people and systems to execute the plans; give a few pep talks; and fine-tune the people, systems, and even the plan itself if outcomes are less than optimal. The focus is on the deliberate and thoughtful pursuit of organizational effectiveness and efficiency. But is this how you would describe a company like The Men's Wearhouse or Amazon.com?

The reason your answer is probably no is that the prescriptive view of organizational behavior is incomplete in several important ways. To begin with, organizations are not just production systems; they are also *social* systems. People do not join organizations just to be more efficient and effective. They also join organizations because they want to belong to groups and because they enjoy sharing their efforts with others. As the Greek philosopher Aristotle noted, "Man is by nature a social animal." Aristotle believed that any individual who does not feel the need to join organizations is either "a beast or a god."[9] Since most of us are neither beasts nor gods, good management must acknowledge the fact that the social aspects of an organization are important to its members.

Fayol's functional view of behavior in organizations is also incomplete in that it underestimates the disjointedness of organizational life. Life in organizations is hardly an orderly progression of activities, each following logically from the one preceding it. Finally, defining organizational life in terms of five managerial functions overestimates the extent to which organizations pursue deliberate, planned activities focused on production and effectiveness.

Clearly there is more to organizational life than thoughtful, orderly planning and execution. A complete portrait includes three additional elements: conflict, uncertainty, and complexity.

CONFLICT

Fayol's approach to managing behavior in organizations assumes that all members share identical perceptions, beliefs, and goals. However, according to Jim March, a political scientist and a professor emeritus at Stanford University, we should not expect the members of an organization to be in total agreement. In fact, we should expect **conflict:** differences in perceptions, beliefs, and goals.[10]

The inevitability of conflict in organizations suggests that they are more than just production systems. Organizations are also **political systems**—social systems of individuals or groups that must work together and speak with one voice, even though each has a personal agenda. The idea that organizations are political systems places emphasis on interpersonal relationships and the behavior of individuals in groups. In addition, two tasks involved in managing organizational behavior become more significant. First, because organizations consist of groups and individuals with inconsistent and con-

---

9. Aristotle. (328 B.C.). *Politics.*
10. March, J. G. (1962). Business firm as political coalition. *Journal of Politics, 24,* 662–678.

Sources of Uncertainty	■ FIGURE 1-3

Internal

Individual:	Perceptions
	Goals/motivations
Organizational:	Means–ends relationships
	Organizational goals
	Responsibility/authority

External

Constant changes:	In the workforce
	In values and expectations
	In technology
	In the legal environment

flicting goals, managers must recognize that conflict management is an important organizational task. Along these lines, one study of managers' behavior found that managers spend a substantial part of each day discussing apparently irrelevant topics with their superiors, subordinates, and coworkers.[11] The researchers labeled this activity "socializing and politicking," thereby suggesting that its purpose is building rapport, relationships, and allegiances to weather the storms when conflicts arose. Second, political decision-making processes hold the potential of undermining organizational efficiency and effectiveness. Therefore, leadership is important in keeping all the members of an organization focused on the organization's goals, in addition to any personal agendas.

UNCERTAINTY

One of the subtle assumptions of the prescriptive view of management is that there is enough information available for orderly and deliberate planning to take place. But is this a good assumption? In reality, organizations are plagued by uncertainty that makes planning very difficult.[12]

Managing uncertainty therefore is another key component of the challenge of managing organizational behavior. **Uncertainty**—or the feeling of not knowing for sure—exists because people, the organizations of which they are a part, and the environment are not totally predictable. Would a better-motivated workforce make a difference? Would new incentive or training programs help? What values are important to a particular worker? History or research may suggest answers to these questions, but in practice the answers are available only through trial-and-error. As shown in Figure 1-3, uncertainty comes from a variety of internal and external sources.

INTERNAL SOURCES OF UNCERTAINTY. Much of the uncertainty individuals face both inside and outside organizations arises from *perceptions*—the collecting of information from the environment. The behaviors of fellow workers can be a constant source of confusion. Was that friendly greeting by my supervisor a sign that I have been doing a good job? Or did my supervisor just have a good time at the company party last night? The inputs we receive

---

11. Kotter, J. P. (1982). *The general managers*. New York: The Free Press.
12. Cyert, R. M., & March, J. G. (1963). *A behavioral theory of the firm*. Englewood Cliffs, NJ: Prentice Hall.

from the environment have meaning only as a result of how we interpret those inputs. If our interpretations are wrong, our actions will be wrong as well.

Uncertainty also exists concerning our understanding of *means–ends* relationships. In other words, we evaluate, albeit not always consciously, the probability that an outcome (the end) will occur if an action (the means) is taken. For example, will replacing the internal human resources function with an outsourced shared services center ensure that our employees get the same service? Will our human resources department be better able to focus on strategic, as opposed to clerical, tasks?

Goals within organizations may also be uncertain. Individuals may not know what they are trying to achieve in their jobs, or what they are told they are trying to achieve may change from day to day. Similarly, different members of an organization may have different ideas of the organization's goals. Or the goals may have to be changed as a result of changes in the organization's environment. Imagine how difficult planning is when the organization's goals are not stable or agreed on!

EXTERNAL SOURCES OF UNCERTAINTY. Much of the uncertainty managers face occurs because of the constantly changing and evolving environment in which the organization functions. The role of the environment is discussed in greater detail in chapter 13; for now, it is important to note several primary sources of external uncertainty that the modern manager must keep in mind.

Changes in the Workforce. As if the management of organizational behavior were not complex enough, managers must deal with changes in the kinds of people who become employees. The U.S. Census Bureau estimates that between 1998 and 2008, the labor force will grow at a rate of approximately 12%, to a total of 17 million workers.[13]

The composition of the U.S. workforce, including age distribution, is also changing. By 2008 40% of the labor force is expected to be older than 45, up from 33% in 1998. Also in this period, the percentage of workers in the post-baby boom generation, including GenXers, is expected to decrease from 51% to 44%.[14] The resulting increase in the median age of employees will have a significant impact on organizations and their operations.

The U.S. workforce is also becoming increasingly diverse, as a result of steady influxes of women and minorities. The rate at which women enter the labor force is expected to continue to increase, and the rate for men is expected to correspondingly diminish. By 2008 women are expected to represent 48% of the labor force.[15]

While the number of Blacks entering the workforce will remain about the same, Hispanics are entering the workforce in large numbers. Only 7.4% of the U.S. workforce in 1988 and 11% in 1998, Hispanics are expected to account for 13% by 2008.[16] Asians are also changing the face of U.S. labor. Individuals of Asian descent represented 3% of the workforce in 1990 and 4% in 1998, and they may represent 5% in 2008.[17]

Changes in Workers' Values and Expectations. As the face of the U.S. workforce has changed, so too have workers' values and expectations. First,

13. Charting the projections: 1998–2008. (1999–2000, Winter). *Occupational Outlook Quarterly, 3.*
14. Charting the projections, *3.*
15. Charting the projections, *3.*
16. Charting the projecitons, *38.*
17. Charting the projections, *38.*

INTERNATIONAL FOCUS ON MANAGEMENT CHALLENGES

THE MIDDLE WAY. The view that management problems remain the same over time but that their solutions differ from country to country isn't popular in an age in which business is supposed to be globalizing. Global businesses must look for global management solutions. Businesses have home countries that stand for values that are functional, even essential, for their effectiveness and corporate identity. Supranational organizations without a home country, like various UN agencies, suffer from poor efficiency and effectiveness.

Multinational organizations—private, public, and nongovernment—stand for values that originated in their home country and that will not be shared equally with their employees and managers from other national origins. Multinational organizations are kept together by shared practices, not by shared values. Philippe d'Iribarne once remarked that international cooperation consists of doing things together, even if each partner does them for a different reason.

Values are specific to national cultures; they are never universal. If there is one moral principle that can be offered as a candidate for a universal value and as a must for organizations aspiring to be global, it is the principle of moderation: Seek a middle way. This principle is independently found in the teachings of three contemporaries who revolutionized human thinking in the fifth century BC: Buddha, Confucius, and Socrates. The rationale of the middle way is that any virtue becomes a sin when extended too far. Fields of application of this principle can be chosen at will: merging, privatization, outsourcing, downsizing, just-in-time management, total quality management, teleworking, lobbying, executive compensation, and whatever other fad the new millennium has in store for us.

Source: Excerpted from Hoffstede, G. (1999, Summer). Problems remain, but theories will change: The universal and the specific in twenty-first-century global management. *Organizational Dynamics, 28*(1), 34–44.

today's workers want work to be meaningful and involving, not just a means to a paycheck. GenXers are notorious for this view, but employers are seeing this shift in values in workers of every generation, including the baby boomers.

Second, workers seem to be more interested in fitting work into their overall lives than in devoting their lives to an organization. The adage "I live to work, not work to live" is quickly becoming antiquated.

Along with its changing values, the modern workforce has changing expectations. Gone are the days when employees felt grateful for a job. Today they feel a sense of entitlement. Employees feel entitled to certain rights, such as privacy and fair treatment, and even to work that is interesting and challenging. Finally, workers are demanding flexibility in their work schedules, so that they can better enjoy life beyond the workplace.[18]

Changes in Global Competition. As workers' demographics and values are changing, the nature of competition is changing as well. Every company must be willing to explore global markets, even if its current operations are limited to a domestic manufacturing plant. To be successful in today's marketplace, people are the key. Global competition also requires finding "the middle way," as Geert Hofstede discusses in the "INTERNATIONAL FOCUS ON: Management Challenges. It also means selecting and training people

---

18. Baltes, B. B., Briggs, T. E., Huff, J. W., Wright, J. A., & Neuman, G. A. (1999). Flexible and compressed workweek schedules: A meta-analysis of their effects on work-related criteria. *Journal of Applied Psychology, 84*, 496–513.

who are willing to take on global challenges. As Jack Welch, chief executive officer, General Electric, noted

> The Jack Welch of the future cannot be like me. I spent my entire career in the U.S. The next head of General Electric will be somebody who spent time in Bombay, in Hong Kong, in Buenos Aires. We have to send our best and brightest overseas and make sure they have the training that will allow them to be the global leaders who will make GE flourish in the future.[19]

As Welch's statement illustrates, today more than ever organizations must direct their attention to the development of future leaders who can manage companies in any and all markets.

Changes in Technology. In 1967 computers were bulky boxes of poorly understood electronic hardware. Today managers and administrative staff throughout American industry can't remember (or were too young to know) what it was like to work without computers, let alone the Internet, intranets, electronic organizers, e-mail, modems, and the like.

Additionally, technological changes are creating new ways to work, and even new ways to think about what constitutes an organization. Today, some workers simply dial in to offices, as noted in "TECHNOLOGY FOCUS ON: Changes in the Workforce."

Many employees have embraced technological alternatives to commuting to offices every day. In a recent report that surveyed over 1,000 organizations, it was found that 66% of organizations offered flexible work schedules and 21% offered compressed work schedules.[20] If managers hope to help their organizations meet their efficiency and effectiveness goals, they must remain keenly aware of technology, for it's changing every day.

Changes in Law. The legal environment in which organizations function represents another source of uncertainty. Laws influence such day-to-day workings of organizations as hiring (the Equal Employment Opportunities Act and the Americans with Disabilities Act), compensation (the Equal Pay Act), and maintenance (the Occupational Safety and Health Act and the Family and Medical Leave Act). In addition, many of the rights that employees take for granted, such as the right to form unions for the purpose of collective bargaining, are codified into law.

As U.S. society has become increasingly litigious, an ever-larger number of laws have been written with the goal of protecting employees' rights. Since 1900 the legal environment in which organizations must function has evolved from one in which the emphasis was on the rights of management, to one in which the emphasis is on the rights of unions, to one in which the emphasis is on the rights of the individual employee. Further, ethical standards have changed, leading to the passage of laws governing the behavior of organizations and their members (such as laws against insider trading).

All these evolving elements in an organization's external environment combine with the internal sources of uncertainty described previously to create a business world in which few things seem certain. As a result, man-

---

19. Black, J. S., Gregersen, H. B., Mendenhall, M. E., & Stroh, L. K. (1999). *Globalizing people through international assignments.* Reading MA: Addison-Wesley.
20. Baltes, B. B., et al., p. 496.

TECHNOLOGY FOCUS ON
CHANGES IN THE WORKFORCE

TELECOMMUTING. Jack Nilles coined the term *telecommuting* while stuck in traffic in Los Angeles. It's not surprising then that telecommuting initially caught on in densely populated areas, such as Southern California, where traffic congestion and pollution are problems.

In the 1980s, as companies focused on cost cutting, some managers saw telecommuting as a means to reduce the cost of maintaining expensive office space. More recently, it's become a tool to attract and retain top personnel in fields with limited labor supplies.

Over the years, the substitution of computer-based technology for physical travel has led to a number of alternative work forms. In addition to home-based telecommuting, these include satellite centers, neighborhood work centers, and mobile working. Together, these alternatives constitute "teleworking." What they have in common is that in-person supervision has been replaced by remote managing, face-to-face communication by telecommunications-mediated communication, on-site working by off-site or multiple-site working, and, in the case of groups, side-by-side collaboration by virtual teamwork.

Estimates of the number of telecommuters in the United States vary, but most figures range from three to nine million people (3% to 8% of the workforce). These figures include people who work from home at least several days per month. Many forecasters predict that these numbers will continue to rise, and some even suggest that telecommuters could represent as much as 57% of the workforce someday. These numbers become startling and critical for managers as they attempt to accept the challenge of managing organizations in the fast-changing technological world.

Source: Excerpted from Kurland, N. B., & Bailey, D. E. (1999, Autumn). Telework: The advantages and challenges of working here, there, anywhere, and anytime. *Organizational Dynamics, 28*(2), 53–68.

agers often behave in ways that bear little resemblance to Fayol's characterization of organizations in terms of deliberate and orderly planning and execution.[21]

COMPLEXITY

With all the conflict and uncertainty that managers must face, it should come as no surprise that complexity is also a defining feature of life in organizations. **Complexity** refers to the overwhelming number of concerns that managers must keep track of and manage. Part of this complexity arises from the fact that any organization is really two organizations: the formal organization and the informal organization. As shown in Figure 1-4, the formal organization consists of the procedures and structures suggested by the functional approach to managing behavior in organizations. In effect, the formal organization represents the organization's perceptions, beliefs, and goals. Yet the formal organization is only the tip of the iceberg.

The informal organization represents the rest of the iceberg. The informal organization encompasses interpersonal realities (such as employees' personal goals, perceptions, and beliefs). These realities are not typically part of the organization's action plan, yet they exert a strong influence on the organization. To achieve optimal efficiency and effectiveness, these characteristics must be taken into account in managing employees' behavior.

21. Cyert, R. M., & March, J. G. (1963). *A behavioral theory of the firm.*

In any organization there are really two organizations: (1) the formal organization, consisting of the formal reporting relationships, rules, and procedures; and (2) the informal organization, consisting of what really goes on in the organization, including beliefs and social relationships.

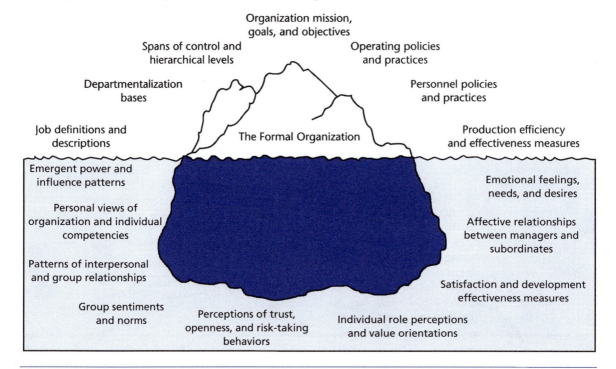

Source: Selfridge, R. J., & Sokolik, S. L. (1975). A comprehensive view of organizational development. *MSU Business Topics, 47.*

The complexity of work organizations is perhaps best captured in a quote by Leonard Sayles, an emeritus professor at Columbia Business School:

> [The manager] is like a symphony orchestra conductor, endeavoring to maintain a melodious performance in which the contributions of the various instruments are coordinated and sequenced, patterned, and paced, while the orchestra members are having various personal difficulties, stagehands are moving music stands, alternating excessive heat and cold are creating audience and instrument problems, and the sponsor of the concert is insisting on irrational changes in the program.[22]

This quote emphasizes the disjointed complexity of organizational behavior and the difference between what organizations are formally supposed to be versus what informally they are. Managers are like jugglers, trying to

---

22. L. R. Sayles (1964) *Managerial Behavior.* New York: McGraw-Hill.

balance many balls at once—including the conflicts of a diverse workforce and the uncertainties of new technologies and a global business environment. Managing the complexity of organizational behavior is a critical component of the management challenge.

SUMMARY

The conflict, uncertainty, and complexity of organizational behavior stand in stark contrast to the prescriptive view of managerial life as deliberate and orderly. Probably the truth falls somewhere between the prescriptive and the descriptive perspectives. The prescriptive (or functional) approach is valuable in that it provides a description of management behavior in the best of all possible organizations. Unfortunately, no manager works in such an environment.

Despite recent technological innovations designed to make work more efficient and effective, organizations are highly complex. Conflict is inevitable, and the only certainties a manager can depend on are that nothing is certain and that everything is changing.

Astute managers recognize the critical role of human behavior in determining an organization's overall success. Managing an organization's human resources to achieve effectiveness and efficiency in the face of complexity, conflict, uncertainty, and constant change is the challenge of organizational behavior. Preparing you to meet that challenge is the goal of this book.

KEY TERMS

Commanding
Complexity
Conflict
Coordinating
Controlling
Effectiveness
Efficiency

Managerial functions
Organization
Organizational behavior
Organizing
Planning
Political systems
Uncertainty

DISCUSSION QUESTIONS

1 What is an organization? Why do people become members of organizations? Think of some organizations to which you belong. Why did you join these organizations? Think of an organization of which you are no longer a member. Why did you leave it?

2 What are the differences between efficiency and effectiveness? Why are Fayol's managerial functions an incomplete description of how organizations pursue these goals?

3 Consider your class as an organization. What sources of uncertainty exist for you as a student? What sources exist for your instructor? What goals do you and your instructor share? What goals might you and your instructor have that are incompatible?

ON YOUR OWN

The Organizational Behavior IQ Test   Please fill out the following questionnaire. Your instructor will provide you with information about the meaning of your responses.

On the following pages are 24 pairs of statements. For each pair, circle the letter preceding the statement that you think is most accurate. Circle *only one* letter in each pair.

After you have circled the letter, indicate how certain you are of your choice by writing 1, 2, 3, or 4 on the line in front of each item according to the following procedure:

Write 1 if you are *very uncertain* that your choice is correct.
Write 2 if you are *somewhat uncertain* that your choice is correct.
Write 3 if you are *somewhat certain* that your choice is correct.
Write 4 if you are *very certain* that your choice is correct.

Do not skip any pairs.

_____   **1 a** A supervisor is well advised to treat, as much a possible, all members of his or her group exactly the same way.

b A supervisor is well advised to adjust his or her behavior according to the unique characteristics of the members of her or her group.

_____   **2 a** Generally speaking, individual motivation is greatest if the person has set goals for himself or herself that are *difficult* to achieve.

b Generally speaking, individual motivation is greatest if the person has set goals for himself or herself that are *easy* to achieve.

_____   **3 a** A major reason organizations are not as productive as they could be these days is that managers are too concerned with managing the workgroup rather than the individual.

b A major reason organizations are not as productive as they could be these days is that managers are too concerned with managing the individual rather than the workgroup.

_____   **4 a** Supervisors who sometime prior to becoming a supervisor have performed the job of the people they are currently supervising are apt to be *more* effective supervisors than those who have never performed that particular job.

b Supervisors who sometime prior to becoming a supervisor have performed the job of the people they are currently supervising are apt to be *less* effective supervisors than those who have never performed that particular job.

_____   **5 a** On almost every matter relevant to the work, managers are well advised to be completely honest and open with their subordinates.

b There are very few matters in the workplace where managers are well advised to be completely honest and open with their subordinates.

_____   **6 a** On almost every matter relevant to the work, managers are well advised to be completely honest and open with their superiors.

b There are very few matters in the workplace where managers are well advised to be completely honest and open with their superiors.

_____   **7 a** One's *need for power* is a better predictor of managerial advancement than one's *motivation to do the work well.*

b One's *motivation to do the work well* is a better predictor of managerial advancement than one's *need for power.*

_____   **8 a** When people fail at something, they try harder the next time.

b When people fail at something, they quit trying.

_____   **9 a** Performing well as a manager depends most on how much *education* you have.

b Performing well as a manager depends most on how much *experience* you have.

_____ **10 a** The most effective leaders are those who give more emphasis to *getting the work done* than they do to *relating to people*.

b The most effective leaders are those who give more emphasis to *relating to people* than they do to *getting the work done*.

_____ **11 a** It is very important for a leader to "stick to his or her guns."

b It is *not* very important for a leader to "stick to his or her guns."

_____ **12 a** *Pay* is the most important factor in determining how hard people work.

b The *nature of the task people are doing* is the most important factor in determining how hard people work.

_____ **13 a** *Pay* is the most important factor in determining how satisfied people are at work.

b The *nature of the task people are doing* is the most important factor in determining how satisfied people are at work.

_____ **14 a** Generally speaking, the top-level executives of major corporations can be expected to make decisions that *maximize the best interests of the organization* as a whole.

b Generally speaking, the top-level executives of major corporations can be expected to make decisions that *make them look good (or at least not look bad)*, even if the interests of the organization as a whole are not maximized.

_____ **15 a** Generally speaking, it is correct to say that a person's *attitudes cause his or her behavior*.

b Generally speaking, it is correct to say that a person's *attitudes are primarily rationalizations for his or her behavior*.

_____ **16 a** Satisfied workers produce more than workers who are not satisfied.

b Satisfied workers produce no more than workers who are not satisfied.

_____ **17 a** Generally speaking, the *structure* of an organization determines the *technology it uses*.

b Generally speaking, the *technology* of an organization determines the structure of the organization.

_____ **18 a** The statement "A manager's authority needs to be commensurate with his or her responsibility" is practically speaking a *very meaningful statement*.

b The statement "A manager's authority needs to be commensurate with his or her responsibility" is practically speaking a *basically meaningless statement*.

_____ **19 a** A major reason for the relative decline in U.S. productivity is that the division of labor and job specialization *have gone too far*.

b A major reason for the relative decline in U.S. productivity is that the division of labor and job specialization *have not been carried far enough*.

_____ **20 a** The notion that most semiskilled workers desire work that is interesting and meaningful is most likely *incorrect*.

b The notion that most semiskilled workers desire work that is interesting and meaningful is most likely *correct*.

_____ **21 a** People welcome change for the better.

b Even if change is for the better, people will resist it.

_____ **22 a** Leaders are born, not made.

b Leaders are made, not born.

_____ **23 a** Groups make better decisions than individuals.

b Individuals make better decisions than groups.

_____ **24 a** Generally speaking, the largest corporations would be more efficient if they were *larger*.

b Generally speaking, the largest corporations would be more efficient if they were *smaller*.

Source: Weinberg, R., & Nord, W. (1982). Coping with "It's All Common Sense." *Exchange, 7,* 32–33.

CLOSING CASE   CHAPTER 1

THE MANAGER'S MEMO

FROM: R. Williams, Executive VP, Operations
TO: P. Harris, Manager, Greenbay Mill, Paper Division
RE: Third-Quarter Performance

Having just reviewed Greenbay Mill's third-quarter performance, I am extremely concerned about its YTD safety results. The mill's quality and productivity results are excellent—strong evidence that you and your employees are on target in meeting the mill's objectives. However, I can find no explanation whatsoever for the mill's poor safety record—currently the worst of all our plants in the nation. To operate at peak effectiveness and efficiency, product quality and productivity cannot be our only concerns; safety must be a paramount concern as well.

Our corporation's number-one mission is to provide a safe work environment for our associates. As you know, all the mill managers agreed to work toward a 15% improvement in lost-time accidents (LTAs) and reportable accidents. Not only is Greenbay's safety record not improving, but, judging by its YTD performance, it is likely to have more injuries and LTAs than ever. Your most recent excuse—that the mill's relations with the union have reached an all-time low—is not an acceptable explanation.

Reversing this poor record must be a high priority. I therefore direct you and your staff to prepare an action plan designed to reverse your safety performance record before the end of the year. I will expect this action plan on my desk within the week.

If you need corporate assistance in this matter, please let us know.

CASE DISCUSSION QUESTIONS

Assume that you are the recipient of this memo. How would you proceed? How might you consider Fayol's management functions in your planning? How would the concepts of conflict, uncertainty, and complexity factor into your action plan?

EXERCISE   PART ONE: Bridge Building

For this exercise, your instructor will divide the class into groups of about 8 to 10 students. One group will act as observers; the remaining groups will be "bridge builders."

The task of each bridge-building group is to build a bridge spanning two desks in the classroom. Your instructor will give each bridge-building group a package of "construction materials." This package will contain:

- 5 straws
- 1 newspaper
- 2 pencils
- 1 blue felt-tip pen
- 5 rubber bands
- 1 box of paper clips
- 1 red felt-tip pen
- 1 pad of sticky notes

Additionally, your instructor will have a pair of scissors, a roll of tape, and a stapler for the bridge-building groups to share.

The bridge-building groups will have about 15 minutes to construct their bridges. At the end of the allotted construction time, all bridge builders will leave the classroom so that the observer group can evaluate the constructed bridges. Using the evaluation form provided, the observer group will evaluate the bridges on the basis of five criteria: length, width, height, strength, and beauty.

The observer group will also have responsibility for observing the *processes of group interaction* that occur as the bridge-building groups build their bridges. Your instructor will provide the observer group members with an observation checklist for that purpose.

Evaluation Form: Bridge Building

Evaluate each bridge on the following criteria (circle a number):

1 Length
(1)   (2)   (3)   (4)   (5)   (6)   (7)   (8)   (9)   (10)
Very Poor   Outstanding

2 Width
(1)   (2)   (3)   (4)   (5)   (6)   (7)   (8)   (9)   (10)
Very Poor   Outstanding

3 Height
(1)   (2)   (3)   (4)   (5)   (6)   (7)   (8)   (9)   (10)
Very Poor   Outstanding

4 Strength
(1)   (2)   (3)   (4)   (5)   (6)   (7)   (8)   (9)   (10)
Very Poor   Outstanding

5 Beauty
(1)   (2)   (3)   (4)   (5)   (6)   (7)   (8)   (9)   (10)
Very Poor   Outstanding

CASE PART ONE: The Ultimate Frisbee Team's Dilemma

Harry, Jere, George, and Bob L. were students at Centerville University who enjoyed playing Ultimate Frisbee, a game requiring two teams of seven. Because it was hard to round up 14 players every time they wanted to play, they decided to start a regular team. They hoped to get together some potentially good frisbee players and teach them how to play Ultimate. They realized that they would need to publicize the team. Jere spoke to a reporter from the school newspaper, and a short article appeared about the team (see Exhibit 1). In the interview, Jere stated, "The team is open to all students, especially girls." Any of the four students could have spoken to the reporter, but Jere took the initiative. Jere also announced a practice through the newspaper. Eleven people came to that initial practice: Jere, Fred, Roger (Fred's roommate), Jim H., Jean, Bob L., George, Pete C., Pete R., Paul, and Harry. Jere took their names, addresses, and telephone numbers and announced that

Source: Cohen, A., Fink, S., Gadon, H., & Willits, R. (Eds.). (1988). *Effective behavior in organizations,* 4th ed. (pp. 910–915). Homewood, IL: Irwin.

"Ultimate Frisbee" Arrives with Spring
By Janice M. Dupre

Springtime is just around the corner, and for Frisbee lovers it's time to warm up the old throwing arm.

This spring a group of Frisbee enthusiasts is trying to get together a frisbee team at Centerville University (CU). The originator of the team is Jere Harris.

Many people are familiar with the Frisbee as a simple plastic disc used for throwing around on the beach. But an official game is played with a Frisbee. It's called Ultimate Frisbee, and it's like soccer in many ways.

"In Ultimate Frisbee there are seven players per team on the field. There is a kickoff, but you can't run with the frisbee in your hand," explains Harris. "It's an extremely fast game, with two 24-minute halfs."

According to Harris, a Middle States Frisbee League is now being formed by a student from Amenon College. Colleges that already have teams and will hopefully be joining the league include Western Reserve, Ohio Wesleyan, Wayne University, and Clarke. One of the best frisbee teams in the area is the New Hampton College team.

In past years individuals from CU have gotten together to play other schools, but there never has been an official team. "I've been playing frisbee all my life, but I'd never heard of the Ultimate Frisbee until a friend of mine told me about the game last year. It's really a fast-moving game with lots of collisions because the Frisbee is always in the air with everyone diving for it," said Harris, a junior hospital administration major.

Ultimate Frisbee is by no means a gentle game. At this moment Bob LaPointe, future cocaptain of the forming CU team, had a dislocated shoulder from a Frisbee game he recently played in.

The friend who introduced the game to Jere Harris last year was a graduate of Columbia High School in New Jersey, which is where the first Ultimate Frisbee game was played.

"The Columbia High team can beat any team in the nation," said Harris. It won more than 30 games at the national tournament in Michigan last year. Columbia High School also publishes the Ultimate Frisbee rule book.

Each year a national Frisbee tournament is held at Copperhopper, Michigan. Hundreds of Ultimate Frisbee teams from the United States and Canada take part in the tournament. But the game of Frisbee is not confined to North America; it's very popular overseas, and according to Harris, it is just being introduced to China.

So far the CU frisbee team comprises about 10 members. Harris is hoping to get the team off the ground and start practicing soon. He is planning to announce practices as soon as he can arrange a time in the indoor tract and as soon as the weather is nice.

"Frisbee is open to women," stresses Harris. "To play, you don't have to be a super Frisbee thrower; you just have to be able to throw and catch the Frisbee and to run."

Along with all the food, energy, and political crises, there is also a Frisbee crisis. Frisbees are made with plastics, and because there is a plastic shortage, Frisbees are an endangered species. Harris said that the major Frisbee companies such as Whamo are urging people to buy their Frisbees now because soon they will be hard to come by. But until that time comes, Frisbees will continue to fly in the sky on warm spring days at Centerville.

practices would be held at 4 p.m. on Tuesdays and Thursdays (at a time that was convenient for Jere). It wasn't clear why Jere should be the one to decide this, but because Jere was taking names, he was the one the newcomers asked.

At the second practice some new people showed up: Chas, Alex, Bert, and Gene (all of whom lived together), and Bob M., Linda, Sharon, and Jack. However, some people from the first practice didn't come back because they had conflicting classes. Jere took these new people's names and toyed with the idea of taking attendance, but nothing came of it because, as he said to his roommate, "I didn't want to turn people off or make them feel they had to come." However, many players made a mental note of who was there and who wasn't. Different people came and went like this at each practice thereafter.

Jere and the others who knew how to play Ultimate spent the first few practices teaching the others. Jere dominated the direction of these early practices, but after a short time the rest of the players were as good, and some were even better. Everyone had a lot of fun learning and playing. Jack and Chas were two players who stood out at practice. Jack (a grad student) was calm and collected, never became angry, and always played fairly. Chas had been the captain of his high school football team and always organized the team he was on, deciding who should play and who should sit out.

Jere dealt with much of the administrative work, such as announcing to the school radio station and newspaper where and when practices would be held. No one asked Jere to do this, but attendance was sporadic and he hoped to get new people to fill the gaps at practice. However, response to the newspaper and radio announcements was minimal; consequently, Jere felt there should be an organizational meeting at night that he hoped would generate interest and attract more players. At the next practice Jere announced the meeting and explained that its purpose was also to set up officers, dues, and so forth. Jack had 200 fliers printed up, and he and Chas posted them around campus.

Jere came to the meeting late and found that strong opposition had developed against dues and against organization in general. Jere tried to explain that in order to receive funding from the university or to use university vehicles, the team must be organized with officers and a constitution; he said that the sports director for the university had told him this. A vote on the dues barely passed, and several members left the meeting, vowing they had quit. Jere followed them into the hall, pleading with them to be sensible, but he could overhear two other members saying, "So what, we don't need them anyway." A debate ensued for a few minutes, and Jere called an end to the meeting, putting off a vote on a captain because he feared it would create further division among the team, since either Jere, Jack, or Chas might have made a good captain. Many new people who had shown up at the meeting explained that they couldn't make practices as currently scheduled. Jere shrugged and said he'd try to set up alternate practices; however, he ever did it.

A new group of players arrived after about 10 practices: Stan, Reggie, Mark, Bill T., and Howie. They always came and left together, and they often played on the same team. They were good players and talked about the coming games and their anticipated roles in them. Reggie asked Jere at his first practice, "Do you think I'll start the first game?" Jere just shrugged.

■ **EXHIBIT 2**

Name	Attendance[a]	Initial Appearance	Ability[a]	Age	Class	Showed Up for Bus
Jack	Regular	2nd practice	A	23	Grad.	XX
Fred	Regular	1st practice	A	19	Fresh.	XX
Jere[b]	Regular	1st practice	B	20	Jr.	XX
Jean	Regular	1st practice	C	19	Soph.	XX
Harry[b]	Regular	1st practice	A	21	Sr.	XX
Roger	Sporadic	1st practice	B	21	Sr.	XX
Reggie	Regular	10th practice	A	18	Fresh.	XX
Mark	Regular	10th practice	A	18	Fresh.	XX
Howie	Regular	10th practice	A	18	Fresh.	XX
Stan	Regular	10th practice	A	19	Fresh.	XX
Paul	Sporadic	1st practice	B	19	Soph.	XX
Jim H.	Regular	1st practice	A	19	Jr.	XX
Chas	Regular	2nd practice	A	20	Soph.	XX
Gene	Sporadic	2nd practice	B	20	Soph.	XX
Bert	Sporadic	2nd practice	B	19	Soph.	XX
Sharon	Regular	2nd practice	C	20	Jr.	XX
Linda	Sporadic	2nd practice	C	18	Fresh.	XX
George[b]	Regular	1st practice	A	19	Soph.	XX
Bob L.[b]	Sporadic	1st practice	B	19	Soph.	XX
Bob M.	Sporadic	2nd practice	B	20	Jr.	XX
Pete C.	Sporadic	1st practice	B	19	Fresh.	XX
Bill T.	Regular	10th practice	C	19	Soph.	XX
Alex	Sporadic	2nd practice	C	19	Soph.	
Pete R.	Sporadic	1st practice	C	18	Fresh.	XX

[a]Based on Jere's "mental notes."
[b]Founders of the team.

By this time more than 20 people had come out for the team, including 3 women (see Exhibit 2). The players fell into five friendship groups, as shown in Exhibit 3. Practices became hard and competitive, and a lot of the fun that had been evident in the beginning seemed to disappear. One day Jere enraged Sharon by taking the Frisbee away from her and throwing it himself. She started to walk off the field, but Jere called her back and the two had an argument in the middle of the field, where everyone could see and hear it. Sharon stayed at practice but was silent the rest of the day.

As the date for the fist game drew near, all the dues money was used to rent a 15-seat bus for the 50-mile trip to the other school. The day before

■ **EXHIBIT 3**   **Subgroups (with the spokesperson for each listed first)**

Group A: Jere, Harry, Bob L., George
Group B: Chas, Gene, Alex, Bert
Group C: Jack, Jean Linda, Sharon, Jim H.
Group D: Stan, Reggie, Mark, Howie, Bill T.
Group E: Fred, Roger, Pete C., Paul

All the rest of the students are independent, coming under no group.

the game, about 12 people attended a meeting to discuss travel plans. Jack brought a letter written by Sharon. It was addressed to the team, but started:

Dear Jack:

The incident at this afternoon's practice was the last straw, but I would like to impress that it was far from the only one. I'm writing this to you because you are the only one on the team who ever gave me any encouragement or made me feel like a real live person and not a bumbling incompetent.

I joined the Frisbee team because I enjoy playing vigorous Frisbee in the comradeship of others and because I wanted to develop my own skill and confidence; but none of these is achievable under the present conditions.

How can I enjoy and concentrate on the game when not a minute goes by that I must force myself to ignore and rise above degrading and humiliating sexist treatment? It's often said that a female, be it a filly race horse or me on the Frisbee team, must be three times as good as a male in order to be considered equal. Nothing truer has ever been said. Even Jere, who's practiced with me so much and encouraged my progress, turns overtly sexist in the presence of his teammates. Certainly the issues are not completely imagined in my mind—ask the other female players.

I am not against competitiveness as long as the competition element stimulates constant improvement. But when point-making takes priority over the freedom to make mistakes or try new things, then I think something is wrong. Maybe, if anyone cares, you could let them in on this. . . .

With this Sharon announced her resignation from the team. The team received the letter with much debate, and some players refused to read the letter. Jack sided with the opinions stated in the letter and was joined in this opinion by many of the original members, including the two remaining women. Jere remained silent, unable to side with one view or the other.

Obviously, some choice had to be made about who would go on the bus. Group D insisted on "sending down the best 15," in which case all of them would be among the 15 to go. Group C said, "Take those who have come to

Comparative Lists of Who Should Go to the Game	■ EXHIBIT 4

Jack's List	Group D's List
Jere	Reggie
Jack	Mark
Fred	Howie
Jean	Stan
Roger	Paul
Jim H.	Jere
Sharon	Jack
Linda	Fred
Bob L.	Roger
George	Jim H.
Harry	Chas
Paul	Gene
Pete R.	Bert
Chas	George
Gene	Harry

the most practices." Jere felt this was the fairest solution, but it was hard to implement because no one was sure who had attended how many practices.

Jere, Jack, and Stan sat down and wrote up several lists of 15 (see Exhibit 4), but none was acceptable to all the groups. Jere put off making any decision; several people got quite sore. Jere felt caught in the middle, and he could not shrug it off. He tried to act as the moderator of the dispute but kept saying, "Does anyone have any ideas?" Argument continued and people began to leave very upset when no decision was reached. Jere felt that he had been responsible for letting the scene get out of hand.

The day of the game came, and 19 people stood out near the bus. Everyone wondered what to do. Some expressed the opinion that a captain should be elected to make the decision.

QUESTIONS FOR DISCUSSION

1 Why has the Ultimate Frisbee team had so much trouble getting organized?

2 Think about the traditional management function of planning, organizing, staffing, and controlling. Has the Ultimate Frisbee team failed to do any or all of these?

3 How have uncertainty, conflict, and complexity contributed to the Ultimate Frisbee team's dilemma?

PART

2

Individual Behavior

CHAPTER 2

Foundations: Perception, Attitudes, and Personality

THE CRISIS AT TEXACO

It's known as "The Crisis" around Texaco's sprawling office headquarters in a leafy suburb north of New York City. It was the embarrassing and expensive saga that forced the oil giant to cut a hefty $175 million check to settle a racial discrimination lawsuit filed by some of the company's African-American employees, the largest such settlement ever.

During The Crisis, as Texaco was accused of prejudice against its minority employees, its stock plunged more than $3 per share in the days after the details were revealed, stripping nearly $1 billion from the company's market capitalization. Texaco was pilloried nationwide. Several major shareholders—including New York State Controller Carl McCall, whose state is one of the company's biggest investors—even called Texaco's chief executive officer (CEO) Peter Bijur personally and wondered aloud whether they should remain invested in Texaco. Right or wrong, guilty as charged or not, company officials knew they were staring at a potential disaster.

"Then I decided that I was going to use this as an opportunity to make us a better company," said Bijur. And that is exactly what he did. Bijur set real goals with real timetables and issued several edicts designed to shake up a culture that had long stifled attitudes toward minority retention and advancement.

It's worth noting that the company's transformation took place during rough economic times for Texaco and the entire oil patch. During all of 1998 and through the first quarter of 1999, the company was savaged by historically low crude oil and natural gas prices. Revenues tumbled 32% in 1998, to $31.7 billion, as earnings dropped 79% to $578 million. Heads rolled. Texaco trimmed employment worldwide from 27,000 to 18,500.

So, just how far has Texaco come? Here are a few numbers worth noting: In 1998 minorities accounted for nearly 4 in 10 new hires at Texaco and for more than 20% of promotions. During the first six months of 1999, minorities accounted for 44% of new hires and 22% of promotions. In 1996 company officials vowed to spend at least $1 billion with minority- and women-owned vendors—or about 15% of overall spending—before 2001. They passed the halfway mark two years into the program, spending $528 million

Source: Excerpted from Labich, K. (1999, September 6). No more crude at Texaco. *Fortune,* p. 205–212.

with minority- and women-owned vendors during 1997 and 1998. (Black and Hispanic firms received $135 million of that total.) Bijur, an aggressive, fast-talking, 33-year company veteran, also made several high-profile hires at key executive positions, a clear signal that Texaco's leadership—the "top of the house," in industry parlance—was not immune to dramatic change.

It's all noble stuff, but none of the programs and directives would be effective if failure to make satisfactory progress toward the goals went without consequence. So Bijur also told Texaco's top executives and managers that their career trajectories would be directly linked to their success in implementing the new initiatives. All bosses were to be subjected to lengthy 360-degree annual evaluations, which would include diversity issues, and compensation would be tied to their performance in, as Bijur puts it, "creating openness and inclusion in the workplace."

Yet Bijur isn't ready to declare victory (white men, after all, still account for nearly 80% of company executives), though he's clearly satisfied with what he sees as concrete signs of a cultural shift. "Now," he says, "we treat all people with the utmost respect—that is a real achievement." It appears as if the stereotypes that created The Crisis are finally dissipating.

INTRODUCTION

Organizations are made up of individuals who are trying to combine their efforts for mutual benefit, much as the people of Texaco are working toward a more inclusive environment. The better managers understand how and why individuals act the way they do—for example, the better they understand the idiosyncrasies of individual generations—the better they can help these individuals work together efficiently and effectively. This has always been a valuable skill that some managers are better at than others. However, as the workforce becomes increasingly more diverse and conducting business abroad becomes ever more common, developing this skill has become not only valuable but essential.

Psychologist Kurt Lewin was eager to quantify individual behavior, and, as part of his attempt to do so, he proposed the following equation, which captures the most fundamental principle of individual behavior[1]:

$$B = f(P, S)$$

According to this equation, all individual behavior (B) can be explained as a function (f) of (that is, is caused by) something inside the person (P) and something outside the person in the situation (S), or context. In terms of Lewin's equation, a manager is challenged to understand two things: what people bring to the organization (P) and what situations (S) must be created in the organization in order to encourage appropriate behaviors (B).

This chapter provides the foundation for answering that management challenge. The chapter begins by exploring how individuals come to know the situations (S) in which they find themselves—the processes of perception. Then the chapter focuses on two important aspects of what individuals bring to organizations (P): their attitudes and their personality.

---

1. Lewin, K. (1970). Behavior and development as a function of the total situation. In L. Carmichael (Ed.), *Manual of child psychology* (pp. 791–844). New York: Wiley.

THE PROCESS OF PERCEPTION

Perception is an individual's window to the world. People first learn about the world through a neurological process called *sensation*. When you put your hand on a hot stove or someone calls your name, your nervous system comes alive, and nerve endings send signals to your brain. At that point, however, there is still no meaning attached to what is occurring. Perception is the process of attaching meaning to the neurological sensations the body is experiencing. Perception is an *active* process in which the perceiver plays an important role.

Much as an artist interprets an image when painting a picture, the process of perception is a process of interpretation. More specifically, it is a process of selecting, interpreting, and giving meaning to the world. Figure 2-1 illustrates the three components that comprise this process—attention, construction, and interpretation of sensory inputs.

ATTENTION

It is easy to forget that our sensory systems are constantly bombarded with a wide variety of inputs or messages. In the workplace, we are exposed to colleagues, customers, e-mail, voicemail, pagers, meetings, newspapers, and ma-

■ FIGURE 2-1

The Processes of Perception

Perception is an active process in which the perceiver plays an important role. The perceiver selectively attends to sensory inputs, constructs a representation of the inputs, and then interprets the construction. Both the perceiver and the source of the sensory inputs—either the object of perception or the context in which the perception occurs—can influence this process. Perceptions then become essential influences on subsequent actions of the perceiver.

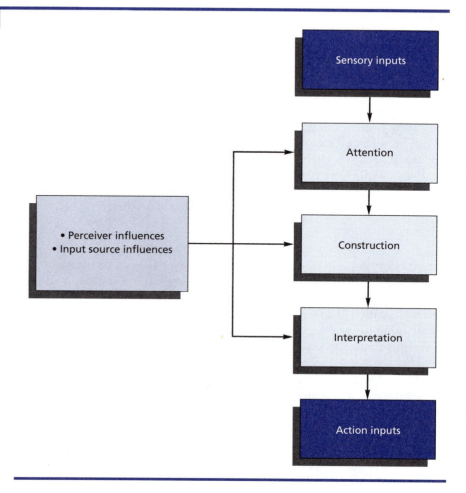

chinery. Our **attention**—where we choose to direct our sensory input system—is a scarce resource that we must direct and ration.

Psychological research has repeatedly demonstrated the limitations of the human sensory input system. Imagine yourself walking along the street. A car drives by. You are in a position to notice the license plate, features of the car, and characteristics of the driver. But do you actually perceive these things? Although we are exposed to an infinite number of sensory inputs, at any given moment we can focus ourselves on only a limited number of them. We can attend to only a limited selection, a sample of all the inputs we are receiving, and hope the sample is representative. Some of the directing and rationing of our attention comes from within—from our expectations and agendas, for instance. But this sampling of our attention is influenced by both internal and external stimuli, by our own expectations and agendas, as well as the sources of the stimuli themselves.

For example, if the car in the earlier example didn't have any distinguishing characteristics, the car would go unnoticed. If, however, the car was full of noisy teenagers playing loud music (unlike other cars), we are likely to take notice. This process of selecting among a number of available sensory inputs is called **accommodation.** Accommodation occurs when a perceiver ignores a sensory input because the input is unchanging. With so many sensory inputs to choose from, the inputs that do not grab your attention immediately are the first to be ignored. Accommodation, however, is only one of several processes that determine which sensory inputs are processed. Other influences by the perceiver and from the input source are discussed in the following sections.

PERCEIVER INFLUENCES. A perceiver's attention can be influenced tremendously by theories that the perceiver harbors about the way the world works. For example, at Texaco a manager's perceptions about the managerial effectiveness of women and minorities could seriously—prior to The Crisis—influence whether they chose minority- or women-owned vendors. New policies implemented after The Crisis, however, have seriously altered the Texaco managers' behaviors. If the minorities and women are successful vendors, this experience may alter the Texaco managers' perceptions of women and minorities as well. Regardless, a manager who believes that being a minority or female negatively influences a person's business capabilities will be more likely to notice (attend to) whether a vendor is minority or female owned.

The needs and motivations of a perceiver can have a similar influence on the rationing of attention. A hungry individual entering a dining room will probably notice what kinds of foods are available. Needs and motivations also can lead someone to observe objects or events carefully enough to pick up important nuances and distinctions that would otherwise be missed. An aspiring junior executive, for example, is likely to pay extra attention to the boss's actions (and perhaps thereby gain important insights into the boss's behavior) in the hopes of gleaning hints about how to get promoted.

Because our attention is finite, there are times when we focus on unimportant characteristics or information and miss the more relevant content. This happens frequently in job interviews, with the result that the interviewer misses critical information that could help him or her predict the job success or failure of the candidate. For example, an interviewer may attend to an applicant's age, race, or gender, while overlooking other, more important

No doubt your eye was drawn to this picture when you first turned the page. The picture's distinctive patterns make it particularly salient, or eye catching. Without the correct perceptual set, however, it would take you a few seconds to arrive at a correct perception of the picture. It's the S&P 500 Index trading pit on the floor of the Chicago Mercantile Exchange.

details about the individual. To minimize this problem, we must have a way to decide which inputs to attend to and which to ignore, whether we're conducting a job interview or performing other business activities. Most of us begin with good theories—ways in which we make sense of the world around us. Only then are we likely to attend to the most valuable sensory inputs.

INPUT SOURCE INFLUENCES. As noted in the job candidate example, sometimes a characteristic of the source object or event, called an **input source influence,** is particularly eye catching and commands the perceiver's attention. Several characteristics in particular are likely to make the source object or event more salient.

Because they are different from what surrounds them, new and novel sensory inputs demand attention, as do objects and images that are particularly vivid and bright.

Personal perspective can also profoundly influence which sensory inputs are considered. Thus, an individual's own contributions to a project or event are much more salient than the contributions of others. You never miss what you yourself contribute, but you may miss what others contribute. It is not surprising then that when asked to evaluate the portion of their contribution to a joint project, members of a group routinely provide answers that total more than 100%. We all think we do more than our fair share because our share is more salient to us than others' contributions.

■ **FIGURE 2-2**   **Differences in Perception between Supervisors and Subordinates**

Supervisors and subordinates have different needs, different expectations, and different perspectives (that is, different input sources), so it is no surprise that their perceptions regarding their own supervisor-subordinate relationship differ in significantly important ways. The difference in perception can lead to conflict. The chart below shows significant mean differences in perception of the supervisor and the subordinate when viewed from each perspective.

Relationship Dimension	Supervisor's Perception (Mean)	Subordinate's Perception (Mean)
1 Does the subordinate know where he or she stands?	3.22	3.81
2 How well does the supervisor understand the subordinate's job problems and needs?	4.42	4.00
3 How well does the supervisor recognize the subordinate's potential?	4.30	3.93
4 Chances that the supervisor would use his or her power to help solve the subordinate's work-related problems?	4.54	4.10
5 Chances that the supervisor would bail out the subordinate at his or her expense?	3.47	4.30
6 Chances that the supervisor would defend the subordinate's decisions even when he or she is not present?	4.00	4.30
7 Overall relationship?	4.25	4.2

Source: Adapted from Varma, A., & Srinivas, E. S. (2000). The relationship between leader-member exchange and subordinate satisfaction with supervisors: A comparative study of U.S. and Indian employees. Proceedings of the Second Asia Academy of Management Meeting (Singapore, December).

Differences in personal perspective can go a long way toward explaining how conflict occurs in organizations; for example, consider the consequences of the differences between supervisor and subordinate perceptions shown in Figure 2-2. Although both supervisor and subordinate agree on the strength of the relationship (4.25 on a 5-point scale), they significantly disagree on other important aspects of the relationship (for example, subordinate's potential, whether the supervisor would "bail" out the subordinate in a difficult situation, understanding of the subordinate's problems and needs). All these differences in perception can lead to future conflicts between them.

Source characteristics have their greatest influence on attention under conditions of **information overload,** when there are too many attention-grabbing sensory inputs. In familiar surroundings, in which many features of the environment are well known and require little attention, plenty of attention is available for new or unusual objects or events. In novel situations, in which someone doesn't have prior knowledge about where to direct attention to the numerous unusual inputs, novel characteristics of the objects and events (for instance, motion, vividness) are likely to command the most attention.

CONSTRUCTION

After sensory inputs have been selected for further processing, the perceiver uses them to construct a representation of the event or object being attended to. The **construction** process organizes and edits the sensory inputs in a way that makes them potentially meaningful. Like our attention, this process is subject to both perceiver and input source influences.

PERCEIVER INFLUENCES. One of the strongest influences on the construction process of perception is the perceiver's **perceptual set**—in other words, the expectations that the perceiver brings to the task of perception. What a perceiver expects or wants to see plays a major role in the perception he or she constructs.

Research by Nobel Prize winner Herbert Simon describes a graphic case study involving the effects of perceptual set.[2] The case study describes the problems faced by the CEO of a major corporation. After reading the case, a group of executives from different departments of major companies were asked to analyze the cause of the CEO's problems. Not surprisingly, each executive perceived the cause to be within his or her specialty. The marketing executives, for example, saw a marketing problem, the finance executives saw a finance problem, and so on. Simon's research demonstrates how we are influenced by our expectations. In this study, each executive brought to the task a perceptual set—his or her own business specialty—which, in turn, determined his or her perception of the CEO's problems. One can recognize how in Texaco managers, untrained and inexperienced with inclusion efforts, failed to develop and promote qualified women and minorities. Another example of the influence of perceptual set on constructions, in the domain of college sports, is shown in "FOCUS ON: Perceiver Influences on Construction."

Interestingly, recent research by Janice Beyer and her associates shapes this theory further. When working with 137 master's of business administration (MBA) students from a large southwestern university, their findings

2. Simon, H. (1945). *Administrative behavior.* New York: Macmillan.

FOCUS ON PERCEIVER INFLUENCES ON CONSTRUCTION

THEY SAW A GAME. The role of perceiver motivations in constructing perceptions is regularly on display when a perceiver's self-image is on the line. For example, if a perceiver identifies with a sports team—takes pride in the team's wins and wallows in misery when the team loses—the perceiver has a vested interest in the team's actions being right and good. This vested interest dramatically affects constructed perceptions about the team's actions, as demonstrated in the following study of fan reactions to a football game:

> Anyone who has observed the spectators at athletic events can't help noticing that two apparently reasonable people can experience a play in football or basketball in very different ways as a function of having been "tuned" by different expectations and purposes. This fact of experience was illustrated by a case study of a football game. It so happened that Dartmouth and Princeton played each other in football one November afternoon. The game turned out to be very rough, and tempers flared both during and after the game. Im-

mediately following the game, partisans for both schools made accusations that the other school had played rough and dirty football. The school papers, the school alumni magazines, and a number of metropolitan newspapers highly publicized the whole affair. There was clearly a very real disagreement as to what had actually happened during the game. What is of special interest . . . were the results of showing a movie of the game to a group of Dartmouth students and a group of Princeton students. Keeping in mind that an identical movie was shown to both groups of students, it is interesting to [note] the number of infractions perceived in the same film by two groups of people with different loyalties and different expectations. Students . . . tended to see the team from the other university as having committed the most infractions.

Source: Excerpted from Schneider, D. J., Hastorf, A. H., & Ellsworth, P. C. (1979). *Person perception.* Reading, MA: Addison-Wesley, p. 4.

---

showed that when an individual's work experience does influence his or her information processing, it may actually be due to the person's *not* perceiving *unrelated* areas.[3] The individual appears to put blinders around his or her perceptual set and fails to see other areas or possibilities. For example, a marketing executive may see a marketing problem because he selectively imperceived—that is, excluded from his perceptual set—the finance and accounting areas.

Another, more dangerous, form of a perceptual set is prejudice. Prejudice is the tendency of an individual to prejudge the actions of another individual according to a set of beliefs, and as we can see through the Texaco example, it can have serious ramifications. Research by Martin Greller and Linda Stroh shows that if an executive believes that older workers are less technologically astute than younger workers, the executive will be likely to perceive all the technological problems older workers encounter as a function of their age, and ultimately be prejudiced against older workers and

---

3. Beyer, J. M., George, E., Glick, W. H., & Pugliese, D. (1997). The selective perception of managers revisited. *Academy of Management Journal, 40*(3), 716–737.

their ability to use technology.[4] As we shall see, perceptual sets influence not only perceptual constructions but also the meanings people attach to these constructions.

INPUT SOURCE INFLUENCES. Characteristics of the source of sensory inputs—the object or event being perceived—also can influence the perceptual construction process. Three examples of such influences are contrast, anchoring-and-adjustment, and halo effects. All three arise when one sensory input influences the construction of perceptions of other sensory inputs.

Contrast effects occur when an individual sees something as larger or smaller than it really is because he or she is comparing the object or event to a very small or very large reference point. Think how you would feel about a $3,000 increase in your annual salary. If your last increase was only $1,000, this raise would seem generous by comparison. However, if you learned that a coworker received a $10,000 increase, your $3,000 would seem paltry. Of course, $3,000 is $3,000. It's the contrast with other reference points—either $1,000 or $10,000—that makes the raise seem large or small.

Anchoring-and-adjustment effects are the flip side of contrast effects. Contrast effects occur when we construct two sensory inputs as more dissimilar than they really are; anchoring-and-adjustment effects occur when our perceptual system constructs two sensory inputs to be more *similar* than they should be. Imagine that you are trying to assign a value to something—for instance, how much a particular employee should be paid. A friend suggests that you pay the new employee $50,000, which you reject as too high. This suggestion, even though you rejected it, nevertheless has an effect on your thinking. Knowing that the suggested amount is too high, you would adjust away from it (lower) in formulating your perception of what would be fair. However, research has repeatedly demonstrated that adjustments of this sort are almost always skewed or biased. In this case, insufficient adjustment down from the $50,000 suggestion would result in the new employee getting a higher salary than he or she would have otherwise. If the suggested salary had been $5,000, you would have rejected it as well and adjusted upward. However, again, the adjustment would have been insufficient, producing a bias to perceive a lower salary as fair.

Interestingly, the ability of an anchor (such as a suggested salary) to influence perceptual construction does not seem to depend on whether the clue is sensible. In one research study of anchoring-and-adjustment effects, students were asked to estimate the proportion of African countries in the United Nations (UN). Before making their estimates, each student was given a number to consider from one spin of a "wheel of fortune." Obviously this random number could not be a useful clue in deciding the correct proportion of African countries in the UN. Nevertheless, the numbers the students obtained from their spins clearly influenced their estimates.[5]

Halo effects also influence sensory inputs by influencing when the perception of an object or event on one dimension influences the construction of perceptions of that object or event on other dimensions. A physically attractive individual, for instance, may be perceived as more competent than a

---

4. Greller, M. M., & Stroh, L. K. (1995). Careers in midlife and beyond: A fallow field in need of sustenance. *Journal of Vocational Behavior, 47,* 232–247.

5. Tversky, A., & Kahneman, D. (1974). Judgment under uncertainty: Heuristics and biases. *Science, 185,* 1124–1131.

worker who is less physically attractive. Why? Because physical attractiveness is a positive attribute and therefore creates a positive halo. Other traits of the attractive individual (such as his or her ability or accomplishments) are perceived as more positive because of the positive halo.

Contrast, anchoring-and-adjustment, and "halo" effects all are examples of how one sensory input can influence the constructed perception of another. These effects arise, of course, as a reaction to uncertainty. Your perception of your own age is not likely to be influenced by anchoring and adjustment. Nor is your perception of your physical attractiveness likely to influence your perception of your age. Your age is something you know. However, you can only construct perceptions of most things.

The perceptual construction process is an uncertain one because you never know if you are seeing things the way they really are. This uncertainty makes perceptual construction vulnerable to influence.

INTERPRETATION

The processes of selection and construction provide the perceiver with only a representation of an object or event. The object or event still has no meaning to the individual. The final stage, in which the perceiver attaches meaning to the object or event, is known as **interpretation.**

One process people use to assign meaning to actions and their outcomes—to interpret—is **attribution.** Attribution is the process of perceiving the causes of actions and outcomes. For example, when a foreman yells at a worker, what caused the yelling? Was it something the worker did? something the worker didn't do? something the foreman ate? Perhaps the foreman just likes to yell at everyone. Needless to say, these are important distinctions. Should the worker take the yelling as important criticism, write it off as evidence that the foreman is having a bad day, or conclude that yelling is something everyone on this job needs to learn to live with? Determining whether the foreman is yelling (as opposed to talking normally) is a matter of attention and construction. Yelling in and of itself is not an important sensory input. The *meaning* of the yelling is what counts.

Attributions are particularly useful because they provide models for how the people around us function, what their motives are, and what determines their behavior, as discussed in the "INTERNATIONAL FOCUS ON: Attribution Theory." These models in turn reduce our uncertainty in social interactions. If we understand how others are likely to behave and why, we can use this knowledge to achieve our goals. Attributions help us to understand cause-and-effect relationships such as what caused the foreman to yell and therefore to predict when he is likely to yell again. Attributions also enable us to predict the future behavior of others based on our understanding of the causes of their past and present behavior. Attributions, then, are critical to formulating action plans for the future.

PROCESSES OF ATTRIBUTION. Psychologist Harold Kelley, the founding father of the theory of attribution, stated that the central principle of attribution is **covariation.** Covariation is when "an effect is attributed to that condition which is present when the effect is present and absent when the effect is absent."[6] In this instance, the condition is said to covary with the

6. Kelley, H. H. (1967). Attribution theory in social psychology. In D. Levine (Ed.), *Nebraska symposium on motivation*, volume 15 (pp. 192–240). Lincoln, NE: University of Nebraska Press.

INTERNATIONAL FOCUS ON ATTRIBUTION THEORY

THE INTERNATIONAL SCENE. Researchers have found that just as individuals differ in the attributes that define their personalities, so too cultures differ in the attributes they exhibit. One trait in which cultures are not the same is the degree to which they are individualist or collectivist. In individualist cultures (for example, Australia, Great Britain, the United States), the focus is on the self; the achievements of individuals are emphasized over those of the group or community. In collectivist cultures (for example, China, India, Taiwan), the focus is much more on the community.

These observations have led to a closely related question: Do individualist cultures and collectivist cultures differ in how they attribute behavior? As more and more managers take positions in cultures different from their own, knowing this answer has taken on practical, compelling interest. Understanding the locals' behavior can mean the difference between success and failure in a foreign assignment.

Recent research has demonstrated that in fact individualist and collectivist cultures do differ in their attributions for behavior, but that people in both kinds of cultures view personality and behavior as being closely correlated. The research indicates that individualists come to more dispositional (that is, personality-based) attributions for behavior, whereas collectivists are likely to rely more on situational (that is, environment-based) explanations. It is increasingly important, therefore, for managers working in different cultures to perceive workers' behaviors in the context of the culture in which they live. What might be seen as appropriate in the United States, for example, might not be appropriate in Japan, and vice versa.

Source: Adapted from Trompenaars, F. (1998). *Riding the waves of culture: Understanding diversity in global business.* New York: McGraw-Hill; Krull, D. S., Loy, M. H., Lin, J., Wang, C., Chen, S., & Zhao, X. (1999). The fundamental attribution error: Correspondence bias in individualist and collectivist cultures. *Personality & Social Psychology Bulletin, 25,* 1208–1219.

effect. Conditions that covary with an effect are often perceived to cause the effect. For example, if a worker's performance is good (the effect) when the worker is supervised (the condition) but poor when the worker isn't supervised, then the supervision will be perceived as the cause of the worker's good performance. People judge covariation in three ways: via distinctiveness, consensus, and consistency.

Imagine that your boss has just complimented you (the effect) on a report that you recently submitted. You are wondering what to make of this compliment. What meaning should you attach to your boss's remark, and what implications does that meaning hold for your future behavior? Was the quality of your report the cause of your boss's compliment? To sort out this uncertainty, you would want to note whether the compliment was *distinctive*: Does your boss compliment people all the time, or is this a rare event?

Another way in which people judge covariance is via *consensus*—whether the condition produces the same effect for other people. Assume that your boss's compliment was distinctive and therefore merits further search for a cause. If other people read the report and also complimented it, you would have evidence that there is covariation between the report and the compliment across people—in other words, consensus that the quality of the report (the condition) caused the compliment (the effect).

Finally, you might look at the *consistency* of your boss's compliments across time and situations. Does your boss compliment you for all your reports, or did she single out this report in particular? Has she complimented you on other reports on the same topic? Has she complimented you for

■ **FIGURE 2-3** | **Attributions**

Our attributions, or explanations, for events (that is, actions and their outcomes) are critical to our responses to those events. This table provides a framework for our attributions and the responses those attributions occasion. For example, we are likely to punish an employee who failed at an assignment if we think he or she didn't make an effort. On the other hand, we may help an employee who failed if we think he or she is lacking a certain ability.

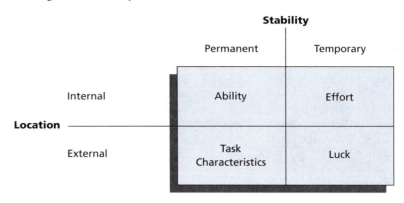

Source: Weiner, B. (1975). *Achievement motivation and attribution theory.* Morristown, NJ: General Learning Press.

other reports written in this same style? These questions are all aimed at isolating the cause of the boss's compliment by finding consistencies between the appearance of the effect and plausible causes.

Attributions are important because different attributions merit different responses. Figure 2-3 provides a framework for the different types of attributions you might arrive at for a subordinate's performance. This framework has two dimensions: location of the cause and stability of the cause. Location can be internal (the individual) or external (outside the individual); stability can be permanent or temporary. As shown in the figure, these two dimensions yield four different causes for behaviors: luck, effort, task characteristics, and ability/personality. Each cause carries with it a different recommendation for action.

The framework of possible attributions also suggests how we come to understand the personality of another individual. Personality is used to describe the tendency of an individual to behave consistently across situations and across time. We attribute an individual's behaviors to stable internal causes when that individual behaves similarly across situations and across time, and unlike other people. In effect, personality is the cause assigned to consistent behavior that cannot be explained otherwise.

PERCEIVER INFLUENCES. Attribution is not the discovery of true causes of behavior; rather, it is an individual's interpretation of the likely causes of behavior and outcomes. Attribution represents the attempts of an individual to make causal sense of the world. Unfortunately, like the perceptual processes of attention and construction, attribution is subject to influences.

One important source of attributional influence is personal perspective. When we observe the behaviors of another individual, the most salient plausible cause of that individual's behavior is that individual. When we ourselves act, our own persons are not a salient component of the scene. In fact, most

RESEARCH IN ACTION
TO GET SHIPPED ABROAD, WOMEN MUST OVERCOME PREJUDICE AT HOME

Linda K. Stroh, Professor of Human Resources and Industrial Relations, Loyola University Chicago; *lstroh@luc.edu*

When it comes to corporate assignments overseas, women have a problem: They are often overlooked as candidates. As a result, although they represent about half the global workforce, women account for less than 12% of managers and other employees on global assignments. My colleagues, Arup Varma, Loyola University and Stacey Valy-Durbin, Fort James Corporation, and I examined the reasons. We sampled 341 female expatriates, repatriates, and inpatriates from 60 multinational companies that were members of the International Personnel Association (IPA), an association of 60 of the top multinationals in the United States and Canada. Our findings suggest that women are underrepresented on international assignments because many male managers perceive that women aren't interested in or won't be effective in overseas positions. The managers in the study cited dual-career complications, gender prejudice in many host countries, and the risk of sexual harassment as justification for male managers' perceptions.

Our study shows, however, that women are in fact just as interested as men in international assignments and just as effective once they're in them. Further, the traits considered crucial for success in conducting business overseas—knowing when to be passive, being a team player, and soliciting a variety of perspectives—are more often associated with women's management styles than with men's. So how can women overcome their supervisors' misperceptions? According to our study findings, women need to take the responsibility to make sure managers know they're interested in going overseas. They should also demonstrate their ability to be cultural chameleons and that they have their family's strong support. Findings further suggested that male supervisors must shed their misperceptions that women do not want to go on international assignments and that women may not be effective managers in cross-cultural settings.

In addition, because women are often perceived to be less mobile than men, they need to be particularly vocal in expressing their interest in overseas assignments during meetings and performance reviews. They should also find mentors with international experience and seek out assignments that require international travel and project teams that include international divisions. When study findings were reported to these 60 multinational companies, Sven Grasshoff, vice president, international HR, for Citibank, and former chair of the IPA, summarized the policy changes that would occur in his organization: Women would be included in the recruiting and selection process, and women would have the first right of refusal before being dropped from the pool of potential candidates for an international assignment. Grasshoff stresses that other company members of the IPA must also address female managers' concerns aggressively, if they intend to have the best candidates for their overseas assignments.

of us rarely see ourselves behaving at all. Instead, we see only the environment to which we are responding.

Furthermore, we see our own behaviors in a variety of different settings, such as at home, at work, and at play. This is not true of many of the other individuals with whom we interact; typically, we see them only in considerably more limited circumstances. We see some people only at work, for instance. As a result, the diversity of circumstances in which we observe their behaviors is quite limited. We may mistakenly see their behavior as consistent across circumstances, when in fact their behavior is consistent only over the extremely limited set of circumstances associated with work.

These consequences of personal perspective—the salience of others as plausible causes of their behaviors and the limited diversity of circumstances in which to view others' behaviors—give rise to an important perceptual bias known as the **fundamental attribution error.**[7] The fundamental attribution error is the tendency of a perceiver to see others' behaviors as caused primarily by stable, internal characteristics (such as personality) while seeing one's own behavior primarily as a response to environmental circumstances. The fundamental attribution error suggests that explanations for actions will typically take the form "I did it because the circumstances demanded it; he did it because that's the kind of person he is."

The fundamental attribution error is important in the context of organizational behavior because of the role that a supervisor's attributions play in evaluating employee behaviors. Supervisors are likely to conclude that a subordinate's behavior reveals something about the subordinate and therefore is worthy of blame or praise. In contrast, the subordinate is likely to believe that that same behavior is simply a sensible reaction to environmental cues—what anyone would have done under the same circumstances.

INPUT SOURCE INFLUENCES. Sometimes we forget that other people represent a significant feature of the perceptual process in which actions and consequences occur. Because others often are present when we are trying to interpret ambiguous sensory inputs, others' actions can also influence our perceptions. If a classmate says that a test you and she just took was difficult, you may be disposed to also see the test as having been difficult, especially if you weren't sure what to think. In effect, the comments and opinions of others can anchor our perceptions and judgments. This process is called *social comparison*, and it is discussed in greater detail in Chapter 7.

ATTITUDES

If an individual's perception is his or her window to the world, then attitudes are the world's window to that individual. **Attitudes** are predispositions to respond in consistent ways to certain people, groups, ideas, or situations.[8] Figure 2-4 suggests that attitudes are simply a reflection of our perceptions of a situation. We perceive something in our organization—a conflict, for example. That perception leads us to have beliefs, which we evaluate against our belief systems and values. For example, in the Texaco Crisis, employees, stockholders and even the general public became aware of (perceived) a severe form of prejudice, and most likely therefore created beliefs about the organization—that they were racist, an "old boys' club," and so on.

Our **belief system** is our stored set of theories and expectations about how and why the world works; our **values** represent our core understanding of what is important to us. This leads us to have **affects**—favorable or unfavorable evaluations of our beliefs—about the conflict. In turn, the beliefs and affects predispose us to act in a particular way concerning the conflict.

7. Jones, E. E., & Nisbett, R. E. (1972). The actor and the observer: Divergent perceptions of the causes of behavior. In E. E. Jones et al. (Eds.), *Ambition: Perceiving the causes of behavior* Morristown, NJ: General Learning Press.

8. George, J. M., & Jones, G. R. (1997). Experiencing work: Values, attitudes, and moods. *Human Relations, 50,* 393–416.

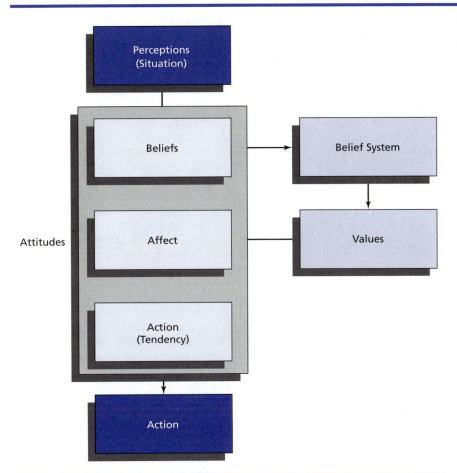

■ **FIGURE 2-4**

Attitudes

Attitudes represent an evaluation of our perceptions against our internal belief systems and values. Attitudes include beliefs, affect, and tendencies to act.

For example, consider the attitude you have toward committees. Perhaps you avoid committees (a tendency to act) because you have negative feelings about them (an affect) and you think that committees are a waste of time (a belief). You probably feel that they are a waste of time because you can't accomplish other tasks during the time they monopolize (beliefs about your beliefs), and it is more important to do other things (the value you attach to those beliefs). Thus, our attitudes are not just a reflection of our perceptions, but they also reflect our belief system and our values.

Because values are relatively stable and enduring personal characteristics, it should not be surprising that some of our attitudes—for instance, our satisfaction with our jobs—also turn out to be quite stable over many years. The "TECHNOLOGY FOCUS ON: Attitudes" further looks at attitudes, specifically in today's workplace.

SELF-PERCEPTION

Unfortunately, even this may be too simple an explanation of how our attitudes develop. Figure 2-4 suggests that we always perceive, form attitudes, and then act accordingly—that actions are a result of attitudes. Sometimes, however, uncertainty, complexity, and conflict may reverse this causal chain. Sometimes we act and only later try to understand why we did so—what our

TECHNOLOGY FOCUS ON
ATTITUDES

WITH LABOR IN SHORT SUPPLY, COMPANIES ARE PULLING OUT ALL THE STOPS FOR EMPLOYEES. So what's the state of the workplace at the turn of the 21st century? One might suggest that our attitudes have changed significantly. Go to Orange County, California, where 20-somethings Jennifer Withers, an administrative assistant, and her husband, Dave, a programmer at electronics firm Odetics, cashed in stock options for a down payment on a townhouse. Or go to New York, where management consultant Susan Sweet just had her Christmas cards hand addressed and a billing dispute with a dry cleaner resolved through a concierge service provided by her employer, Ernst & Young.

Welcome to the brave new workplace, as revealed in *Fortune's* third annual survey to determine the 100 Best Companies to Work for in America. In an ultratight labor market, compa-

nies primp to woo and retain talent, and struggle to make the lists that have become so valuable.

The growth of new hot technology firms is often considered responsible for this competitive labor market. The technology firms typically have more casual work environments, more opportunity for greater earnings, and more of an entrepreneurial spirit—all characteristics that are increasingly more appealing to workers. See for yourself. Here's a snapshot of the 100 Best Companies to work for: They're in 20 different fields and in 30 states; however, a whopping 42 are in information technology or financial services. There are also stars in retailing, pipe manufacturing, supermarkets, the jam business, and even law firms, but most of the best companies to work for are firmly grounded in technology in a major way. Companies in other industries have had to become very creative to compete with the technology firms for talent.

Companies that do right by employees seem to do right by stockholders. Shares of public companies on the 100 Best Companies list rose 37% annualized over the past 3 years, compared with a 25% increase in the S&P 500. Is it a coincidence that these public companies did so much better than the S&P index? Maybe. But the list does reflect a fundamental change in the economy. A century ago the most valuable U.S. corporation was U.S. Steel, whose primary assets were smokestack factories. Today's most valuable corporations are those whose most valuable assets go home every night (e.g. Microsoft, Intel). Companies that want those assets to return every morning must pay attention to the attitudes in the workplace and how they are perceived both internally and externally.

Source: Excerpted from Levering, R., & Moskowitz, M. (2000, January 10). The 100 best companies to work for: With labor in short supply, these companies are pulling out all the stops for employees. *Fortune, 141,* 82–110.

attitude must have been. In this case, we evaluate our own action to form an attitude. When we examine our own actions in this way, we are engaging in **self-perception.** We are trying to make sense of our own behaviors, a process known as *rationalization.*

Rationalization occurs in a couple different ways. One way is through a **self-serving bias**—the tendency of individuals to attribute the causes of actions or their outcomes in a way that reflects well on them or absolves them from responsibility for poor outcomes. Self-serving attributions can take one of two forms:

1 They explain an action as a sensible response to situational demands or constraints. In this case, they admit that the action taken was wrong but excuse it as a sensible reaction to the situation.
2 They explain the action as the result of causes external to the individual (such as the interfering behaviors of others). This form suggests that the action taken might have been correct but that it didn't produce a good outcome for reasons beyond the individual's control.

In one demonstration of self-serving attribution bias, several groups of students played a game in which they were responsible for governing a fictitious nation torn by revolution. Many decisions were required during the game, and the researcher arranged for each group of students to meet with some significant successes and some significant disasters. The researchers found that students tended to place blame for the failures on situational circumstances but claimed responsibility or credit for the successes.[9] (Teachers demonstrate similar self-serving attributional biases when they credit their high-quality instruction for their students' successes but blame the students' lack of effort for their failures.[10]) Research by Gerald Salancik and James Meindl shows that in their annual reports to stockholders, unstable corporations often attribute their past successes and failures in ways that emphasize management's ability to control corporate performance and therefore improve it in the future.[11] This form of self-serving bias can affect the attitudes of stockholders and potential investors, and consequently, their actions.

Self-perception also comes into play when an individual acts quickly and only later reflects on why he or she took a certain action. If we engage in actions that are mysterious even to ourselves (for instance, because we do not wish to admit to our subconscious motives), we arrive at an understanding of our attitudes that explains our actions. Imagine that you do something with a friend that you know you should not do—trading on the stock market based on insider information, for example. After the fact, you might convince yourself that it was important to go along with the friend, rather than admit that you really wanted to take advantage of the insider information. You have rationalized your behavior (that is, made it appear sensible) by deciding what your attitude must have been. If there are environmental forces (such as incentives or requests by powerful others) that could have "caused" our behaviors, we are unlikely to attribute the actions to our own attitudes.

OBJECTIVE SELF-AWARENESS. Self-perception biases can be alleviated by encouraging individuals to see their actions as others would see them. Making an individual more aware of his or her role in causing actions or their consequences is helpful. Distinguishing between one's personal moti-

9. Streufert, S., & Streufert, S. C. (1969). Effect of conceptual structure, failure, and success on attribution of causality and interpersonal attitude. *Journal of Personality and Social Psychology, 11*, 138–147.
10. Johnson, T. J., Feigenbaum, R., & Weiby, M. (1964). Some determinants and consequences of the teacher's perception of causality. *Journal of Educational Psychology, 55*, 237–246.
11. Salancik, G. R., & Meindl, J. R. (1984). Corporate attributions as strategic illusions of management control. *Administrative Sciences Quarterly, 29*, 238–254.

vations or preferences and simple reaction to environmental demands is necessary to alleviate self-perception bias. An actor's awareness of his or her own role in causing behaviors and their consequences is called **objective self-awareness.** Studies have shown that without such awareness individuals make more situational attributions for their actions and consequences, as discussed previously.[12]

What happens, however, when individuals are instead given feedback that highlights their roles in the actions? What happens, for example, when individuals view videotapes of their behavior? Individuals then attribute more of their behaviors and consequences to themselves—to their own attitudes—just as an impartial observer would. Objective self-awareness helps an individual see himself or herself at the center of the action and thereby eliminates a major source of differences between processes of perception applied to the self and to others.

PERSONALITY

Personality has been defined as the characteristics of an individual that cause consistent patterns in that individual's behaviors over time.[13] Personality represents a predisposition to have particular beliefs, attitudes, and behaviors. Although attitudes often change, and values may evolve over time, personality is usually thought of as more enduring and stable. In fact, research shows that personality differences assessed in childhood are valid predictors of career success later in life.[14]

Personality is typically discussed in terms of **traits** or characteristics, such as conservative and imaginative, that are usually expressed as a dimension on which every person can be measured. As relatively enduring characteristics, personality traits are likely to predispose an individual to particular beliefs, attitudes, and behaviors.

THE BIG FIVE PERSONALITY TRAITS

Psychologist Raymond Cattell was the pioneer in the search for a set of universal personality traits.[15] He used direct observations of a large number of people in everyday life and a variety of questionnaires to elicit 16 primary personality traits identified in pairs of polar-opposite words, such as relaxed versus tense and serious versus happy-go-lucky.

However, the most recent development in the search for a universal set of primary personality traits has identified five primary dimensions of personality.[16] This is noteworthy in the context of organizational behavior because researchers believe that an individual's personality influences his or her behav-

12. Wicklund, R. A. (1975). Objective self-awareness. In L. Berkowitz (Ed.), *Advances in experimental social psychology, 8* (pp. 233–273). New York: Academic Press.

13. Pervin, L. A. (1984). *Personality.* New York: Wiley; and Mischel, W. (1986). *Introduction to personality.* New York: Holt, Rinehart & Winston.

14. Judge, T. A., Higgins, C. A., & Thoresen, C. J. (1999). The big five personality traits, general mental ability, and career success across life span. *Personnel Psychology, 52,* 621–652.

15. Cattell, R., Saunders, D., & Stice, G. (1950). *The 16 personality factor questionnaire.* New York: Academic Press; and Cattell, R. (1965). *The scientific analysis of personality.* Baltimore: Penguin.

16. Revelle, W. (1995). Personality processes. *Annual Review of Psychology, 46,* 295–328.

The Five Dimensions of Personality	■ **FIGURE 2-5**

Almost all personality measures can be categorized under these "Big Five" personality traits:

1 **Extraversion**—Sociable, talkative, assertive, ambitious, active
2 **Emotional stability**—Calm, secure, not nervous
3 **Agreeableness**—Considerate, cooperative, trusting
4 **Openness to experience**—Imaginative, artistically sensitive, intellectual
5 **Conscientiousness**—Responsible, dependable, organized, achievement oriented

Source: Mount, M. K., Barrick, M. R., & Strauss, J. P. (1999). The joint relationship of conscientiousness and ability with performance: Test of the interaction hypothesis. *Journal of Management, 25,* 707–721.

ior in a work setting.[17] Referred to as the "Big Five," these traits include extraversion/intraversion, emotional stability, agreeableness, openness to experience, and conscientiousness,[18] and they are defined in Figure 2-5. Research in the 1990s supports the generalizability of these traits across almost every culture and suggests that they remain fairly stable over a person's lifetime.[19]

In fact, in a study of 123 pairs of identical twins and 127 pairs of fraternal twins conducted by Kerry Jang, W. John Livesley, and Philip Vernon, the big five traits were shown to be largely—between 40% and 60%—inheritable.[20] The researchers addressed both genetic and environmental factors in an effort to better understand the origin of a person's personality structure (that is, the five dimensions of personality). An individual attempting to choose a career could infer from this research that he or she should look at the traits he or she has demonstrated throughout life—perhaps even witnessed his or her parents—to identify the perfect match. Research by Jennifer Chatman, David Caldwell, and Charles O'Reilly builds on this notion by suggesting that to find the perfect fit between an individual and a career, one should consider the relationship between personality and behavior in a certain situation, and understand that success or failure can be predicted based on this interplay.[21] For example, conscientiousness might be more important in some jobs, such as accounting, where openness might be more critical in others, such as research and development.

Similarly, personality dimensions of emotional stability and conscientiousness have been shown to be good predictors of job performance.[22]

---

17. See, for example, Judge, T. A., Locke, E. A., Durham, C. C., & Kluger, A. N. (1998). Dispositional effects on job and life satisfaction: The role of core evaluations. *Journal of Applied Psychology, 83*(1), 17–34; and Hudiburg, R. A., Pashaj, I., & Wolfe, R. (1999). Preliminary investigation of computer stress and the big five personality factors. *Psychological Reports, 85,* 473–480.
18. Digman, J. M. (1990). Personality structure: Emergence of the five-factor model. *Annual Review of Psychology, 41,* 417–440.
19. Judge, T. A., et al. (1999).
20. Jang, K. L., Livesley, W. J., & Vernon, P. A. (1996). Heritability of the big five personality dimensions and their facets: A twin study. *Journal of Personality, 64,* 577–591.
21. Chatman, J. A., Caldwell, D, F., & O'Reilly, C. A. (1999). Managerial personality and performance: A semi-idiographic approach. *Journal of Research in Personality, 33,* 514–545.
22. Barrick, M. R., Mount, M. K., & Judge, T. A. (in press). The FFM personality dimensions and job performance: A meta-analysis of meta-analysis. *The International Journal of Selection and Assessment.*

Research by Tim Judge and associates revealed that all of the Big Five personality traits, combined with intelligence, are significant and positive predictors of career success, as long as career success is measured at two levels: the intrinsic level, through a subjective assessment of job satisfaction, and the extrinsic level, through an objective, observable assessment (for example, pay, movement up the hierarchy).[23] High conscientiousness is related to intrinsic success. Low neuroticism (high emotional stability), low agreeableness, high extraversion, high conscientiousness, and high cognitive ability are related to extrinsic success. Research has also shown that these traits are good predictors of career success over an individual's life span—even over a period of 50 years.

The practical implications of these studies become apparent when one considers that career success is dependent on job and organizational success. The traits that make an individual successful in a career are the same traits that make him or her successful in a job; thus, they are the traits that contribute to organizational success as well. Therefore, if in an organization hires employees who demonstrate great emotional stability and conscientiousness, the likelihood of success for both the organization and the individuals will be likely to be high.

ORGANIZATIONAL PERSONALITY TRAITS

Many organizational researchers have been less interested in deriving primary personality traits than in identifying specific personality characteristics that predict organizational outcomes. Two characteristics that have been of particular interest to organizational researchers are locus of control and self-esteem, both of which have been shown to have moderating effects on important organizational outcomes, such as job satisfaction.[24]

Locus of control is the degree to which people think they can control the consequential events in their lives.[25] An individual who has a strong internal locus of control believes (for the most part) that he or she can control these important events. In contrast, an individual who has a strong external locus of control believes that important events are (for the most part) beyond his or her control; for instance, they are controlled by fate, chance, or other people. Studies have found that individuals with an internal locus of control are more satisfied with their jobs, more interested in opportunities to participate in organizational decision making, and more likely to be managers.[26] Managers high on internal locus of control also have been shown to adjust more easily to international transfers.[27]

Self-esteem refers to the amount of self-respect an individual has for himself or herself and can affect organizational outcomes. An individual with high self-esteem has a strong belief in his or her self-worth and generally

---

23. Judge, T. A., et al. (1999).

24. Judge, T. A., Locke, E. A., Durham, C. C., & Kluger, A. N. (1998). Dispositional effects on job and life satisfaction: The role of core evaluations. *Journal of Applied Psychology, 83,* 17–34.

25. Rotter, J. B. (1966). Generalized expectancies for internal versus external control of reinforcement. *Psychological Monographs* (80), 1–28.

26. Mitchell, T. R., Smyser, C. M., & Weed, S. E. (1975, September). Locus of control: Supervision and work satisfaction. *Academy of Management Journal,* 623–631; and Renn, R. W., & Vandenberg, R. J. (1966). Differences in employee attitudes and behaviors based on Rotter's (1966) internal–external locus of control: Are they valid? *Human Relations, 44,* 1161–1178.

27. Black, J. S., Gregersen, H. B., Mendenhall, M. E., & Stroh, L. K. (1999). *Globalizing people through international assignments.* Reading, MA: Addison-Wesley.

isn't easily influenced by others.[28] Research by Edwin Locke, Kyle McClear, and Don Knight found that self-esteem is related to job satisfaction.[29] Similarly, Tim Judge and Edward Locke noted that high levels of self-esteem are related to one's satisfaction with their life.[30] People with high levels of self-esteem put a *positive spin* on life events and the circumstances they encounter. Judge and Locke suggested that this is well illustrated by mystery writer P. D. James's *Shroud for a Nightingale*, where Sister Rolfe describes Detective Dagliesh as "a man who could never imagine himself at a disadvantage in any company since he was secure in his private world, possessed of that core of inner self-esteem which is the *basis* of happiness."[31]

Most researchers agree that for a match between an individual and an organization to be effective, there must be a good fit between the individual's and the organization's personalities. Evaluating whether the match is likely to be a good one is best measured as a function of both the traits of the person and those of the organization.[32]

Throughout this book we address additional personality traits as they relate to topics under discussion. For example, Chapter 3 looks at need for achievement and theories of motivation, and Chapter 4 addresses risk propensity in relationship to decision making.

PREDICTING INDIVIDUAL BEHAVIOR

Personality is a useful concept to the extent that measuring an individual's personality enables us to predict that individual's behaviors over time and across situations. To date, researchers generally have had only modest success in using personality assessment instruments to predict how people will behave.[33] However, the controversy over the use of personality assessments in organizations has led to two interesting developments.

The first development regarding personality assessments is the notion that there are strong and weak situations.[34] A **strong situation** is one in which the demands are likely to cause everyone to behave in the same way. A **weak situation,** by contrast, is one in which the appropriate behavior is not at all obvious and in which people are pretty much free to decide for themselves what to do.

A lecture is an example of a strong situation; most students, regardless of their personality, are likely to sit quietly and listen because that's what the

28. Northcraft, G. B., & Ashford, S. J. (1990). The preservation of self in everyday life: The effects of performance expectations and feedback context on feedback inquiry. *Organizational Behavior and Human Decision Processes, 47,* 42–64.

29. Locke, E. A., McClear, K., & Knight, D. (1996). Self-esteem and work. In C. L. Cooper & I. Robertson (Eds.), *International review of industrial/organizational psychology* (Vol. 11, pp. 1–32). New York: Wiley.

30. Judge, T. A., & Locke, E. A. (1993). Effect of dysfunctional thought processes on subjective well-being and job satisfaction. *Journal of Applied Psychology, 78,* 475–490.

31. James, P. D. (1987). *P. D. James: Three complete novels.* New York: Avenel Books, pp. 603–604; and Judge, T. A., & Locke, E. A. (1993).

32. Chatman, J. A., & Barsade, S. G. (1995). Personality, organizational culture, and cooperation: Evidence from a business simulation. *Administrative Science Quarterly, 40,* 423–443.

33. See, for example, Ozer, D. J. (1999). Four principles for personality assessment. In L. A. Pervin & O. P. John (Eds.), *Handbook of personality: Theory and research* (pp. 671–686). New York: The Guilford Press; and Mischel, W. (1986). *Introduction to personality.* New York: Holt, Rinehart & Winston.

34. Davis-Blake, A., & Pfeffer, J. (1989). Just a mirage: The search for dispositional effects in organizational research. *Academy of Management Review, 14,* 385–400.

situation demands. Social gatherings, on the other hand, are weak situations, where a wide variety of behaviors could be appropriate.

Personality traits are more likely to be predictive of behavior in weak situations than in strong situations. Thus, an individual's behavior at a social gathering is much more likely to reflect that individual's personality than would that same individual's behavior at a lecture. Knowing whether a situation is strong or weak can help us understand whether personality will be useful in predicting individual behavior.

The second development in the effects of personality in organizations is the idea of using personality as a **moderating variable** in explaining individual behavior.[35] A moderating variable does not by itself influence behavior; rather, a moderating variable influences the effect of *another* variable on behavior. An example of a moderating variable is the personality trait *growth need strength* (GNS).[36] GNS refers to an individual's interest in growing and developing on the job and has been used to predict how individuals will behave at work. For instance, information technology companies use the concept to retain and motivate their employees. (GNS is discussed in more detail in Chapter 11.)

Together, understanding of strong versus weak situations and the possible moderating role of personality traits have rekindled interest in the usefulness of personality in predicting organizational behavior.

PERSON PERCEPTION

Because what people bring to an organization (for instance, their attitudes and personality) is important in determining their behaviors, understanding the attitudes and personalities of other people is a primary perceptual task for all members of organizations. Where do our impressions of other organizational members come from? The answer is that we develop our perceptions of others from both evidence we gather about the person and beliefs we have about the evidence we gather. Often this building process involves stereotypes.

SOCIAL IDENTITY THEORY

Social identity theory plays a large part in how we perceive ourselves and other organizational members. According to **social identity theory,** individuals classify themselves and others into various categories, such as race, age, gender, religious affiliation, professional membership, and so on.[37]

A person's self-perception is built around his or her personal identity (characteristics such as physical attributes, psychological traits, abilities, and interests) and social identity (the perception of belonging to a certain social group).[38] An example of personal identity might be an individual partially

35. Weiss, H. M., & Adler, S. (1984). Personality and organizational behavior. In B. Staw & L. Cummings (Eds.), *Research in organizational behavior* (Vol. 6, pp. 1–50). Greenwich, CT: JAI.

36. Hackman, J. R., & Oldham, G. R. (1974). *The job diagnostic survey: An instrument for the diagnosis of jobs and the evaluation of job redesign projects* (Tech. Rep. No. 4). New Haven, CT: Yale University, Department of Administrative Sciences.

37. Ashforth, B. E., & Mael, F. (1989). Social identity theory and the organization. *Academy of Management Review, 14*(1), 20–39.

38. Ashforth, B. E., & Mael, F. (1989).

identifying himself or herself with a specific talent or interest, such as being the only person to balloon around the world. Social identity can be illustrated through identification with a particular political party, or as a specific profession, such as "I am a teacher" or "I am a democrat." These categorizations help us to locate or define ourselves in the social environment.

However, these perceptions apply not only to our self-perceptions, but also to our perceptions of others. Social identity is a process driven by comparisons; we define ourselves by comparing ourselves with people in other social groups.[39] To do this we tend to generalize across traits and create homogenous groups, which then become the foundation for many of the stereotypes we build and maintain. Individuals sharing a social category, also referred to as an "in group," are assumed to share similar values and interests, and they often favor members of their own group over those in an "out group."[40]

Sherry Schneider and Gregory Northcraft used social identity theory to explain the dilemma organizations have in attaining and maintaining workforce diversity.[41] Based on the idea that individuals perceive their needs, desires, values, and perspectives as mutually exclusive from those of members of different social groups, rather than potentially congruent or complementary, Schneider and Northcraft strongly suggested that for organizations to be successful they must "correctly align employees' perceptions."[42]

As noted previously, when we strive to define ourselves based on our similarities to or differences from others, the result can be the development of stereotypes. Next, we discuss the concept of stereotypes and the often inappropriate uses of these beliefs.

STEREOTYPES

A **stereotype** is a complex set of expectations and beliefs associated with specific personal characteristics, such as gender, age, race, or occupation. The opening vignette describes some of the stereotypes once held by employees at Texaco. Both minorities and women were targeted by these prejudices. In addition, the "FOCUS ON: Person Perception" shows that people hold a variety of stereotypes associated with different generations, some of which might be flawed.

According to stereotypes, if you know just one characteristic about an individual, then that characteristic brings forth an entire set of beliefs and expectations about that individual. Knowing that an individual is an investment banker, for instance, may suggest that the individual is arrogant, impatient, self-centered, and highly focused on money.

Where do such stereotypes come from? Some come from personal experience, such as meetings with a few investment bankers who were self-centered. Stereotypes also develop based on other people's opinions. Your friends may have told you that investment bankers are arrogant and impatient.

39. Jackson, J. W., & Smith, E. R. (1999). Conceptualizing social identity: A new framework and evidence for the impact of different dimensions. *Personality & Social Psychology Bulletin, 25*(1), 120–135.

40. Schneider, S. K., & Northcraft, G. B. (1999). Three social dilemmas of workforce diversity in organizations: A social identity perspective. *Human Relations, 52*, 1445–1467.

41. Schneider, S. K., & Northcraft, G. B. (1999).

42. Northcraft, G. B., Polzer, J., Neale, M., & Kramer, R. (1995). Diversity, social identity, and performance: Emergent social dynamics in cross-functional teams. In S. Jackson & M. Ruderman (Eds.), *Diversity in work teams* (pp. 69–96). Washington DC: APA Press.

GENERATIONAL STEREOTYPES. Each generation that comes along is a mystery to marketers, advertisers, the media, parents, and teachers. Whether they're baby boomers or in Generation X, Y, or Z, those in the "new generation" are likely to behave somewhat differently from their parents' generation is used to. For marketers and advertisers, the neverending problem is how to sell to them. For corporations the challenge is how to successfully motivate and manage them, particularly the GenXers that are now entering management roles. Equally important, corporations must figure out how to attract and retain them.

Given that a lot of corporate success is riding on corporations developing an understanding of GenXers, it's not surprising that researchers have been investigating what makes them tick. Until recently, GenXers in corporate America have been portrayed in wildly general terms as self-absorbed and impatient. How true are these stereotypes? That was one of the questions Yankelovich Partners set out to answer when it studied a group of 104 senior executives over the age of 35 and 152 GenXers working in business, between the ages of 21 and 34.

Although any generalizations about a group as large as a generation need to be accepted cautiously, GenXers do seem to exhibit some traits that set them apart from their parents and other people who are older than they. In fact, GenXers are an entrepreneurial, independent lot, and although hard working, they tend to be less loyal to their companies than older executives. A whopping 90% believe they could easily find new jobs if they wanted.

Somewhat surprisingly, GenXers perform well in and seek out situations that are stable and highly structured; however, they might want to bend the rules occasionally, too. Based on these findings, we would expect them to fit best in a work environment with clear expectations and clear rewards.

What about some of the other stereotypes that can affect the perceptions of GenXers in the workplace—that GenXers are impatient and self-absorbed, for example? Like many stereotypes, there's some truth in this one. GenXers do seem most comfortable working at a fast pace. One explanation is that they are the first generation to grow up in an age of electronic communication. On the positive side, their fast pace makes them very good multitaskers. As a group, they also seem to care more about the needs of individuals over the good of the group. This would seem to follow from their entrepreneurial spirit.

As GenXers move up the corporate ladder, corporations would be wise to take these characteristics into account. They shouldn't forget the generations following the GenXers, though, for they are now entering the workforce, too.

Sources: Adapted from Strategic new research on Generation X: Invaluable to the future of corporate leadership. (1999, September 30). *Business Wire*; Strategic new research on Generation X: Invaluable to the future of corporate leadership. (1999, September 30); Strategic new research on Generation X: Invaluable to the future of corporate leadership. (1999, September 30).

The accuracy of stereotypes is always problematic. Obviously, not all investment bankers are arrogant, impatient, self-centered, and money focused. Further, having a stereotypic view of a person or group leads us to assume that individuals have characteristics (because of the stereotype's influence on our attention, construction, and interpretation of that person) that are not really there. So why do we have stereotypes at all? There are two reasons: as a way of minimizing uncertainty and as a form of projection.

UNCERTAINTY. When you meet a new member of an organization for the first time, you have no idea how that person will act. Will he or she be trustworthy? Responsible? Will the new person be fun to work with? You cannot know these things until you have worked with the new person for a while and gotten to know him or her better.

But what do you do in the meantime? Getting to know someone means working together and sharing experiences. To do this, you must make some assumptions about how that person is likely to act. For example, it is difficult to determine what a new young male worker will consider "forward" behavior. Would you, as a woman, be perceived as "obnoxiously aggressive" if you asked him out to lunch his first day on the job? If you act too friendly, will he think that before long you'll want to borrow money from him? To interact with the individual at all, you have to make some inferences about him based on whatever small amount of information you have. The question is not *whether* you should assume anything about the new person, but *how much* you should assume.

Stereotypes carry with them many assumptions about people. But just because your first impressions about people are based on stereotypes doesn't mean you have to act on those beliefs. For many of us, stereotypes simply provide a way to learn about another person by providing a series of hypotheses to test. If the new colleague is an investment banker, you might watch at lunch and see if he is impatient with the waiter or obsessed about the bill.

SELF-FULFILLING PROPHECIES. The problem with having hypotheses about a person is that there is no way to test them objectively. Consequently, hypotheses about how a person is likely to act—even innocent and tentative hypotheses—give rise to self-fulfilling prophecies.[43] A **self-fulfilling prophecy** occurs when an expectation about how someone is likely to act causes that person to confirm the hypothesis or fulfill the expectation.[44] Self-fulfilling prophecies were popularized by a stage play called *Pygmalion*. In the play, an English lord made (and won) a bet that a common servant girl would blossom into a beautiful and sophisticated princess if she were treated as one. Therefore, the *Pygmalion effect* describes the dynamic in which an individual lives up to another's high expectations.[45]

There are two kinds of self-fulfilling prophecies: passive and active. In the case of a passive self-fulfilling prophecy, the perceiver's expectations do not actually change the target individual's behaviors; all that changes is the perceiver's perceptions of that behavior. If a perceiver expects investment bankers to be arrogant and meets an investment banker, the perceiver's attention will be biased to search for evidence of arrogance, and the perceiver will be more likely to construct and interpret ambiguous actions as arrogance. The expectation of arrogance will likely be fulfilled because the expectation will drive the attention, construction, and interpretation processes. And, not coincidentally, confirmation that an investment banker was arrogant would strengthen the stereotype that all investment bankers are arrogant and make it even more likely, based on passive self-fulfilling prophecy, that the stereotype will be confirmed in the future.

Active self-fulfilling prophecies are more dynamic. In this case, the perceiver's expectations actually result in a change in the behavior of the target individual so that the perceiver's expectations are fulfilled.

---

43. Rosenthal, R., & Jacobson, L. (1968). *Pygmalion in the classroom.* New York: Holt, Rinehart & Winston.
44. Snyder, M., & Stukas, A. A. (1999). Interpersonal processes: The interplay of cognitive, motivational, and behavioral activities in social interaction. *Annual Review of Psychology,* 273–303.
45. Manzoni, J., & Barsoux, J. (1998). The set-up-to-fail syndrome. *Harvard Business Review,* 76(2), 101–113.

Consider what happens when a supervisor has high expectations for a new worker. The supervisor is friendly toward the worker, gives the worker opportunities to assume responsibility, and checks on the new worker to see if things are going well or if he or she needs assistance. If the new worker fouls something up, the supervisor will see the failure as a learning experience and urge the new worker to shrug it off. In fact, the supervisor is likely to see failures not as the new worker's fault but as evidence of his or her own failure. In short, because of his positive expectations, the supervisor is likely to ensure that the work environment is supportive and includes every possible opportunity to succeed. This positive climate would not likely be lost on the new worker, which is why expectations become *actively* self-fulfilling. If treating the new worker makes a difference in his or her performance (as a result, for instance, of the supervisor's confidence), then providing a supportive climate with high expectations will yield performance that fulfills the supervisor's high expectations.

Compare this scenario with what happens if the supervisor has *low* expectations for the new worker, which Jean-Francois Manzoni and Jean-Louis Barsoux refer to as the "set-up-to-fail syndrome."[46] They suggest that the poor performance of a worker might be caused by the manager rather than by a lack of skill, experience, or motivation. Indeed, the manager may be trying to motivate the employee, but ends up making his or her performance worse. If the supervisor doesn't trust the new worker to do a good job, the supervisor will probably watch the new worker constantly. All this attention may make the new worker nervous and thereby more likely to fail on the job. In this case, the new worker will also fulfill the supervisor's expectations, albeit by performing poorly. Douglas McGregor summed up the problem of self-fulfilling prophecies succinctly when he said that in our attitudes toward our subordinates "we may be caught in a web of our own weaving."[47]

Self-fulfilling prophecies highlight the importance of *first impressions* in perception. The first information received about an individual may evoke expectations (for instance, a stereotype) that lead (through self-fulfilling prophecies) to their own confirmation. It should not be surprising, then, that corporations are willing to spend millions of dollars annually on image advertising aimed at creating a positive image of their organization. Over time, this image, that the company is friendly and helpful or likes children, for example, becomes an expectation that leads customers to experience positive self-fulfilling prophecies (or so the organization hopes) when they interact with the organization or read about it in the news.

The potency of first impressions also explains why clothing is accorded so much attention in corporate circles. John Molloy's dictum that "the clothes make the man" forced people to realize that clothing is an important component of any first impression.[48] One of the first things most people learn about a new member of an organization is the way the person dresses. When a new person first enters the hallowed halls of the organization, how the person is dressed is immediately salient, perhaps as salient as the person's gender or race, and certainly more salient than his or her educational background or work experience.

---

46. Manzoni, J., & Barsoux, J. (1998).
47. McGregor, D. (1960). *The human side of enterprise.* New York: McGraw-Hill, p. 42.
48. Molloy, J. T. (1975). *Dress for success.* New York: P.H. Wyden.

Blue pinstriped suits convey a certain image—of power, knowledge, and seriousness—that can significantly influence later perceptions of and actions toward a new member of an organization. While the dictates of fashion may change as executives move up the corporate ladder, the role of clothing in shaping those important first impressions remains a constant. Clothing is one way to manage uncertainty when we are forming first impressions.

PROJECTION. In addition to helping us sort out how to deal with a new person and uncertainties, stereotypes serve symbolic purposes by providing us with clues about what we would like to think is true, rather than what is true, about a new person. For example, unfavorable stereotypes about new MBAs in an organization may symbolize the feelings of the organization's "old guard" toward the organization's new generation of managers. If the non-MBA workers are jealous of the successes of the new MBAs, envious of their higher salaries, and upset that the new MBAs didn't have to "work their way up from the shop floor," these feelings may surface in negative stereotypes. In this example, the non-MBA workers' negative stereotypes do not reflect actual characteristics of the new MBAs (though, through self-fulfilling prophecies, they certainly could!). Rather, the non-MBA workers are projecting their negative feelings onto their image of the new MBAs.

If stereotypes serve symbolic functions, it should not be surprising that mismatches occur between behaviors and (apparent) beliefs.[49] The negative stereotype may represent people's attempt to let off steam in a way that they would never direct at any individual. Alternatively, negative stereotypes often present such horrible images that actual individuals provide a stark contrast. The new person can then be treated as an exception to the stereotype—an MBA who is "one of the guys," for example. This allows the stereotype to remain intact and to continue to fulfill its symbolic function while enabling the new employees' coworkers to treat the new person according to beliefs about his or her other characteristics.

The failure of women and African Americans to attain positions of corporate leadership in the 1960s and 1970s is a stark reminder of the damaging consequences of unfavorable stereotypes. Further, unfavorable stereotypes always claim more victims than just those individuals discriminated against. The organizations that allow stereotypes to be the basis of their personnel decisions are also casualties, as they forgo the valuable contributions of the individuals they erroneously reject, and perhaps lose millions of dollars, as was the case with Texaco.

SUMMARY

Perception is the prelude to action in organizations. Before we can act—before we can even decide what action to take—we must perceive what is going on around us.

Perception is an active process. Perceptions are the product of a process of selection, construction, and interpretation by the perceiver. First, the perceiver must sample inputs from the infinitely complex environment. After a manageable set of inputs has been selected, a representation of what is going

---

49. LaPiere, R. T. (1934). Attitudes and action. *Social Forces, 13,* 230–237.

on must be constructed. Finally, this representation must be interpreted to give it meaning. These meaningful representations of reality subsequently affect our decisions and actions.

Because perception is an active process, it is susceptible to a variety of external and internal influences, including the perceiver's theories, beliefs, and expectations. These influence (and sometimes bias) all three components of the perception process. In fact, without some preconceptions, perceptions could not occur at all. Characteristics of the objects of perception, as well as the context in which perception occurs, also influence the outcome of the process.

Our attitudes are shaped via a process of evaluation of our perceptions, including our beliefs, affects, and a tendency to act. Sometimes our attitudes come from observing and trying to understand our own behaviors. Other people's attitudes also provide a window for understanding them.

Our personalities consist of the characteristics that lead us to behave in consistent ways over time. Personality is typically discussed in terms of traits, such as locus of control. Personality and attitudes both figure prominently in our attempts to perceive and understand other individuals in organizations.

Having an accurate understanding of the effects of perceptions, attitudes, and personality on human behavior is a key to addressing the management challenge.

KEY TERMS

Accommodation	Moderating variable
Affect	Objective self-awareness
Anchoring-and-adjustment effect	Perception
Attention	Perceptual set
Attitude	Personality
Attribution	Self-esteem
Belief system	Self-fulfilling prophecy
Construction	Self-perception
Contrast effect	Self-serving bias
Covariation	Social identity theory
Fundamental attribution error	Stereotype
Halo effect	Strong situation
Information overload	Trait
Input source influence	Values
Interpretation	Weak situation
Locus of control	

DISCUSSION QUESTIONS

1 In what ways is perception an *active* rather than a *passive* process?

2 Why are good theories about reality a necessary prerequisite to accurate perceptions of reality?

3 Which of the following statements is more defensible, given the view of perception developed in this chapter: "A little knowledge is a dangerous thing," or "A little knowledge is a necessary thing"?

4 Drawing on only your understanding of the perceptual process, provide three explanations for the phrase, "There's no accounting for taste."

5 In what way might the attributions we make about the consequences of our behaviors be more important than the consequences themselves?

6 How are our perceptions of our own actions different from our perceptions of the actions of others?

7 How do attitudes and personality provide similar explanations for why individuals behave consistently over time? How do they differ? Why are people more likely to use attitudes and personality to explain *others'* behaviors than to explain their *own* behaviors?

ON YOUR OWN

Locus of Control   For each of the following 10 statements, indicate your agreement or disagreement by using the following scale:

1 = strongly agree
2 = agree
3 = slightly agree
4 = neither agree nor disagree
5 = slightly disagree
6 = disagree
7 = strongly disagree

_____   **1** People's misfortunes result from their mistakes.
_____   **2** Getting a good job depends mainly on being in the right place at the right time.
_____   **3** In the long run, people get the respect they deserve.
_____   **4** Many times I feel that I have little influence over the things that happen to me.
_____   **5** Most misfortunes are the result of lack of ability, ignorance, laziness, or all three.
_____   **6** Most people don't realize the extent to which their lives are controlled by accidental happenings.
_____   **7** Capable people who fail to become leaders have not taken advantage of their opportunities.
_____   **8** Who gets to be the boss depends of who was lucky enough to be in the right place at the right time.
_____   **9** Becoming a success is a matter of hard work. Luck has little or nothing to do with it.
_____   **10** The world is run by the few people in power, and there is not much any individual can do about it.

To determine your locus of control, subtract each of your responses to the even-numbered questions from 8. (For instance, if you answered 5 for Question 10, your final score for Question 10 would be $8 - 5 = 3$.) Add the total of your corrected scores for the even-numbered questions to the total of your actual responses to the odd-numbered questions. The lower your score, the more internal your locus of control; the higher your score, the more external your locus of control.

Source: Adapted from Rotter, J. B. (1966) Generalized expectancies for internal versus external control of reinforcement. *Psychological Monographs: General and Applied (80)*1, 1–28.

CLOSING CASE   CHAPTER 2

THE MANAGER'S MEMO

FROM: P. Clydesdale, President
TO: A. Jablonski, Comptroller
RE: Reports from the Finance Department

I am getting tired of being bombarded with incomprehensible reports from the Finance Department. Your hotshot MBAs may think they are impressing me with their fancy words and long columns of numbers, but they are just telling me they are too big for their britches.

Just last week, I received five more reports from different members of your staff. One report was 23 pages long. When do these people think I have time to read this stuff?

Long as the reports are, they are woefully short on policy ideas. So what if gross margin return on investment is up 3% over the last quarter? What does that tell us about our business of selling fire-fighting equipment? Believe me, having started this business from scratch, I could tell your pinstriped people a lot about fire-fighting equipment!

Please establish some guidelines to stem this tidal wave of paper, and then let me know what you've done.

CASE DISCUSSION QUESTIONS

Assume that you are the comptroller, and respond to the president's memo. In setting guidelines that will meet the president's needs, consider what you have learned about perception. In writing your response, try to follow any relevant guidelines you have set for your staff members to follow in their writing.

CHAPTER

3

Learning and Motivation

THE MARINE CORPS: A 21st-CENTURY LEARNING ORGANIZATION

The U.S. Marine Corps has always been a learning organization, but on May 17, 1999, it took a giant step toward expanding its learning capacity. On that day, it signed a contract with Pennsylvania State University to establish the Marine Corps Research University (MCRL1). The contract enables the Marine Corps to use Penn State's multidisciplinary research and education capabilities to address the complex issues facing the Marine Corps in the 21st century—in essence to expand its mission of teaching, research, and public service. The implications of this initiative are significant; it has the potential to make the Marine Corps one of the most effective learning organizations in the country.

Among the areas targeted are emerging, commercially available technologies, as well as missiles, mass-destruction weapons, satellite imagery, and directed energy weapons. Additionally, the Marine Corps will study the domestic scene. Societal and legal changes, as well as internal motivation, could significantly affect the ability of the Marine Corps to recruit, interact with the media, and perform other duties. As Defense Intelligence Agency director Lt. General Patrick M. Hughes has said, "One of the key issues we must guard against is technology surprise."

Today's business—and military—environment is unforgiving of slow learners. Being an effective learning organization is critical. One has to look no further than the Marine Corps's rich history of innovation and execution—amphibious warfare, close-air support, helo operations, and marine expeditionary unit development—to see how they effectively translate knowledge into rapid action. It's clear that the Marine Corps is a learning organization; however, it takes this concept one step further, and also understands the importance of learning fast—faster than the other guys!

Source: Excerpted from Herbert D. B., & Madrid, R. R. (2000, April). The new Marine Corps Research University: The 21st-century learning organization. *Marine Corps Gazette,* pp. 54–56.

THE LEARNING ORGANIZATION

Peter Senge, in his best-seller *The Fifth Discipline*, popularized the concept of the learning organization:

> The organizations that will truly excel in the future will be the organizations that discover how to tap people's commitment and capacity at all levels in an organization.... The learning organization is my view of what a corporation can and should be.[1]

In doing so, Senge also revolutionized business ideals and what it means for an organization to be effective. According to Senge, a **learning organization** continually strives to expand its storehouse of knowledge,[2] in order to more effectively create, innovate, and adapt to the changing challenges of the business environment. Everyone understands that it is important that employees learn how to do their jobs, but Senge made people realize that in the best organizations this learning should never stop. At the individual level, this means employees need to be continuously learning new skills and putting those skills to good use. The foundation for this learning is motivation that makes a workforce energized, engaged, and excited about work.

Forward-thinking organizations such as the Marine Corps recognize the importance of developing as learning organizations. In today's globally competitive business environment, learning is the key to continued success. Figure 3-1 will help you diagnose whether your organization is a learning organization.

Measures of Organizational Learning Disabilities   ■ FIGURE 3-1

Is your organization in a learning rut? Do managers and employees continually focus on the here and now instead of looking toward the future? If you answer yes to any of the following, your organization may have a learning disability:

1 "If it ain't broke, don't fix it" represents the general attitude here pretty well.

2 We're not very good at finding/creating new markets.

3 In general, our work procedures have functioned well, so we see little need of pervasive change.

4 Groups and departments in this organization function fairly interdependently, without much integration.

5 We have had trouble ensuring that our actions are consistent with organizational goals.

6 Good ideas tend to disappear if they are not put to regular use.

7 Even though individuals learn here, this learning is not transmitted up the organizational levels.

8 We aren't very good at determining the causes of unexpectedly low and high levels of performance.

Source: Yeung, A. K., Ulrich, D. O., Nason, S. W., & Glinow, M. A. V. (1999). *Organizational learning capability*. New York: Oxford University Press, p. 188.

1. Senge, P. M. (1990). *The fifth discipline: The art and practice of the learning organization*. New York: Doubleday, p. 4.
2. Senge, p. 14.

Like the Marine Corps, many organizations—including Intel, AT&T, Procter & Gamble, and Coopers & Lybrand—are working hard to cure themselves of learning disabilities[3] and become effective learning organizations. As noted in "FOCUS ON: Learning Organizations," many organizations are sending their executives back to school—to learn from both the school and each other!

Some organizations have discovered that this new emphasis on continuous learning can lead to a potential problem. What does the organization do with all the knowledge it has acquired? Ideally, the organization develops skills in **knowledge management**—the ability to retrieve, capture, combine, create, distribute, and secure knowledge.[4] Knowledge management is a critical skill for a learning organization.[5] After all, an organization cannot learn from knowledge it doesn't know it has. A study conducted by Arthur Andersen found that 59% of managers thought the company managed knowledge poorly, and some employees reported that knowledge was not managed at all.[6] To remedy this inability to manage knowledge, many organizations have created the position chief knowledge officer (CKO); this individual's whole job is to initiate programs that catalog, coordinate, and make accessible what an organization has learned.[7]

THE CRITICAL ROLE OF MOTIVATION

Learning organizations represent something of an ideal in pushing the envelope of learning and motivation. However, even less forward-looking organizations still struggle with the key question that learning organizations are addressing: How do we keep our workers motivated to perform in the present and learn for the future? That particular challenge is the focus of this chapter.

Understanding how and why employees are motivated is critical if the manager hopes to capture a worker's full potential to learn and perform. Motivating workers to learn and perform at their best is a complex and difficult challenge for the manager. To begin with, no two employees—not even two employees doing the same job—are alike. At any point in time, different employees will have different needs and different desires. Further, what motivates an employee to do his or her work today and to do it well may not motivate that same employee the next year, the next week, or even the next hour. At the same time, motivated employees represent tremendous promise. When workers are motivated, performance, learning, and satisfaction can all improve dramatically. Everyone benefits.

This chapter explores two pieces of the challenge of motivating employees. First, improving the welfare or even the profits of the organization is sometimes not enough of an incentive to motivate workers. Employees need to feel that they are enhancing their own welfare as well. This chapter identifies

---

3. Senge, p. 4.

4. Liebowitz, J. (2000). *Building organizational intelligence: A knowledge management primer.* Boca Raton, FL: CRC Press, p. 1.

5. Buckley, P. J., & Carter, M. J. (1999). Managing cross-border complementary knowledge. *International Studies of Management & Organization, 29,* 80–104.

6. Allee, V. (1997). *The knowledge evolution: Expanding organizational intelligence.* Boston: Butterworth-Heinemann, p. 8.

7. Earl, M. J., & Scott, I. A. (1999). Opinion: What is a chief knowledge officer? *Sloan Management Review, 40*(2), 29–38.

FOCUS ON
LEARNING ORGANIZATIONS

EXECUTIVES RETURN TO SCHOOL TO PERFECT SKILLS AND MINGLE. Faced with an array of new challenges, increasing numbers of executives are returning to classrooms to brush up on traditional management skills and to learn new ones. Business schools are cashing in on their interest by catering to an array of tastes and needs.

At the University of Chicago, enrollment in this type of course has grown sixfold since the program began in 1996. IMD, based in Lausanne, Switzerland, enrolled about 4,000 executives in 22 different programs in 1999, and it derives 80% of its revenue from executive education courses.

At Harvard Business School, enrollment in executive education jumped 80% in the past five years and now accounts for about 25% of the school's total revenue. In 1999 about 5,000 executives and managers attended one of Harvard's executive programs, which vary in length from 3 days to 10 weeks at costs ranging from $4,000 to nearly $50,000. Several hundred more people participated in courses custom designed for particular companies.

"In this booming economy, businesses can afford this," said Richard Vietor, senior associate dean for executive education at Harvard. What's more, managers from China, India, Mexico, Brazil and elsewhere are rushing "to learn Western business practices," he said. Add to that the changes occurring in technology, and there's so much demand among managers for education that "we no longer have the faculty or dormitory space to meet it," said Vietor. Because few managers can afford to break away from work for weeks at a time, most opt for 5-day or weeklong courses on particular topics, such as finance, e-commerce, or general management.

For many, the biggest benefit of executive programs is the opportunity to meet and mingle with other managers, particularly those who share similar experiences. They prefer getting practical help with problems they face on their jobs, rather than more theoretical learning.

"You can study lessons from a book, but lessons from life are more valuable," said Claude Boruchowitch, manager of major accounts and government for Minolta in Brussels, who attended the IMD program. "I could talk about problems and solutions to problems with people who work in very different industries than mine but, like me, must work globally."

Harvard offers a 4-day program for women executives that addresses a range of general business topics, from marketing to finance strategy, and draws women from diverse industries who have shared problems finding mentors, balancing their professional and personal lives, and breaking through the glass ceiling.

After the programs have finished, executives usually stay connected with both the school and their classmates—through e-mail and occasional alumni events. Naturally, deeper bonds tend to be forged among managers who enroll in programs that last a month or longer.

"Our business isn't a small microcosm anymore—and living with and talking to managers from abroad about what they are going through was extremely beneficial," says Bob Fenech, senior vice president of electric generation at Consumers Energy (Jackson, Michigan), who spent 10 weeks at Harvard's Advanced Management Program.

The longer-term classes also signal a company's commitment to helping a promising executive. IMD's 10-week program for executive development targets fast-trackers in their 30s and 40s who have been identified as "future leaders of their companies," said Nirmalya Kumar, a professor of marketing and e-commerce who cochairs the program. "They have to be that for their companies to invest this kind of money in them."

several **content theories of motivation.** These theories attempt to explain what workers want and need and therefore what tools managers can use to create a successful learning environment.

Second, to motivate employees, their actions must be properly *directed*. This implies that the employees learn what needs to be done and how and when to do it. **Process theories of motivation** focus on the ways in which managers can use their knowledge of their subordinates' needs and desires to motivate appropriate learning and performance. Taken together, content theories and process theories provide managers with the building blocks for creating a learning organization.

CONTENT THEORIES: HOW TO ENERGIZE BEHAVIOR

Motives, needs, wishes, and desires are all terms used (for the most part interchangeably) to explain what energizes workers' behaviors. In some cases these terms refer to physiological necessities (such as the need for food and water); in other cases they refer to outcomes individuals might desire but that they could certainly live without (such as power and a sense of achievement).

Content theories of human motivation attempt to explain what motivates workers to accomplish work tasks. Because different people seem to have different, constantly changing needs, wishes, and desires, managers need a framework for understanding their subordinates' motives, how likely these motives are to be acted on, and how these motives are likely to evolve over time. We will examine several content theories of motivation, including Maslow's needs-hierarchy theory and several popular revisions to it. We will examine the basic tenets of each theory and each theory's unique contribution to our understanding of human motivation and organizational learning. As you shall see, our understanding of motivation has changed significantly over time.

MASLOW'S NEEDS-HIERARCHY THEORY

Before the 1940s, economic theories of worker motivation dominated, even in the field of psychology. That changed with the work of Abraham Maslow, whose **needs-hierarchy theory** was the prototype among several hierarchical theories of human motivation.

Maslow's theory was based on several assumptions. First, Maslow believed that human wants and needs could be divided into at least five distinct categories[8]:

1 **Basic physiological needs.** These include hunger, thirst, and sex drives.
2 **Safety needs.** Concern about protection from physical sources of harm, including shelter from the weather.
3 **Belonging/affiliation needs.** The need for interpersonal relationships with others that include personal liking, affection, care, and support.

---

8. Maslow, A. H. (1943, July). A theory of human motivation. *Psychological Review*, 370–396.

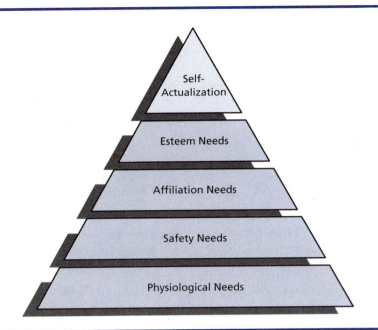

■ **FIGURE 3-2**

Maslow's Hierarchy of Needs

Maslow's needs hierarchy explains differences in needs among employees and across time. According to Maslow's theory, employees turn their attention to higher-order needs only after lower-order needs have been fulfilled.

4 Esteem needs. The need for respect, positive regard, status, and recognition from others.

5 Self-actualization needs. The need to fulfill one's potential—to be all that one can be.

Second, as shown in Figure 3-2, Maslow believed that individuals pursued these needs in a specific hierarchical order. For instance, because physiological needs are the most basic, individuals focus first on their fulfillment. According to Maslow, only after these needs had been met would an individual turn his or her attention to the fulfillment of needs further up on the needs hierarchy.

Despite the intuitive appeal of Maslow's research, subsequent research has not been kind to Maslow's theory. Critics claim that his work does not enjoy a lot of scientific support.[9–11] Many studies suggest that workers distinguish only between broad categories of lower-order and higher-order needs.[12] Nevertheless, Maslow's needs-hierarchy theory has encouraged organizations to begin thinking broadly about what motivates their employees and has laid the foundation for subsequent research on noneconomic sources of employee motivation.

OTHER CONTENT THEORIES

Over the years, motivational theorists have tried to build on and improve Maslow's hierarchy. Next we will discuss three such theories.

9. Heylighen, F. (1992). A cognitive systematic reconstruction of Maslow's theory of self-actualization. *Behavioral Science, 37,* 39–58.

10. Schott, R., & Maslow, A. (1992). Humanistic psychology, and organization leadership: A Jungian perspective. *Journal of Humanistic Psychology, 32,* 106–120.

11. Wahba, M., & Bridwell, L. (1976). Maslow reconsidered: A review of research on the need hierarchy theory. *Organizational Behavior and Human Performance, 15,* 212–240.

12. Wahba & Bridwell, pp. 212–240.

ERG THEORY. Clay **Alderfer's ERG theory,** for example, revised Maslow's five categories of needs into three broader ones:[13]

1 **Existence.** The basic physiological needs (hunger and thirst) and protection from physical danger.
2 **Relatedness.** Social and affiliation needs and the need for respect and positive regard from others.
3 **Growth.** The need to develop and realize one's potential.

Alderfer further proposed that when circumstances prevent a higher-order need from being fulfilled, an individual shifts his or her attention to fulfillment of needs lower down the hierarchy. Alderfer also contended that, as needs become fulfilled, some needs become more, rather than less, important.[14]

TWO-FACTOR THEORY. Fredrick Herzberg offered another revision of Maslow's hierarchy, in the form of his **two-factor theory.**[15] Herzberg framed his theory in terms of two categories that affect work satisfaction:

1 **Hygiene factors.** A broad category of working conditions, including safety and the amount of pay, quality of supervision, and social environment of work.
2 **Motivators.** Factors associated with the performance of work, such as recognition for a job well done, achievement, autonomy, and responsibility.

An important conclusion of Herzberg's work is that the determinants of job satisfaction and dissatisfaction are not the same. According to Herzberg, dissatisfaction results when the work setting does not fulfill the worker's basic needs, or **hygiene factors.** For example, a worker who is worried about safety on the job cannot devote attention to the task at hand and therefore cannot do a good job. However, fulfillment of these needs does not satisfy workers, but only prevents dissatisfaction. Satisfaction depends on a second set of factors, which Herzberg labeled **motivators.** One might assume that these motivators would be universal. In fact, as noted in "INTERNATIONAL FOCUS ON: Motivators" research has revealed that they differ across countries.

LEARNED NEEDS THEORY. David McClelland's research offers a different perspective on the contents of motivation. **McClelland's Needs Theory** focused on three categories of needs:

1 **Need for affiliation.** Concern with establishing and maintaining social relationships.
2 **Need for power.** Concern with reputation, responsibility, influence, and impact.
3 **Need for achievement.** Concern with establishing and maintaining high levels of performance quality.

13. Alderfer, C. P. (1969). An empirical test of a new theory of human needs. *Organizational Behavior and Human Performance, 4,* 141–175.
14. Wanous, J. P., & Zwany, A. (1977). A cross-sectional test of need hierarchy theory. *Organization Behavior and Human Performance, 18,* 78–97; Alderfer, C. P., Kaplan, R. E., & Smith, K. K. (1974). The effect of variations in relatedness need satisfaction on relatedness desires. *Administrative Sciences Quarterly, 19,* 507–532.
15. Herzberg, F. (1966). *Work and the nature of man.* Cleveland, OH: World.

Source: Excerpted from Fisher, C. D., & Yuan, A. X. Y. (1998, June). What motivates employees? A comparison of U.S. and Chinese responses. *International Journal of Human Resource Management, 9*(3), 516–528.

INTERNATIONAL FOCUS ON MOTIVATORS

WHAT MAKES A JOB SATISFYING IS DIFFERENT IN THE UNITED STATES AND CHINA. Differences in employees' preferences in job attributes appear to differ across cultures, probably because of differences in history, economy, and political and management systems. To the extent that this is true, it behooves managers and designers of motivation systems to learn the preferences of local employees. This and other findings of a set of studies on Chinese and U.S. workers should be of major concern to managers in multinational corporations and in organizations looking to expand overseas.

Based on studies of employees of a major hotel in Shanghai and of two studies on what motivates U.S. employees, researchers have found that U.S. workers are much more motivated by interesting work and appreciation for a job well done. Chinese workers, on the other hand, are more motivated by good wages and good working conditions.

Based on these studies, Chinese workers seem to have far more material concerns than U.S. workers. The two groups of Americans ranked highest on intrinsic factors, whereas they ranked very low on social concerns. By contrast, both intrinsic and social factors were of only moderate concern to the Chinese workers.

The message of these studies can be summarized in one recommendation: Don't assume that what motivates workers in one place will motivate workers in another place.

McClelland's approach to motivation differs from that of the other content theories in that McClelland emphasized that affiliation, power, and achievement are **learned needs.** In a dramatic demonstration that needs can be learned, McClelland attempted to improve the economy in Kakinada, India, by training 50 businesspeople to have greater needs for achievement. The training group was encouraged to imagine positive outcomes of aggressive investment strategies, to imagine how these strategies would fulfill personal needs, and to set goals.

The trained businesspeople invested more money in local business ventures, started more new businesses, participated in more community development activities, and created more new jobs in the community than their untrained counterparts.[16] However, these effects were not long lasting, perhaps because of a lack of cultural support for personal achievement in Kakinada.[17]

IMPLICATIONS OF CONTENT THEORIES

To a student new to the field of organizational behavior, the content theories of motivation we have discussed—several different needs-hierarchy theories and McClelland's learned needs theory—probably seem like two or three theories too many. Each of these theories (compared in Figure 3-3) has been questioned by researchers. For example, researchers Maureen Ambrose

16. McClelland, D. C., & Winter, D. G. (1971). *Motivating economic achievement.* New York: The Free Press.
17. Misra, S., & Kanungo, R. N. (1994). Bases of work motivation in developing societies: A framework for performance management. In R. N. Kanungo & M. Mendonca (Eds.), *Work motivation: Models for developing countries* (pp. 27–48). Newbury Park, CA: Sage.

■ **FIGURE 3-3**   A Comparison of Four Content Theories of Motivation

Although a variety of content theories of motivation have been developed, the sources of motivation proposed in each bear many similarities. According to all these theories, individuals have both self-development and social affiliation needs. Only in McClelland's theory of learned needs is the importance of basic physiological needs not emphasized.

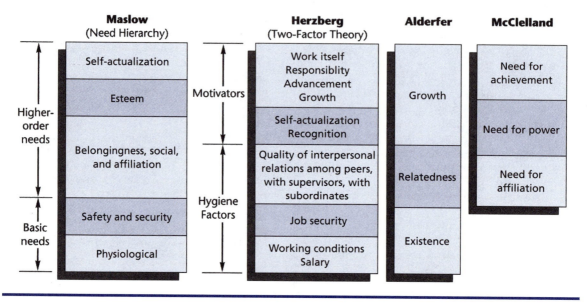

and Carol Kulik found that kibbutz workers prefer jobs that satisfy higher-order needs over jobs that provide for convenience or good physical conditions,[18] which seems to contradict needs-hierarchy theories. Other researchers have found that none of these content theories seem to apply equally well to all organizations.[19] Of the four content theories of motivation we have considered, McClelland's has probably received the most consistent support.[20]

Nevertheless, each theory has advanced our understanding of how to motivate workers. Needs-hierarchy theories highlighted the importance of noneconomic needs, such as Maslow's self-esteem needs and Alderfer's relatedness needs. Similarly, Herzberg's motivators have been found to account for the success of quality improvement programs,[21] and—as noted in "Technology Focus On: Content Theories"—have helped us understand what factors motivate telecommuters. Finally, McClelland's theory drove home the idea that some needs are learned.

---

18. Ambrose M. L., & Kulik, C. T. (1999). Old friends, new faces: Motivation research in the 1990's. *Journal of Management, 25,* 231–292.

19. Wanous, J. P. & Zwany, A. (1977). A cross-sectional test of need hierarchy theory. *Organizational Behavior and Human Performance, 18,* 78–97.

20. Steers, R. M., & Braunstein, N. D. (1976). A behaviorally based measure of manifest needs in work settings. *Journal of Vocational Behavior, 9,* 251–266; French, E. (1955). Some characteristics of achievement motivation. *Journal of Experimental Psychology, 50,* 232–236.

21. Utley, D. R., Westbrook, J., & Turner, S. (1997). The relationship between Herzberg's two-factor theory and quality improvement implementation. *Engineering Management Journal, 9*(3), 5–13.

TECHNOLOGY FOCUS ON
CONTENT THEORIES

MOTIVATING TELECOMMUTERS. Employment is undergoing a transformation that may cause as much dislocation as the move from farms to factories. Many forms of alternative work arrangements—flextime, home offices, hoteling, remote managing, mobile work, and telecommuting, to name a few—have been created to accommodate knowledge workers. Do traditional theories of motivation have any application in the information age? Pamela Knight and Jerry Westbrook examined that very issue.

Of the telecommuters Knight and Westbrook studied, 100% stated that they were satisfied overall with their positions as telecommuters, and more than 50% said that they would not take a job that didn't allow them to telecommute. Equally important, the telecommuters were motivated by their need or desire for achievement/accomplishment, recognition, work itself, responsibility, advancement, and growth—the same motivators Herzberg identified.

In addition, the respondents identified several other factors that they felt motivated them to do their jobs. Flexibility and control over their work, lives, and schedules, were shown to be solid motivators. Work overload was shown to be a hygiene factor. Telecommuters complained that because their work boundaries were not well defined, and they were sometimes overloaded with many small jobs that they were expected to "work in-between" normal tasks.

In this study, company policy, supervision, interpersonal relations, and personal factors showed up as motivators rather than as hygiene factors. This shift appears to be due largely to the fact that telecommuters, unlike traditional knowledge workers, place exceptionally high value on their working arrangements and, consequently, on their company's policy of allowing telecommuting, their supervisors' willingness to cooperate, their interpersonal relationships with customers and peers, and a host of other personal factors.

This research suggests that managers should be aware of the importance to telecommuters of flexibility and control, built on a foundation of improved communications with management and coworkers. Taking advantage of the fact that company policy, supervision, interpersonal relations, and personal factors have been found to motivate telecommuters could be valuable in recruiting and maintaining workers. Employers should also be sensitive to the fact that work overload can become a serious impediment to satisfaction; in particular, a telecommuter should not be expected to work more hours than non-telecommuters just because the telecommuter has the flexibility to do so.

Source: Excerpted from Knight, P., & Westbrook, J. (1999). Comparing employees in traditional job structures versus telecommuting jobs using Herzberg's hygienes and motivators. *Engineering Management Journal, 11*(1), 15–20.

In short, although they have not all been consistently supported, content theories of motivation provide managers with two thoughts to consider as they help their companies become learning organizations. First, content theories of motivation serve as a reminder that there is no such thing as an ideal job; a job is ideal only for the person who is motivated by what that job has to offer. Second, it's important to remember that the individual features of a job have an effect on a worker's motivation only to the extent that the worker wants or needs more of what the job offers. This conclusion has led some management theorists to suggest that it is important when selecting new employees to find individuals whose needs fit those of the job.[22] (Chapter 12 will further explore the relationship between job design and motivation.)

---

22. Lawler, E. E., III, (1974, Summer). For a more effective organization—Match the job to the man. *Organizational Dynamics*, 3.

RESEARCH IN ACTION
HIGH-PERFORMANCE ORGANIZATIONS

Edward E. Lawler III, University of Southern California;
elawler@marshall.usc.edu

In the early 1970s I began a series of studies that were focused on team-based high-performance manufacturing facilities in the United States. At that time there was great concern about the viability of U.S. manufacturing because many U.S. corporations were losing out to Japanese and European competitors who had lower costs and better quality. An American answer to this international threat was needed.

I had previously done work on employee involvement, work design, and motivation, and I felt strongly that better organization design and management represented the key to creating more competitive manufacturing organizations. I began working with Procter & Gamble, General Foods, Corning, General Electric, and several other companies that wanted to create team-based plants that emphasized employee involve-

ment. After these plants became operational, I had the chance to do attitude surveys of their employees as well as to assess their productivity and financial performance. The results were quite positive. The team-based high-performance plants without exception outperformed their traditionally managed competitors because of their high levels of employee motivation and learning.

The result of the early work on high-performance plants has now spread to a wide range of organizations. Today the high-performance management approach is used by most U.S. manufacturers. As practiced, today's high-performance approach typically includes team-based production, rewards for learning, problem-solving groups, flat organization structures, performance-based bonuses, and continuous improvement efforts.

PROCESS THEORIES: ACQUIRING AND DIRECTING BEHAVIOR

When a manager knows his or her subordinates' needs, the next challenge is to use that knowledge to direct those workers to behave appropriately—to maximize each employee's learning and performance. Process theories concern how managers can use their knowledge about their subordinates' needs to provide effective direction for those employees. Process theories also provide the foundation for many of the specific management techniques (such as goal setting and job design) that will be the focus of Part IV of this book.

The challenge in providing effective direction boils down to ensuring that workers are energized to both learn appropriate work behaviors and to perform them. In this section two types of learning are examined: simple learning and complex learning.

SIMPLE LEARNING

Conditioning, amounts to building good habits, or automatic, routine behaviors, and is one of the simplest forms of learning. Automatically cleaning one's machines at the beginning of a shift is a good example. Through conditioning, workers learn which simple behaviors (ones they already know how to perform) will be rewarded. In many cases, performing these tasks is inconvenient and does not produce short-term personal benefits, but it can produce long-term benefits for the organization. Ensuring that workers perform these behaviors, through the process of conditioning, is therefore a critical management task.

THE "LAW OF EFFECT." How are workers conditioned to have good work habits? To answer this question, it helps to understand the **law of effect.** The law of effect is the primary principle managers use to build good work habits, and states:

> Of several responses to the same situation, those that are accompanied or closely followed by satisfaction . . . will be more likely to recur; those which are accompanied or closely followed by discomfort . . . will be less likely to occur.[23]

Central to the law of effect are the concepts of **contingency** and **consequences.** If good consequences are contingent on (follow) a behavior, the probability of that behavior occurring again will be strengthened until it eventually becomes a habit or routine. If bad consequences are contingent on (follow) a behavior, the probability of that behavior occurring again is weakened; the behavior will be avoided and will not become routine. Simply stated, the law of effect says that behaviors are a function of the consequences they produce.

REINFORCEMENT THEORY. How can the law of effect be put into practice to direct workers' behaviors in a learning organization? The answer is simple: by reinforcing appropriate behaviors and not reinforcing (and sometimes even punishing) inappropriate behaviors. **Reinforcement** increases the probability that an action will occur again in the future. As discussed in Figure 3-4, managers reinforce desired behaviors by giving employees something they want or need (or by taking away something the worker dislikes) when the worker behaves appropriately.

The opposite of reinforcement, **punishment,** is an action that a worker finds distasteful (for example, suspending or demoting the worker) taken in response to inappropriate behavior. Punishment is most appropriate when it is used to put an immediate stop to counterproductive behavior (for example, suspending an employee who shows up for work drunk). As a result of its negative connotations, punishment tends to build an interpersonal wall between the punisher and the worker. Even so, research has found that managers *perceive* punishment as instrumental in achieving respect and learning. These objectives are much broader than just changing attitudes or behaviors.[24]

OB-MOD. The systematic application of conditioning and reinforcement theory to the management of organizational behavior is known as **organizational behavior modification (OB-Mod).** OB-Mod encompasses the important aspects of conditioning and reinforcement theory in a simple framework that a manager can apply to any behavior problem in a learning

---

23. Thorndike, E. L. (1911). *Animal intelligence.* New York: Macmillan, p. 244.
24. Butterfield, K. D., Trevino, L. K., & Ball, G. A. (1996). Punishment from the manager's perspective: A grounded investigation and inductive model. *Academy of Management Journal, 39,* 1479–1512.

■ **FIGURE 3-4** | **Reinforcement Schedules and Their Effects on Behavior**

Different schedules of reinforcement have dramatically different effects on behavior. Continuous reinforcement means rewarding a subordinate after every correct behavior and is the fastest way to teach someone a new behavior. Variable reinforcement schedules (variable ratio or variable interval) reward correct behaviors only occasionally and promote their persistence even when rewards are not available.

Schedule	Description	When Applied to Individual	When Removed by Manager	Organizational Example
Continuous	Reinforcer follows every response	Fastest method for establishing new behavior	Fastest method to cause extinction of new behavior	Praise after every response, immediate recognition of every response
Fixed Interval	Response after specific time period is reinforced	Some inconsistency in response frequencies	Faster extinction of motivated behavior than variable schedules	Weekly, bimonthly, monthly paycheck
Variable interval	Response after varying period of time (an average) is reinforced	Produces high rate of steady responses	Slower extinction of motivated behavior than fixed schedules	Transfers, promotions, recognition
Fixed ratio	A fixed number of responses must occur before reinforcement	Some inconsistency in response frequencies	Faster extinction of motivated behavior than variable schedules	Piece rate, commission on units sold
Variable ratio	A varying number (average) of responses must occur before reinforcement	Can produce high rate of response that is steady and resists extinction	Slower extinction of motivated behavior than fixed schedules	Bonus, award, time off

Source: Behling, O., Schnesheim, C., and Tolliver, J. (1974) Present Theories and New Directions in Theories of Work Effort, *Journal of Supplement Abstract Science of the American Psychological Assocation, 57.*

organization. Five steps are used to establish an OB-Mod behavior-change program[25]:

1 **Define the target behavior.** This must be a clear and unequivocal statement of the desired behavior. For example, "be at work on time" would be defined explicitly as "checked in, work smock on, at workbench, and ready to begin work when the plant time clock reads 8:00 a.m." The manager must be able to state the desired performance in terms of precise events.

2 **Measure the frequency of behavior.** The success of a change effort needs to be measured against a baseline of normal performance. This is important so that both management and the worker will be able to tell whether progress is being made and when to reinforce the behavior.

3 **Set reasonable performance goals.** If behavior is to be changed, give the employee a goal to think about and shoot for. (The importance of goals in motivating work behavior is discussed in detail in Chapter 12.)

4 **Monitor the behavior.** Keep track of the frequency of appropriate behavior. Requiring the subordinate to collect this information will help maintain the subordinate's involvement in the behavior-change effort.

25. Luthans, F., & Kreitner, R. (1985). *Organizational behavior modification and beyond.* Glenview, IL: Scott, Foresman.

5 Administer rewards. Because OB-Mod is based on conditioning and reinforcement theory, the final and most important step is to reward appropriate behaviors. The manager must reward acceptable progress toward or achievement of the performance goals. This increases the likelihood that these desired behaviors will become habits.

Has OB-Mod proven successful? Research has provided mixed results. Critics have claimed that OB-Mod has too narrow a scope because it emphasizes only *observable* and *measurable* performance.[26]

A 20-year review of OB-Mod research, conducted by Alexander Stajkovic and Fred Luthans, presented an interesting mix of results.[27] On average, OB-Mod programs produced a 17% performance improvement in such areas as productivity, performance, customer service, absenteeism, tardiness, and safety. These results were more likely to be found in manufacturing settings (33% increase) than in service settings (13% increase). In addition, Stajkovic and Luthans found that manufacturing workers were as likely to be motivated by nonfinancial interventions (such as praise) as by financial reinforcement. By contrast, in the service organizations, the financial reinforcers resulted in stronger effects. These findings demonstrate that, as stated previously, what motivates one person to work at top capacity may not motivate another person.

COMPLEX LEARNING

Unlike conditioned learning, **complex learning** involves behaviors that occur only with substantial training and practice. The golf swing is a good example of a skill that requires complex learning. How would you condition someone to swing a golf club correctly? You could punish the person when he or she executes a poor swing and reinforce the person for good swings. Unfortunately, making a good swing is such a complex behavior that you could wait forever before the golfer executes a good swing, especially if your student were just learning to play golf. So what might you do instead? Two options are considered here: successive approximation and social learning.

SUCCESSIVE APPROXIMATION. Conditioning can be used to facilitate complex learning. Because appropriate behavior is unlikely to occur when someone is first learning a complex skill, successively better approximations, rather than "perfect" behavior, is reinforced. This is called reinforcement through **successive approximation.**

One variant of successive approximation is *shaping*. With shaping, only desired behavior is reinforced, but the requirements for reinforcement become more stringent over time. Shaping a golf swing, for instance, would entail reinforcing almost any swing initially, and then only reasonable approximations of the correct swing, and then only good approximations of the correct swing, and finally only the correct swing. As the reinforcement criteria become more stringent, the learner's behavior is fine-tuned, until only desired behavior is reinforced.

26. Stajkovic, A. D., & Luthans, F. (1997, October). A meta-analysis of the effects of organizational behavior modification on task performance, 1975–95. *Academy of Management Journal, 40,* 1122–1149.

27. Stajkovic & Luthans, A meta-analysis of the effects of organizational behavior modification on task performance.

Another form of successive-approximation conditioning is called *chaining*. In chaining, the desired complex behavior is broken down into component behaviors; successively more complete demonstrations of the desired behavior chain are reinforced until, finally, the desired behavior is acquired. A golf swing, for instance, could be broken down into five parts: the address, the take-away, the back swing, the down swing, and the follow-through. To chain a correct golf swing, you would start by reinforcing only a good address; then a good address and a take-away; then a good address, a good take-away, and a good back swing; and so on, until you were reinforcing only good examples of the entire swing.

In practice, chaining and shaping are often used together. Extremely complex work behaviors can be broken down into components and (using chaining) acquired one component at a time. Within the process of learning each component, shaping may be used to encourage acquisition of the desired behavior.

SOCIAL LEARNING. Largely ignored to this point in our discussion is the role of workers' cognitions (thoughts) in acquiring and performing appropriate work behaviors. The image of learning offered by conditioning and reinforcement theorists is learning by doing or learning by trial and error. Workers try behaviors and acquire appropriate behaviors when they are reinforced for trying them. A major criticism of behaviorist approaches to learning is that they ignore the fact that workers learn many behaviors without ever doing them, just by observing others engaged in these behaviors. This is also true of golfers, who watch others in the hopes of getting pointers.

Learning by observing is a focus of psychologist Albert Bandura's **social learning theory.**[28] Social learning theory states that people learn from watching others, and the likelihood that the learned behavior will be repeated is determined by modeling—displaying those behaviors that have been observed and avoiding behaviors that are seen as producing negative outcomes. For example, if an employee sees a coworker get punished for making too many personal phone calls, he or she is likely to learn that management will not accept abuse of phone privileges.

Social learning theory can also be applied to group learning. Sandra Robinson and Anne O'Leary-Kelly found a "monkey see, monkey do" relationship between employees and their coworkers.[29] Openness to learning also appears to enhance the likelihood of learning taking place. For example, managers who were open to learning about different cultures before being transferred overseas (that is, they were open to modeling) also showed greater interest in the culture of their host country while they were expatriates.[30]

An additional aspect of social learning theory, **self-reinforcement**—punishing or rewarding oneself in the hopes of acquiring desired actions—is important in understanding Bandura's theory. For self-reinforcement to take place, an individual must put off acquiring a readily available reward until

---

28. Bandura, A. (1977). *Social learning theory.* Englewood Cliffs, NJ: Prentice Hall.
29. Robinson, S. L., & O'Leary-Kelly, A. M. (1998). Monkey see, monkey do: The influence of work groups on the antisocial behavior of employees. *Academy of Management Journal, 41,* 658–672.
30. Caligiuri, P. M. (2000). Selecting expatriates for personality characteristics: A moderating effect of personality on the relationship between host national contact and cross-cultural adjustment. *Management International Review, 40*(1), 61–80.

some goal has been achieved. For example, you might decide against going out to lunch with your team until after you complete a project for your boss.

Vicarious learning, learning by observing others, is yet another form of social learning. Vicarious learning includes acquiring complex behaviors modeled by others (such as a golf swing) or learning which behaviors (simple or complex) will be reinforced, which will not, and which will be punished.

Behavior acquisition through vicarious learning is different from behavior acquisition through conditioning. Acquisition of appropriate behaviors through conditioning can occur through what is essentially "muscle memory." Imagine that you engage in an appropriate behavior and the behavior is reinforced. The reinforcement strengthens the probability that you will repeat the same component motions of the behavior the next time you get a chance. In the case of vicarious learning, someone else is engaging in the behavior, so that muscle memory cannot take place. The appropriate behavior is stored symbolically, rather than in the form of component motions, in the brain.[31] You observe someone engaging in a behavior, and the observation creates an image in your mind that you retain. If you think or talk about this image or about the behavior itself, the words you think or speak also are retained as verbal representations. These verbal representations and images then serve as templates (road maps or instructions) that will help you engage in the appropriate behavior later on.

Vicarious learning is limited, however. Watching another individual engage in a complex behavior provides a symbolic representation of a gross approximation of the behavior. However, symbolic representations are exactly that—gross. Often, observing the subtle nuances of the behavior is difficult or impossible. Observation may provide a good first approximation of the behavior, but reinforcement of successively better approximations is required to fine-tune the component motions.

Interestingly, the sequence of these two types of learning—vicarious learning first and conditioning later—is sometimes reversed to further fine-tune complex behaviors. Some work behaviors are so foreign to new workers—that the workers are able to perform tasks only in the most gross or general way. Under these circumstances, workers' further vicarious observation of others or of themselves (for instance, by watching themselves on videotape) may be helpful. Observation of their behavior at this point may reveal differences in how the behavior is being performed and how it should be performed. In such cases, vicarious learning and conditioning become complementary components on the road to complete and satisfactory acquisition of desired behavior. The next section further discusses the importance of cognition to the learning process.

COGNITIVE QUALIFICATIONS

If a manager knows what workers need and makes the fulfillment of those needs contingent on appropriate behaviors, will appropriate behaviors occur? If top managers at the Marine Corps (discussed in the first few paragraphs of this chapter) merely made their demands known and knew the needs of the Corps's members, would it have been possible for the Marine

---

31. Wood, R., & Bandura, A. (1989). Social cognitive theory of organizational management. *Academy of Management Review, 14,* 361–384.

Corps to proceed as successfully as it has in meeting its target goals? Unfortunately, no. As Bandura has noted, this is far too simple a view of human behavior:

> A theory that denies that thoughts can regulate actions does not lend itself readily to the explanation of human behavior. Although cognitive activities are disavowed in the law-of-effect framework, their role in causal sequences cannot be eliminated.[32]

From our discussion of process theories, one question still needs to be answered: If workers have acquired appropriate work behaviors, and outcomes desired by the workers have been made contingent on the execution of these behaviors, can workers' thoughts and beliefs still prevent them from engaging in appropriate behavior? The answer is very much yes. Two cognitions (that is, beliefs and thoughts) in particular often stand in the way of maximum performance: expectancy and justice.

EXPECTANCY

The basic principles of **expectancy theory** are summarized in an early statement about the theory:

> If a worker seeks high productivity as a path leading to the attainment of one or more of his personal goals, he will tend to be a high producer. Conversely, if he sees low productivity as a path to the achievement of his goals he will tend to be a low producer.[33]

The differences between this expectancy view of motivation and the law of effect are both subtle and striking. The law of effect states that if managers make desired consequences contingent on appropriate behavior, appropriate behaviors will occur. In contrast, expectancy theory suggests that it is not enough that desired consequences are contingent upon appropriate behavior (law of effect); the worker must also *believe* that the consequences are desirable, *believe* that the behavior will produce these consequences, and *believe* that he or she can execute the desired behavior.

The differences between law-of-effect and expectancy theories of work motivation are portrayed in Figure 3-5. The blue boxes in the figure illustrate a simple conditioning model of motivation. If a worker desires contingent consequences, the consequences will reinforce the worker's behavior, making that behavior more likely to occur again.

The black boxes in Figure 3-5 illustrate the expectancy model of motivation, including three "belief" components: valence, instrumentality, and expectancy.

Valence refers to the value of the consequences of a behavior, as perceived by the worker. It is important to note that what workers *actually* need can be different from what workers *think* they need. For better or for worse, what people *think* they need is what they are willing to work for.

Instrumentality refers to how much the worker believes that attaining these levels of performance will produce desired personal outcomes (such as monetary rewards or praise). If the worker believes that performance is not

---

32. Bandura, *Social learning theory*, p. 10.
33. Georgopoulos, B. S., Mahoney, G. M., & Jones, N. W. (1957). A path–goal approach to productivity. *Journal of Applied Psychology, 41,* 346.

Expectancy Theory   ■ **FIGURE 3-5**

Expectancy theory captures the important role of cognitions in motivation. A worker may be capable of superior performance, and superior performance, may be rewarded. But if the worker does not *believe* that he or she can do the work, or that the work will be rewarded, he or she will not be motivated to perform at satisfactory levels.

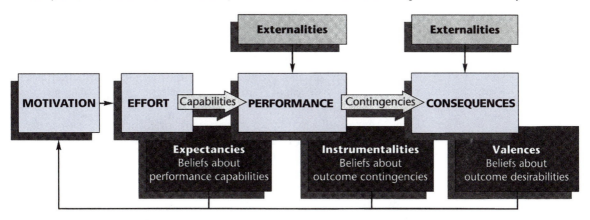

really contingent on effort, or that the desired rewards are not really contingent on performance, the worker will not be motivated to engage in appropriate behavior, even if it really would produce the desired consequences. The worker's *beliefs* about these contingencies are more important than the contingencies themselves.

Expectancy refers to how much the worker believes that, through his or her own efforts, he or she is capable of producing the required levels of performance. For example, **self-efficacy** is the belief that engaging in appropriate work behaviors will produce required levels of performance.[34] Workers with high self-efficacy believe that (a) they have the ability needed, (b) they are capable of making the effort necessary to produce a required level of performance, and (c) no outside influences will prevent them from attaining the required level of performance. In contrast, workers with low self-efficacy believe that no matter how hard they try, something (insufficient ability, inadequate effort, or outside interference) will prevent them from reaching their performance goals.

A worker's self-efficacy is a perception and therefore can be wrong. On one hand, a worker who achieves the required level of performance may attribute the success to luck. On the other hand, a worker who fails to reach the required level of performance may identify excuses for the failure (such as interference from other workers, lack of time, or even lack of personal effort) that enable the worker to continue to believe that the required performance level is well within reach. In either case, the worker's high level of self-efficacy stands in stark contrast to the latest consequences of his or her performance.

34. See, for example, Bandura, A. (1999). Social cognitive theory of personality. In L. A. Pervin and O. P. John (Eds.), *Handbook of personality: Theory and research* (pp. 154–196). New York: Guilford; Gist, M. E., & Mitchell, T. R. (1992). Self-efficacy: A theoretical analysis of its determinants and malleability. *Academy of Management Review, 17,* 183–211.

Nonetheless, having a high level of self-efficacy can be tremendously useful. Workers with high levels of self-efficacy are likely to persevere in the face of failure and to continue with a successful strategy that accidentally produced poor performance. In contrast, workers with low levels of self-efficacy are likely to reevaluate their approach to a problem, find ways to exert greater effort, or perhaps convince themselves that assistance (perhaps in the form of additional training) is necessary.

Research has shown that workers with high self-efficacy are more likely than others to succeed in their careers.[35] Research has also shown that the theory provides a dynamic description of organizational performance[36]: Self-efficacy can affect performance and rewards, which, in turn, can influence self-efficacy, and so on.[37]

Finally, **externalities** refer to determinants of a worker's performance—or determinants of the consequences of those behaviors—that are beyond the worker's control. Examples of externalities include the behaviors of coworkers in a workgroup and the reliability of a worker's machine. Externalities can disrupt a worker's perceived connection between effort, performance, and desired consequences.

Research has provided considerable support for the expectancy theory. In a study of international students, for instance, expectancy theory was used to accurately predict academic effort.[38] Research has also shown that expectancy theory can aid organizations in motivating employees to act ethically,[39] and managers in a variety of corporate arenas use the theory as the basis for interpreting, assessing, and evaluating employee behavior.[40] The most comprehensive research on expectancy theory to date is a review of 77 studies on the subject by Wendelien Van Eerde and Henk Thierry.[41] These researchers discovered that attitudinal components of motivation (valence, instrumentality, and expectancy) are also very useful predictors of workplace behavior.

JUSTICE

Expectancy theory concerns how workers answer the question Can I obtain the outcomes I want at work? In contrast, justice concerns instead are about the question If I can get the outcomes I want, will those outcomes be fair? Individuals who perceive their outcomes to be unjust (unfair) become dissatisfied and engage in actions aimed at restoring their sense of fairness.[42]

35. Gianakos, I. (1999). Patterns of career choice and career decision-making self-efficacy. *Journal of Vocational Behavior, 54,* 244–258.

36. Lindsley, D. H., Brass, D. J., & Thomas, J. B. (1995). Efficacy–performance spirals: A multilevel perspective. *Academy of Management Review, 20,* 645–678.

37. Stajkovic, A. D., & Luthans, F. (1998). Social cognitive theory and self-efficacy: Going beyond traditional motivational and behavioral approaches. *Organizational Dynamics, 26*(4), 62–74.

38. Geiger, M. A., Cooper, E. A., Hussain, I., O'Connell, B. T., et al. (1998). Cross-cultural comparisons: Using expectancy theory to assess student motivation—An international replication. *Issues in Accounting Education, 13,* 139ff.

39. Fudge, R. S., & Schlacter, J. L. (1999). Motivating employees to act ethically: An expectancy theory approach. *Journal of Business Ethics, 18,* 295–304.

40. Ambrose & Kulik, Old friends, new faces.

41. Van Eerde, W., & Thierry, H. (1996). Vroom's expectancy models and work-related criteria: A meta-analysis. *Journal of Applied Psychology, 81,* 575–586.

42. Ambrose & Kulik, Old friends, new faces.

In experiments with monkeys in the 1930s, animal psychologist Edward Tolman provided a first glimpse at the importance of justice concerns in motivating behavior.[43] As part of his work aimed at finding out whether monkeys recognized symbols, Tolman put different symbols on each of several cups. Then, over many trials, he consistently put bananas under the cup with a particular symbol and observed whether the monkey used the symbol to find the banana.

As the story goes, one day Tolman tried to substitute monkey chow for the banana under the cup. Monkeys like monkey chow, but monkeys *love* bananas. So what happened when Tolman's clever monkey picked the correct symbol and turned over the cup only to find monkey chow? Just like any self-respecting human being under the same circumstances, the monkey got hysterical, threw a temper tantrum, and refused to play Tolman's game anymore.

Why was this outcome so upsetting for the monkey? Why would it be upsetting if it happened to you? The consequences were desirable, and the contingencies were not violated. The problem was that the outcome wasn't fair. The monkey had been led to believe he *deserved* a banana for the difficult task of identifying the correct symbol. When you deserve a banana, getting paid off in monkey chow just isn't fair.

Two types of justice concerns influence employee motivation: distributive justice concerns and procedural justice concerns. **Distributive justice** concerns have to do with the fairness of the outcomes received; **procedural justice** concerns have to do with the fairness of the process by which those outcomes were determined.

DISTRIBUTIVE JUSTICE. A lot of what we know about workers' distributive justice concerns is captured in **equity theory.** Equity theory views behavior as a process in which workers exchange appropriate work behaviors for desired consequences. This means workers are aware of more than just which behaviors are appropriate and which desired consequences they will merit. It means that workers also are aware of the *relationship* between appropriate behaviors and desired consequences, of just how much need fulfillment they receive in exchange for a specified amount of appropriate behavior.

J. Stacey Adams developed and tested the ideas underlying equity theory while working as a researcher with the General Electric Company in Crotonville, New York. Adams found that workers strive to maintain equity in their exchange relationship at work; when they perceive inequity, they strive to reestablish an equitable exchange arrangement.[44]

JUDGING EQUITY. Equity is a function of the perceived *ratio* between the effort (inputs) a worker puts into a job and the outcomes (consequences) he or she receives in exchange. For instance, if you worked 4 hours (your input) and received $60 in exchange (your outcome), your equity ratio (outcomes/inputs) would be 60/4, or 15. In practice, of course, equity ratio calculations are much more abstract and complex. Possible work inputs might include such factors as initiative, effort, enthusiasm, education, experience, and accountability (Figure 3-6). In addition to pay, outcomes might include

---

43. Tolman, E. C. (1932). *Purpose behavior in animals and men.* New York: Century.
44. Adams, J. S. (1963). Toward an understanding of inequity. *Journal of Abnormal and Social Psychology, 67,* 422–436.

■ FIGURE 3-6	Possible Inputs and Outcomes Considered in Equity Calculations

An individual decides whether the consequences contingent upon work behaviors are equitable by comparing work outcomes (the rewards received from the work) to work inputs (what the worker brings to or puts into the job). Work outcomes include both those extrinsic rewards provided by the organization, such as wages, and rewards intrinsic to the job, such as the possibility of personal growth and development.

Inputs	Outcomes
Quality of work performed	Job security
Reliability	Pay
Acceptance of responsibility	Competent supervisor
Job knowledge	Possibility of growth
Cooperation with others	Fair supervisor
Self-improvement	Recognition
Attitude	Adequate working conditions
Quantity of work performed	Interpersonal relations with
Initiative	Supervisor
Adaptability-versatility	Peers
Judgment	Adequate planning/management
Intelligence	Adequate personnel policies
Experience	Amount of work
Personal appearance	Responsibility
Oral communication skills	Advancement
Education	Routine work
Written communication skills	Status
Personal involvement with work	Difficult work
	Personal life

Source: Belcher, D. W. & Atchinson, T. J. (1970). "Equity Theory and Compensation Policy, *Personnel Administration 33*(3), 28; Belcher and Atchinson, (1971) Equity, Rewards, and Compensation Administration, *Personnel Administration 34*(2), 34.

such factors as acknowledgement of contributions, respect, growth, and advancement.[45]

A critical issue in equity calculations is how a worker decides whether a particular outcome/input exchange ratio is or is not fair. A worker makes this decision by comparing the input/exchange ratio to other exchange ratios, such as personal or absolute standards, the ratios of other workers in the organization, and the ratios of other workers outside the organization. Personal standards might include an individual's living costs; thus, a job that did not cover living expenses would be perceived as inequitably compensated. Absolute standards would include the federally established minimum wage. If comparisons were made to the ratios of workers within the organization or to the ratios of workers in other organizations, the comparison might be with the ratios of workers who have the same or similar jobs or equal seniority, or jobs with similar selection requirements. Equity comparisons are usually made on the basis of what comparisons are salient and available. In any case, it is important to remember that equity judgments are based on *percep-*

45. Belcher, D. W., & Atchinson, T. J. (1970). Equity theory and compensation policy. *Personnel Administration, 33*, 28; and Belcher, D. W., & Atchinson, T. J. (1971). Equity, rewards, and compensation administration. *Personnel Administration, 34*, 34.

tions and therefore are susceptible to error. As noted in Chapter 2, workers generally *overestimate* their own contributions at work relative to other workers; workers see more of what they themselves accomplish and contribute, and less of what others do. This tends to lead to judgments of inequitable treatment.

Many organizations have attempted to prevent judgments of inequitable compensation by keeping compensation levels secret. Unfortunately, keeping pay levels secret only makes matters worse. Workers then tend to *overestimate* other workers' compensation levels, fostering perceptions of inequity.[46]

If an organization is compensating its employees equitably, its best defense against accusations of inequity is open communication. Ensuring that the performance-review system leads workers to develop accurate perceptions of their work contributions and that well-publicized rules state the relationship between workers' contributions and compensation should reduce the probability of workers developing inaccurate perceptions about how others are being compensated.

There is growing evidence that a significant difference exists between the ways that women and men arrive at equity judgments. Although some women just starting their careers have better credentials for first jobs than their male counterparts (for example, higher GPAs, better verbal skills), men generally perceive themselves as bringing more or better inputs to their jobs. Men also have higher performance expectations than women, even in female-dominated occupations. Further, although women value pay and promotion as much as men, they do place more value on nonfinancial job outcomes (such as interpersonal relationships). Not surprisingly, then, because women often perceive themselves to be offering fewer or less valued inputs and are willing to count more outputs as compensations of a job, women tend to view lower pay than their male counterparts as more equitable than would men.[47]

RESTORING EQUITY. How do workers react to perceived inequities in the workplace? In cases of *over-reward*, the worker believes that he or she is receiving *more* compensation than he or she deserves. According to equity theory, over-reward can be distressing. On the interpersonal level, it can lead to anxiety that rivalries will erupt with lower-compensated coworkers. It can also lead to insecurity that at some time the earnings level will drop.[48] Workers often react to over-reward by increasing their inputs. For example, research has shown that workers who believe they are being paid too much per completed unit on a piecework compensation schedule will increase the quality of the units they produce. By raising the quality, not only are the workers increasing their personal work contributions, but they are also justifying the overpayment.

Because equity judgments are perceptions of the ratio of work contributions to the value of the consequences received, over-reward may be justified simply by adjusting perceptions. If workers think they are overpaid, the easiest

46. Lawler, E. E. (1971). *Pay and organizational effectiveness: A psychological view.* New York: McGraw-Hill.

47. Jackson, L. A., Gardner, P. D., & Sullivan, L. A. (1992). Explaining gender differences in self-pay expectations: Social comparison standards and perceptions of fair pay. *Journal of Applied Psychology, 77,* 651–663.

48. Jacques, E. (1961). *Equitable payment.* New York: Wiley, pp. 142–143.

path to reconciling this inequity is to become convinced either that their work contributions were more substantial than they believed or that the consequences received were not (upon reflection) nearly as valuable as initially suspected. In sum, workers often sort out over-reward inequities by convincing themselves that their work merited the extra compensation after all.

Inequity judgments arising from *under-reward* pose a more serious threat. Perceptions among workers that they are underpaid have been linked with absenteeism, turnover, and even sabotage. Any of these responses could prove disastrously expensive for an organization. Research has also found that such factors as a high level of job involvement and intolerance for absenteeism by coworkers may mitigate these factors.[49] How a worker resolves the perception that he or she is under-rewarded may depend on the organization's ability to provide additional financial incentives.

PROCEDURAL JUSTICE.   Whereas distributive justice and equity focus on outcomes, procedural justice focuses on how those outcomes are determined.[50] **Procedural justice theory** suggests that workers are more satisfied with the outcomes they receive at work when they believe that the *processes* used to determine those outcomes are fair. Workers are therefore motivated by both their perception that the process used to determine outcomes is fair as well as the outcomes themselves.

Six procedures are believed to increase workers' perceptions of fairness:

1 **Consistency.** Procedures must be consistent to ensure fairness. Inconsistent procedures may engender feelings of injustice.
2 **Bias suppression.** Procedures must be developed and implemented independently of the self-interests of those who develop and implement them.
3 **Rule of accuracy.** Procedures must be based on accurate information.
4 **Rule of correctability.** Procedures must allow room for correcting decisions once they are made and perceived as wrong.
5 **Rule of representativeness.** Procedures must integrate the interests of all parties involved in the process.
6 **Rule of ethicality.** Procedures must follow moral and ethical standards.[51]

Procedural justice has been linked to several critical work outcomes, including job satisfaction.[52] When employees feel that they are receiving fair treatment, they also tend to trust their employers and the organization managers, and they are more likely to demonstrate commitment to their companies.[53]

---

49. Yperen, N. W. V., Hagedoorn, M., Geurts, S. A. E. (1996). Intent to leave and absenteeism as reactions to perceived inequity: The role of psychological and social constraints. *Journal of Occupational and Organizational Psychology, 69*, 367–372.

50. Korsgaard, M. A., Schweiger, D. M., & Sapienza, H. J. (1995). Building commitment, attachment, and trust in strategic decision-making teams: The role of procedural justice. *Academy of Management Journal, 38*, 60–84.

51. Beugre, C. D. (1998). *Managing fairness in organizations.* Westport, CT: Quorum Books, pp. 29–30.

52. Lawler, *Pay and organizational effectiveness.*

53. Mowday, R. T., Porter, L. W., & Steers, R. M. (1982). *Employee–organization linkages: The psychology of commitment, absenteeism, and turnover.* New York: Academic Press.

In summary, motivating a workforce is not just about managing the consequences and contingencies of the work environment. It is also about managing employees' perceptions of those consequences and contingencies.

SUMMARY

Energizing and directing workers to learn and perform appropriate behaviors is important in any organization. Motivating workers to perform efficiently and effectively is especially important to becoming a learning organization. In learning organizations, commitment to acquiring new skills and experimenting with new procedures is often a survival technique in this globally competitive business environment.

The study of motivation can be traced to early content theories that focused on workers' basic needs and desires. Subsequent process theories of motivation shifted the focus to directing workers' efforts toward the fulfillment of organizational needs. The assumption was that workers would pursue such objectives when fulfillment of their personal needs was contingent on appropriate work behaviors.

With the growth of cognitive theories of motivation, the focus shifted once again, this time to the role of workers' beliefs in determining whether appropriate behavior would take place. A worker will pursue a desired consequence only if he or she expects to get it and considers the cost fair. Perceptions about expectancies and justice play important roles in a worker's decision to engage in appropriate work behaviors.

The various approaches to motivation discussed in this chapter are important because they provide managers with critical building blocks for motivating the learning and performance of a workforce. The specific application of these theories to management tasks is the focus of Part IV of this book.

KEY TERMS

Alderfer's ERG theory
Complex learning
Conditioning
Consequence
Content theories of motivation
Contingency
Distributive justice
Equity theory
Expectancy
Expectancy theory
Externality
Herzberg's two-factor theory
Hygiene factor
Instrumentality
Knowledge management
Law of effect
Learned needs
Learning organization

Maslow's needs-hierarchy theory
McClelland's needs theory
Motivators
Needs-hierarchy theory
Organizational behavior modification
  (OB-Mod)
Procedural justice
Procedural justice theory
Process theories of motivation
Punishment
Reinforcement
Self-efficacy
Self-reinforcement
Social learning theory
Successive approximation
Two-factor theory
Valence
Vicarious learning

DISCUSSION QUESTIONS

1 Given your understanding of the principles of motivation, does following the adage "Spare the rod and spoil the child" sound like a sensible approach to raising children? Does it sound like a sensible approach to managing workers?

2 Is compassion incompatible with the principles of motivation? Why or why not?

3 Compare and contrast the assumptions underlying the content theories of motivation discussed in this chapter. Why hasn't one theory simply "won out" as the best?

4 Why is conditioning (or behaviorism) an inadequate explanation for how complex behaviors are learned?

5 Why is it difficult to predict whether a worker's performance of appropriate work behaviors will be undermined by equity or expectancy concerns? How can a manager prevent equity and expectancy concerns from undermining appropriate behaviors?

6 Why is it important to avoid the use of punishment as a means of directing work behaviors?

ON YOUR OWN

Assessing Your Work Motivation   This exercise assesses your own work needs and motivations. First, fill out the following questionnaire. Scoring instructions will be provided by your instructor. Next, take a look at the woman in the photograph (provided by your instructor). Is she relaxing, worrying, or daydreaming? What is going through the woman's mind? Write a one-paragraph description of what you think is going on.

   This test is projective, meaning that the respondent projects his or her inner feelings onto the picture. There is no right answer to the question What is going through the woman's mind? The picture is intended to be ambiguous, so that the respondent's answer will reflect what he or she is feeling. Projective tests have been used extensively to assess affiliation, power, and achievement motives.

Motivation Questionnaire   This questionnaire assesses the relative importance of several job characteristics. For each characteristic below, circle the number on the scale that represents your feelings about the statement (1 = very unimportant to 7 = very important). Answer based on your feelings concerning your most recent job or the job you currently hold.

1 The feeling of self-esteem a person gets from being in that job	1 2 3 4 5 6 7
2 The opportunity for personal growth and development in that job	1 2 3 4 5 6 7
3 The prestige of the job inside the company (that is, regard received from others in the company)	1 2 3 4 5 6 7
4 The opportunity for independent thought and action in that job	1 2 3 4 5 6 7
5 The feeling of security in that job	1 2 3 4 5 6 7
6 The feeling of self-fulfillment a person gets from being in that position (that is, the feeling of being able to use one's own unique capabilities, realizing one's potential)	1 2 3 4 5 6 7
7 The prestige of the job outside the company (that is, the regard received from others not in the company)	1 2 3 4 5 6 7
8 The feeling of worthwhile accomplishment in that job	1 2 3 4 5 6 7

9 The opportunity in that job to give help to   1 2 3 4 5 6 7
other people
10 The opportunity in that job for participation   1 2 3 4 5 6 7
in the setting of goals
11 The opportunity in that job for participation in   1 2 3 4 5 6 7
the determination of methods and procedures
12 The authority connected with the job   1 2 3 4 5 6 7
13 The opportunity to develop close friendships   1 2 3 4 5 6 7
in the job

Now that you have completed the questionnaire, score it as follows:

Rating for question 5 = ___. Divide by 1 = ___security.
Add ratings for questions 9 and 13 = ___. Divide by 2 = ___social.
Add ratings for questions 1, 3, and 7 = ___. Divide by 3 = ___esteem.
Add ratings for questions 4, 10, 11, and 12 = ___. Divide by 4 = ___autonomy.
Add ratings for questions 2, 6, and 8 = ___. Divide by 3 = ___self-actualization.

How do your scores compare with the scores of managers working in organizations? Your instructor has national norms for presidents, vice presidents, and upper-middle-level, lower-middle-level, and lower-level managers with whom you can compare your mean scores.

Source: Porter, L. W. (1964). *Organizational patterns of managerial job attitudes.* New York: American Foundation for Management Research, pp. 17, 19.

CLOSING CASE   CHAPTER 3

THE MANAGER'S MEMO

FROM: A. D. Williams, Plant Manager, Millennium Computers
TO: B. G. Simpson, Production Manager, Millennium Computers
RE: Need for Strategy to Increase Production

Brad, as you know, sales of our Computer Pro laptop have been extremely good. Millennium is quickly moving into the number-one position in the competitive laptop market. Unfortunately, production is not keeping pace with demand. As you know, failure to deliver product in a timely fashion to the marketplace is a sure-fire route to destroying our hard-earned reputation. As you also know, as a startup company, we are limited in the capital available for expansion. Ensuring our competitive advantage—if not Millennium's very survival—depends on our increasing production while maintaining costs.

Currently, even with three shifts per day, 6 days a week, production is 30% lower than sales forecasts. The only solution is to motivate our production associates to significantly increase their output. Your future with Millennium, as well as the future of the company itself, depends on achieving this change in work behavior.

By Friday of this week, please provide me with your department's strategy for increasing production by 20% by the end of this quarter and for continued improvement throughout subsequent quarters.

I know that one of your strengths is in motivating our employees. I'm counting on you to get swift, desirable results.

CASE DISCUSSION QUESTIONS

Assume that you are Brad Simpson, the production manager to whom this memo was written. Write a response to plant manager A. D. Williams in which you describe your plans for motivating Millennium's production associates to increase output of its Computer Pro laptop. Refer to the motivation theories and research described in this chapter, as well as the concept of a learning organization, to support your strategy.

CHAPTER 4

Individual Decision Making

DECISION TO BOMB IRAQ MEETS WITH GREAT CONTROVERSY

Considered by many to be "the most powerful man on earth," the president of the United States makes decisions that affect not only residents of the United States but of the world. Is it any wonder that President Clinton's decision to bomb Iraq on December 16, 1998, on the eve of his impeachment vote, was met with a great deal of criticism?

Two basic assumptions underpinned the critics' arguments: First, the president's approval ratings would rise following the bombing because the public generally supports the president in times of crisis; second, military action would serve to deflect attention from the Monica Lewinsky scandal and President Clinton's impeachment trial. In short, the president's detractors claimed that his decision to bomb Iraq was personally driven.

Not surprisingly, the president and his supporters defended the decision equally strenuously. "What I did was the right thing for the country," the president said. "How could the president not have gone forward?" argued a senior White House official. Whether as president or in less powerful positions, employees are constantly called upon to make decisions, some of which may affect the viability of their organizations. In this chapter, we will examine the processes of individual decision making and the psychological and cognitive factors that go into the selection of one choice over another.

Sources: Dunham, R. S., Crock, S., & Borrus, A. (1998, December 28). How bombing Iraq may deepen the divide in Washington. *Business Week,* p. 77; McFeatters, A. (1998, December 18). Clinton denies airstrike tied to impeachment amid criticism of timing, president says he did "right thing for the country." *Milwaukee Journal Sentinel,* p. 15; Ratnesar, R. (1998, December 28). What good did it do? The air assault battered Iraq, but it hasn't wiped out the threat posed by Saddam's secret lethal arsenal. *Time Magazine,* p. 68.

INTRODUCTION

The complete cycle of organizational decision making, of which individual decision making is one of four components, is illustrated in Figure 4-1. These four components can be described as follows:

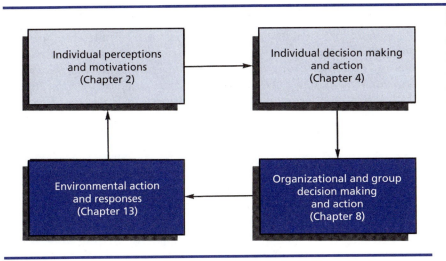

Organizational Decision Making

Organizational decision making is cyclical. Individuals (1) think and (2) choose. Individual choices add up to (3) organizational choices, which invite (4) environmental responses. In turn, these responses influence individual thought.

- **Individual perceptions and motivations.** Decision making begins when individuals perceive a discrepancy between how their organization could or should be and how it actually is. This perceived difference between what is and what could or should be precipitates decision making and action.
- **Individual decision making and action.** Individuals respond to perceived discrepancies by making decisions and taking actions. This chapter focuses on the nature and importance of these individual decisions in the larger organizational context.
- **Organizational and group decision making and action.** The process through which individuals' choices and actions come together to produce group or organizational choices and actions—group decision making, for instance—is the focus of Part III of this book. Note that at the group or organizational level, good decisions do not always produce good actions. When lots of people are involved, even good decisions can be implemented incorrectly.
- **Environmental action and responses.** Finally, the larger environment in which the organization functions responds to behavioral changes. The importance of the environment and its responses to and influences on organizations is the focus of Part V of this book.

MAKING DECISIONS

The focus of this chapter is the individual decision-making component of organizational decision making. Decisions are responses to problems—differences between what is and what could or should be. These problems can vary in importance from figuring out which job you should accept after graduation to deciding which brand of toothpaste to buy. The vignette at the beginning of this chapter tells of a difficult decision that faced President Clinton—whether to bomb Iraq. The president's decision could be considered one of great importance, especially since it would significantly affect the lives of many individuals.

THE RATIONAL MODEL: SIX STEPS OF DECISION MAKING

One commonly accepted model of decision making is often referred to as the rational model.[1] The notion is that decisions are based on **rationality,** or a careful and calculated choice to maximize value given in assessment of alternatives and their consequences. In Western society, the term *rationality* also denotes high-quality decision making uninfluenced by irrelevant or fleeting considerations. The rational model proposes that a decision maker goes through the following six steps before reaching a decision:

1 **Recognize and define the problem.** Perceiving a discrepancy between what is and what could or should be is called *problem recognition* and provides the foundation for all individual decision making.

Defining the problem correctly is critical to successful individual decision making. However, because problem recognition is a perceptual process, managers do not always accurately assess the problems at hand. There are several reasons they make this mistake: (a) They define the problem by available solutions, (b) they focus on aspects of problems they know they can solve and ignore larger, more difficult, issues, or (c) they diagnose problems in terms of the most obvious symptoms. In other words, they get sidetracked by tangential issues and by their beliefs about what problems they know they can solve.

2 **Identify and weight the criteria.** The rational decision maker identifies criteria necessary to make a decision. Given that most decisions require accomplishing more than one objective, the criteria must also be weighted to determine the relevant value of each identified criterion.

3 **Search for information.** If a perceived discrepancy is important, then the decision maker will implement a third stage of the decision-making process: determining why the problem occurred. This involves gathering information about the problem or discrepancy and possible ways to solve it. At the end of this process, the decision maker should have a clear understanding of the problem and should have collected sufficient information to begin the fourth phase of the decision-making process.

4 **Generate alternatives.** In this phase of individual decision making, the decision maker develops or identifies potential courses of action. This phase requires transforming the information that was previously gathered into a set of alternatives. Identifying these alternatives is a difficult task that requires considerable creativity and mental flexibility.

Frequently, managers spend too little time on this phase because they are willing to choose from among the available alternatives before they have generated a diverse range of options. Theoretically, managers should continue to generate alternatives until the potential for improving on the choices is too small to justify the added expense. Often, managers are willing to stop generating alternatives at the first sign that they have a potentially acceptable solution.

5 **Compute the optimal decision.** When a sufficient number of alternatives have been identified, it's time to evaluate them and make a choice. Either the decision maker can compare each alternative to every other alternative, or the decision maker can weigh each alternative in the con-

---

1. See, for an example, Bazerman, M. H. (1998). *Judgment in managerial decision making* (4th ed.). New York: Wiley, pp. 3–4; and Huber, G. (1980). *Managerial decision making.* Glenview, IL: Scott, Foreman).

text of the desired goal. Although both methods have their strong points, the more clearly defined the problem and its antecedents (or causes) and the more specific the alternatives, the better the eventual choice.

6 **Implement and assess the decision.** When a choice has been made, the decision maker must implement the decision. The process of making a choice is important, but decisions are worthless unless implemented. For example, if President Clinton had made a decision but did not follow through in implementing it, his credibility as a decision maker would have been questioned by the public. Decision makers are remiss if they do nothing to implement a decision after having devoted time, energy, and organizational resources to identifying an appropriate course of action. Decision makers are also remiss if they make no attempt to assess the appropriateness of the chosen course of action.

After implementing the choice, the decision maker should monitor the outcome to determine what changes have occurred. Did the discrepancy between desired and actual states disappear? If not, perhaps the real problem was not solved. The information about the problem may have been incomplete, or the wrong alternative may have been selected. Do changes need to be made in how alternatives are evaluated? Perhaps the decision was not correctly implemented. Regardless of the cause, if the decision does not resolve the discrepancy, then the process may have to begin again. Figure 4-2 illustrates this complete cycle of individual decision making.

This six-phase process represents an ideal to which decision makers aspire; however, it is a difficult (if not an impossible) ideal to achieve. To be a rational decision maker, a manager would have to compile a complete list of all the possible solutions to a problem and their consequences. The manager would have to know how the world (or at least the organization and its environment) would be affected by each alternative. Even when making apparently simple decisions, this places substantial demands on the information-collection, storage, and integration powers of individual decision makers. In fact, these demands are so great that they typically exceed the capabilities of

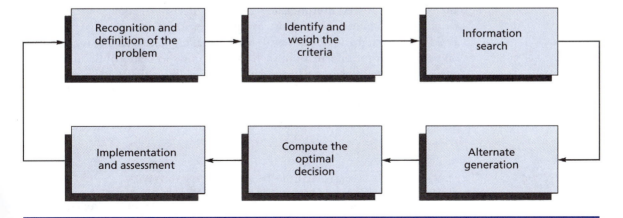

The Individual Decision-making Process   ■ **FIGURE 4-2**

Individual decision making, as organizational decision making, can be represented as a feedback cycle.

Recognition and definition of the problem	→	Identify and weigh the criteria	→	Information search

Implementation and assessment	←	Compute the optimal decision	←	Alternate generation

the human mind. Thus, although rationality is an attractive ideal, actual decision making typically falls short of rationality in the following ways[2]:

1 To make a totally rational decision requires complete knowledge and anticipation of the consequences that will follow each choice. In practice, knowledge is always incomplete.

2 Because the consequences of actions occur in the future, they can only be imagined. In attaching preference or value to a particular outcome, decision makers must rely on their imagination rather than experience, and, as a result, the attractiveness of a consequence can be anticipated only imperfectly. Only by actually experiencing a consequence can we typically know our preference for that outcome.

3 Making a totally rational decision requires choosing from among all possible alternatives. However, the number of alternative actions in any situation is unlimited. In practice, decision makers have the time to consider only a few of the infinite possibilities.

4 Human decision makers can retain only a relatively small amount of information in memory.

5 The limited information-processing capabilities of decision makers constrain their ability to perform the necessary calculations (even given all the necessary information) that would lead to making the best decisions from among all the alternatives.

6 Rationality assumes that decision makers have a stable, specifiable, and consistent hierarchy of needs and motivations. As noted in Chapter 3, however, human needs and goals change over time, and individuals and organizations often simultaneously pursue apparently incompatible objectives.

Given these limitations on any decision maker's abilities, it should not be surprising that decision making in the real world often falls short of the rational ideal. However, because rationality is such an attractive goal, individuals are hesitant to give up their perceptions of themselves as rational decision makers. Much of the research on managers as decision makers has been based on self-reports of how they claim they make decisions. Typically, they describe a process of individual decision making that closely follows the six-phase rational cycle.

When actual behavior has been systematically observed, however, quite a different picture emerges. In contrast with the perception that managers sit in their offices, carefully consider information and alternatives, and make calculated choices, observation indicates that their decision-making processes fall far short of the ideal. One study, for example, found that managers tend to avoid hard (systematic or analytical) data in making decisions and tend to rely on softer forms of information, such as gossip or speculation.[3] Because managers make hundreds of decisions daily, it seems likely that even approximating the demands of rational decision making is beyond reach. A different decision-making model is required to capture the actual decision behavior of managers.

2. March, J. G., & Simon, H. A. (1958). *Organizations.* New York: Wiley.

3. Mintzberg, H. (1975, July/August). The manager's job: Folklore and fact. *Harvard Business Review*, pp. 49–61; and How top managers manage their time. (1990, June 4). *Fortune*, pp. 250–262.

| **Decision Making Quiz** | ■ **FIGURE 4-3** |

1 The following 10 corporations were ranked by *Fortune* magazine as among the 500 largest U.S.-based firms based on sales volume for 1995:
A Black and Decker, Dean Foods, McGraw-Hill, Owens-Corning, Pennzoil
B American International Group, Albertson's, McKesson, USX, Pricecostco
Which group of five organizations (A or B) had the largest total sales volume?

2 The best student in my MBA class this past semester writes poetry and is rather shy and small in stature. What was the student's undergraduate major:
A Chinese studies?
B Psychology?

3 Which is riskier:
A Flying in a commercial airliner on a 400-mile trip
B Driving a car on a 400-mile trip?

4 Are there more words in the English language that
A Begin with the letter *r*
B Have *r* as the third letter?

5 On one day in a large metropolitan hospital, eight births were recorded by gender in the order of their arrival. Which of the following orders of births (B = boy, G = girl) was most likely to be reported?
A BBBBBBBB
B BBBBGGGG
C BGBBGGGB

6 A large car manufacturer his recently been hit with a number of economic difficulties, and it appears as if three plants need to be closed and 6,000 employees laid off. The vice president of production has been exploring ways to avoid this crisis. She has developed two plans:
A Plan A will save one of the three plants and 2,000 jobs.
B Plan B has a one-third probability of saving all three plants and all 6,000 jobs, but it has a two-thirds probability of saving no plants and no jobs.
Which plan would you select?

Source: Bazerman, *Judgment in managerial decision making* (4th ed.), pp. 11–41; and Bazerman, M. H. (1990). *Judgment in managerial decision making* (2nd ed.). New York: Wiley.

THE BOUNDED RATIONALITY MODEL

The rational model of decision making describes how a decision should be made, rather than how managers actually make decisions. In his Nobel Prize–winning work, economist Herbert Simon suggested that, given the limitations of human information processing, prescriptions for how decisions should be made (such as the six-step process illustrated in Figure 4-3) are far less useful for understanding and predicting individual decision-making behavior than are descriptions of how decisions are made.[4] As an alternative to the rational model, Simon proposed what he called the *bounded rationality model*. A descriptive model, Simon's bounded rationality model diverges from the rational ideal in four important ways: It characterizes actual individual decision-making behavior as based on a limited perspective, the sequential evaluation of alternatives, satisficing, and the use of judgmental heuristics.

LIMITED PERSPECTIVE. Simon's model assumes that actual decision makers manage the demands of information processing by limiting the scope

---

4. Simon, H. A. (1957). *Administrative behavior.* New York: Macmillan.

of decisions. The assumption is that not all alternatives are considered and not all goals are accommodated. Instead, the focus of the choice is limited to a manageable subset of goals, alternatives, and consequences. Further, the decision maker may pursue multiple and conflicting goals simultaneously. To reconcile the differences, decision making is compartmentalized. At one time, one decision may be seen to help achieve one goal, whereas at another time, another decision may be seen to help achieve another, mutually exclusive, goal.

Consider, for example, a department head who issues a travel policy at the beginning of the fiscal year. The policy, designed to promote departmental budgetary goals, states that reimbursement for all company-sponsored travel will be limited to $1,500. However, 2 weeks after the policy is put in place, an employee known for his "squeaky wheel" behavior requests reimbursement of $1,650 for a trip. After three meetings with the employee, the department head finally approves the request. On the one hand, the decision satisfies the department head's need to limit further interactions with the troublesome employee—an important goal—but, on the other hand, it's at the cost of violating the first goal of careful fiscal management. Limited-scope decision making reduces information-searching and -processing demands and makes decision making manageable. Though, as the department head quickly discovered, it clearly has its costs.

SEQUENTIAL EVALUATION OF ALTERNATIVES. The second way in which the bounded rationality model deviates from the normative rational model is in its assumptions about how alternatives are evaluated. According to Simon, rather than simultaneously considering all possible alternatives and their consequences and choosing the best alternative, actual decision makers evaluate alternatives sequentially.

For example, two alternatives may be considered and the better one is chosen. That alternative may then be compared to another alternative. This "pair-wise" comparison requires considerably less mental activity than comparing a number of alternatives simultaneously. In fact, a study of decision making in personnel selections found that individuals who evaluated candidates sequentially took significantly less time than those who evaluated the same number of candidates simultaneously.[5]

SATISFICING. Theoretically, a decision maker could continue making pair-wise comparisons of all possible alternatives until the optimal solution emerged. However, given the number of decisions that need to be made and the amount of time that would be consumed in such extended comparisons, another goal—taking timely action—must take precedence. Since the costs of finding an optimal course of action are too dear, decision makers must be willing to forgo the best solution in favor of one that is acceptable. Thus, decision makers **satisfice** (derived from *satisfy* and *suffice*) and choose the one that produces an outcome that is "good enough."

JUDGMENTAL HEURISTICS AND BIASES. The fourth way in which the bounded rationality model differs from the rational model is in its use of judgmental heuristics. **Judgmental heuristics,** or summaries of past experiences, are used as rules of thumb, or shortcuts, to reduce the information-processing demands on decision makers. Increasingly significant in strategic decision making, heuristics have been reported to be used both individually

---

5. Huber, V. L., Neale, M. A., & Northcraft, G. B. (1987). Decision bias and personnel selection strategies. *Organizational Behavior and Human Decision Processes, 40,* 136–147.

and in combination with other strategies to reach acceptable decisions.[6] For the most part, using heuristics saves the decision maker mental energy but can result in systematically biased outcomes. Two examples of judgmental heuristics are availability and representativeness.

Availability. The first example of a judgmental heuristic is availability. Availability means that decision makers often assess the frequency or likelihood of an event occurring based on how easily they can remember it or how easily it becomes available.[7] This "rule" assumes that frequently occurring events are familiar to us and thus easy to recall. Familiar events often *are* more easily recalled than less frequent events.

Biased outcomes can result from dependence on the availability heuristic when the ease of recall is influenced by factors unrelated to the actual frequency of an event's occurrence. Problem 1 in Figure 4-3 provides an example of the use of the **availability bias.** Most people choose Group A, even though B is really the correct choice. The corporations represented by Group B in Problem 1 have more than twice the sales volume of the companies listed in Group A. However, because the first group contains consumer firms, consumers are more likely to be familiar with them. For Problem 3, driving a car on a 400-mile trip is actually much riskier than flying 400 miles on a commercial airliner. However, media attention to airplane crashes has made them quite vivid in our memories. Little attention is given to automobile accidents, probably partially because they are so common.

The common response to Problem 4 is that more words in the English language begin with *r* than have *r* as the third letter. In fact, a rather extensive list of words begin with the letter *r*. However, considerably more words have *r* as their third letter. In deciding how to answer this question, you probably tried to come up with a list of words that begin with *r* and another list that have *r* as the third letter. Because of the way in which we store information in memory, it is much easier to generate examples of words beginning with *r*. If we think of our memory as analogous to a card catalogue in the library, it is very easy to come up with all sorts of *r* words (just as it would be easy to generate authors from the card catalogue whose last name is Woolf). The card catalogue would be of little use in trying to identify words with *r* as the third letter (just as it would not help in trying to find authors whose first name is Virginia). Neither the catalogue nor our memories is designed to store and retrieve information in that way.

Representativeness. The second example of a judgmental heuristic is representativeness. **Representativeness** is a decision heuristic which says that an outcome should resemble its cause. Managers assess the likelihood of an event occurring based on related occurrences. For example, they predict the success of a new product based on the similarity of that product to past successful and unsuccessful product types.

Most people think that the student described in Problem 2 in Figure 4-3 must have majored in Chinese studies (Answer A). In fact, the correct answer is B, psychology. In deciding to select the first option, respondents ignore important base-rate information—the overall probability that something will occur, all else being equal. The base-rate probability that an MBA student

6. Krabuanrat, K., & Phelps, R. (1998). Heuristics and rationality in strategic decision making: An exploratory study. *Journal of Business Research, 41,* 83–93.

7. Tversky, A., & Kahneman, D. (1974). Judgement under uncertainty: Heuristics and biases. *Science, 185,* 453–463.

majored in psychology is always higher than the probability that he or she majored in Chinese studies, simply because there are far more psychology majors than Chinese studies majors. Thus, in this case, respondents ignore the rational choice and let their stereotypical views of Asians (that they are short in stature, studious, and shy) influence their decision.

Bias also influences most respondents' answers to Problem 5, to which the most common response is C. When asked why they choose this answer, most people say that the birth order looked random, whereas the first and second options looked too ordered. Actually, all three birth orders are equally likely to occur. The sequences—in this case, eight births—are too small for a totally random process to express itself, because of what is called the "law of small numbers." The overall assumption respondents make—that boys and girls are born in about equal numbers—is true for large samples of births. However, one can no longer make that assumption when one is talking about a small sample, such as eight births. In this case, the chances are equally good that the birth order will be eight boys or four boys followed by four girls. In other words, the births will not necessarily follow a specific order (or specific lack of order). To come to any other conclusion, one must assume, as many respondents do, that a relationship exists between one birth and the next, when actually each birth is an independent event.

The belief that events have some sort of "memory" is rampant in the bias known as the *gambler's fallacy*. Assuming a fair (untampered-with) roulette wheel, how would you bet on the next spin—red or black—if the ball just landed on a red number 10 times in a row? If your answer is black, you're not alone. Many betters would do the same, thinking that a black number was somehow due. However, since the number of black numbers and red numbers is exactly the same, the objective probability that the ball will land on red or black is exactly the same. Although you may remember where the ball landed, the ball doesn't; each roll is completely independent of the next. The gambler's fallacy may be wrong, but it definitely has intuitive appeal.

THE INTUITIVE MODEL

Another model that has been used to explain the decision-making process is the intuitive model. Intuition, which professionals use to make decisions,[8] has been defined in terms of several conceptualizations: (a) as a personality trait; (b) as an unconscious process, as opposed to analysis, which is assumed to occur separately on the conscious level; (c) as a set of actions that the decision maker chooses to employ; and (d) as a function of experience from having made many similar decisions.[9]

Although the intuitive model offers an alternative to the rational model, managers should use their intuition with caution. On the one hand, by following their intuition, managers can make decisions rapidly based on comparatively little information. On the other hand, the outcome of the decision is not likely to be better than if they used another decision-making model.[10]

It is important that we recognize that our intuition is often imperfect. Our culture and past experiences are strong influences on the decisions we

---

8. Burke, L. A., & Miller, M. K. (1999). Taking the mystery out of intuitive decision making. *Academy of Management Executive, 13*(4), 91–99.

9. Behling, O., & Eckel, N. L. (1991). Making sense out of intuition. *Academy of Management Executive, 5*(1), 46–54.

10. Burke & Miller, pp. 91–99.

reach using the intuitive model. Consequently, intuition may have been a more effective tool for decision making when our workforce was more homogenous and our experiences more similar. For example, in the 1960s, white male managers supervised white male subordinates producing products for a relatively homogeneous consumer market. Currently, however, with the highly heterogeneous workforce and consumer market, using one's intuition may be increasingly less effective.

DECISION MAKING UNDER UNCERTAINTY

A basic premise of the **bounded rationality** perspective is that decision makers cannot possibly consider, evaluate, and integrate all means–ends information. As a result, all decisions carry some element of **uncertainty** or **risk.** President Clinton's decision to bomb Iraq was considered risky in the sense that it carried the uncertainty of how the public would view his decision. Both uncertainty and risk suggest that the consequences of an action must be understood in the context of their perceived likelihood of occurrence. In other words, a particular action may produce a desired consequence, but at the risk of other uncertain consequences. We often express our uncertainty in phrases such as "Chances are," "It seems likely that," and "I bet." Formally, uncertainty is expressed through probabilities. As used in the field of statistics, probability is a measure of the likelihood that a particular event will occur.

Under some circumstances, our confidence in a particular probability may be very high. Most people would agree, for example, that when a fair coin is tossed, there is a 50% probability that it will come up heads. However, few people would agree that the Dow Jones Industrial Average (DJIA) will be higher than 16,000 on March 30, 2010. The difference is that in the case of the DJIA, we are being asked to forecast the future without knowing all the factors that could affect it. When dealing with cards, coins, gambling, and games, it is much easier to produce accurate probabilities for specific events because we can identify all the possible outcomes and all the processes that could affect them. Even if the probability is low, it is knowable. For example, the probabilities of being dealt certain hands in a poker game are illustrated in Figure 4-4.

Chances of Being Dealt Different Poker Hands	■ FIGURE 4-4

In poker, the probability of being dealt a pair (two of the same card—for instance, two kings) is one in 2.5, or 40%. If you were offered \$1 if you could deal yourself one pair, your expected value would be (\$1 × .4) + (\$0 × .6) = \$.40.

Straight flush	1 in	64,974
Four of a kind	1 in	4,165
Full house	1 in	694
Flush	1 in	509
Straight	1 in	256
Three of a kind	1 in	48
Two pairs	1 in	21
One pair	1 in	2.5
No pairs	1 in	2

Source: Excerpt from Jacoby, O. (1981). *Oswald Jacoby on Poker.* Garden City, N.Y.: Doubleday.

■ **FIGURE 4-5**   **Framing a Decision**

Some choices bring out our aversion to risk; others bring out our attraction to it. When we have sure gains to protect (as in Scenario 1 below), we are likely to avoid risks. When we are facing possible losses (as in Scenario 2), we are likely to take chances to avoid these losses or break even.

1 You can (A) have $10,000,000 for sure (expected value = $10,000,000) or (B) flip a fair coin and receive $22,000,000 if heads appears and nothing if tails appears (expected value = $11,000,000). The expected-value rule would pick B. What would you do?

2 You are being sued for $5,000 and estimate a 50% chance of losing the case (expected value = −$2,500). However, the other side is willing to accept an out-of-court settlement of $2,400 (expected value = $2,400). Ignoring attorney fees, court costs, aggravation, and such, would you (A) fight the case or (B) settle out of court? The expected value decision rule would lead you to settle out of court.

Source: Bazerman, *Judgment in managerial decision making* (4th ed.), p. 46.

REACTIONS TO RISK. Decision makers' reactions to risk and uncertainty often do not reflect careful consideration of the consequences of alternatives. The rational ideal for decision making under uncertainty is to select the alternative with the highest expected value. The **expected value** of an action is the value assigned to each possible consequence of the action, multiplied by the probabilities that each of these possible consequences will occur.

Do decision makers rely on expected-value calculations when they make decisions? For the first scenario presented in Figure 4-5, the "rational" decision is to select the alternative with the highest expected value. For Option A, the expected value (EV) of taking the $10,000,000 is the outcome ($10,000,000) multiplied by the probability of that outcome (100%), or $10,000,000. For Option B, the expected value is the sum of the two possible outcomes ($22,000,000 and $0 million), each multiplied by the probability of their occurrence (50% and 50%), or:

$$EV = (\$22,000,000 \times 50\%) + (\$0 \text{ million} \times 50\%) = \$11,000,000.$$

Surprisingly, the most common response is A, even though A results in a smaller expected value. One explanation is that the typical decision maker is not **risk neutral.** Choosing the option with the highest expected value is a risk-neutral decision—it assumes that the decision maker is indifferent between risky and certain outcomes if they have the same expected value. However, in many situations, **risk-averse** decision makers ignore the expected-value solution and choose the option associated with less risk. The decision maker is willing to pay a premium (the $1,000,000 difference in the first situation) to avoid the risk of the $22,000,000 gamble. Paying such a premium to avoid risk is a common practice. The enormous size of the insurance industry is evidence of that.[11]

Risk-seeking behavior is just the opposite of risk-averse behavior. That is, a decision maker is risk seeking when he or she pays a premium to experience risk, such as gambling in Las Vegas. Because objectively the odds of winning are in favor of the "house," the risk-neutral (or expected-value) de-

11. Holloway, C. (1979). *Decision making under uncertainty: Models and choices.* Englewood Cliffs, NJ: Prentice Hall.

cision would be not to play. Given the odds and the inherent risk, the risk-averse decision also would be not to play. However, as a visit to any Las Vegas casino reveals, a large number of individuals make the risk-seeking choice. In making such decisions, the risk or uncertainty that accompanies the decision options influences the final selection.

RISK IN ORGANIZATIONS. What is an appropriate level of risk taking in an organization? It depends on whom you ask. Stockholders or owners of the company may have their own view, and, as a rule of thumb, lower-level managers generally are more risk averse than upper-level managers. According to managers, their risk strategies mirror their best interests rather than the best interests of the company.[12] Although, ultimately, organizational influences may win out, personal and organizational biases can also pull the decision maker in opposite directions.[13] As noted at the beginning of this chapter, this was the dilemma that President Clinton confronted when he was deciding whether to bomb Iraq. To his critics, he was guided not by organizational motives, but by personal biases.

How, then, can an organization influence the risk strategies of its managers in the direction of the company's best interests? In some cases, communicating the level of acceptable risk to the employees may generate a more consistent risk policy. In other cases, the incentive structure may need to be changed. If incentives are based on the individual's and not the company's success, then individuals are more likely to make decisions consistent with their own best interests. The task, then, is to make the best interests of the organization and the best interests of the individual consistent. In Chapter 12 we will consider in detail the importance and impact of incentive and compensation systems on organizational performance. In the following sections, however, we will address two ways in which individuals deal with uncertainty in organizations when making decisions: framing and escalation.

Framing. **Framing** is defined as a judgmental heuristic that decision makers use to deal with risk such that they become increasingly likely to take risks when confronting potential losses and increasingly likely to avoid risks when confronting possible gains. Used correctly, framing significantly influences the number of favorable choices individuals make.[14] In Problem 6 in Figure 4-4, the typical response is to select A. However, let's reconsider the problem, replacing the two original choices with the following choices:

- Plan C will result in the loss of two of the three plants and 4,000 jobs.
- Plan D has a two-thirds probability of resulting in the loss of all three plants and all 6,000 jobs, but it has a one-third probability of resulting in the loss of no plants and no jobs.

Which plan would you select? If you closely compare Plans A and B to Plans C and D, you will discover that they are exactly the same. Plans A and C both result in the loss of two plants (and 4,000 jobs) and the saving of one plant (and 2,000 jobs). Plans B and D both represent gambles—a 1-in-3 chance that all the plants and jobs will be saved and a 2-in-3 chance that all the

12. MacCrimmon, K., & Wehrung, D. (1986). *Taking risks: The management of uncertainty.* New York: The Free Press.
13. Carroll, J. (1998). Evaluations of risk: Do organizational or individual biases prevail? *Academy of Management Executive, 12*(4), 129–130.
14. Biswas, T. (1997). *Decision-making under uncertainty.* New York: St. Martin's Press, p. 8.

plants and jobs will be lost. Yet, when individuals see only Plans C and D, they typically choose Plan D. Although both sets of plans represent the same two options, changing how they are described—from potential gains (jobs and plants saved) to potential losses (jobs and plants lost)—is sufficient to influence people in their choice of the risk-averse Plan A or the riskier Plan D. Why?

There is a fundamental difference in decision makers' responses to gains and losses. When we are confronted with the choice of losing $10,000 for certain or taking a gamble with an equal expected value, we are likely to take the gamble rather than incur the pain of certain loss. It seems that the pain associated with losing, say, $10,000 is greater than the pleasure associated with gaining the same amount. As the potential losses get larger, we are likely to become more and more risky in our behavior. Conversely, as the potential gains get larger, we are likely to forgo more and more of them for the comfort of certainty.

Escalation. In some cases, a manager may decide to commit resources to a failing cause based on the (slim) hope that there will be a dramatic positive change. This is called **escalation**.[15] Everyday examples of such behavior are commonplace. Do you continue to put more money into your old car? How long do you wait for an elevator? How long do you persist in getting a degree after you realize there is no hope of getting a job after graduation? How many more resources do you commit to a failing marriage? Thus, escalation is the continuing commitment to a previous decision, when a "rational" decision maker would withdraw. Some of these decisions in the escalation process are made based on assumptions because there is uncertainty of the future outcome when making the decision.

For escalation to occur, unrecoverable—that is, "sunk," or historical—resources must already have been committed to the cause. Objectively, a decision maker should be concerned only with the future costs and benefits associated with a particular course of action. Thus, whether you have invested 1 or 10 years in your current relationship, the primary consideration should be its future costs versus its future benefits. This future-oriented perspective is likely to lead to a more optimal outcome.

In accounting, one of the major prescriptions for decision makers is to ignore sunk costs. When we are involved in accounting tasks, it is quite easy to implement this rule. It is a lot harder when we are confronted with similar unrecoverable costs in our daily lives. In avoiding certain loss, a decision maker may discount negative information in an attempt to justify the original decision. And, in committing additional resources, the decision maker may believe that the downturn is temporary—that contributing more resources increases the chance that the initial decision will be proved correct. Unfortunately, such rationalizations may be very risky to the health of an organization.

Escalation has also been examined cross-culturally. These studies have shown that culture is an important moderator of escalation in decision making. The implication is that one's escalation of commitment to a cause is determined not only by the specifics of the situation but also by cultural norms characterized by such attributes as masculinity, individualism, power distance, and uncertainty avoidance.[16]

15. Staw, B. M. (1976). Knee-deep in the big muddy: A study of escalating commitment to a chosen course of action. *Organizational Behavior and Group Performance, 16*, 27–44.

16. Geiger, S. W., Robertson, C. J., & Irwin, J. G. (1998). The impact of cultural values on escalation of commitment. *International Journal of Organizational Analysis, 6*(2), 165–176.

INTERNATIONAL FOCUS ON ESCALATION

EURO DISNEY. In April 1992 Euro Disney opened its gates just outside Paris. Within a year, however, the future for Mickey and his friends looked bleak. Euro Disney was already in the throes of financial troubles. With each passing fiscal quarter, stock prices and earnings continued to fall. By November 1993, less than 2 years after opening, Euro Disney had lost more than $900 million.

Several explanations were given for the unanticipated failure. First, cultural differences between France and the United States were blamed for the rough start. Second, at the time the park opened, Europe was in an economic recession; park visitors simply weren't willing to spend money in the park. And, third, the hotels Euro Disney had built and intended to sell were not attracting buyers.

In an effort to keep Euro Disney operating, the Walt Disney Company, which had 49% ownership, invested $175 million. With the influx of capital, the park managed to stay open through March 1994. Meanwhile, beginning in January 1994, negotiations began between Euro Disney, its 60 creditor banks, the Walt Disney Company, and the French government, aimed at restructuring a debt of $3.6 billion. This was followed by "Challenge 1994"—a major overhaul of operations, in hopes of devising a new strategic approach to the park's marketing campaign and employee staffing.

Finally, after operating for more than 3 years, Euro Disney brought in its first profits. But at what cost? Would the truly rational decision maker have given up on ever hoping to make French Mickey and his friends smile? And, if so, at what point should that decision have been made?

It is easy to see from this example how one decision seems to lead to another decision and so on. The situation can become troublesome when future decisions are based on assumptions or past incorrect decisions, as happened in this case. Although Disney eventually began making profits, this may not be the outcome in all escalation situations. If, for example, Euro Disney would have had to close its doors, the reason could have been attributed to either a series of bad business decisions or escalation.

Sources: Brett, J. M. (2000). *Negotiating across cultures*. San Francisco: Jossey-Bass; Mickey's trip to trouble: Unsuccessful theme park could be closed. (1994, February 14). *Newsweek*, p. 34; Heuslein, W. (1994, January 3). The mouse that roars and roars. *Forbes*, p. 174; and Bernoth, A. (1995, November 12). Smiles return to magic kingdom: Euro Disney. *Times of London*.

As illustrated in "INTERNATIONAL FOCUS ON: Escalation," victims of escalation do not include opportunity costs in their mental arithmetic. Opportunity costs are the costs associated with using resources inefficiently. Unlike out-of-pocket expenses, which are vivid and salient in nature, opportunity costs are passive, abstract, and in the future. These costs are incurred as a result of the passage of time. Ignoring them makes continuing a failing project appear like a more positive decision and abandoning the project appear more negative.

Escalation is insidious, but following these recommendations can help reduce its influence[17]:

- Set limits on your involvement and commitment in advance, and stick to those limits.
- Avoid looking to other people to see what you should do, since they are likely to be escalating their commitment inappropriately.

17. Brockner, J., & Rubin, J. (1985). *Entrapment in Escalating Conflicts*. New York: Springer-Verlag.

- Actively reevaluate why you are continuing your commitment (escalation is often a function of impression management—we want other people to think that we know what we are doing).
- Remind yourself of the costs involved; people tend to ignore the opportunity costs or the costs of continuing.

TYPES OF DECISIONS

If rationality is only an unattainable dream of decision makers, what determines how carefully a decision maker attempts to follow the rational model versus when (for instance) he or she uses heuristics? What determines how bounded a decision maker's efforts are likely to be?

Individual decisions cover a wide range of issues of varying importance to an organization. At one extreme are the decisions that can be made quickly, almost without the appearance of conscious thought. At the other extreme are the decisions that involve many groups and considerable organizational resources. What influences the amount of cognitive and organizational resources allocated to making a decision? Most significant is the importance of the decision to the individual and to the organization.

The amount of time and resources spent on any decision-making process is a function of three factors: the significance of the problem, the irreversibility of the solution, and the accountability of the decision maker.[18] The more important the decision to the individual or the organization, the more irreversible the solution once implemented; and the greater the responsibility of the decision maker for the actual decision, the more organized, analytic, and purposeful the decision maker is in making a choice. Decisions that are trivial or easily reversible result in less organized decision-making strategies.

The familiarity of a decision also influences the resources devoted to it. The routine problems that face corporate decision makers allow the use of standard operating procedures, rules, and policies as substitutes for comprehensive decision making. If the same problem recurs regularly (for example, how much travel money to allow for business trips), a policy can be established, thus eliminating the need for decision making. The policy, or "automatic" decision, greatly reduces information-processing demands. Without standard operating procedures, rules, and policies to direct the daily activity of organizational actors, it is unlikely that managers could ever cope with the minute-to-minute demands for decisions necessary to produce the goods or services demanded by the organization's customers.

Often, the selection of an appropriate outcome depends, in large part, on whether the decision maker perceives the outcome to be attractive. Closely related to this perception is whether the decision maker perceives the outcome to be fair. The general notion of fairness encompasses many different inputs into the decision-making process and therefore deserves serious consideration. In the next section, we will consider this broad concept as it relates to perceptions of justice or fairness in organizations, as well as the importance of fairness and ethics in managerial decision making.

---

18. McAllister, D. W., Mitchell, T. R., & Beach, L. R. (1979). The contingency model for the selection of decision strategies: An empirical test of the effects of significance, accountability, and reversibility. *Organizational Behavior and Human Performance, 24,* 228–244.

RESEARCH IN ACTION
THE IMPOSSIBILITY OF AUDITOR INDEPENDENCE

Max Bazerman, Harvard University; *mbazerman@hbs.edu*

During the year 2000, the U.S. Securities and Exchange Commission (SEC) held hearings on the question of whether auditing firms were sufficiently unbiased to offer independent assessments on the accuracy of corporate financial statements. During the 1990s, increasing concern had developed as a result of auditors investing in the firms that they audited as well as an increase in the number of consulting practices owned by the same firms that performed "independent" audits. Much of the discussion focused on whether investments and the desire to sell consulting services corrupted auditors.

A colleague of mine, George Loewenstein, Carnegie Mellon University, and I appeared before the SEC to argue that the fundamental problem was not corruption but psychological bias. We argued that auditor bias was likely to occur as a result of self-serving biases that were unintentional and hence unconscious. Specifically, we said that the bias was not limited to a few corrupt auditors, but that it would affect most auditors as a result of psychological processes common to all people.

When people are asked to make impartial judgments on the basis of complex information, having an incentive to give a positive audit report based on investments, consulting relationships, or the desire to remain the auditor of that firm in the future makes it impossible to assume that audits are independent under the current system. Rather, auditor judgments are likely to be biased in favor of their own and their clients' interests. The only way to eliminate the self-serving bias, and hence to ensure auditing independence, is to eliminate all incentives to provide a favorable audit.

During the SEC hearings, Loewenstein and I argued that external users of audits were paying a huge price for the lack of independence that results from human biases. Consequently, auditors should not be allowed to invest in their clients' firms and should not be allowed to provide consulting services. Furthermore, we need to replace the current process, whereby firms may choose their own auditors. Without changes, self-serving biases will continue to prohibit the possibility of auditor independence.

FAIRNESS AS A COMPONENT OF DECISION MAKING

Fairness is an important consideration in any discussion of individual decision making, for two main reasons. First, individuals make decisions in part based on what they think is fair; second, individuals, such as employees, who are affected by those decisions also have perceptions about whether those decisions were fair.

Although it is often easy to determine whether we have been treated fairly, it is much more difficult to determine what others perceive as fair. When we are personally involved in a situation, "fair" becomes biased due to egocentrism and self-serving bias. **Egocentrism** occurs when perceptions of fairness are biased in a self-serving manner.[19] In short, we tend to confuse that which is self-gratifying or rewarding with what is truly fair, moral, or even ethical. Max Bazerman, Kimberly Morgan, and George Loewenstein found that auditors, despite their best efforts to place the interests of external users above those of the client and to maintain objectivity, may be unable to

---

19. Bazerman, M. H. (2002). *Judgment in managerial decision making* (5th ed.). New York: Wiley.

overcome this self-serving bias which tends to produce decisions in favor of a "client" (see Max Bazerman's "Research in Action: The Impossibility of Auditor Independence"[20]).

When our expectations of fair treatment are not met, we often experience a strong emotional response. Consider this experience of an assistant brand manager for a Fortune 500 consumer products firm[21]:

> So often I am filled with so much rage and anger because of how I am treated . . . the broken promises and lies by my bosses, the undeserved recognition that others receive, or when I feel as manipulated as an accounting entry into our current fiscal year budget. . . . You know sometimes you want to grab them and shake them so hard that it hurts them as much as you feel hurt. . . . All I want here is a fair deal. . . . Yeah, I know there is no justice, but that makes it all the worse. With every day, it seems that revenge is becoming my only *real* option to gain some sense of justice.

Unfair practices run the gamut from minor to severe in organizations. Likewise, employee responses can range from minor (griping) to critical (destroying valuable company records) to dangerous (revenge through physical violence).

INTERACTIONAL JUSTICE

Researchers have identified several issues that relate to employees' perceptions of fairness in the workplace. These include **distributive justice** (whether they believe rewards or benefits are distributed fairly),[22] **procedural justice** (whether they perceive the process by which these rewards are distributed is fair),[23] and **interactional** (or interpersonal) **justice** (whether they feel the quality of the interpersonal treatment they receive is fair).[24] Managers may have little to say about organizational rewards (distributive justice) or how they are allocated (procedural justice), but they often have considerable discretion concerning the treatment their employees receive (interactional justice). For example, managers may be told that only a certain percentage of their employees may be given an outstanding rating and the concomitant salary increase. Thus, managers may be unable to reward employees equitably for their productivity. Similarly, organizational policies may restrict managers' ability to get feedback from employees when completing performance evaluations. However, even when organizational impediments to fair treatment exist, whether employees feel justly or unjustly

20. Bazerman, M. H., Morgan, K. P. & Lowenstein, G. F. (1997, Summer). The impossibility of auditor independence. *Sloan Management Review, 38*(4), 89–94.
21. Bies, R. J. (1987). The predicament of injustice: The management of moral outrage. In B. M. Staw & L. L. Cummings (Eds.), *Research in organizational behavior* (Vol. 9, p. 290). Greenwich, CT: JAI.
22. See for example, Homans, G. C. (1961). *Social behavior: Its elementary forms.* New York: Harcourt Brace.
23. See for example, Thibaut, J., & Walker, L. (1975). *Procedural justice.* Hillsdale, NJ: Laurence Erlbaum Associates.
24. See for example, Tyler, T. R., & Bies, R. J. (1988). Beyond formal procedures: The interpersonal context of procedural justice. *Advances in applied social psychology: Business settings.* New York: Laurence Erlbaum Associates; and Bies, R. J., & Moag, J. S. (1986). Interactional justice: Communication criteria of fairness. In M. H. Bazerman, R. J. Lewicki, & B. Sheppard (Eds.), *Research on negotiations in organizations* (Vol. 1, pp. 43–55). Greenwich, CT: JAI.

treated will depend in large measure on the interpersonal treatment they receive from their managers and on whether management uses its discretionary authority properly.[25]

INTERPERSONAL TREATMENT. In evaluating the quality of interpersonal treatment, individuals focus on whether they were treated politely and respectfully and whether management followed general principles of ethical conduct. In one study, students were asked whether they were treated fairly or unfairly in job interviews. Students believed they were treated fairly to the extent that the interviewer was candid and honest, provided timely feedback about whether they would be made a job offer, treated them with respect, focused on appropriate topics and avoided such inappropriate issues as gender, race, and marital status, and provided appropriate justification concerning whether to hire them.[26]

USE OF DISCRETIONARY POWER. As noted previously, the use of discretionary power is critical area in which managers can influence employees' perceptions about whether they are being treated fairly. For example, employees perceive decisions as being more fair when they participate in making them. Alternatively, employees are likely to become outraged if they discover that their opinions are not taken seriously—in other words, that their participation is a sham. In fact, employees tend to react more negatively if they are led to believe that their opinions are valued than if their views are never even solicited.[27]

Employees' perceptions of fairness are also significantly influenced by what they assume to be their managers' intents. Thus, employees are likely to discount even fair procedures if they believe a manager is using these procedures to advance his or her own interests and thus benefiting personally. And, as in the case of participation, if workers are given an opportunity to voice their objections to a procedure and are subsequently ignored, they will view the procedure as even more unfair than they would have had they never been given the opportunity to complain.

The context in which individuals are allowed to express their beliefs about the justice of a procedure can also alter whether they believe it is fair. For instance, the order of the items on a survey (the context) had a significant effect on how students assessed the fairness of the grading procedure in an organizational behavior class.[28] This research can be applied to professional settings as well. When surveying employees regarding company policy and procedures, for example, perceptions of fairness are likely to be influenced by the context in which the information is collected.

Because the perceived fairness of an outcome or a procedure may differ from its objective fairness, managing impressions of organizational justice is critical to being perceived as just. In other words, managers should be

---

25. Tyler & Bies, Beyond formal procedures.

26. Bies, R. J. (1999). Identifying principles of interactional justice: The case of corporate recruiting. In *Moving Beyond Equity Theory: New Directions for Research on Justice in Organizations.* Symposium conducted by the Academy of Management, Chicago, IL.

27. Cohen, R. (1986). Power and justice in intergroup relations. In H. Bierhoff, R. Cohen, & J. Greenberg (Eds.), *Justice in social relations.* New York: Plenum.

28. Harrison, D. A., McLaughlin, M. E., & Coalter, T. M. (1995). Do context effects really matter? Psychometric and cognitive evidence in organizational justice perceptions. *Academy of Management Journal Best Papers Proceedings 1995*, 375–379.

FOCUS ON LOOKING FAIR

WHAT DO MANAGERS DO TO APPEAR FAIR?

Jerald Greenberg asked 815 managers to describe the one thing they thought they did to make their subordinates think management treated them fairly. Two kinds of acts were mentioned repeatedly; the managers said that to create the perception that they were being just, they had engaged in *behavioral acts* (things done to look fair) and *social accounts* (things said to look fair).

Eighty-one percent of the respondents said that managers could enhance their reputations as being fair by announcing pay raises and promotions publicly—a behavioral act focused on outcomes. Fifty-one percent mentioned allowing workers to participate in decision making—also a behavioral act focused on process.

Forty-three percent of the managers said that of the social accounts mentioned, examining why certain work assignments were made would enhance their reputations as being fair. An even higher percentage—76%—said that explaining how such decisions as pay raises were determined would have an equally positive effect.

Greenberg suggests that one of the most interesting aspects of this survey was the extent to which the managers were aware of having used entitlement tactics to manage employees' perceptions of fairness.

Source: Adapted from Greenberg, J. (1996). *The quest for justice on the job: Essays and experiments.* Thousand Oaks, CA: Sage, pp. 95–101.

concerned not only with *being* fair but with *looking* fair when making decisions that affect their employees.[29]

Managers use several tactics to reinforce employees' perceptions of fairness. Among these are defensive tactics, such as using excuses ("Economic conditions necessitate my decision"), justifications ("I am punishing you for your own good"), and apologies ("I'm sorry I have to give you such a low rating"). These tactics distance managers from their responsibility for their actions.

Other tactics are more proactive. These include **entitling** and **enhancement**. Entitling tactics—the opposite of excuses—are aimed at gaining responsibility for positive events and their consequences.[30] "FOCUS ON: Looking Fair" illustrates a number of ways in which managers increase their perceived responsibility for fair outcomes and, thus, their perception of being fair. One of the most interesting findings of the research on which this "FOCUS ON" is based is that individuals are more likely to perceive a decision as being fair if they had a say in making it than if they had no involvement in the process at all.

Enhancements, the opposite of justifications, are aimed at augmenting the positive consequences of one's behavior.[31] That is, a manager frames his or her behavior in such a way as to make it appear more fair or positive than it objectively is. One way individuals do this is by leaking information about their actions to opinion leaders, thereby biasing the interpretation of an

29. Greenberg, J. (1990). Looking fair versus being fair: Managing impressions of organizational justice. In B. M. Staw & L. L. Cummings (Eds.), *Research in organizational behavior* (*Vol. 12*). Greenwich, CT: JAI.

30. D'Arcy, E. (1963). *Human acts: An essay on their moral evaluation.* New York: Oxford University Press.

31. Schlenker, B. R. (1980). *Impression management: The self-concept, social identity, and interpersonal relations:* Belmont, CA: Brooks/Cole.

event.[32] They may also use informal communication channels to disperse specific interpretations of events.[33]

Both public and private benefits accrue to managers who have a reputation for being fair. Their self-esteem and self-concept are likely to be enhanced, and, they are likely to have a broader power base. Further, the perception that a manager is fair encourages compliance on the part of subordinates. Such a manager is likely to experience fewer challenges to his or her authority and be rated as more credible and trustworthy than would another manager.

However, there are certain liabilities as well. If fairness is an integral part of a manager's identity, then hints of unfairness in this person will be more damaging than they would be to another manager for whom fairness was not so salient an issue.[34]

How, then, should a manager behave so as to appear fair? One obvious answer is that he or she should allocate valued resources among employees fairly. But by what criteria should these resources be allocated?[35] One option is to adhere to a norm of equality—each party gets the same amount of the benefit. Another option is to distribute resources based on the respective input of the relevant parties such that their ratios of contributions to rewards are equal. Finally, the relative need of the parties can be used as the determinant.[36]

The importance of equality as a norm of fairness should not be underestimated. Those who would be disadvantaged if some other allocation rule were invoked (such as equity—each based on his or her contribution—or relative need) typically propose sharing equally.

But what happens when the self-interest of one party interferes with the interests or rights of another party or of the society or organization as a whole? In other words, what is the significance of ethics in the context of individual decision making? Is the ability to be fair in making decisions consistent with good, ethical decision making? We will examine this complex question in the next section.

ETHICAL DECISION MAKING

Ethics can significantly affect not only perceptions of fairness but also how decisions are made. Researchers have studied the concept of self-interest as it relates to ethical decision making. One of the earliest scholars to justify this concept as a basis for action was Adam Smith. Smith believed that the general welfare of the society was promoted as a side effect of people's self-interest. People would work harder for their own self-interests than if they were made to contribute directly to society.[37]

32. Bies, R. J. (1987). The predicament of injustice: The management of moral outrage. In B. M. Staw & L. L. Cummings (Eds.), *Research in organizational behavior* (Vol. 9, pp. 289–319). Greenwich, CT: JAI.

33. Tyler & Bies, Beyond formal procedures.

34. Cohen, Power and justice in intergroup relations.

35. Franke, R. H. (1988). *Passions with reason.* New York: Norton.

36. Adams, J. S. (1965). Inequity in social exchange. In L. Berkowitz (Ed.), *Advances in experimental social psychology* (Vol. 2). New York: Academic Press; Deutsch, M. (1975). Equity, equality, and need: What determines which value will be used as the basis of distributive justice? *Journal of Social Issues, 31,* 137–149; and Deutsch, M. (1984). *Distributice justice.* New Haven, CT: Yale University Press.

37. Buccholz, R. (1986). Isn't it all a matter of self-interest? *Business ethics series* (Vol. V). Chicago: Loyola Marymount.

■ **FIGURE 4-6**   **The Tragedy of the Commons**

A common grazing area is used freely by a town's dairy farmers. Increasing the number of cattle grazed in the area is obviously in the best interest of any particular farmer. However, if all the farmers keep increasing their herds, they will eventually overgraze the commons. Ultimately, they will kill the grass and diminish the collective interest; that is, they will reduce the value of the commons to the group as a whole as well as to themselves as individuals. What should the individual farmer do?

Source: Hardin, G. R. (1968). The tragedy of the commons. *Science, 162*, 1243–1248.

Justifying decisions in light of self-interest is compelling. Think back to the example at the beginning of this chapter. How strong a role do you think self-interest played in President Clinton's decision to bomb Iraq?

On one hand, it is unlikely that our capitalist system would function if individuals were truly altruistic and pursued the interests of others to the detriment of their own interests. In addition, people are likely to be more highly motivated if they are encouraged to pursue their own self-interests. On the other hand, a distinction needs to be made between short-term, or immediate, self-interest and long-term, or enlightened, self-interest. When Smith described self-interest, he was referring to the long-term view.[38] The conflict between these two perspectives is often referred to as a *social dilemma*—that is, when the best long-term interests of the individual (and, simultaneously, the society) conflict with the immediate interests of the individual. This dilemma describes exactly what President Clinton must have been going through in the hours leading up to the Iraq bombing. As pointed out earlier, one of the greatest criticisms of his decision was that it was driven mainly by his immediate self-interests.

A common example of a social dilemma, the tragedy of commons, is provided in Figure 4-6. Obviously, it is in the best interest of the individual to graze as many dairy cattle as possible. However, with this strategy, the land quickly becomes unusable for the entire village.

The tragedy of the commons is not an unusual problem. Consider the typical example in the study group or group project of the **free rider,** who exhibits an unwillingness to contribute to the larger good. It is in the free rider's short-term self-interest not to contribute his or her fair share, especially if no one can tell if the individual is making an effort to contribute. However, although opting to be a free rider is initially attractive, let's con-

38. Smith, A. (1937). *The Wealth of Nations*. New York: Modern Library.

sider some of the outcomes that may result. First, if all the group members chose this option, thousands of students in hundreds of colleges would receive poor grades and miss out on a useful learning experience. Second, the individual who chooses this option may enjoy the benefits of receiving a grade without incurring the cost of contributing, but what happens if this person's behavior becomes public knowledge? The free rider may end up without a group to share the burden of future group projects.

Given these facts, why do some individuals opt for short-term gain to the exclusion of long-term benefits? Why choose short-term benefits even in the face of considerable long-term costs? Three factors promote this type of short-term decision. First, referring to the earlier discussion of the availability heuristic, immediate benefits are more likely to be vivid and salient. Time-delayed costs or benefits are likely to be less available. Thus, when deciding the likely outcome of a choice, decision makers sometimes discount the probability of incurring long-term costs or benefits. Consequently, decision makers will evaluate the short-term benefits as being more attractive than either the long-term costs or rewards.[39]

Second, decision makers may opt for choices that maximize short-term gain out of ignorance or because of limited cognitive capabilities. That is, from the perspective of their bounded rationality, the information search may not have been sufficient for the decision maker to choose the "enlightened" alternative. Just as a fish swimming into a baited net does not know that escape is impossible, the decision maker may not possess the cognitive capabilities to make the what-if analysis needed to maximize the long-term value of a complex decision.

Finally, short-term benefits may be very rewarding early on. However, these benefits may become less and less rewarding over time, until they are eventually punishing. Examples of such rewards in everyday life include drug and alcohol abuse, extramarital affairs, and excessive consumption of natural resources.

MANAGING ORGANIZATIONAL ETHICS

Since organizational as well as personal ethics affect how individuals make decisions, it is important for managers to "manage" those ethics as they do other resources. It is also important for organizations to be clear about what those ethical structures are so that decisions made in the organization will be ethically acceptable.

Research indicates that most companies have formal ethical structures. A 1995 study of corporate ethics practices, for example, found that 78% of Fortune 100 companies had codes of ethics, 51% had telephone lines for reporting ethical concerns, and 30% had offices that dealt with ethical and legal compliance.[40] Additionally, according to the 1994 National Business Ethics Survey conducted by the Ethics Resource Center, not only do many

---

39. Neale, M. A. (1984). The effect of negotiation and arbitration cost salience on bargainer behavior: The role of arbitrator and constituency in negotiator judgment. *Organizational Behavior and Human Performance, 36,* 97–111; and Platt, J. (1973, August). Social traps. *American Psychologist,* 641–651.

40. Weaver, G. R., Trevino, L. K., & Cochran, P. L. (1999). Corporate ethics practices in the mid-1990's: An empirical study of the Fortune 1000. *Journal of Business Ethics, 18,* 283–294; and Weaver, G. R., Trevino, L. K., & Cochran, P. L. (1999). Corporate ethics programs as control systems: Influences of executive commitment and environmental factors. *Academy of Management Executive, 42*(1), 41–57.

companies have corporate ethics programs, but these programs are broad in scope.[41]

Corporate ethics is becoming more of a focus in countries other than the United States as well. A 1999 survey of Canadian executives, for example, found that 27% of organizations trained their staff in ethical decision making—up from 21% in 1997.[42] Likewise, many Asian, African, and Latin American business leaders believe that achieving a more ethical business climate is the next step toward becoming a more integral part of the global economy.[43] Consider, for example, the following quote from researchers, Theodore Purcell and James Weber:

> Institutionalizing ethics may sound ponderous, but its meaning is straightforward. It means getting ethics formally and explicitly into daily business life. It means getting ethics into company policy formation at the board and top management levels and through a formal code, getting ethics into all daily decision making and work practices down the line, at all levels of employment. It means grafting a new branch on the corporate decision tree—a branch that reads "right/wrong."[44]

Although there appears to be increasing emphasis on corporate ethics, employees express doubt about whether ethical behavior is rewarded in the workplace. Many employees are also skeptical about the ethical commitment and behavior of their coworkers.[45] This skepticism is understandable in light of several unfortunate incidents. In January 2000, for instance, a computer hacker stole and then listed thousands of credit card numbers on a Web site when the Internet music retailer from which he stole the numbers refused to pay a $100,000 ransom.[46] And in October 1999, 13 wholesalers and 8 inspectors—more than half the Department of Agriculture's inspection team—were charged with bribery. It was estimated that members of the team regularly took bribes in return for downgrading quality labels on produce.[47] Reports of unethical behavior among employees is also surfacing in Japan. In January 2000 a former employee of the country's largest company-loan group, Nichiei, was sentenced to a jail term of 18 months, which was later suspended, for advising a customer to sell his body parts to repay a loan.[48]

As managers interact with more employees and associates from cultures with different beliefs about what is standard ethical behavior, specifying what constitutes ethical conduct is increasingly the organization's responsibility. Given the frequent occurrences of blatantly unethical and often illegal be-

41. Ethics Resource Center. (1994). *1994 national business ethics survey* [Online]. URL: www.ethics.org/1994survey.html

42. Gibb-Clark, M. (1999, March 23). Rules seen as key to an ethical business: KPMG's annual survey finds that unexplained expectations, deadline pressures, and individual ambitions are the biggest obstacles to a company behaving properly. *The Globe and Mail*, p. B11.

43. Berenbeim, R. E. (2000, January 1). Rooting out corruption around the world. *Across the Board, 37*, 71.

44. Purcell, T. V., & Weber, J. (1979). *Institutionalizing corporate ethics: A case history* (Special Study No. 71). New York: Presidents Association of American Management Associations.

45. Buccholz, Isn't it all a matter of self-interest?

46. Hacker takes credit-card numbers. (2000, January 11). *The Washington Post*, p. E02.

47. Kappstatter, B. (1999, November 11). Big chill hunts Point Terminal/Arrests, indictments put loans on hold. *New York Daily News*, p. 1.

48. Tett, G. (2000, January 20). Nichiei "eyeball scandal" results in suspended sentence. *Financial Times*, p. 18.

havior in large and highly respected organizations, promoting ethical conduct—that is, the institutionalization of ethics—has never been more critical.

INSTITUTIONALIZING ETHICS

Within organizations, ethical principles can be institutionalized in a variety of ways. The goal of such activities is to ensure that ethical concerns are considered in the same routine manner as legal, financial, and marketing matters. To put this another way, the objective becomes ensuring that even when decisions are not made fairly, they are made ethically. Over the past 20 years, U.S. businesses have implemented several structures and activities with this goal in mind.[49]

Some corporations have permanent board-level committees that monitor the ethical behavior of the organization. These committees, often called social responsibility or public policy committees, are charged with developing ethics policies, evaluating company or employee actions, and/or investigating and adjudicating policy violations. Other organizations have codes of ethics that describe the organization's general value system and purpose and provide guidelines for decision making that are consistent with these principles.

Yet another method gaining popularity is ethics training programs. These can take the form of communication systems, such as hotlines employees can call to report abuses or obtain guidance or—as described in "TECHNOLOGY FOCUS ON: Ethical Behavior"—online programs. Regardless of the medium, the goal is to avoid embarrassing public-relations problems, raise employee morale and productivity, and increase the overall level of honesty.

Broadening our perspective from the organization to the larger society, an interesting cycle becomes evident. Ethical issues for organizations and individuals are those for which there are no clear-cut societywide mandates, such as laws or regulations. Business ethics, then, encompasses practices and behavior that are not covered by legal principles.

These practices are constantly changing, and what is typically an ethical agenda at one time becomes, in subsequent years, the focus of legislation. For example, protection of the environment was an ethical and a moral issue beginning in the 1950s, and the first major environmental legislation was passed in the 1960s. Concern about unethical behavior on the part of U.S. firms operating in foreign countries was an ethical issue in the 1960s, and Congress passed the Foreign Corrupt Practices Act in the 1970s. Issues of workplace safety and employment discrimination were ethical problems in the 1960s, resulting in major legislation in the 1970s. Concerns in the 1970s about sexual harassment in the workplace led to the passage of laws aimed at preventing the problem, beginning in the 1980s. Concerns in the 1980s about fair treatment of disabled workers led to the passage of the Americans with Disabilities Act in 1992. More recently, legal and ethical issues have focused on technological advances. For example, is it ethical for an organization to have access to employees' e-mail? One might surmise that these types of ethical concerns may result in future legislation over behaviors related to technology.

However, one should not ignore ethical issues until they have been codified into law. Quite the contrary. Without laws to guide them, individuals

---

49. Weaver, Trevino, & Cochran, Corporate ethics practices in the mid-1990's.

TECHNOLOGY FOCUS ON
ETHICAL BEHAVIOR

TRACKING AND TRAINING ETHICS ELEC-TRONICALLY AT LOCKHEED MARTIN. On the eve of its merger with Martin Marietta, aero-space giant Lockheed agreed to pay a fine of $24.8 million and plead guilty to conspiring to violate U.S. antibribery laws. Lockheed admitted that in 1990 it had paid $1 million to a lawmaker in Egypt in exchange for help in selling its C-130 aircraft in that country. As a repercussion of this scandal, Lockheed has directed serious attention to auditing, recording, and perfecting measure-ment of employee morals.

Today, many of Lockheed Martin's 160,000 employees receive online training in topics rang-ing from sexual harassment to insider trading. During the 45-minute interactive sessions, em-ployees encounter such pointed questions as "Which is the best means of addressing harass-ment when it first occurs?"

Lockheed Martin's online program also en-ables the company to track wrongdoing within the organization. For example, data are com-piled on the number of employees who have been terminated for ethics violations in given pe-riods of time and on the nature of the allega-tions. In the first 6 months of 1999, for example, 4.8% of the ethics allegations involved conflicts of interest, and 8.9% involved security and mis-use of assets.

Lockheed Martin is realistic about its efforts. Although the company doesn't expect employ-ees to be overly excited about compliance train-ing, employees have warmed up to the pro-gram, especially now that it's offered online. In the past, employees had to check out CD-ROMs or visit special workstations to meet their training requirements. Nonetheless, Lockheed Martin's goal is to tackle ethical matters with the preci-sion it directs toward designing and constructing F-16 fighter jets.

Source: Adapted from McCarthy, M. J. (1999, October 21). How one firm tracks ethics electronically. *The Wall Street Journal*, p. B1.

are responsible for making their own decisions about what constitutes appro-priate ethical behavior.

CREATIVITY

A final aspect of individual decision making is the idea-generating process known as **creativity.** In the past, most people believed that creativity was something a person is born with. Recent research, however, suggests other-wise. The process is now viewed as one of mental gymnastics. Creative em-ployees initiate problem solving in order to benefit their companies, and they develop techniques for accomplishing tasks efficiently.[50]

Companies are beginning to realize the benefits of promoting creativity. This is especially important as companies become increasingly diverse and competitive. Supporting creativity enables them to continually improve and develop. Jerry Hirshberg, president of Nissan Design International, under-stands this concept. When his employees reached a stumbling block in the design of the Pathfinder, he took them to the premiere of the move *The Si-lence of the Lambs.* "The cost to Nissan for our truancy was 50 movie tickets,

---

50. Robinson, A. G., & Stern, S. (1997). *Corporate creativity: How innovation and improvement ac-tually happen.* San Francisco: Berrett-Koehler, p. 11.

50 bags of popcorn, and about 50 extra minutes of lunchtime," he recalled. "The payoff was a flood of ideas for an international product representing hundreds of millions of dollars in development investment."[51]

A number of methods are used to encourage creativity, but four pre-scriptions are common to most creativity training programs:

1 Make sure you thoroughly understand the problem you are trying to solve or the decision you are trying to make. Sometimes problems elude solutions or decision making becomes more difficult because the problems are poorly defined.
2 Relax. Stress reduces creative ability.
3 Try to think in terms of analogies or metaphors. For example, how is this problem similar to problems you have solved previously? If that doesn't help, try thinking about the problem as a paradox and find an analogy that solves it. In general, the idea is to break out of rigid think-ing patterns that may block new ideas.
4 Pay attention to daydreams. Try to put together an image or a piece of in-formation that is outside the problem. Reconciling the two can force the mind to make new connections. For example, try consulting the dictio-nary. This worked for a greeting-card company. Combining the word *shrink* and the business (greeting cards) led to the development of business card-sized greetings that could be slipped into lunch boxes and shirt pock-ets. Creativity can be cultivated. To do so, a decision maker must look at things in new and different ways. Creativity is a form of decision making that requires heuristics rather than logical, comprehensive calculation.

SUMMARY

Because human beings make thousands of decisions every day, the process of decision making appears to be deceptively simple. On closer examination, however, it becomes clear that when done well, decision making is often dif-ficult and time-consuming. Although we would like to perceive our decision-making processes as rational, we are unable to meet the cognitive and infor-mation demands necessary to always reach optimal solutions.

Although the demands of rationality exceed the capabilities of human decision makers, we must still strive to make rational decisions. Decision makers use four means to adapt to their limitations: They conduct local rather than comprehensive alternative searches; they evaluate alternatives se-quentially rather than simultaneously; they satisfice rather than optimize; and they use judgmental heuristics to reduce the demands of information processing.

Attempts to improve our decision-making skills are made more difficult by the uncertain nature of our environment. Not knowing for certain what outcome will result from a particular alternative, we are forced to include el-ements of risk in our mental calculations. Expected value models and deci-sion trees are useful mechanisms when probabilities are clear and outcomes can be assigned different values or utilities. However, many decision

---

51. Caudron, S. (1998). Corporate creativity comes of age. *Training and development, 52*(5), 50–55.

processes are not clear-cut. Even when an expected-value calculation or a decision tree identifies a dominant solution, the decision maker may not select that option. To understand how decisions are made, other factors, such as the risk preferences of decision makers—as well as probabilities and preferences—need to be considered.

Given the inevitability of flawed decision making, how can we make better decisions? First, we must consider the ethical implications of decisions at the individual, organizational, and societal levels. Second, to ensure that ethical considerations become a routine part of organizational decision making, organizations may need to institute board-level committees to tackle ethical issues, adopt official codes of ethics, or implement ethics training for employees. In addition to these organizational efforts, society sometimes needs to legislate conduct, thereby relegating ethical issues to the domain of law.

Developing one's creativity is often useful in increasing one's ability to solve problems or make decision. Creativity is an idea-generating process that can aid employees in making decisions.

KEY TERMS

Availability bias
Bounded rationality
Creativity
Distributive justice
Egocentrism
Enhancement
Entitling
Escalation
Expected value
Framing
Free rider

Interactional justice
Judgmental heuristics
Procedural justice
Rationality
Representativeness
Risk
Risk averse
Risk neutral
Risk seeking
Satisfice
Uncertainty

DISCUSSION QUESTIONS

1 Think about your general strategies for making a decision. How do those you use to make a decision about your choice of breakfast foods differ from those you use to determine what computer you will purchase? What are some of the critical differences in these very different decisions?

2 Even if we did have the cognitive mechanisms necessary to make optimal choices, why might we choose not to engage in a rational decision strategy?

3 What are the three ways in which an individual can achieve a "great" outcome? What differentiates the expert from the novice, if both can achieve great outcomes?

4 What is your general attitude toward risk? List some situations in which you are willing to take risks. List some situations in which you are not willing to take risks. In what general ways do these two groups of situations differ?

5 Ethical dilemmas can occur at all levels of organizations. Why is it difficult for individ-

uals who are low in the organizational hierarchy to confront such issues? Why is it difficult for individuals who are high in the hierarchy to address these ethical concerns?

6 Why is it important that managers consider how employees will judge the fairness of their decisions? How can judgments of fairness and unfairness influence employees' willingness to perform?

7 Consider the following poem:

> I am not free.
> Nor want to be.
> I produce my claim to humanity

Through my willingness to accept
The unjustified demands
Of duty.*

What approach to decision making is implied by this poem? What are the implications for a manager? Would you want this person working for you?

8 Why might it be important for people to believe that they take action on the basis of rational decisions?

---

*March, J. G. (1974). *Academic Notes*. London: Poets' and Painters' Press.

ON YOUR OWN

The Wall Street Journal **Workplace-Ethics Quiz**   The spread of technology into the workplace has given rise to a variety of new ethical questions, and many old ones still linger. Compare your answers with those of the U.S. workers surveyed.

Office Technology
1 Is it wrong to use company e-mail for personal reasons?
   Yes   No
2 Is it wrong to use office equipment to help your children or spouse do schoolwork?
   Yes   No
3 Is it wrong to play computer games on office equipment during the workday?
   Yes   No
4 Is it wrong to use office equipment to do Internet shopping?
   Yes   No
5 Is it unethical to blame an error you made on a technological glitch?
   Yes   No
6 Is it unethical to visit pornographic Web sites using office equipment?
   Yes   No

Gifts and Entertainment
7 What's the value at which a gift from a supplier or client becomes troubling?
   $25 $50 $100
8 Is a $50 gift to a boss unacceptable?
   Yes   No
9 Is a $50 gift from the boss unacceptable?
   Yes   No
10 Is it okay to take a $200 pair of football tickets from a supplier?
   Yes   No
11 Is it okay to take a $120 pair of theater tickets from a supplier?
   Yes   No

Sources: The Wall Street Journal workplace-ethics quiz. (1999, October 21). *The Wall Street Journal*, p. B1; Ethics Officer Association, Belmont, MA; and Ethical Leadership Group, Wilmette, IL.

12 Is it okay to take a $100 holiday food basket from a supplier?
Yes No

13 Is it okay to take a $25 gift certificate from a supplier?
Yes No

14 Can you accept a $75 prize won at a raffle at a supplier's conference?
Yes No

Truth and Lies

15 Because of on-the-job pressure, have you ever abused or lied about sick days?
Yes No

16 Because of on-the-job pressure, have you ever taken credit for someone else's work or idea?
Yes No

The following are the results of the survey, given to a cross-section of workers at large companies throughout the United States.

1 34% said writing personal e-mails on company computers is wrong.
2 37% said using office equipment for schoolwork is wrong.
3 49% said playing computer games at work is wrong.
4 54% said Internet shopping at work is wrong.
5 61% said it's unethical to blame an error on technology.
6 87% said it's unethical to visit pornographic sites at work.
7 33% said $25 is the amount at which a gift from a supplier or client becomes troubling, 33% said $50, and 33% said $100.
8 35% said a $50 gift to the boss is unacceptable.
9 12% said a $50 gift from the boss is unacceptable.
10 70% said it's unacceptable to take the $200 football tickets.
11 70% said it's unacceptable to take the $120 theater tickets.
12 35% said it's unacceptable to take the $100 food basket.
13 45% said it's unacceptable to take the $25 gift certificate.
14 40% said it's unacceptable to take the $75 raffle prize.
15 11% reported that they lie about sick days.
16 4% reported that they take credit for the work or ideas of others.

CLOSING CASE   CHAPTER 4

THE MANAGER'S MEMO

FROM: P. Dawson, Purchasing Manager
TO: F. Baumgartner, Vice President, Small-Cars Division
RE: Alternative Supplier of Seat Belts

The representative of a potential supplier has informed me that his company can supply us with seat belts made of a new material. The primary advantage of using this supplier is that the new material is less expensive. At our present rate of production, switching to this manufacturer could save our company $3 million a year.

According to the sales rep, the new seat belts are like the standard ones in every way except that they are slightly less strong. In crash tests, the seat belts tear apart in 1 in 10,000 tests. This seems like minimal risk, although the standard seat belts never tear apart in crash tests. (As an aside, I checked with the legal department and learned that the average settlement for a death of a driver of one of our cars when we were held liable is $1 million).

Considering the competitive pressure we are under, this alternative supplier may be a wise choice. I am, of course, aware that the company is considering closing the Mill City plant in order to cut costs. Perhaps the savings from this alternative supplier would enable us to keep the plant open, saving 500 to 1,000 jobs.

Please let me know whether you want to try the new seat belts in your division's cars.

CASE DISUSSION QUESTIONS

Based on what you have learned about individual decision making, assume that you are the vice president of the Small-Cars Division, and write a memo describing your decision. Consider whether your decision is a rational one and, if it is not, why is it not.

CHAPTER 5

Conflict in Organizations

CAN THE MARRIAGE OF DAIMLER-BENZ AND CHRYSLER SUCCEED?

In May 1998 two corporate giants in the world of auto manufacturing made an equally giant announcement: Daimler-Benz AG and Chrysler Corporation were about to undergo a $130 billion merger. Much debate ensued over the cultural conflicts that were certain to arise. Some pundits even speculated that the cultural conflict would cause the new entity to fail. Could Daimler avoid the fate of other foreign buyers who failed after spending billions in mergers with U.S. companies?

Research has shown that as many as 50% of mergers fail. Many of these failures occur because of disagreements among executives, differences in structural philosophy, and the inability of employees to mix and work together collectively. These conflicts can lead to exorbitant losses of money. Such was the case when Rogaine maker Pharmacia merged with Upjohn. After the $13 million merger in 1995, the new company suffered 3 years of declining profits.

According to analysts, critical to DaimlerChrysler's success will be whether the new company's executives, particularly the executives and cross-cultural teams, can collaborate and work through the cultural, strategic, and power-related conflicts that will inevitably occur. If so, DaimlerChrysler may avoid the fate of many other merged organizations.

Sources: Quinones, E. R. (1998, May 7). From Autobahn to Motown in corporate culture, Daimler and Chrysler are more than an ocean apart, analysts say. *Boston Globe,* p. C1; Jebb, F., & Arnold, W. (1998, August 17). Business: Great synergies . . . what about the people? *The European,* p. 19–20; Quinones, From Autobahn to Motown in corporate culture.

INTRODUCTION

Companies undergoing monumental change, such as Daimler-Benz and Chrysler, inevitably experience conflicts over resources and uncertainty concerning the future, often leading to stress among employees. This chapter examines some of the forms of conflict that can arise in organizations large and small and their impact on organizations and their members.

INTRAORGANIZATIONAL CLASHES

Conflicts occur in an organization when individuals' interests are incompatible with the interests of others in the organization or with the goals of the organization itself. The consequences can be serious, including turnover of critical employees and even, as in the case of some mergers, failure of the organization. Conflict becomes a critical determinant of success in the face of perceived or real **resource scarcity**—a lack of resources (such as food, love, attention, cars, clothes, autonomy, recognition, and opportunities) for everyone to accomplish his or her goals. Under these conditions, individuals must compete with others for a share of whatever scarce resources exist. Similar competition can occur among family members and friends and among social groups.

Conflict does not always lead to competition. It arises when two individuals (or groups) perceive their goals to be mutually exclusive—that is, if one party gets what he or she wants, the other cannot.

Although managers are sometimes guilty of creating conflict, more often they are expected to manage it. Of the 10 managerial roles identified by Henry Mintzberg, 3 relate specifically to conflict management: disturbance handler, negotiator, and resource allocator.[1] Research indicates that, on average, managers spend more than 20% of their workdays in some form of conflict-management activity.[2]

Mary Parker Follett was the first management theorist to highlight the role of conflict in organizational behavior. Her work during the 1920s contrasted markedly with the mechanistic perspectives of her more famous contemporaries, such as Frederick Taylor. Taylor and others focused on ways to structure organizations to avoid conflict, whereas Follett believed that conflict was inevitable and was even necessary for effective organizational performance. Much of her theorizing now serves as the basis for current perspectives on managing conflict in the workplace.[3]

It is important to remember that although the members of all organizations are destined to be involved in a variety of conflicts and competitions, conflict is neither uniformly bad nor always undesirable. As noted in Chapter 1, individuals with differing perceptions, beliefs, and goals are often the precursors of conflict. Such differences are both inevitable and healthy. When managed effectively, multiple and conflicting perspectives on a problem can lead to creative solutions and insights. As with many other human conditions, conflict in the extreme—that is, when it is poorly managed and leads to hostility and infighting—is destructive. As important as it is to react when conflict has become destructive, managers need to remember that too little conflict may be a sign of serious organizational or group problems as well.

---

1. Mintzberg, H. (1973). *The nature of managerial work.* New York: Harper & Row.
2. See, for example, Baron, R. A. (1989). Personality and organizational conflict: Effects of the Type A behavior pattern and self-monitoring. *Organizational Behavior and Human Decision Processes, 44,* 281–296; and Thomas, K., & Schmidt, W. (1976). A survey of managerial interests with respect to conflict. *Academy of Management Journal, 19,* 315–318.
3. Follett, M. P. (1982). Constructive conflict. In E. M. Fox & L. Urwick (Eds.), *Dynamic administration: The collected papers of Mary Parker Follett* (pp. 1–20). New York: Hippocrene.

■ **FIGURE 5-1**

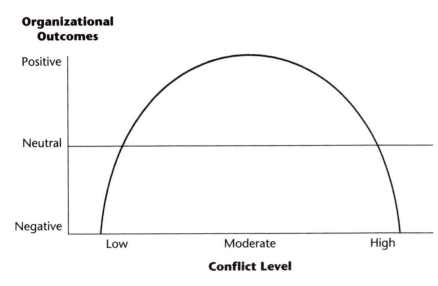

Organizational Outcomes

Conflict Level

Relationship between Intensity of Conflict and Organizational Outcomes

Conflict occurs because people differ in their perceptions, beliefs, and goals in the context of scarcity. Some conflict in organizations is inevitable; however, if managed appropriately, it can prove to be useful and healthy.

Source: Brown, L. D. (1983). *Managing conflict at organizational interfaces.* Reading, MA: Addison-Wesley.

Figure 5-1 depicts the relationship between levels of conflict and organizational outcomes.

U.S. society provides ample examples of situations in which there is too much conflict, but examples of situations in which there is too little are much more difficult to find. Yet the results can be equally deleterious. In his book *Groupthink*, Irving Janis suggested that when too little conflict is expressed in important decision-making bodies, the result can be disastrous decisions in areas such as foreign policy.[4] When too little conflict is expressed in a special task force, for instance, quite possibly either conflicts are being suppressed or the group is lacking in perspectives diverse enough to generate insightful, high-quality decisions.

When there is too much conflict in an organization, it can arouse anxiety in employees and lead to lower rates of job satisfaction, decreased productivity, increased turnover, and reduced information sharing and creative risk taking. The climate may become characterized by mistrust or defeat. Effectively managed, however, conflict promotes creative problem solving and the search for new ways of doing business. It increases employee interest and clarifies individual decisions and perceptions. Conflict also decreases individuals' motivation to agree to decisions without thinking.[5]

In addition to its motivating and involving aspects, conflict can point to problem areas and signal the need for change. It can enable a variety of perspectives to be brought to bear in finding solutions to problems and in identifying new directions for the organization.[6] Thus, the successful manager is

4. Janis, I. (1982). *Groupthink: Psychological studies of policy decisions and fiascoes.* Boston: Houghton Mifflin.

5. Jehn, K. (1995). A multimethod examination of the benefits and detriments of intragroup conflict. *Administration Science Quarterly, 40,* 256–282.

6. Jehn, A multimethod examination of the benefits and detriments of intragroup conflict.

not someone who eliminates conflict but rather someone who maintains it at moderate levels so that individual and organizational goals can be achieved. However, managers must face the challenge of dealing with conflict from numerous sources. Next, we will examine potential sources of conflict.

INTRAPERSONAL CONFLICT

When conflict exists at an individual level, it can take the form of *intrapersonal* conflict (conflict within an individual) or interpersonal conflict (conflict between individuals). In the case of intrapersonal conflict, choosing one goal and selecting the appropriate alternative to maximize this goal removes other alternatives from consideration. For example, in deciding to go to graduate school, an applicant must eventually make a choice of one particular program, thus eliminating other schools from consideration. The amount of conflict that surfaces in these decisions depends on the attractiveness of each choice. Three common types of intrapersonal goal conflict have been identified, each representing different levels of attractiveness among options.

Approach–approach conflict occurs when an individual must choose between two equally attractive alternatives, such as two outstanding job offers. On first blush, this may seem to be an ideal situation. However, if both alternatives are equally attractive, then choosing between them may be difficult. Fortunately, this type of conflict is not long lasting because we are often able to find reasons one option is more attractive than the other—if only by just a little bit. Once this happens, then the slightly preferred option is chosen.

Unfortunately, approach–approach conflict does not always end there. Often, after the choice is made, "decision regret" occurs.[7] The option not chosen then becomes more attractive, simply because it was not chosen. Decision regret may lead to reconsideration of the positive aspects of the chosen option and make it difficult to justify and validate the decision made.

Avoidance–avoidance conflict is created when we are faced with two equally unattractive choices, both with negative outcomes. For example, an employee may be faced with choosing between excessive company-related travel and a demotion. As with approach–approach conflict, this is difficult to resolve because it represents a choice between two like outcomes.

Approach–avoidance conflict is the most common type of intrapersonal conflict and occurs when we have to choose an option with both good and bad outcomes. For example, a person may have to choose between his or her current job and a great position in a bad location. The intensity of the approach–avoidance conflict increases as (a) the number of alternatives increases, (b) the attraction/aversion of the outcomes remains about equal, and (c) the issues increase in importance. If the conflict becomes too extreme, individuals may remove themselves from the conflict by refusing to make a decision. This response probably is not very functional but is quite common. Being confronted with any of these types of choices is difficult. The more

---

7. Bell, D. *Regret in decision making under uncertainty* (working paper). Boston: Harvard Univer-

FOCUS ON
INTERPERSONAL CONFLICT

THE PRISONER'S DILEMMA.   Two suspects are taken into custody and separated. The district attorney (DA) is certain they are guilty of a crime but does not have sufficient evidence to convict them. She points out the alternatives to both prisoners—to confess to the crime that the police are sure they committed or not to confess. If neither confesses, then the DA will prosecute both of them on a minor charge for which they will both receive minor punishments. If both confess, they will be prosecuted, but she will recommend less than the most severe sentence. If one turns "state's evidence" and confesses and the other does not, the confessor will receive a small sentence, but the other will receive the maximum sentence. Each prisoner must make his decision *without* communicating with or knowing what the other is doing. The possible outcomes in years in prison are shown here:

	Keep Quiet	Confess
Keep Quiet	5, 5	15, 1
Confess	1, 15	10, 10

such choices we have to make, the greater the intrapersonal conflict we may have to manage.

CONFLICT BETWEEN INDIVIDUALS

Interpersonal conflict arises when two or more people have incompatible goals, ideas, feelings, or ways of behaving. There are two common forms of interpersonal conflict[8]:

- *Relationship conflict* occurs when members of a group are personally incompatible. Typically, tension, animosity, and annoyance are expressed.
- *Task conflict* occurs when the members of a group cannot agree about the tasks they are expected to perform. Differences in ideas, perspectives, and opinions about how to proceed are likely to arise.

The prisoner's dilemma, discussed in "Focus On: Interpersonal Conflict," is often used to illustrate the nature of conflict.[9]

Recent research by Karen Jehn examined relationship conflict and task conflict more closely.[10] After surveying 93% of the employees at the international headquarters of a large freight transportation firm, Jehn showed that relationship conflict was detrimental to the functioning of the group, regardless of the type of task the members were performing. However, task conflict was shown to have both negative and positive effects. Low levels of task-related conflict were viewed as being necessary for effective group functioning, whereas high levels were shown to have detrimental effects on productive workgroup processes.

The prisoner's dilemma illustrates two basic points about interpersonal conflict. First, the parties in a dispute are often interdependent—that is,

---

8. Jehn, A multimethod examination of the benefits and detriments of intragroup conflict.
9. Rapaport, A., & Chammah, A. (1965). *Prisoner's dilemma: A study in conflict and cooperation.* Ann Arbor: University of Michigan Press.
10. Jehn, A multimethod examination of the benefits and detriments of intragroup conflict.

the choices one party makes influence the outcomes and choices of the other party. Second, individual and joint outcomes may be mutually exclusive. The dominant (best) individual outcome results when the individual confesses. The dominant joint outcome occurs when both parties remain silent. Thus, the crux of the prisoner's dilemma is whether to maximize the individual or the joint outcome—which, of course, depends on what the other party will do.

CONFLICT BETWEEN GROUPS

It would be simple if what we know about interpersonal conflict could easily be applied directly to groups. However, although much of what we know about dyadic (two-person) conflict can be applied to groups, group conflict involves more than just summing the conflicts and motives of the individual actors. We will go into considerably more detail about groups in Chapters 6 and 8; for now, it is important to consider the added dimensions groups bring to the management of conflict.

Group conflict can occur within a group (intragroup) or between groups (intergroup). In day-to-day activities, it is often difficult to separate the effects of each of these forms of conflict, since groups rarely exist in isolation. Intragroup conflict occurs primarily because groups exert considerable influence on individual members. This influence usually takes the form of shaping individuals' behavior into a form acceptable to the group. Individual members may resist, resulting in conflicting goals ("What is the nature or focus of our group?"), ideas ("What does this group stand for?" "What does it mean for me to be a part of the group?"), emotions ("How do I feel about being a part of this group?"), and behaviors ("How are we to accomplish our goals?").

Intergroup conflict can also alter what is occurring within a particular group. In a study of interactions within and between groups, Muzafer Sherif found that when two groups are in conflict, behaviors within the groups change in the following predictable ways[11]:

- Group cohesiveness increases.
- Task orientation increases.
- Loyalty to the group increases.
- Acceptance of autocratic leadership increases.

In short, intergroup conflict leads to more cohesion or unification and enables a group to better cope with external threats. Additionally, Sherif noted that conflict between groups often produces a "we/they" mentality that reveals itself in

- Distorted perceptions and goals.
- Negative stereotypes about the other group.
- Reduced communication with the other group.

Sherif and his colleagues collected much of their data on group conflict at a summer camp. Known as the Robber's Cave experiments, Sherif's camp studies provide the basis for much of what we know about intergroup com-

---

11. Muzafir, S. (1977). *Intergroup conflict and cooperation.* Norman, OK: University Book Exchange.

FOCUS ON
GROUP-LEVEL CONFLICT

THE ROBBER'S CAVE EXPERIMENTS. Set up specifically for these experiments, the Robber's Cave boys' camp recruited participants from different schools (to eliminate previous acquaintances) and screened for both physical and psychological health. During the first days of camp, the boys were allowed to develop friends spontaneously through a variety of campwide activities. The boys were then housed in two cabins. The population of each was designed so that about two thirds of each camper's best friends were in the other cabin.

Within a few days, the pattern of interaction shifted dramatically. The boys tended to interact almost exclusively with their cabin mates, and shared norms about group activities began to develop.

The researchers then arranged a series of competitive activities (such as football, baseball, and tug-of-war) in which the boys in each cabin were pitted against each other. To increase the conflict, prizes were awarded to the winning team. During this time, the researchers

noted that campers became hostile toward and stereotyped the behavior of members of the other cabin; they even planned ambushes and raids. New leaders emerged who were effective in combat, and intragroup solidarity increased dramatically.

The researchers also devised situations specifically designed to promote intergroup conflict. At a campwide party, for instance, one group (the Red Devils) was allowed to arrive considerably earlier than the other group (the Bulldogs). In addition, half the party refreshments were fresh and appealing; the other refreshments were old and unappetizing. Because of the general level of competition between the groups, the Red Devils consumed most of the inviting food, leaving the unappealing food for their adversaries. When the Bulldogs arrived, they were so annoyed that the incipient conflict escalated from name-calling to a full-scale food fight.

Source: Muzafir, S. (1977). *Intergroup conflict and cooperation.* Norman, OK: University Book Exchange.

petition, whether among adolescents or adults. These experiments are described in more detail in "FOCUS ON: Group-Level Conflict."

CONFLICT WITHIN ORGANIZATIONS

At the organizational level, both group and individual conflict regularly occur. The organization provides an arena for the conflict, and it also defines the relationships and interdependencies among the disputants. A number of patterns of conflict are possible: between two individuals, between an individual and a group, between two groups, or among two or more groups. Further, conflicts can occur at the same level of the organization's hierarchy (between disputants of equal status) or across levels of the organization (between supervisor and subordinate, for example).

A conflict between two people at different levels of an organization is referred to as a **vertical conflict.** The primary basis for such a conflict is the difference in power. For example, the senior managers at Daimler-Benz are likely to have very different personal and organizational expectations than assembly-line workers in the same organization, especially those at Chrysler. These expectations can color experiences, beliefs, and interests, making the groups appear to be incompatible and potentially causing the merger to fail.

A conflict between two people at similar levels in an organization is referred to as a **horizontal conflict.** The more organizational units come into

RESEARCH IN ACTION
DIVERSITY, CONFLICT, AND TEAM PERFORMANCE

Margaret Neale, Stanford University; Graduate School of Business
neale_margaret@gsb.stanford.edu

Recent research has found that diversity among employees can generate better performance when it comes to out-of-the-ordinary creative tasks. The study of diversity in the workplace has taken on new importance as changing economics prompt many companies to downsize and restructure into flatter, more decentralized entities.

The result is that today's corporations are built around teams that must find answers to novel and complicated business issues. These teams bring together diverse groups of people who incorporate a variety of backgrounds, ideas, and personalities.

People tend to think of diversity as simply demographic: a matter of color, gender, or age. However, groups can be disparate in many ways. Diversity is also based on informational differences, reflecting a person's education and experience, as well as on values or goals that can influence what one perceives to be the mission of something as small as a single meeting or as large as a whole company. Diversity among employees can create better performance when it comes to out-of-the-ordinary creative tasks such as product development or cracking new markets, and managers have been trying to increase diversity to achieve the benefits of innovation and fresh ideas. Recently, Karen Jehn of the University of Pennsylvania's Wharton School, Gregory Northcraft of the University of Illinois, and I (from Stanford's Graduate School of Business) studied the effects of each kind of diversity on group performance.

From our results, it is clear that diversity (of any kind) does not have a direct performance effect. It turns out that different types of diversity generate various sorts of conflict—and how the team handles the conflict influences how well it will perform.

Our research shows that informational diversity stirred constructive conflict, or debate, around the task at hand. That is, people deliberate about the best course of action. This is the type of conflict that absolutely should be fostered in organizations. On the other hand, demographic diversity can sometimes precipitate interpersonal conflict. This is the kind of conflict people should fear. It is the type of conflict that is personal: I don't like what you do or how you do it; I don't like you. It is this type of conflict that can destroy a team.

The third type of diversity is based on goals and values, and it actually generates both types of conflict. This is the most potentially damaging of all the diversities. Without value-goal homogeneity, a team can accomplish little. But when a team recognizes and accepts a goal, it makes problems easier to deal with because each person knows the intentions of the others are the same.

In our field research, we studied a relocation company with work teams. We measured different types of diversity by surveying employees. We also obtained actual group performance data and supervisor assessments of how various teams were doing in terms of on-time delivery and services rendered. We found that the effects of diversity (both positive and negative) were more pronounced during complicated tasks that required the interdependent work of several group members.

contact with each other, the more dependent they are on each other; and the smaller the amount of available resources, the greater the probability for horizontal conflict.[12]

Line–staff conflict is also a common organizational occurrence. Line employees are directly involved in producing the organization's product, so they often have more direct influence in an organization. In contrast, staff

---

12. Thomas, K. (1976). Conflict and conflict management. In M. Dunnette (Ed.), *Handbook of industrial and organizational psychology* (pp. 889–936). Chicago: Rand McNally.

employees are not directly involved in production but provide technical and advisory assistance to the line. How much influence staff employees can have on the line is often subject to line employees' discretion. The groups often have very different perspectives, goals, and statuses, creating many opportunities for conflict.

Role conflict is a special form of organizational conflict. A role is a set of activities associated with a particular position. These activities are determined by the expectations of other members of the organization (usually supervisors and coworkers), who make up the role set. Role conflict occurs when two or more role-specific activities are incompatible.[13] In such cases, any attempt to comply with one set of expectations makes it impossible or difficult to comply with the other set. Unlike other forms of conflict, role conflict is organizationally based. That is, it exists because the expectations for the performance of the job (as defined by the role set) do not coincide with the perception of what constitutes appropriate job-related activities of either the occupant of the role or other members of the role set.

MANAGING CONFLICT

By now it should be obvious that conflict is common, whether we are by ourselves, with friends or relatives, or in workgroups. What is important from both a personal and a managerial perspective is how effectively the conflict is managed. In this time of megamergers, the successful management of conflict before, during, and after a merger can result in millions, if not billions, of dollars saved. Needless to say, in the case of a merger like that of Daimler-Benz and Chrysler, the heads of the companies must hope that their managers will be able to manage conflict successfully.

STRATEGIES FOR RESOLVING INTERPERSONAL CONFLICTS

If you find yourself in a dispute with another individual, you'll have several strategies from which to choose for resolving the conflict. Figure 5-2 illustrates five common strategies: competing, avoiding, accommodating, collaborating, and compromising. Notice that these strategies are based on differing levels of concern with maximizing your own needs and those of the other party. Which strategy you select will depend on where within the figure's two-dimensional space your interests lie.

If your primary concern is with getting what you want out of the exchange, then two strategies are likely to be most useful: competing and collaborating. If you are unconcerned with the needs of the other party, **competing** may be most appropriate. Other situations when you might need to compete include emergencies or crises, when the other party is untrustworthy, or when you are sure of the correct solution.

If considering the other party's concerns is as important as considering your own, then **collaborating** may be a better option. Collaborating is particularly useful when the issue is too important to compromise, when you are trying to engender commitment among the parties to the dispute, or when you are trying to gain insight. It is also effective when dealing with people

---

13. Katz, D., & Kahn, R. L. (1978). *The social psychology of organizations*. New York: Wiley.

■ FIGURE 5-2

A Two-Dimensional Model of Conflict Behavior

Strategies for reducing interpersonal conflict can be characterized by the individual's concern with his or her own needs versus the needs of the other party. Variations along these dimensions can give rise to five distinct styles of conflict resolution.

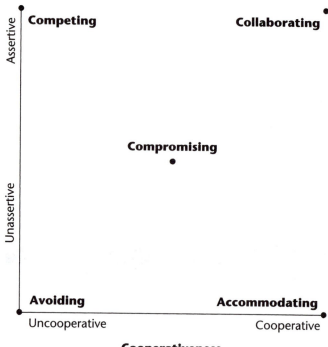

Assertiveness
(Attempting to satisfy one's own concerns)

Assertive   **Competing**   **Collaborating**

Unassertive   **Compromising**

Avoiding   **Accommodating**
Uncooperative   Cooperative

Cooperativeness
(Attempting to satisfy the other party's concerns)

Source: Thomas, Conflict and conflict management. p. 900.

from other cultures, as it helps the parties involved in the dispute focus on keeping cultural differences in perspective.[14]

If you have little concern for your position or for the position and desires of the other party, then **avoiding** the conflict may be your best option. Situations under which this might be the wisest decision are when the issue is trivial or you are seriously outmatched by your opponent. Avoidance may also be the best course of action if others can better handle the problem, people need time to cool down and regain perspective, or the disruption that may occur from confronting the problem is greater than the potential benefit from solving it.

There are likely to be occasions when the other party's issues have priority. If you find out that the position you have been arguing is wrong or you wish to minimize a losing position, you may choose to give in. Perhaps by **accommodating** to the other party, you can earn "social credits" for your next interaction ("You have convinced me on this one, but just remember that you owe me one.").

Finally, if both sets of goals are important but not worth the potential disruption that would occur if the parties used aggressive tactics, then a **compromising** strategy may be most effective. Perhaps a quick, temporary

14. Black, J. S., Gregersen, H. B., Mendenhall, M. E., & Stroh, L. K. (1999). *Globalizing people through international assignments.* Reading, MA: Addison-Wesley.

TECHNOLOGY FOCUS ON NEGOTIATION

AUTOMATED NEGOTIATING IS BECOMING CRITICAL TO E-COMMERCE. Automated negotiation is quickly becoming one of the most critical components of business-to-business (B2B) e-commerce. In fact, say leaders in the B2B world, this online strategy is a prerequisite for seizing the potential multi-trillion-dollar B2B e-commerce market. Although current B2B e-commerce technologies support the buying and selling of commodities, production goods that are strategic to the bottom line represent the enormous untapped side of B2B e-commerce—80% or more of the overall B2B market.

Panelists speaking at a teleconference briefing hosted by TradeAccess, a pioneer in negotiation technology, revealed that currently available technologies for B2B e-commerce, including auctions, shopping carts, and exchanges, do not address the fundamental requirements for trading production goods globally. Buyers and sellers trade in these goods via complex, tiered, ongoing commercial relationships that require the negotiation of dozens of issues. Jeff Conklin, founder and CEO of TradeAccess, noted,

> This new e-commerce market segment is vast and still untapped because today's systems were not designed to meet the fundamental requirements of buyers and sellers of production goods for ongoing sustainable commercial relationships. With production goods, transactions exist only within the framework of commercial relationships. Enabling market makers to offer automated online negotiation is the key to unlocking vast new global B2B e-commerce opportunities.

Source: Adapted from B2B marketplaces need negotiation capabilities to seize multi-trillion dollar global market for production goods. (2000, April 4). *PR Newswire,* www.prnewswire.com.

solution is needed, or other tactics don't seem to be working. Compromising—a solution that enables the disputants to "split the difference"—is the strategy with which most of us have the most experience. Compromise is the strategy many families use to solve the "last-piece-of-pie-and-two-children-want-it" dilemma. The solution: One child cuts the piece of pie into two, and the other child selects the first piece.

Conflict and conflict management represent very broad categories of behavior—so broad that it is often difficult to grasp exactly how to implement a particular strategy. To understand the usefulness of the five strategies, it is important to place them in a specific context. Given the nature of organizations and Western society, negotiation is a particularly fruitful conflict-resolution mechanism.

NEGOTIATION. Negotiation is the process whereby two or more parties decide what each will give and take in an exchange between them.[15] This definition highlights (1) the interpersonal nature of negotiation, (2) the dependency of the parties, and (3) the goal—namely, to allocate limited resources. In the global business environment, negotiation is generally the most effective method for arriving at win-win solutions.[16] As illustrated in "TECHNOLOGY FOCUS ON: Negotiation," this process has spread to the Web, where it is used in global business-to-business e-commerce.

15. Rubin, J. Z., & Brown, B. R. (1975). *The social psychology of bargaining and negotiation.* New York: Academic Press.

16. Adler, N. J. (1997). *International dimensions of organizational behavior.* Cincinnati, OH: South-Western College Publishing.

Negotiation is a process in which the parties decide what each will give and take. Generally, it involves parties who are interdependent and who have roughly equal power. Negotiating a new contract between workers and management might best be handled using integrative techniques whereby both can gain.

Unlike other conflict-management techniques, negotiation involves a dispute with or between two or more parties that are in approximately equal power positions. Further, negotiation involves the division of tangible and intangible resources through a sequential evaluation of alternatives. In an attempt to manage conflict through negotiations, both parties (either explicitly or implicitly) prefer to search for a mutually acceptable solution rather than to fight openly, give in, break off interaction, or have their dispute resolved by someone of higher authority.[17]

The next section examines specific information negotiators must have about opponents' interests, priorities, and alternatives to produce high-quality negotiated agreements.

NEGOTIATING RATIONALLY.[18] The goal of negotiating is to arrive at a *good* agreement. Far too often individuals substitute the goal of arriving at *any* agreement. Thus, it is critical for a negotiator to know what a good agreement or contract is and what it is not. To differentiate between these outcomes, negotiators need to know their alternatives (i.e., the Best Alternative To a Negotiated Agreement [BATNA]), as well as the *reservation price*. BATNA represents the disputants' best alternative should no agreement be reached. The reservation price is the least they would accept—the point at which the negotiators become indifferent to accepting the offered deal or an impasse.[19]

People typically begin negotiating with some idea of what they hope to get, but knowing the reservation price is often more important. While BATNAs and reservation prices are similar in many respects, they are also different. If you are trying to negotiate the purchase price of a new car, for instance, your BATNA may be to continue riding your bicycle to school. Your reservation price may be the price offered to you for a similar car at another dealership. Your BATNA is outside the current negotiation—your option if there is "no deal"; your reservation price is within the negotiation—your bottom line.

Specifying one's own BATNA and reservation price is not enough. A rational negotiator also tries to discern those of his or her opponent. While this may be difficult information to obtain, one should make as good an estimate as possible, knowing that the actual negotiation interaction will provide additional opportunities to gather information about the opponent.

Next, a good negotiator identifies, to the extent possible, the true issues in the negotiation and how important each issue is to each of the parties. The basis for true integrative agreements is that the parties are willing to make trade-offs. That is, they are willing to *make* concessions on issues that are less important so as to *obtain* concessions on issues that are more important.

Regardless of the negotiating situation, identifying the alternatives, issues, and preferences of both parties is critical to reaching good agreements. This information can facilitate the negotiator's assessment of which of the two opposing strategies to focus on: integrating or enlarging the available pool of resources versus distributing or claiming as large a share of that pool as possible.

17. Lewicki, R. J., & Litterer, J. R. (1985). *Negotiation.* Homewood, IL: Irwin.

18. This section relies considerably on a book by Bazerman, M. H., & Neale, M. A. (1992). *Negotiating rationally.* New York: The Free Press

19. Blount, S., Thomas-Hunt, M. C., & Neale, M. A. (1996). The price is right—Or is it? A reference point model of two-party price negotiations. *Organizational Behavior and Human Decision Processes, 68*(1), 1–12.

Depending on the desires of the parties, negotiation can incorporate all the conflict-management tactics previously described. One may choose to avoid certain issues or provocations, one may give in on certain issues (usually with the expectation that the other party will be accommodating on other issues), or one may state one's position and resist conceding. These strategies are part and parcel of the two dominant types of negotiation—distributive negotiation and integrative negotiation.

Distributive negotiation is the type of negotiation that we most commonly expect to encounter. In distributive negotiation, the parties must decide how to allocate a fixed amount of resources, preferences for which are typically opposite and equal. The assumption is that every time one party wins, the other must give up something of equal value. The perception of a fixed pie leads the negotiators to behave competitively and contentiously. As a result, the parties see each other as adversaries, as "me against you." Both must concede or compromise, and, therefore, neither wins completely. Then again, neither loses everything. Of course, splitting the difference, or compromising, is sometimes silly, as suggested by the cartoon in Figure 5-3.

As suggested by our earlier description of compromising, distributive negotiation is a style of conflict management best implemented under the following conditions:

■ No ongoing relationship or potential for one exists—the interaction is a one-shot deal.
■ A quick, simple solution to the conflict is needed.
■ The parties have mutually incompatible goals.

■ **FIGURE 5-3**

Splitting the difference, while a simple strategy, does not always produce the best results.

Their community property had been
equally divided. Still, neither one of
them was happy with the divorce settlement.

Source: RUBES by Leigh Rubin. By permission of Leigh Rubin and Creator's Syndicate, Inc.

| ■ **FIGURE 5-4** | **Integrative Division of Resources** |

Integrative agreements arise when two parties find that their needs and resources are *complementary*. In this cartoon, a single ice-cream bar provides dessert for two: the ice cream for the man and the wooden stick for the beaver. Both the man and the beaver seem to want the ice-cream bar, but they really want different parts of the treat.

Source: Frank and Ernest, reprinted by permission of NEA, Inc.

What about conflict between supervisors and subordinates, coworkers, spouses, friends, and family groups? Many of these interactions are characterized by the potential for, or the existence of, long-term relationships, compatible goals, and longer time horizons for discovering solutions. When these conditions exist, distributive negotiation is an inappropriate technique. Rather than an adversarial perspective, an advocacy, or cooperative, orientation works better.

Integrative negotiation is different from distributive negotiation in that one party can win without the other having to lose. The assumption is that by using creative problem solving, the resources can be expanded. Thus, the parties need not compete directly with each other. Since, in this case, neither party is the enemy or the adversary of the other, the disputants may be more willing to share concerns, ideas, and expectations. An example of an integrative division of resources is illustrated in Figure 5-4.

Integrative negotiation also has its demands. For it to succeed, both participants must have high aspirations or goals (for the attainment of the "right" solution), a problem-solving orientation (both parties must perceive themselves as allies against the problem), and a sufficient level of trust to share information.[20]

Although achieving positive results with integrative negotiation is more difficult than with distributive negotiation, the benefits are considerable. Agreements reached integratively are generally more stable than those reached distributively, and they strengthen the relationship between the parties. Integrative bargaining may also be the only way to reach an agreement when the individuals involved have high aspirations and resist conceding on important issues.[21]

Figure 5-5 illustrates the differences between distributive and integrative negotiation.

Each of us has a great deal of experience with and skill in distributive negotiation. It is easy to envision an opponent as the source of a conflict. It is

20. Pruitt, D. G. (1983). Integrative agreements: Nature and consequences. In M. H. Bazerman & R. J. Lewicki (Eds.), *Negotiating in organizations.* Beverly Hills, CA: Sage.
21. Pruitt, Integrative agreements.

	Distributive	**Integrative**
Payoff Structure	Fixed amount of resources to be divided	Variable amount of resources to be divided
Primary Motivation	To gain at the expense of the other	To maximize joint outcomes
Interests	Diametrically opposed	Convergent or congruent
Relationships	Short term	Long term

Distributive versus Integrative Negotiation ■ **FIGURE 5-5**

Integrative agreements—in which both parties win—are difficult to achieve. However, they tend to be more stable than distributive agreements and to strengthen the long-term relationship between the disputing parties.

much more difficult to develop and maintain the level of trust required to view the other party as a collaborator (with whom information may be freely shared) and to view the issue over which we disagree as the enemy. An all-too-common response is to view all negotiations as adversarial processes. Thus, learning how to reframe negotiations—as integrative, not distributive, processes—is important in developing strategies for resolving conflicts.

Dealing with a conflict from an integrative perspective is often more difficult than approaching it from a distributive perspective. Keeping the following five tactics in mind should help[22]:

1 **Superordinate goals.** A primary difference between distributive and integrative negotiation is that, in the latter, the relationship between the parties is important. With a good relationship, it is therefore much easier to develop goals that supersede the short-term conflict the parties are experiencing. Members of organizations have an explicit superordinate goal—to resolve the conflict in the organization's best interest. Acknowledging this goal can enhance the parties' perceptions that they are aligned in achieving the superordinate goal—in other words, that they are advocates rather than adversaries.

2 **Separate the people from the problem.** It is very difficult not to personalize a problem or conflict. As suggested earlier, one of the critical differences between integrative and distributive negotiation is how the parties perceive each other. To see the other party as an advocate rather than as an adversary is critical to developing the trust needed to achieve integrative agreements.

3 **Focus on interests, not on positions.** Positions are demands the negotiator makes. Interests underlie demands or positions. Positions may be one-dimensional, but individuals typically have multiple interests. Often shared and different (although not incompatible), interests underlie incompatible positions.

4 **Invent options for mutual gain.** This is the basis for expanding the resource pie. All too often, however, individuals ignore the opportunity for

22. See, for example, Anderson, T. (1992, May). Step into my parlor: A survey of strategies and techniques for effective negotiation. *Business Horizons, 35*(3), 71–76; and Fischer, R., & Ury, W. (1981). *Getting to yes.* Boston: Houghton Mifflin.

mutual gain because they assume that the resource pie has a fixed number of pieces. To invent options for mutual gain, participants must be willing to think creatively. They must separate the act of creating alternatives (brainstorming) from judging those alternatives. They must go beyond obvious issues or positions and look for broader solutions. In the search for mutual gain, the task is to get the other side to make the decision you want. Thus, you need to make it as easy as possible for the disputants to agree. Understand their perspective, search for precedents, and develop proposals to which they can respond with a single word: yes.

5 **Use objective criteria.** No matter how integrative the parties may be, they are likely to have some incompatible interests. Rather than see these disagreements as contests of will, it is often more productive to focus on what is fair. Framing disagreements as searches for fair standards is likely to be much more fruitful than focusing on who will win. Deciding what is fair requires both parties to understand the criteria for judging fairness. Each party must be reasonable and open.

Even with the best of intentions and when the negotiated settlement is in both parties' best interests, reaching agreement is sometimes difficult. A host of intervening variables can cripple even the most well-intentioned set of negotiators. As illustrated in "INTERNATIONAL FOCUS ON: Interpersonal Conflict," what has leads up to a conflict is that everyone assumes that his or her perceptions represent an "objective reality." Lee Ross and Andrew Ward called this **naive realism.**[23] Ross and Ward noted that recognizing naïve realism can be extremely helpful in avoiding erroneous assumptions about the values adhered to by others.

COGNITIVE BIASES AND NEGOTIATION. In Chapter 4, we identified a number of heuristics, or cognitive shortcuts, which, when used inappropriately, result in systematically biased decisions. In recent years, considerable research has demonstrated the impact of some of these biases—framing, anchoring and adjustment, and availability—on negotiators' behavior.[24]

As you may recall, the first bias—the *framing* heuristic—is associated with the risk inherent in an individual's decisions.[25] That is, when a decision is framed in terms of potential gains, the decision maker is more likely to choose the risk-averse option. When the decision is framed in terms of potential losses, the decision maker is likely to choose the riskier option. In negotiation, this tendency can be translated into an increased willingness to reach agreement in the former case and a resistance to reach agreement in the latter.

Any potential agreement can be valued in two different ways: A negotiator can consider what is being gained from the new agreement (how much better it is than the old agreement, for example) or what is being given up to get the new agreement. Researchers have shown that individuals who perceive the outcome of a negotiation in terms of what they have to gain are

23. Ross, L., & Ward, A. (1996). Naïve realism in everyday life: Implications for social conflict and misunderstanding. In E. S. Reed, E. Turiel, & T. Brown (Eds.), *Values and knowledge* (pp. 103–135), Mahwah, NJ: Lawrence Erlbaum Associates.

24. Neale, M. A., & Bazerman, M. (1991). *Cognition and rationality in negotiation.* New York: The Free Press.

25. Kahneman, D., & Tversky, A. (1979). Prospect theory: An analysis of decisions under risk. *Econometrica, 47,* 263–291.

INTERNATIONAL FOCUS ON
INTERPERSONAL CONFLICT

SAVING FACE. Avoiding interpersonal conflicts is hard enough when our beliefs and values are like those of our coworkers. But imagine how difficult maintaining harmony can be when the groups to which we belong include a mix of members, some of whom look nothing like us, talk differently, and have different worldviews. This is exactly the situation confronting multicultural teams in the workplace, whether they're in the United States, Japan, or China.

The members of our social groups who look like us, talk like us, and agree with our views reinforce our sense of who we are and what we know. In other words, they confirm our social identity. The Chinese call this process *giving face*. In contrast, team members who look different, talk different, and/or disagree with us can threaten our social identity. Interpersonal conflict in a multicultural team occurs when our social identity is threatened, whether there is a basis for this feeling of being threatened or not.

Because we generally want to maintain positive social identities, we attempt to save face when our social identity is threatened. One way we do this is by engaging in enthnocentric thinking. Such thinking was readily apparent in a recent study involving French and U.S. managers. When the managers realized how differently they approached problem solving, each group

focused on the most favorable characteristics of its approach. The French managers argued that their way was the best because they had arrived at the right answer. The U.S. managers argued that their way was best because there was no single right answer, and they didn't want to waste time looking for it.

Another way to save face and maintain a positive social identity is by exerting pressure for social conformity. European and U.S. managers in a drug-certification project took this approach. Each subgroup tried to convince the other to adopt its way, arguing that it was the *right* way for the environment. Of course, both groups were right: Their way *was* the right way for their environment. But the team's task was to identify synergistic ways to deal with both European *and* U.S. environments.

Neither ethnocentric thinking nor pressure for social conformity is a solution to interpersonal conflict in multicultural teams. Ethnocentric thinking can bring teams to a halt, if neither group accepts the other's approach and so no decisions are made, no problems are solved, or no synergies are discovered. The results can be equally negative when teams use pressure to conform, if neither side gives in to the pressure.

Source: Adapted from Brett, J. M. (in press). *Negotiating across cultures.* San Francisco: Jossey-Bass.

more willing to reach agreement than those who perceive it in terms of potential losses. For example, individuals who were told to maximize profits (gains) in their negotiation reached agreements more easily than those who were told to minimize expenses (losses).[26] Thus, simply altering how the negotiation is presented can significantly influence how the negotiators behave.

The second bias that has been examined in the context of negotiation is the *anchoring-and-adjustment* effect, which we discussed in Chapter 2 as a building block of the perception process. This heuristic suggests that people will use a piece of information as a basis on which to make a judgment or decision but will not use that information sufficiently to arrive at the correct answer.

The anchoring-and-adjustment heuristic is the basis for research which suggests that the level of an initial offer is highly correlated with the level of the final agreement. The more extreme the initial offer, the more extreme the final agreement. For example, when real estate agents were asked to assess a

---

26. Bazerman, M. H., & Neale, M. A. (1992). *Negotiating rationally.* New York: The Free Press.

piece of residential property, the seller's listing price significantly influenced the realtors' estimate of the property's value. The higher the price, the higher the real estate agents perceived the value of the property to be.[27] This was true whether the asking price was higher or lower than the appraised value of the property. From these results, one can surmise that negotiators are also influenced by the anchor of the party's initial offer; this is so much the case that it can color the final valuation of the negotiated commodity or product.

The third bias—the *availability* heuristic—occurs when individuals attempt to judge the likelihood that an event will occur in the future based on its previous occurrence. The rule here becomes "that which is most easily remembered occurs most frequently."[28] While it is true that frequently occurring events are familiar to us, it is not always true that familiar events occur frequently. Consider the negotiator who is representing a constituency. The consequences of not meeting the constituency's expectations (loss of status or position, evaluation anxiety, and so forth) may be very clear to the negotiator. In determining the strategy to be used, the negotiator is likely to overestimate the probability that those costs will be incurred. The costs are more vivid to the negotiator because they are costs he or she would personally bear. Further, the more the negotiator overestimates the probability of these costs occurring, the more likely the negotiator is to behave in a competitive manner and to be unwilling to concede on issues for fear of how the constituency will respond.[29]

Many other heuristics can systematically bias a negotiator's behavior and subsequent agreements. However, this sampling illustrates the importance of giving serious consideration to the ways in which the negotiator can cripple the prospect for reaching a high-quality agreement. The barriers to good negotiated agreements are many, and the organizational and individual costs of reaching poor agreements can be high.

CULTURE AND NEGOTIATION.[30] Both psychological and institutional aspects of culture—the unique character of a group—can have significant effects on the progress of negotiations. Cultural values, for example, shape what issues are more and less important and influence the negotiators' priorities. Cultural norms define what behaviors are appropriate and inappropriate and influence the strategies negotiators use.

Cultural differences in negotiation strategy—perhaps incompatible motivations or uses of influences or information—can lead to inefficiency and unrealized integrative potential. At the same time, cultural differences in priorities can increase the potential that an integrative agreement will be reached.

Lorna Doucet and Karen Jehn expanded on these ideas in their study of Americans living and working in China.[31] Doucet and Jehn staged their

27. Northcraft, G. B., & Neale, M. A. (1987). Experts, amateurs, and real estate: An anchoring-and-adjustment perspective on property pricing decisions. *Organizational Behavior and Human Decision Processes, 39*, 84–97.

28. Tversky, A., & Kahneman, D. (1973). Availability: A heuristic for judging frequency and probability. *Cognitive Psychology, 5*, 207–232.

29. Neale, M. A. (1984). The effects of negotiation and arbitration cost on bargainer behavior: The role of arbitrator and constituency on negotiator judgement. *Organizational Behavior and Human Performance, 34*, 97–111.

30. Brett, J. M. (2001). *Negotiating globally: How to negotiate deals, resolve disputes, and make decisions across cultural boundaries.* San Francisco, CA: Jossey-Bass.

31. Doucet, L., & Jehn, K. A. (1997). Analyzing harsh words in a sensitive setting: American expatriates in communist China. *Journal of Organizational Behavior, 18*, 559–582.

study in an international joint venture—an especially fertile ground for conflict. They examined both intracultural conflicts (among members of the same culture) and intercultural conflict (among members of different cultures). Their findings suggest that Americans working in Sino–American ventures express more hostility in their conflicts with other Americans than in their conflicts with their Chinese counterparts. Americans may behave more hostilely toward other Americans because this is the accepted cultural norm, and they may behave less hostilely toward their Chinese coworkers as a result of intercultural influences, including the Chinese cultural norm of saving face and maintaining harmony.

ORGANIZATIONAL CONFLICT MANAGEMENT

Organizations can be structured in ways that help alleviate conflict. Two structures are discussed; formal structures and informal structures. Formal structures include liaisons, organizational slack, and ombudsmen or employee/client/customer representatives, whose task is to resolve conflict at the organization's internal and external boundaries. Informal structures to resolve conflict focus primarily on the manager as dispute resolver.

FORMAL ORGANIZATIONAL ROLES. Because conflict is commonly associated with scarce resources and interdependencies, one way organizations can reduce the potential for conflict is to reduce the interaction among groups and the competition for resources. This can be accomplished by having what are known as slack resources and buffers. Having **slack,** or excess, resources minimizes conflict because slack resources reduce the amount of interaction that is necessary. For example, if two departments are sequentially interdependent, having excess inventory of A's output (slack) insulates or buffers B from A. However, many organizations can't afford to have slack. Therefore, it is important to consider having not only excess inventory or product, but also people, as **buffers.**[32] For example, in an organization with a matrix structure (described in Chapter 14), the project manager often serves this function. Acting as a liaison or linking pin, this individual integrates the activities of two interdependent organizational units or groups.

A different form of the linking-pin role is that of the organizational **ombudsman.** Whereas a linking pin generally integrates the activities of two interdependent units, an ombudsman typically focuses on conflict at the employee–organizational boundary. An ombudsman provides a formal mechanism for employee grievances to be aired. In some situations, ombudsmen can be significantly effective during negotiations in influencing disputants' offers.[33] In some institutions, the ombudsman also offers a means for clients or customers to make their dissatisfactions known.[34]

The duties of an ombudsman usually include interpreting policy, counseling, resolving disputes, and providing feedback and identifying potential

---

32. Floyd, S. W., & Lane, P. J. (2000). Strategizing throughout the organization: Management role conflict in strategic renewal. *Academy of Management Review, 25*(1), 154–177.
33. Arnold, J. A., & O'Connor, K. M. (1999). Ombudspersons or peers? The effect of third-party expertise and recommendations on negotiation. *Journal of Applied Psychology, 84,* 776–785.
34. Kolb, D. M. (1987). Who are organizational third parties and what do they do? In R. J. Lewicki, B. Sheppard, & M. H. Bazerman (Eds.), *Research on negotiation in organizations.* Greenwich, CT: JAI.

| ■ **FIGURE 5-6** | **Individuals Engaged in Informal Dispute Resolution** |

Many roles in society, including the following, focus largely on conflict resolution:

Go-betweens (messengers)	Matchmakers
Lawyers	Brokers
Auditors	Agents (insurance agents, real
Managerial consultants	estate agents)
Marriage counselors	Umpires
Psychotherapists	Parents
Special envoys	Dictators
Priests and rabbis	Law enforcement officials
Village elders	International monitors
Elected representatives	Regulatory agencies
Auctioneers	International courts of law

Source: Kaufman, S., & Duncan, G. T. (1988). Third-party intervention: A theoretical framework. In M. A. Rahim (Ed.), *Managing conflict: An interdisciplinary approach.* New York: Praeger.

problem areas to senior management.[35] For example, at McDonnell Aircraft in St. Louis, Missouri, and at Douglas Aircraft in Long Beach, California, most of the ombudsmen's cases concern corporate disputes such as conflicts with supervisors, arguments over promotions and transfers, and misunderstandings about benefits. Most such problems can be sorted out with a direct call to the department head involved, without invoking higher authority. A few problems, however, involve whistle blowing on the safety of a product design or the billing of a defense contract.

INFORMAL ORGANIZATIONAL ROLES. An ombudsman has a formal role as a dispute resolver. However, this formal designation does not limit the role that others in the organization play in reducing or managing conflict. Because conflict in group and organizational life is so common, formal structures or procedures often do not adequately meet the demand for conflict resolution. As a result, a variety of individuals assume the role of dispute resolver or intervenor. The manager is an excellent example of someone who spends a great deal of time managing conflict, although conflict resolution is not usually considered a formal aspect of the job description. Figure 5-6 presents a list of other potential third-party intervenors.

Managers often serve as third parties to conflicts. In this case, the manager is neither directly involved in the conflict nor is one of the disputants. This role is not limited to managers, however. The legal system, for example, is a formal system for **third-party intervention.** Judges resolve conflicts between private parties in civil courts or between representatives of public and private parties in criminal courts. Within the context of industrial relations, third parties may resolve differences between labor and management through mediation, arbitration, or factfinding. Each type of third-party intervention is used in different, specific ways.

Arbitration functions much like the U.S. judicial system. After hearing both sides of a dispute, a neutral third party, called an arbitrator, determines

---

35. Rowe, M. P. (1984). The non-union complaint system at MIT: An upward-feedback model. *Alternatives to the High Cost of Litigation, 2,* 10–18.

Differences between Managerial & Institutional Third-Party Roles		■ FIGURE 5-7
Dimension	**Institutional Third Parties**	**Managers As Third Parties**
	Dispute Characteristic	
Construal of disputes	Disputes exist and involve parties with competing claims, often with a basis in law or prior agreement.	Conflict is a problem of misunderstanding that demands a rational solution.
Boundaries of dispute	Dispute is well demarcated and isolated from other activities of parties.	Dispute is embedded in an ongoing stream of activity.
Point of intervention	Third party sought, often as a last effort at dispute resolution.	Intervention frequently early, at the initiative of the manager.
	Third-Party Role	
Involvement in dispute	Disinterested third party. Principal concern is for resolution.	Frequently a part of the problem, with concern for his or her own and the organization's best interests.
Authority	Limited authority circumscribed by role as a mediator or an arbitrator.	Wide range of authority, without clear demarcation of the third-party role.
Cultural expectations	Expected to act as conflict solver involved in recognized conflicts of interest.	Expected to act as decision maker involved in differences of opinions over best direction for organization.
Frequency of exposure	Limited exposure to parties, typically only once.	Frequent interaction with parties within many roles. Often dealt with similar problem in the past.

a final, binding outcome. In marked contrast, in **mediation** the neutral third party has no authority to force a solution on the disputants; rather, the mediator helps the parties reach their own solution. Finally, in **factfinding,** the neutral third party determines a reasonable solution to the conflict based on evidence the parties have presented. However, as in mediation, the parties are not bound to follow the recommendation.

Unlike formal third parties or organizational ombudsmen who have prescribed ways of interacting with disputants, managers have considerably more leeway in choosing their dispute-resolution tactics. Managers differ from formal third-party intervenors in many other ways as well, as summarized in Figure 5-7.

MANAGERIAL DISPUTE INTERVENTION

Unlike formal third-party intervention in organizational disputes, which usually involves bringing in a mediator, a factfinder, or an arbitrator, managers have considerable flexibility in the tactics they can use to resolve organizational conflicts. They sometimes function as arbitrators (judges) or mediators, and they can also serve as inquisitors, avoiders, delegators, and providers of impetus. Each of these types of intervention is described as follows:

1 Judges exert high degrees of control over the outcome of conflicts but not over the process by which conflicts are resolved. Judges typically allow both sides to present whatever facts, evidence, or arguments they desire, and then decide the outcome of the conflict. They have the power to enforce that decision on the disputants.

2 Inquisitors exert high degrees of control over both the outcome and the process of conflict resolution. They direct the presentation of evidence, ask questions, act as referees, and call for evidence that is not willingly offered. Like judges, inquisitors decide the outcome of conflicts and enforce those decisions on the disputants.

3 Mediators exert high degrees of control over the process of conflict resolution but not over its outcome. A mediator may separate the parties, interview them, and bring them back together. A mediator may also separate the parties and ferry proposals back and forth between them to help them forge their own solution.

4 Avoiders, **delegators,** and the **"providing impetus" tactic** exert low degrees of control over both the process and the outcome of conflict resolution. Avoiders prefer to find ways to ignore the conflict or minimize its importance. Delegators recognize that the conflict exists but try to return responsibility for its solution to the disputants or to get someone else to accept responsibility. The providing-impetus tactic (also known as the kick-in-the-pants style) delegates the conflict back to the parties with a threat—"Either resolve this yourselves, or the manager will resolve the problem—and nobody will like that solution!"

Managers who have resolved a variety of disputes are observed using the inquisitorial style most often, followed by the judging and providing-impetus styles. They also report using mediation frequently but in fact seldom give the disputants any real control over the outcomes. Research suggests that they are more likely to use strategies in which they control the outcome when (a) there are time pressures, (b) the disputants are not likely to work together in the future, and (c) the settlement has broad implications for the resolution of other disputes.[36]

Researchers may understand what managers do in conflict situations, but they do not suggest that these are the correct or optimal responses. Describing managers' behavior and endorsing it as correct are very different. Roy Lewicki, Blair Sheppard, and their colleagues have proposed and tested a contingency model of managerial intervention. Based on their results, they believe that a manager should choose an intervention strategy based on what the manager wishes to accomplish in addition to resolving the dispute. Which of the following is the objective:

1 The conflict should be resolved quickly (efficiency).
2 The optimal solution should be chosen (effectiveness).
3 The disputants should be satisfied with the outcome (satisfaction).
4 The disputants should perceive the outcome as just (fairness).

Figure 5-8 describes these four outcomes in more detail.

Whether the manager attempts to control the outcome of the conflict or the manner in which the conflict is resolved determines which intervention objective will result. Figure 5-9 illustrates the relationship between concern

36. Lewicki, R. J., & Sheppard, B. (1985). Choosing how to intervene: Factors affecting the use of process and outcome control in third-party dispute intervention. *Journal of Occupational Behavior, 6,* 49–64.

| Managerial Dispute Intervention Outcomes | ■ FIGURE 5-8 |

Efficiency: To solve the problem with a minimum expenditure of resources—third-party time, disputant time, capital outlay, and so on. Solving the problem quickly would be an example of procedural efficiency.

Effectiveness: To solve the problem so it is solved well and stays solved. Making sure that the third party listens to all parties that have a relevant perspective on the conflict is an example of procedural effectiveness; brainstorming to determine the best possible solution—one that will work or one that will not bring the parties back to the manager with the same dispute—is an example of outcome effectiveness.

Satisfaction: To solve the problem so that the parties are satisfied with the solution. Giving all sides an opportunity to present their cases and having the disputants play a critical role in the development of the actual solution are examples of procedures that enhance participant satisfaction.

Fairness: To solve the problem so that the parties believe the outcome is fair (by some specific standard—equality, equity, and so on). Hearing both sides, applying rules consistently, and treating both disputants in a similar manner are mechanisms that promote the perception of fairness.

with process or outcome control and the four intervention objectives. If the manager cares most about efficiency—simply reaching a solution, any solution—and wishes to have control over how the outcome is reached, then the manager should use an inquisitorial style. If the manager does not want control over either the process or the outcome, then the appropriate strategy would be avoiding, delegating, or providing impetus.

If getting the best or optimal solution to the conflict (effectiveness) is the manager's primary objective, the choice of intervention strategy would be between using the inquisitorial style and that of a judge. If how the solution is determined is at issue, the inquisitorial style would be more appropriate. If the manager has little concern about controlling the conflict-resolution process, then the best choice would probably be to act like a judge.

| Strengths of Intervention Strategies | ■ FIGURE 5-9 |

Conflict intervention strategies differ in the extent to which they exert control over the process and outcomes of disputes. These differences, in turn, result in maximizing a variety of conflict-resolution goals, such as participant satisfaction.

		Third Party Controls the Outcome	
		Yes	No
Third Party Controls the Process	Yes	Efficiency Effectiveness	Satisfaction Fairness
	No	Fairness Effectiveness	Efficiency

When a manager's greatest concern is that the disputants be satisfied with the resolution, then the only correct intervention strategy is mediation. This goal may be important when commitment to the solution is critical for its successful implementation.

Finally, if the manager wants to ensure that the disputants perceive the solution to the conflict to be fair, then the manager has a choice of strategies. If the manager's goal is to control the solution, then intervening as a judge is best. This strategy has the additional benefit of being associated with effective solutions. Alternatively, if the manager is not concerned with the exact nature of the final solution, then mediation may be more appropriate. Because mediation promotes both participant satisfaction and the perception of fairness, it is the form of intervention most desired by disputants. It gives them the greatest control over the solution, while providing them with an incentive to reach agreement (via the involvement of the mediator).

Managers seem to understand the attractiveness of mediation because they report using this strategy to a greater extent with subordinates than they actually do. However, managers find giving up control difficult. In fact, research has demonstrated that low-level managers are more likely to use intervention strategies that emphasize control over outcome. The higher the manager is in an organization, the more likely the manager is to use mediation.[37]

SUMMARY

Conflict is an organizational reality. One reason conflict is so inevitable is that managers and the other employees in an organization are constantly competing for scarce resources. Thus, an important management task is to maintain an optimal level of conflict, given the unique characteristics of the organization and the individuals who compose it.

How well one copes with conflict depends on a variety of factors. Understanding conflict and its impact on individuals and groups increases a person's ability to predict its outcomes and make interventions when appropriate. Further, once conflict is viewed as a common organizational process rather than an aberration, its presence becomes much less stressful. Finally, the more conflict management is viewed as a necessary managerial skill, the more structural alternatives will be implemented to address conflict in the organization.

Structural forms of conflict management are found primarily in organizations that exist in constantly changing environments and that have high intraorganizational interdependencies. However, regardless of the nature of the organization, managers are expected to intervene as third parties in the management of a great deal of conflict. On average, managers spend one fifth of each workday on some form of conflict-related activity. Given the ex-

---

37. Pinkley, Robin L., Brittain, Jack W., Neale, Margaret A., & Northcraft, Gregory B. (1995). Managerial third party dispute intervention: An inductive analysis of intervenor strategy selection. *Journal of Applied Psychology, 80,* 386–402; and (working paper).

tensive time crunch all managers face, increasing their effectiveness in managing conflict gives them more time to focus on the company's primary goal—producing the product or providing the service that is the company's reason to exist.

At the same time, increasing one's skills means more than simply finding a way (any way) to resolve a dispute for now. Rather, to resolve a conflict effectively, the manager must understand the nature of the conflict and his or her objective in resolving it. Identifying the objectives or goals of the conflict intervention enables the manager to choose the intervention style that will best achieve those goals.

KEY TERMS

Accommodating
Approach–approach conflict
Approach–avoidance conflict
Arbitration
Avoidance–avoidance conflict
Avoiding
Buffer
Collaborating
Competing
Compromising
Delegator
Distributive negotiation
Factfinding

Horizontal conflict
Integrative negotiation
Line–staff conflict
Mediation
Negotiation
Ombudsman
"Providing impetus" tactic
Resource scarcity
Role conflict
Slack
Third-party intervention
Vertical conflict

DISCUSSION QUESTIONS

1 In common usage, the term *conflict* has a negative connotation. Within an organizational setting, however, conflict is a necessary, even critical, resource of the successful manager. What is it about conflict that makes it so useful to organizations while being perceived as negative by the general public?

2 What indicators might warn a manager in a large organization that excessive, nonfunctional conflict exists?

3 Managers are often required to intervene in conflicts within and between their departments and other organizational entities. What specific skills would a manager need in order to accomplish this role successfully?

4 Although managers report using mediation techniques extensively, direct observations of managerial interventions indicate that they rely more on controlling strategies. What is it that makes mediation attractive to managers yet a strategy that they don't often implement (except possibly at higher organizational levels)?

5 What effects does intergroup conflict have on the groups themselves?

6 What are some examples of organizational slack? How do these examples buffer the organization from conflict?

ON YOUR OWN

Conflict Questionnaire   This questionnaire helps you to understand your responses and behavior when confronted with situations in which your wishes differ from those of another person. For each of the following statements, think about how likely you would be to respond in the way described. Check the rating that best corresponds to your response.

	Very Unlikely	Unlikely	Likely	Very Likely
1 I am usually firm in pursuing my goals.	_____	_____	_____	_____
2 I try to make my position win.	_____	_____	_____	_____
3 I give up some points in exchange for others.	_____	_____	_____	_____
4 I fell that differences are not always worth worrying about.	_____	_____	_____	_____
5 I try to find a position that is between the other person's and mine.	_____	_____	_____	_____
6 In approaching negotiation, I try to consider the other person's wishes.	_____	_____	_____	_____
7 I try to show the logic and benefits of my position.	_____	_____	_____	_____
8 I always lean toward a direct discussion of the problem.	_____	_____	_____	_____
9 I try to find a fair combination of gains and losses for both of us.	_____	_____	_____	_____
10 I attempt to work through our differences immediately.	_____	_____	_____	_____
11 I try to avoid creating unpleasantness for myself.	_____	_____	_____	_____
12 I might try to sooth the other's feelings and preserve our relationship.	_____	_____	_____	_____
13 I attempt to get all concerns and issues out immediately.	_____	_____	_____	_____
14 I sometimes avoid taking positions that create controversy.	_____	_____	_____	_____
15 I try not to hurt the other's feelings.	_____	_____	_____	_____

SCORING: Very Unlikely = 1; Unlikely 2; Likely 3; Very Likely 4.

Competing:	Item 1 ___	Item 2 ___	Item 7 ___	TOTAL ___
Collaborating:	8 ___	10 ___	13 ___	TOTAL ___
Compromising:	3 ___	5 ___	9 ___	TOTAL ___
Avoiding:	4 ___	11 ___	14 ___	TOTAL ___
Accommodating:	6 ___	12 ___	15 ___	TOTAL ___

Conflict-Handling Modes	Appropriate Situations
Competing	1 When quick, decisive action is vital, such as emergencies.
	2 On important issues on which unpopular actions need implementation, such as cost cutting, discipline.
	3 On issues vital to organizational welfare when you know you are right.
	4 Against people who take advantage of noncompetitive situations.
Collaborating	1 To find an integrative solution when both sets of concerns are too important to compromise.
	2 When your objective is to learn.
	3 To merge insights from people with different perspectives.
	4 To gain commitment by incorporating concerns into a consensus.
	5 To work through feelings that have interfered with a relationship.
Compromising	1 When goals are important but not worth the effort or potential disruption of more assertive modes.
	2 When opponents with equal power are committed to mutually exclusive goals.
	3 To achieve temporary settlement of complex issues.
	4 To arrive at expedient solutions under time pressures.
	5 As a backup when collaboration or competition is unsuccessful.
Avoiding	1 When an issue is trivial or more important issues are pressing.
	2 When you perceive no chance of satisfying your concerns.
	3 When potential disruption outweighs the benefits of resolution.
	4 To let people cool down and regain perspective.
	5 When gathering information supersedes an immediate decision.
	6 When others can resolve the conflict more effectively.
	7 When issues seem tangential or symptomatic of other issues.
Accommodating	1 When you find you are wrong—to allow a better position to be heard, to learn, and to show your reasonableness.
	2 When issues are more important to others than to yourself—to satisfy others and maintain cooperation.
	3 To build social credits for later issues.
	4 To minimize a loss when you are outmatched and losing.
	5 When harmony and stability are especially important.
	6 To allow subordinates to develop by learning from mistakes.

Source: Thomas, K. W. (1977). Toward multi-dimensional values in teaching: The example of conflict behaviors. *Academy of Management Review, 2,* 487.

CLOSING CASE   CHAPTER 5

THE MANAGER'S MEMO

FROM: F. Cunningham, Manager, Cookie Sales Force
TO: P. Rodriguez, Vice President, Cookie Division
RE: Problems with Engineering

I think we have a problem with the division's chief manufacturing engineer, Bill Lee. It seems to have started in the meeting where we launched our new novelty shaped graham crackers, TeleGrahams.

  At the meeting, Angela Boskins, who is in charge of sales for this product, was excited about our expectation that we can exceed our initial sales projections by 200%. This would involve opening a second production facility in the Southeast within 3 months.

  As Angela was explaining the favorable results of our test marketing, Bill said, "When are we going to talk about the bugs in the production process that are causing us to burn 25% of the product?" Well, as Angela explained, consumers in the test markets have been satisfied with the product as it is, so we can go ahead with launching the product and work out the bugs later. But Bill just stormed out of the room, shouting something about how we always expect production to work miracles.

  I don't know what his problem is; you'd think he'd be excited about doubling production. I guess he's just a typical engineer—more concerned about his machinery than about the big picture.

  I tried to call Bill today to smooth things over, but he was out sick. Maybe you can talk to him. Or maybe if we just ignore him, he'll get over his attitude problem. What, if anything, do you think I should do?

CASE DISCUSSION QUESTIONS

Assume that you are the vice president, and respond to the manager's memo. Try to infer the real nature of this conflict, and determine your goals for intervention. Use those goals as the basis for choosing an intervention style and phrasing your response. If you think it will help you achieve your goals for resolving this conflict, also write a memo to Bill Lee, the chief manufacturing engineer.

EXERCISE   PART TWO: Carter Racing (A)

What Should We Do?

John Carter was not sure what to do, but his brother and partner, Fred Carter, was on the phone and needed a decision. Should they run in the race or not? It had been a successful season so far, but the Pocono race was important because of the prize money and TV exposure it promised. The first

Source: Copyright 1986 by Jack W. Brittain & Sim B. Sitkin. Entered into The Stanford Case System by permission of the authors.

year had been hard because the team was trying to make a name for itself. It had run a lot of small races to get this shot at the big time. A successful outing could mean more sponsors, a chance to start making some profits for a change, and the luxury of racing only in major events. On the other hand, if the team suffered another engine failure on national television. . . .

Just thinking about the team's engine problems made John wince. The team had blown the engine 7 times in 24 outings this season, with various degrees of damage to the engine and car. No one could figure out why. It took a lot of sponsor money to replace a $20,000 racing engine, and the wasted entry fees were no small matter either. John and Fred had everything they owned riding on Carter Racing. This season had to be a success.

Paul Edwards, the engine mechanic, was guessing that the engine problem was related to ambient air temperature. He argued that when the weather was cold, the different expansion rates for the head and block were damaging the head gasket and causing the engine failures. It had been below freezing last night, which meant a cold morning for starting the race.

Tom Burns, the chief mechanic, did not agree with Paul's "gut feeling" and had data to support his position (see Exhibit 1). He pointed out that gasket failures had occurred at all temperatures, which meant temperature was not the issue. Tome has been racing for 20 years and believed that luck was

---

■ Note from Tom Burns   ■ EXHIBIT 1

John,
I got the data on the gasket failures from Paul. We have run 24 races this season with temperatures at race time ranging from 53° to 82°. Paul had a good idea in suggesting that we look into this, but, as you can see, this is not our problem. I tested the data for a correlation between temperature and gasket failures and found no relationship.

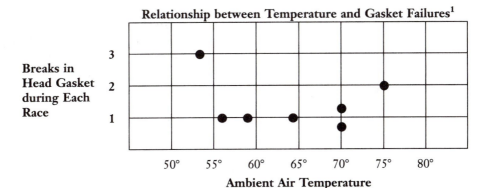

Relationship between Temperature and Gasket Failures[1]

Breaks in Head Gasket during Each Race

Ambient Air Temperature

In comparison with some of the other teams, we have done extremely well this season. We have finished 62.5% of the races, and when we finished we were in the top five 80% of the time. I am not happy with the engine problems, but I will take the four first-place finishes and 50% rate of finishing in the money[2] over seven engines any day. If we continue to run like this, we will have our pick of sponsors.

Tom

---

1. Each point is for a single race. A gasket can have multiple breaks, any of which may produce an engine failure.
2. The top five finishers in a race are "in the money."

an important element in success. He had argued this view when he and John discussed the problem last week: "In racing, you are pushing the limits of what is known. You cannot expect to have everything under control. If you want to win, you have to take risks. Everybody in racing knows it. The drivers have their lives on the line, I have a career that hangs on every race, and you have every dime tied up in the business. That's the thrill—beating the odds and winning." Last night over dinner he had forcefully added to this argument what he called Burns's First Law of Racing: "Nobody ever won a race sitting in the pits."

John, Fred, and Tom had discussed Carter Racing's situation the previous evening. This first season had been a success from a racing standpoint, with the team's car finishing in the top five in 12 of the 15 races it completed. As a result, the sponsorship offers critical to the team's business success were starting to come in. A big break had come two weeks ago, after the Dunham race, where the team scored its fourth first-place finish. Goodstone Tire had finally decided that Carter Racing deserved its sponsorship at Pocono—worth a much-needed $40,000—and was considering a full season contract for next year if the team's car finished in the top five in the Pocono race. The Goodstone sponsorship was worth $1 million per year, plus incentives. John and Fred had gotten a favorable response from Goodstone's racing program director last week, when they had presented their plans for the next season, but it was clear that this support depended on the visibility they generated in this race.

"John, we only have another hour to decide," Fred said over the phone. "If we withdraw now, we can get back half the $15,000 entry and try to recoup some of our losses next season. We will lose Goodstone, they'll want $25,000 of their money back, and we end up the season $50,000 in the hole. If we run and finish in the top five, we have Goodstone in our pocket and can add another car next season. You know as well as I do, however, that if we run and lose another engine, we are back at square one next season. We will lose the tire sponsorship, and a blown engine is going to lose us the oil contract. No oil company wants a national TV audience to see a smoker being dragged off the track with its name plastered all over it. The oil sponsorship is $500,000 that we cannot live without. Think about it—call Paul and Tom if you want—but I need a decision in an hour."

John hung up the phone and looked out the window at the crisp, fall sky. The temperature sign across the street flashed "40 DEGREES AT 9:23 AM."

Carter Racing (B)

"Get Paul Edwards for me." John was calling to get this engine mechanic's opinion on whether they should run. The data Tom put together indicated that temperature was not the problem, but John wanted to get Paul's direct assessment.

Paul Edwards was a classic "gas station mechanic." His fingernails were permanently blackened by grease, and his coveralls never stayed clean for more than two minutes on Saturday mornings. He had been knocking around the professional circuit for 10 years, after having dropped out of school at 16 to follow sprint car racing. He lacked the sophisticated engineering training that was getting more common in racing, but he did know racing engines.

John had discussed the gasket problem with Paul 2 days ago. As he waited for Paul to come to the phone, he reflected on their previous conversation. Paul was a man of few words and was not given to overstatement. He said, "The way I see it, the turbo pressure during warm-up—in conjunction with the different expansion rates for the head and block—is doing a number on us." This was his personal opinion on the cause of the engine failures; he would never represent it as anything else.

It was the same story John had heard 20 times, but it did not match Tom's data. "Paul, we have chewed this over before. How do you know this is the problem? When we ran at Riverside, the temperature was 75°, and we still lost the gasket and engine."

"I am not sure what happened at Riverside," Paul had replied. "I am not sure that temperature is the problem, but it is the only thing I can figure out. It is definitely the gaskets that are blowing out and causing the engine to go."

Part of Carter Racing's success was due to a unique turbo-charging system that Tom and John had developed. They had come up with a new head design that allowed them to get more turbo pressure to the engine while maintaining fuel consumption at a fairly constant level. By casting the head and turbo bodies in a high-strength aircraft alloy, they had also saved almost 50 pounds of weight. The alloy they were using was not as temperature sensitive as the material in the engine block, but the head gasket should be able to handle the different expansion rates.

John could hear the sounds of race day in the background as Paul approached the phone. "Hello, John," he said, obviously excited. "The Goodstone coveralls just got here. We are talking some fine threads. No sew-on patches from these guys. The logo's on the back, and our names are stitched right into the material. I guess this means we get to keep 'em. Course, I got some grease on mine already, so they probably won't want 'em back anyway."

"I'm glad you like them," John said. "I need to get some information from you. What are we doing about the gasket failure business?"

"The car is set to go. We have been using a different seating procedure since Slippery Rock and have had no problems for two races. Tom says the Goodstone deal is set as long as we finish in the money today. The guys in the shop want this bad. Goostone is a class act. They can make us the number-one team on the circuit if they decide to take us on."

CASE PART TWO: The Case of the Disputed Arches

A complex, technical description of a yieldable arch roof support is not required. Centuries ago, the Greeks knew that the more pressure put on a keystone, the stronger it became. This concept has numerous applications, including as mine haulage roof supports. I had worked five years as a union miner and acquired a mining engineering degree. Nobody was going to fool *me* about yieldable arches.

Joe Bond was a motorman who was smarter than his job required; he was a troublemaker. Nobody could fool me about Joe Bond either.

This case was prepared by G. R. Spindler, under the supervision of David L. Bradford, as the basis for class discussion rather than to illustrate either effective or ineffective handling of an administrative situation. Reprinted by permission of Stanford University Graduate School of Business. Copyright 1980 by the Board of Trustees of the Leland Stanford Junior University.

I was 24 years old and had recently become superintendent of the Bunker Mine. The average age of the union employees at Bunker was 46. I had just been left a note that Bond, who worked the midnight shift, had complained about the condition of some of the arches. He demanded that the arches be replaced. Rumor was that he would cause trouble if they were not replaced. Fact was that I was being tested.

James Franklin, the mine foreman of 27 years and a man much respected by the union, looked at the arches. Frank Randall, the federal mine inspector, looked at the arches. I looked at the arches. We all agreed: Even though they showed signs of taking pressure, the arches were safe. Furthermore, replacing the arches would require closing the haulage, and therefore the mine, for about four days.

I left a polite note for Joe Bond, which was to be given to him by the midnight shift foreman. I thanked Joe for his suggestion, his attention to matters of safety, and his wisdom in reporting these matters to management. However, the arches in question did appear to be perfectly safe. I would continue to watch them and perhaps change them at the first convenient opportunity.

The midnight shift foreman called to tell me that Joe had received the note and had promptly gone into the waiting room and announced that management was trying to get him killed. Then he went home, and the rest of the shift had followed close behind. The mine was on strike.

I hurriedly phoned the union safety committee and met them at the mine at 2:30 a.m. The safety committee asked me to show them the arches in question. I had a better idea, I said. If these arches were as unsafe as claimed, that fact should be immediately obvious to so well-trained and experienced a group as the safety committee. I would accompany them down the entire length of the haulage, and *they* could tell *me* where the bad arches were.

Two trips up and down the haulage produced a half dozen wrong guesses. At the end of the second trip one member of the safety committee told me to stop messing around and just show them the arches in question.

I pointed out the exact cause of Joe Bond's complaint to the committee. They reluctantly admitted that the arches didn't look too bad to them. They indicated that they would take the matter under advisement and let me know their recommendation.

The day shift worked, much to the disgust of the midnight shift. There was an unwritten union rule that no one could work until the shift that initiated a strike decided to return. The afternoon shift would be the problem. The youngest, most volatile employees were on the afternoon shift, and I felt that they would be inclined to rekindle the strike. To forestall this, James Franklin and I went into the waiting room to talk to the men on the afternoon shift as they arrived.

James haltingly and cautiously explained the situation to the afternoon shift. He refused to definitely disclaim any hazard, saying only that although he didn't believe there was one, he couldn't guarantee anything and there was no substitute for a man's own best judgment in this type of matter. I finally lost patience with him and declared that I would guarantee that there was no hazard, and I could see no point in anyone losing a day's pay because of one troublemaker.

After talking among themselves, the afternoon shift decided to continue the strike. This established a two-to-one vote and guaranteed that tomorrow, the day shift also would not work.

At this point I had my first consultation with my supervisor, Mike Beanch. Mike was known for giving in to union pressure, and the union lacked respect for him because of it. After a lengthy conversation, I convinced Mike that we should resist the demands to replace the arches.

Thus began what promised to be a long strike. Every day I met with the safety committee in an attempt to prove the safety of the arches and find some way to get the men back to work. Every day I was encouraged and congratulated by the line foreman who worked under me for finally standing up to the union and restoring dignity to management. Every day Mike got more nervous.

During one meeting with the safety committee, when Joe Bond was present, I was asked if I had referred to Joe as a troublemaker. I replied that I certainly had, and I said that I had every belief that even Joe didn't think any hazard existed—that he simply did not want to work and chose to penalize everyone else's paycheck along with his own.

Halfway through the second week of the strike, Mike called me. "We have a new wrinkle in the union's demands," he said. "They've backed down. They no longer insist that the arches be replaced. I've just finished talking to the safety committee on the phone."

I was a little miffed that the safety committee was talking to Mike directly—bypassing me—but I ignored this for the present.

"They are coming back to work, then," I said.

"No," Mike replied. "Now they won't come back to work until you are fired."

QUESTIONS FOR DISCUSSION

1 How would you characterize the motivations of the case writer? What are Joe Bond's motivations in this case? Do any of these motivations change over the course of the case?

2 What is really in dispute in this case? Does it change from the beginning to the end of the

case? How have the writer's attempts to resolve this conflict made it worse?

3 Are there some important differences in perception in this case? How are they contributing to the problem?

PART 3

Behavior in Groups

CHAPTER 6

Groups and Teams

CONSULTING IN THE KITCHEN

The tension was so thick you could cut it with a high-carbon chef's knife. At one stove, three cooks bickered over the grits cakes. At another, an onion shortage was under way. Across the kitchen, the salt was missing, a saucier had lost her spoon, and the executive chef was staving off a seasonings crisis.

A bad night at Lutece? No, it's just an ordinary day in the life of the latest fad in industrial motivation: cooking school for dysfunctional management teams. On a recent day, a group of Mississippi advertising executives has come to a palatial kitchen at the Viking Culinary Arts Center to master the art of "team building" by learning how to cook together.

Companies are paying top dollar to management consultants who follow a recipe of one part cooking technique and two parts pop psychology as a way to improve morale and productivity. Just as survival simulation games and outdoor adventure courses were once popular team-building techniques, the kitchen exercises are supposed to foster trust and communication.

One thing the corporate cooking classes often foster is a culinary three-ring circus. Still, companies such as Viacom's MTV, Nickelodeon networks, the giant credit-card issuer FCC National Bank; Bank One's First USA; and Sun Microsystems are eating them up. "It's the trendy thing to do," said Bill Reynolds, the Culinary Arts Center's associate vice president of continuing education. The kitchen is a good place to improve teamwork, he said, because "there are a lot of things that can go wrong."

That's what the Ramey Agency discovered when 10 of its 55 employees showed up for class at this cooking school run by Viking Range Corporation, whose $8,000 stove is a status symbol for foodies.

Communication problems were evident from the first recipe: Jalapeno Cheese Grits Cake with Shrimp, Tomatillo Sauce, and Mirliton Corn Rel-

Source: Excerpted from Daspin, E. (2000, April 5). Managers & managing: Memo to team: This needs salt!—*The Wall Street Journal Europe*, p. 30.

ish. "It was like team building in reverse," said Wilson Wong, a management consultant who observed the action and provided analysis afterward.

The Southwestern-style appetizer should have taken 45 minutes to prepare. Instead, with half the people in the kitchen ricocheting around, searching for ingredients and tools and the other half arguing over the best way to prepare the dish, they clocked an hour and a half.

"They had to communicate or get in trouble, and they got in trouble," said Mr. Wong, a founder of the consulting firm Jackson, Wong & Associates, which helped devise the class.

The consultants who promote the cooking classes as excellent team-building exercises maintain that they offer some uniquely pungent links to the workplace. The fact that a product—say, Roasted Chicken with Toasted Riso and Braised Mustard Greens—is being produced in real time makes the work easy to evaluate and the class more like real life. "Maybe the person who can't break the egg will start seeing others in a new way," said Rick Phillips, who leads the HMS-Culinary Institute team-building courses. Phillips and the HMS-Culinary Institute charge $450 per person for their team building program.

INTRODUCTION

Groups and communication in groups are the building blocks of organizations and of social life. When people get together and talk in groups, things can happen. The challenge of group dynamics, therefore, is learning how to manage the energy of groups, whether in the kitchen, office, or manufacturing plant.

This chapter explores the nature of individual behavior in groups and teams, including the structuring, development, and improvement of group and team interaction. A model of communication is also presented, which highlights the importance of effective communication to successful group and team functioning.

THE NATURE OF GROUPS

A **group** is "an organized system of two or more individuals who are interrelated so that the system performs some function, has a standard set of role relationships among its members, and has a set of norms that regulate the function of the group and each of its members."[1]

There are two important features to this definition. First, groups have a function—they serve a purpose. People do not simply come together to come together. People come together to accomplish something. Second, groups have structure. Groups must be organized to pursue their functions effectively. Some groups, such as task forces, have formal structures. These groups exist as legitimate, documented subunits of larger organizations. Their structures exist on paper in the form of charters or handbooks. Other groups, such as study groups, are informal. These groups exist only in the minds of their members, who may know the group's structure only implicitly.

---

1. McDavid, J. W., & Harari, M. (1968). *Social psychology: Individuals, groups, and societies.* New York: Harper & Row, p. 237.

In either case, there must be rules that govern the conduct of group members. Each member of the group must have tasks or duties to perform in the service of the group's function, or the group may find that there are too many cooks in the kitchen.

Why do people join groups? What are individuals hoping to obtain through groups that they could not obtain alone? The reasons people join groups fall into two general categories—group membership as means and group membership as ends:

- **Means.** As we noted in the Introduction of this book, one important reason people come together and form groups (and join those groups into organizations) is that groups can be an important *means* to accomplishing desired outcomes. In particular, groups can enhance individual effectiveness and efficiency. This can be good for each of the individual members of the group, as well as for any larger organization of which the group is a part. A neighborhood watch may form because no one individual can police an entire neighborhood alone. A carpool may form because it's more efficient to have only one person drive to work each day. Groups enable individuals to pool their resources and increase their individual productivity by taking advantage of economies of scale.
- **Ends.** Individuals also join groups because group interactions can be desirable outcomes (or *ends*) in and of themselves. Someone may join a carpool because it saves gasoline and time, but that carpool also provides companionship and interesting conversation. A student may join a study group to improve his or her grades, but the interaction of the study group also provides an intimate social circle with which to commiserate when the demands of the classroom become overwhelming. The processes of group interaction represent more to group members than just the means to accomplishing difficult tasks. Group interaction itself provides important rewards.

THE STRUCTURING OF GROUP INTERACTION

From a means perspective, groups are useful only if the interaction of group members produces something greater than the sum of all the individuals' efforts. Group interaction must be structured so that group members coordinate their actions in the cooperative pursuit of both their individual objectives and the group's objectives. The structure of group interaction is apparent in the rules and roles that define acceptable behavior in the group.

RULES. Group rules can be formal or informal. Formal policies are explicitly agreed upon by the group members and may even be written down—for example, how often or at what time of day the group will meet. Many groups structure their meetings according to Robert's Rules of Order. These well-known rules specify in writing who may talk and when, and how disagreements will be settled by discussion and vote. As technology has become increasingly important in our lives, these formal rules are changing, as illustrated in "TECHNOLOGY FOCUS ON: Groups and Teams."

Group rules can also be informal. Informal, unstated rules that govern and regulate group behavior are called **norms**. Some groups have norms about what is appropriate to wear to meetings. Often, they have norms about lateness or absence. For example, particularly in the United States, it may be

TECHNOLOGY FOCUS ON
GROUPS AND TEAMS

COMPUTER EMERGENCY RESPONSE TEAMS. Computer emergency response teams (CERTs) were unheard of 10 years ago, yet they represent the workgroup of the future. This new form of knowledge group was created to identify attacks on the Internet and to provide solutions to these attacks. An attack represents an illegal attempt to steal information (e.g., financial) from transactions on the Internet.

The first CERT was launched at the Software Engineering Institute at Carnegie Mellon University. Today, this work is conducted in the following way:

1 Individuals monitor for attacks.
2 When the evidence indicates that an attack is becoming severe, a CERT is convened to discuss whether there should be action.
3 Action comes in the form of an advisory, which is a document sent to a user's community, warning about the attack and identifying immediate and longer-term remedies.

The advisories must be carefully worded to provide enough information to users while not giving information that might lead to more attacks. New CERTs are constituted for each advisory. When people are not working on teams, they may be working with vendors to improve systems to prevent future attacks.

The military is one of the most common places to find these teams, as they are deployed to maintain the security of government networks. In fact, the U.S. Department of Defense is considering establishing a 400-person joint integrated virtual organization that would allow reservists to focus on information operations and information security.

Sources: Excerpted from Goodman, P. S., & Rousseau, D. M. (2000). CERT [Online]. URL: www.workvideos.com; Lawlor, M. (2000, March). Military leaders formulate virtual organization plans. *Signal,* 27–29.

---

the norm for group members to call ahead to warn the group if they are going to be more than 10 minutes late for a meeting.

Some groups also have norms prohibiting criticism of group decisions to "outsiders"—people who are not members of the group. This type of norm demonstrates an important difference between norms and explicit group policies. A group might feel uneasy about adopting an explicit rule against airing group dissension outside the group. Nevertheless, an informal rule of this sort may be necessary for group members to feel free to voice dissenting or controversial positions during group discussions, or if it is important for the group to appear united in its opinions to outsiders.

Knowing a group's rules for social interaction and playing by them is often critical if a newcomer wants to make good first impressions and establish healthy long-term relationships with U.S. members of the group. Nowhere is this more apparent than when U.S. managers conduct business abroad. As noted in "INTERNATIONAL FOCUS ON: Rules and Norms," the rules that govern social interaction in other countries are often very different from the norms practiced at home. Managers traveling abroad are well advised to learn the local rules of social interaction, so as to avoid accidentally insulting their foreign hosts.

ROLES. Whereas rules delineate the proper behaviors of all members in a group, **roles** define the set of behaviors appropriate to particular *positions* occupied by specific individuals. Roles also specify authority relationships, including who in the group has the right to call meetings, set agendas, and

INTERNATIONAL FOCUS ON
RULES AND NORMS

STRANGERS IN STRANGE LANDS. Rules and norms can facilitate smooth and productive social interaction only when individuals are aware of them. Within a country, there may be subtle differences in social conventions among regions, or even among organizations within a region. But these differences pale in comparison to the differences across countries. Consider some of the rules for social interaction in the Arab Middle East.

The Arab concept of privacy is quite different from that held by most Americans. Americans new to the Middle East may schedule a confidential meeting to discuss classified company business, only to find their Arab host's office filled with friends, relatives, and professional associates at the appointed hour. But finding *anything* in the Middle East at the appointed hour is no small triumph because in general, Arabs view time as a continuous flow of events in which past, present, and future blur together. If unanticipated events prevent an Arab from meeting agreed-upon deadlines, it's the immutable will of Allah. As one frustrated U.S. oil company executive put it, "Arab clocks have no hands."

Hospitality is also an important aspect of Arab social interaction rules. To ancient Bedouins, from whom modern Arabs take many cultural cues, the purpose of hospitality was to strengthen group ties, vital to security in a tenuous nomadic existence in the harsh desert. Today, Arab hospitality is still a two-way street: a show of mutual respect, reciprocity, and delicately balanced obligations between host and guest, who will then, in a future situation, become guest and host. Not only do Arabs feel obligated to be generous to their guests, but for a guest to *refuse* such generosity is an insult, a rejection of bonding to the group with which the host is aligned. When the situation is reversed, the former guest is expected to play the host with equal, but not greater, hospitality, so as not to create an imbalance in the relationship.

When you're offered something by an Arab colleague—be it coffee, tea, nuts, dates, an invitation to dinner, or even a gift—Arab rules of politeness dictate that you should accept it. Whether you want it is irrelevant. The symbolic meaning of the offer and your acceptance matter, not the content of the offer or your desire to receive it. And your playing by the rules in a foreign country matters when it comes to the locals' acceptance of you.

Sources: Nydell, M. K. (1996). *Understanding Arabs: A guide for Westerners.* Yarmouth, MA: Intercultural Press; and Chesanow, N. (1985). A thousand and one Arabian nights. *World-Class Executive* (pp. 110–147). New York: Rawson Associates.

assign tasks to group members. Social psychologist Erving Goffman contended that roles (like rules) smooth interaction in groups.[2] Roles allow us to know what we should be doing and what to expect from others. Like rules, the roles that structure the interaction of group members can be formal or informal.

In work organizations, formal roles are specified by job descriptions. **Job descriptions** are written documents that specify what duties individuals must perform, to whom individuals must report, and what goals individuals must attain—in short, their role in the organization. Job descriptions are very useful because they decrease an individual's uncertainty about what to do to fulfill the group's needs and expectations.

Many groups (especially informal ones) do not have job descriptions. Roles instead evolve or are negotiated informally as the group develops. Some role assignments evolve during group development as particular strengths and talents of group members are revealed. As we shall see in

---

2. Goffman, E. (1959). *The presentation of self in everyday life.* New York: Doubleday Anchor.

Chapter 9, most groups have at least two leadership roles: a task leader (who focuses on getting the group's goals accomplished) and a socioemotional (relations-oriented) leader (who focuses on maintaining harmony and good working relationships within the group). Whereas task leadership is often decided formally (e.g., by vote of the group members or appointment from a higher source), socioemotional leadership emerges (and even changes) as the group develops and matures.

Roles are specific to particular positions within particular groups. The role an individual occupies in one group may be completely different from the role that same individual occupies in other groups. Figure 6-1 identifies a variety of roles that one individual might assume in different groups and relationships.

Because all of us simultaneously occupy different roles, *role conflict* is always a potential problem. Role conflict occurs when the behaviors dictated by one role conflict with the behaviors dictated by another. The coach of a

■ FIGURE 6-1

One Person = Many Roles

Every person assumes many different roles. At home, an individual might be a parent or spouse, and at work a supervisor or subordinate (or both). Each of these roles carries with it prescriptions for behaviors and expectations on the part of others (for example, your boss expects you to obey, and your spouse expects you to be supportive and affectionate). These roles help us know what to do—and help others know what to expect from us.

Source: Wrightsman, L. A. (1977). *Social psychology* (2nd ed.). Monterey, CA: Brooks/Cole, p. 17.

company softball team may find himself in a quandary about how to address his boss if his boss tries out for the team. Is the boss still "Ms. Perkins" on the softball field (as she is in the office), or is she "Janet"? And if she's "Janet" on the softball field, is she now "Janet" in the office?

An important component of most roles is status. **Status** refers to the position of a role in a social hierarchy and is a source of power for a role holder. The amount of status that a role commands is the amount of personal worth, respect, prestige, and deference that the role provides *any* individual occupying that role. High-status individuals can influence the behaviors of a group because of their revered positions. Similarly, members of the group view high-status individuals as opinion leaders.

The power that high-status individuals exert over low-status group members is sensible when status reflects ability or expertise. For example, senior students at a university (high-status role holders) are likely to be extremely knowledgeable and thereby worthy of the deference freshman students accord them. The role of university professor carries even more status, though this status may be less reflective of a particular expertise if the group's primary task is one of advising students on university-specific policies if the professor has been on campus for only a few days and is therefore ignorant of such campus policies, norms, and procedures.

Interestingly, undeserved status may be no less powerful than earned status. In courtroom trials, jurors from high-status occupations disproportionately influence final jury decisions, even though the high-status occupation may make the individual no more capable than others of rendering a just verdict.[3]

MAINTAINING GROUP ADAPTABILITY. Rules and roles are important for coordinating and regulating group interaction, as shown in the opening vignette describing groups preparing appetizers. After all, in the absence of roles and rules, there is typically chaos and a low probability of effective group functioning. This does not mean, however, that all rules and roles are universally good for a group. Rules and roles improve the effectiveness of group functioning precisely because they constrain the behaviors of group members, thereby allowing predictability and coordination of group behavior. But, although a little constraint is not only good but also *necessary* for a group to function effectively, too much constraint can prove disastrous.

In an article titled "The Technology of Foolishness," political scientist and organizational behavior professor Jim March suggested that rules and roles can constrain a group's creativity and flexibility.[4] This constraint, in turn, can hinder the group's adaptability to changing demands and opportunities. Norms and roles represent prescriptions for behavior—prescriptions that summarize past learning about how the group can best function. For example, a norm may previously have been established for group members to bring food to meetings. The food makes it possible for the group to work during the noon hour without anyone missing lunch. The food also informalizes the meetings, thereby encouraging open discussion. Having a norm about bringing food allows these advantages to occur at every meeting with-

3. Strodtbeck, F. L., James, R. M., & Hawkins, D. (1957). Social status in jury deliberations, *American Journal of Sociology, 22*, 713–719.
4. March, J. G. (1988). The technology of foolishness. *Decisions and Organizations.* Oxford, Basil Blackwell, 253–265.

out members having to figure out a new way to accomplish them. What the norm also does, however, is to discourage anyone from figuring out a *better* way of accomplishing these same (and, admittedly, valuable) benefits. This can prove extremely important if circumstances change so that rules that were appropriate for regulating group behavior in the past are no longer appropriate. When a norm has been established, group members will hesitate to break the norm and risk sanctions by the group.

March suggested that it is important for group members occasionally to "act out" and violate group rules and roles. In most cases, violating these rules and roles will result in poor outcomes for the group. Sometimes, however, it will reveal that a norm or policy was ill advised in the first place, that circumstances have changed, or that there is simply a better way of doing things. Only violation of a rule or role can show why the rule or role is still appropriate, if in fact it still is. Unfortunately, unless a group member is willing to risk sanctions by the group, violations of rules and roles will not occur. Thus, while rules and roles capture past learning about effective group functioning, they may also stand in the way of continual learning and adaptation by the group.

Idiosyncrasy credits provide a way for individuals in groups to be creative within the necessary constraints of rules and roles. **Idiosyncrasy credits** are allowances given to group members to violate group rules and roles.[5] If someone has proved to be a good group member—has largely gone along with the behavioral prescriptions of the group's rules and roles—that individual will be *allowed* to violate the group's rules and norms without incurring extreme sanctions. That individual's actions are not likely, on balance, to be seen as a threat to the group. In contrast, an individual new to the group or one who has consistently violated rules and roles in the past is likely to be seen as a threat to the integrity of the group. Because rules and roles are important to maintaining the group's coordination and stability, this individual's behavior is unlikely to be tolerated. Thus, group members accumulate idiosyncrasy credits by demonstrating their group loyalty. Idiosyncrasy credits also provide a mechanism by which group members can challenge and reaffirm the continuing appropriateness of group rules and roles.

STAGES OF GROUP DEVELOPMENT

The rules and roles that structure group interaction do not simply exist. Groups must evolve and develop rules and roles over time. Many theories have been offered to explain how groups develop.[6] We will examine two of them: the five-stages perspective and the punctuated-equilibrium model.

THE FIVE-STAGES PERSPECTIVE. The **five-stages perspective** is probably the best-known theory of how groups develop over time. This perspective proposes that groups pass through five distinct phases as they develop: forming, storming, norming, performing, and adjourning.[7]

5. Hollander, E. P. (1958). Conformity, status, and idiosyncrasy credits. *Psychological Review,* 65, 117–127.

6. Wanous, J. P., Reichers, A. E., & Malik, S. D. (1984). Organizational socialization and group development: Toward and integrative perspective. *Academy of Management Review,* 9, 670–683.

7. Tuckman, B. W., & Jensen, M. A. C. (1977). Stages of small group development revisited. *Group and Organization Studies,* 2, 419–427.

Two important points should be kept in mind when considering the stages of group development. First, groups sometimes move back and forth among these stages. As noted earlier, it is not unusual for a group to find that all of its conflicts were not settled initially. In such cases, a second or even third phase of differentiation may occur, until critical conflicts are ironed out. Second, the transitions from one stage to the next may not be obvious to the group members themselves. In fact, much of the negotiation of roles and rules may be quite implicit.

Forming. When groups first come together, the members must get acquainted as well as determine the basis for group membership. **Forming** includes learning the traits and strengths of each member as well as what distinguishes a member from a nonmember. If participation in the group is voluntary, individuals decide during formation if membership is necessary or whether this group is likely to fulfill their needs. Preliminary identification of a leader usually occurs at this stage as well.

Storming. When group members have had an opportunity to assess the human resources available in a group, several battles must be fought; this is the **storming** stage. First, the group must decide what its goals and priorities will be. A study group might ask whether its only purpose is to study or whether it should fulfill an important social function as well. If the group is to have a social function, as well as a study function, how will these two goals be reconciled? Are there other functions? Can the group fulfill its functions without creating problems for its members?

The second battle arises because the group must structure interactions to ensure effective functioning. It becomes important to determine who will fulfill which roles. Disagreements that are not handled now typically force the group back to this stage later in its development.

Norming. After group functions have been (at least tentatively) decided on and roles have been assigned, the tone of the interactions changes. Group members are working toward a common purpose, and the group has identified the human resources it needs to fulfill that purpose. During the **norming** stage, the group members define a set of rules and roles to coordinate group interactions and make pursuit of the goals effective.

Performing. After a group has identified its rules and roles, it has a structure within which to pursue its goals, and the group has reached maturity. If further conflicts surface, the structure (roles and rules) should lead to nondisruptive resolution of the conflicts. This is the **performing** stage.

Adjourning. Some time after a group has reached maturity, it may make sense for the group to disband, or **adjourning.** Some groups adjourn because their time is up; a CEO-advisory group, for instance, disbands when the CEO's term of office expires, or when the CEO quits or is fired. Groups may also choose to adjourn because they have outlived their usefulness—for example, if the group has lost critical members or found a solution to the problem it was convened to address (or even has realized that there is no solution). Finally, a group may adjourn prematurely if it fails to develop adequately—for instance, if it cannot manage conflicts.

THE PUNCTUATED-EQUILIBRIUM MODEL. Not all groups develop according to the five-stages model. According to another theory, project teams that have a fixed time frame in which to accomplish a task tend to develop through a process known as the **punctuated equilibrium model**.[8]

According to the punctuated-equilibrium model of group development, the tone for a project team (how it will interact, what approach it will take to the project, what its goals will be) is set in the team's first meeting. The project team stays with these arrangements (regardless of their efficiency or effectiveness) until approximately the midpoint of the time frame for completion of the project. At about this time, a "revolution" occurs in the team's approach to its project. The team breaks out of its inertia and generates a new set of agreements and arrangements that carry the team through to the project's completion.

According to this model, the team's closing meetings also depart from previous meetings. Typically, final meetings are focused on preparing the work of the project team for external consumption.

THE ROLE OF TIME. The difference between the five-stages and punctuated-equilibrium models is the role of time. Groups without a deadline for completion of their work may progress and develop according to the internal needs of the group or the needs of the group's members. Indeed, such groups may fail precisely because they reach a development stage beyond which they cannot progress. According to the punctuated-equilibrium model, the development of a project team working under a time deadline is not a function of the group's internal needs to develop effective group functioning. Instead, its development is triggered by the deadline imposed on the team and by the need for completion of the project by that deadline.

THE NATURE OF TEAMS

In the management literature, the term *team* is often used interchangeably with the term *group*; however, we would like to make a distinction. Earlier we defined a group as two or more individuals who have come together to perform a function; they represent individual efforts coordinated within an existing system.[9] In contrast, although a team is also a group, in a team the members are mutually accountable for the product or service they produce or provide.[10] "FOCUS ON: Teams" provides details on what makes a group a team. In addition, Figure 6-2 illustrates some of the differences between teams and groups.

TYPES OF TEAMS

There are hundreds of types of teams. Among the most common are work teams, parallel teams, project teams, and management teams.[11]

8. Gersick, C. J. G. (1994, February). Pacing strategic change: The case of a new venture. *Academy of Management Journal, 37*(1), 9–45; Gersick, C. J. G. (1988). Time and transition in work teams: Toward a new model of group development. *Academy of Management Journal, 31*, 9–41.

9. Cleland, D. I. (1996). *Strategic management of teams.* New York: Wiley, p. 38.

10. Mohrman, S. A., Cohen, S. G., & Mohrman, A. M., Jr. (1995). *Designing team-based organizations: New forms for knowledge work.* San Francisco: Jossey-Bass, p. 39.

11. Cohen, S. G., & Bailey, D. E. (1997). What makes teams work: Group effectiveness research

FOCUS ON TEAMS

"TEAM DOCTORS, REPORT TO ER". If teams are the cure, what's the disease? These days, teams are offered as the answer to whatever ails an organization, from lousy customer service to bloated bureaucracy. But all too often, teams fail because of what ails *them*. Usually, this includes an assortment of aches and pains that sap performance and confidence, eventually landing even good teams in the intensive care unit.

Typically, brain-dead senior executives authorize a team without questioning whether the project really needs one. Team members wonder, Why are we here? Often it's because some new-paradigm guru told the company's higher-ups that teams are hot. But this is the real world, and it turns out that the project should have been divided among individuals, with a single leader who has real clout riding shotgun. Too late, team members discover that the team is superfluous.

Jon Katzenbach, a director at the Dallas office of McKinsey & Company, has become the nation's best-known team doctor by helping scores of high-profile companies—such as Citicorp, General Electric, and Mobil Oil—use teams wisely. Yet Katzenbach is a big believer in not forming teams.

"Teams are neither efficient nor orderly groupings," he argued, "and teamwork is rarely the fastest way for a group with a capable leader to get where it's going—particularly if the leader has been there before."

The next time you're assigned to a team, use Katzenbach's diagnostic checklist to determine whether the team is better off dead. Among the questions it addresses are whether the project really requires collective work. If the work can be divided among, say, eight people who do their parts and leave it to the leader to integrate those parts, then a team adds no real value.

"Team performance is all about doing real work together," said Katzenbach. "And working collectively as a real team means having a small number of people with complementary skills who are committed to a common purpose and to common performance goals, and who hold themselves mutually accountable."

Do team members lead various aspects of the project? If the team leader makes all the critical decisions, you're not on a team—you're on a "single-leader unit."

This nonteam, said Katzenbach, "has a strong leader who knows the marketplace, who's disciplined about setting high performance standards, and who benefits from a well-designed system for assessing individual results. When these conditions exist, real team efforts are often unneeded."

Do people in the group hold one another accountable? If people answer to the boss instead of to one another, it's not a real team.

"A critical litmus test for a real team is whether there's mutual accountability," said Katzenbach. "It's best characterized by the phrase 'we hold each other accountable'—not 'the boss holds us accountable.' Mutual accountability reflects the higher degree of commitment that the members of a real team demonstrate."

Source: Excerpted from Fishetti, M. (1998, March). "Team doctors, report to ER": Is your team headed for intensive care? Our specialists offer prescriptions for the five illnesses that can afflict even the best teams. *Fast Company, 13,* 170–177.

WORK TEAMS. Unlike many teams that are set up for the duration of a project, work teams are ongoing work units.[12] In the past, these were most often led by a supervisor who made the majority of the decisions. More recently, such teams have been **self-managed teams**, meaning that the team assumes the tasks of the former supervisor. Team members are cross-trained to perform any task the team requires, including—but not limited to—performing work functions, setting schedules, ordering materials, and coordinating with other groups.[13] Many well-known companies, such as General

---

12. Cohen, & Bailey, What makes teams work.
13. Barker, J. R. (1999). *The discipline of teamwork.* Thousand Oaks, CA: Sage.

Differences between Groups and Teams	■ FIGURE 6-2

Teams	Groups
■ Shared authority and responsibility	■ Limited sharing of authority and responsibility
■ All members share leadership	■ Leadership rests with one or a few individuals
■ Individual and team accountability	■ Individual accountability
■ Shared results and rewards	■ Modest sharing of results and awards
■ High degree of self-direction	■ Limited self-direction
■ Members work together to produce results	■ Results are produced by individual effort

Source: Cleland, *Strategic management of teams,* p. 38.

Motors, Xerox, PepsiCo, and Motorola, have introduced self-managed teams in an effort to improve productivity and quality.

PARALLEL TEAMS. Parallel teams literally work parallel to the organization, performing problem-solving and improvement-oriented tasks that the regular organization is not equipped or structured to handle. Often referred to as task forces or quality improvement teams, parallel teams include people from across functions or work units. They typically have limited authority and can make recommendations only to individuals higher in the organizational hierarchy.[14]

PROJECT TEAMS. Project teams exist for relatively short periods of time for the purpose of producing a one-time product or service. Often, project teams consist of individuals from different and diverse disciplines or functions so as to increase the range of specialized knowledge and, consequently, chance of success.[15] In developing a new product, for example, team members might include operations specialists, financial analysts, and engineers. Once the product is produced, team members either return to their original unit or move on to a new project.

MANAGEMENT TEAMS. Management teams coordinate collective output by managing and providing direction to the interdependent subunits they are responsible for.[16] In a car manufacturing facility, for example, such a team would manage the production of an entire car.

At the top of the organization, the executive management team manages the firm's overall performance and provides strategic direction. In increasingly complex and rapidly changing environments, top management teams (TMTs) are becoming common. Among their strengths are the members' extensive experience and expertise and their willingness to share in the responsibility for the success of the organization.[17]

HIGH-PERFORMANCE TEAMS. Within these four types of teams is a variation called the *high-performance team.* As the name suggests, high-performance teams perform at significantly higher-than-normal levels,

---

14. Barker, *The discipline of teamwork.*
15. Barker, *The discipline of teamwork.*
16. Mohrman, Cohen, & Mohrman, *Designing team-based organizations.*
17. Cohen, & Bailey, What makes teams work.

■ **FIGURE 6-3**	**Typical Characteristics of the Four Styles of Team Members**

Contributor:	Responsible, authoritative, reliable, proficient, and organized
Collaborator:	Forward-looking, goal directed, accommodating, flexible, and imaginative
Communicator:	Supportive, considerate, relaxed, enthusiastic, and tactful
Challenger:	Honest, outspoken, principled, ethical, and adventurous

Source: Parker, *Team players and teamwork,* p. 164.

making them exceptionally effective. Characteristics of high-performance teams include members' commitment to values, trust, respect, caring, collaboration, meaningful recognition and rewards, and integration into the organization as a whole.[18] Johnsonville Foods in Sheboygan Falls, Wisconsin, is an excellent example of an organization that supports high-performance team-based activities. At Johnsonville Foods, teams not only enjoy autonomy and access to resources, but also receive ongoing training.[19]

STYLES AMONG TEAM MEMBERS

Research suggests that team members generally manifest one of four types of personalities: the contributor, the collaborator, the communicator, and the challenger.[20] Typically, an individual most noticeably displays one of these styles, but has the capacity to develop all four.[21] Figure 6-3 presents qualities of these four styles.

CONTRIBUTOR. The contributor is a task-oriented team member. Having gathered all the necessary information, the contributor enjoys sharing technical data and other details about how to proceed. The contributor's standards are high, and he or she pushes others to have high standards and to use resources wisely.

COLLABORATOR. The collaborator is a goal-oriented, big-picture person. The collaborator's focus is primarily on the vision or mission of the organization, but he or she is flexible and able to work outside that role if necessary.

COMMUNICATOR. The communicator is a process-oriented person. A good listener, the communicator is also good at such other people skills as conflict resolution and consensus building. The communicator is often the person who ensures that the team has an informal, comfortable environment in which to work.

CHALLENGER. The challenger is the team member who questions members of the team, is willing to disagree with the leader, and encourages members to take well-calculated risks.

Although we have emphasized here that teams and groups are separate entities, they subscribe to the same rules and norms. In the rest of the chap-

---

18. Harari, O. (1995). The dream team. *Management Review, 84,* 29–31.
19. Harari, The dream team.
20. Parker, G. M. (1996). *Team players and teamwork.* San Francisco: Jossey-Bass, pp. 63–86.
21. Kline, T. (1999). *Remaking teams: The revolutionary research-based guide that puts theory into practice.* San Francisco: Jossey-Bass.

RESEARCH IN ACTION
MEASURING CROSS-FUNCTIONAL TEAM EXPERTISE AT OUTDOOR LIVING COMPANY

John R. Austin, University of Washington–Bothell; *austinj@u.washington.edu*

By most measures, Outdoor Living Company's transition to a cross-functional team structure was a success. Outdoor Living manufactures and sells a wide array of outdoor sporting goods and clothing. In 1995, in hopes of improving communication and speeding up product development time, 27 newly formed cross-functional teams assumed product line management responsibility. Since then, product development time had been reduced, employee turnover is down, and senior management has reported having to moderate fewer disputes between departments. However, the team members continued to struggle with questions regarding team development. The cross-functional team structure was an improvement over the previous functional structure, but the team members wanted to know how to improve their performance. Benchmarking against each other was of limited value because each team faced a unique market and had different manufacturing requirements for its products. In annual surveys, team members reported decreased satisfaction with their teams' work processes and frustration with team communication. The team coordinator and trainer began looking for a way to improve the functioning of even the most successful teams.

At this time, I was brought in as an outside consultant. After conducting preliminary interviews with team members and senior managers, I developed a survey to measure how well team members were using the expertise of their fellow team members. Team member expertise could be task expertise (such as financial planning skills, manufacturing knowledge, graphic design) or social expertise (such as close ties with important team stakeholders). The survey also measured the extent to which the team members were willing to go outside their team for help when needed. I theorized that the most successful teams were better able than others to identify and use the available team expertise resources when faced with difficult problems. The results of the surveys supported this hypothesis. Higher-performing teams tended to have a more complete understanding of team expertise resources. Members of the higher-performing teams were also more likely go outside the team for help.

The cross-functional teams received the aggregated survey results, and team members were given an opportunity to discuss the study with me. Terri Mansfield, Outdoor Living's senior organization development manager at the time of the study, reported several changes that were direct results of the study. Most of the teams have assigned a team member to track team expertise and stakeholder connections. This team member attempts to ensure that available team expertise is used and that team members receive updates about new sources of expertise that become available. One team reported that this process enabled it to discover some stakeholder ties while developing a new product. The team leader estimated that the use of these new information resources cut several weeks off the product development cycle. The annual team member survey now includes two questions regarding team expertise. One question asks if team members feel that their expertise is being put to good use by the team. A second question asks if team members have a working understanding of their fellow team members' expertise. In the two years after completion of this study, the cross-functional teams continued to meet or exceed most of their team goals. Results from the annual team surveys reveal that team members have a high level of confidence in the abilities of their team and are satisfied with their team's development.

ter, we will use the terms interchangeably, as is done in much of the management literature.

BUILDING EFFECTIVE GROUPS AND TEAMS

The challenge of managing groups and teams in organizations is to get members to go along with good rules and roles, to communicate openly about the bad ones, and to consider carefully the questions about rules and roles offered by their fellow group members. This section briefly explores this important challenge from two perspectives. First, a model is presented that details the characteristics of effective groups and teams. Second, a technique is described that is used to improve team functioning in organizations.

CHARACTERISTICS OF SUCCESSFUL GROUPS AND TEAMS

Successful groups and teams typically share five characteristics: group objectives, role differentiation, rule clarity, membership, and communication. These characteristics support the team's composition and ultimate performance.

GROUP OBJECTIVES.   The goals, purposes, and functions that a group or team is trying to achieve are its **group objectives.** For a group or team to be successful, its goals must be specific. Vague goals lead to vague attempts to pursue them. Specific goals get everyone working in the same direction and sharing the same priorities.

It is important that the entire team share the group objectives. It is no help to group functioning if some members of the group have specific but different beliefs about where the group is headed and why. All group members should have the *same* goals in mind, even if some of the members don't completely agree with these objectives.

Finally, very successful groups and teams figure out ways to integrate individual and group goals. When group and individual goals are integrated, group actions become more than just the price individuals must pay for access to fulfillment of individual goals. Group actions also become the path to individual goal fulfillment. The "jigsaw classroom" in Austin, Texas, illustrates the importance of individual and group goal integration. Jigsaw classrooms put into practice a grade-school instructional technique that was based on building cooperative student learning teams:

> In a jigsaw classroom, small student-directed groups replace the teacher-dominated lecture method; students serve as the principal sources of information and reinforcement for one another. Students are placed in small groups of five or six for about an hour each day. The day's lesson is divided up into as many segments as there are group members and each student is given a unique part. Each member is then responsible for learning the assigned segment well enough to teach it to the others. Since group members can only learn a lesson in its entirety by pooling all their knowledge, interdependence is established.[22]

22. Aronson, E., & Yates, S. (1983). Cooperation in the classroom: The impact of the jigsaw method on interethnic relations, classroom performance, and self-esteem. In H. Blumberg, A. Hare, V. Kent, & M. Davies (Eds.), *Small groups and social interaction* 1. New York: Wiley.

The jigsaw classroom was devised to combat racial prejudice during de-segregation efforts in Texas. In jigsaw classrooms, cooperation, and thereby group achievement, was the only effective path to individual achievement, in stark contrast to most U.S. elementary schools, which typically reward individual over group achievement. Students in jigsaw classrooms in Austin learned their classroom lessons better, *and* they learned the value of teamwork and coordinated group efforts toward shared goals. Students in jigsaw classrooms were also better able to understand other students' perspectives, leading to decreased racial prejudice and misunderstanding in the schools.

More recent research by Sherry Schneider and Greg Northcraft has linked the idea of the jigsaw classroom to cross-functional teams. Schneider and Northcraft found that by virtue of the diversity of skill sets represented, teams, like jigsaw classrooms, have the potential to increase intergroup cooperation.[23]

ROLE DIFFERENTIATION. Members of successful groups and teams know more than just what the group or team is trying to accomplish. Each member also has a role that specifies his or her contribution. Appropriate **role differentiation** occurs in two ways. First, all group and team members should have a clear idea of their own roles—their own duties and responsibilities in the organization and how they contribute to the realization of the group's goals. Second, the roles assigned to each member of the group or team should reflect individual strengths and interests. It is not enough that each member has a role and knows what it is. As much as possible, each role should maximize group members' opportunities to contribute to fulfillment of the group's, the organization's, *and* their individual objectives.

RULE CLARITY. All members of the group should agree on the formal rules and informal norms that structure interactions within the group or team. These rules and norms include authority (task assignment) and reporting relationships. As discussed earlier in the chapter, rules are critical to the coordination of group member activities. If appropriate rules are not agreed on or are not known, they cannot control and direct group and team interaction.

MEMBERSHIP. Successful groups and teams strike an appropriate balance among similarities and differences in their members' values and backgrounds. A certain amount of variety in perspectives is important to ensure a healthy amount of controversy and conflict in the group or team. However, too much controversy and conflict can lead to hostility and to the eventual breakup of the group. Rules for membership and participation in group and team activities also need to be clear.

COMMUNICATION. All successful groups and teams have adequate channels of communication. Good communication is a group's first line of defense against threats to its survival, whether from external or internal sources. No matter how well objectives are selected and shared, rules and roles made clear, and membership constructed, circumstances are bound to change. Good channels of communication are important if the group is to adapt to new challenges and remain successful over time.

---

23. Schneider, S. K., & Northcraft, G. B. (1999). Three social dilemmas of workforce diversity in organizations: A social identity perspective. *Human Relations, 52,* 1445–1467.

■ **FIGURE 6-4** **Three Categories of Diversity**

Category	Definition	Example
Informational diversity	Differences in knowledge bases and perspectives that members bring to the group.	A difference in educational background
Social category diversity	Explicit differences in social category membership, such as race, gender, and ethnicity.	A difference in race
Value diversity	When members differ in terms of what they think the group's real task, goal, target, or mission should be.	A difference in values held

Source: Jehn, Northcraft, & Neale, Why differences make a difference.

TEAM COMPOSITION

When building groups and teams, an important component of performance is composition. Teams can be *homogeneous* (e.g., members have similar experiences, values, norms, expertise, or even ethnicity) or *heterogeneous* (e.g., members have differences in experiences or values). The diversity present in heterogeneous groups is shown in Figure 6-4 as informational diversity, social category diversity, and value diversity.

Interestingly, research presents conflicting findings regarding the relationship between diversity and performance. Some research suggests that diverse groups outperform homogeneous groups, and other research shows that homogeneous groups are better performers.[24] P. Christopher Earley and Elaine Mosakowski interviewed and observed five teams in the Pacific Rim, working for a multinational clothing producer. They found that both homogenous and highly heterogeneous teams outperform moderately heterogeneous teams over time, suggesting that modestly diverse groups are the most problematic.[25]

Research by Katherine Williams and Charles O'Reilly also examined composition in groups.[26] From their review of 40 years of research on diversity in organizations and examination of 80 studies, Williams and O'Reilly claimed that although diversity in groups may have positive effects on group performance, diversity is likely to hinder group performance if organizations do not take action to counterbalance negative effects. They pointed to information and decision studies which predict that diversity in organizations has positive effects (e.g., avoid groupthink, increase quality and quantity of deci-

24. Jehn, K. A., Northcraft, G. B., & Neale, M. A. (1999). Why differences make a difference: A field study of diversity, conflict, and performance in workgroups. *Administrative Science Quarterly, 44*, 741–763.

25. Earley, P. C., & Mosakowski, E. (2000). Creating hybrid team cultures: An empirical test of transnational team functioning. *Academy of Management Journal, 43*, 26–49.

26. Williams, K. Y., & O'Reilly, C. A., III. (1998). Demography and diversity in Organizations: A review of 40 years of research. *Research in Organizational Behavior, 20*, 77–140.

sion making). Yet, they noted that most research supports social categorization and similarity/attraction theories which predict that most people prefer working in groups with people who are more, rather than less, like themselves. Consequently, individuals in heterogeneous groups may set up barriers that work to the detriment of effective group behavior. Therefore, management's challenge is to develop innovative ways to downplay the negative effects of diversity in order to realize the potential positivve effects on group performance. Often making group members more conscious of differences in thinking that can result from diverse backgrounds is a strong first step.

Recent research by Karen Jehn, Gregory Northcraft, and Margaret Neale provides yet another perspective on team composition. These authors suggested that distinguishing among different *types* of diversity and their *effects* may reconcile many of the inconsistencies found in the literature related to composition and performance.[27] Their research found that value diversity, not the commonly assumed social category diversity, has the most significant influence on both performance and morale. In addition, they found that diversity does not have a direct effect on performance, but conflict does have both positive and negative effects on performance. Their research clarified previous research in this area by showing that heterogeneous groups have more conflict throughout the group processes, yet this conflict leads to better workgroup performance whereas homogeneous groups experience lower levels of conflict throughout the group process, but the result may be lower levels of performance. For further details on this research, see the RESEARCH IN ACTION section in Chapter 5.

TEAM DEVELOPMENT

This chapter begins by noting that groups and teams are essentially collections of individuals whose interactions are structured to fulfill functions, whether these be independent or mutually accountable. This chapter's opening vignette notes that companies pay consultants huge sums of money to help them build successful teams. As outlined in this chapter, a successful group or team has a good understanding of its functions (objectives) and an appropriate structure (in the form of role differentiation, rule clarity, membership, and communication) for achieving them.

How do groups and teams come to possess these important characteristics? Some groups achieve them through natural evolution. Other groups get a helping hand by participating in team-development activities.

Team development is defined as "an inward look by the team at its own performance, behavior, and culture for the purposes of deleting dysfunctional behaviors and strengthening functional ones."[28] Team-development activities teach team members valuable skills related to working and getting along with others. These skills become the foundation for team effectiveness. All team-development (or team-building) activities share some important functions: diagnosis, change, and development.

DIAGNOSIS. Team development always includes activities that focus on identifying functional and dysfunctional aspects of the group's interactions.

27. Jehn, Northcraft, & Neale, Why differences make a difference.
28. French, W., & Bell, C. (1978). *Organizational development: Behavioral science interventions for organizational improvement.* Englewood Cliffs, NJ: Prentice Hall.

Typically, the roles and rules for group interaction are examined and their appropriateness openly questioned. Often group members are asked to complete diagnostic questionnaires. The questionnaire might ask, for instance: How *clear* are the group's goals? How much *consensus* is there around the group's goals? The results of the questionnaire are then fed back to the group and used to stimulate awareness and discussion of problems concerning any of the five dimensions (group objectives, role differentiation, role clarity, membership, and communication) of effective group interaction.

CHANGE. After a group has identified its problems, the members of the group must work together to remove impediments to effective functioning. Naturally, attempts to make changes will prove successful only if diagnosis has been careful and thorough. The immediate identification of obvious behavior problems rarely provides a complete diagnosis of deficiencies in the group's interactions. The "maintaining conditions" that have allowed this problem to persist or grow must also be examined and questioned.

DEVELOPMENT. Successful group development goes beyond identifying and repairing dysfunctional interactions. The need for group-development activities in the first place suggests that a group is not adequately self-diagnostic. Successful **group development** therefore does more than just solve interaction problems. It also creates a system for identifying and resolving *future* problems.

Role therapy is one example of a group-development activity. In role therapy an external group process consultant leads the team in defining the individual roles in the group. Role therapy also creates opportunities to clarify the group's overall objectives and rules and to enhance channels of communication within the group.

Through a cycle of analysis, modeling, and coaching by the process consultant, role therapy achieves two important objectives. First, sources of role problems are identified publicly so that the group can begin to work toward their resolution. Second, group communication processes are improved so that in the future the group can identify, acknowledge, and resolve role problems on its own.

Role therapy is only one of a variety of techniques that organizations use to develop more effective group functioning. Several other techniques are discussed in Chapter 15.

COMMUNICATION IN GROUPS AND TEAMS

Communication is the transmitting of information and understanding by one group member to another through the use of symbols.[29] Communication is probably the most visible of all group activities, and it is critical to effective group functioning. As noted in this chapter's opening vignette, effective communication is the difference between an effective and a dysfunctional team.

---

29. Ivancevich, J. M., & Matteson, M. T. (1987). *Organizational behavior and management.* Plano, TX: BPI, p. 632.

Communications Model	■ **FIGURE 6-5**

Communication is essentially a perceptual process. The sender must encode intended meaning to create messages. The receiver then decodes the messages to obtain perceived meaning. Effective communication depends on the sender and the receiver sharing an understanding of the rules used to encode meaning into messages.

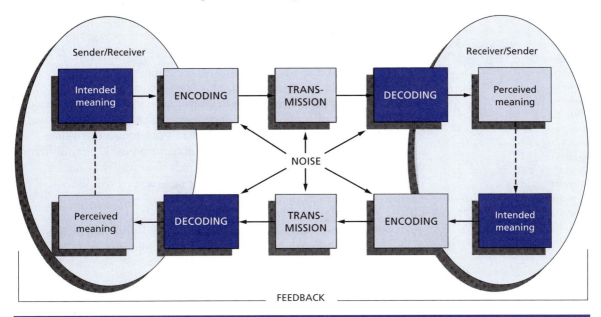

Research has repeatedly shown that groups and organizations spend enormous amounts of time communicating. In some occupations, more than half of all time on the job is spent communicating; for some managerial positions, the figure can reach almost 70%.[30] Research also indicates that it is essential that managers not only communicate well but that their success is, in large measure, determined by their communication skills.[31]

The remainder of this chapter addresses the important topic of communication in groups and teams. We begin by describing the basic processes of communication, including nonverbal communication, communication styles, and the important differences between formal and informal communication in organizations. The chapter closes by examining barriers to communication and suggesting some techniques for improving communicator effectiveness.

BASIC COMMUNICATION PROCESSES

As shown in Figure 6-5, effective communication between individuals (the sender and the receiver) involves many steps, including encoding, decoding, and feedback.

---

30. Luthans, F., & Larsen, J. K. (1986). How managers really communicate. *Human Relations*, *39*, 161–178; and MacLeod, L., Scriven, J., & Stanford, W. F. (1992). Gender and management-level differences in the oral communication patterns of bank managers. *Journal of Business Communication*, *29*, 343–365.
31. Penley, L. E., Alexander, E. R., Jernigan, I. E., & Henwood, C. I. (1991). Communication abilities of managers: The relationship to performance. *Journal of Management*, *17*, 57–76.

ENCODING. Intended meaning is the thought or idea that the sender would like to convey to the receiver. In order to transmit this intended meaning, the sender must encode it. **Encoding** is the three-part process of creating a message for the receiver to receive:

1 First, the sender must select some contents of the intended meaning to transmit. To do this, the sender must decide what the receiver knows, what the receiver will assume, and what else must be conveyed.

2 Second, the sender must select a communication medium and channel (or channels) through which to transmit the intended meaning. For instance, will the communication be verbal or written? If verbal, will other channels (nonverbal gestures or voice inflections, for instance) be used? The importance of communication medium and channel selection was immortalized forever by Marshall McLuhan's pronouncement that "the medium is the message."[32] McLuhan's comment serves as a reminder that medium and channel selections themselves convey information. An e-mail communicates something different from a personal phone call or a face-to-face discussion, even if the words are the same.

3 Finally, the sender must translate the contents selected for the message into symbols. Communication symbols are agreed-upon representations of meaning. Spoken words, for instance, are appropriate symbols for verbal communication.

DECODING. After the message is transmitted, the receiver must decode it. During **decoding** the receiver attempts to reverse the encoding process and extract meaning from a message. The success of decoding is dependent on the sender and the receiver agreeing on the meanings of communication symbols. The perceived meaning that the receiver extracts from a message will not resemble the sender's intended meaning if the symbols used have different meanings for the sender and the receiver.

FEEDBACK. The final stage of communication is **feedback**—the receiver's reaction to the sender's message and the perceived meaning of that message. Feedback is critical to effective communication because it helps the sender know if the receiver correctly decoded the intended meaning of the initial message.

NOISE. As noted in Figure 6-5, effective communication can be disrupted by noise. **Noise** refers to any characteristics in the immediate context or the communicating individuals that might interfere with the communication process, such as the noise level in the room, loss of hearing, and even stress levels.

NONVERBAL COMMUNICATION

Nowhere is the importance of perception to communication in groups and teams more apparent than in understanding nonverbal communication. **Nonverbal communication** refers to any form of interpersonal communication other than formal verbal language. It typically includes facial cues, hand or arm gestures, and body positioning. Clothing can be used to send nonverbal signals as well—for example, when a male colleague buttons up his

---

32. McLuhan, M. (1967). *The medium is the message.* New York: Random House.

shirt and tightens his tie to signal that a meeting is all business. People also surround themselves with objects (such as fancy cars, walnut desks, and corner offices) that communicate who they are—or who they would like to be.

Nonverbal communication channels often are used to supplement verbal communication by highlighting or reinforcing parts of a verbal message. However, nonverbal communication is generally more uncertain than verbal communication, both in meaning and in likelihood of receipt. Some perceivers may not attend to attempts at nonverbal communication or may completely misunderstand them. What is the meaning of a wink at the end of a sentence? What does it mean if a speaker turns away when sending a message? Additionally, when communication occurs over the phone, via a fax, or on a virtual team, the individual does not have the benefits of face-to-face interaction, as illustrated in "TECHNOLOGY FOCUS ON: Communication."

TECHNOLOGY FOCUS ON
COMMUNICATION

VIRTUAL TEAMS. When it comes to virtual working, we need to know the new rules of communication. How do managers manage people they rarely meet face to face?

"Virtual workers are a bit like spacemen," claimed Peter Wingrave of IBM Europe's Design and Workplace Strategy Group. "While out walking in space, the umbilical chord through which they communicate with the space craft is crucial." At IBM there are Europe-wide, dawn-to-dusk information technology and human resources help desks, a personal counseling service, secretarial support for each virtual team, and training on the management of remote workers.

Management becomes far more complex when staff are no longer around on a regular basis, added Wingrave. "You have to make judgments on whether a weekly phone call is enough to keep in touch, or whether a face-to-face meeting would be advisable," he said.

Barbara Reeves, of Boeing, emphasized the importance of extending people issues into the training of virtual workers. When she launched Boeing's flexible work scheme 4 years ago, training tended to concentrate on the mechanics of the scheme and use of technology. Now, much of this can be gleaned from two Web-based training units.

Face-to-face training has shifted in focus to subjects such as protocols for remote contact between teleworkers and motivation and produc-

tivity. Originally, for instance, workers were asked to log their activities, even when not bound to do so by a client contract. It was supposed to measure productivity, but it simply added to paperwork. Now, where there is no obligation to keep a log, productivity is measured through setting targets and reviewing delivery. As all veterans of telework will tell you, a shift from measuring inputs to outputs is fundamental to managing flexible workers.

In its pilot stage, Boeing held meetings between teleworkers. These proved so valuable, with colleagues jointly "solving" many of the technical and personal problems that arose ("How do I tackle a neighbor who keeps calling during work hours?"), that they have remained in place.

"Regular face-to-face meetings—even if they are just social—are important," said Louis Wustemann, editor of *Flexible Working*, whose staff, not unexpectedly, are widely dispersed. If remote methods of communication don't work, things start to go wrong quickly, he said. He pointed out that you must learn when it is proper to contact particular people at home according to their routine. Another rule is never to give bad news or deal with tricky human resources issues over the phone.

Source: Excerpted from How to manage people you never see; Sheena Vernon on the ways teleworkers talk to each other. (1999, October 24). *The Independent*, p. 3.

■ **FIGURE 6-6**

The Johari Window

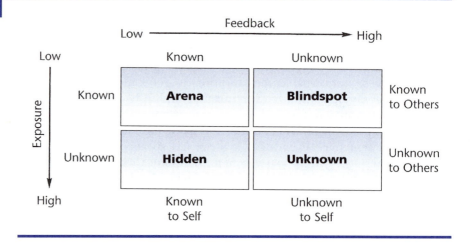

COMMUNICATION STYLES

People differ in the ways they choose to communicate with others. We all know individuals who rely on face-to-face discussions, and others who utilize e-mail and voicemail almost exclusively. Developed by Drs. Joseph Luft and Harry Ingham (after whom it was named), the **Johari Window** has received widespread use by management trainers as a device for assessing and categorizing managers' communication styles. As shown in Figure 6-6, the Johari Window classifies an individual's tendencies to facilitate or hinder interpersonal communication along two dimensions: exposure and feedback.[33] **Exposure** is the extent to which an individual openly and candidly divulges feelings and information when trying to communicate. *Feedback* is the extent to which an individual successfully elicits exposure from others.

These two dimensions of communication—exposure and feedback—give rise to four distinct components of interpersonal communication. As shown in Figure 6-6, the *arena* represents information that is known to the manager and known to others. In the best of all worlds, all communication would be in the arena. A manager would be open and candid in discussions with others team members, and in turn those other members would be open and candid in discussions with the manager. The more information that falls in the arena, the more effective the communication.

The second cell of the Johari Window is the *blindspot*. Information in the blindspot is known to others but not known to the manager. Blindspots occur when a manager does not communicate enough, does not listen well when communicating, or antagonizes others so that they don't provide the manager with feedback.

Components of communication become *hidden* when a manager fails (intentionally or unintentionally) to provide information to others. Hidden information can cause problems, particularly if the manager incorrectly assumes that everyone already knows it. Finally, information may be *unknown* to both the manager and others. This information is not intentionally being held back, but it nevertheless remains uncommunicated.

---

33. Hall, J. (1973, Spring). Communication revisited. *California Management Review*, 30–48.

Differences in the extent to which managers' communication skills and abilities result in arena, blindspot, hidden, and unknown information give rise to four distinct communication styles:

- *Type A* communicators are low in both exposure and feedback. Type A managers would be characterized as uncommunicative, terse, and even aloof or impersonal. Type A communication results in both hidden information and blindspots.
- *Type B* communicators are also low in exposure, but they are high in feedback. Type B managers constantly seek out information, but they rarely provide information in exchange. Type B communication results in hidden information.

     Managers low in exposure (Type A or Type B communicators) basically don't trust others with important information. Low-exposure communication is particularly ineffective when paired with high feedback because it results in continual requests for information.
- *Type C* communicators are high in exposure but low in feedback. Type C managers are typically perceived as being autocratic or arrogant. They provide lots of information but rarely request the opinions of others. They are likely to be perceived as not valuing others' opinions and perspectives. Type C communication tends to create blindspots.
- *Type D* communicators are high on both exposure and feedback. Most of their information is arena information, and they tend to communicate effectively.

In addition to whether they provide and seek information, communicators differ in their use of physical space, eye contact, and touching. For example, Mexicans often address colleagues with a hug and then stand or sit very close while they're talking; further, they often touch their associate on the arm or shoulder. By contrast, Americans and Germans tend to be more comfortable greeting each other with a handshake, and when they converse there is usually at least 3 feet of space between the parties and no touching.[34] Men and women also differ in their communication styles, and, like cultural differences, gender differences sometimes diminish communication effectiveness. The "On Your Own" exercise at the end of this chapter includes an instrument to help you assess your own communication style.

BARRIERS TO COMMUNICATION

As mentioned previously, communication is essentially a perceptual process. Receivers must attend to, construct, and interpret communication symbols to arrive at a meaning for a message. Many communication failures can be explained as problems of perception. We will consider two examples of communication problems here: problems with attention and problems with interpretation.

ATTENTION AND INFORMATION OVERLOAD. One of the biggest barriers to effective communication is information overload, which occurs when there is more information available than the receiver can decode. In perceptual terms, this is a problem of limited attention. Managers are buried

---

34. Morrison, T., Conaway, W. A., & Borden, G. A. (1994). *Kiss, bow, or shake hands: How to do business in sixty countries.* Holbrook, MA: Adams Media.

under an avalanche of information transmitted to them daily from a variety of sources, such as subordinates, superiors, e-mail, and newspapers. Much of this communication may be redundant or of little or no immediate value to the manager. No manager can attend to all the available information to decide what is important and what is not. The manager must select which messages to decode. Given that uncertainty is a defining characteristic of organizations, the receiver will not always know which messages are the most important. Thus, the first barrier to effective communication is that any single message may not even be received.

Another influence on a manager's attention is the individual's frame of reference. One study demonstrated that managers' communication activities are dramatically influenced simply by whether a situation is labeled a crisis or a challenge. When managers perceive a situation to be a crisis, they ask fewer questions then they normally would, listen less carefully to individuals not involved in the crisis, and are less interested in hearing what others not involved in the crisis have to say.[35]

Additionally, anything that can increase the salience of a message will make it more likely to be received. For instance, presentations are often presented in unusual formats or colors to attract and maintain the audience's attention.

Motivations of the receiver—the individual for whom the communication is intended—also play a role in what gets attention. Consequently, communication attempts from above are usually attended to more carefully than are those from below.

INTERPRETATION AND DECODING. Figure 6-7 suggests that for information to be communicated accurately, the rules behind the encoding of the message must be shared by the information decoder. The receiver must share the sender's views about what aspects of the intended message need to be transmitted, and the receiver must share the sender's beliefs about the meanings attached to communication symbols and channels. In the communication failure shown in Figure 6-7, the scientists have attended to and built appropriate constructions of the dolphins' messages. However, the scientists do not know the rules for decoding the message: They have not figured out that the dolphins are speaking Spanish. In other words, simply attending to the correct symbols and constructing a correct representation does not ensure communication if the receiver cannot accurately decode the communication attempts.

When two communicators literally are not speaking the same language, the importance of shared encoding/decoding rules seems obvious. The importance of sharing rules may be less obvious, however, when two people *seem* to be speaking the same language but really are not. There is a story about a plumber who wrote to the government to find out if it was safe to use hydrochloric acid to unclog drains. The government responded that "the efficacy of hydrochloric acid is indisputable, but the corrosive residue is incompatible with metallic permanence." What the government meant, of course, was that hydrochloric acid "eats the heck out of pipes"—a message that would have been significantly more understandable to a plumber.[36]

---

35. Tjosvold, D. (1984). Effects of crisis orientation on managers' approach to controversy in decision making. *Academy of Management Journal, 27,* 130–138.

36. Wexley, K. N., & Yukl, G. A. (1977). *Organizational behavior and personnel psychology.* Homewood, IL: Irwin.

■ **FIGURE 6-7**

"Matthews ... we're getting another one of those strange 'aw blah es span yol' sounds."

Barriers to Communication

A perceiver may construct a correct representation of incoming sensory inputs but still miss the message by not interpreting it correctly, as the scientists in this cartoon have done. Perceivers often need to read between the lines—terpret meaning beyond what is explicitly said, perhaps based on nonverbal cues. A shared set of rules and expectations is essential if this type of communication is to be effective.

Source: THE FAR SIDE copyright 1985 FARWORKS, INC. Distributed by UNIVERSAL PRESS SYNDICATE.

Every occupation or profession—in fact, every group of people—uses special words or attaches special meanings to common words. These words are called jargon. A group's **jargon** reflects its common experiences and history and allows the simple communication of complex meanings by group members. Unfortunately, jargon also requires shared understanding and shared experiences to be interpreted correctly.

IMPROVING COMMUNICATOR EFFECTIVENESS

Because communication is essentially a perceptual process, to improve communication, one must increase the probability that the receiver will accurately perceive (that is, attend to and decode) a sender's communication attempt. Three keys to improving the receiver's perceptual accuracy are through sender empathy, active listening, and media selection.

SENDER EMPATHY. For communication to be effective, the sender must empathize with the receiver. **Empathy** is the ability of one individual to appreciate another's perspective. Obviously, if the receiver speaks only Spanish, a message in English is unlikely to convey the intended meaning. Even within the same language, however, empathy can help a sender ensure that the intended meaning is the one received. Which channels is the receiver likely to attend to? What meaning will the receiver attach to the choice of a particular communication medium? Will the receiver attach the same meanings to our symbols as we do?

Senders often fail to realize that subtle shades of meaning can be quite group specific and embedded in personal experience. Does "participative management" have the same meaning for employees at Hewlett-Packard and those at General Motors? Because their companies' participative management programs are different, the term will have different meanings for employees of these two companies. Consequently, use of the term *participative management* in a message to an employee of either company will require some clarification. Further, to be correctly understood, the clarifications probably will need to be different, depending on which company the receiver is from.

Effective communication requires that the sender realize and adjust to how a receiver is likely to decode messages. Effective communication requires that the sender appreciate the receiver's perspective and tailor messages to fit the receiver's ability to decode them.

ACTIVE LISTENING. Active listening is the mirror image of sender empathy. A sender who has empathy accepts responsibility for ensuring proper transmission of intended meaning. **Active listening** involves the receiver accepting responsibility for ensuring the proper transmission of the intended meaning by actively assisting the sender in clarifying the meaning of the message.[37]

This assistance on the part of the receiver can take three forms. First, the receiver can simply work harder at listening. It's easy to think—incorrectly—that the sender is supposed to do all the work. Some specific suggestions for improving communication by working harder at listening are listed in Figure 6-8. Second, a receiver can use feedback to check the appropriateness of decoding strategies even as a message is transmitted. For instance, if a sender uses a symbol whose meaning is ambiguous, the receiver can request more information about the sender's use of the term. ("By *participative management*, did you have in mind something like suggestion boxes or employee committees?") Third, a receiver can help clarify the meaning of a message by reflecting the received meaning back to the sender. ("It seems like you're very angry about what's happened. Is that right?") Providing feedback gives the sender an opportunity to try again if a message was not received as the sender intended. Of course, feedback is itself another message and therefore susceptible to lost meaning when the sender (now acting as a receiver) decodes it.

Active listening represents a form of **two-way communication**—communication in which receivers can return messages to senders. Research has shown that one-way communication, in which the receiver cannot return messages to the sender, is more efficient and less threatening for the sender. However, it is also less effective and more frustrating for the receiver.[38] Communication is about transmitting meaning, and two-way communication provides the best opportunity for the sender's intended meaning to be perceived by the receiver.

MEDIA SELECTION. An important consideration in sending a message is deciding which communication medium is most appropriate. **Information**

---

37. Rogers, C. R., & Farson, R. F. (1984). Active listening. In D. Kolb, I. Rubin, & J. McIntrye (Eds.), *Organizational psychology: Readings on human behavior in organizations* (pp. 255–267). Englewood Cliffs, NJ: Prentice Hall.
38. Leavitt, H. J., & Mueller, R. A. (1951, November). Some effects of feedback on communications. *Human Relations*, 401–410.

		■ **FIGURE 6-8**
Ten Keys to Effective Listening		

These keys are a positive guideline to better listening. In fact, they're at the heart of developing better habits that could last a lifetime.

Keys to Effective Listening	The Bad Listener	The Good Listener
1 Find areas of interest	Tunes out dry subjects	Opportunitizes: asks "What's in it for me?"
2 Judge content, not delivery	Tunes out if delivery is poor	Judges content; skips over delivery errors
3 Hold your fire	Tends to enter into arguments	Doesn't judge until comprehension is complete
4 Listen for ideas	Listens for facts	Listens for central themes
5 Be flexible	Takes intensive notes using only one system	Takes fewer notes; uses several different systems, depending on the speaker
6 Work at listening	Shows no energy output; fakes attention	Works hard; exhibits active body state
7 Resist distractions	Is distracted easily	Fights or avoids distractions; tolerates bad habits; knows how to concentrate
8 Exercise your mind	Resists difficult expository material; seeks light, recreational material	Uses heavier material as exercise for the mind
9 Keep your mind open	Reacts to emotional words	Interprets color words; does not get hung up on them
10 Capitalize on the fact that *thought* is faster than speech	Tends to daydream with slow speakers	Challenges, anticipates, mentally summarizes, weighs the evidence, and listens between the lines to the tone of the speaker's voice

Source: Steil, L. K. (1986, July/August). How well do you listen? *Executive Female,* 37.

richness is the information-carrying capacity of an item of data.[39] When the communication of a single item of data (e.g., a wink) conveys substantial new understanding, that communication is information rich. As shown in Figure 6-9, communication media vary in their information richness. Information richness is determined by such factors as the number of channels utilized in the communication medium and the opportunities for and speed of feedback.

Face-to-face communication is highly information rich because it utilizes multiple channels (words, facial gestures, body language) to reinforce a message. Face-to-face communication also provides opportunities for immediate feedback. Written communication is lower in information richness because it lacks the support of multiple, meaning-confirming channels, and feedback is slower.

39. Daft, R. L., & Lengel, R. H. (1984). Information richness: A new approach to managerial behavior and organization design. In B. Staw & L. Cummings (Eds.), *Research in organizational behavior* 6 (pp. 191–233). Greenwich, CT: JAI.

■ **FIGURE 6-9** | **The Relationship between Information Medium and Information Richness**

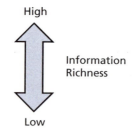

High

Information Richness

Low

Information Medium

Face-to-face communication
Telephone
E-mail and voicemail
Written documents (letters, memos, bulletins, etc.)

Source: Webster, J., & Trevino, L. K. (1995). Rational and social theories as complementary explanations of communication media choices: Two policy-capturing studies. *Academy of Management Journal, 38,* 1544–1572.

Recent research indicates that whether one selects an appropriate communication medium is based both on the level of information richness matched to the complexity of the issue and on the social influences involved.[40] *Media richness theory* suggests that effective communication is most likely to occur when the information richness of the communication medium matches the complexity of the issue.[41] On the one hand, for low-complexity issues, a communication medium low in information richness will suffice; using an information-rich medium in this circumstance may waste valuable time and communicate more information than necessary (i.e., overload). For example, a brief e-mail announcing the time of a weekly team meeting is probably more effective than personally calling each team member to tell him or her the time. On the other hand, highly complex issues demand information-rich communication media to help receivers fully understand the meaning of the messages. A corporate reorganization announced through a written memo, for example, would be unlikely to adequately clarify in everyone's minds exactly what was going to happen and why. To communicate this complex information would require a face-to-face question-and-answer session, with all the opportunities for clarification this type of situation implies.

Complementing media richness theory, *social influence theory* suggests that the norms of one's workgroup and the attitudes and behavior of one's coworkers and supervisors influence an individual's decision to use such new media as e-mail, voicemail, and videoconferencing.[42] Individuals may choose electronic media more frequently to send everything from a joke to a formal

40. Webster, & Trevino, Rational and social theories as complementary explanations of communication media choices.

41. Daft, & Lengel, Information richness.

42. Webster, Trevino, Rational and social theories as complementary explanations of communication media choices.

contract, not because the medium matches the task, but rather because their colleagues and peers are doing so.

SUMMARY

Groups (or teams) and communication are the building blocks of organizations. People come together and talk because groups provide the means to desired ends and because group interaction is a desired end in itself. Group and team behavior are governed by rules and roles that evolve as groups and teams develop. Development activities (such as role therapy) improve the quality of a group's rules and roles so that the benefits of interaction can be realized.

Communication is the most visible of all group and team activities and is critical to effective functioning. Good communication involves the encoding and transmission of intended meaning by a sender and the decoding and feedback of perceived meaning by a receiver. People differ in the ways they choose to communicate, in how open they are, and in how much they elicit feedback from others. Communication can be improved in organizations and groups if senders and receivers become more sensitive to the other side's perspective, when receivers practice active listening, and when communicators select media appropriate to their message.

KEY TERMS

Active listening
Adjourning
Communication
Decoding
Empathy
Encoding
Exposure
Feedback
Five-stages perspective
Forming
Group
Group development
Group objectives
Idiosyncrasy credits
Information richness
Jargon

Job description
Johari Window
Noise
Nonverbal communication
Norm
Norming
Performing
Punctuated-equilibrium model
Role
Role differentiation
Role therapy
Self-managed team
Status
Storming
Team development
Two-way communication

DISCUSSION QUESTIONS

1 What would social interaction be like without rules and roles?

2 Think of a group to which you belong. In what ways is your membership in this group a means to an end? In what ways is your membership in this group an end in and of itself?

3 What are the stages of group development outlined in this chapter? How do each of these stages contribute to the effective functioning of the group?

4 What can senders do to improve communication effectiveness? What can receivers do?

Interpersonal Communications Survey This survey is designed to assess your understanding of and behavior in your interpersonal communications practices. There are no right or wrong responses. Rather, the requested response is simply the one that comes closest to representing your practices.

For each item on the survey, you are requested to indicate which of the alternative reactions would be more characteristic of the way *you* would handle the situation described. Some alternatives may be equally characteristic of you or equally uncharacteristic. Although this is a possibility, please choose the alternative that is *relatively* more characteristic of you. For each item, you will have 5 points that you may distribute in any of the following combinations, where 5 = most characteristic and 0 = least characteristic:

	A	*B*
1	5	0
2	4	1
3	3	2
4	2	3
5	1	4
6	0	5

Thus, there are six possible combinations for responding to the pair of alternatives presented to you with each survey item. *Be sure the numbers you assign to each pair sum to 5.*

To the extent possible, please relate each situation in the survey to your own personal experience. As used throughout this survey, the words *he, him,* and *his* include both the masculine and feminine genders unless specifically stated.

1 If a friend of mine had a personality conflict with a mutual acquaintance of ours with whom it was important for him to get along, I would:

    ____ **A** Tell my friend that I felt he was partially responsible for any problems with this other person and try to let him know how the person was being affected by him.

    ____ **B** Not get involved because I would not be able to continue to get along with both of them once I had entered into the conflict.

2 If one of my friends and I had a heated argument in the past and I realized that he was ill at ease around me from that time on, I would:

    ____ **A** Avoid making things worse by discussing his behavior and just let the whole thing drop.

    ____ **B** Bring up his behavior and ask him how he felt the argument had affected our relationship.

3 If a friend began to avoid me and act in an aloof and withdrawn manner, I would:

    ____ **A** Tell him about his behavior and suggest that he tell me what was on his mind.

    ____ **B** Follow his lead and keep our contacts brief and aloof since that seems to be what he wants.

4 If two of my friends and I were talking and one of my friends slipped and brought up a personal problem of mine that involved the other friend, I would:

    ____ **A** Change the subject and signal my friend to do the same.

    ____ **B** Fill in my uninformed friend on what the other friend was talking about and suggest that we go into it later.

5 If a friend were to tell me that, in his opinion, I was doing things that made me less effective than I might be in social situations, I would:

    ____ **A** Ask him to spell out or describe what he has observed and suggest changes I might make.

    ____ **B** Resent the criticism and let him know why I behave the way I do.

6 If one of my friends aspired to an office in our student organization for which I felt he was unqualified and if he had been tentatively assigned to that position by the president of the student organization, I would:

____ **A** Not mention my misgivings to either my friend or the president and let them handle it in their own way.

____ **B** Tell my friend and the president of my misgivings and then leave the final decision up to them.

7 If I felt that one of my friends was being unfair to me and his other friends, but none of them had mentioned anything about it, I would:

____ **A** Ask several of those people how they perceived the situation to see it they felt he was being unfair.

____ **B** Not ask the others how they perceived our friend but wait for them to bring it up to me.

8 If I were preoccupied with some personal matters and a friend told me that I had become irritated with him and others and that I was jumping on him for unimportant things, I would:

____ **A** Tell him I was preoccupied and would probably be on edge a while and would prefer not to be bothered.

____ **B** Listen to his complaints but not try to explain my actions to him.

9 If I had heard some friends discussing an ugly rumor about a friend of mine that I knew could hurt him and he asked me what I knew about it, if anything, I would:

____ **A** Say I didn't know anything about it and tell him no one would believe a rumor like that anyway.

____ **B** Tell him exactly what I had heard, when I had heard it, and from whom I had heard it.

10 If a friend pointed out the fact that I had a personality conflict with another friend with whom it was important for me to get along, I would:

____ **A** Consider his comments out of line and tell him I didn't want to discuss the matter any further.

____ **B** Talk about it openly with him to find out how my behavior was being affected by this.

11 If my relationship with a friend had been damaged by repeated arguments on an issue of importance to us both, I would:

____ **A** Be cautious in my conversations with him so the issue would not come up again to worsen our relationship.

____ **B** Point to the problems the controversy was causing in our relationship and suggest that we discuss it until we get it resolved.

12 If in a personal discussion with a friend about his problems and behavior, he suddenly suggested that we discuss my problems and behavior as well as his own, I would:

____ **A** Try to keep the discussion away from me by suggesting that other, closer friends often talked to me about such matters.

____ **B** Welcome the opportunity to hear what he felt about me and encourage his comments.

13 If a friend of mine began to tell me about his hostile feelings about another fiend whom he felt was being unkind to others (and I wholeheartedly agreed), I would:

____ **A** Listen and also express my own feelings to him so he would know where I stood.

____ **B** Listen but not express my own negative views and opinions because he might repeat what I said to him in confidence.

14 If I thought an ugly rumor was being spread about me and suspected that one of my friends had quite likely heard it, I would:

____ **A** Avoid mentioning the issue and leave it to him to tell me about it if he wanted to.

____ **B** Risk putting him on the spot by asking him directly what he knew about the matter.

15 If I had observed a friend in social situations and thought that he was doing a number of things that hurt his relationships, I would:

____ **A** Risk being seen as a busybody and tell him what I had observed and my reactions to it.

____ **B** Keep my opinions to myself, rather than be seen as interfering in things that are none of my business.

16 If two friends and I were talking and one of them inadvertently mentioned a personal problem that involved me but of which I knew nothing, I would:

____ A Press them for information about the problem and their opinions about it.

____ B Leave it up to my friends to tell me or not tell me, letting them change the subject if they wished.

17 If a friend seemed to be preoccupied and began to jump on me for seemingly unimportant things and to become irritated with me and others without real cause, I would:

____ A Treat him with kid gloves for a while, on the assumption that he was having some temporary personal problems that were none of my business.

____ B Try to talk to him about it and point out to him how his behavior was affecting people.

18 If I had begun to dislike certain habits of a friend to the point that it was interfering with my enjoying his company, I would:

____ A Say nothing to him directly but let him know my feelings by ignoring him whenever his annoying habits were obvious.

____ B Get my feelings out in the open and clear the air so that we could continue our friendship comfortably and enjoyable.

19 In discussing social behavior with one of my more sensitive friends, I would:

____ A Avoid mentioning his flaws and weaknesses so as not to hurt his feelings.

____ B Focus on his flaws and weaknesses so he could improve his interpersonal skills.

20 If I knew I might be assigned to an important position in our group and my friends' attitudes toward me had become rather negative, I would:

____ A Discuss my shortcomings with my friends so I could see where to improve.

____ B Try to figure out my own shortcomings by myself so I could improve.

Scoring Key

In this survey, there are 10 questions that deal with your receptivity to feedback and 10 that are concerned with your willingness to self-disclose. Transfer your scores from each item to this scoring key. Add the scores in each column. Next, transfer these scores to the following figure by drawing a vertical line through the feedback score and a horizontal line through the self-disclosure line.

Receptivity to Feedback	**Willingness to Self-Disclose**
2 B _____	1 A _____
3 A _____	4 B _____
5 A _____	6 B _____
7 A _____	9 B _____
8 B _____	11 B _____
10 B _____	13 A _____
12 B _____	15 A _____
14 B _____	17 B _____
16 A _____	18 B _____
20 A _____	19 B _____
Total: _____	Total: _____

Personal Openness to Interpersonal Communications

As suggested through this figure, higher scores on *receptivity to feedback* and *willingness to self-disclose* indicate a greater willingness to engage in personal openness in interpersonal communications. Of course, we need to be mindful of the situational factors that may influence our personal predispositions to be relatively more open or closed in interpersonal communications.

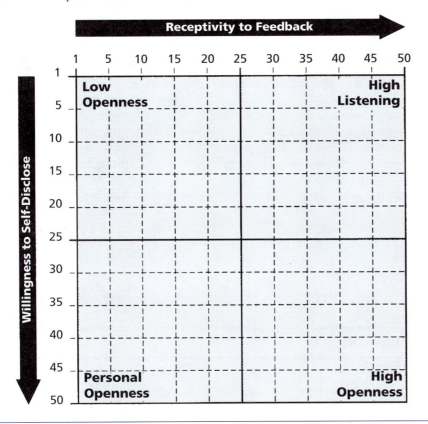

Source: D. Roberts, formerly manager of training, LTV Missiles and Electronics Group, Grand Prairie, TX; and Hellriegel, D., Slocum, J. W., & Woodman, R. W. (1992). *Organizational behavior* (6th ed., pp. 454–457). St. Paul, MN: West.

CLOSING CASE   CHAPTER 6

THE MANAGER'S MEMO

FROM: H. Barbieri, Vice President, Consumer Electronics Division
TO: B. Jones, Production Manager
RE: Quality First program

I think it's time to look at a new approach to our Quality First program. We've had the suggestion box out for a year, and so far we've received only two suggestions for quality improvements, of which only one was of any value. Several supervisors have confidentially informed me that their subordinates have some great ideas. Why aren't we hearing any?

How about a group approach? We can divide the employees into teams that can meet to come up with ideas for improving the quality of our products and production process.

I'd like you to prepare a plan for these groups. How should they operate? How often should they meet? Should the teams be divided into engineers, production workers, maintenance personnel, and so on, or should each team include a variety of workers? What problems can we anticipate with this format, and how should we resolve them?

These questions are meant as a starting point. If you have other ideas or concerns, please include them in your plan.

CASE DISCUSSION QUESTIONS

Assume that you are the production manager and respond to the vice president's memorandum with a memo outlining ways to open up the lines of communication. Use as many of the concepts in the chapter as you can to develop a complete plan.

CHAPTER 7

Power, Politics, and Influence

IS POWER THE LAST DIRTY WORD?

Has power become a dirty word in the English language? According to Harvard professor Rosabeth Kanter, not only is power a dirty word but it's "America's last dirty word." Most people prefer to shy away from politics in the office—or so they say.

Whether we like it or not, some jockeying for power is inevitable when people work together. Differing individual needs, limited resources and rewards, and inequitable or unfair distribution give rise to dissatisfaction, conflict, and scuffles in organizations. When employees attempt to exert power or influence, politics is said to be taking place.

Who then are those people, found in offices across America, for whom office politics is an everyday part of life? Generally, we know, for instance, that they tend to be ambitious individuals who have a healthy liking or need for power. However, unlike other ambitious individuals, they tend to be less capable than their peers. They are driven by strong selfish motives or insecurities and feel forced to safeguard their jobs.

However, especially in the hands of managers, some power is not only welcome but necessary. Without the appropriate use of power, or authority from the top, how would managers get things done? Likewise, when managers fail to exercise authority (or position power), subordinates either become paralyzed or engage in unproductive bickering. Chaos and low productivity become the order of the day.

Thus, an important component of the manager's job is to ensure an appropriate balance of power. Often this requires that the manager "nip office

Source: Adapted from Long, W. P. (1999, March 28). Managing problems: Nipping office politics in the bud. *New Straits Times*, p. 42.

politics in the bud" while ensuring that he or she retains an appropriate amount of power or authority to get things done.

INTRODUCTION

An important part of understanding the role that groups play in organizations is understanding how and why individuals behave differently in groups and teams than they behave when alone. These differences go beyond the constraints on behavior created by roles and rules in group interactions. In groups and organizations, *other group members* are potent influences on individuals' thoughts and behaviors. In this chapter, we consider two facets of this influence: the apparent and direct persuasion that results from the exercise of power in groups and organizations and the subtle influence *other group members* exert in the social context.

POLITICS AND POWER

As noted in Chapter 1, political conflict is a defining characteristic of organizational behavior. **Political conflicts** occur when individual members of an organization use their power to pursue *personal* (rather than organizational) agendas. Ultimately, political conflicts are settled based on the distribution of power.

Political behavior, or politicking, is simply part and parcel of working together with others. There are no "right" goals or objectives for groups to pursue; there may not even be a "best" way to pursue agreed-upon goals. There are only the goals and the means for reaching them that each member of the group prefers. As we saw in Chapter 3, these preferences are quite likely to conflict. Using your power to push a group (or an organization) in the direction you prefer—a direction where the group's goals will match your personal goals—is neither right nor wrong; it is just politics. As illustrated in "INTERNATIONAL FOCUS ON: Politics," politics becomes truly wrong only when it turns into corruption and is used to pursue personal goals *at the expense* of the goals of the organization.

Political scientist Robert Dahl has defined power as follows: "A has power over B to the extent that he can get B to do something B would not otherwise do."[1] There are two parts to this definition. First, power is something between or among people. No one simply has power; an individual (or a group) has power *over* another individual or group. *Power is part of the relationships among people* and therefore exists only as a characteristic of a social system (such as a group or an organization). Outside that social system, the power relationships may dissolve.

In addition to locating power in the relationships among people, Dahl's definition emphasizes that power refers to the capacity of one individual to change the attitudes or actions of another individual. In a power relationship one individual is able to influence the thoughts of another or to *control* that other individual's behavior. Influence and control are outcomes; power makes those outcomes occur.

---

1. Dahl, R. (1957, July). The concept of power. *Behavioral Science*, 202–203.

INTERNATIONAL FOCUS ON POLITICS

INTRODUCTION OF THE EURO TAINTED BY POLITICAL CORRUPTION. The financial scandals engulfing the German Christian Democrats represented the last piece of a complex jigsaw puzzle concerning the creation of the euro, the single European currency, in the early 1990s. The picture that has emerged is not a pretty one; it points to the fact that many of the major players who forced the euro on to the statute books were abusing their power. In 1992, for example, President Mitterrand of France may have ordered the secret payment of £9 million from the oil company Elf-Aquitaine to the Christian Democrats, headed by his friend Helmut Kohl.

For years, British pro-Europeans have been arguing that the British political system is too adversarial and Britain needs a more consensual system, like Germany's. Yet, as Germans are now realizing to their dismay, it was their system that enabled the corruption to take place. Because Kohl was notorious for intervening into the tiniest details of party management, he was able to create a huge reserve of party members who depended exclusively on him for advancement and who were unlikely to question what he did.

The "Kohl system" thus made a mockery of parliamentary rule because he was sustained in power by people he controlled. It may be a tragedy for German democracy that its most distinguished political party has been shown to be a fraud; it is a European tragedy that others should have been duped into copying the German model.

Source: Excerpted from Laughland, J. (2000, January 25). Many key players who forced the euro on to the statute book were crooks. *Times of London,* p. 1F.

SOCIAL EXCHANGE

How does power work? The **theory of social exchange** offers one simple explanation:

> Social behavior is an exchange of goods, material goods but also nonmaterial ones, such as symbols of approval or prestige. Persons that give much to others try to get much from them, and persons that get much from others are under pressure to give much to them. The process of influence tends to work out at an equilibrium to a balance of the exchanges.[2]

According to this theory, power occurs because of resource dependence. A **resource dependence** occurs when one individual needs or desperately wants something (the resource) that another individual possesses. The person who wants or needs the resource is dependent on the person who has it. In the terms of social exchange, power or influence occurs when individuals who need or desire the resource take possession of it *in exchange for* changes in their personal thoughts (influence) or actions (control).

Politics is one obvious demonstration of power, but power can also be exercised in more subtle ways through implicit resource exchanges. Dale Carnegie courses teach sales personnel how to influence and control potential customers by offering them something in addition to the product

---

2. Homans, G. C. (1958). Social behavior as exchange. *American Journal of Sociology, 63,* 597–606.

that is valuable to the customer and that the sales force has in unlimited quantities—compliments. In effect, the sales force exchanges compliments for successful sales.[3]

Just because power is a form of resource exchange does not mean that the exchange is fair or that what the parties exchange is equal. When power is exercised, both sides receive something in the transaction. However, as Aristotle noted:

> The benefits that one party receives and is entitled to claim from the other are not the same on either side. . . . The better of the two parties, for instance, or the more useful or otherwise superior as the case may be, should receive more affection than he bestows; since when the affect rendered is proportional to desert, this produces equality.[4]

In effect, the social exchanges in power transactions are governed by supply and demand; the benefit each party receives in the exchange will reflect the relative power of the two parties. More powerful individuals can give less and expect to get back more.

SLACK

If resource dependence and social exchange explain why and when power works, then **slack** explains why and when it doesn't. In the book *Equality*, political philosopher R. H. Tawney noted that to destroy power, "nothing more is required than to be indifferent to its threats and to prefer other goods to those which it promises."[5] Slack, as discussed in Chapter 5, refers to any overabundance of a resource that decreases an individual's or a group's dependence for it on any other individual or group.[6] If power represents the capacity of one individual to influence or control a second individual, slack represents the capacity of that second individual to resist.

Slack comes in two forms: stockpiles and alternative sources. **Stockpiles** are quantities of a resource (nest eggs) set aside for future use; **alternative sources** are other ways to fulfill a resource dependence, thereby reducing an individual's dependence on any one source. If your boss makes an unreasonable request, you could go along with the request in order to preserve your job. If you have a nest egg, you have a little slack. You know that, even if you wake up unemployed tomorrow morning, the rent will get paid and you will eat (at least for a while). The nest egg reduces your resource dependence on the boss and thereby allows you to resist the boss's attempts to influence or control you.

The other form of slack—alternative sources—also could allow you to refuse your boss's unreasonable request. In this case, you could have an alternative source of employment. Knowing that another source of income is readily available reduces your dependence on your current boss for income.

---

3. Carnegie, D. (1936). *How to win friends and influence people.* New York: Simon & Schuster.

4. Aristotle. (1975). *The nichomachean ethic.* Boston: Reidel.

5. Tawney, R. H. (1961). *Equality.* New York: Capricorn.

6. Nohria, N., & Gulati, R. (1996). Is slack good or bad for innovation? *Academy of Management Journal, 39,* 1245–1264.

■ **FIGURE 7-1**	**Sources of Power**

Individual power in organizations can come from a variety of sources. Structural sources of power refer to power that an organization gives an individual, such as authority to give orders to others in the organization. Personal sources of power come from characteristics of individuals, such as charisma or expertise in a field.

Structural Sources

Reward power	The capacity to dispense rewards
Coercion power	The capacity to dispense punishments
Task interdependence	Power that accrues naturally to a particular role in an organization
Legitimate power	Authority; the right to give orders

Personal Sources

Expert power	Possession of valuable information or status
Referent power	Power stemming from the desire of others to imitate an individual

It is often easier for us to see how we depend on others than to see how they depend on us. We may have slack and not know it. When we find out how easy it is to find a new job (if it is easy), no boss will ever again be able to control or influence us by suggesting that he or she has a resource—namely, a job—that we need. Perception thus plays a key role in the exercise of power. You must perceive that you are dependent on another individual for that individual to have power over you.

SOURCES OF POWER

What kinds of resources do individuals have to exchange? What gives them power within the office and the social environment? Figure 7-1 presents six sources of power.[7] Of these six sources of power, reward and coercion are the two basic sources. They arise in the control of rewards and punishments, respectively. The other four sources of power—expert, legitimate, referent, and task interdependence—refer to organizational forms of reward and punishment.

REWARD POWER. **Reward power** occurs when one individual possesses resources that another individual desires and has the ability to reward the second person in exchange for the desired behavior.

Reward power is based on the law of effect, which is discussed in Chapter 3. If a particular behavior is followed by a reward, the individual will be more likely to engage in that behavior again. A supervisor can encourage subordinates to engage in appropriate work behaviors by making desired rewards contingent on those behaviors. In this way, the supervisor exercises power over the subordinates.

Reward power is a two-way street. If a supervisor rewards a subordinate for a job well done, the subordinate in turn may work harder, which rewards the supervisor for rewarding the subordinate. When this reward cycle is set in motion, it becomes increasingly more likely that the subordinate will re-

---

7. French, J. R. P., & Raven, B. (1959). The bases of social power. In D. Cartwright (Ed.), *Studies in social power* (pp. 150–167). Ann Arbor, MI: Institute for Social Research.

peat appropriate work behavior and, in turn, that the supervisor will reward the subordinate's behavior in the future.

COERCION POWER. **Coercion** is the threat of punishment for *not* engaging in appropriate behaviors. Coercion can be based on material forms of punishment, such as fines or the docking of pay. Coercion also can refer to less material forms of punishment, such as rejection. For instance, an individual may feel coerced into getting along with his or her workgroup or team if he or she fears rejection or ridicule for voicing a lone dissenting opinion. In organizations, termination of employment or suspension is a threat used to coerce employees. Naturally, threats work best when there is no fear of retribution.

As mentioned in Chapter 3, in the discussion on the use of punishment in organizations, coercion is effective under only limited circumstances. An employee who works only to avoid termination is not likely to be an enthusiastic contributor in the workplace. In fact, he or she may even react like a cornered animal by fighting back. Goofing off while the boss isn't looking, taking liberties with office supplies, and sabotaging work are all ways in which subordinates try to give back to a supervisor what the supervisor gave them—trouble. Coercion is occasionally an effective form of power in organizational settings, but only in a very shortsighted sense.

EXPERT POWER. Experts are highly experienced or highly trained in a field. **Expert power** refers to a person's willingness to defer to experts and to be swayed by their opinions. The two main components of expert power are information and status.

Expert power comes into play when an individual possesses special information, knowledge, or an ability that another individual needs. A stockbroker, for instance, may have a dizzying array of financial-analysis information. The information that the stockbroker chooses to share with clients, and the manner in which that information is presented, will have a tremendous impact on the decisions the clients make.

In organizations, power from special information or a special ability is not always reflected on the organizational chart. Certainly the top executives possess certain knowledge that gives them the power to influence the beliefs and actions of those below them. However, executives often complain that they don't know what's going on in the lower ranks. Middle managers or first-line supervisors are privy to that information. Thus, these managers and supervisors possess information that gives them power over the top executives—and, as a result, the ability to sway the top executives' beliefs and actions.

The other form of expert power comes from an individual's status as a source of special information or ability. Experts have impressive credentials, such as a doctorate, a medical degree, a law degree, or another great amount of experience or ability. These credentials *imply* the possession of knowledge or ability, which makes others believe that the experts' opinions are particularly trustworthy or informative. Expert status thus elicits deference and respect.

There is an important paradox in the idea that information represents power—expert power—in organizations. Managers are rewarded when their subordinates perform well. Subordinates who have less information can do less and will be less productive. A manager who shares information transforms the power of that information into power for his or her subordinates.

The manager **empowers** the subordinates to reward the manager with better performance. The point of having power is to accomplish things, to positively influence others. Sometimes giving that power away—empowering others—is the best way to use power productively.

LEGITIMATE POWER. One of the most pervasive forms of power in organizations is **legitimate power**—the *right* to give orders. This means that the organization has given an individual the authority to exercise control over the behavior of others for their own good and for the good of the organization.

Why does legitimate power work? Why would a subordinate obey the orders of the boss? Authority (or legitimate power) is often simply an implicit form of reward, coercion, or expert power. If your boss tells you to make a sales call, you could sit down and decide for yourself if the ordered action is a good idea. However, if you decide to disregard the order, you risk the eventual loss of a valued reward that the boss controls—such as a bonus—or face immediate punishment—such as termination for insubordination (failure to follow orders).

Alternatively, the boss may be the boss because he or she is smarter or more experienced than you are, and not following the boss's orders will result in the loss of an important sale. If you truly believe that the sales call is unwarranted but decide to make it anyway, you may be reacting to the implicit control the boss exercises over rewards, punishments, and important information.

There are also relatively subtle reasons to obey the boss, and these have to do with the survival of social systems. People join social systems such as organizations because they offer advantages over going it alone. Failure to obey orders is a challenge not only to the particular order given but also to the social system itself. If the system has advantages, then challenging the system means you risk losing those advantages. While it may be overstating the case, the logical consequences of disobedience are anarchy, the eventual destruction of the system, and the loss of any advantages the system provides. If an organization is to avoid the trap of having all bosses and no subordinates, a little obedience clearly is a good thing.

Unquestioned obedience is just as clearly not a good thing. Decision makers can be wrong, just as rules and norms can be wrong. The dangers of unquestioned obedience to authority—and the compelling nature of legitimate power—were dramatically demonstrated in "FOCUS ON: Obedience to Authority."

TASK INTERDEPENDENCE. Sociologist Michael Crozier has identified a source of power that accrues to a particular job (or group of jobs) in an organization because of task interdependence. **Task interdependence** occurs when two or more employees must depend on each other to complete assigned tasks.

The power dynamics between executives and their assistants illustrate power from task interdependence. After the executive has given an order, he or she actually becomes dependent on the assistant to complete the task correctly and on time. Certainly the executive has the power to replace the assistant if the task is done poorly or late. Unfortunately for the executive, firing the assistant is not equivalent to getting a task done well and on time. The organization gives the executive legitimate power over the assistant; the arrangements for getting work done give the assistant task interdependence power over the executive. Legitimate power comes with the job description; task interdependence power comes with the territory.

FOCUS ON
OBEDIENCE TO AUTHORITY

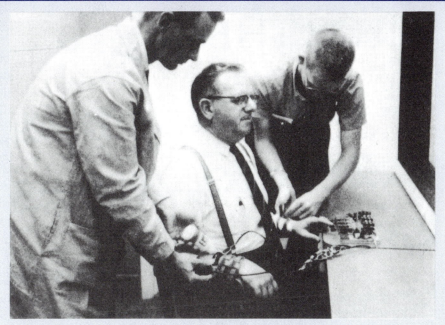

EXPLORING THE ORIGINS OF OBEDIENCE.
Researcher Stanley Milgram was particularly interested in why, during wartime conditions such as those in Germany during World War II, individuals often commit atrocities that they excuse as simply "following orders". Milgram's study involved two participants working together: a teacher and a learner. The participants drew lots to see who would be the learner and who would be the teacher. In fact, the drawing was arranged so that one of Milgram's assistants always drew the role of learner.

After the drawing, the assistant took the learner into an adjacent room and connected the learner to an electric shock apparatus. The real participant was informed that his job would be to administer a word-pair memory task for the learner to learn. After each incorrect response, the teacher was to punish the learner by administering a shock. The teacher was then given a sample 45-volt shock. At this point the teacher was seated at a simulated shock generator, with an array of switches and labels corresponding to shocks ranging from 15 volts ("slight shock") to 450 volts ("danger: severe shock").

The teacher was told to give the learner one shock for each incorrect response and to increase the voltage of the shocks for each succeeding incorrect answer. (In fact, no shocks were administered at all.)

The learner's responses had been carefully orchestrated, and they were the same for each new teacher. The learner gave many incorrect responses, so the teacher had to administer many shocks. And with the shocks came the apparent painful suffering of the learner.

The teacher participants were volunteers and could have quit at any time. In fact, many subjects did register complaints during the procedure. Many were obviously tense and anxious during the experiment and demonstrated concern about and sympathy for the learner. These complaints and concerns were met by a simple comment from the experimenter that "the experiment requires that you continue." That command was enough for 62% of the subjects (620 of 1,000 subjects) to remain obedient and to administer shocks all the way to the end of the range on the generator, to a protesting and eventually ominously silent learner.

If a lot of obedience is a good thing in organizations, a little disobedience is not only good but necessary. If someone is giving the wrong orders, the organization's survival could just as easily depend on workers disobeying those orders as on their obeying them.

Summarized from Katz, D., & Kahn, L. (1966). *The social psychology of organizations.* New York: Wiley.

REFERENT POWER. Perhaps the most mysterious form of power is **referent power.** Jill has referent power over Jack when Jack willingly imitates or obeys Jill because Jack identifies with or admires her. Identifying with an individual means seeing in that individual traits that you think you have or that you would like to have. For example, many young people dress like the rock stars or sports heroes they aspire to be like. The young people communicate their aspirations by imitating their heroes in fashion and behavior.

One form of referent power derives from charisma. **Charisma** is a personal style that captures people's attention, hearts, and imaginations. A person is thought to have charisma when he or she seems to possess the characteristics that define the model person for many admirers. Thus, an individual's charisma will be quite specific to a particular reference group. An individual will have charisma not because of personal characteristics but because of a fit between those characteristics and those desired or admired by others.[8] For instance, T. E. Lawrence (better known as the legendary "Lawrence of Arabia") possessed certain characteristics that made him an admired leader of the Arabs during World War I. By contrast, his personal style was unappealing in his home country of England, where his political aspirations failed upon his return. (Charisma is discussed in more detail in Chapter 9.)

Referent power is more like expert power than like the other sources of power. Both are based almost exclusively on *personal* characteristics. A person is an expert because of background credentials or experience; a person has charisma because that person's personality traits match what the people think they need. In both cases, power derives from the individual. On the other hand, reward, coercion, task interdependence, and legitimate power are primarily *structural* sources of potential influence. The ability to dispense rewards and punishments, or the authority to act as if one could do so, arises from work relationships rather than from personal traits.

USING POWER: STRATEGIES AND TACTICS

Any member of an organization has access to some sources of power. It is somewhat unclear, however, how individuals can make effective use of the power they have—to perhaps navigate their way through the office politics. This section reviews several ways participants in organizations—even those far down the organizational hierarchy—can individually mobilize their powers. These power tactics are summarized in Figure 7-2.

EXCHANGE AND PRESSURE. Assume that you are a newly hired executive assistant in a large industrial corporation. How can you get things proceeding to your satisfaction? There are two ways: (a) identify which valuable resources (e.g., information, rewards, punishments) are already at your disposal, or (b) go out and capture some resources that are available for you to control. When an individual has identified or captured a valued resource, the most obvious power tactic available is exchange. *Exchange* means offering to trade what you control (e.g., your vote at a meeting, your expertise using a complex new piece of software) for something you want (e.g., a better office, a cushy job assignment).

The most important and abundant resource often available to lower-level members of an organization is effort. The higher individuals are in an

8. MacGinnis, J. (1976). *Heroes.* New York: Viking.

Power Tactics	■ FIGURE 7-2

Exchange	The person makes an explicit or implicit promise that you will receive rewards or tangible benefits if you comply with a request or support a proposal.
Pressure	The person uses demands, threats, or intimidation to convince you to comply.
Ingratiation	The person seeks to get you to do something by invoking reciprocity for a favor or compliment.
Rational Persuasion	The person uses logical arguments and factual evidence to persuade you that a proposal or request is likely to result in the attainment of your objectives.
Inspirational Appeals	The person makes an emotional request that appeals to your values and ideals.
Personal Appeals	The person appeals to feelings of loyalty and friendship when asking for something.
Consultation	The person seeks your participation in making a decision or planning how to implement a proposed policy to provide you ownership and gain your support.
Legitimating Tactics	The person seeks to establish legitimacy of a request by claiming the authority or right to make it, or by verifying that it is consistent with organizational policies, rules, practices, or traditions.
Coalition Tactics	The person seeks the aid of others to persuade you to do something or uses the support of others as an argument for you to comply.

Source: Yukl, G. (1998). *Leadership in organizations* (4th ed.). Upper Saddle River, NJ: Prentice Hall, p. 208.

organization, the busier they are and the less time they have to deal with problems below them in the hierarchy. This is an advantage for lower-level employees. They can trade their time and effort for things they want. Effort thus provides power when it represents a valuable and scarce resource.

Individuals are using power to pressure when they threaten to withdraw valuable resources rather than offering to exchange them. The difference between exchange and pressure is like the difference between reward power and coercion. If lower-level employees continue to pursue an issue, eventually it will become less expensive for those above them to let the lower-level employees have their way rather than lose the time necessary to dissuade them or even meet with these employees. Persistent effort carries the implicit threat of continuing to be a nuisance until demands are met. Similarly, if your effort and persistence are sufficiently unique and valuable to an organization (e.g., your persistent hard work), you can also exert pressure by threatening to withdraw your effort.

INGRATIATION. Lower-level participants in an organization may also use ingratiation as a power tactic.[9] *Ingratiation* occurs when an individual does

9. Jones, E. E. (1964). *Ingratiation.* New York: Appleton-Century-Crofts.

nice things for someone in the hope of making that individual feel a sense of obligation to return the favor. Subordinates can ingratiate themselves with the boss by supporting the boss's ideas in group meetings, going out of their way to do little things for the boss, or even playing up to the boss with compliments and gifts.

Ingratiation is a powerful influence tactic because social exchange transactions are governed by the norm of reciprocity. The *norm of reciprocity* states that if someone does something nice for you, you are obligated by social convention to return the favor, even if you didn't want it in the first place. Cicero noted, "There is no duty more indispensable than returning a kindness . . . all men distrust one forgetful of a benefit."[10]

Reciprocation is quite different from compensation (direct payment for services rendered). In fact, any attempt to repay a kindness quickly and directly in order to avoid obligation "is unseemly and conveys distrust."[11] The norm of reciprocity not only entails repayment of a previous kindness, it often suggests an *ongoing exchange relationship* in which favors are traded. If I scratch your back, I expect that at some point you will scratch mine and that exchanges of this sort are part of our ongoing relationship.

Ingratiation represents something of a perversion of the reciprocity norm. The norm of reciprocity allows low-power individuals to give others in the organization things they may not want or need and to expect something in return. Ingratiation creates an obligation of repayment.

RATIONAL PERSUASION. *Rational persuasion* is another power tactic used to influence others. This tactic involves convincing someone that a particular behavior is "logically" the best course of action because it is the most likely to accomplish that individual's personal objectives. Rational persuasion works for the same reason that expert power works—because it suggests that a request is logically in your best interests. When you use rational persuasion, you don't even need to personally control the resource another individual wants in order to influence that individual. You need only convince the individual that the course of action you prefer is in his or her best interests. Thus, informing a new coworker that your organization values and rewards cooperation and "team players" can be an effective way to elicit assistance.

INSPIRATIONAL AND PERSONAL APPEALS. *Inspirational* appeal occurs when you invoke an individual's self-image and values in the context of a request (for example, "A good citizen would help me with this"). Inspirational appeals work because they threaten an individual's self-image (e.g., as a good citizen) if he or she does not comply.

Similarly, *personal appeals* involve asking someone to do a favor for you based on friendship or loyalty. For this influence tactic to be effective, the person must like you or feel a sense of loyalty to you. Personal appeals work because friendship implies potentially valuable past and future exchanges of favors. Personal appeals are often used when the favor is "beyond the call of duty."

CONSULTATION. The most subtle power tactic in groups and organizations is consultation. *Consultation* occurs when someone gains your support for a course of action by letting you participate in planning it. Participation

---

10. Gouldner, A. (1960). The norm of reciprocity. *American Sociologial Review, 25,* 161–178.
11. Blau, P. (1964). *Exchange and power in social life.* New York: Wiley.

in planning creates ownership of and commitment to a course of action. When handled skillfully, consultation is really co-opting; it provides an individual with the illusion of participating in planning a course of action without providing any real opportunities to shape or alter the plan.

LEGITIMATING TACTICS. Finally, individuals are using *legitimating tactics* when they invoke the right or authority to make requests of higher-ups in the organization based on an implicit or explicit psychological contract. For example, an individual might make reference to a quotation from an executive's recent speech, or implicit promises made during employee orientation, as a way of convincing his or her supervisor that a request is legitimate and should be honored. Such requests are unlikely to be questioned if they concern routine duties; they are more likely to be scrutinized if the request is unusual.

COALITION TACTICS. In the end, all the sources of power discussed so far share an assumption that the person being persuaded doesn't have alternative sources for the resources at stake. After all, a boss who has lots of fawning subordinates may not be very persuaded by a single employee's threats to his or her self-image. It should not be surprising, then, that the most important source of power for lower-level members of organizations is not one source of power, but the union of many through the formation of coalitions. A **coalition** is a collection of individuals who have banded together, thereby combining their individual sources of power.

As the members of the Tagi alliance found in the hit television show *Survivor*, coalitions are the secret to power in organizations. When you join a coalition, your individual power is increased by the power of the others in the group. If you have one vote in an election, you cannot elect anyone on your own. But if you can gather together a large group of voters (each with one vote), those voters can decide who gets elected. Similarly, one disgruntled employee exercising the power to disrupt work by walking off the job may have little or no effect; several thousand employees walking out simultaneously can move mountains.

Coalitions represent a form of power *sharing* and, consequently, joining one incurs some costs. If you are a middle manager in a large corporation, undoubtedly you have some sources of power at your disposal, but who is going to listen to your one lone voice? You don't have enough power to effect a major change in corporate policy by yourself. Perhaps you could find some other managers who want the same change. Then it would be more than just your one voice; then your voice would have the strength of numbers behind it.

One of the problems with this strategy, of course, is that finding other managers who want *exactly* what you want may be difficult. Under these conditions, you could form a compromise coalition. In Chapter 5 we define a compromise decision as one in which each of two or more parties gives a little to reach an agreement. The parties don't get exactly what they want, but they get something better than they would have had they not compromised. Likewise, in a **compromise coalition,** all the members of the coalition are interested in the same issues, but they don't all get exactly what they want. The members of the coalition *compromise* on what each wants to make sure that the coalition gets something for its effort.

Perhaps you think that 6 weeks of maternity leave at half pay would be appropriate. Someone else thinks that 3 weeks at full pay would be best.

Both of you agree that *anything* is better than the company's current policy of 2 weeks at half pay. So the two of you compromise on 4 weeks at three-fourths pay. It is not really what either of you wanted, but you both prefer this alternative to the company's idea. And by finding a way to agree, you can now both put your sources of power behind the one compromise suggestion.

Sometimes coalitions form for reasons other than shared interests. In the case of **logrolling,** for example, members of the coalition lend each other power so that each can pursue interests not shared by other coalition members. If you were the only manager in the company interested in changing the maternity leave policy, the only way to get other managers to join your coalition would be to give them something to get them to join. And what do you have to give? Your limited sources of power, of course.

Imagine that you found an employee (we'll call him Sam) who didn't care about maternity leave but cared dearly about getting the company to sponsor a softball league. Assuming that you had no strong opinions about softball leagues, the two of you could logroll a coalition. You would support Sam's initiatives on company softball leagues in exchange for Sam's support of your proposed changes to the company's maternity leave policy. Both proposals would have the strength of two people behind them, even though only one employee was interested in each proposal. As you might imagine, logrolls can produce strange organizational bedfellows.

The cost of joining a compromise coalition is the compromise of your initiative; the cost of joining a logroll coalition is your obligation to support issues in the future in which you have no interest. Both forms of coalitions have costs, although the costs differ. Nevertheless, recent research by Jeffrey Polzer, Elizabeth Mannix, and Margaret Neale shows that building coalitions is an especially effective way to gain power during group negotiations.[12]

CONSEQUENCES OF THE USE OF POWER

Two major problems can surface when managers or others in power exert their power. One problem has to do with people's perceptions when it is obvious that someone is taking advantage of his or her power. Similarly, the relationship between the powerful and the powerless often depends more on the way power is used than on its outcomes. The other problem occurs when power becomes an addiction, which can lead to abuses of power, including sexual harassment.

PERCEPTIONS OF POWER USERS.
Social scientist D. J. Moberg noted that the consequences of using power in organizations can depend on the motive that the objects of power plays attribute to the power holders.[13] Toni Falbo explored this problem by asking 141 students to each write an essay titled "How I Get My Way."[14] The essays were scored for the use of 16 general power tactics. Each student was rated by other students on 6 dimen-

12. Polzer, J. T., Mannix, E. A., & Neale, M. A. (1998). Interest alignment and coalitions in multiparty negotiation. *Academy of Management Journal, 41,* 42–54.

13. Moberg, D. J. (1977). *Organizational politics: Perspectives from attribution theory.* Paper presented at the annual meeting of the American Institute of Decision Sciences, Chicago.

14. Falbo, T. (1977). Multidimensional scaling of power strategies. *Journal of Personality and Social Psychology, 35,* 537–547.

sions: consideration, friendliness, quality of self-expression, honesty, desirability as a participant (in another discussion group), and liking.

Falbo found that power tactics can be described along two major dimensions: direct/indirect and rational/nonrational. Tactics along the direct/indirect dimension concern whether the attempt to influence is oriented toward changing an individual (direct) or getting an individual to *choose* to change (indirect); tactics along the rational/nonrational dimension concern whether the attempt entails providing good reasons for the change (rational) or not (nonrational). In general, Falbo found that power users who used indirect and rational tactics (such as consultation and rational persuasion) were perceived much more favorably than were those who used direct and nonrational tactics (such as pressure or personal appeals).

A major limitation of Falbo's work is that it measured only how power users were *perceived*. It is entirely possible that direct and nonrational power tactics may be tremendously effective in the short run. However, if power holders who employ such tactics arouse negative perceptions in others, the tactics spell disaster in the long run.

ADDICTIVENESS OF POWER. The second major problem with the use of power concerns its addictiveness. Two anthropologists described this problem quite well after observing men in the primitive Indian village of Karimpur:

> If you were to take one of the most harmless men in the village and put him in the watchman's place, he would be a rascal within six months. . . . The sense of power and sudden popularity which a man experiences on finding himself an agent of power is in itself a danger.[15]

This transformation occurs in a series of steps. First, the availability of power leads to its use. Second, the use of power fuels the perception that the person wielding the power has control over others, often eclipsing any realization of the *shared* resource dependency of all social exchanges. Third, this perception of control in turn leads power users to view themselves as more worthy and others as less worthy of taking control. Finally, power users come to believe that their use of power is justified and appropriate and that others are incapable of self-control or governance.[16]

In effect, a power user comes to see the use of power as appropriate and even necessary because others are weak and unworthy, even when the source of the power is a resource-dependency relationship. Often, this distorted belief that others are unworthy encourages the power user to use more direct and nonrational power tactics, such as coercion. It may also lead to abuses of power such as sexual harassment, as noted in "FOCUS ON: Abusers of Power." These tactics invoke angry reactions, and the demise of the power user often follows. Thus, to summarize, when the addictiveness of power causes the power holder to lose sight of the symmetry of resource dependencies, the power user's dark side emerges, and, eventually, he or she loses power.

---

15. Wiser, W., & Wiser, C. (1967). *Behind mind walls*. Berkeley: University of California Press.
16. Kipnis, D. (1976). *The powerholders*. Chicago: University of Chicago Press.

FOCUS ON
ABUSERS OF POWER

SEXUAL HARASSMENT AS A POWER PLAY.
Sexual harassment provides a graphic example of the way that power holders can become addicted to their power and wield it inappropriately to meet personal goals. As actor Michael Douglas noted in the hit movie *Disclosure*, sexual harassment is all about power because control over valuable resources (e.g., employment) is what gives sexual harassers the opportunity to harass. The definition of this abuse of power is fairly broad. According to the 1980 Equal Employment Opportunity Commission guidelines, conduct is defined as sexual harassment if it is verbal or physical and of a sexual nature or if any of the following conditions apply:

■ Submission to such conduct is made either explicitly or implicitly a term or condition of an individual's employment.
■ Submission to or rejection of such conduct by an individual is used as the basis for employment decisions affecting such individuals.

■ Such conduct has the purpose or effect of substantially interfering with an individual's work performance or creating an intimidating, hostile, or offensive work environment.

Although it appears to occur most often in supervisor–subordinate relationships, sexual harassment also takes place between coworkers and peers. A consequence of differences in power based on organizational position, sexual harassment affects both men and women, individuals in every race and class, and individuals in countries around the world. In the United States at least, sexual harassment also affects victims' employers, who are legally responsible for employees who abuse power in this way.

Sources: Rospenda, K. M., Richman, J. A., & Nawyn, S. J. (1998). Doing power: The confluence of gender, race, and class in contrapower sexual harassment. *Gender & Society, 12*(1), 40–61; and Novit, M. S. (1982), January/February). Employer liability for employee misconduct: Two common law doctrines. *Personnel,* 11–18.

GROUPS AS SOCIAL CONTEXT

As discussed in the opening paragraphs of this chapter, office politics are as much a reality of organizational life as coffee breaks and meetings. Office politics concern *intentional* efforts by groups in an organization to marshal their sources of power.

However, people are also part of the **social context** of organizations, and as such are also able to exert considerable influence that is unintended but nevertheless dramatic. In the following sections, we will concentrate on two ways in which groups can exert unintentional influence: by influencing judgment and by influencing behavior.

SOCIAL CONTEXT AND JUDGMENT

One way to examine the most subtle but most powerful form of influence groups exert is from the perspective of **social comparison theory.**[17] According to social comparison theory, the opinions and actions of other people are a major influence on our perceptions and beliefs about the world around us. When we construct a perception, judgment, or belief about the world, we check its accuracy by comparing it to the perceptions and judgments constructed by others around us. If our perceptions and judgments match those

17. Festinger, L. (1954). A theory of social comparison. *Human Relations,* 7, 117–140.

of these other people, everything is fine. But what happens when we construct beliefs, perceptions, and judgments that differ from those of others? The following fictional account demonstrates the acquisition of a workgroup norm:

> You are a newly hired worker on the assembly line at Mega Manufacturing. Your supervisor spends the morning introducing you around and explaining your new job to you—how to work the machinery at your workstation, where to get raw materials when you run out, when you can take breaks, and so on. She winds up the morning by noting that she would like you to think about shooting for 50 complete units per day as a performance goal. Then she sends you off to lunch with your assembly-line coworkers.
>
> At lunch some of the old hands on the line seem friendly enough and ask if you have any questions about the job. You mention that you are wondering about keeping up with the daily quota of 50 units suggested by your supervisor. At this point the old hands laugh. They reassure you that it's the job of the supervisor to talk about completing 50 units per day but that no one really expects you to do that much. They claim that the supervisor usually seems pleased with 40. One of the old hands even notes that if you did make 50, it would make some of the older workers (for whom even 35 units is a challenge) look bad.
>
> Late in the afternoon, your supervisor stops by to see how you are doing and asks whether, in your judgment, you think you will be able to keep up a 50-units-per-day pace.

As suggested by this story, workgroup norms often dictate more than just what behaviors are appropriate. They may also dictate what thoughts are appropriate—what perceptions, beliefs, or judgments about possible performance levels are allowed. If you were the worker in the story, what would you say to your supervisor at this point about your ability to keep up a 50-units-per-day pace? And how would your coworkers' comments at lunch influence your answer?

One possibility is that you might treat your coworkers' comments as evidence. If you have worked the assembly line for a couple hours before the supervisor comes around, you might already have a good idea of what is possible and what is not. Let's say you think that producing 50 units per day is possible. In the back of your mind, of course, are the old hands' comments that the normal target for the group is really 40. At this point you might think to yourself, "These coworkers are reasonable people, and while their perceptions may not be entirely accurate, mine may not be entirely accurate either." In the end, you would adjust your estimate to reflect the old hands' input and report to your supervisor that you will shoot for 46.

What if there is so much uncertainty that individuals have no faith in their own judgments? What if, after several hours on the assembly line, the worker in the example still has no idea of what a reasonable production target is? What roles would the opinions of the coworkers play in this case?

When the perception or judgment process is extremely uncertain, other people's opinions can strongly anchor judgment, even subconsciously. The existence of **social anchoring** of judgment was convincingly demonstrated in a series of studies concerned with **bystander apathy**—why observers fail to lend assistance in emergency situations. The scenario for a typical by-stander apathy study is described here:

> You have been asked to participate in a research study at your university. You report as requested. The experimenter seats you in a small room at a desk, gives you a short background questionnaire to complete, and leaves the room while you fill it out. After working on the questionnaire for about 5 minutes, you notice that some wisps of smoke seem to be coming out of a vent in the room. What do you do?[18]

It seems obvious that if you are alone in the room, you should get up to investigate the smoke. Perhaps you would leave the room to sound the alarm or seek assistance. But what if other subjects are in the room with you, also filling out the questionnaire?

The key to understanding human reactions to this situation is that the meaning of the smoke is *highly uncertain*. It could be an emergency, but then maybe it's just dust blowing out of an air-conditioning vent or something equally harmless. You don't know, just as when you join a new organization, you don't know what behaviors are regulated by the organization's rules and roles. Under conditions of high uncertainty, we allow others to anchor our judgments, often without even knowing we are doing so.

In a test of this scenario, subjects who were alone in the room were likely to judge the smoke to be a potential emergency; 75% investigated the situation. However, if the real subject was with other subjects who had been told to ignore the smoke, only 10% of the subjects got up to investigate. The unresponsiveness of the others in the room anchors the uncertain judgment of the subject.

The difference between accepting someone else's evidence and accepting the anchoring effects of social comparison is a subtle but important one. When we accept someone else's judgments as evidence, we are still aware of our own opinion and are attempting to reconcile the differences between our judgments, beliefs, or perceptions and those of others we trust. There is a conscious awareness of the differences in judgment, and we feel the need to understand the origins of those differences. In contrast, anchoring effects often catch us unaware. The real subjects in the bystander apathy study probably didn't realize the extent to which their judgments were being influenced by the behavior of others. Their perception of the experience was that it was not an emergency.

Returning to the example of the assembly-line worker, under circumstances of uncertainty, the worker would be likely to increase the production target he told his supervisor. Using the old hands' opinions as evidence, he would judge 50 units to be possible but hedge his estimate to 46 in deference to the possibility that his coworkers knew something he didn't. If he was really uncertain about what was possible, he would be more likely to anchor his judgments based on the estimates of the old hands; thus, he would report that 40 units was about right, and he would honestly believe it was.

As a final thought on how groups influence judgment, remember that both forms of influence—evidential and anchoring—play important roles in ensuring appropriate group functioning. This may explain why mentoring

18. Latane, B., & Darley, J. (1970). *The unresponsive bystander: Why doesn't he help?* New York: Appleton-Century-Crofts.

RESEARCH IN ACTION
MENTORING: A WAY TO LEARN TO NAVIGATE ORGANIZATIONS

Stacy Blake-Beard, Harvard University; *stacy_blake@harvard.edu*

For those who are traditionally outside the corridors of power—such as women and people of color—mentoring may provide a way to gain access to the opportunities and resources that are used to determine who moves ahead in organizations. The formal mentoring program sponsored by the Financial Women's Association (FWA) with the Murray Bergtraum High School for Business Careers provided an excellent opportunity to benchmark one such successful formal mentoring program.

The FWA High School Mentoring Program is a 14-year partnership between the women of the FWA and young women attending Murray Bergtraum High School. Eileen McGowan, a research associate at Harvard University, and I explored the mutual benefits and challenges experienced by high-powered women in the financial services industry and the multicultural high school students with whom they are paired in a formal mentoring program.

We found that the mentoring program was beneficial to both mentors and protégés, but in very different ways. The mentoring relationships served as a way to broaden the students' horizons, both literally and figuratively, acting as a mechanism to expand the range of options open to the students as they considered moving beyond high school and into organizations in the real world. The students also gained access to the considerable college preparation activities that the FWA incorporates into its program as well as employment opportunities from FWA members whose organizations needed student help.

The mentors also gained greatly from their involvement. Many of them talked about how much they appreciated the opportunity to pass on information based on their organizational experiences; in short, the mentoring relationship was a *generative* experience for these mentors.

One policy change that we proposed for the program was related to the structure of relationships; the small "pod" model. The pods serve as an intermediary layer between individual pairs and the entire membership. The pods could be constructed, whenever possible, of experienced and inexperienced mentors mentoring each other. This would allow for small groups of mentors to meet more frequently and in more intimate gatherings. The extra value to these pods is that they could supply additional support for the mentors and for the dyads as well. The lessons gained from the FWA High School Mentoring Program are invaluable as more corporations build partnerships with schools via formal mentoring programs.

programs (such as the one described in the "RESEARCH IN ACTION: Mentoring" box) can be so critical to organizational success. A group's roles and rules represent a summary of the group's past learning. They allow newcomers to produce high-quality behaviors and judgments immediately, without a lot of unnecessary trial-and-error learning. Thus, exerting influence by offering evidence and anchoring are important mechanisms by which a group teaches newcomers what the group has learned. If the group has learned well, everyone benefits when the newcomer falls in line with the old hands; in this case, a little social influence is a good thing. If the group has learned poorly, a little "foolishness" (ignoring the old hands) can be a good thing, too.

SOCIAL CONTEXT AND BEHAVIOR

Groups can also influence the behaviors of members directly. We will consider several examples of direct influence: conformity, social facilitation, and social loafing.

■ **FIGURE 7-3**   **The Asch Study: Which Test Line Matches the Target?**

The Asch experiment demonstrated the power of group influence. In this figure, it seems obvious that test line B is the best match for the target line. However, if several of your friends all claimed that test line C was the closest match, what would go through your mind? Would you begin to doubt your judgment? Would you perhaps go along to avoid looking foolish if they just happened to be right?

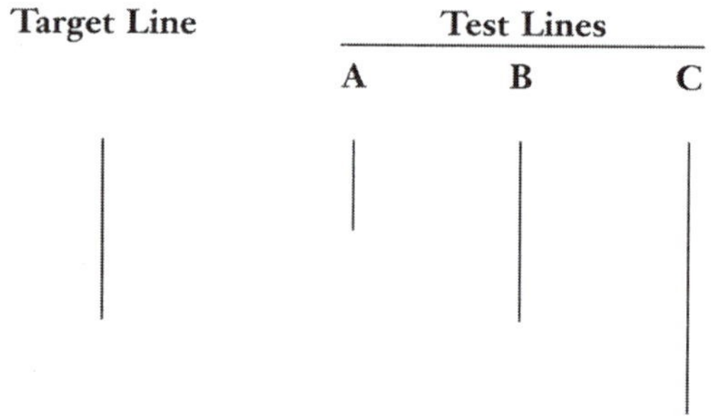

Target Line   **Test Lines**

                              A   B   C

CONFORMITY. Conformity represents a form of social comparison beyond social anchoring. **Conformity** occurs when an individual engages in a behavior or admits to a belief that the group encourages, even though the individual believes that the behavior or belief is incorrect or inappropriate. Conformity does not occur because the judgments of others provide good evidence for behaving or believing a certain way and does not occur because an individual is uncertain about his or her judgment. Rather, conformity occurs simply because an individual wants to go along with a group. Conformity occurs when an individual is concerned that a group has selected a course of action that is inappropriate but fails to say so.

The following psychological experiment, known as the Asch study, provides a classic example of the effects of conformity[19]:

> You are invited to participate in a research study. You report at the appointed hour and are ushered into a room with six other participants. The seven of you are seated in a row (you occupy the last chair in the row), and you are told that this will be a study of your ability to make visual judgments of size. For each judgment, a machine will project four lines on the wall. One line will be the target line, and you must judge which of the test lines (A, B, or C) best matches the target (see Figure 7-3).
>
> The experiment seems quite boring. For the first six trials, it seems obvious which test line matches the target, and there is no disagreement at all among the participants. The seventh target line is just like the one shown in Figure 7-4 and just as easy to match as the others have been, so you are quite surprised when the first subject responds C—an obviously wrong answer. Before you can even ponder why this has occurred, however, the other five participants each give their responses—also C and also obviously wrong. At this point it is your turn to respond. The other six all have agreed on C, but you *know* the correct answer is B. How do you respond?

19. Asch, S. E. (1956). *Studies of independence and conformity: A minority of one against a unanimous majority.* Psychological Monographs, *70*, whole #16.

The key to understanding the importance of the Asch study is to realize that the subjects have little or no sense of uncertainty about the correct answer. Subjects *know* that the correct answer is B. When presented with the target and test lines in the absence of other respondents, subjects virtually never make mistakes. What that seventh subject in the experiment doesn't know, of course, is that the first six respondents have been told to answer C on the seventh trial of the study. How does that seventh subject respond in the face of a unanimous but obviously incorrect majority? About one third of the time the seventh subject goes along with the group and says C is the answer.

It's important to bear in mind that whereas the processes by which groups use anchoring and evidence to influence behavior are similar, conformity is really quite different. In using others' opinions as evidence, we have a good idea of what is correct but are willing to consider and incorporate the opinions of more experienced others. In using others' opinions as anchors, we know that we really don't know what is correct and are open to influence (perhaps without knowing it) of more experienced others. In the case of conformity, however, we know what is correct but don't voice that opinion and act as if we are in agreement with the group. Instead, we defer to, or conform to, the behavior or beliefs of the group.

What causes people to conform? First, the individual may want to avoid conflict with the group. In the case of the new assembly-line worker, it has been made clear that 40 units is the agreed-upon target. By violating this norm, the worker risks the wrath of the group members, perhaps by exposing their collusive attempts to keep down management's performance expectations and protect less able workers.

Second, by disagreeing with the majority, the individual risks being labeled a deviant. Depending on the individual's reasons for joining the group, he may value being accepted more than being right. Disagreement may not be the fastest path to making new friends, especially if it is seen as an attempt to show up his coworkers. Most of all, by disagreeing, he risks rejection by the group—no doubt in part for being a deviant troublemaker.

Normally we think of mistakes in judgment—a poor hiring decision, a bad investment, or a sloppy report—as leading to formal sanctions by the organization. However, conformity raises the specter of informal, even intangible, sanctions that quietly and implicitly enforce workgroup norms. It is worth noting that in the Asch study, it does not seem that acceptance or rejection by the group should have been a big concern for the subjects. Nevertheless, group influence was apparent.

This influence becomes tragic when the norms the workgroup implicitly enforce run contrary to the best interests of the organization as a whole and therefore prove contrary to the group's long-term interests. The assembly-line workers who promote the illusion to management that 40 units per day is the maximum they can produce may one day find that this target is not enough to justify keeping the plant open. Perhaps more to the point, the silencing effects of conformity beg a question: How many imaginative and useful ideas have never been suggested, and, therefore, how many organizations and workgroups have never been able to take advantage of them? How many great innovations have never been made because workers believed there was only one way to do something—the company's way?

Other people's opinions become particularly influential when those individuals are similar to us. We don't find it unusual for someone to voice different judgments or beliefs if that person has a different background, makes different assumptions, or entertains different motivations as the basis for perceptual or judgmental constructions. In fact, if you can find reasonable explanations for differences between your judgments and those of others, the opinions of the others will exert little influence on your opinions. Thus, when the older workers suggest that a target of 50 units isn't possible, you may think that for them 50 really isn't possible, even if it is for you. However, when you can't find an obvious basis for a difference of opinion, you may become quite alarmed and adjust your judgment, or behavior, or expect the other person to do so.

SOCIAL FACILITATION. When the mere presence of other individuals (e.g., other group members) spurs an individual to exert greater effort, **social facilitation** has occurred.[20] Norman Triplett was first credited with exploring social facilitation in 1897. Triplett noticed that world records in sports such as cycling were always set during events when many riders were competing against each other and almost never when athletes were competing only against themselves or the clock. Triplett concluded that world-class athletes derived extra energy from the mere presence of competitors.[21]

Where does this extra energy Triplett observed come from? One possibility is that the mere presence of other individuals arouses fears of failing and then being evaluated negatively by the other group members who are watching.[22] According to this explanation, the extra energy provided by the mere presence of others is a form of arousal that comes from fear or anxiety. Another possibility is that the presence of the others is a distraction. If the other people are working on the same task, their actions might provide clues for the individual about how to improve performance. If the other people are just observing the individual, their facial expressions provide valuable feedback about how well the individual is doing. The individual feels conflict because, on the one hand, he or she wants to concentrate on the task, but on the other hand, he or she wants to look at the other people. This internal conflict becomes a source of arousal from which the individual derives extra energy.[23]

Social facilitation refers to increases in an individual's supply of *energy*—not necessarily to improvement in performance. Research on social facilitation has shown that the extra arousal derived from the presence of others positively affects performance only if the behaviors necessary for high-quality performance are well learned or the task is very simple.[24] In other words, arousal increases the probability of dominant responses. If the task is well learned or simple, high-quality responses are likely to be dominant, and social facilitation simply increases the probability of those responses, leading to

20. Griffith, T. L., Fichman, M., & Moreland, R. L. (1989). Social loafing and social facilitation: An empirical test of the cognitive-motivational model of performance. *Basic and Applied Social Psychology, 10,* 253–271.

21. Triplett, N. (1898). The dynamogenic factors in pacemaking and competition. *American Journal of Psychology, 9,* 507–533.

22. Cottrell, N. B., Wack, D. L., Sekerak, G. S., & Rittle, R. H. (1968). Social facilitation of dominant responses by the presence of an audience and the mere exposure of others. *Journal of Personality and Social Psychology, 9,* 245–250.

23. Sanders, G. G. (1981). Driven by distraction: An integrative review of social facilitation theory and research. *Journal of Experimental Social Psychology, 17,* 227–251; and Baron, R. S. (1985). Distraction-conflict theory: Progress and problems. In L. Berkowitz (Ed.), *Advances in experimental social psychology.* San Franciso: Academic Press.

24. Zajonc, R. B. (1965). Social facilitation. Science, *149,* 269–274.

enhanced performance. If the task is difficult or unfamiliar, correct responses are not likely to be dominant. In this case, arousal from social facilitation may increase the probability of *incorrect* behaviors, thereby leading to worse performance. Thus, social facilitation cuts both ways. The presence of others increases an individual's arousal level; whether performance is improved or hurt depends on how difficult or unfamiliar the task is.

SOCIAL LOAFING. **Social loafing** occurs when individuals decrease the amount of effort they put into a task—that is, loaf—while doing that task with other people. The important word here is *with*. Social loafing occurs when several people are working on the same task together, so that it is difficult (if not impossible) to tell who is doing a given amount of the work.

A German psychologist named Ringelmann first identified the phenomenon of social loafing. He noticed that in strength tasks such as tug-of-war, the effort exerted by the team never added up to the sum of the effort each individual was capable of exerting alone.[25] Social loafing was later demonstrated over a variety of tasks. In one study the researchers told a group of subjects to scream into individual microphones as loud as possible, first one at a time, and then together. By hooking up sensors to each of the microphones, the researchers were able to show that each subject screamed much louder when he or she was screaming alone than when screaming as part of a group.[26]

Social loafing is thought to occur because of a **diffusion of responsibility** in groups. When group members work together on a single task and it is difficult to determine who is working hard and who is not, responsibility for the outcome is diffused—or shared—over the entire group.[27] Whether the outcome is considered a success or a failure, group members share the credit relatively equally. This decreases the incentive for any individual to work hard because there is only a loose connection between effort and the outcome for the group or the individual. Extra effort may have little or no effect on the outcome for the group and will have absolutely no effect on the credit for the outcome that an individual receives (as long as the individual *appears* to be trying hard). The result is a kind of free-rider problem whereby each individual slacks off a little bit, and in the end the performance of the entire group suffers.

In extreme cases, diffusion of responsibility can lead to deindividuation. **Deindividuation** occurs when the personal identities of group members—and therefore the responsibility they feel for their actions—are submerged in the group's identity. Consider an important difference between the tug-of-war game mentioned earlier and an infamous incident during the Vietnam War: the My Lai massacre. In a tug-of-war, if someone in the game isn't working as hard as possible, no one knows because the collective action is made up of many smaller individual behaviors that cannot be examined separately. There is only one action—the pulling of the rope. In the My Lai massacre of the civilian population of a small village in Vietnam, the collective action (the massacre) was also made up of many individual actions. Hypothetically, the death of each villager was an individual action that could have

25. Moede, W. Die (1927). Richtlinien der Leistungs-Psychologie. *Industrielle Psychotechnik, 4,* 193–207.

26. Latane, B., Williams, K., & Karkins, S. (1979). Many hands make light the work: The causes and consequences of social loafing. *Journal of Personality and Social Psychology, 37,* 822–832.

27. Wagner, J., III. (1995). Studies of individualism–collectivism: Effects on cooperation in groups. *Academy of Management Journal, 38,* 152–172.

been attributed to an individual soldier. But in practice this did not happen. No one claimed to know anything more than that American soldiers massacred the villagers, and to any observer of the incident, any soldier would have looked pretty much like any other. There were no individuals involved, only group members acting not as individuals but as members of the group.

Anonymity is an important part of the process of deindividuation. Mobs often engage in behaviors that no individual alone would consider, such as lynching an untried suspect. There is only the mob and the mob's actions—no individual responsibility for the actions. If the mob's actions are bad, they are certainly not felt to be the fault of any individual. Similarly, exceedingly cruel, humiliating, and even inhuman treatment of others apparently becomes acceptable when everyone else is doing it under the guise of initiation rites and rituals.[28] Obviously, diffusion of responsibility is an important part of deindividuation.

GROUP CHARACTERISTICS AND INFLUENCE

Some groups or groups in certain social settings are more likely than others to exert strong influence (power) on members' judgment and behavior. We close this chapter by briefly examining two characteristics that dramatically affect a group's social context and, therefore, its influence: its cohesiveness and size.

GROUP COHESIVENESS

In general, more cohesive groups—those in which the members want to remain together as a group—are more productive than others, but that does not mean that group cohesiveness is an unqualified asset.[29] The pressure to conform is much more intense in highly cohesive groups than in others,[30] and group members are more likely to trust the opinions of other group members and less willing to risk rejection by the group for disagreeing.

A group is more cohesive when the group's goals are compatible with the individual goals of the group's members, the group members support each other, and the group's leader encourages effective participation by all group members.[31] Cohesiveness further increases when group members build personal relationships with one another.[32] Personal relationships promote a sense of closeness and also provide group members with the information necessary to work closely and effectively with each other. Members of cohesive groups are also less likely to engage in back-biting and the sort of office politicking highlighted in the opening paragraphs of this chapter.

---

28. Reilly, R. (1991, September 14). What is the Citadel? *Sports Illustrated, 70–79*; and Strr, M. (1991, May 13). The night of the taming: Tales of hazing and beatings at a military academy. *Newsweek, 37.*

29. Napier, R. W., & Gershenfeld, M. K. (1989). *Groups: Theory and experience.* Palo Alto, CA: Houghton Mifflin, p. 151; and Norris, D., & Niebuhr, R. (1980). Group variables and gaming success. *Simulation and Games, 11,* 301–312.

30. Festinger, L., & Thibaut, J. (1951). Interpersonal communication in small groups. *Journal of Abnormal and Social Psychology, 16,* 92–99.

31. Cartwright, D., & Zander, A. (1968). *Group dynamics: Research and theory.* New York: Harper & Row.

32. Napier, & Gershenfeld, *Groups.*

Possible Channels of Communication (by group size)	■ FIGURE 7-4

Number of Group Members	Number of Possible Channels of Communications
2	1
3	3
4	6
5	10
6	15
7	21
8	28
9	36
10	45

Not surprisingly, a group whose goals match those of the organization of which it is a part is likely to make important contributions to the organization. However, if the goals of the group and the organization are out of step with one another, the group, by dint of its cohesiveness, may become a formidable renegade coalition.

GROUP SIZE

One of the most important consequences of a group's size is its effect on communication among group members. When there are many members in a group, the number of possible channels of communication increases dramatically. As shown in Figure 7-4, doubling the size of a group from 3 to 6 participants increases the number of possible two-person channels of communication from 3 to 15—a fivefold increase! Thus, in a group of 7 or 8, all-channel communication would be used only rarely.

Small groups provide more opportunities for individuals to make significant contributions to group activities and discussions among group members, which can lead to higher morale among group members overall.[33] However, in groups with more than five members, members often complain that the group is too large, probably because there isn't enough time for everyone to participate actively in discussions.[34] Typically, this leads the group to break into cliques,[35] which can quickly become voting coalitions.

As the size of a group increases, the connectedness among members decreases,[36] which can lead to increases in social loafing, bystander apathy, and even deindividuation.[37] Larger groups also promote more conformity, since there are more peers to exert pressure on any individual to conform.[38]

---

33. Huberman, S. (1987). Making Jewish leaders. *Journal of Jewish Communal Service, 64,* 32–41.
34. Gentry, G. (1980). Group size and attitudes toward the simulation experience. *Simulation and Games, 11,* 451–460.
35. Mamali, C., & Paun, G. (1982). Group size and the genesis of subgroups: Objective restrictions. *Revue Roumaine des Sciences Sociales—Serie de Psychologie, 26,* 139–148.
36. Napier, & Gershenfeld, *Groups,* pp. 38–41.
37. See, for instance, Pantin, H., & Carver, C. (1982). Induced competence and the bystander effect. *Journal of Applied Social Psychology, 12,* 100–111.
38. Gerard, H. B., Wilhelmy, R. A., & Conolley, E. S. (1968). Conformity and group size: *Journal of Personality and Social Psychology, 8,* 79–82.

On the other side of the coin, the effects of social facilitation increase with group size, and having more members means that there are more opportunities during group discussions to consider more perspectives and more knowledge. Thus, the real issue is not group size per se but whether a group is managed well enough that its size is an asset rather than a liability.

SUMMARY

Power and politics are forms of influence in which the resource dependencies of two individuals allow one to change, influence, or control the beliefs or actions of the other. In groups and organizations, other group members can be potent influences on individuals' thoughts and behaviors. In power plays, both sides receive something; the more powerful person simply receives more for less. One way individuals can insulate or protect themselves from power plays is by having slack.

Power arises when an individual, a group, or an organization controls two basic resources—rewards and punishments. Expert, legitimate, referent, and task interdependence power all refer to forms of control that organizations wield over rewards and punishments.

Even the lowliest member of an organization has access to some forms of power. He or she could join a coalition, for example. Coalitions offer the most important tactic for acquiring influence. By sharing power in a coalition, relatively powerless individuals can achieve more than they could by using their individual power alone.

Certain power tactics—particularly direct and nonrational attempts to influence others, including sexual harassment—are poorly received in organizations. Their use cannot only destroy relationships but eventually undermine the power of the power holder.

As this chapter points out, it is important to remember that behavior in a group and an organization takes place in a social context—in other words, in the presence of other individuals. The opinions and actions of these other people can exert dramatic—if often unintended—power over our beliefs and behaviors.

KEY TERMS

Alternative source
Bystander apathy
Charisma
Coalition
Coercion
Compromise coalition
Conformity
Deindividuation
Diffusion of responsibility
Expert power
Legitimate power
Logrolling

Political conflict
Referent power
Resource dependency
Reward power
Social anchoring
Social comparison theory
Social context
Social facilitation
Social loafing
Stockpile
Task interdependence
Theory of social exchange

DISCUSSION QUESTIONS

1 Imagine that the students and the instructor in a university course are unhappy with the way the course is going. What sources of power are available to the students to effect change in the classroom? What sources of power are available to the instructor? Who is more powerful in this setting—the students or the instructor?

2 What does it mean to say that *all* exercises of power are examples of exchanges? When a supervisor gives an order to a subordinate in an organizational setting, what is being exchanged?

3 Why are coalitions such an important way for lower-level participants in organizations to mobilize their power?

4 What is meant by the phrase "those who govern do so at the consent of those governed"? What source of power does this describe?

5 What sources of power depend on the existence of an organization? What sources of power are personal? What does it mean to say that reward power and coercion are the two basic forms of power?

6 How do complexity, conflict, and uncertainty, as defining characteristics of organizational behavior, contribute to a group's ability to influence an individual?

7 Are group influences on judgment and group influences on behavior equally likely to occur at each of the different stages of group development, as discussed in Chapter 6?

ON YOUR OWN

Social Power Inventory

Introduction   The questionnaire in this exercise is designed to measure your predisposition to be responsive to certain forms of social power. In responding to these questions, you will learn something about the types of power that you are most responsive to, or least responsive to, depending on who is exercising the power.

Procedure

Step 1: 5 Minutes   Identify three different people who have influence over you. One must be a teacher, a second may be a roommate or spouse, a third may be a boss. Others might include friends, business associates, parents, or people whom you negotiate with regularly. Specify the three people you have identified:

■ Person 1: _____
■ Person 2: _____
■ Person 3: _____

Step 2: 20 Minutes   For *each* of the three people, work completely through the following questionnaire with that person in mind. For each of the questions, pick A or B, depending on which one of the two best describes the way that the person affects you. Make sure to pick one answer, even if neither is a very good response.

Step 3: 30 Minutes   Your instructor will hand out a scoring key. Follow the key in order to score your questionnaire.

Source: Questionnaire developed by David W. Jamieson, & Kenneth W. Thomas, as it appeared in Lewicki, R. J., & Litterer, J. A. (1985). *Negotiation: Readings, exercises, and cases.* Homewood, IL: Irwin, pp. 490–493.

Person 1	Person 2	Person 3	

_____   _____   _____   **1 A** I sometimes do what that person says in order to get something I want.

          B I sometimes have to go along to avoid trouble.

_____   _____   _____   **2 A** That person always convinces me with his or her reasoning.

          B I sometimes do things for that person because I admire him or her.

_____   _____   _____   **3 A** That person might do good things for me in return.

          B I don't know as much about it as that person does.

_____   _____   _____   **4 A** That person's suggestions always make sense.

          B I could receive things I want from that person.

_____   _____   _____   **5 A** I want that person to like me.

          B I often feel that it is legitimate for that person to influence my behavior.

_____   _____   _____   **6 A** I take his or her word for things.

          B I sometimes try to avoid trouble by doing what that person asks.

_____   _____   _____   **7 A** That person has the right to tell me what to do.

          B That person is able to harm me in some way.

_____   _____   _____   **8 A** That person knows better.

          B I will receive something I want.

_____   _____   _____   **9 A** That person's friendship is important to me.

          B That person seems fairly intelligent.

_____   _____   _____   **10 A** The reasoning of the request usually agrees with my way of thinking.

          B That person is in a position to legitimately ask things of me.

_____   _____   _____   **11 A** I will receive something I want.

          B I sometimes go along with that person to make him or her happy.

_____   _____   _____   **12 A** That person's knowledge usually makes him or her right.

          B I feel that person has the right to ask things of me.

_____   _____   _____   **13 A** I want that person to like me.

          B I sometimes have to go along to avoid trouble.

_____   _____   _____   **14 A** I would sometimes like to get things from that person.

          B Sometimes I feel that person might do something unpleasant to those who do not do what is suggested.

_____   _____   _____   **15 A** That person's suggestions always makes sense.

          B I do what is asked to keep that person from taking actions that could be unpleasant for me.

_____   _____   _____   **16 A** That person should be listened to.

          B That person's friendship is important to me.

_____   _____   _____   **17 A** That person can do things that I would not like.

          B That person always knows what he or she is doing.

_____   _____   _____   **18 A** I sometimes have to go along in order to get things I need.

          B I often feel that it is legitimate for that person to influence my behavior.

_____   _____   _____   **19 A** The request is sometimes appropriate, considering that person's position.

          B At times, that person's suggestions make sense.

_____   _____   _____   **20 A** I sometimes do so because I feel that person is my friend.
  B That person's expertise makes him or her likely to be right.

_____   _____   _____   **21 A** That person has the right to tell me what to do.
  B That person could do something unpleasant to me.

_____   _____   _____   **22 A** That person is able to do things that benefit me.
  B That person always convinces me with his or her reasoning.

_____   _____   _____   **23 A** That other person's position permits him or her to require things of me.
  B That person's knowledge usually makes him or her right.

_____   _____   _____   **24 A** I trust that person's judgment.
  B I agree with what that person says.

_____   _____   _____   **25 A** Sometimes I feel that person might do something that is unpleasant to those who do not do what he or she suggests.
  B I always do what is asked because that person's ideas are compelling.

_____   _____   _____   **26 A** That person might help me get what I want.
  B It would not be proper sometimes for me to do otherwise.

_____   _____   _____   **27 A** That person can make things uncomfortable for me if I don't comply.
  B I do what is asked to make that person happy.

_____   _____   _____   **28 A** I would like to be his or her friend.
  B That person can help me.

_____   _____   _____   **29 A** That person always gives me good reasons for doing it.
  B I sometimes do what is asked to gain that person's friendship.

_____   _____   _____   **30 A** What that person says seems to be appropriate.
  B That person has had a lot of experience and usually knows best.

Discussion Questions

1 What was your score for each of the different forms of power?

Scoring Key

	Expert	Legitimate	Coercive	Reward	Referent	Informational
Person 1						
Person 2						
Person 3						

2 Find others in the class who rated the same type of person (teacher, parent, roommate, and so on). How do your scores compare with theirs, with respect to the types of people who are most and least influential? Why do you suppose this is so?

3 How do the situations that these people are in—for example, their objectives and your objectives, the differences in your ages, the kind of resources they control and what you want, and so on—affect the kind of power they are likely to use and the kind of power that has an impact on you? Explain.

4 If you were the powerful party in these situations, would you try to use different forms of power from those now being used? Explain.

5 As a power user yourself, which forms of power are you most comfortable using? least comfortable using? in which situations?

CLOSING CASE   CHAPTER 7

THE MANAGER'S MEMO

FROM: E. Grainger, Vice President
TO: F. Blackstone, President
RE: Potentially Damaging Resignation

Pat McDonnell has just submitted her resignation to me, effective in 2 weeks. Because Pat was responsible for designing *Galaxy Detective*, our most successful video game to date, this departure will be a great loss for the company.

I am particularly concerned because a major distributor of children's games and video products has just asked us to submit a bid to produce another game similar to the one Pat designed. I believe that two other companies are also bidding on this contract.

As you know, *Galaxy Detective* currently represents over 90% of our business. I am afraid that, without Pat, our ability to produce similar products will be seriously compromised, at the very time when getting new products into the market is extremely important.

Pat has hinted that for a substantial raise plus a stock interest in the company, she would reconsider her decision to resign from the company. To me, this sounds vaguely like blackmail. I find these tactics unpleasantly coercive. What do you advise that I tell Pat?

CASE DISCUSSION QUESTIONS

Assume that you are the president, and write a response to the vice president's memorandum. What power does Pat McDonnell have relative to the company? What power, if any, does the company have relative to Pat? Use your answers to these questions and your knowledge about power to guide you in considering the alternatives available to the company.

CHAPTER 8

Group Decision Making

ELECTRONIC MEETINGS

Twenty-four KPMG (Peat Marwick) senior managers, all tapped for the partnership track in the accounting giant's state and local tax (SALT) services, are seated around a table in a hotel conference room, collectively addressing the question "What are the most significant leadership issues you are facing as a manager in the KPMG SALT practice?" In 8 minutes, the group identifies 130 leadership issues. And it does so without uttering a single word.

Welcome to a new kind of meeting: the electronic or computer-mediated meeting, where individuals, even while sitting cheek to jowl, communicate via networked computers. Marketed as groupware, this technology is designed to facilitate decision making by teams and knowledge management. According to Douglas S. Griffin, managing director of D.S. Griffen & Associates in Scottsdale, Arizona, using PCs allows for more ideas and quick, reliable, computer-assisted skimming of the cream. In addition, the electronic meetings are self-documenting in that a complete record of a meeting, graphs and tables included, can be compiled and distributed immediately, which can aid future meetings.

"Anonymity is another powerful feature of the meetings," says Maryam Alavi, chairperson of information systems at the Robert H. Smith School of Business at the University of Maryland at College Park. "People get brutally honest and provide negative feedback more freely and frequently through this technology."

Anonymity, however, has a negative side as well because it means that a good idea may not be credited to its originator. Additionally, the process is

Source: Excerpted from Grossman, J. (1998, June). The sounds of silence. *Sky*; and Bartimo, J. (1990, June 11). At these shouting matches no one says a word. *Business Week*, 78.

unnatural to those who may not have quick keyboard skills. Despite these shortcomings, Alavi still believes computer-mediated meetings have a bright future.

Critics claim it's not as good as face-to-face oral communication, but some said that about the telephone, too!

INTRODUCTION: THE NATURE OF GROUP DECISION MAKING

When individuals meet for the purpose of solving problems and making decisions (whether the meetings are electronic meetings as mentioned above, or traditional face-to-face meetings), the group is generally more productive and effective than its individual members would be. What is it about groups that gives rise to such extraordinary levels of performance?

WHY MAKE DECISIONS IN GROUPS?

When it comes to making decisions, groups have some obvious advantages over individuals. One advantage is that, because groups are composed of a number of individuals, they reflect a range of perspectives on any given issue. Also, unlike individuals, groups have the potential for **resource pooling.** Collectively, the group has more information than do any of its members. Consequently, individuals can fill in the knowledge gaps of other group members.

Group members also can stimulate and encourage each other. This mutual influence process is called **synergy.** Individuals working alone on a problem tend to persist in viewing the problem in a particular way. This mind-set can cause the individual to become stuck and unable to solve the problem. Individuals in a group have the same tendency, but, because a number of different approaches are represented, group members more easily move out of their solution ruts. The information contributed by one member of the group may catalyze another member's thinking or alter its direction, indirectly aiding each individual's contributions to the solution of the problem at hand.

Yet another advantage of groups is that, because of the number of different skills represented, individual members have the luxury of working on parts of a problem. Groups offer the opportunity for specialization of labor, which is unavailable to individual decision makers. The **diversity** of the group—the heterogeneity of its members with respect to their personalities, gender, attitudes, background, and experience levels—can also positively alter the group's effectiveness at decision making.[1] The diversity of the individual group members may heighten the level of creativity and thus increase the number of ideas available to the group. The "Focus On: Groups" shows how Ford Motor Company benefits from diverse groups in its organization.

The benefits of group decision making are not limited solely to the solution-generation stage. Many solutions depend on the commitment of the decision makers for successful implementation. When more people are involved in decision making, a larger number of people feel responsible for

---

1. Guzzo, R. A., & Dickson, M. W. (1996). Teams in organizations: Recent research on performance and effectiveness. *Annual Review of Psychology, 47,* 307–338.

FOCUS ON GROUPS

INCLUSION AT FORD. Ford always tries to hire people from diverse backgrounds because good decisions are made when people with different perspectives work together to solve a problem.

If you have a diverse workforce, then you know that the customer's point of view will always be represented in the decision making process. When Ford created the Windstar minivan, many women were both on the design team and on the marketing committee; this was good because the Windstar is driven mostly by women. When making the final decisions on design, Ford included feedback from a variety of sources. For example, on Take Our Daughters to Work Day, kids gave feedback on Ford products. Ford also has a car-lease program for employees, and it asked the spouses of the lessees for their thoughts about various cars. If Ford didn't in-clude that kind of input in group decision processes, it would miss out on a host of good ideas.

For example, with the Windstar, Ford created "sleeping-baby mode" for the overhead light. One of the women on the Windstar electrical team has young children, and she said that her car's overhead light always wakes her children after a night drive. So, when we designed the Windstar, we provided an option for having only the floor lighting turn on when the door is opened.

It is clear the inclusion of a diverse group of ideas and people on the Windstar team had a positive effect on the decisions related to the final product.

Source: Excerpted from Rosenfeld, J. (2000, April). Here's an idea. *Fast Company, 33,* 102.

---

making the solution work, making implementation easier. Thus, a low-quality solution that has good group commitment can be more effective than a high-quality solution that lacks such commitment.[2]

Group decisions are also likely to be better understood. This is in part because those involved in making the decision are likely to be the same people ensuring its successful implementation. By contrast, when a decision is made by an individual, the decision needs to be relayed to the implementing parties. In some cases, failure to convey the solution (poor communication) effectively can reduce its attractiveness and create even greater problems than the one the solution was designed to solve. For example, after attending a seminar on motivating employees, a company chief executive officer (CEO) may decide to replace the current seniority-based compensation system with a merit-based system. Regardless of the wisdom of this decision, employees may believe that the company is just trying to make them work harder for less money—that the company does not really care about them but cares only about its bottom line. The only person to whom this particular decision belongs is the CEO of the company. If the decision had resulted from group interaction, the sense of ownership would have been much more widespread. Now the result of the CEO's decision may be lowered morale and reduced productivity, even though the CEO intended to give the workers more direct rewards for their productivity.

If the CEO had included others in the decision-making process, the likelihood of this type of failure would have been reduced. The individuals implementing the system would have understood not only why a particular

---

2. Maier, N. R. F. (1967). Assets and liabilities in group problem solving: The need for an integrative function. *Psychological Review, 74,* 239–249.

compensation package was chosen but also why alternative systems were ruled out. Executive meetings are a common method for involving individuals in company decision making.

TRANSACTIVE MEMORY

As "FOCUS ON: Groups" suggests, successful communication of ideas in teams is an important aspect of high-performing teams. Most successful teams include not only a demographically diverse group of employees, but also employees from a variety of functional areas within the organization (see further discussion of cross-functional teams in Chapter 6). Recent research related to cross-functional team effectiveness has focused on transactive memory systems.[3] A **transactive memory** system refers to the combination of knowledge related to each individual within a team and the teams' awareness of who knows what.[4] Research in this area has shown that group performance is optimized when team members have a transactive memory system in place.[5]

As noted earlier, an assumption based on the use of teams or groups is that members of a team are more able to deal with complex problems than are individuals because team members are able to pool their knowledge. For cross-functional teams to be effective, team members must often understand the total process of operations within the organization (e.g., manufacturing, procurement, research and development) in addition to maintaining their own technical-specific expertise.[6] Cross-functional teams add value to organizations when team members are able to integrate specific individual technical knowledge and develop team knowledge.[7] It is not surprising that recent research indicates that the most effective teams are not necessarily those that have the most diverse set of knowledge, but rather those that are most able to integrate individual specific knowledge within the team.[8] Recall from the "Research in Action" in Chapter 6 that high-performing teams tended to have a more complete understanding of their expertise resources—their transactive memory—than do their lower performing counterparts.

Recently researchers have focused on expanding transactive memory systems to include team members' accessibility of knowledge from outside the group[9]—that is, knowledge of how to find knowledge, which includes

---

3. Austin, J. R. (2000). *Knowing what and whom other people know: Linking transactive memory with external connections in organizational groups.* Paper presented to the Academy of Management, Organization Behavior Division, Toronto; Moreland, R. L. (1999). Transactive memory: Learning who knows what in work groups and organizations. In L. L. Thompson, J. M. Levine, & D. M. Messick (Eds.), *Shared cognition in organizations: The management of knowledge* (pp. 3–31). Mahwah, NJ: Lawrence Erlbaum Associates; and Gruenfeld, D. H., Mannix, E. A., Williams, K. Y., & Neale, M. A. (1996). Group composition and decision making: How member familiarity and information distribution affect process and performance. *Organizational Behavior and Human Decision Processes, 67,* 1–15.

4. Wegner, D. M. (1986). Transactive memory: A contemporary analysis of the group mind. In B. Mullen & G. R. Goethals (Eds.), *Theories of group behavior* (pp. 185–205). New York: Springer-Verlag.

5. Fisher, K., & Fisher, M. D. (1998). *The distributed mind: Achieving high performance through the collective intelligence of knowledge work teams.* New York: AMACOM.

6. Austin, *Knowing what and whom other people know.*

7. Gruenfeld, Mannix, Williams, & Neale. *Group composition and decision making.*

8. Austin, *Knowing what and whom other people know.*

9. Moreland, *Transactive memory.*

knowing who knows whom. John Austin claimed that for cross-functional teams to be effective, it is not only important that members know who knows what, but also that they know whom others know; Austin called this **situated expertise.** Situated expertise includes the group's transactive memory system and an understanding of group members' external ties. For example, groups that have external ties possess a large pool of expertise from which to draw when faced with a problem.[10] Situated expertise becomes important when we consider that the strength of a group is grounded not only in what members do while working within the group but also in what members do while working outside the group.[11] For teams to be effective, team members must have an accurate account of group knowledge that includes knowing what other members know as well as who they know.

Austin's research shows that groups are less effective if these knowledge resources are not used when team members are solving problems in non-group settings. In particular, higher levels of the group's situated expertise are related to higher levels of performance (e.g., greater collaborative efforts, lower turnover, greater use of external resources to solve problems). This research emphasizes the importance of training team members to develop transactive memory systems that include accessing external resources in problem solving efforts.

TYPES OF GROUP DECISIONS

Given the advantages of group decision making suggested so far and the number of skilled individuals in a typical organization, perhaps all decisions should be made by groups. Yet, many decisions are made by only one or two key individuals. So if group decision making has so many benefits, why isn't it used much more in organizations? There are several reasons for this, and one is that not all types of decisions can benefit from the unique contributions of a group.

Group decision making is usually superior to individual decision making when judgments need to be made about uncertain events. Such decisions are primarily concerned with quality outcomes and usually have the following characteristics:

- The potential benefits are substantial, the costs of error are high, and it is difficult to reverse or salvage a poor decision after action has begun.
- Information is incomplete or uncertain.
- Many feasible alternatives exist.
- Identifying the optimal alternative is difficult.
- Feedback about results from the chosen alternative will not be available until long after the decision has been implemented.[12]

When solving a problem involves generating many or unique ideas, recalling information accurately, and evaluating ambiguous or uncertain situations, then a group is likely to outperform individuals. As pointed out in this chapter's

---

10. Austin, *Knowing what and whom other people know*, p. 7.

11. Austin, *Knowing what and whom other people know*.

12 Zand, D. E. (1974). Collateral organizations: A new strategy. *Journal of Applied Behavioral Science, 10,* 63–89.

opening vignette, using a group produced more than 100 ideas in about 8 minutes. One individual would probably not have arrived at so many suggestions in such a short period of time. If group members can perform their jobs relatively independently of each other, individual decision making is probably appropriate. If, however, group members are interdependent and must cooperate with each other, then effective performance is likely to hinge on their ability to coordinate their decisions.[13]

Groups have been shown to produce judgmental decisions of generally higher quality than individuals,[14] but the need for high-quality decisions is not the sole reason to involve a group. Another important factor is whether acceptance of the decision is necessary for its successful implementation. As mentioned previously, a major benefit of group decision making is that members of the organization are usually more willing to accept a decision for which they participated in the decision-making process.

PARTICIPATIVE DECISION MAKING

Should organizations involve their employees in the decision-making process? This question has been debated for decades. The main point of contention is whether participative decision making results in higher performance.

Just as certain decisions are better suited to group decision making, the decision to involve others in the decision-making process also depends on a number of factors. These include such issues as the abilities of the group members, their willingness to search for and share information, and the nature of the decision to be made. Research indicates that if we ignore these considerations, participative decision making results in no increases in productivity, yet it may have an impact on employee satisfaction.[15]

Participative decision making can be categorized by various dimensions. The first is the basis for including the employee in the decision-making process. A primary rationale is that individuals have a right to take part in making decisions that will affect their jobs and, thus, their lives.

The second dimension is the structure of the employee participation, which may be formal or informal. Formal decision-making structures have rules about who participates, which decisions are open to discussion, and the process to be used in making the decisions. Informal structures have fewer and less explicit rules.[16] If an employee is elected to represent other workers on a work-safety committee, the employee's role in the decision-making process is as a formal participant. However, if the supervisor asks the employee's opinion on a particular work-safety issue, the employee's role is informal; it is based not on the employee's position but on his or her personal relationship with the supervisor.

13. Sashkin, M. (1976). Changing toward participative management approaches: A model and methods. *Academy of Management Review, 1,* 75–86.

14. Murnighan, J. K. (1981). Group decision making: What strategy should you use? *Management Review,* 55–62; and Laughlin, P., & McGlynn, R. (1986). Collective induction: Mutual group and individual influence by exchange of hypotheses and evidence. *Journal of Experimental Social Psychology, 22,* 567–589.

15. Locke, E. A. & Schweiger, D. M. (1979). Participative decision making: One more look. *Research in Organizational Behavior, 1,* 265–339.

16. Black, S. J., & Gregersen, H. B. (1997). Participative decision-making: An integration of multiple dimensions. *Human Relations, 50,* 859–879.

The third dimension is whether the participation is direct or indirect. As members of a quality circle, individuals have the opportunity to make their views known directly. Alternatively, when people vote for representatives (who, in turn, participate directly in decision making), they are indirect participants in the decision-making process.

Finally, the fourth dimension of employee participation is whether it is voluntary or involuntary. Participation can be forced through laws, government regulation, or decree. When a union is certified, for example, both management and labor must participate in contract negotiations. Before creating policies, many government regulations require citizen input. Thus, because of the nature of the political system, people must, at times, participate in decision making, regardless of their unique desires or preferences.

Employee characteristics also influence whether employee participation is useful. If employees have no knowledge of or interest in a decision, their input will probably do little to improve its outcome. In fact, expecting employees to participate in making decisions about which they have little knowledge or concern can increase their sense of frustration. Similarly, having too much participation can lead to lower performance, stress, and dissatisfaction.[17]

In some instances, however, participation is useful in increasing both employee satisfaction and performance. Employees are most likely to be satisfied when they participate in decision making that leads to a favorable outcome.[18] In a manufacturing plant, for example, employees are likely to be more satisfied with the implementation of a new pay structure if they have been allowed to have input in the decision-making process.[19]

PROBLEMS WITH GROUP DECISION MAKING

Although participative decision making has great potential for improving morale and performance in organizations, it also has inherent pitfalls. One obvious concern is that groups take considerably more time to reach decisions than do individuals. This is because group decision making involves increased demands for information processing, rules, and complex interpersonal processes.[20]

GREATER COMPLEXITY

INFORMATION-PROCESSING DEMANDS. Any decision involves complex processes, but the complexity is multiplied when more parties are involved.[21] Having more decision makers may mean that there are greater op-

17. Hespe, G., & Wall, T. (1976). The demand for participation among employees. *Human Relations, 29,* 411–429.
18. Black & Gregersen, Participative decision-making.
19. Black & Gregersen, Participative decision-making.
20. Bazerman, M. H., Mannix, E. A., & Thompson, L. L. (1988). Groups as mixed motive negotiations. In E. J. Lawler & B. Markovsky (Eds.), *Advances in group processes: Theory and research* (Vol. 5). Greenwich, CT: JAI.
21. Bazerman, M. H. (1998). *Judgment in managerial decision making.* (4th ed., p. 153). New York: Wiley.

portunities for creative solutions, but it can also generate greater cognitive demands on each member of the group.

DECISION-MAKING RULES. Individuals in groups must decide such issues as how dissenting opinions will be incorporated into a group decision. In addition, there must be rules such as whether decisions require consensus, a majority, and so on, all of which can influence the decision-making process.

Groups can make decisions in a number of ways, including by a lack of response.[22] In this case, any alternative for which no one voices a preference is dropped from consideration. The idea for which there is support is the one that is accepted.

Groups can also reach a decision by authority rule. In this case, the leader of the group makes the decision based on discussion in the group. The group plays an advisory role to the decision maker.

In yet another arrangement, a small subset of the group's membership convinces the other members of the group to accept an alternative it favors. This is also known as *railroading* a decision.

A common way that groups reach decisions is by majority rule, whose primary mechanism is voting. The problem here is that there are clear winners and losers. The losers may feel left out, given that they did not support the decision that was made, which may lead to difficulties in its implementation.

Finally, the last two mechanisms by which groups can make decisions are consensus and unanimity. Although these mechanisms are similar in outcome—all group members accept the final decision—in reaching consensus, the group acknowledges that there may be dissension among members of the group. By contrast, unanimity occurs when all group members agree on the course of action to be taken.

Each of these approaches to decision making has benefits and costs. If a group member knows that to get a particular solution to a problem, the members of the group need to convince the majority, that member's strategy is likely to be very different than if all members of the group must reach an agreement (unanimity).[23]

COMPLEX INTERPERSONAL PROCESSES. The greater the number of individuals involved in the decision-making process, the wider the range of skills, abilities, and knowledge available to produce an effective solution. However, the larger the group, the greater the potential number of interpersonal relationships. In a larger group, subgroups and coalitions are likely to form, and there is increased potential for conflict.[24] Culture can also have an effect on the dynamics of group decision making, as highlighted in "INTERNATIONAL FOCUS ON: Decision Making."

As mentioned previously, decisions requiring judgments about uncertain events or widespread acceptance are prime candidates for group decision making; the benefits of the final decision are worth the additional complexity involved in getting a group to make the decision. However, groups are often required to make a variety of decisions, whether or not the final result merits

22. Thompson, L. L., Mannix, E. A., & Bazerman, M. H. (1988). Group negotiation: Effects of decision rule, agenda, and aspiration. *Journal of Personality and Social Psychology, 54*, 86–95.
23. Thompson, Mannix, & Bazerman, Group negotiation.
24. Goleman, D. (1988, June 7). Why meetings sometimes don't work. *New York Times*, p. B1.

INTERNATIONAL FOCUS ON DECISION MAKING

GROUP DECISION MAKING IN MEXICO. In the traditional Mexican workplace, managers made the vast majority of decisions, set goals, and resolved conflicts, and workers expected to be given instructions and decision making to be based on status roles. The highly centralized nature of decision making in traditional Mexican companies, many of which were controlled by individual families, reflected Mexico's past and the hierarchical nature of the society.

Paternalistic and hierarchical, management in these traditional companies was at odds with the behaviors of delegation, trust, support, and information sharing required by management in a self-managed work team environment. Nonetheless, leading companies in Mexico have implemented team-based work systems, and many other Mexican companies have explored these techniques as a possible way to increase their competitiveness.

Not surprisingly, the implementation of self-managed work teams has proved to be a challenge for Mexican managers and workers. One of the most apparent cultural hurdles is that some Mexican managers have difficulty accepting the philosophy of power sharing that underlies self-managed teamwork and thus the behavioral requirements of information sharing and trust.

Further, while favoring a collectivist environment, Mexican workers place strong value on minimizing confrontation and individual risk taking. As a result, they tend to be hesitant to confront one another or to express disagreement that could be interpreted as personal criticism. Although this preference is conducive to collaboration, confrontation is often a necessary ingredient of successful teamwork.

Although team-based work systems are a common occurrence in U.S. organizations, their use cannot be assumed in companies all over the world. This is the situation with Mexican organizations that are in the process of implementing such work systems. Due to the traditional hierarchical structure of Mexican organizations, it is not surprising that implementing a work team environment has confronted some obstacles.

Source: Excerpted from Nicholls, C. E., Lane, H. W., & Brechu, M. B. (1999). Taking self-managed teams to Mexico. *Academy of Management Executive, 13*(3), 15–27.

---

the group's attention. Consider the following classic example of a family decision about whether to take a trip to Abilene:

> The July afternoon in Coleman, Texas, was particularly hot—104 degrees, as measured by the Walgreen's Rexall Ex-Lax temperature gauge. In addition, the wind was blowing fine-grained West Texas topsoil through the house. But the afternoon was still tolerable— even potentially enjoyable. There was a fan going on the back porch; there was cold lemonade; and finally there was entertainment. Dominoes. Perfect for the conditions. The game required little more physical exertion than an occasional mumbled comment, "shuffle 'em," and an unhurried movement of the arm to place the spots in the appropriate perspective on the table. All in all, it had the makings of an agreeable Sunday afternoon in Coleman—that is, until my father-in-law suddenly said, "Let's get in the car and go to Abilene and have dinner in the cafeteria."
>
> I thought: What, go to Abilene? Fifty-three miles? In a dust storm and heat? In an un-air-conditioned 1958 Buick?
>
> But my wife chimed in with "Sounds like a great idea. I'd like to go. How about you, Jerry?" Since my own preferences were obviously out of step with the rest, I replied, "Sounds good to me," and added, "I just hope your mother wants to go."

"Of course I want to go," said my mother-in-law. "I haven't been to Abilene in a long time."

So into the car and off to Abilene we went. My predictions were fulfilled. The heat was brutal. We were coated with a fine layer of dust that was cemented with perspiration by the time we arrived. The food at the cafeteria provided first-rate testimonial material for antacid commercials.

Some four hours and 106 miles later, we returned to Coleman, hot and exhausted. We sat in front of the fan for a long time in silence. Then, both to be sociable and to break the silence, I said, "It was a great trip, wasn't it?"

No one spoke.

Finally, my mother-in-law said, with some irritation, "Well, to tell the truth, I really didn't enjoy it much and would rather have stayed here. I just went along because the three of you were so enthusiastic about going. I wouldn't have gone if you all hadn't pressured me into it."

I couldn't believe it. "What do you mean, 'you all'?" I said. "Don't put me in the 'you all' group. I was delighted to be doing what we were doing. I only went to satisfy the rest of you. You're the culprits."

My wife looked shocked. "Don't call me a culprit. You and Daddy and Momma were the ones who wanted to go. I just went along to be sociable and to keep you happy. I would have had to be crazy to go out in heat like that."

Her father entered the conversation abruptly. "Hell!" he said.

He proceeded to expand on what was already absolutely clear. "Listen, I never wanted to go to Abilene. I just thought you might be bored. You visit so seldom I wanted to be sure you enjoyed it. I would have preferred to play another game of dominoes and eat the leftovers in the icebox."

After the outburst of recrimination, we all sat back in silence. Here we were, four reasonably sensible people who, of our own volition, had just taken a 106-mile trip across a godforsaken desert in a furnace-like temperature through a cloudlike dust storm to eat unpalatable food at a hole-in-the-wall cafeteria in Abilene, when none of us had really wanted to go. In fact, to be more accurate, we'd done just the opposite of what we wanted to do. The whole situation simply did not make sense.[25]

Although larger groups have a higher potential for conflict than do smaller groups, such conflict can be a double-edged sword. On the one hand, when managed properly, conflict can be functional to the team's decision-making process. Research has shown, for instance, that conflict can improve the quality of decision making because more solutions are identified and considered. On the other hand, conflict among group members can create negative feelings, dissatisfaction, and less cooperation in the group.[26]

25. Harvey, J. (1974, Summer). Managing agreements in organizations: The Abilene paradox. *Organizational Dynamics*, 63–80.

26. Brockmann, E. (1996). Removing the paradox of conflict from group decisions. *Academy of Management Executive, 10*(2), 61–62.

Dilemmas such as the one experienced by the family that took the trip to Abilene are typical of problems that can derail even the best of workgroups when faced with conflict. The resources of taking the trip may be minimal, but the same factors can work to offset the benefits of groups in making decisions.

GROUPTHINK

The family described in the preceding section took the trip to Abilene because of groupthink. First described by Irving Janis, **groupthink** occurs in highly cohesive groups in which the members have lost some of their willingness and ability to critically evaluate one another's ideas.[27] Groupthink involves an overemphasis on agreement and consensus and an unwillingness to critically evaluate alternative courses of action.

Examples of groupthink are found throughout U.S. history. The lack of preparedness of the U.S. Naval Forces for the Japanese attack on Pearl Harbor, President Kennedy's handling of the Bay of Pigs, and many of the roads paved for U.S. entry into and continued involvement in the Vietnam War are a few salient examples. By studying such examples, Janis identified a number of symptoms that should signal decision makers to a potential "groupthink situation." See Figure 8-1 for a summarization of Janis's work.

CHOICE-SHIFT EFFECTS

Consider the following situation: You are one of six members of the research and development advisory committee for a large computer software company. During your monthly meeting, your task is to determine which projects are to be funded. One of the decisions facing your group in tomorrow's meeting is whether to fund a $12.2 million request for the development of a new accounting software program. The product is predicted to be so much better than the competition that the company will generate a minimum 50% return on its investment in the first 2 years of production. Other projects are also competing for resource dollars, but their expected rates of return are between 10% and 20%. What minimum probability for success would you consider necessary to invest the money in the accounting software product? Should this decision be made by a group or by an individual? That is, which approach will result in a higher probability of success for the company?

In such cases, research suggests that groups behave in a more risky manner than would the average individual member of the group.[28] The group as a whole and each individual in it will be more willing to accept greater levels of risk after group discussion than before it. This is known as the **risky shift.**

27. Janis, I. (1982). *Victims of groupthink: A psychological study of foreign policy decisions and fiascoes.* Boston: Houghton Mifflin.

28. Stoner, A. (1961). *A comparison of individual and group decisions involving risk.* Unpublished master's thesis, Massachusetts Institute of Technology, Sloan School of Industrial Management, Cambridge, MA; and Lamm, H., & Myers, D. G. (1978). Group-induced polarization of attitudes and behavior. In L. Berkowitz (Ed.), *Group-induced polarization of attitudes and behavior* (Vol. 11). New York: Academic Press.

Groupthink	■ **FIGURE 8-1**

Groupthink occurs when the members of a highly cohesive group lose their willingness to evaluate each other's inputs critically. The symptoms of groupthink listed here can be avoided by following several procedural guidelines for appropriate group discussion and choices.

Symptoms of Groupthink:

■ **Illusions of invulnerability:** Members of the group overemphasize the strength of the group and feel that they are beyond criticism or attack. This symptom leads the group to approve risky actions about which individual members might have serious concerns.

■ **Illusions of unanimity:** Group members accept consensus prematurely, without testing whether all members really agree. Silence is often taken for agreement.

■ **Illusions of group morality:** Members feel that the group is "right" and above reproach by outside members. Thus, members feel no need to debate ethical issues.

■ **Stereotyping of the "enemy" as weak, evil, or stupid:** Members do not realistically examine their competitors, and they oversimplify their motives. The stated aims of outside groups or anticipated reactions of outsiders are not considered.

■ **Self-censorship by members:** Members refuse to communicate concerns to others because they fear disturbing the consensus.

■ **Mind-guarding:** Some members take responsibility to ensure that negative feedback does not reach influential group members.

■ **Direct pressure:** In the unlikely event that a note of caution or concern is interjected, other members quickly respond with pressure to bring the deviant back into line.

Guidelines for Avoiding Groupthink:

■ Assign each group member the role of critical evaluator and encourage the sharing of objections.

■ As the leader, avoid clear statements about your preferred solution or decision.

■ Create subgroups or subcommittees, each working on the same problem.

■ Require that members of the group make use of the information available to them through their subordinates, peers, and networks.

■ Invite outside experts to observe and evaluate group processes and outcomes.

■ Assign a member to play the devil's advocate role at each meeting.

■ Focus on alternative scenarios for the motivation and intentions of competitors.

■ After the group reaches consensus, reexamine the next (but unchosen) alternative, comparing it to the chosen course of action.

Source: Janis, I. L. (1982). *Groupthink* (2nd ed.). Boston: Houghton Mifflin.

Yet groups do not always make such shifts. In fact, documentation indicates that just the opposite can occur—namely, a **cautious shift.** A cautious shift occurs when group members make less risky decisions than would the average individual member.

Research suggests that individuals shift to more extreme positions following group discussion because members holding the dominant view (either risky or cautious) exchange information during the discussion and are exposed to views they had not previously considered. Further, individuals

RESEARCH IN ACTION
GROUP DECISION MAKING AND INTERCULTURAL RELATIONS

Maddy Janssens, Katholieke Universiteit Leuven;
Maddy.Janssens@econ.kuleuven.ac.be

The HR manager of a Belgian-based multinational pharmaceutical company contacted Jeanne M. Brett (of Northwestern University), Ludo Keunen (a management consultant), and me to undertake a study on group decision making and intercultural relations between the different national groups within the company.

Based on the data gathered, we identified four issues that influenced decision making in intercultural teams and formulated these issues as challenges for management. The first challenge was to find a new equilibrium with respect to internationalization. Until then the company had adopted a multiregional approach, leaving a high degree of autonomy to the different affiliates. Consequently, there were high costs and no synergies between different regions, particularly in the areas of marketing and research and development. Both the United States and Japan were growing in importance as regions within the organization, and this transition of power seemed to lead to job as well as status insecurities for the employees in Brussels.

Managing these insecurities was a second identified challenge. Belgian employees felt that their jobs were not secure because they feared that R&D would be relocated to the U.S., as had happened in some other pharmaceutical companies. These insecurities led to the third challenge—being aware of language and nationality as tools of the power game. Although English is the business language of the company, it was not the native language of most employees. Consequently, even people who were quite fluent in the working language sometimes had difficulties understanding the subtle nuances of expression. This led to misinterpretations and attributions of other people as being blunt, rude, and insincere.

The last challenge we identified referred to the need to legitimize cultural and contextual differences. Because the U.S. operates in a much more strict regulatory environment than Belgium, the Americans expected very high-quality standards, which were not always met by Belgian reports. Belgian team members approached the task pragmatically and wanted to rely on informal relationships to get things done, whereas the U.S. team members preferred to rely strictly on formal procedures and channels.

The findings of this study led to several changes in this company. First, the CEO asked us to write a brochure on valuing cultural diversity in which we described critical intercultural skills. This brochure was distributed to all high-level managers, with the purpose of increasing awareness about the potential pitfalls and synergies of cultural differences. Simultaneously, the human resources department organized training programs about remote management, with attention to the use of information technology. The strategic committee became more internationalized, eventually having two American, one Dutch, one Swiss, one Japanese, one German, and three Belgian team members. The company is currently pursuing a policy of short-term international assignments of up to 3 months in several locations as a way for employees to learn to better understand the different cultures. The human resources department also organized succession planning, in which upper management from all over the world was evaluated by an international decision-making body. This evaluation will lead to managers' transfer or promotion to different places in the world, depending on their skills.

may shift their perspectives so as to be more in synch with the group's attitudes. If the group favors risk, then the individual may see the advantages of being perceived as being even more risk seeking than the group, thus being seen as being idiosyncratic.[29]

However, these notions do little to aid managers in predicting whether a group will tend toward a cautious or a risky shift. Research has suggested a different explanation for this choice-shift phenomenon that incorporates the decision biases discussed in Chapter 4.[30] It seems that whether groups shift toward risk or toward caution depends on how the decision is framed. They tend to become less cautious in positively framed situations and more cautious in negatively framed situations.[31] For example, when an individual considers a decision involving potential gains, he or she is risk averse rather than risk neutral. Thus, a group in this situation may appear to be shifting toward risk when, in reality, it is simply behaving in a risk-neutral manner.

The same logic can apply to the cautious shift. When individuals are confronted with decisions involving potential losses, they are risk seeking rather than risk neutral. Groups may appear to be less risky when, in fact, they are simply behaving in a risk-neutral manner. Although these findings are tentative, they are compatible with the belief that group decision making is often superior to individual decision making. The broad topic of whether group decision making can reduce the vulnerability of decision makers to cognitive bias is beginning to receive attention.[32]

SOLUTIONS IN GROUP DECISION MAKING

There are several ways in which a manager can make decisions. He or she may unilaterally make the decision based solely on the information at hand, unilaterally make the decision but solicit input on the problem from others, or involve others in both providing input and making the actual decision. Because the goal of a manager is to make a good decision—one that is timely, acceptable, implementable, and high in quality—it is critical that the manager be able to use these three levels of participative decision making when they are most appropriate and most likely to produce a good decision.

WHEN TO USE GROUP DECISION MAKING

LEVELS OF PARTICIPATION IN DECISION MAKING. Victor Vroom and Philip Yetton have developed guidelines to help managers choose the most appropriate decision-making methods in a variety of situations encountered

29. Burnstein, E. (1983). Persuasion as argument processing. In M. Brandstatter, J. Davis, & G. Stocker-Kreschgauer (Eds.), *Group decision process.* London: Academic Press.

30. Neale, M. A., Bazerman, M. H., Northcraft, G. B., & Alperson, C. A. (1986). Choice shift's effects in group decisions: A decision bias perspective. *International Journal of Small Group Research 2,* 33–42.

31. Bazerman, M. H. (1998). *Judgment in managerial decision making* (4th ed.), New York: Wiley, p. 149.

32. Neale, Bazerman, Northcraft, & Alperson, Choice shift's effects in group decisions.

in daily activities. They divide the three levels of participative decision making as follows:

1 Authoritative
   - ■ **AI.** In this, the most authoritarian decision-making level, the manager solves the problem or makes the decision based on information available at that time.
   - ■ **AII.** The manager obtains the necessary information from subordinates or peers and then makes the decision.
2 Consultative
   - ■ **CI.** The manager conveys the problem to relevant peers or subordinates, soliciting their ideas and suggestions without bringing them together as a group. Although the other group members have input, the manager makes the decision, which may or may not reflect the others' influence.
   - ■ **CII.** The manager conveys the problem to subordinates or peers, soliciting their ideas and suggestions as a group. While the group members may collectively make suggestions and provide input, the manager still makes the decision, which may or may not reflect the input of the group.
3 Group Decision Making
   - ■ **G.** The manager conveys the problem to subordinates and peers as a group, and the group, through consensus, determines the final solution.

From the manager's perspective, then, the first aspect of making a decision is deciding who will be in the cast of characters that determines the solution. Consider the following problem:

> You are the head of the staff unit reporting to the vice president of finance. He has asked you to provide a report on the firm's current portfolio to include recommendations for changes in the selection criteria currently used. Doubts have been raised about the efficiency of the existing system, given current market conditions, and there is considerable dissatisfaction with the prevailing rates of return.
>
> You plan to write a report, but at the moment, you are quite perplexed about the approach you should take. Your own specialty is the bond market, and it is quite clear to you that a detailed knowledge of the equity market—which you lack—would greatly enhance the value of the report. Fortunately, four members of your staff are specialists in different segments of the equity market. Together, they possess a vast amount of knowledge about the intricacies of investment. However, they seldom agree on the best way to achieve anything when it comes to the stock market. Although they are obviously conscientious and knowledgeable, they have major differences when it comes to investment philosophy and strategy.
>
> You have six weeks before the report is due. You have already begun to familiarize yourself with the firm's current portfolio and have been provided by management with a specific set of constraints that any portfolio must satisfy. Your immediate problem is to come up with some alternatives to the firm's present practices

| **Problem Characteristics and Diagnostic Questions in the Vroom and Yetton Model** | ■ **FIGURE 8-2** |

1 The importance of the quality of the decision:
   Is there a quality requirement such that one solution is likely to be more rational than another?
2 The extent to which the leader possesses sufficient information or expertise to make a high-quality decision alone:
   Do I have sufficient information to make a high-quality decision?
3 The extent to which the problem is structured:
   Is the problem structured? Do I know what information is required and where it is located?
4 The extent to which acceptance or commitment on the part of the subordinates is critical to the effective implementation of the decision:
   Is acceptance of the decision by subordinates critical to effective implementation? Can I do it without their support?
5 The probability that my autocratic decision will receive acceptance by subordinates:
   If I were to make the decision by myself, is it reasonably certain that it will be accepted by my subordinates?
6 The extent to which the subordinates are motivated to attain the organizational goals as represented in statement of the problem:
   Do subordinates share the organization goals to be obtained in solving this problem? Or do they have personal considerations that might dominate?
7 The extent to which subordinates are likely to be in conflict over preferred solutions:
   Is conflict among subordinates likely in preferred solutions?

Source: Vroom, & Yetton, *Leadership and decision making.*

and select the most promising for detailed analysis in your report. Given this problem, would you make your decision using AI, AII, CI, CII, or G?[33]

PROBLEM CHARACTERISTICS. Vroom and Yetton suggested that the correct level of participation in decision making depends on various characteristics of the problem at hand.[34] They identified seven characteristics that can be used to diagnose the problem and to determine what level of decision making should be used. The seven characteristics and their associated questions are listed in Figure 8-2. These characteristics are arranged in the form of questions on a decision tree. The end of each path identifies the optimal level of participation recommended. The full decision tree is illustrated in Figure 8-3. Although each path ends with a specific level of participation, Vroom and Yetton suggested that when there is enough time, the manager may choose an option in the feasible set that lends itself to greater participation by subordinates. That is, when the decision suggests that an autocratic solution is appropriate, the manager may use a more participative style—C or G; when a consultative solution is appropriate, the manager may also use G.

33. Vroom, V. H., & Yetton, P. (1973). *Leadership and decision making.* Pittsburgh, PA: University of Pittsburg Press.
34. Vroom, & Yetton, *Leadership and decision making.*

■ **FIGURE 8-3** | **Decision Tree for Determining Appropriate Decision Strategy**

1 Does the problem possess a quality requirement?
2 Do I have sufficient information to make a high-quality decision?
3 Is the problem structured?
4 Is acceptance of the decision by subordinates important for effective implementation?
5 If I were to make the decision by myself, am I reasonably certain that my subordinates will accept it?
6 Do subordinates share the organizational goals to be attained in solving this problem?
7 Is conflict among subordinates likely in preferred solutions?

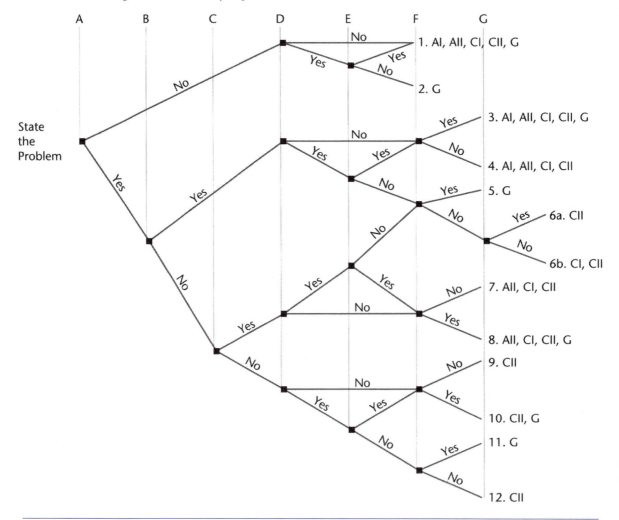

Source: Vroom, & Yetton, *Leadership and decision making.*

Now let's consider the problem facing you, the manager. Examining the problem from the perspective of the Vroom and Yetton decision tree in Figure 8–3, the first question concerns a quality requirement: Is one solution likely to be significantly better than others? In the case of the stock portfolio, the answer is yes. The second question concerns whether you have sufficient information to make the decision on your own. Clearly, you do not. Since the problem is not a structured one, the last question you will have to answer is whether acceptance by subordinates is critical to implementation. Because your superiors will implement the decision, acceptance of the solution by subordinates is irrelevant. This particular path ends after the fourth question and indicates that you should use the CII level of participation. Thus, you should involve subordinates as a group to offer ideas and suggestions, but make the final decision as to the preferred stock portfolio selection criteria yourself.

Vroom and Yetton found that managers who had been trained to use these problem characteristics to diagnose the optimal level of participation in decision making were better able to classify decision problems and choose appropriate levels of participation than were managers without such training.[35] Evidence also indicates that the effectiveness of decision making increases when managers are skilled at determining their correct levels of participation.[36]

THE VROOM-JAGO MODEL OF PARTICIPATION IN DECISION MAKING.[37]
Vroom and Arthur Jago presented an extended and more complex version of the Vroom-Yetton model. The new model extends the Vroom-Yetton model in two ways. First, the manager must consider 12 situational characteristics instead of 7, increasing the levels of situational analysis. Additionally, instead of the original yes/no question format in the Vroom-Yetton model, the Vroom-Jago model presents 10 of the characteristics on a 5-point scale, which increases the precision of the evaluation. A study of three separate samples of manager-reported decisions using the Vroom-Jago model found that the new model is also a valid model for decision making.

HOW TO USE GROUP DECISION MAKING

After the number of individuals to be involved in making a decision has been determined, the next step is to determine how the group is to reach a decision. In selecting a particular group decision-making process, the intent is to minimize the liabilities of groups and maximize their benefits. Three techniques are described here: brainstorming, nominal group technique, and the Delphi technique.[38]

BRAINSTORMING. An advertising executive developed the process of **brainstorming** more than 40 years ago as a means of enhancing creativity by encouraging the free discussion and exchange of ideas. Participants in brainstorming sessions are encouraged to produce as many and as creative a set of ideas or alternatives as possible, and they are simultaneously prohibited from being critical of the ideas being generated. The opening vignette in this chapter is an example of a group using computer software to brainstorm ideas. As noted in that vignette, an electronic meeting is an especially good

35. Vroom, A new look in managerial decision making, pp. 66–80.

36. See, for example, Vroom, V. H., & Jago, A. G. (1978). On the validity of the Vroom-Yetton model. *Journal of Applied Psychology, 63*, 151–162; and Filed, R. H. (1982). A test of the Vroom-Yetton normative model of leadership. *Journal of Applied Psychology, 67*, 523–532.

37. Field, R. H. G., & Andrews, J. P. (1998). Testing the incremental validity of the Vroom-Jago versus the Vroom-Yetton models of participation in decision making. *Journal of Behavioral Decision Making, 11*, 251–261.

38. See, for example, Osborn, A. F. (1957). *Applied imagination.* New York: Scribner's; and Delbecq, A. L., Van de Ven, A. L. & Gustafson, D. H. (1975). *Group techniques for program planning: A guide to nominal groups and Delphi techniques.* Glenview, IL: Scott, Foresman.

TECHNOLOGY FOCUS ON PIGGYBACKING

INVENTION AT MCI. Vinton Cerf, senior vice president for internet architecture and technology at MCI WorldCom is a proponent of the jujitsu method of innovation. Jujitsu teaches you to take advantage of your opponent's momentum. Cerf likes to take advantage of what already exists—to grab the intellectual momentum and then use it to advance an application into the mainstream. When Cerf and Robert Kahn were creating TCP/IP (a set of protocols that makes it possible to link various networks around the world), they decided not to require the networks that support it to change in any way. Instead, they took advantage of what already existed and thereby avoided adding another layer of complexity.

People often take the view that standardization is the enemy of creativity. But standards help make creativity possible by allowing for the establishment of an infrastructure, which then leads to enormous entrepreneurialism, creativity, and competitiveness.

When it comes to innovation, the question is not how to innovate but how to invite ideas. How do you invite your brain to encounter thoughts that you might not otherwise encounter? Creative people let their minds wander, and they mix ideas freely. Innovation often comes from unexpected juxtapositions, from connecting subjects that aren't necessarily related.

Another way to generate ideas is to treat a problem as though it were generic. If you're experiencing a particular problem, odds are that other people are experiencing it, too. Generate a solution, and you may have an innovation.

Source: Excerpted from Rosenfeld, J. (2000, April). Here's an idea. *Fast Company, 33,* 106.

way to maintain objectivity of ideas, as the sources of the ideas can remain anonymous. When practiced correctly, brainstorming separates the evaluative stage from the idea-generation stage of decision making. The basic structure of a brainstorming session is determined by four rules[39]:

1 **No criticism!** Adverse judgments about your own or others' ideas are to be withheld.
2 **"Freewheeling" is invited.** No idea is too wild or crazy. The more creative or unusual the idea, the better.
3 **Quantity is desired**. Generate as many ideas as possible. The greater the number of ideas, the greater the likelihood that one will work.
4 **"Piggybacking" is encouraged.** Participants should build on the ideas and suggestions of others. Combining and extending other ideas is a critical aspect of successful brainstorming.

As illustrated in "TECHNOLOGY FOCUS ON: Piggybacking," building on the ideas of others is an important business strategy.

The primary intent of brainstorming is to reduce participants' fears of criticism and provide multiple sources of stimulation for creative problem solving. In general, brainstorming works to improve the quantity and quality of ideas or alternatives generated. However, for brainstorming to work, evaluation and criticism must be suppressed until all ideas are on the table.[40]

Recent research has led researchers to conclude that face-to-face brainstorming is not as effective as once believed. In particular, the researchers

---

39. See, for example, Osborn, *Applied imagination;* and Delbecq, Van de Ven, & Gustafson, *Group techniques for program planning.*
40. Parnes, S. J., Noller, R. B., & Biondi, A. M. (1977). *A guide to creative action.* New York: Scribner's.

pointed to three factors that contributes to a loss of productivity. They label the first factor *evaluation apprehension*—namely, members of the group may become concerned about what other members will think, leading to a reluctance to express ideas. The second factor that can inhibit brainstorming is free-riding or social loafing. Research has demonstrated that individuals in groups tend to put less effort into solving a problem than do individuals who are attempting to solve a problem on their own. Finally, production blocking can occur. In other words, while listening to others talk, individuals may stop generating ideas, thus hampering constructive thinking.[41]

As noted in the opening vignette, electronic brainstorming has been gaining attention as an alternative to face-to-face brainstorming. Individuals work on a problem simultaneously, communicating via computer. Participants can therefore see what others are suggesting as solutions but don't have to wait their turns to respond. Electronic brainstorming produces more ideas per person than face-to-face brainstorming, and individual loss of productivity does not seem to be a problem.[42]

NOMINAL GROUP TECHNIQUE. Whereas brainstorming focuses on generating new and creative ideas, the **nominal group technique (NGT)** focuses on generating alternatives and selecting among them. Conducted within the context of a group meeting, NGT includes the following steps:

1 Individuals silently and independently write down their ideas and alternative solutions to a stated problem.
2 All members take turns presenting their ideas, and these ideas are recorded on a chart or chalkboard.
3 The ideas are discussed only in terms of clarification. Evaluative comments are not allowed.
4 A written voting procedure is used to rank the alternatives.

The exact voting procedure is determined in advance, and the alternative that receives the most votes is selected. One advantage of this technique is that it restricts conflict and promotes acceptance. However, it appears that the quality of the decision may not be as high with NGT as when brainstorming is used. In addition, because conflict is not expressed, a synthesis of views does not occur.[43] Although NGT has some drawbacks, it can be a very useful process in groups in which there is considerable inhibition, hostility, or a dominant individual.

THE DELPHI TECHNIQUE. For situations in which group members cannot meet face-to-face, the RAND Corporation developed a group decision-making technique that offers many of the benefits of face-to-face interaction. Like NGT, the **Delphi technique** minimizes the effects of different levels of status and influence on group decision making, but it does not require that the group members convene in the same physical space. Instead of reporting

---

41. Sutton, R. I., & Hargadon, A. (1996). Brainstorming groups in context: Effectiveness in a product design firm. *Administrative Science Quarterly, 41,* 685–719.
42. Sutton, & Hargadon, Brainstorming groups in context.
43. Amason, A. C. (1996). Distinguishing the effects of functional and dysfunctional conflict on strategic decision making: Resolving a paradox for top management teams. *Academy of Management Journal, 39,* 123–149; and Van de Ven, A. H., & Delbecq, A. L. (1974). The effectiveness of nominal, Delphi, and interacting group decision making processes. *Academy of Management Journal, 17,* 605–621.

and recording alternatives as in NGT, participants answer a series of questionnaires. A group might use the Delphi technique as follows:

1 The first questionnaire distributed to members identifies the problem and asks for alternative solutions to it.
2 The Delphi coordinator summarizes the solutions, and the summary is returned to participants in the form of a second questionnaire specifically designed to identify areas requiring further clarification and consideration.
3 The results of the second questionnaire are presented to the participants, who rate the various alternatives presented.
4 Members' ratings are tabulated, and a summary of the data and resulting decision is returned to the participants.

COMPARING GROUP DECISION-MAKING TECHNIQUES. NGT and the Delphi technique are very similar to one another. The primary differences lie in whether all the members of the group are physically present. The Delphi technique enables group members to remain anonymous (which is very helpful for particularly sensitive issues), but it requires considerably more time than NGT.

Group members who interact often spend much time developing interpersonal relationships, discussing tangential issues, and maintaining pressure for conformity. They also may be unduly influenced by the status, persuasiveness, or seniority of various group members.[44] Thus, when a manager is confronted with a problem in which the generation of creative alternatives is critical and criticism must be held to a minimum, NGT or the Delphi technique may be most appropriate.

As with any management technique, managers should not ignore the potential pitfalls of these methods. In using these two methods of group decision making, managers run three risks. First, because there is no opportunity for discussion and clarification, group members may lack understanding about the problem or the final solution. Second, it is difficult to arrive at a truly creative solution using these techniques because the ideas of the minority are usually not clarified. Third, because of the lack of face-to-face interaction, group members may not develop much or any commitment to the solution.[45]

Groups have a great deal to offer management in producing good decisions. However, it is important to bear in mind both the advantages and disadvantages of group decision making. The three methods discussed here are based on the notion that the effectiveness of group decision making is equal to the potential effectiveness of the combined inputs of the members, minus the losses in effectiveness that follow from the group processes plus the gains in effectiveness from group processes.[46] In other words:

Actual Effectiveness = Potential Effectiveness − Process Losses + Process Gains

44. Huber, G. P. (1980). *Managerial decision making.* Glenview, IL: Scott, Foresman.
45. Bartunek, J., & Murnighan, K. (1984). Nominal group techniques. *Group and Organizational Studies 9,* 417–432.
46. Hackman, J. R., & Morris, C. G. (1975). Group tasks, group interaction process, and group performance effectiveness. In L. Berkowitz (Ed.), *Advances in experimental social psychology* (Vol. 7). New York: Academic Press.

In this equation, *process gains* include many of the benefits of group decision making outlined early in this chapter, such as synergy, resource pooling, and task specialization. *Process losses* are the costs of group decision making, such as groupthink, undue social influence, and time.

WHY GROUP DECISION MAKING WORKS[47]

Since the Hawthorne studies that demonstrated the power of the informal structure of the work group, managers and organizational scholars have known that groups can have a profound influence on productivity. Why, then, has group decision making been so consistently avoided in favor of individual decision making?

A primary reason for this bias lies in the rationality notion, which assumes that the individual is the elemental unit of an organization. This traditional view of the dominance of the individual is consistent with the assumptions underlying much of U.S. culture. That is, great value and importance are placed on individual achievement. From the individual's perspective, organizations merely represent arenas in which to compete for individual recognition and satisfaction. At the same time, organizations need to control, or at least direct, individuals to meet common organizational objectives. In combination, the divergent orientations—the individual's, to achieve personal fulfillment, coupled with the organization's, to mold and direct activity—leads to constant tension between the organization and the individual.

With the discovery that groups could positively influence individual performance, groups took on new importance. Management began to see them as a way to relieve or reduce the tension between the individual and the organization, coordinate individual activities, and discipline and control nonconforming group members. However, organizations were not designed around groups. Rather, groups were tacked on to existing organizational structures—and these structures were based on the individual, not on the group. Groups tended to be slow and too democratic. In-groups formed that were hard for outsiders to penetrate, and groups diffused responsibility for decision making. Although management could never completely remove groups as a source of influence on organizational members, their importance in the structure of the organization remained ancillary. It is as if "someone had insisted that automobiles be designed to fit the existing terrain rather than build roads to adapt to the automobile."[48]

What might be the advantages of an organization designed around groups? First, this would reduce the need for organizational control, since the groups would supervise their members. Second, individuals would have many fewer units with which to interact. Rather than interact with each individual on the traditional organizational chart, group members would interact with many fewer units or groups, although each unit would be larger. Finally, the organization would realize such routine benefits of group interactions as increased cohesiveness, motivation, and commitment, and higher-quality decisions.

---

47. Much of this discussion is based on Leavitt, H. (1975). Suppose we took groups seriously. . . . In E. L. Cass & F. G. Zimmer (Eds.), *Man and work in society*. New York: Van Nostrand Reinhold.

48. Much of this discussion is based on Leavitt, Suppose we took groups seriously. . . .

What must happen for organizations to take advantage of the potential productivity and decision benefits of groups? Must organizations be restructured, and, if so, how? To begin with, such organizations would have to select, train, pay, evaluate, and promote groups rather than individuals. In addition, jobs would have to be designed for groups, and an entire group would be at risk for termination or relocation if it did not meet performance expectations.

Although these ideas initially go against our notions of how organizations should function, managing groups might actually be a lot easier than managing individuals. For example, it would probably be easier for upper-level management to evaluate the performance of a workgroup than of an individual. Compensating individuals based on group performance would increase the collaboration and cooperation among group members.[49] Thus, the likelihood of yoking productivity contributions to rewards might be greater because group members would have considerable opportunity to observe each other and would be much closer than a supervisor to the activities involved in producing the good or service.

SUMMARY

Groups foster increased communication, commitment, development, and ownership of a problem and solution. Groups are often able to outperform individuals in making decisions, particularly when the quality and acceptability of the decision are important.

Whether employees should participate in decision making—even when it does not directly affect them—is also an important consideration in group decision making. In deciding when to use participative decision making, a manager must consider the structure of employee participation and whether it is voluntary.

Additionally, group decision making is not without difficulties. The more individuals are involved in coming up with a solution, the more information each individual member must process, the more complex the rules governing decision acceptance, and the more complex the interpersonal processes. As a result, groups require considerably more time and resources to make decisions than do individuals.

Groups may also be influenced by factors that do not affect individuals, such as groupthink or choice shift. Groupthink occurs primarily among highly cohesive groups and results in a decision process that emphasizes conformity and suppresses criticism. Choice-shift effects indicate that groups may be either more or less drawn to risk than their average individual members.

Deciding when to take advantage of the benefits of group decision making and when to rely on an individual decision making is an important component in solving organizational problems. Vroom and Yetton developed guidelines for determining whether a group or an individual is the most appropriate decision maker. If the decision requires acceptance by subordinates, if one alternative is qualitatively better than another, and if the group possesses information necessary for the selection of an alternative, then group decision making is likely to be the preferred option.

---

49. Deutsch, M. (1975). Equity, equality, and need: What determines which will be used as the basis of distributive justice? *Journal of Social Issues, 31,* 137–149.

After deciding who should make the decision, a manager must decide how the decision is to be made. Three methods of group decision making are described in this chapter—brainstorming, NGT, and the Delphi technique. All three of these techniques separate the creative, idea-generation process from the critical, idea-evaluative phase of decision making.

KEY TERMS

Brainstorming
Cautious shift
Delphi technique
Diversity
Groupthink
Nominal group technique (NGT)

Resource pooling
Risky shift
Situated expertise
Synergy
Transactive memory

DISCUSSION QUESTIONS

1 Consider the decision-making process in a group project you are involved in. What are some benefits that you as an individual experienced that related directly to the group and its decision-making process? What are some liabilities you as an individual incurred?

2 When groups convene to make decisions, one of their first acts typically is to determine how a decision will be made. What type of decision rule is likely to encourage the greatest amount of information exchange? the most political behavior? coalition formation among group members? high commitment to the decision? Why?

3 Even when it is in the best interests of a manager to involve subordinates in decision making, he or she often makes decisions au-tocratically. What are some reasons managers choose autocratic decision making over group decision making, regardless of the quality of the outcome?

4 What are the advantages and disadvantages of brainstorming?

5 Why might a manager choose to collect group members' suggestions and preferences using the Delphi technique rather than NGT?

6 Groupthink is typically viewed as a group decision-making error. In what types of groups or situations might a manager encourage groupthink?

7 What are some of the major advantages and disadvantages to managing by groups?

ON YOUR OWN

Applying the Vroom-Yetton Model   In the discussion of when to use group decision making, we presented an example of a managerial problem and used the Vroom-Yetton model of decision making to determine who should be involved in the decision-making process. The following is a problem scenario. Should the manager in the case use an autocratic (AI or AII), consultative (CI or CII), or group (G) decision-making process?

Source: Vroom, V. H., & Yetton, P. W. (1973). *Leadership and decision making.* Pittsburg, PA: University of Pittsburgh Press.

Scenario

You are supervising the work of 12 engineers. Their formal training and work experience are very similar, which means you can use them interchangeably on projects. Yesterday, your manager informed you that a request had been received from an overseas affiliate for 4 engineers to go abroad on extended loan for a period of 6 to 8 months. For a number of reasons, you agreed that this request should be met from your group.

All you engineers are capable of handling this assignment, and from the standpoint of present and future projects, there is no particular reason why any one should be retained over any other. The problem is somewhat complicated by the fact that the overseas assignment is in what is generally regarded in the company as an undesirable assignment.

CLOSING CASE   CHAPTER 8

THE MANAGER'S MEMO

FROM: P. Dorian, Administrator
TO: J. Sternberg, MD
RE: Ethics Task Force

I have been considering your request that the hospital convene an ethics panel whenever we receive a request that some or all treatment be withheld from a patient who is presumed to be dying.

I can't help but be concerned by the idea of tying up the time of a doctor, a nurse, a social worker, a chaplain, family members, and possibly others every time we need to make such a decision. Obviously, this could be costly.

When I started in the business, we took it for granted that doctors made all the decisions about treatment—with the okay of the patient and family members, of course. I'm afraid I don't understand the benefits of the change you are proposing. What do we gain from all the time we would have to invest?

CASE DISCUSSION QUESTIONS

Assume that you are Dr. Sternberg, and respond to the hospital administrator's memo. Support your position with what you have learned about when and how group decision making can be beneficial. Who will benefit most from the group process in this situation?

Who will bear most of the costs and disadvantages? If you wish, you can assume that you have changed your mind about recommending the formation of a task force. If so, use material from the chapter to support this new viewpoint.

CHAPTER 9

Leadership

CARLY FIORINA PROVIDES THE LEADERSHIP JOLT THAT HP NEEDED

Carly Fiorina's name is undoubtedly not as familiar to most people as that of Sandra Day O'Connor, the first woman U.S. Supreme Court justice, or Geraldine Ferraro, the first woman to run for vice president. However, Fiorina's achievement is equally—maybe even more—striking. In July 1999 Fiorina was awarded the highest-ranking position at computer giant Hewlett Packard (HP). This fact alone would have put her in the annals of business history, but what elevated Fiorina's accomplishment to historical proportions was that, in taking the helm at HP, Fiorina became the first women chief executive officer (CEO) of a Dow 30 company.

Fiorina, known for her work with technology and corporate makeovers, was brought in to revolutionize HP from a slow-moving engineering company to an Internet champion. Fiorina is a strong leader who inspires her employees to greatness. One of her mass voicemails announced, "It's a new start for HP . . ."

Fiorina's best leadership characteristic is that she performs. She is not afraid of challenges at the top. As she reviewed HP's annual report she stated, "Some people will have to leave. We need people who like the pace, can deal at a high level, can handle greater ambiguity and risk. . . . I am not afraid" claimed Ms. Fiorina.

Source: Excerpted from Greenfield, K. (1999, August 2). What glass ceiling? Carly Fiorina takes over Hewlett-Packard, becoming the first woman CEO of a Dow 30 firm. *Time Magazine, 154*(5), 72; and Hardy, Q. (1999, December). The cult of Carly: Hewlett Packard, Silicon Valley's first garage startup, was raised on humility and consensus but over time grew insular, self-satisfied, and sclerotic. It needed a good jolt. Carly Fiorina is delivering it. *Forbes, 164*(14), 138–144.

INTRODUCTION

In previous chapters, we examined group decision making and the phenomenon of power and influence. The focus was on how group behavior influences the individual and how one individual can influence another individual. In this chapter, the focus shifts, and we look at how one individual can influence the behavior of groups.

Most of us would agree that the success of any venture, whether it be a large corporation—such as Hewlett Packard in the opening vignette—or a small startup, is largely a function of the leadership abilities of its identified leader. This is clearly shown in "INTERNATIONAL FOCUS ON: The Benefits of Leadership." However, agreeing on the definition of leadership is considerably more difficult. Commonly used definitions of leadership focus on a host of factors that we will consider in this chapter, including the leader's traits, behaviors, influence over other people, interaction patterns, role relationships,

INTERNATIONAL FOCUS ON
THE BENEFITS OF LEADERSHIP

PAYING CEOs WELL HELPS ECONOMIES THRIVE. Shareholders often complain about the large compensation packages of some leaders of U.S. corporations. But are U.S. CEOs, as a group, really overpaid? To answer that question, it is important to investigate how their pay affects the overall U.S. economy. And, as it turns out, when pay is linked to performance, compensating corporate leaders well is crucial to ensuring that the United States is the most competitive country in the world.

To understand why this is so, a comparison of the freedoms and expectations accorded U.S. and non-U.S. corporate leaders is useful. In Japan, for example, pay programs are fixed and employment is often guaranteed. Among the effects of these cultural mainstays have been stifled competition and a weakened economy. One explanation for this weakened economy is that, unlike American leaders, Japanese executives have no economic incentive to deal with difficult management decisions, such as layoffs, even when faced with serious regional economic problems, such as those that confronted Asia in the 1990s. Moreover, top executives in Japan are not paid to act autonomously; they are expected to be loyal to members of their *keiretsu* (conglomerate), regardless of the impact on their own company. In short, they are not paid to be strong leaders.

Other mainstays of Japanese corporate culture, such as lifetime employment (*nenko*) and

pay for seniority (*shushin koyo*), discourage entrepreneurial spirit. These ingrained policies also discourage the kind of risks U.S. CEOs take to improve a company's productivity.

By comparison, in the United States, executive compensation is often linked closely to the performance of the company's stock—a key reform of the past decade. This motivates CEOs to improve corporate performance and therefore their own compensation, but it also succeeds in bolstering the competitive advantage of U.S. companies. When necessary, U.S. companies use aggressive stock incentives, mergers, and occasionally even layoffs to increase shareholder value and overall job security.

It is little wonder then, that even amid the cries of U.S. critics, companies in other countries are moving toward U.S.-style compensation programs. In so doing, they are beginning to recognize the need for strong executive leaders who are willing, when necessary, to make tough, unpopular decisions. These companies are also recognizing that, in the long run, a performance-based economy can guarantee a healthy labor market and deliver more value for consumers and more profits for investors.

Source: Adapted from Kay, I. T. (1998, February 23). Manager's journal: High CEO pay helps the U.S. economy thrive. *Wall Street Journal*, A22.

and incumbency in administrative positions.[1] Here we begin by defining **leadership** according to the outcomes it achieves: the ability to influence employees to go above and beyond mechanical compliance with the routine directives of the organization.[2]

Some key questions to keep in mind throughout this chapter are Is leadership obsolete in today's modern organizations? and has the emergence of "dot.coms" and self-managed teams eliminated the need for leadership? To begin answering these questions, we first consider the difference between formal and informal leadership.

FORMAL AND INFORMAL LEADERSHIP

There are two major types of leaders: formal and informal. Formal leaders differ from informal leaders in their organizational legitimacy. For example, the person occupying the role of executive vice president of sales has a formal leadership role. Fiorina occupies such a formal role as CEO of HP. However, just because someone is assigned a formal leadership role does not guarantee that the person will be the only leader of a group. Other persons often emerge to fill the gaps. These informal leaders influence group members for reasons beyond their formal organizational assignment.

Typically, informal leaders contribute to group performance by providing special expertise or skills, being unusually involved in activities necessary for group performance, and/or actively participating in group discussions. Specifically, informal leaders are likely to be those perceived to (a) aid the group's attainment of its goals because of direct knowledge or expertise or indirect influence of those with the necessary knowledge or expertise; (b) volunteer relatively more time to pursuing the group's task; or (c) be more visible in group discussions by contributing ideas and suggestions. Contributing high-quality suggestions significantly increases the perceived influence group members believe the informal leader exerts.[3]

LEADERSHIP AS A MANAGERIAL ROLE

In our quest to more fully understand leadership, confusion sometimes arises between the role of a *leader* and the role of a *manager*. Yet the activities of these two roles can differ radically. In some groups, the manager is the leader; in other groups, the manager performs functions separate from the tasks traditionally described as leadership activities. For example, the manager may be involved in developing and securing the necessary budget for the group's activities. Although this is clearly not a leadership function, it is critical to the effective functioning of the group. Figure 9-1 clarifies the distinction between the roles of managers and leaders in carrying out organizational objectives.

The primary reason for continuing to study the evolution of leadership has been to identify the differences between good and poor leaders. Social

---

1. Yukl, G. (1998). *Leadership in organizations* (4th ed.). Englewood Cliffs, NJ: Prentice Hall.
2. Katz, D., & Kahn, R. L. (1978). *The social psychology of organizations.* New York: Wiley.
3. Sorrentino, R. M., & Boutillier, R. G. (1975). The effect of quantity and quality of verbal interaction on rating of leadership ability. *Journal of Experimental Social Psychology, 11,* 403–411.

A Comparison of Managers and Leaders ■ FIGURE 9-1

Often the roles of managers and leaders in an organization are not clearly understood. Frequently, the assumption is that managers and leaders are the same. Although this is sometimes the case, managers and leaders often approach organizational tasks and objectives differently.

	Managers	**Leaders**
Creating an agenda	Planning and budgeting	Establishing direction
Developing a human network for achieving the agenda	Organizing and staffing	Aligning people
Executing the agenda	Controlling and problem solving	Motivating and inspiring
Outcomes	Predictability and order	Change

Source: Kotter, J. P. (1990). *A force for change: How leadership differs from management.* New York: The Free Press.

scientists and practitioners have approached the idea of effective leadership from a number of directions; in fact, Amazon.com offers 1,400 hardcover books with the word *leadership* in the title.[4] This overwhelming amount of literature has produced a variety of perspectives. Several are discussed in this chapter, including one expert's view in "FOCUS ON: Ineffective Leaders."

FOCUS ON
INEFFECTIVE LEADERS

RAMBOS IN PINSTRIPES. For more than a decade, executive-development consultant Richard Hagberg has been advising chief executives on the fine points of leadership. His firm, the Hagberg Consulting Group, has compiled a database on the characteristics of 511 CEOs that delivers insights into why so many fail to inspire loyalty among their troops. One of Hagberg's most revealing conclusions is that the number of "Rambos in pinstripes" is increasing. According to Hagberg, whereas in 1991 half his CEO clients were classified as loners, by 1996, the figure had risen to almost 70%.

As a group, CEOs are good at developing visions, but frequently their strategy isn't widely understood; it seems that many CEOs have poor communication skills. As a result, leaders can get confused and frustrated because their subordinates aren't doing what they think they've told them to do. They consequently become critical and suspicious of others.

Not surprisingly, people often find it difficult to disagree with these Rambo-like leaders. Subordinates stop giving them bad news, so that the CEOs lose out on the benefits of give-and-take conversations. This creates even more barriers, and ultimately, teamwork, which you need in any corporation, suffers.

So, although Rambo may be a successful leader on the screen, this leadership style is rarely effective in the board room.

Source: Excerpted from Rambos in pinstripes: Why so many CEOs are lousy. (1996, June 24). *Fortune, 133*(12), 147.

4. Krohe, J. (2000, January). Leadership books: Why do we buy them? *Across the Board, 37*(1), 18.

The great-person theory of leadership contends that certain individuals, such as Nelson Mandela, or Martin Luther King, Jr., possess traits that set them apart as leaders, regardless of the situations in which they find themselves.

UNIVERSAL APPROACHES TO LEADERSHIP

One popular perspective on leadership is that leaders are leaders because of some enduring aspect of their personality or behavior. That is, regardless of the situation in which these individuals find themselves, their leadership abilities will emerge. The primary consideration here, however, is whether such leadership is a function of the individual or the way in which that individual behaves.

The "great person" theory was among the earliest theories on leadership, and it remains the most intuitively appealing. According to this popular perspective, certain individuals are destined to become leaders because they possess a constellation of personality characteristics that separates them from others—their followers. They point to individuals such as Nelson Mandela, Martin Luther King, Jr., Winston Churchill, and Indira Gandhi as examples of individuals who would have been leaders regardless of the situations in which they found themselves.

TRANSFORMATIONAL VERSUS TRANSACTIONAL LEADERSHIP

The great-person perspective on leadership makes the implicit assumption that such individuals are transformational leaders as opposed to transactional leaders; they motivate by providing followers with rewards for their behavior. **Transformational leaders** (such as Fiorina at HP) arouse intense feelings and generate turbulent one-to-one relationships with their followers. They are inspirational and concerned with ideas rather than processes. They heighten expectations and engender excitement. They are likely to be dramatic and unpredictable.

Transformational leaders rely on such personal sources of power as referent power, discussed in Chapter 7. They motivate their followers to do more as a group than they originally intended by transforming the group's expectations. Such processes of transformation occur when the leader:

- Raises the level of follower awareness, consciousness, and commitment to designated outcomes as well as knowledge of how to achieve these outcomes
- Encourages followers to transcend their self-interests for the sake of the organization
- Alters the followers' needs or expands their wants.

Transformational leaders have an almost magical appeal for their followers. As Thomas J. Watson did at IBM and George Patton did for the Third Army, they identify ways for their followers to achieve superordinate goals. Through their appeal, they are able to transform organizations and their participants. Self-confidence and self-esteem, low internal conflict, self-determination, and enthusiasm all contribute to the success of transformational leaders.[5] They have the ability both to conceive and to articulate goals that lift people out of their petty preoccupations.[6] Such leaders unite people to seek goals worthy of their best efforts.

5. See, for example, Bass, B. M. (1985). *Leadership and performance beyond expectations.* New York: The Free Press.

6. Bennis, W. G., & Nanus, B. (1985). *Leaders: The strategies for taking charge.* New York: Harper & Row.

In contrast, **transactional leaders** motivate followers by exchanging rewards for services. By relying on coercive and reward power, they:

- ■ Recognize what subordinates want from their work and try to see that they get it (if their performance warrants it)
- ■ Exchange rewards and promises of rewards for subordinates' effort
- ■ Are responsive to subordinates' immediate self-interests if they get the job done.[7]

In short, transactional leaders focus on situational determinants of leadership (which are discussed in greater detail later in this chapter).

Which type of leadership—transformational or transactional—is best for an organization? Which leaders produce better results? Does leadership style even have a direct effect on organizational performance? Research has found evidence that transformational leadership has a greater positive effect on overall organizational performance than does transactional leadership.[8] In addition, the effects of transformational leadership are mostly seen in long-term gains rather than in short-term performance.[9] However, the presence of a transformational leader alone does not guarantee results. Research has shown that the effectiveness of transformational leaders is influenced by such contextual factors as employee receptiveness to the leadership type, company culture, and organizational structure.[10] Therefore, it is important to consider all aspects of the organization in choosing and developing leaders.

CHARISMATIC LEADERSHIP. In light of the earlier discussion of the differences between managers and leaders, one could say that transactional leaders are more like managers, making sure tasks are done right, whereas transformational leaders are what we generally refer to as *leaders*. David Berlew described transformational leadership as Stage 3, or **charismatic leadership.** He differentiated it from two other stages (or types): Stage 1, custodial leadership, and Stage 2, managerial leadership.[11]

According to Berlew, in Stage 1, **custodial leadership,** the focus is on improving working conditions, compensation, and fringe benefits. By contrast, in Stage 2, **managerial leadership,** the emphasis is more on providing subordinates with work that is less routine and more challenging, building cohesive work teams, and giving employees more say in decisions that affect them directly. The first two stages of leadership seem much more consistent with what we consider to be transactional leadership. In contrast, Stage 3 leaders are what Berlew termed *charismatic.* These transformational leaders use their leadership abilities to develop a common vision of what could be, to discover or create opportunities, and to strengthen organizational members' control of their destinies.

---

7. Bass, *Leadership and performance beyond expectations.*

8. Geyer, A. L., & Steyrer, J. M. (1998, July). Transformational leadership and objective performance in banks. *Applied Psychology: An International Review, 47,* 397–420.

9. Geyer & Steyrer, , Transformational leadership and objective performance in banks.

10. Pawar, B. S., & Eastman, K. K. (1997, January). The nature and implications of contextual influences on transformational leadership: A conceptual examination. *Academy of Management Review,* 80–109.

11. Berlew, D. E. (1979). Leadership and organizational excitement. In A. Kolb, I. M. Rubin, & J. M. McIntyre (Eds.), *Organizational psychology: A book of readings.* Englewood Cliffs, NJ: Prentice Hall.

FOCUS ON
CHARISMATIC LEADERS

WHY EMPLOYEES LOVE WORKING FOR SOME COMPANIES. Many of the best companies to work for are run by powerful, visionary leaders. Andy Grove of Intel and Larry Bossidy of AlliedSignal are among the most demanding bosses in business, yet workers seem to feel inspired rather than oppressed by them.

Non-celebrities who run many lesser-known companies have the same effect. These include Herb Kelleher, the CEO of Southwest Airlines. Kelleher spends his business life making sure his employees believe in him and in the operation he has muscled into the top tier of a savagely competitive industry. He smokes, he arm-wrestles, he drinks large quantities of Wild Turkey, he raps in music videos, and it's only slight hyperbole to say nearly all his employees worship the ground he walks on. But even he can't match the act of devotion displayed for Dave Duffield, the founder and CEO of software maker PeopleSoft. A few years ago employees formed a garage band and decided to call it The Raving Daves.

Remarkably, the well-worn story of Mary Kay Ash also retains its power to inspire. Those who know her well—and almost all who work for Mary Kay Incorporated seem to think they do—describe her as a corporate Everywoman. Pushed aside by her male superiors as a saleswoman in the 1950s, she quit her job and built a sales organization intended to empower other women.

Though Mary Kay herself is a millionaire many times over, the people who work for her marvel at her ability to remain accessible. Before she suffered a stroke in 1996, she used to invite employees to her home for tea several times a year.

What is the common trait among these effective leaders? They inspire employees not just to work hard and succeed but also to become mini-versions of the leaders themselves. "People understand that for Mary Kay, it was all about fulfilling a mission that was bigger than just her," says an employee who works at corporate headquarters. "They've increased their own self-esteem by being around her, and they want to pass that on to others the same way she did."

Source: Lieber, R. B. (1998). Why employees love these companies. *Fortune, 137*(1), 72–74.

By inspiring and leading employees to develop specific goals and self-efficacy, charismatic leaders have positive effects on employees' motivation and, consequently, positively impact employees' performance.[12] Research has shown that employees view leaders who have sacrificed in some way as more charismatic than leaders who have always benefited. This trait in turn enables charismatic leaders to have even more influence over their followers,[13] as is evident in "FOCUS ON: Charismatic Leaders."

In addition to identifying a common vision and giving meaning to an organization and its activities, the charismatic leader also must empower followers—make them feel stronger, more confident, more in control of their destinies, and more competent. Berlew suggested that charismatic leaders engender this feeling of power among their followers by having high expectations of them, rewarding good performance rather than punishing poor performance, encouraging collaboration among individuals, helping only when asked, and creating success experiences for followers.[14]

---

12. Kirkpatrick, S. A., & Locke, E. A. (1996). Direct and indirect effects of three core charismatic leadership components on performance and attitudes. *Journal of Applied Psychology, 81*(11), 36–51.

13. Yorges, S. L., Weiss, H. M., & Strickland, O. J. (1999). The effect of leader outcomes on influence, attributions, and perceptions of charisma. *Journal of Applied Psychology, 84*, 428–436.

14. Berlew, Leadership and organizational excitement.

LEADER IDENTIFICATION. Because of the attraction and effectiveness of transformational leaders, behavioral scientists have searched for ways to identify them. Thousands of studies have investigated the impact on leadership potential of demographic characteristics (such as height, weight, and age), social characteristics (such as educational level, socioeconomic background, grades, appearance, and popularity), and personality characteristics (such as dominance, introversion–extroversion, initiative, and cooperation). However, the search for specific factors that clearly and consistently predict which individuals will be effective transformational leaders has not been overly successful. Thus, although the great-person perspective has considerable intuitive appeal (especially given the success of such transformational leaders as John F. Kennedy and Vladimir Lenin), research provides only minimal support for this theory.

However, a constellation of traits seem to distinguish business leaders from followers, effective from ineffective leaders, and higher-status from lower-status leaders. These characteristics include drive, the desire to lead, integrity, self-confidence, intelligence, and knowledge of the business.[15] Additionally, research has indicated that effective leaders have a high level of emotional intelligence.[16] **Emotional intelligence** can be defined as one's ability to effectively deal with ambiguity and use sound judgment in performing a job.[17]

In an effort to help companies identify individuals with leadership potential, many major corporations turn for help to assessment centers. First developed by the Office of Strategic Services in World War II to select spies, assessment centers test leadership potential by using role-playing exercises, psychological tests, simulations, and management games that measure managerial talent. The accuracy of these centers' selections is quite impressive. For example, tests conducted for AT&T correctly identified 78% of the individuals who reached middle management. Equally significant, of the individuals who did not reach middle-management positions within 10 years of the evaluation, the tests had correctly identified 95%.[18]

Another way in which corporations identify leadership potential is with personality testing, which is usually a less expensive alternative to testing at an assessment center. Personality testing and the services of an assessment center are sometimes used together.[19]

The personalities of effective leaders has also been the subject of rigorous academic research, such as that of Finn Havaleschka of Denmark. Havaleschka's research provides evidence that the personality of an executive(s)

15. Kirkpatrick, S. A., & Locke, E. A. (1991, May). Leadership: Do traits matter? *Academy of Management Executive, 5*(2), 48–60.

16. Gregersen, H. B., Morrison, A. J., & Black, S. B. (1998). Developing leaders for the global frontier. *Sloan Management Review, 40*(1), 21–32; and Goleman, D. A. (1998). What makes a leader? *Harvard Business Review, 76,* 92–102.

17. Andersen, A. (2000, April). *Building global leaders.* Paper presented at the meeting of the International Personnel Association, St. Petersburg, FL; and Barling, J., Slater, F., & Kelloway, E. K. (2000). Transformational leadership and emotional intelligence: An exploratory study. *Leadership & Organization Development Journal, 21,* 157–161.

18. Bray, D. W., & Grant, D. L. (1966). The assessment center in the measurement of potential for business management. [Monograph] *Psychological Monographs, 80*(17).

19. Goffin, R. D., Rothstein, M. T., & Johnston, N. G. (1996). Personality testing and the assessment center: Incremental validity for managerial selection. *Journal of Applied Psychology, 81,* 746–756.

(and the personalities of his or her team members) greatly influences the company's chances for success or failure in the market.[20] For example, research shows that successful leadership is highly correlated with a leader's propensity to extraversion and openness. These findings are applied equally to men and women.[21]

One of the most widely researched aspects of personality and leadership is the big five factors of personality (neuroticism, extraversion, openness to experience, agreeableness, and conscientiousness—as discussed in Chapter 2), and its ability to predict leaders. In fact, greater empirical support has been found for the five-factor model (in predicting leaders) than for the popular Myers-Briggs Type Indicator (MBTI).[22] But research has also found that for looking at charismatic leaders, a proactive personality scale (e.g., measuring the ability to change the organization's environment, to show initiative, and to persevere) is a better predictor of charismatic leadership than even the big five personality factors.[23]

THE BEHAVIOR APPROACH TO LEADERSHIP

In the late 1940s, research on leaders began to focus less on their personality and demographic characteristics and more on their behavior. Like the great-person theory, this research was appealing for several reasons. First, examining behaviors rather than traits made it possible to study not only formal leaders in stable leadership positions but informal leaders as well. Second, focusing on behavior opened up the possibility of training leaders, not just identifying them. Finally, this focus enabled researchers to more closely examine the exchange relationship between leaders and followers. For example, a leader may give a group direction, coordination, legitimacy, and access to valued resources. Followers then reciprocate with resources of their own, such as compliance and deference.[24]

Despite the less-than-strong statistical support for the idea that leaders exhibit certain common behaviors, the notion continues to be appealing. Further, the behavioral approach has served as the foundation for many leadership training programs. Robert Blake and Jane Mouton, for example, have developed what they call a **managerial grid.** Shown in Figure 9-2, this grid reflects what Blake and his colleagues believe are the two dimensions of a leader's behavior—concern for production (task-oriented leadership) and concern for people (socioemotional leadership). They believe that the only management style that will result in superior performance is a team-oriented style that combines high production with a high concern for people (team management). According to Blake and his associates, this style elicits high-quality performance from highly committed followers who share a common

20. Havaleschka, F. (1999). Personality and leadership: A benchmark study of success and failure. *Leadership & Organization Development Journal, 20,* 114–132.

21. Lindley, L. D., & Borgen, F. H. (2000, August). Personal style scales of the Strong interest inventory: Linking personality and interests. *Journal of Vocational Behavior, 57*(1), 22–41.

22. Cannella, A. A., & Monroe, M. J. (1997, May). Contrasting perspectives on strategic leaders: Toward a more realistic view of top managers. *Journal of Management,* 213–237.

23. Crant, J. M., & Bateman, T. S. (2000, February). Charismatic leadership viewed from above: The impact of proactive personality. *Journal of Organizational Behavior, 21,* 63–75.

24. Hollander, E. P. (1978). *Leadership dynamics: A practical guide to effective relationships.* New York: The Free Press/Macmillan.

The Managerial Grid

The managerial grid is a variation of the two-dimensional perspective of leader behavior. These two dimensions result in five distinct leadership styles.

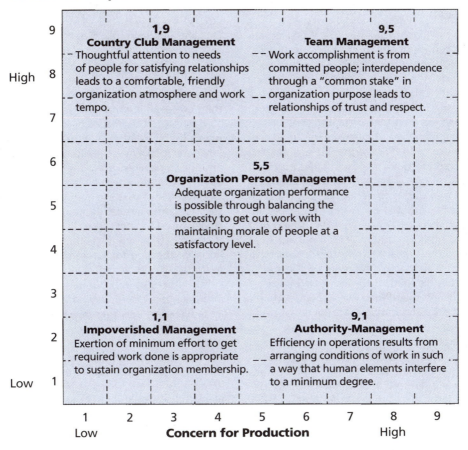

Concern for People

	1,9 **Country Club Management** Thoughtful attention to needs of people for satisfying relationships leads to a comfortable, friendly organization atmosphere and work tempo.	**9,5** **Team Management** Work accomplishment is from committed people; interdependence through a "common stake" in organization purpose leads to relationships of trust and respect.
	5,5 **Organization Person Management** Adequate organization performance is possible through balancing the necessity to get out work with maintaining morale of people at a satisfactory level.	
	1,1 **Impoverished Management** Exertion of minimum effort to get required work done is appropriate to sustain organization membership.	**9,1** **Authority-Management** Efficiency in operations results from arranging conditions of work in such a way that human elements interfere to a minimum degree.

Concern for Production

Source: Blake, R. R., & Mouton, J. S. (1978). *The new managerial grid.* Houston, TX: Gulf Publishing.

purpose. The team leader uses mutual trust and respect to accomplish both individual and organizational goals.[25]

Although companies have spent large amounts of money training managers in Blake and Mouton's team-management style, once again, researchers found little empirical support for the existence of a relationship between leadership style and such factors as productivity, absenteeism, and turnover.[26]

The fruitless search for a universal approach to leadership led researchers to reformulate their questions, which then led to the development of the contingency theories of leadership.

25. Blake, R. R., & Mouton, J. S. (1978). *The new managerial grid.* Houston, TX: Gulf Publishing.
26. Korman, A. K. (1966). Consideration, initiating structure, and organizational criteria: A review. *Personnel Psychology, 19,* 349–361.

RESEARCH IN ACTION
BUILDING GLOBAL LEADERS

J. Stewart Black, University of Michigan; *SBlackGLI@aol.com*

In examining global leadership, my colleagues, Hal Gregersen (Brigham Young University), Allen Morrison (University of Western Ontario), and I wanted to get the perspective of current leaders charged with global responsibilities but also have them identify future global leaders—prototypes or exemplars—within their organizations.

Consequently, we interviewed senior executives in more than 55 companies around the world. Forty individuals were identified as exemplars of future global leaders. We asked subjects essentially two questions: What are the capabilities of successful global leadership? and How are those capabilities best developed? We found that about two thirds of large multinational firms felt that they did not have the number or quality of global leaders that would be required for the future. Second, we found that about two thirds of the capabilities mentioned were common, regardless of industry, nationality, functional background, and so on. One third were unique to an industry, a company culture, the national origin of the firm, and the like. Of the common capabilities, inquisitiveness was at the core. If you are not naturally interested in and curious about differences, then those differences simply overwhelm you in positions of global responsibility. The other capabilities were business and organizational savvy, the ability to connect emotionally with others, personal integrity, embracing of uncertainty, and balancing of competing demands.

Despite differences in age, ethnicity, nationality, functional responsibilities, industry, and so on, 8 out of 10 interviewees gave the identical response when asked what was the most powerful global leadership developmental experience in their lives—an international assignment.

Based on this research, companies such as Exxon-Mobil Aviation, Suncor Energy, and Cemex have changed what they look for in future leaders, the capabilities they focus training on, and how they utilize international assignments in the identification and development of future global leaders. For example, although most companies already used business savvy as a criterion, few had given much thought to the necessity of emotional connection for future global leaders. However, the world for most companies is getting larger—not smaller. Companies are expanding into countries where they have never been before and increasing their presence in established countries to a degree never imagined before. For executives, this translates into a bigger world—one in which command-and-control does not work. As one executive said, "Even though 99.9% of the employees report up to me, the world is a big place to hide. By the time I find out that they are not going along with company policy or strategy in Russia or wherever, it's too late. It takes goodwill to get people in far-flung places to cooperate. Goodwill comes from an emotional connection with you, not a reporting line of authority."

CONTINGENCY APPROACHES TO LEADERSHIP

Rather than search for a Holy Grail of executive behaviors, researchers in the past 4 decades have turned their attention to the situations in which most leaders find themselves. In today's environment, these situations are changing rapidly, as illustrated in "TECHNOLOGY FOCUS ON: Leadership." Investigation in this area requires an understanding of situational differences, or *contingencies* (such as the nature of the task, subordinates' attributes, and group characteristics), and from this understanding three theories have evolved: the contingency model of leadership, the path–goal model, and the situational leadership model.

THE CONTINGENCY MODEL

The earliest theory specifically called a contingency theory was Fred Fiedler's **contingency model of leadership.** Fiedler's basic assumption was

TECHNOLOGY FOCUS ON LEADERSHIP

LEADERS.COM. What does leadership mean in the digital economy, where organizations are as decentralized and as networked as the Web itself? What does leadership mean when the pace of change is so rapid that decisions are made with minimal information? And what does leadership mean when the people in an organization both demand more independence and require more guidance? Are Internet-based leaders a different breed?

According to Ruthann Quindlen, a partner at Institutional Venture Partners (IVP), every leader today has to unlearn one lesson that was drilled into each one of them: You gather data so that you can make considered decisions. You can't do that on Internet time. If your instinct is to wait, ponder, and perfect, then you're dead. In practice, that means that leaders have to hit the undo key without flinching, to try something and see if it works—and, if it doesn't, to change it fast.

Jay Walker, founder and vice chairman of Priceline.com, concurs that being a leader in an Internet business requires constant conceptual reinvention. Internet businesses don't have the luxury of narrowly defining a task at hand. They have to envision a future in which customers are going to behave in new ways because new solutions have become available. The real challenge for any leader in this environment is to execute solutions to problems. And forget about today's problems. You've got to focus constantly on the next generation of problems. If, for example, you really believe that you're going to double your business every year, then you've got to hire ahead of the curve. If you wait until you're actually doing that much business, you'll be too late.

Source: Excerpted from LaBarre, P. (1999, June). Leaders.com: Unit of one. *Fast Company;* volume 25, 95–96.

that the effectiveness of a leader's behavior is determined by the nature of the situation he or she confronts. To determine leadership styles, Fiedler developed the **least-preferred coworker (LPC) scale**, reproduced in Figure 9-3.

Consistent with previous work on leaders' behavior, Fiedler's scale measures two basic styles of behavior: task-oriented and relationship-oriented behavior. Research conducted by Fiedler and Rice[27] suggests that leaders who score low on the LPC scale emphasize completing tasks—even at the expense of interpersonal relationships—and gain self-esteem through task completion. In contrast, leaders who score high on the scale derive satisfaction and a sense of accomplishment from relationships with others. Fiedler argued that the importance of the LPC scale was in ferreting out an individual's ability to overlook negative traits in followers. According to Fiedler, individuals who are unable to overlook such traits because of their potential influence on future task accomplishment are likely to be task oriented. Those who can maintain a strong relationship with an individual, regardless of his or her negative traits, are likely to be relationship oriented.

After an individual's leadership style is ascertained, it is then important to diagnose the particular situation in which the leader works. Because Fiedler believed that leadership style was a trait—a stable personality characteristic—he suggested that organizations assign leaders based on a fit between their LPC scale and the situation. He thought that it was considerably

27. Fiedler, F. E. (1967). A theory of leadership effectiveness. New York: McGraw-Hill; Rice, R. W. (1978). Construct validity of the least preferred co-worker scale. *Psychological Relations, 85*, 106–118.

■ **FIGURE 9-3** **The LPC Scale**

Fiedler's contingency model of leadership contends that situational characteristics determine which leadership traits or skills are effective. Fiedler developed the LPC scale to measure an individual's leadership skills. This scale produces scores between 18 and 144. Low-LPC leaders are usually described as those scoring below 58 points. High-LPC leaders score 64 or more points

Directions: Think of all the people with whom you have ever worked, and then think of the person with whom you could work least well. This person may be someone with whom you work now or with whom you have worked in the past. This does not have to be the person you liked least well; it should be the person with whom you had the most difficulty getting a job done.

Describe this person on the scale that follows by placing an X in the appropriate space.

Look at the words at both ends of the line before you mark your X. *There are no right or wrong answers.* Work rapidly; your first answer is likely to be the best. Do not omit any items, and mark each item only once. Now describe the person with whom you can work least well.

Scoring

Left	8	7	6	5	4	3	2	1	Right	Score
Pleasant	8	7	6	5	4	3	2	1	Unpleasant	___
Friendly	8	7	6	5	4	3	2	1	Unfriendly	___
Rejecting	1	2	3	4	5	6	7	8	Accepting	___
Tense	1	2	3	4	5	6	7	8	Relaxed	___
Distant	1	2	3	4	5	6	7	8	Close	___
Cold	1	2	3	4	5	6	7	8	Warm	___
Supportive	8	7	6	5	4	3	2	1	Hostile	___
Boring	1	2	3	4	5	6	7	8	Interesting	___
Quarrelsome	1	2	3	4	5	6	7	8	Harmonious	___
Gloomy	1	2	3	4	5	6	7	8	Cheerful	___
Open	8	7	6	5	4	3	2	1	Guarded	___
Backbiting	1	2	3	4	5	6	7	8	Loyal	___
Untrustworthy	1	2	3	4	5	6	7	8	Trustworthy	___
Considerate	8	7	6	5	4	3	2	1	Inconsiderate	___
Nasty	1	2	3	4	5	6	7	8	Nice	___
Agreeable	8	7	6	5	4	3	2	1	Disagreeable	___
Insincere	1	2	3	4	5	6	7	8	Sincere	___
Kind	8	7	6	5	4	3	2	1	Unkind	___
									Total	___

Source: Fiedler, F. E., Chemers, M. M., & Mahar, L. (1976). *Improving leadership effectiveness.* New York: Wiley.

easier (and more appropriate) for individuals to find situations that required their leadership style than to change their style to fit a situation.

Fiedler identified three situational characteristics that influenced whether a high-LPC or low-LPC leader would be more effective:

1 **Leader–member relations.** The extent to which the group trusts and respects the leader and will follow the leader's directions.
2 **Task structure.** The degree to which a task is clearly specified and defined, as opposed to unstructured and ambiguous.
3 **Position power.** The extent to which the leader has official power or the potential or actual ability to influence others in a desired direction because of the leader's position in the hierarchy.

Unlike some of the other theories of leadership, research has supported Fiedler's approach. However, critics have noted that the LPC does not directly measure leader behavior but instead measures an individual's *feelings* about a coworker. This, coupled with a lack of consistent scores among individuals who complete the scale on different occasions, has called into question the usefulness of the LPC scale. Nonetheless, the concept of the contingency model of leadership is useful. Although Fiedler and his colleagues are clearly wedded to a contingency model of leadership and the importance of a situation–style fit, they have made it obvious that very different styles of leadership can be effective in different organizations.

THE PATH–GOAL MODEL

In contrast to Fiedler's view that specific individuals should be chosen to be leaders based on the match between their leadership style and the situation, the notion of contingency suggests that leaders *can and should* adapt their styles, depending on the situational demands. Specifically, from this perspective, the task of a leader is to strengthen subordinates' expectancy links.[28] (The idea of expectancy links is derived from expectancy theory, discussed in Chapter 3.) Expectancy links are subordinates' perceptions of the extent to which a tie or link exists between effort, performance, and desired outcomes. An effective leader (a) encourages subordinates' desires for outcomes over which the leader has some control; (b) ensures that performance is rewarded as expected (i.e., that the link between performance and expected outcome is strong); (c) coaches and directs subordinates along the path of successful performance; (d) helps subordinates clarify expectations (i.e., set goals, specify organizational expectations, identify the route to successful job performance); (e) ensures that the necessary resources (e.g., skills, equipment, training) for successful task performance are available to subordinates; and (f) develops subordinates' extrinsic and intrinsic motivational forces. To the extent that the leader is able to accomplish these tasks, the **path–goal model** of leadership suggests that subordinates will:

- Experience high job satisfaction because the path to job performance and subsequent rewards is more direct.
- Accept the leader because the leader aids in the attainment of valued rewards.
- Become motivated. They will come to believe that they are performing the task required of them and that, in doing so, they will receive valued rewards.

---

28. House, R. J., & Mitchell, T. R. (1974). A path–goal theory of leadership. *Journal of Contemporary Business, 3,* 81–97.

CHOOSING A LEADERSHIP STYLE. The path–goal theory identifies four styles of behavior that leaders demonstrate: directive, supportive, achievement oriented, and participative. The first two styles are similar to the task-oriented and socioemotional behavior described by other leadership theorists. The third style, achievement-oriented leadership, focuses on performance, goal setting, and other aspects consistent with McClelland's theories of motivation (discussed in Chapter 3). The fourth leadership style, participative, focuses on behaviors that enlist subordinates in the decision-making process. Examples of these specific behaviors are outlined in Figure 9-4.

In determining which leadership style to implement, the path–goal approach suggests that both subordinate and situational characteristics are important. It is important to consider the characteristics of subordinates, such as their level of authoritarianism (rigidity), locus of control, and level of ability. According to the path–goal theory, the greater the subordinates' perception of their abilities relative to task demands, the less willing they are to accept a directive style of leadership. The more authoritarian the subordinates, the more likely they are to accept a directive style of leadership. And individuals with an internal locus of control (who believe that rewards are contingent on their behavior—that they control what happens to them) are more satisfied with a participative style of leadership than are those with an exter-

| ■ **FIGURE 9-4** | **Leader Behavior Dimensions in House and Mitchell's Path–Goal Model** |

The path–goal theory outlines four styles of leader behavior. The theory suggests that both subordinate and situational characteristics are important determinants of the appropriate style a leader should adapt. The styles vary along the following dimensions:

Leader Directiveness
■ Letting subordinates know what is expected
■ Providing specific guidance as to what should be done and how
■ Making the leader's part in the group understood
■ Scheduling work to be done
■ Maintaining definite standards of performance

Leader Supportiveness
■ Showing concern for the status and well-being of subordinates
■ Doing little things to make work more pleasant
■ Treating subordinates as equals
■ Being friendly and approachable

Leader Achievement-Orientedness
■ Setting challenging goals
■ Expecting subordinates to perform at their highest levels
■ Showing a high degree of confidence in subordinates
■ Constantly emphasizing excellence in performance

Leader Participativevness
■ Consulting with subordinates
■ Soliciting subordinates' suggestions
■ Taking subordinates' suggestions seriously

Source: House & Mitchell, A path–goal theory of leadership.

Effective Leadership Styles under Certain Conditions: Prediction from the Path–Goal Theory of Leadership   ■ **FIGURE 9-5**

According to path–goal theory, characteristics of subordinates that determine appropriate leadership style include social and achievement needs; situational determinants include the nature of the task.

	Leadership Styles			
Sample Situational Characteristics	**Directive**	**Supportive**	**Achievement**	**Participative**
Task				
Structured	No	Yes	Yes	Yes
Unstructured	Yes	No	Yes	No
Clear goals	No	Yes	No	Yes
Ambiguous goals	Yes	No	Yes	No
Subordinates				
Skilled in task	No	Yes	Yes	Yes
Unskilled in task	Yes	No	Yes	No
High achievement needs	No	No	Yes	No
High social needs	No	Yes	No	Yes
Formal Authority				
Extensive	No	Yes	Yes	Yes
Limited	Yes	Yes	Yes	Yes
Workgroup				
Strong social network	Yes	No	Yes	Yes
Experienced in collaboration	No	No	No	Yes
Organizational Culture				
Supports participation	No	No	No	Yes
Achievement oriented	No	No	Yes	No

Source: Wofford, J. C., & Srinivasan, T. N. (1983). Experimental tests of the leader–environment–follower interaction theory of leadership. *Organizational Behavior and Human Performance, 32,* 35–54.

nal locus of control (who believe that their behaviors have little to do with the rewards they receive—that fate controls their destinies).

Similarly, the situational or environmental variables to consider, according to path–goal theory, include the nature of the task, the formal authority structure of the organization, and the relationship norms within the organization. The more unstructured or ambiguous the task, the more likely subordinates are to be satisfied with a directive style of leadership. Finally, the more structured the task, the more important a supportive leadership style is to subordinates' performance and satisfaction.[29]

Figure 9-5 illustrates the situations in which each of the leadership styles results in positive outcomes. Subordinates with a high need for achievement, for example, respond satisfactorily only to a leader using an achievement-oriented leadership style.[30]

29. House, R. J., & Dessler, G. (1974). The path–goal theory of leadership: Some post hoc and a priori tests. In J. G. Hunt & L. L. Larson (Eds.), *Contingency approaches to leadership.* Carbondale, IL: Southern Illinois University Press.

30. Wofford & Srinivasan, Experimental tests of the leader–environment–follower interaction theory of leadership.

The path–goal theory of leadership provides some specific, testable predictions about leader effectiveness. Unfortunately, research has provided only marginal support for some of these predictions. For example, there is consistent evidence that subordinates are more satisfied performing in a structured situation when the leader demonstrates a supportive style of leadership. However, the findings are mixed when the leadership style is directive and the task situation is highly structured. Sometimes subordinates' satisfaction suffers; sometimes subordinates' satisfaction is enhanced.[31]

THE SITUATIONAL LEADERSHIP MODEL

A third, and currently popular, contingency theory is Paul Hersey and Ken Blanchard's **situational leadership model.** This model suggests that leaders are effective when they use the most appropriate leadership style for the situation they face. Effective leaders, therefore, vary their style according to the readiness of their followers—that is, how willing and able their followers are to perform a task.[32]

Like Blake and Mouton, Hersey and Blanchard have developed a grid that they have divided into four leadership styles—telling, selling, participating, and delegating—according to task and relationship. Participating, for example, is a low-task, high-relationship style.

Although very popular, the situational leadership model has received little empirical support. However, it has reinforced the ideas that leadership behavior is flexible and adaptable and that leaders should look for opportunities to develop their subordinates along the entire readiness continuum.[33]

LEADERSHIP THEORY EVOLVES. The evolution of leadership theory from a trait or behavior approach to a contingency perspective is critical to our understanding of the complex phenomenon of leadership. Just as the need theorists discussed in Chapter 3 have provided us with the insight that people are different from one another and their needs and motivations cannot neatly fit into simple economic models, the contingency theories of leadership have illuminated the association between appropriate leadership style and task characteristics.

Unfortunately, contingency theories of leadership have not answered all our questions about leadership. In fact, such models are primarily descriptive—that is, they describe which leadership style is best associated with which task or situation. However, they leave gaps in our understanding of leadership. For example, does the leader influence the subordinate, or does the subordinate's behavior subtly influence and shape the leader's behavior? What impact do leaders' perceptions of their subordinates have on their choice of leadership style? What characteristics of the task, the subordinates, or the situation make leaders more or less necessary? Finally, are there substitutes for leadership, such as work arrangements that make leadership less necessary?

31. Yukl, *Leadership in organizations*; Schriecheim, C. A., & Denisi, A. (1981). Task dimensions as moderators of the effects of instrumental leadership: A two-sample replicated test of the path–goal leadership theory. *Journal of Applied Psychology, 66*, 589–597; and Indvik, J. (1986). Path–goal theory of leadership: A meta-analysis. *Proceedings of the Academy of Management Meetings, 46*, 189–192.

32. Hersey, P., & Blanchard, K. (1996, January). Great ideas revisited: Revisiting the life-cycle theory of leadership. *Training & Development, 50*(1), 42–47.

33. Yukl, *Leadership in organizations*.

ALTERNATIVE THEORIES OF LEADERSHIP

Researchers have begun to fill in some of the gaps by examining leadership from different and relatively novel perspectives. For the most part, the resulting theories do not assume that leadership exists as an objective and consistent construct. Rather, the assumption is that leadership is a *social construction* of reality—a way that people talk about the relationships among employees in organizations. From this perspective, leaders and their behavior cannot exist independently from the task, situational, and subordinate components of the environment in which the task takes place.

THE LEADER–MEMBER EXCHANGE MODEL

In the behavior theories of leadership discussed previously in this chapter, the leader's behavior is assumed to be consistent across all subordinates. By contrast, in the **leader–member exchange (LMX) model** the focus is on the differential patterns of interaction between leaders and subordinates. An extension of exchange theory, it suggests that the leader does not interact with the group as a whole. Rather, the leader has unique relationships with each workgroup member, and the nature of these dyadic (two-person) relationships determines the behaviors of the leader's subordinates.[34]

One way in which these relationships have been categorized is by whether group members are in in-groups or out-groups, which, in turn, depends on that individual's association with the leader. Members of the in-group typically share common interests with the leader and are part of the leader's communication and support network. Likewise, members of the out-group have less in common with the leader and are less likely to support or associate with the leader.

Membership in the in-group leads to better understanding between the subordinate and the leader. As supervisors become more knowledgeable about the specific strengths and weaknesses of their in-group subordinates, they are likely to express more faith in their performance potential and judgment than in those of out-group members. The competitive advantage of in-group membership thus becomes a self-fulfilling prophecy. Differences in the performance potential of in-group and out-group members may be low initially, but they are magnified over time. If a task is critical or complex, for example, the supervisor is more likely to assign it to an individual in whom that supervisor has more trust. Particularly valued assignments go to members of the in-group—who "deserve" to be rewarded. Out-group members are likely to be assigned the remaining tasks—those that are repetitive, unimportant, and repugnant.

Over time, not only will the assignments of the out-group members be unchallenging, but these subordinates' performance will deteriorate, thus completing the cycle of the self-fulfilling prophecy. Ultimately, both the employees' perceptions of their capabilities and those of their leaders will be seriously eroded. Job satisfaction will be low and turnover high.

---

34. Varma, A., & Stroh, L. K. (2001). Impact of the gender composition of supervisor-subordinate dyads on performance evaluation. *Human Resource Journal*, 40. Graen, G., & Minami, T. (1972). Dysfunctional leadership styles. *Organizational behavior and human performance*, 7, 216–236; and Duchon, D., Green, S., & Taber, T. (1986). Vertical dyad linkage: A longitudinal assessment of antecedents, measures, and consequences. *Journal of Applied Psychology*, 71, 56–60.

This self-fulfilling prophecy certainly provides beneficial outcomes for the individual, supervisor, and organization as a whole. Studies consistently support a positive correlation between LMX and supervisor satisfaction, organizational commitment, and overall employee satisfaction. Research also supports a negative correlation between LMX and turnover.[35]

Given human nature, the development of in-groups and out-groups is difficult to avoid in organizational settings. However, such a split does not necessarily have to be damaging to workgroup effectiveness. Two instances in which the existence of in-groups and out-groups may not hurt overall performance are tasks that do not require a great deal of coordination among groups and tasks that can be accomplished with the skills of a few exceptional individuals. Overall performance can be seriously hampered, however, if there is overreliance on a small portion of the workforce to the exclusion of other members.

As suggested in Chapter 8, one of the advantages of group decision making is that it uses the unique knowledge and skills of all group members. Ensuring that all employees are given the opportunity to take on challenging tasks has equally long-term benefits. To ensure fair distribution of work assignments, leaders should regularly examine their patterns in assignments and reinforcement. In addition, they should occasionally behave counter to their instincts and assign challenging and critical tasks to subordinates in whom they do not have total confidence.

That a leader's perception of a subordinate influences the leader's behavior and, in turn, influences the subordinate's behavior should not come as a surprise. The processes of mutual influence identified in equity theories (Chapter 3) and negotiation (Chapter 5) are described in other chapters of this book. The notion that a subordinate's performance may be more influenced by his or her leader's perceptions and subsequent behavior than by innate ability and skill is also critical to the second alternative theory of leadership, the attribution model.

THE ATTRIBUTION MODEL OF LEADERSHIP

The **attribution model of leadership** is different from other leadership models in that it deals specifically with perceptions and subsequent behaviors of organizational actors. This model has two facets: (a) leader attributions for and reactions to poor performance by subordinates and (b) observer attributions for and reactions to poor performance by the leader. Similar to the LMX model, it is based on the notion that leaders and followers are involved in a process whereby they influence one another's behavior.

LEADER ATTRIBUTIONS. In the daily performance of work, a leader obtains information about subordinates and their behaviors. Based on this information, the leader makes a determination—an attribution—of the cause of each subordinate's behaviors and selects strategies to deal with poor per-

---

35. Wayne, S. J., Liden, R. C., Kraimer, M. L., & Graf, I. K. (1999). The role of human capital, motivation and supervisor sponsorship in predicting career success. *Journal of Organizational Behavior, 20,* 577–595; Liden, R. C., & Maslyn, J. M. (1998). Multidimensionality of leader–member exchange: An empirical assessment through scale development. *Journal of Management, 24*(1), 43–72; and Gerstner, C. R., & Day, D. V. (1997). Meta-analytic review of leader–member exchange theory: Correlates and construct issues. *Journal of Applied Psychology, 82,* 827–844.

The Attribution Model of Leader Behavior ■ **FIGURE 9-6**

As with the LMX model, the attribution model of leadership emphasizes the mutal influence of leaders and followers. The core of this model is attributions for and reactions to poor performance by either the leader or followers.

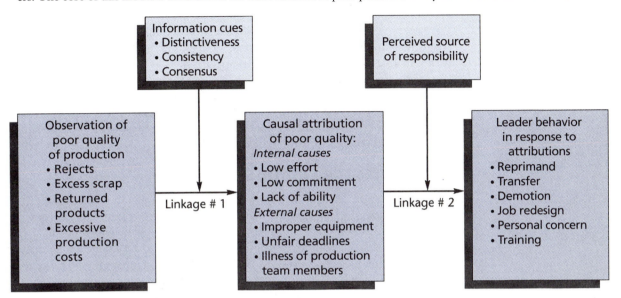

Source: Mitchell, T. R., & Wood, R. E. (1979). An empirical test of an attributional model of leader's responses to poor performance. In R. C. Huseman (Ed.), *Academy of Management Proceedings, 39*, 94–106.

formers. The leader's attributions, as much as each subordinate's behavior, determine how the leader responds to poor performers.

As detailed in Chapter 2, attributions are based on three dimensions of behavior: distinctiveness, consensus, and consistency. These three dimensions help leaders identify an external (situational) or internal (personal) cause for an employee's poor performance.

This attribution is critical to leader–follower relations. A subordinate whose successes or failures are attributed to personal traits such as skill or natural ability will have very different interactions with the leader than will a subordinate whose successes or failures are attributed to environmental factors, such as luck.[36] These attributions can influence many different facets of a leader's behavior, as illustrated in Figure 9-6.

OBSERVER ATTRIBUTIONS. Leaders often are given credit for an organization's successes and blamed for its failures, regardless of whether they deserve the credit or blame. One study found that when observers were told that a workgroup had performed well, they concluded that the leader had been more consistent and provided more task structure than the leader did when the workgroup performed poorly.[37]

36. Mitchell, T. R., Green, S. G., & Wood, R. E. (1981). An attribution model of leadership and the poor performance subordinate: Development and validation. In L. L. Cummings & B. M. Straw (Eds.), *Research in organizational behavior* (vol. 3, pp. 197–234). Greenwich, CT: JAI.
37. Larson, J. R., Lingle, J. H., & Scerbo, M. M. (1984). The impact of performance cues on leader-behavior ratings: The role of selective information availability and probabilistic response bias. *Organizational Behavior and Human Performance, 33*, 323–349.

From this perspective, successful leaders are those who associate themselves with successes and dissociate themselves from failures—who figure out where the group is heading and arrive there first. When they know that a group or division is about to improve because of economic cycles, successful leaders visibly and vividly associate themselves with that group and its performance. When failure is imminent, successful leaders distance themselves from the actions of that group, perhaps going so far as to transfer to another group or to a completely different organization.

Both the attributional model and the LMX model assume that the perception of hierarchical leadership and its subsequent influence are important for organizational performance. A third and final perspective suggests that many characteristics—individual, organizational, and task—have the capacity to serve as substitutes for leadership.

SUBSTITUTES FOR LEADERSHIP

Inherent in many of the theories introduced in this chapter is the assumption that leadership makes a difference. Although it is generally accepted that no one leadership trait will be effective in all situations, the focus in most modern theories of leadership is on determining the situational contingencies in which a particular style of leadership will be most effective. Sometimes, however, hierarchical leadership does not have its intended influence. Even some of the more traditional leadership theories, such as path–goal theory, suggest that when both paths and goals are clear, attempts by the leader to clarify them will be redundant and subordinates will see such efforts as imposing unnecessary, close control.[38] Such close control may enhance performance, but it will reduce participant satisfaction as well. Action on the part of the leader will be perceived as redundant in such situations. A number of research studies now go further, arguing that the leader's behavior is irrelevant in many situations, as is discussed in "Focus On: A Substitute for Leadership."

Occasionally, situational factors appear to neutralize or substitute for the formal leader's ability to influence workgroup satisfaction or performance.[39] Such factors, called **neutralizers of leadership,** paralyze, destroy, or counteract the effectiveness of the leader's behaviors, making it impossible for the leader to have an impact. A **substitute for leadership** makes behavior on the part of the leader not only impossible but also unnecessary. Thus, all substitutes are neutralizers, but all neutralizers are not necessarily substitutes for leadership. For example, a professional orientation (i.e., a commitment to a profession rather than to an organization) is more a substitute for leadership than it is a neutralizer. Individuals who are seriously committed to their professions care more about horizontal than vertical relationships, give considerable credence to peer reviews and evaluations rather than to hierarchical evaluations, and tend to develop relationships outside the employing organization.[40] Alternatively, hierarchical leadership is neutralized when work is

38. House & Mitchell, A path–goal theory of leadership.
39. Kerr, S. (1977). Substitutes for leadership: Implications for organizational design. *Organizational Administrative Science, 8,* 135–146.
40. Filley, A. C., House, R. J., & Kerr, S. (1976). *Managerial processes and organizational behavior.* Glenview, IL: Scott, Foresman.

FOCUS ON
A SUBSTITUTE FOR LEADERSHIP

IS LEADERSHIP OBSOLETE IN SELF-MANAGED TEAMS?   One would think that the art of leadership is dead within self-managed teams (SMTs). However, the reality is that leadership is not obsolete—just different. The John Wayne model of leadership won't work here. What's needed now is a different model of leadership, one that demands more skills than ever before.

This new leadership in SMTs often starts with the team members themselves. Team members share or rotate leadership and hold themselves mutually responsible for a set of performance goals, an approach to their work, and deliverables that reflect the company's mission and business plan. As a result, companies such as Levi Strauss and 3M have found that SMTs inspire members to connect with the company's vision in a very personal way.

And what becomes of the former manager/ John Wayne leader? In many well-functioning SMTs, that person keeps projects on track and ensures that everyone is working with the same information, understands the business vision, and has set appropriate goals. They explain the jobs to be accomplished, assist the team in performing tasks, and review end products. Gradually, he or she relinquishes certain decision-making and conflict-resolution responsibilities as the team members gain skill and competence in their leadership abilities. The former leader serves more as a coach and an adviser as the team matures, but he or she always remains a member of the team, participating in decisions and supplying expertise, knowledge, and resources.

Therefore, *self-managed* does not mean "without a leader." Rather, it implies self-leadership and self-accountability—two traits that will aid in the success of any self-managed team.

Source: Bennis, W. (1998, March). Leading teams. *Executive Excellence, 15*(3), 6; and Moravec, M., Johannessen, O. J., & Hjelmas, T. A. (1998, June). The well-managed SMT. *Management Review, 87*(6), 56–58.

very standardized, machine paced, or serially interdependent. In these situations, the employee has little autonomy or ability to be influenced by leader behaviors.

Leadership substitutes or neutralizers are also often aspects of a task that employees and employers alike seek. For example, task-provided performance feedback can supplant a leader's usefulness. Because task-provided feedback is the most immediate, accurate, and intrinsically motivating source of performance information, a leader's ability to influence employee performance through performance evaluation may pale in comparison. Organizations are therefore encouraged to ensure the inclusion of such mechanisms as task-provided feedback, peer evaluation systems, or goal setting in their daily activities. If the organization is to benefit from these substitutes, it is essential that they be incorporated into the routine of the firm.

The concept of substitutes for and neutralizers of hierarchical leadership is interesting. On the one hand, it is unlikely that any organization will have so many such factors that leadership will be rendered useless. On the other hand, it is equally unlikely that such factors will be so rare that followers will be forced to rely exclusively on leaders. Thus, in attempting to better understand the impact of leaders and their behaviors, it is important to consider when leadership is useful as well as when it is irrelevant or harmful to organizational performance.

VISION.   One common way organizations substitute for leadership is through using a **balanced scorecard** to concretely capture organizational vision for

■ **FIGURE 9-7** **The Balanced Scorecard**

A balanced scorecard is an effective tool to use as a substitute for leadership. By understanding the financial, customer, internal business, and innovation and learning perspectives, managers can lead their organizations to shared visions. Here we present an example of a balanced scorecard from ECI, a semiconductor company.

Financial Perspective

Goals/Vision	Measures
1 Survive	1 Cash flow
2 Succeed	2 Quarterly sales growth and operating income by division
3 Prosper	3 Increased market share and ROE

Customer Perspective

Goals/Vision	Measures
1 New products	1 Percentage of sales from new products
2 Responsive supply	2 On-time delivery
3 Customer partnership	3 Number of cooperative engineering efforts

Internal Business Perspective

Goals/Vision	Measures
1 Technology capability	1 Manufacturing geometry versus competition
2 Manufacturing excellence	2 Cycle-time unit-cost yield
3 New product introduction	3 Actual introduction schedule versus plan

Innovation and Learning Perspective

Goals/Vision	Measures
1 Technology leadership	1 Time to generate next generation
2 Manufacturing learning	2 Process time to maturity
3 Time to market	3 New product introduction versus competition

Source: Kaplan & Norton, *Harvard Business Review, 76.*

managers who lack charisma and other leadership abilities. **Vision** is a view of what the organization wishes to become.[41] By providing the organization's vision to employees, corporations can create specific goals for employees that demonstrate the way their own personal goals (interests) align with the organization's goals. Research has shown that most multinational executives share their visions with their employees to gain greater employee commitment in their organizations.[42]

Top managers often use the balanced scorecard as a comprehensive snapshot of the organization, incorporating four main perspectives—financial perspective (How do shareholders view us?), customer perspective (How do customers view us?), internal business perspective (In what areas do we need

41. Nirenberg, J. (1997). *Power tools: A leader's guide to the latest management thinking.* Singapore: Prentice Hall, p. 48.

42. Rowden, R. W. (1999). The relationship between charismatic leadership behaviors and organizational commitment. *Leadership & Organization Development Journal, 21,* 30–35; and Darling, J. R. (1999). Organizational excellence and leadership strategies: Principles followed by top multinational executives. *Leadership & Organization Development Journal, 20,* 309–321.

to excel?), and the innovation and learning perspective (How can we continuously improve and add value?).[43] An example of a balanced scorecard is shown in Figure 9-7.

As you can see in Figure 9-7, a balanced scorecard can be an effective leadership tool by turning a company's general vision into more specific, meaningful measures of success.[44] This scorecard is particularly useful when organizations are looking to implement change. Beginning with the end in mind, creating visions with results—driven concepts can aid managers in obtaining desired results in shorter periods.[45] Thus, by using the balanced scorecard together with a visionary perspective, organizations can ensure that they will be ready to confront the management challenges that lie ahead.

SUMMARY

Leadership is a broad and difficult topic within organizational behavior. Early in its history, leadership research focused on whether a set of unique personality and demographic characteristics differentiated leaders from followers. As this method proved less than useful, the emphasis shifted to a search for universal traits and behaviors that leaders exhibited. The contingency approach next gained attention, assuming that effective leadership is contingent on, or varies depending on, the specific situation.

What was still needed was a theory of leadership that placed responsibility on organizational leaders. Thus emerged the path–goal theory, which assumes that a leader's effectiveness is influenced by several situational components. The leader's task is to make the paths to performance and rewards for performance clearly visible to subordinates. This perspective allowed the leader more flexibility in responding to organizational demands but, along with its predecessors, there was an implicit assumption that leadership was a construct that could be identified and studied separately from other organizational influences—particularly those of subordinates.

Other views of leadership have emerged as well, such as the LMX model, which suggests that, while important, leadership is by no means one dimensional. According to this view, the same behavior on the part of a leader can influence subordinates in a variety of ways, depending on whether the subordinates are members of in-groups or out-groups. The primary assumption of this model is that leadership is interactive.

The attribution model of leadership is an extension of the LMX model in which the emphasis is on the idea that leadership exists because people (subordinates and leaders alike) have certain expectations about how individuals will behave. Thus, what people perceive reality to be is often more important than what is. In other words, as leaders develop opinions and ideas (attributions) about the behavior of their subordinates, those subordinates begin to behave consistently with those attributions, regardless of the veracity of the attributions. Similarly, subordinates make attributions about their superiors/leaders, and those attributions influence the leaders' ability to effectively influence their subordinates' performance.

43. Kaplan, R. S., & Norton, D. P. (1992). The balanced scorecard—Measures that drive performance. *Harvard Business Review, 70*, 71–79.

44. Kaplan & Norton, *Harvard Business Review*, 73.

45. Schaffer, R. H., & Thompson, H. A. (1992). Successful change programs begin with results. *Harvard Business Review, 70*, 80–89.

The final model of leadership presented here assumes that the usefulness of leadership depends on whether there are substitutes for or neutralizers of leadership. That is, the greater the presence of particular task, subordinate, and organizational characteristics (such as intrinsically satisfying work, ability, experience, and inflexibility), the less relevant or necessary the role of the leader.

We opened this chapter questioning whether leadership would become obsolete, given the greater use of variant managerial structures such as SMTs and the many changes in modern organizations. The material in this chapter clearly suggests that, if anything, modern organizations are in even greater need than ever of more and better leaders.

Regardless of the particular perspective one endorses, leadership is likely to continue to attract researchers and organizational theorists. It is an intriguing topic, and it is an important influence on behavior in organizations.

KEY TERMS

Attribution model of leadership
Balanced scorecard
Charismatic leadership
Contingency model of leadership
Custodial leadership
Emotional intelligence
Leader–member exchange (LMX) model
Leadership
Least-preferred coworker (LPC) scale

Managerial grid
Managerial leadership
Neutralizers of leadership
Path–goal model
Situational leadership model
Substitute for leadership
Transactional leader
Transformational leader
Vision

DISCUSSION QUESTIONS

1 The current wisdom—based on leadership theories—is that effective leaders must be flexible. What, if any, potential problems might there be with adopting this perspective?

2 Although they are very different, Fiedler's contingency theory of leadership and House and Mitchell's path–goal model of leadership are both categorized as contingency models. What does the term *contingency* really mean in these contexts?

3 Based on your knowledge of leadership theory, how would you go about selecting an effective leader from a group of managers? What is an effective leader?

4 Why should managers be sensitive to the existence of substitutes for leadership in their organizations? How might such substitutes enhance or detract from the managers' leadership efforts?

ON YOUR OWN

T-P Leadership Questionnaire: An Assessment of Style   Some leaders deal with general directions, leaving details to subordinates. Other leaders focus on specific details, with the expectation that subordinates will carry out orders. Depending on the situation, both approaches may be effective. The

Source: The T-P Leadership Questionnaire was adapted from Ritchie, J. B. & Thompson, P. (1984). *Organization and people.* New York: West. Copyright 1969 by the American Educational Research Association. Adapted by permission of the publisher.

important issue is whether someone is able to identify relevant dimensions of a situation and behave accordingly. Through this questionnaire, you can identify your relative emphasis on two dimensions of leadership: task orientation and people orientation. These are not opposite orientations, and an individual can rate high or low on either or both.

Directions: The following items describe aspects of leadership behavior. Respond to each item according to the way you would most likely act if you were the leader of a workgroup. Circle whether you would most likely behave in the described way always (A), frequently (F), occasionally (O), seldom (S), or never (N).

A F O S N	**1**	I would most likely act as the spokesperson of the group.
A F O S N	**2**	I would encourage overtime work.
A F O S N	**3**	I would allow members complete freedom in their work.
A F O S N	**4**	I would encourage the use of uniform procedures.
A F O S N	**5**	I would permit members to use their own judgment in solving problems.
A F O S N	**6**	I would stress being ahead of competing groups.
A F O S N	**7**	I would speak as a representative of the group.
A F O S N	**8**	I would needle members for greater effort.
A F O S N	**9**	I would try out my ideas in the group.
A F O S N	**10**	I would let members do their work the way they think best.
A F O S N	**11**	I would be working hard for a promotion.
A F O S N	**12**	I would tolerate postponement and uncertainty.
A F O S N	**13**	I would speak for the group if there were visitors present.
A F O S N	**14**	I would keep the work moving at a rapid pace.
A F O S N	**15**	I would turn the members loose on a job and let them go to it.
A F O S N	**16**	I would settle conflicts when they occur in the group.
A F O S N	**17**	I would get swamped by details.
A F O S N	**18**	I would represent the group at outside meetings.
A F O S N	**19**	I would be reluctant to allow the members any freedom of action.
A F O S N	**20**	I would decide what should be done and how it should be done.
A F O S N	**21**	I would push for increased production.
A F O S N	**22**	I would let some members have authority.
A F O S N	**23**	Things would usually turn out as I had predicted.
A F O S N	**24**	I would allow the group a high degree of initiative.
A F O S N	**25**	I would assign group members to particular tasks.
A F O S N	**26**	I would be willing to make changes.
A F O S N	**27**	I would ask the members to work harder.
A F O S N	**28**	I would trust the group members to exercise good judgment.
A F O S N	**29**	I would schedule the work to be done.
A F O S N	**30**	I would refuse to explain my actions.
A F O S N	**31**	I would persuade others that my ideas are to their advantage.
A F O S N	**32**	I would permit the group to set its own pace.
A F O S N	**33**	I would urge the group to beat its previous record.
A F O S N	**34**	I would act without consulting the group.
A F O S N	**35**	I would ask that group members follow standard rules and regulations.

T_____ P_____

Scoring

The T- P Leadership Questionnaire is scored as follows:

a Circle the item number for items 8, 12, 17, 18, 19, 30, 34, and 35.

b Write the number 1 in front of *a circled item number* if you responded S (seldom) or N (never) to that item.

c Also, write a number 1 in front of *item numbers not circled* if you responded A (always) or F (frequently).

d Circle the number 1s that you have written in front of the following items: 3, 5, 8, 10, 15, 18, 19, 22, 24, 26, 28, 30, 32, 34, and 35.

e *Count the circled number 1s.* This is your score for concern for people. Record the score in the blank following the letter P at the end of the questionnaire.

f *Count uncircled number 1s.* This is your score for concern for task. Record this number in the blank following the letter T.

CLOSING CASE   CHAPTER 9

THE MANAGER'S MEMO

FROM: I. Rand, President
TO: T. Meyers, Vice President, Human Resources
RE: Leadership Development Program

To support our plans to open 10 new stores over the next 5 years, I think we need a program to develop future store managers. I would like your support in creating a leadership development program.

   This program would have two phases: (a) identifying employees with leadership potential and (b) developing in them the skills that make a person a good leader.

   Please submit to me your recommendations for how to carry out each phase of this program. If you submit these recommendations in the form of a general outline of what the program should include, we can discuss the details in a meeting next week.

CASE DISCUSSION QUESTIONS

Assume that you are the vice president of the human resources division, and write a response to the president's memo. Use the material in the chapter as a resource for outlining a program you think will most likely succeed in meeting the president's objectives. Consider also the type of leadership most likely to be important in a store manager.

EXERCISE   PART THREE: The Desert Survival Situation

The situation described in this exercise is based on more than 2,000 actual cases in which men and women lived or died, depending on the survival decisions they made. Your "life" or "death" will depend on how well your group

Source: Lafferty, J. C., Eady, P. M., & Pond, A. W. (1974). *The Desert Survival Situation: A Group Decision Making Experience for Examining and Increasing Individual and Team Effectiveness,* 8th ed. Grosse Pointe Park, M1-Experimental Learning Methods. Used with permission.

can share its present knowledge of a relatively unfamiliar problem so that the team can make decisions that will lead to your survival.

When instructed, read about the situation and complete step 1 without discussing it with the rest of the group.

The Situation

It is approximately 10:00 a.m. in mid-August, and you have just crash-landed in the Sonora Desert in the U.S. Southwest. The light twin-engine plane, containing the bodies of the pilot and the copilot, has completely burned. Only the air frame remains. None of the rest of you has been injured.

The pilot was unable to notify anyone of your position before the crash. However, he had indicated before impact that you were 70 miles south–southwest from a mining camp that is the nearest known habitation and that you were approximately 65 miles off the course that was filed in your VTR flight plan.

The immediate area is quite flat and, except for occasional barrel and saguaro cacti, appears to be rather barren. The last weather report indicated that the temperature would reach 110° that day, which means that the temperature at ground level would be 130°. You are dressed in lightweight clothing: short-sleeved shirts, pants, socks, and street shoes. Everyone has a handkerchief. Collectively, your pockets contain $2.83 in change, $85.00 in bills, a pack of cigarettes, and a ballpoint pen.

Your Task

Before the plane caught fire, your group was able to salvage the 15 items listed in the following table. Your task is to rank these items according to their importance to your survival, 1 = *the most important* to 15 = *the least important*.

You may assume the following:

1 The number of survivors is the same as the number of people on your team.
2 You are the actual people in the situation.
3 The team has agreed to stick together.
4 All items are in good condition.

Step 1   Each member of the team is to individually rank each item. Do not discuss the situation or problem until each member has finished his or her ranking.

Step 2   After everyone has finished the individual ranking, rank-order the 15 items as a team. After the discussion begins, do not change your individual ranking. Your instructor will inform you how much time you have to complete this step.

Item	Step 1: Your Individual Ranking	Step 2: The Team's Ranking	Step 3: Survival Expert's Ranking	Step 4: Difference Between Step 1 and Step 3	Step 5: Difference Between Step 2 and Step 3
Flashlight	_____	_____	_____	_____	_____
Jackknife	_____	_____	_____	_____	_____
Sectional air map of the area	_____	_____	_____	_____	_____
Plastic raincoat (large size)	_____	_____	_____	_____	_____
Magnetic compass	_____	_____	_____	_____	_____
Compress kit with gauze	_____	_____	_____	_____	_____
.45-caliber pistol (loaded)	_____	_____	_____	_____	_____
Parachute (red and white)	_____	_____	_____	_____	_____
Bottle of salt tablets (1,000 tablets)	_____	_____	_____	_____	_____
1 quart of water per person	_____	_____	_____	_____	_____
A book titled *Edible Animals of the Desert*	_____	_____	_____	_____	_____
A pair of sunglasses per person	_____	_____	_____	_____	_____
2 quarts of 180-proof vodka	_____	_____	_____	_____	_____
1 topcoat per person	_____	_____	_____	_____	_____
A cosmetic mirror	_____	_____	_____	_____	_____

Totals
(the lower the score, the better)   _____   _____

Your Score, Step 4   Team Score, Step 5

Please complete the following steps and insert the scores under your team's number.

	Team Number					
	1	2	3	4	5	6
Step 6: **Average individual score** Add up all the individual scores (step 4) on the team and divide by the number of people on the team	____	____	____	____	____	____
Step 7: **Team score**	____	____	____	____	____	____
Step 8: **Gain score** The difference between the team score and the average individual score. If the team score is lower than the average individual score, then gain is +. If the team score is higher than the average individual score, then the gain is >.	____	____	____	____	____	____
Step 9: **Lowest individual score on the team**	____	____	____	____	____	____
Step 10: **Number of individual scores lower than the team score**	____	____	____	____	____	____

CASE   PART THREE: The Making of a Bad Cop

What makes a police officer go sour? I can tell you. I was a Denver police officer until not long ago. Then I quit so I could hold my head up.

Don't get me wrong. I'm not trying to shift the burden of responsibility for the burglaries, break-ins, safe jobs, and that sort of thing. This is bad, *very* bad.

My concern is about the individual officer—the hard-working, basically honest guy. For most, being a cop starts out as an honorable, decent way of making a living. Then, as the pressures mount, the guy becomes disillusioned. Before long, he's walking down the road that, for some, leads to the penitentiary.

Let's back up a little. The trouble really starts with how you get to be a policeman in Denver. It's a cinch. They ask the predictable questions—"Why do you want to become a police officer?"—and just about everybody gives the predictable answer: "I want to help people." They take five or ten minutes to spot the sadist, the psychopath, the guy with an eye for an easy buck. They weed some out, but some get through.

Source: Reprinted by permission of *The Denver Post.*

The police academy is point No. 2 in my bill of particulars. It's a fine thing in a way. You meet the cream of the police department. Your expectations soar. But how well are you really prepared? You have six hectic weeks in which to learn all about the criminal laws you have sworn to enforce, to assimilate the rules of evidence, methods of arbitration, use of firearms, mob and riot control, first aid (including some basic obstetrics), public relations, and so on.

And even this early there is a slight sour note. You knew, of course, that you had to provide your own uniforms, your own hat, shoes, pistol, and bullets. What you didn't know was that you don't just choose a tailor shop for price and get the job done, you're sent to a place by the police department—always the same establishment—and you have to pay the price even though the work may be ill fitting.

There's also something intangible that's not on the formal agenda. You begin to learn that the police department is a fraternity into which you are not automatically accepted by your peers. You have to earn your way in; you have to establish that you are all right. If the rookie's fortunate, he gets little signs that he's been making a good impression. It may happen like this: An older cop stops at a bar, comes out with packages of cigarettes. He explains that this is part of the job, getting cigarettes free from proprietors to resell, and that as a part of the rookie's training it's his turn to "make the butts."

So he goes into a skid-row bar and stands uncomfortably at the end waiting for the bartender to acknowledge his presence and disdainfully toss him two packages of butts. A hint of shame takes hold. But he tells himself this is unusual, that in six months, after he's off probation, he will be the upright officer he meant to be.

One thing leads to another, and after six months the rookies have become conditioned to accept free meals, a few packages of cigarettes, turkeys at Thanksgiving, and liquor at Christmas from respectable people in the district.

The rule book forbids all this. But it's winked at on all levels. So the rookies say to themselves that this is a far cry from stealing, and they can still be good policemen. Besides, their fellow officers are beginning to accept them as good guys. This becomes more and more important as the young officers begin to sense hostility toward them in the community. Other negative aspects of the job also build up, like the people they come in contact with: thieves, con artists, narcotics addicts, and out-and-out nuts.

Off the job the officer's associations narrow. Sometimes, when he tries to mix with neighbors, he senses a kind of strain. When he's introduced to someone, the guy is likely to say, "This is John Jones. He's a police officer." And someone is likely to tell you that there are a few guys in uniform he hates.

It's no wonder the officer begins to think of himself as a member of the smallest minority group in the community. The idea gradually sinks in that the only people who understand him, that he can be close to, are his fellow officers.

But that isn't the whole story. An officer lives with tensions and with fears. Part of the tensions come from the incredible monotony. Part come from the manifold fears. Paramount is the physical fear that he will get hurt to the point where he can't go on working, or that he will be killed. But his biggest fear is that he will show fear. This is the reason he will rush heedlessly in on a cornered burglar or an armed maniac if a couple other officers are present.

He is now at the stage when he wants to be one of the guys. And then one night his car is sent to check on a "Code 16"—a silent burglar alarm.

By the time the officer and his partner get to the scene, the burglar's gone. They call the proprietor. He comes down to look things over. And maybe he says, "Boys, this is covered by insurance, so why don't you take a jacket for your wife, or a pair of shoes." And maybe the officer takes a jacket, just because his partner does. Or maybe the proprietor doesn't come down. But after they get back in the car his partner pulls out four $10 bills and hands him two. "Burglar got careless," says the partner.

Mind you, not all officers do this. But for others it's just a few short steps to participating in and planning crimes. And what has happened to a few could happen to others.

Questions for Discussion

From what you have read and learned in Part Three, what decision-making, leader, group, and political influences contribute to the making of a bad cop? What recommendations would you make to restructure the selection, training, and apprenticeship processes to reduce the likelihood that a police rookie will "go bad"?

PART

4

Managing for Performance

CHAPTER 10

Organizational Entry and Socialization

Lone Star One, Arizona One, Shamu II and the traditional Southwest colors.

SOUTHWEST AIRLINES: WINNING THE WAR FOR TALENT

The Southwest Airlines behavior-based, conversational style of interviewing puts people at ease, claimed human resources director Libby Sartain, whose official title, vice president of people, is intended to do the same. She said, "People feel like they are talking to a friend, and sometimes they tell us the most unbelievable things." Sartain recalled one candidate who, when asked how he dealt with prior difficulties with his co-workers, admitted to having stabbed one with a screwdriver.

But more than screening tools for unlikely violent behavior, Southwest's interview process brings out indicators of how successfully a candidate will fit into the company's storied, customer-focused culture. After 10 years of analyzing the behavior of Southwest's own employees, Sartain and her staff have calibrated their questions to test for the specific needs and requirements of each job, as well as for shared attributes such as common sense, judgment, and decision-making skills.

Last year's 5,000 new hires came from an initial pool of 160,000 applicants, of whom 70,000 were interviewed. The time and money spent on the hiring process has resulted in a turnover rate of only 9% (6% for upper management), by far the lowest in the industry. It has also enabled Southwest to maintain a strong, unified culture in the face of enormous growth, and to groom management talent within the company. Fewer than five "outsiders" hold senior management positions at the airline, and many managers began their careers in entry-level positions.

Beginning with the selection process, it is apparent that Southwest Airlines takes great care to find employees that fit into the organization. It

Source: Excerpted from Stein, N. (2000, May 29). Winning the war to keep top talent. *Fortune,* 132–138.

clearly recognizes the importance of socializing employees to build strong commitments to the organization, and the result is a strong company culture with payoffs to the bottom line.

INTRODUCTION

How does a new employee learn the organizational ropes? What distinguishes an established member of an organization from a new hire? Because it is clear that the development of a committed employee requires more than having him or her simply accept the job, the purpose of this chapter is to examine some of the factors that influence an individual's association with and commitment to an organization. The intent is to give you a beginning point for thinking about how an individual becomes an organizational member. Starting with the selection process, we will examine critical issues related to how organizations choose individuals and how individuals choose organizations. However, this is just the first step in becoming a member of an organization.

After an individual joins an organization, the next step is to link the organization and the individual—to commit the individual to the goals, expectations, and aspirations of the organization. In this chapter we discuss how organizational commitment is transmitted from one member to another via the organization's culture.

ENTRY INTO AN ORGANIZATION: THE ORGANIZATION'S PERSPECTIVE

Employing the best individuals is critical to an organization's performance. If all applicants for a job were able to perform equally well, then selection would require little more than hiring the right number of "warm bodies." However, in the vast majority of cases, *who* is hired makes a big difference. In fact, research on productivity suggests that a high-ability worker will be two to three times as productive as a low-ability worker.[1] Thus, the benefits of identifying and then hiring the best-qualified candidate for a job can be considerable.

PERSON–ORGANIZATION FIT

As highlighted in the opening vignette, finding the right employee at Southwest is a matter of fit—between the person and the job as well as between the person and the organization. The importance of such a fit stems from the organization's need for shared outlooks or a common purpose among its members and the individual's need to be comfortable in his or her work environment. **Person–organization fit** can thus be defined as the compatibility between an individual and the organization for which he or she works. This fit includes of personal characteristics of the employee that add to the

---

1. Mackworth, N. H. (1947). High incentives versus hot and humid atmospheres in a physical effort task. *British Journal of Psychology, 38,* 90–102; and Schmidt, J. L., & Hunter, J. E. (1983). Individual differences in productivity: An empirical test of estimates derived from studies of selection procedure utility. *Journal of Applied Psychology, 68,* 407–414.

organizational environment, as well as characteristics that complement characteristics of other employees.[2]

Person–organization fit can be assessed during the interview process,[3] as interviewing provides an opportunity for both the organization and the individual to assess the characteristics of the other party. The interviewer can examine an applicant's personal characteristics and organizational suitability. In addition, applicants can gain valuable information about how well they would fit into the organization. The organizational culture and structure of the company are two things the applicant can keep in mind when assessing his or her fit with the organization.

Whether there is a good person–organization fit has important implications for both organizational outcomes and the individual well-being of the employee.[4] For example, a good fit between the values of the employee and those of the organization has been shown to predict job satisfaction and organizational commitment.[5] Because tasks will be completed most efficiently by an employee who fits with the organization, such a fit may also be correlated with improved performance.

In addition to improved performance, good person–organization fit affects intentions to quit and the turnover rate in the organization.[6] The keen attention Southwest Airlines pays to person–organization fit during the selection and hiring process enhances the likelihood that employees will remain with the organization. Southwest's turnover rate, as pointed out in the opening vignette, is the lowest in the industry, due in part to the company's goal of ensuring a fit between the applicants and the organization.

Selection of individuals who are underqualified or overqualified for their positions is one of many possible reasons for a lack of fit. Some researchers suggest that hiring over- or underqualified employees may be on the rise. For example, research by Karen Jehn, Linda Stroh, and Mary Ann Von Glinow shows that when one member of a dual-career couple accepts a new position or is transferred to a new location, the other person may have to settle for a less-than-desirable position. Consequently, with the increase in the number of dual-income couples, research has shown that there has been a concomitant increase in the number of overqualified applicants for many jobs.[7] Organizations may be especially tempted to hire an overqualified worker, thinking that there may be positive benefits associated with hiring an overqualified person. However, research suggests that this may be an er-

2. Kristof, A. L. (1996). Person–organization fit: An integrative review of its conceptualizations, measurement, and implications. *Personnel Psychology, 49*(1), 1–49.

3. Cable, D. M., & Judge, T. A. (1997). Interviewers' perceptions of person–organization fit and organizational selection decisions. *Journal of Applied Psychology, 82*, 546–561.

4. Vianen, V., & Annelies, E. M. (2000, Spring). Person–organization fit: The match between newcomers' and recruiters' preferences for organizational cultures. *Personnel Psychology, 53*(1), 113–149.

5. Vianen & Annelies, Person–organization fit; and O'Reilly, C. A., Chatman, J., & Caldwell, D. F. (1991). People and organizational culture: A profile comparison to assessing person–organization fit. *Academy of Management Journal, 34*, 487–516.

6. Saks, A. M., & Ashforth, B. E. (1997). A longitudinal investigation of the relationship between job information sources, applicant perceptions of fit, and work outcomes. *Personnel Journal, 50*, 305–426.

7. Jehn, K. A., Stroh, L. K., & Von Glinow, M. A. (1997). The commuting couple: Oxymoron or career freedom? In Y. Altman (Ed.), *Careers in the new millennium* (pp. 163–178). Brussels, Belgium: Academic Cooperative.

Major Steps in the Employee Selection Process	■ **FIGURE 10-1**

Selecting the right employee for a job entails three steps. Job analysis catalogs the tasks in a job and the skills required of job incumbents. Next, assessment procedures that test applicants for these skills must be developed. Finally, the assessment procedures must identify qualified applicants.

Job Analysis
(Identification of Tasks Performed, and Skills and Abilities Required)
↓
Development and Validation of Assessment Devices to Measure Knowledge,
Skills, and Abilities
↓
Use of Assessment Devices in Processing of Applicants

Source: Gatewood, & Feild, *Human resource selection,* p. 18.

roneous assumption and that organizations should be very cautious when hiring either over- or underqualified workers.[8] Therefore, selection and placement become critical as organizations may find it especially difficult to retain over- and underqualified employees.

SELECTION AND PLACEMENT

One of the best ways an organization can enhance the fit between the organization and its employees is through the selection process.[9] **Selection** can be viewed as a matching process in which organizations seek out (recruit) specific individuals, and individuals select from among a variety of organizations. For an organization, selection is the process of collecting and evaluating information about an individual before deciding whether to extend an offer of employment.[10] Because a mismatch incurs high costs associated with rapid turnover, lower performance levels, and friction between an employee and the organization, ensuring a good match between the individual's talents and needs and the organization's demands should be a high priority.[11]

As illustrated in Figure 10-1, three steps are necessary for a good selection process: job analysis, selection of assessment devices, and processing of applicants via screening, interviewing, and testing of the applicant pool. The selection process is most likely to succeed in identifying interested, qualified candidates and be worth its costs when the process is valid, when there are more qualified applicants than positions to fill, and when a small percentage of applicants become successful hires.

JOB ANALYSIS.   The logical way for an organization to ensure a good person–job fit is to begin with a thorough understanding of the position to be filled. **Job analysis** is the gathering of information about the tasks, activities,

8. Stroh, L. K., Gregersen, H. B., & Black, J. S. (1998). Closing the gap: Expectations vs. realities among repatriates. *Journal of World Business, 33,* 111–124.

9. Chatman, J. A. (1991). Matching people and organizations. *Administrative Science Quarterly, 36,* 459–484.

10. Gatewood, R. D., & Feild, H. S. (1998). *Human resource selection.* (4th ed.). Fort Worth, TX: Dryden Press.

11. Kotter, J. P. (1973). The psychological contract. *California Management Review, 15,* 91–99.

results (products or services), equipment, materials, and working conditions that characterize a job.[12]

The primary purpose of a job analysis is to determine the job dimensions (aspects of the job essential for good performance) and critical worker characteristics needed in successful job incumbents. For example, promptness, low absenteeism, or participation in an advanced training program may be important job dimensions. Worker characteristics include the specific knowledge, skills, and abilities that an individual must possess to qualify for the position.

In addition to specifying who should be recruited, the job analysis aids in the organization's performance appraisal, training, and compensation functions. Only by knowing the skills the position requires can the organization effectively train and promote employees. A good job analysis evaluates the relative worth of a position to the organization and helps to ensure that each position is compensated appropriately relative to other positions in the organization.

IDENTIFICATION OF ASSESSMENT DEVICES. Assessment devices used in the selection process can include application forms, references, intelligence tests, special ability tests, personality tests, work simulation exercises, and selection interviews.[13] Although not all of these devices are used in every selection decision, empirical or anecdotal evidence supports the use of most of them in different situations.[14] The critical factor in deciding which devices to use in a particular situation is the ability of the devices to differentiate among applicants and, given the litigious environment in which selection takes place, their defensibility in a court setting. Adequate selection techniques should be based on the devices' validity and reliability to differentiate among job applicants. In addition, these assessment devices must show the utility of each technique assessed for a particular job. Such devices need to be designed so that they are not biased and so that they do not discriminate against potential applicants on the basis of unrelated job attributes such as age, race, gender, or ethnicity. (Chapter 12 includes an extended discussion of the legal and regulatory environment and its impact on organizations.)

Because particular jobs require certain skills, abilities, and knowledge, the process used to screen applicants should identify individuals who possess those particular traits and abilities. For example, Southwest Airlines conducts a conversational interview, using behavior-based questions. An example of a behavior-based question that Southwest might use is, "When have you experienced conflict with a coworker and how have you handled that situation?" When the organization understands both the position (through the job analysis) and how to measure worker characteristics (through assessment devices), it is ready to identify and evaluate applicants.

---

12. Gatewood & Feild, *Human resource selection.*

13. Chatman, Matching people and organizations.

14. See, for example, Guion, R. (1991). Personnel assessment, selection, and placement. In M. Dunnette & L. Hough (Eds.), *Handbook of industrial and organizational psychology* (pp. 327–398). Palo Alto, CA: Consulting Psychologists Press; Andrews, K., Schmitt, W., & Schneider, B. (1983). Current issues in personnel selection. In K. Rowland & G. Ferris (Eds.), *Research in personnel and human resource management* (Vol. 1, pp. 85–126). Greenwich, CT: JAI; and Holland, J. (1973). *Making vocational choices: A theory of careers.* Englewood Cliffs, NJ: Prentice Hall.

TECHNOLOGY FOCUS ON RECRUITING

INTERNET RECRUITING CATCHING ON FOR JOBS AT ALL LEVELS. Frustrated by the slow turnaround and expense of advertising in local-market newspapers, corporate recruiters are turning to the Internet to mine talent from around the world. Recruiting sites such as Monster.com (*www.monster.com*), HotJobs.com (*www.hotjobs.com*), and Career Mosaic (*www.careermosaic.com*) get hundreds of thousands of hits each month from job seekers and recruiters.

The Internet offers a fast, easy way to reach a broad audience of job seekers, said Doreen Collins, manager of staffing and quality initiatives at General Electric's (GE's) home office in Fairfield, Connecticut. The company has more than 2,000 job openings listed at its GE Careers.com web page. "We post the majority of our job openings at the site, whether they are entry-level or mid-career positions," said Steve Poole, GE's manager of recruiting and staffing services. GE also posts at Monster.com, HotJobs.com, Career Mosaic, and other online recruiting sites. Like GE, most other large companies have a job openings web page.

"The Internet makes jobs available to a worldwide audience," said Collins. "And we can get a job posting out any time, any day." By recruiting online, added Poole, GE finds people who may not live in the city where the job is, but would relocate for the right opportunity.

Of the 15,000 résumés GE receives monthly, roughly half are now submitted online. The résumés are automatically stored in a database, and skill searches are used to match jobs to candidates. Paper résumés are stored in the same database, but someone must first run them through a scanner, says Poole. Online résumés can be searched instantly.

Recruiting via the Internet allows organizations to identify applicants in a speedy and time-efficient manner. Additionally, depending on the company's needs and the type of applicants the company wants to attract, the Internet may be used to target those specific individuals, thus eliminating a large number of unqualified applicants.

Source: Excerpted from Fister, S. (1999). Online recruiting: Good, fast and cheap? *Training, 36*(5), 26–28.

IDENTIFICATION AND PROCESSING OF APPLICANTS. Applicants can be identified through a number of mechanisms, including the classified sections of newspapers and journals, personal contacts and references, executive-search firms, employment agencies, college and university placement centers, outplacement services, and as "TECHNOLOGY FOCUS ON: Recruiting" discusses, the Internet. Figure 10-2 further describes each of these venues.

Research suggests that the means by which an employee is recruited is an important factor in predicting the employee's future performance. This research shows that candidates who apply directly to organizations or are recruited at professional meetings or conventions seem to be more dependable, are absent from work less often, and report higher levels of job satisfaction and involvement than employees who are recruited through newspaper ads or college placement offices.[15] One reason for this difference may be that individuals who apply to the organization directly or who are recruited at professional meetings and conventions are likely to have more accurate

---

15. Williams, C. R., Labig, C. E., & Stone, T. H. (1993). Recruitment sources and posthire outcomes for job applicants and new hires: A test of two hypotheses. *Journal of Applied Psychology, 78,* 163–172; and Rynes, S. (1991). Recruitment, job choice, and post hire consequences. In M. Dunnette & L. Hough (Eds.), *Handbook of industrial organizational psychology.* Palo Alto, CA: Consulting Psychologists Press.

■ **FIGURE 10-2**	**Source of Identification of Applicants**

- ■ *Executive search firms*, **"headhunter":** Under contract to organizations to find candidates for specific jobs.
- ■ *Current employees*: Provide employers with an inexpensive method for identifying potential candidates.
- ■ *Private employment agencies*: Charge fees for their services, which include advertising job openings, screening applications, and conducting initial interviews.
- ■ *Government employment agencies*: Assist employers in employee testing, job analysis and evaluation, and community wage surveys.
- ■ *Outplacement firms*: Typical activities include job counseling and job placement for employees who have been laid off.

information about positions than are individuals who are recruited through newspaper advertisements or college placement offices. Thus, from the perspective of the organization, providing accurate information about positions may increase the likelihood of achieving good person–organization fit.

ENTRY INTO AN ORGANIZATION: THE INDIVIDUAL'S PERSPECTIVE

While the organization is processing job applicants, individual applicants are processing the organization. That is, they are simultaneously determining whether this is an organization they would like to join. Two mechanisms help an individual understand the organization so that they can make such a decision: the realistic job preview and the psychological contract.

THE REALISTIC JOB PREVIEW

In seeking positions, job candidates sometimes have unrealistically high expectations about organizations.[16] If these expectations are not met, the employee may experience low job satisfaction early in his or her tenure with the organization and may even leave the company.[17] One way to avoid such unrealistic expectations is through the use of a realistic job preview.[18]

A **realistic job preview** is a mechanism used by organizations to present both the desirable and undesirable aspects of a job and the organization so that potential employees have complete and accurate information. Specific attributes of what it takes to get the job done, whether positive or negative, should be included in a realistic job preview. This would include, for example, the daily activities required to complete the job. Also, devices such as videotapes, work simulations, and interviews with current jobholders are effective ways to portray realistic job previews to potential applicants.

Realistic job previews are an important step in the socialization and selection process of new employees. Research has indicated that when organi-

---

16. Wanous, J. P., Poland, T. D., Premack, S. L., & Davis K. S. (1992). The effects of met expectations on newcomer attitudes and behaviors: A review and meta-analysis. *Journal of Applied Psychology*, 77, 288–297.

17. Wanous, J. P. (1992). *Organizational entry: Recruitment, selection, orientation, and socialization of newcomers* (2nd ed.). Reading, MA: Addison-Wesley, p. 31.

18. Phillips, J. M. (1998). Effects of realistic job previews on multiple organizational outcomes: A meta-analysis. *Academy of Management Journal, 41,* 673–690.

zations provide realistic job previews, they experience higher performance and lower turnover.[19] Given the costly nature of the selection process (each employee selected is a potential half-million-dollar asset or a half-million-dollar liability to the organization[20]), weeding out the "undecideds" may have considerable long-term benefits for the organization.

A survey of 1,700 U.S. organizations by Aon Consulting found that one third of the organizations used realistic job previews as a part of their overall international assignment strategy.[21] Selection for international assignments must include the assessment of interpersonal and cross-cultural skills of the candidate (as these are often equally important as, if not more important than, the technical skills[22]), and the candidate must have a clear picture—a defined set of expectations—of what the assignment will entail. This increases the likelihood of a good person–job match on the international scene.

Providing a clear picture of an organization and a position is not without risks. The goal is that realistic job previews will assist applicants to essentially self-select themselves into and out of the organization. This means that individuals who are undecided may be persuaded to withdraw their names from consideration, as their view of the organization becomes more realistic.

However, those who ultimately take the position are likely to be more committed to and remain in the position longer.[23] As suggested earlier, candidates who have more complete and accurate information about a position are more likely to succeed in that position.[24] In addition, research shows that an organization's candidness may increase the new recruit's feeling that the organization treats employees fairly.[25]

THE PSYCHOLOGICAL CONTRACT

An individual who accepts a position with an organization enters into a **psychological contract** with his or her employer. This unwritten contract consists of a set of expectations regarding the terms of the exchange relationship between the employee and the organization.[26] Psychological contracts usually concern expectations about such matters as working conditions, work requirements, the level of effort to be expended on the job, as well as the amount and nature of the employer's authority.[27] Psychological contracts differ from other contracts in that they may contain thousands of items; both

19. Phillips, Effects of realistic job previews on multiple organizational outcomes.

20. Podsakoff, P. M., Williams, M. L., & Scott, W. E. (1987). Myths of employee selection systems. In R. S. Schuler, S. A. Youngblood, & V. L. Huber (Eds.), *Readings in personnel and human resource management* (pp. 612–619). New York: West.

21. Frazee, V. (1998, July 1). No common thread in expat selection. *Workforce*, 9.

22. Black, J. S., Gregersen, H. B., Mendenhall, M. E., & Stroh, L. K. (1999). *Globalizing people through international assignments.* Reading, MA: Addison-Wesley.

23. Wanous, J. P. (1977). Organizational entry: The individual's viewpoint. In J. R. Hackman, E. E. Lawler, & L. W. Porter (Eds.), *Perspectives on behavior in organizations.* New York: McGraw-Hill.

24. Breaugh, J. A. (1981). Relationships between recruiting sources and employee performance, absenteeism, and work attitudes. *Academy of Management Journal, 24,* 142–147.

25. Bies, R. J., & Moag, J. (1986). Interactional justice: Communication criteria of fairness. In R. J. Lewicki, M. H. Bazerman, & B. Sheppard (Eds.), *Research on negotiating in organizations* (Vol. 1, pp. 43–55). Greenwich, CT: JAI.

26. Rousseau, D. M. (1995). *Psychological contracts in organizations: Understanding written and unwritten agreements.* Thousand Oaks, CA: Sage, p. 9; and Schein, E. A. (1980). *Organizational psychology.* Englewood Cliffs, NJ: Prentice Hall.

27. Schein, *Organizational psychology.*

RESEARCH IN ACTION
SELECTING THE RIGHT CANDIDATES FOR INTERNATIONAL ASSIGNMENTS

Rosalie L. Tung, Simon Fraser University; *tung@sfu.ca*

The globalization of the world economy means that it is increasingly important for managers to possess a global mind-set. An effective way of developing this perspective is through international assignments. I recently undertook a study, with the assistance of Arthur Andersen, Incorporated, to examine the attitudes and experiences of 409 U.S. expatriates with regard to international assignments.

The following are some of the major findings of this study:

- Most expatriates valued an international assignment because it allowed them to acquire skills and experience usually not available at home.
- The vast majority of expatriates were not guaranteed a job and/or promotion upon return after successful completion of the tour of duty abroad.
- There was no difference in performance between men and women expatriates, regardless of country of assignment (i.e., women were able to perform as well as men in culturally tough environments, including male-dominated societies).
- Most expatriates felt that the assimilation and socialization (i.e., adapting to the norms and

practices of the host society) and integration (i.e., selecting and combining the best of both home and host country norms and practices) modes contributed to effective performance abroad, whereas separation (i.e., maintaining a distance from host country culture and norms) was least conducive to successful performance overseas.
- The family situation played an important role in international assignments, including the decision to accept/reject an international assignment, performance abroad, and choice of mechanisms to cope with the stress and strains associated with living abroad.
- Many expatriates felt that their companies failed to provide them with adequate predeparture training and realistic job previews of what to expect while abroad.

Findings from this study suggest that multinational corporations should give due consideration to the employee's family situation in their selection decision, provide more adequate predeparture training and realistic job previews, and do a better job in reabsorbing repatriates upon their return.

---

parties may have different expectations, since some matters may have been explicitly discussed and others only inferred; and they change as the individual's and the organization's expectations change.[28]

Traditionally, the psychological contract was viewed as committing both sides to a relationship in which employees gave organizations their loyalty, and organizations gave employees steady employment.[29] However, increasingly, management practices are significantly affecting the psychological commitment of employees. Downsizing and restructuring, for example, are making it more difficult to identify what both the employee and the organization are owed in the exchange relationship.

---

28. See, for example, Rousseau, D. M. (1990). New hire perceptions of their own and employees' obligations: A study of psychological contracts. *Journal of Organizational Behavior, 17,* 389–400; and Kotter, J. P. (1973). The psychological contract. *California Management Review, 15,* 91–99.

29. Stroh, L. K., & Reilly, A. H. (1997). Loyalty in an age of downsizing. *Sloan Management Review, 38*(4), 83–88; and Marks, M. E. (1988, September). The disappearing company man. *Psychology Today,* 34–39.

Additionally, organizations are finding it more difficult to fulfill their obligations to employees during downsizing and other turbulent states.[30] Violating the psychological contract of the employee, although not completely detrimental to the employee–organization relationship, can have serious consequences for both the organization and the employee.[31] From the employee's perspective, violation leads to decreased trust of employers and reduced job satisfaction. Employees also might be inclined to reduce their contributions to the organization or to leave the organization altogether.[32]

The individual and organizational consequences of violations of the psychological contract are clear examples of why psychological contracts are necessary for there to be continuing, harmonious relationships between employees and organizations. Because psychological contracts are entered into as individuals join the organization, whether the individuals' expectations about the contract are met is crucial to their ongoing relationship.

ORGANIZATIONAL COMMITMENT

After an organization extends an offer to an applicant and that individual enters into a psychological contract by accepting the offer, the applicant becomes a member of the organization. The applicant must now become educated in and committed to the organization's goals and objectives.

Organizational commitment is the relative strength of an individual's identification with and involvement in a particular organization.[33] Organizational commitment is not simply loyalty to an organization, but an ongoing process through which organizational actors express their concern for the continued success and well-being of the organization of which they are a part.[34]

Recently, however, researchers have proposed that organizational commitment may take many forms.[35] In their three-component model of organizational commitment, Natalie Allen and John Meyer identified and represented three forms of commitment: affective, continuance, and normative.[36] *Affective commitment* is an individual's emotional attachment with (i.e., identification with and involvement in) the organization. *Continuance commitment* refers to the individual's recognition of the benefits of continued organizational mem-

30. Morrison, E. W., & Robinson, S. L. (1997). When employees feel betrayed: A model of how psychological contract violation develops. *Academy of Management Journal, 22,* 226–256; and Stroh, & Reilly, Loyalty in an age of downsizing.

31. Stroh, L. K., & Reilly, A. H. (1997). Rekindling organization loyalty: The impact of career mobility. *Journal of Career Development, 24*(1), 39–54; Rousseau, D. M. (1995). *Psychological contracts in organizations: Understanding written and unwritten agreements.* Thousand Oaks, CA: Sage, p. 111; Morrison & Robinson, When employees feel betrayed.

32. Morrison & Robinson, When employees feel betrayed.

33. Mowday, R. T., Porter, L. W., & Steers, R. M. (1982). *Employee–organization linkages: The psychology of commitment, absenteeism, and turnover.* New York: Academic Press.

34. Stroh, Gregersen, & Black, Closing the gap.

35. Meyer, J. P., Irving, P. G., & Allen, N. J. (1998). Examination of the combined effects of work values and early work experiences on organizational commitment. *Journal of Organizational Behavior, 19,* 29–52.

36. Allen, N. J., & Meyer, J. P. (1996). Affective, continuance, and normative commitment to the organization: An examination of construct validity. *Journal of Vocational Behavior, 49,* 252–276; and Meyer, J. P., & Allen, N. J. (1991). A three-component conceptualization of organizational commitment. *Human Resource Management Review, 1,* 61–89.

bership versus the perceived cost of leaving the organization. Finally, *normative commitment* refers to the employee's feelings of obligation to stay in the organization. All three forms of commitment affect not only employees' willingness to remain with an organization, but their work-related behavior as well.[37]

There are several important reasons an organization should want to increase the level of commitment among its employees. First, research has shown that a positive relationship exists between organizational commitment and employees' job satisfaction, attendance, and motivation.[38] Second, because highly committed employees want to remain associated with the organization and to advance organizational goals, they are less likely to leave and more likely to remain with the organization for longer periods of time. Thus, high levels of organizational commitment are associated with low levels of employee turnover.[39] Meyer and Allen cautioned however, that there is also a "dark side" to commitment in that continuance commitment might reduce turnover, but it may not necessarily improve job performance.[40]

Despite this dark side to organizational commitment, many researchers have recently been focusing on whether organizational commitment influences job performance. Summary findings suggest that commitment to one's supervisors may be more positively related to employee performance than one's commitment to the organization as a whole.[41] Thus, managers must be concerned with employees' commitment not only to the organization as a whole but to different organizational levels or players in the organization.

FACTORS LEADING TO COMMITMENT

What leads individuals to be more or less committed to an organization? To answer this question, we must consider the four major factors leading to commitment: visibility, explicitness, irreversibility, and volition.[42]

VISIBILITY. One of the most simple and straightforward ways to get individuals to commit to an organization is to make their association and contribution to the organization public information (i.e., increase their **visibility**). Behaviors that are secret or unobserved do not have a committing force behind them because they cannot be linked to specific individuals.

One way to make employee contributions public is through internal newsletters. By highlighting an employee's contribution or connection to the

---

37. Meyer, Irving, & Allen, Examination of the combined effects of work values and early work experiences on organizational commitment.

38. Becker, T. E., Billings, R. S., Eveleth, D. M., & Gilbert, N. L. (1996). Foci and bases of employee commitment: Implications for job performance. *Academy of Management Journal, 39*, 464–482.

39. Angle, H., & Perry, J. (1981). An empirical assessment of organizational commitment and organizational effectiveness. *Administrative Science Quarterly, 26*, 1–14; Mowday, R. T., Steers, R. M., & Porter, L. W. (1979). The measurement of organizational commitment. *Journal of Vocational Behavior, 14*, 224–247; Koch, J. L., & Steers, R. M. (1978). Job attachment, satisfaction, and turnover among public employees. *Journal of Vocational Behavior, 12*, 119–128; and Steers, R. M. (1977). Antecedents and outcomes of organizational commitments. *Administrative Science Quarterly, 22*, 46–56.

40. Meyer, J. P., & Allen, N. J. (1997). *Commitment in the workplace: Theory, research and application.* Thousand Oaks, CA: Sage.

41. Becker, Billings, Eveleth, Gilbert, Foci and bases of employee commitment.

42. Salancik, G. R. (1977, Summer). Commitment is too easy! *Organizational Dynamics,* 207–222.

organization in a company newsletter, the employee becomes more linked to the company. The more visible individuals and their contributions, the more committed they are likely to be.

Yet another way to visibly link an employee to an organization is through the use of common uniforms. For example, Southwest Airlines employees wear khaki shorts and red shirts that indicate to outsiders that the employee is associated with the organization, or "connected" to the airline. The uniforms make public the individual's association with Southwest Airlines and align the worker to the company in a very visible way.

EXPLICITNESS. Visibility alone is not sufficient to commit individuals to the organization. It must be combined with explicitness; the more explicit the behavior, the less deniable it is. **Explicitness** is the extent to which the individual cannot deny that the behavior occurred. How explicit the behavior is depends on two factors: its *observability* and its *unequivocality* (equivocality is the difficulty of determining the actual act or behavior). When a behavior cannot be observed but only inferred, it is less explicit.

Consider the example of two employees working on a company project. One of the employees spends significantly more time in the office working on the project where other employees view their behaviors. The second person working on the project works from home, thus the person's behavior is less explicit and observable. Under the concept of explicitness, the individual working in the office will appear more committed to the project because that individual's behaviors are observed as clearly contributing to the completion of the project.

IRREVERSIBILITY. **Irreversibility** means that a behavior is permanent—it cannot easily be revoked or undone. Organizations are aware of the committing aspect of irreversible acts. Thus, many organizations develop programs and work structures that tie individuals to their organizations. Benefits packages, for example, are not transferable from one firm to another. The irreversible loss of these benefits, should an individual choose to leave an organization, commits the individual to continued employment. Job-specific training is also irreversible. Developing an employee's abilities so that they match the unique constellation of an organization's expectations reduces the likelihood that the person will disengage from the organization. Developing work or project teams and fostering collaborations among specific coworkers are other ways to connect workers to the organization. Whether through benefits packages, job-specific training, or team projects, the effect is to entangle the individual in organizational relationships. And the greater the entanglement, the higher the irreversibility and the more costly termination would be to the employee.

VOLITION. **Volition** (a choice to act) and its observable equivalent—personal responsibility—is the fourth mechanism that binds people to actions. Without volition, behaviors are not committing. Enhancing employees' personal responsibility for their actions is critical to establishing and maintaining their commitment to tasks and the organization. A number of organizational interventions acknowledge the importance of personal volition. For example, organizations are beginning to design tasks in ways that increase individuals' personal responsibility for performing or scheduling them. Participative decision making (discussed in Chapter 8) is one example that emphasizes volition or personal responsibility. If a workgroup is involved in making a decision or solving a problem, its members will be more committed to the implementation of that decision or solution than if they were simply informed of it.

As we have seen, visibility, explicitness, irreversibility, and volition are important in the creation of commitment. Further, commitment to the organization and its goals is important because, as noted throughout this section of the chapter, individuals adjust their attitudes and expectations in situations to which they are committed.

FACTORS INFLUENCING COMMITMENT

Although enhancing organizational commitment is an ongoing process, it is probably most critical early in an employee's association with an organization, to ensure continued attachment. Richard Mowday, Lyman Porter, and Richard Steers suggested a number of factors that may increase this level of commitment,[43] including (a) personal factors, such as the employee's initial level of commitment (deriving from initial job expectations, the psychological contract, and so on); (b) organizational factors, such as the employee's initial work experiences and subsequent sense of responsibility; and (c) non-organizational factors, such as the availability of alternative jobs.

Commitment to an organization and its goals is a major factor in predicting performance.[44] Thus, having mechanisms to enhance the development of organizational commitment among new employees is critical. One way in which organizations with high levels of commitment differ from organizations with low levels of commitment is that the former are "strong culture" firms. For employees to be part of a strong culture, they must be educated about the expectations and practices of the organization. The extent of employees' commitment to their jobs and the organization may hinge on their ability to understand, accept, and become a part of the organizational culture.[45]

PERSONAL FACTORS. The primary personal factor is the amount of potential attachment an employee brings to work on the first day—in other words, the employee's propensity to develop a stable attachment to the organization. Some organizations, like Southwest Airlines, assess this stability in the selection process to ensure a greater probability that a new employee will stay with the organization.

ORGANIZATIONAL FACTORS. Organizational factors such as job scope—the job's feedback, autonomy, challenge, and significance—increase behavioral involvement. The ability to participate actively in task-related decision making also influences commitment levels. Likewise, consistency between workgroup and organizational goals will increase commitment to those goals and a person's ultimate commitment to the organization. Finally, organizational characteristics such as concern for employees' interests or

---

43. Mowday, R. T., Porter, L. W., & Steers, R. M. (1982). *Employee-organization linkages: The psychology of commitment, absenteeism, and turnover.* New York: Academic Press; and Meyer, J. P., & Allen, N. J. (1997). *Commitment in the workplace; Theory research and application.* Thousand Oaks, CA: Sage Publications.

44. Eby, L. T., Freeman, D. M., Rush, M. C., & Lance, C. E. (1999). Motivational bases of affective organizational commitment: A partial test of an integrative theoretical model. *Journal of Occupational and Organizational Psychology, 72,* 463–483.

45. Ott, J. S. (1989). *The organizational culture perspective.* Chicago: Dorsey.

employee ownership are also positively associated with increased commitment to the organization.[46]

NONORGANIZATIONAL FACTORS. The primary nonorganizational factor that enhances commitment is the availability of alternatives after the initial choice to join the organization has been made. It seems that the highest level of initial commitment occurs among employees who (a) have insufficient external justification for their initial choice and (b) view the choice as relatively irrevocable; that is, they believe that they have had no subsequent opportunities that would warrant their changing their minds.[47]

ORGANIZATIONAL CULTURE

Every organization has its own **organizational culture**—a system of shared values about what is important and beliefs about how things work that produce the norms and expectations of performance.[48] Applicants and new employees are introduced to company culture from the moment the interview process begins. As pointed out in the opening vignette, Southwest's easygoing interview style gives the applicants a preview to the company's easygoing organizational culture. Unlike Southwest Airlines, however, some organizational cultures are very fragmented and difficult to perceive; like Southwest Airlines, other cultures are very strong, cohesive, and clear to insiders and outsiders alike. Whether weak or strong, an organization's culture has a profound influence on how work gets done. It can affect many aspects of organizational life, from who gets promoted and what decisions are made to how people dress, act, and play at work. "FOCUS ON: Corporate Cultures" highlights the clashes that can occur when a merger unites two companies with radically different cultures. How the employees adjust to the postmerger culture of an organization can have significant effects on whether the organization survives.

STRONG ORGANIZATIONAL CULTURES

There is a widely held notion among managers that organizations with strong cultures enjoy a number of competitive advantages, including high commitment among employees and an ability to respond quickly to changes in the environment.[49] Southwest Airlines is an obvious example of an organization with a strong culture. Others include 3M, Frito-Lay, Disney, Johnson & Johnson, and Procter & Gamble. What distinguishes these companies from other organizations is that they have a widely shared philosophy of norms and values that they have clearly and consistently conveyed to their employees.[50] This clarity and consistency reinforces and extends the corporate norms and values.

46. Steers, R. M. & Rhodes, S. R. (1978). Major influences on employee attendance: A process model. *Psychological Bulletin, 63*, 391–407.

47. O'Reilly, C. A., & Caldwell, D. (1980). Job choice: The impact of intrinsic and extrinsic factors on subsequent satisfaction and commitment. *Journal of Applied Psychology, 65*, 559–565.

48. Black, J. S., Gregersen, H. B., Mendenhall, M. E., & Stroh, L. K. (1999). *Globalizing people through international assignments.* Reading, MA: Addison-Wesley.

49. Peters, T. J., & Waterman, R. H. (1997). *In search of excellence: Lessons from America's best-run companies.* New York: Harper & Row.

50. Powell, G. N. (1998). Reinforcing and extending today's organizations: The simultaneous pursuit of person–organization fit and diversity. *Organizational Dynamics, 26*(3), 50–61.

FOCUS ON CORPORATE CULTURES

DRESS CODES CAN BE AS DIVISIVE AS EXECUTIVE POWER STRUGGLES. When SmithKline Beecham and Glaxo Wellcome called off their planned megamerger in 1998, SmithKline issued a terse news release blaming differences in management philosophy and corporate culture. The business media promptly interpreted the rather fuzzy explanation to mean that the people at the top couldn't agree on who would get the bigger office and wield more power in the new pharmaceutical giant.

But experts who study why mergers fail say corporate culture is much more important than a simple power struggle between executives. It covers, for example, whether the new company will require employees to punch time clocks and whether the head office will call all the shots. If it's not given enough attention before, during, and after a merger, culture can become the rock against which the marriage founders.

The costs of cultural differences are underlined in the experience of Apria Healthcare Group of Costa Mesa, California, formed by the Homedco Group and the Abbey Healthcare Group. Before their merger, Abbey was a decentralized operation, with managers who were used to a lot of au-

tonomy. Homedco was more traditionally structured, and the head office made the decisions. One major issue of contention surfaced when Homedco's managers started asking Abbey pharmacists to punch time clocks, to which they objected. The Homedco dress code—ties for men, pantyhose for women—was equally unpopular. Arguments over pantyhose may not bring down a company, but in Apria's case they have clearly contributed to negative morale.

It's apparent that when these two companies merged, management neglected to deal with the organizational entry and socialization issues necessary to commit the employees in both companies to the new organization. In particular, Homedco began to behave like a "takeover" company and ignored the integration and socialization processes for the employees in the acquired company, Abbey. The lack of attention to the organizational culture "fit" issues between these two companies has created serious setbacks in attaining organizational goals.

Source: Excerpted from Drohan, M. (1998, April 21). Culture clash wrecks marriages/mergers—Dress codes and time clocks are just as divisive as executive power struggles. *The Globe and Mail*, p. B13.

In addition to having a widely shared philosophy, organizations with strong cultures generally display four other characteristics: (a) a view of people as a critical human resource, (b) charismatic leaders and heroes, (c) rituals and ceremonies, and (d) clear expectations about the direction of the organization.[51]

Southwest Airlines, as introduced in the opening vignette, is an organization known for its strong culture.[52] Every employee at Southwest knows that his or her job is to provide excellent customer service while having fun. Southwest spokesperson Kristin Nelson stated, "At Southwest, we will work your tail off, but you will have fun doing it." The company's rituals include flight attendants singing in-flight instructions or advising smokers to light up on the wing since there is no smoking in the aircraft. Herb Kelleher, the CEO and company leader, also supports the company culture with his infamous charismatic personality.

---

51. Deal, T., & Kennedy, A. (1982). *Corporate culture: The rites and rituals of corporate life.* Reading, MA: Addison-Wesley.

52. Stewart, D. (2000). Employees of Dallas-based airline maintain productivity through happiness. *KRTBN Knight-Ridder Tribune Business News: The Daily Oklahoman* [On-line]. URL: *http://ptg.djnr.com/ccroot/asp/publib/story.asp*

PEOPLE AS CRITICAL HUMAN RESOURCES. Organizations with strong company cultures view their people as strategic weapons in the globally competitive environment.[53] They recognize that their people are their greatest assets in the organization. Organizations with strong company cultures view their people as *resources*, not as costs to the organization.

CHARISMATIC LEADERS AND HEROES. In strong company cultures, the guiding philosophy of charismatic leaders will be consistently and widely shared among its employees. Developing the management philosophy of the company and its direction is not a sideline of top management; it is the *essence* of the company. Charismatic or transformational leadership is common, and myths and stories of heroic employees, leaders, and products—which provide tangible role models for employees—are well integrated into a strong organization's oral history.

RITUALS AND CEREMONIES. Strong company cultures also have ingrained rituals and ceremonies that exhibit acceptable and expected behavior. Whether performed daily or annually, ceremonies demonstrate, vividly and potently, what the organization stands for. Ceremonies may include such events as the annual holiday party or sales meeting, but they can also refer to a more complex and expensive process such as the way an organization chooses a new CEO.

CLEAR EXPECTATIONS ABOUT THE DIRECTION OF THE ORGANIZATION. Mission and vision statements are a common method for organizations to clarify the company's expectations and to establish the direction where the company is going. These vision and mission statements are indicators of not only what the company stands for but the overall goal of the organization. Thus, mission and vision statements are the first visible signs of the organizational culture.

A strong organizational culture will shape an employee's commitment to the organization. To further enhance the fit between its culture and its employees, an organization can use three major mechanisms: selection, socialization, and mentoring. We have already addressed selection as a means of bringing in individuals whose values and beliefs are consistent with those of the organization or who can be inculcated with those values. Socialization—the process by which culture is conveyed and commitment is produced—begins when an individual becomes an employee and is discussed in the next section. Finally, the benefits of mentoring to organizational commitment is discussed.

ORGANIZATIONAL SOCIALIZATION

Organizational socialization is the process by which employees learn about and adapt to their workplace, including their new responsibilities and roles and the organization's culture.[54] Socialization molds the new employee to fit the organization.

Through socialization, the employee comes to appreciate the values, abilities, expected behaviors, and social knowledge that are essential for

---

53. Black, Gregersen, Mendenhall, & Stroh, *Globalizing people through international assignments.*
54. Klein, H. J., & Weaver, N. A. (2000). The effectiveness of an organizational-level orientation program in the socialization of new hires. *Personnel Psychology 53*(1), 47–66.

assuming a role in the organization and for participating as an employee. As such, socialization conveys the organization's *culture* and thus is often unique to each organization.

There are times, however, when it becomes necessary to resocialize employees who have been with the organization for some time so as to maintain or reestablish commitment. This is often warranted when a company undergoes major restructuring or change, such as a merger or downsizing. In other cases, such as when employees are sent on foreign assignments, continued commitment may depend on whether the organization socializes employees in the culture of the country to which they are being sent and in preparation for the return home. Unfortunately, given that few companies provide such socialization activities, international assignees often experience disastrous results, as discussed in the "INTERNATIONAL FOCUS ON: Socialization."

Individuals involved with newcomers to an organization should also consider the value of mentors or role models, reward systems, and career paths and career ladders—all of which reinforce the culture and expectations of the organization vis-à-vis its employees. Reward systems are thoroughly discussed in Chapter 12, and the remaining mechanisms are well worth examining in some detail here.

INTERNATIONAL FOCUS ON
SOCIALIZATION

TAKE THIS JOB AND.... At the time Gerald Carson was offered his new job as a general manager of Pittsburgh-based BIGBANK's banking operation in Kuala Lumpur, Malaysia, he was told it would be a gateway to upper management. This was to be BIGBANK's first venture in Asia, and if KL BIGBANK was a success, Carson would be a success as well.

Carson and his family were given only minimal training and information before moving day. The only other general manager of the branch, a bachelor, had just been removed from the assignment, and getting someone to Malaysia was the top priority. As Carson learned later, the previous general manager had been relieved of his duties after being charged, by a person unknown to him, with violation of the "close proximity" law regarding Muslim women. Because Carson was married and had a family, such problems would be unlikely to occur with Carson at the helm. But that didn't mean that Carson and his family would not encounter problems.

In fact, the problems they encountered were significant. The Carsons had an unrealistic preview of life in Malaysia—they actually had no preview at all—and they all experienced severe cases of culture shock. Difficulties at school, communicating with people who spoke another language, and adapting to their new lifestyle resulted in a dysfunctional family situation for the Carsons. Carson also experienced difficulties at work. In particular, he noticed that the local employees went to his assistant, Mahmoud, with their problems instead of coming to him. Eventually, Carson's problems at home and work seemed so overwhelming that he requested a transfer back home. His fax to headquarters in Pittsburgh read: "Take this job and . . ."

Clearly, BIGBANK did a poor job of socializing Carson into the Malaysia operation. Had it done a better job, it would have eliminated yet another costly mistake. One can also question whether the organization used appropriate selection techniques when it chose Carson. Just because Carson was an effective manager in the United States does not mean he would have been equally effective in this cross-cultural setting.

Source: Adapted from Black, J. S., Gregersen, H. B., Mendenhall, M. E., & Stroh, L. K. (1999). *Globalizing people through international assignments.* Reading, MA: Addison-Wesley.

MENTORING

In the context of the workplace, a **mentor** is someone who provides a less experienced employee with advice and support, with the goal of facilitating the junior individual's upward mobility and success in the organization.[55] Mentoring contributes to the establishment of a good fit between the employee and the organization in that senior employees can provide information about historical background on the organization. When used effectively in the socialization process, mentors unite those in the first phase with those in a later phase of their careers. In addition, research has shown mentoring to be positively related to promotions, career mobility, and career satisfaction.[56]

A mentor–protégé relationship is often a formal or at least an acknowledged interchange between an inexperienced and an experienced employee. Mentors provide two primary functions in the organization.[57] First, they model career development behaviors to the protégé through such means as coaching, providing challenging assignments, and protecting the protégé from adverse forces in the organization. Second, they assume psychological roles, by offering personal support, friendship, and role modeling.

Mentoring relationships are not without risks, however. If there is a mismatch between the mentor and protégé, the relationship can be anything but supportive. In a worst-case scenario, an individual may feel pressured into a mentoring role, regardless of his or her level of skill or enthusiasm for this assignment.

It is wise to remember that, in the past, research on mentoring relationships was based on a homogenous workforce. Today's organizations however, have become less homogenous and more diverse than in the past. Taylor Cox and Stacy Blake have found that organizations need to be aware of the cultural differences of their employees in order to remain competitive. Their research indicates that an organization's ability to recruit and retain people from diverse backgrounds may lead to competitive advantages for the organization in terms of cost structures and maintaining quality human resources.[58]

With today's workforce becoming more and more diversified, organizations have indeed realized that the traditional mentoring relationship also has to change. Recently research has shown that some organizations have attempted to offer formal mentoring programs in an attempt to provide minority group members and women with much-needed mentors. These formal mentoring programs usually occur in the form of a voluntary assignment of a mentor with a protégé. Female protégés, for example, can benefit from female mentors because these mentors can assist in overcoming barriers to advancement in the organization.[59] Research by Belle Rose Ragins shows that these formal mentoring relationships are less effective than informal

55. Ragins, B. R. (1997). Diversified mentoring relationships in organizations: A power perspective. *Academy of Management Review, 22,* 482–521.

56. Ragins, B. R., & Scandura, T. A. (1994). Gender differences in expected outcomes of mentoring relationships. *Academy of Management Journal, 37,* 957–971.

57. Ragins, B. R. (1997). Diversified mentoring relationships in organizations: A power perspective. *Academy of Management Review, 22,* 482–521.

58. Cox, T. H., Jr., & Blake, S. (1991). Managing cultural diversity: Implications for organizational competitiveness. *Academy of Management Executive* 5(3), 45–56.

59. Ragins, B. R., Cotton, J. L., & Miller, J. S. (in press). Marginal mentoring: The effects of type of mentor, quality of relationship, and program design on work and career attitudes. *Academy of Management Journal.*

mentoring. The research also points out that whether formal or informal, the quality of the mentoring relationship is the most important determinant of its usefulness to minorities and women in their career development.[60]

Research has also identified another form of mentoring relationship, *diversified mentoring*. In this relationship, the mentor and protégé belong to different membership groups in the organization, which are also associated with power differences in the organization. For example, the mentor and protégé may differ in race, ethnicity, gender, class, physical ability, and sexual orientation. Research on cross-race and cross-gender relationships shows that the processes and outcomes that these relationships go through may differ from the traditional informal mentoring relationship.[61] For example, if the mentor and protégé belong to different power groups, their relationship may be influenced by these differences in power. The diversified mentoring relationships are another result of the organization's reacting to a more heterogeneous workforce.

CAREER PATHS AND CAREER LADDERS

Career paths are job-progression routes along which employees advance through an organization.[62] Although career paths are often designed for particular employees, organizations may develop common "highways." Such routes usually consist of a combination of lateral, downward, and upward moves through the organizational hierarchy. When career paths are formalized, they become career ladders. Thus, a **career ladder** is a specific series of jobs or experiences necessary to advance in an organization. For example, in most airline companies, like Southwest Airlines, a clear career ladder must be followed to achieve the command of an aircraft. An individual qualified to be a pilot must first serve as a navigator and then as a second officer, before advancing to the rank of captain.

The existence of career paths and career ladders plays a role in the socialization of new employees. Employees will benefit most from these paths and ladders in the future, but understanding how one advances in the organization also provides critical information to individuals deciding whether to join a company and newcomers searching for a mentor or role model. In addition to outlining a route to advancement, career paths have a symbolic function. They send a message to employees that the organization is interested in establishing a long-term relationship with them—that the company is committed to them not just for now but for the future. In fact, one major reason for turnover in organizations is the lack of clear opportunities for advancement.[63] By now it should be clear that the process of socialization into an organization and its culture is complex and multifaceted. As the importance of a strong culture has gained wider acceptance, organizations are beginning to recognize that carefully structuring the process by which newcomers are socialized into an organization can pay off not only in higher levels of organizational commitment but also in increased productivity and thus in the financial bottom line.

---

60. Ragins, Diversified mentoring relationships in organizations.
61. Ragins, Diversified mentoring relationships in organizations.
62. Stroh, L. K., & Reilly, A. H. (1999). Gender and careers: Present experiences and emerging trends. In G. Powell (Ed.), *Handbook of gender in organizations* (pp. 307–324). Thousand Oaks, CA: Sage.
63. Brett, J. M., & Stroh, L. K. (1997). Jumping ship: Who does better on the external labor market? *Journal of Applied Psychology, 82,* 331–341.

SUMMARY

This chapter focuses on how individuals become committed members of organizations. The selection and socialization processes help to ensure good person–organization and person–job fits. The selection process is the first contact potential employees have with the organization. A good selection process is critical to identifying a good fit of people for the organization because such individuals may have specific skills and values that are compatible with the organization. From the applicant's perspective, the process of gathering the right kind of information is equally critical to the selection of an appropriate organization. For this process to be effective, the job applicant should receive a realistic job preview on the desirable and undesirable aspects of the job. Clarifying the inducements and the contributions that the organization and the individual will exchange establishes the psychological contract between the individual and the employer.

After the individual accepts an offer of employment, the next task is to commit the individual to the company's goals and expectations. Ensuring such commitment is in the organization's best interest, in that committed employees are more likely than uncommitted employees to remain with the organization and to expend greater effort in the accomplishment of their tasks. The visibility of individuals as organizational members, the explicitness and irreversibility of their choices and behaviors, and the volition or personal responsibility they feel for their actions are all means by which commitment to the organization is generated.

A primary way in which organizations with highly committed employees differ from those with less committed employees is that the former have strong organizational cultures. In addition to having a widely shared philosophy, an organization's culture is composed of four elements: a view of people's critical resources, charismatic leaders and heroes, rituals and ceremonies, and clear expectations about the organization's direction.

Conveying the culture of an organization to newcomers requires a complex process of socialization that includes communicating the organization's goals, norms, and preferred ways of doing things. Mentors and role models, and clearly defined career paths and career ladders are a few of many mechanisms organizations use during this process. With today's increasingly diversified organizations, the traditional mentoring relationship has had to change. Recently, some organizations have tried implementing formal mentoring programs in an attempt to provide minority group members and women with much-needed mentors.

KEY TERMS

Career ladder
Career path
Explicitness
Irreversibility
Job analysis
Mentor
Organizational commitment
Organizational culture

Organizational socialization
Person–organization fit
Psychological contract
Realistic job preview
Selection
Visibility
Volition

DISCUSSION QUESTIONS

1 The selection process in organizations has taken on increasing importance in the past few decades. What factors are responsible for this change?

2 Realistic job previews are one way organizations can convey their expectations of employee performance to potential organizational members. In what ways do realistic job previews facilitate the development of an effective psychological contract?

3 One way in which organizations deal with newcomers is to try to humble them early in their tenure with the company. Why might organizations put their employees through such experiences, and why might the newcomers learn from this and find it useful?

4 In recent years, fraternity hazing has increasingly become a problem on college campuses. In fact, hazing activities have resulted in a number of highly publicized deaths. What is the purpose of hazing? Say that your campus has formed a committee to propose new socialization processes; what would you recommend?

5 What is the difference between organizational commitment and behavioral commitment?

6 Why are socialization activities so important in bringing employees of newly acquired firms up to speed in productivity?

7 Under what conditions might a firm want to maintain a weak culture?

ON YOUR OWN

Alien Invasion Organizational cultures are so ubiquitous that we often overlook the information they can convey to an observer. The trick to deciphering a culture is in learning to read the clues. The following are some examples of clues you can use in examining a company's particular culture: building style, dress code, employee behaviors, company stories or rituals, organizational hierarchy, and company leaders. It is surprising how much of a feel for an organization you can acquire simply by looking and listening carefully.

Consider an organization to which you belong, such as your family, university, or church. Now look at your chosen organization through the eyes (and antennae!) of an alien. Your ability to interact verbally with the organization you are observing is limited. Your objective is to learn about what the organization does when it is going about its normal business. You are to learn as much as you can about the organization by simply observing. Many skilled managers use this ability in sensing what is going on as they walk through their plant or office area. When you have completed your observation of the chosen organization, write a short description of the culture of the organization, focusing on its ideologies, myths, values, and norms of behavior.

Source: D. D. Bowen (1996). Alien invasion: An organizational culture assignment. In R. J. Lewicki, D. D. Bowen, D. T. Hall, & F. S. Hall (Eds.), *Experiences in management and organizational behavior* (4th ed.). New York: Wiley.

CLOSING CASE   CHAPTER 10

THE MANAGER'S MEMO

FROM: H. Roadruck, Vice President, Pickle Production Division
TO: T. Phinney, Production Supervisor
RE: High Turnover

It has become increasingly apparent to me that turnover among the workers in our pickle production division is at an all-time high. Some figures I obtained from the human resources department show that my concerns are justified. Our workforce currently stands at 135; however, that number is dropping steadily, and the number of recent hires is low. The following losses for the past 12 months make this patently clear:

Within 5 years of hiring	6
Within 1 year of hiring	23
Within 6 months of hiring	31
Within 1 month of hiring	97

As these figures show, we are constantly replacing our production workforce. No company can afford to do this. Our wages are already above the industry average, so we cannot even consider paying higher wages.

The numbers suggest that a lot of the people you are hiring are either unqualified or quickly become disillusioned with their jobs. According to the human resources department, some of the workers who have quit have commented that working in our plant is a lot more boring than they were led to believe it would be. One worker commented that he was on the job for a full week before he was even allowed to touch the packaging machine. Another said he was embarrassed to tell his friends that he makes pickles all day.

Please provide some ideas on how you plan to rectify this situation.

CASE DISCUSSION QUESTIONS

Assume that you are the production supervisor, and respond to the vice president's memorandum. Review the concepts in the chapter, and apply the ones you think would be most effective in selecting and assimilating production workers. Be sure to support your recommendations.

CHAPTER
11
Job Design

CHARLENE PEDROLIE REARRANGED FURNITURE AND BOOSTED A BUSINESS

In the mid-1990s, Charlene Pedrolie introduced the latest management methods at Rowe Furniture Corporation. Since then, workers have been organized into "cells," cross-training has been instituted, and four layers of supervision have been wiped out.

Today, output and earnings are surging, making Rowe a hot stock in the furniture group. Results for the second quarter of 2000 show net shipments of $87.7 million, compared to $63.9 million for the same period in 1999. And, gross profits soared from $17.8 million in 1999 to $29.7 million in 2000. The way Pedrolie pulled off this growth teaches a valuable lesson in job design.

Rowe Furniture was stuck midway through a major transformation when it recruited Pedrolie. Rowe's research had shown that people hated upholstered furniture. They wanted a much wider selection than any showroom could display, yet they refused to wait months for special orders. Pedrolie's assignment? To figure out a way to produce a much wider variety of products in much less time, all with no increase in cost.

In her mind, there was little mystery about the method. She would eliminate the inefficient old assembly line. Sewers, gluers, staplers, and stuffers would be brought together in cells of roughly 35 employees. Through cross-training, everyone in the cell would do every job related to making a sofa, instead of just one job on every piece. When a worker had time to spare, he or she would help someone who had fallen behind.

The production workers returned after the plant makeover agog to see their power tools dangling from the ceiling in clusters instead of in long, straight lines. Suddenly they were working alongside—and forced to communicate with—three dozen cell members. Accustomed to having the parts come to them, they began dragging raw materials to their cells and bumping into one another along the way. Productivity fell as staplers learned to glue and gluers to staple.

Thankfully, the passage of a few weeks—and the regular Christmas shutdown—proved therapeutic. As workers returned from vacation to a less frenzied schedule, cells began to function as teams. Workers realized that

Source: Adapted from *The Rowe Companies announces second quarter financial results.* [On-line] (2000, June 14). URL: *http://therowecompanies.com/NEWS.HTM#8;* and Petzinger, T., Jr. (1996, September 13). Charlene Pedrolie rearranged furniture and lifted a business. *The Wall Street Journal,* p. B1.

they could snuff out problems instantly, whereas solutions were slow to come on the old assembly lines.

Most important, shop-floor workers were stunned to see their ideas triggering action, which in turn triggered more ideas. One task force found a better way to stuff pillows. A loading crew made the case for larger truck trailers. Another group created a new revenue source by selling spare kiln capacity to lumber-drying operations.

Today, because of the implementation of a new job design, the plant operates at record productivity and, as one shop worker commented, "Everybody's a lot happier."

INTRODUCTION

Managers today face many challenges in developing healthy and productive workforces. Finding and hiring the right people is only the first step. This chapter addresses the second step: designing jobs and roles for employees that take full advantage of each individual's abilities to contribute to organizations' effectiveness and efficiency. As the example of Rowe Furniture illustrates, job redesign can transform day-to-day production.

This chapter presents three perspectives on the design of jobs: the tradition of work simplification, job characteristics approaches, and workgroup approaches. The chapter concludes by considering several factors that affect the success of all job design efforts.

THE TRADITION OF WORK SIMPLIFICATION

The field of organizational behavior traces its roots to shortcomings of the traditional job design efforts of the early 1900s. Traditional job design—as exemplified by Frederick Taylor's "scientific management" and Henry Ford's assembly line—focused primarily on efficiency. Often this focus led to strategies of **work simplification.** Managers designed tasks to be simple and therefore easily mastered and quickly accomplished. Each worker focused on a small number of very simple tasks, such as screwing several nuts onto several bolts. The basic philosophy was that each worker could quickly become expert at a few tasks and learn to do them repeatedly, with lightning speed and no mistakes.

Consider the range of tasks required to produce a shirt, as portrayed in Figure 11-1. Using a work-simplification strategy, each worker would be assigned one of the three tasks. Each worker would then master one task, in the spirit of efficiency through job specialization.

THE WORK SIMPLIFICATION PARADOX

The philosophy behind work simplification is very appealing, and by some estimates as many as 50% of all manufacturing jobs are still designed on the premise that simpler is better.[1] The routinization and specialization of work are viewed as necessary by these organizations for optimizing efficiency and productivity.[2] However, because the focus of work simplification is increas-

---

1. Lawler, E. E., 111. (1986). *High-involvement management.* London: Jossey-Bass, p. 84.
2. Baytos, K., & Kleiner, B. H. (1995). New developments in job design. *Business Credit, 92*(2), 22–25.

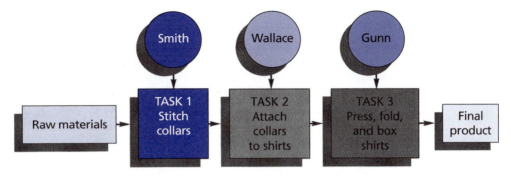

Job Specialization ■ **FIGURE 11-1**

Job specialization is a way of executing work simplification strategies. It aims to make each worker a "specialist" in the job that he or she performs. Here Smith, Wallace, and Gunn are all specialists. Smith stitches collars; Wallace attaches collars to shirts; and Gunn presses, folds, and boxes the shirts.

ing task efficiency, the assumption is that *workers are indifferent* to what they are doing. This is far from the truth; workers are *not* indifferent to the design of their work.

> "Workers are not machines. They may slow or block the functioning of machines to show their dissatisfaction. It is therefore necessary to satisfy their needs and train them in a way that motivates them to do a good job and enjoy it."[3]

As the remainder of this chapter makes clear, job design focused on improving workers' attitudes toward their work can be as important as work simplification in achieving optimal productivity.

In his book *High-Involvement Management*, management theorist Edward Lawler III summarized the effects of work simplification on workers' behaviors:

> The work simplification approach is often associated with (1) low quality because individuals do not care about product quality, (2) low productivity because individuals are not motivated to be productive, and (3) high wages because individuals demand them for repetitive, boring, unsatisfying jobs. In addition, it often leads to high levels of turnover and absenteeism, and therefore overstaffing to replace absentees and people who quit. Further, despite the fact that jobs are relatively simple to learn, training costs may be high because of the high turnover rate. Finally, the social costs are high. Although largely undocumented, it is thought that the dissatisfying nature of simplified, repetitive work causes mental problems, alcohol and substance abuse, and a general alienation from society.[4]

This is the paradox of work simplification: A simple job design may be easy to master and easy to do, but job simplicity often creates feelings of boredom and alienation—resulting in decreased quality and productivity.

Work simplification may alienate the worker. Work simplification has also been shown to result in a loss of workers' loyalty and trust in their organizations

Whatever simplified, routinized jobs might gain in potential efficiency they often lose in boredom and alienation. This woman feels like a part of the machine as she keeps the product flowing along the production line. There is virtually no variation or interest in her day.

3. Theriault, P. (1996). *Work simplification*. Norcross, GA: Engineering & Management Press, p. 4.
4. Lawler, *High-involvement management*.

and loss of loyalty to their immediate supervisors.[5] With work-simplification there is also the risk of *job plateauing*. Job plateauing occurs when work has been mastered and the job has become boring—which can occur very quickly if the job design is simple.[6]

In addition to lost productivity, loss of company loyalty, and job plateauing, work simplification also has been associated with high turnover rates. This is an important concern for organizations. Although some turnover is healthy for organizations, providing a process whereby the workforce is naturally renewed,[7] high turnover can be very disruptive and can result in the loss of valuable employees. This can be extremely costly. Billions of dollars per year are spent because of lost productivity, employee recruitment, socialization, and training due to turnover.[8] For every 10 managerial and professional employees who leave an organization, the company loses an average of $1 million.[9]

The bottom line is that all workers have a reservoir of interest and energy. If this reservoir is not tapped in their jobs, it will be wasted or will surface in other forms—such as counterproductive work behaviors. The challenge of job design is to harness workers' interest and energy and direct it toward the accomplishment of organizational objectives. Next, we consider two approaches to redesigning jobs: redesign focused on the characteristics of individual jobs and workgroup approaches to job redesign.

INDIVIDUAL JOB CHARACTERISTICS

While traditional approaches to job design focused almost exclusively on work simplification, more enlightened approaches have taken into account worker's needs by focusing on individual job characteristics.

THE JOB CHARACTERISTICS MODEL

In search of a way to improve on work simplification strategies, J. Richard Hackman and Greg Oldham proposed the **job characteristics model,** shown in Figure 11-2. Their model identifies three "critical psychological states" that can be designed into jobs: meaningfulness, responsibility for work outcomes, and knowledge of work activity results. A job must foster these three states in workers to achieve such desired outcomes as worker satisfaction and high-quality performance. These critical psychological states are likely to occur when jobs are designed to contain five characteristics: skill variety, task identity, task significance, autonomy, and feedback.

5. Hendry, C., & Jenkins, R. (1997). Psychological contracts and new deals. *Human Resource Management Journal,* 7(1), 38–44.

6. Allen, T. D., Russell, J. E., Poteet, M. L., & Dobbins, G. H. (1999). Learning and development factors related to perceptions of job content and hierarchical plateauing. *Journal of Organizational Behavior,* 20, 1113–1137.

7. Hollenbeck, J. R., & Williams, C. R. (1986). Turnover functionality versus turnover frequency: A note on work attitudes and organizational effectiveness. *Journal of Applied Psychology,* 71, 601–611.

8. Sailors, F. J., & Sylvestre J. (1994). Reduce the cost of employee turnover. *Journal of Compensation & Benefits,* 9(5), 32–34.

9. Fitz-enz, J. (1997, August). It's costly to lose good employees, *Workforce,* 76(8), 50–51.

The Job Characteristics Model ■ FIGURE 11-2

The job characteristics model summarizes the relationships among features that can be designed into jobs (such as skill variety), the psychological effects of these features (such as meaningful work), and the outcomes for workers and organizations (such as productivity and satisfaction).

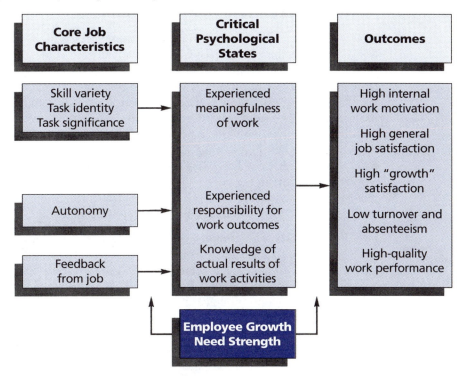

Source: Hackman, J. R., & Oldham, G. R. (1980). *Work redesign.* Reading, MA: Addison-Wesley.

Plenty of anecdotal evidence supports the job characteristics model, and it has unquestionably become the dominant model of job design theory.[10] However, research findings show mixed results. In one study by Joan Rentsch and Robert Steel, the job characteristics model significantly predicted absenteeism over a 6-year period.[11] On the other hand, a review of 30 redesign efforts found that failures occurred as frequently as successes.[12] Even the researchers who developed the model have conceded that although there is support for the model, it would be inappropriate to conclude that it provides a complete picture of the relationship between job characteristics and performance or motivation.[13] Overall, most researchers agree that the model offers important insights into job design. As with most theoretical models, the best predictor of its success is often how well the model is implemented.

10. Evans, M. G., Kiggundu, M. N., & House, R. J. (1979). A partial test and extension of the job characteristic model of motivation. *Organizational Behavior and Human Performance, 24,* 354–381.

11. Rentsch, J. R., & Steel, R. P. (1998, April). Testing the durability of job characteristics as predictors of absenteeism over a six-year period. *Personnel Psychology, 51,* 165–190.

12. Kopelman, R. E. (1985). Job redesign and productivity: A review of the evidence. *National Productivity Review, 4,* 237–255.

13. Hackman & Oldham, *Work redesign.*

Nevertheless, the model does provide a foundation from which managers can begin to redesign jobs in the hopes of improving employee satisfaction and motivation. Next we discuss options, (based on the job characteristics model) that managers can use to enhance individual job characteristics.

JOB CHARACTERISTICS OPTIONS

One way management may attempt to harness workers' interest and energy is by changing the characteristics of individual jobs. This can be accomplished through job rotation, job enlargement, or job enrichment. **Job rotation** allows workers to move to another job (for example, every few months, weeks, days, or even hours), without management needing to change the job itself. **Job enlargement,** on the other hand, *changes* the range of a job—the number of tasks that a worker performs. Job enlargement combines more tasks into a single job (creating a more complex job for the employee). Finally, **job enrichment** harnesses workers' interest and energy by allowing workers to fulfill higher-order needs—such as for achievement and control—through work. Figure 11-3 compares these three job characteristics, and the next sections elaborate on these three concepts.

JOB ROTATION. To conquer the damaging effects of dullness and boredom from job specialization, organizations can turn to job rotation. As shown in Figure 11-4(a), job rotation increases the variety of tasks workers perform by enabling workers to occasionally switch jobs. The first worker does Task 1 (stitching on collars) for a while, moves on to Task 2 (ironing and folding), and finally on to Task 3 (boxing). Rotation, which can occur every week, every day, or even every few hours, breaks up the monotony of doing a single, repetitive task by regularly assigning workers to new tasks.

Job rotation can be accomplished through cross-training. **Cross-training** involves employees learning their coworkers' jobs, and it provides benefits for both individual workers and the organization. For the individual, learning new skills or tasks results in increased variety on the job and thus breaks up the monotony of working on only a small number of tasks, and it provides the worker with challenges to look forward to every day. For management, cross-training provides greater flexibility; if an employee calls in sick or leaves the organization, or if a particular task becomes a temporary bottleneck, work assignments can be shifted around to handle the situation. When implemented well, as at Rowe Furniture, cross-training can be an effective job redesign strategy.

Cross-training also provides an avenue by which management can train personnel to take on supervisory responsibilities. An employee who has been cross-trained on all the jobs in a workgroup is likely to make a better workgroup supervisor than someone who has learned only one task.

Cross-training can have positive effects on a company's financial performance. In a study of 131 U.S. companies conducted by the Texas Center for Productivity and Quality of Work Life, financial performance increased by as much as 40% when multiskilling was combined with other innovative work practices.[14] Some companies view cross-training as such a benefit to their overall performance that they have implemented compensation schemes (known as "pay-for-knowledge" plans) that reward employees for

---

14. Dalton, G. L. (1998, December). The collective stretch. *Management Review, 87*(11), 54–59.

| Comparison of Job Rotation, Job Enlargement, and Job Enrichment | ■ FIGURE 11-3 |

Job rotation, job enlargement, and job enrichment are all ways that an organization can conquer the negative effects of job specialization. Job rotation and job enlargement make jobs more interesting by increasing the variety of skills used, and job enrichment increases the workers' commitment by increasing the decision-making responsibility of the worker.

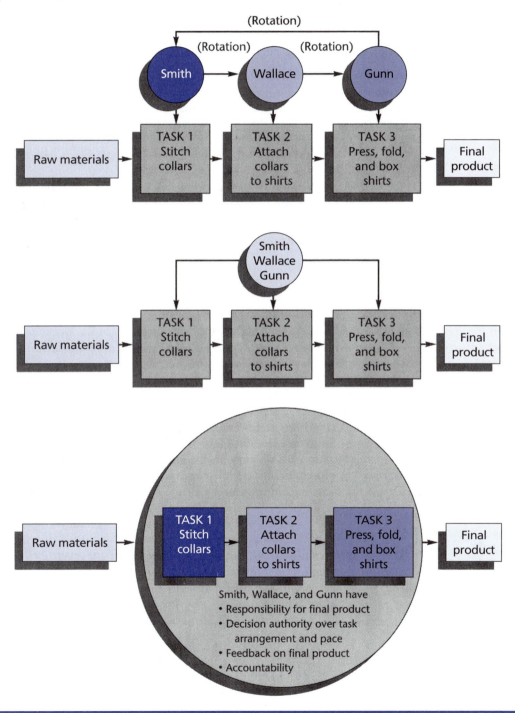

each new skill they acquire. For example, under the United Auto Workers' contract, auto workers are rewarded with increases in their hourly wages for acquiring new auto-assembly skills.[15]

However, managers need to be aware of the potential pitfalls of developing job rotation and cross-training in their organizations. Even unhappy employees may be reluctant to learn another job.[16] They may not see the short- and long-term advantages, or they may not have the confidence to learn a new position.[17] Therefore, managers need to carefully assess the capabilities and wishes of their workers before using job rotation as a solution.

JOB ENLARGEMENT. In contrast to job rotation, where workers are shifted from job to job, job enlargement changes the nature of an individual job itself by adding additional tasks for a worker. Sometimes, it even combines two separate jobs into one job for a single person. In essence, it gives people more tasks to work on.[18] It is based on the simple premise that a job will be more interesting and involving if the worker has a wider range of tasks to perform.

Job enlargement also decreases the probability of alienation and boredom by increasing the variety of skills each worker masters and performs. This was part of the success of the job redesign strategy used at Rowe Furniture. In the example of job enlargement shown in Figure 11-4(b), each worker does all three tasks. Several jobs are combined into one.

Businesses as well as workers profit from job enlargement. First, job enlargement is an effective retention tool, since job content has become as important as compensation in retaining some employees.[19] Also, employees who take on more tasks and broader responsibilities are better problem solvers, more productive, and make more effective decisions in the workplace.[20]

Like Rowe Furniture, General Electric's jet-engine manufacturing facility in Durham, North Carolina, is a job-enlargement convert. At these companies, the monotonous assembly lines are gone, and management has embraced task variety for the workers. Everyone develops the skills to keep jobs stimulating. At the General Electric facility, employees are knowledgeable about all areas, "from the point when parts are uncrated and staged to the moment a team member climbs on a forklift to place the finished engine on a truck for shipment." Workers do the jobs that interest them, and, because there is choice, there is always variety. Job enlargement has positively improved the workers' morale and performance. The turnover rate at the plant is a stunningly low 5% per year.[21]

While job rotation and job enlargement are certainly improvements over work simplification as ways to design jobs, they also have drawbacks. Perhaps most critically, increasing the range of jobs a worker performs does not go far enough in tapping the interests and energies of some workers.

15. Milkovich, G. T., & Newman, J. M. (1999). *Compensation* (6th ed.). Boston: Irwin/McGraw-Hill.

16. Holbeche, L. (1998). *Motivating people in lean organizations.* Oxford, UK: Butterworth-Heinemann, p. 213.

17. Holbeche, *Motivating people in lean organizations.*

18. Nirenberg, J. (1997). *Power tools: a leader's guide to the latest management thinking.* Singapore: Prentice Hall, p. 371.

19. Lee, T. W., Mitchell, T. R., Wise, L., & Fireman, S. (1996, February). An unfolding model of voluntary employee turnover. *Academy of Management Journal, 39*(1), 5–36.

20. Dalton, The collective stretch.

21. Fishman, C. (1999). Engines of democracy. *Fast Company, 28*, pp. 174+.

| **Positive Task-Related Experiences** | ■ **FIGURE 11-4** |

Accountability: Workers should be held responsible for their performance.
Achievement: Workers should feel that they are accomplishing something worthwhile.
Control over resources: If possible, workers should have control over their tasks.
Feedback: Workers should receive clear and direct information regarding their performance.
Personal growth and development: Workers should have the opportunity to learn new skills.
Work pace: Within constraints, workers should be able to set their own work pace.

Source: Herzberg, F. (1974, September/October). The wise old Turk. *Harvard Business Review,* 70–80.

JOB ENRICHMENT. The concept of job enrichment originated in Herzberg's two-factor theory of motivation (discussed in Chapter 3). Herzberg maintained that workers would be interested and involved in work when their jobs provided task-related enrichment opportunities such as achievement, autonomy, and responsibility.[22] A list of such experiences is shown in Figure 11-4. Job enrichment efforts try to include these positive task-related experiences in the design of the job itself.

Job enrichment programs have been shown to be successful in two ways. First, they often lead to improvements in product quality. Managers can expect product defect rates to drop as much as 60% when job enrichment is instituted.[23] In one review of 21 programs, job enrichment improved product quality (as measured by error rates) by an average of 28%.[24] This profound benefit appears to occur because job enrichment increases workers' sense of responsibility for quality. Workers are much more motivated to turn out something they can be proud of.

Second, job enrichment gives workers a broader perspective on their work. When management entrusts workers with responsibility for quality control, quality becomes more important. This broader perspective may lead workers to think of innovations that would never have occurred to them when they were concentrating on just fulfilling the basics of their tasks. Job enrichment also leads to greater job satisfaction. In the review of 21 job enrichment programs cited earlier, employee turnover and absenteeism decreased by an average of 14.5% when job enrichment was instituted. Apparently, workers enjoy being given opportunities for achievement and control on the job.

Research shows that in addition to increasing workers' involvement in their jobs, job enrichment enhances an individual's confidence in his or her ability to perform tasks.[25] Only when individuals are confident in these abilities do they succeed when given greater responsibilities and duties.[26]

22. Herzberg, F. (1966). *Work and the nature of man.* Cleveland, OH: World.
23. Northcraft, G. B., & Ashford, S. J., The preservation of Self in Everday Life: The Effects of Performance Expectations and Feedback Context on Feedback Inquiry, *Organizational Behavior and Human Decision Processes 47*, 42–64.
24. Northcraft & Ashford, *Organizational behavior and human decision processes.*
25. Parker, S. (1998). Enhancing role breadth self-efficacy: The roles of job enrichment and other organizational interventions. *Journal of Applied Psychology, 83*, 835–852.
26. Parker, Enhancing role breadth self-efficacy.

The benefits of job enrichment to an employee are numerous. But how can an organization design jobs that aid in furthering this objective? We will consider four ways job enrichment can be achieved: providing task identity, task significance, decision-making responsibility, and context enrichment.

Task Identity. **Task identity** occurs when a worker is allowed to see a process through from start to finish. The result is a sense of completion and achievement. Naturally, for a worker to take a process through from start to finish, the job must incorporate a fair number of skills. Thus, for task identity to occur, a job must have skill variety. In the opening vignette about Rowe Furniture, it was noted that each production cell completed every job related to making a sofa, from beginning to end. When all employees knew each step in the production process (e.g., how to glue, sew, staple, and stuff the sofas), both production and employee satisfaction increased.

Task Significance. Job enrichment also occurs when management increases **task significance.** A task is significant when a worker can see that whether he or she performs well or poorly makes a difference to someone or something. Task significance often is tied to contact with the consumer of a product or service. Any chance a worker has to experience a customer's appreciation for a job well done will enhance that worker's feeling that the task he or she is performing is significant.

Managers can also increase task significance by showing employees how their efforts and hard work positively impact the organization financially. By openly sharing company profit reports and annual reports, employers can operationalize "hard work" into something more meaningful and tangible.

Often managers supply such information regarding the impact of an employee's work efforts through **feedback**—letting the employee know how well he or she accomplishing tasks. Organizations have found that offering workers feedback can lead to job enrichment and, subsequently, higher job satisfaction and productivity. Providing feedback about their performance also benefits workers psychologically by reducing workers' feelings of uncertainty. When offered in a timely manner, feedback not only helps alert workers to the existence of problems but also help pinpoint their source. Finally, feedback provides workers with the information necessary to make high-quality decisions. The RESEARCH IN ACTION box, Getting Feedback Where It's Needed, shows some of the difficulties related to the feedback process.

Decision-Making Responsibility. Job enrichment often allows workers to take responsibility for decision making on the job. Thus, it can represent the first move by management to share control in the workplace. Managers can increase workers' decision-making responsibility either by allowing them to participate in management decision making (perhaps by soliciting their opinions through problem-solving groups) or by allowing workers limited decision-making autonomy within the scope of their jobs.

Consider again the shirt assembly line example. In Figure 11-3(c), not only does each worker have responsibility for all the component tasks (collar stitching, folding and ironing, and boxing), but each also controls how these tasks are arranged. Should all the collars be stitched on first, then all the folding and ironing done, and finally all the boxing? Perhaps the whole process could be run through in lots of 5 or 10 shirts? Management has delegated these decisions to the workers. The workers control the immediate work environment and have the option of changing the order of the tasks

RESEARCH IN ACTION
GETTING FEEDBACK WHERE IT'S NEEDED

Greg Northcraft, University of Illinois; *northcra@uiuc.edu*

Feedback is a critical resource for organizations. Employees can perform best when they understand how well they are performing. Feedback can also give employees a sense of control, by helping them self-regulate their behavior to achieve their personal goals—and the organization's.

Unfortunately, my research with Susan Ashford has shown that individuals harbor a lot of self-presentation concerns—individuals want to look good in the eyes of their managers and coworkers. Therefore, they are reluctant to seek feedback from their managers if they think that feedback will be negative and make them look bad or will remind the manager that they are not performing well. As a result, the performers that

most need feedback are often the most reluctant to seek it.

Technology may help provide a solution to this problem, by giving employees a way to seek feedback without having to worry about self-presentation concerns. An innovative program at Australia Post (Australia's postal delivery system) has managers post performance results for their workers online. That way, workers can privately view the results without having to worry about self-presentation. This makes it more likely that workers can get the feedback that they want and need to help their performance—and the organization's.

---

when necessary. The workers in Figure 11-3(c) also have responsibility for quality-control decisions regarding the work they produce. Traditionally, a separate worker would perform this task.

Consulting workers about management decisions, such as how to design a new manufacturing line, enhances workers' feelings of control and responsibility. Providing ways for workers to participate in organizational decision making also gives workers the message that management respects their opinions.

For the organization, worker participation opens up a communication channel, enabling management to access an important source of knowledge and innovation—the workers. It's important to remember, however, that taking responsibility on the job or making innovative suggestions may be as foreign an idea to the workers as it used to be to management. Time and even training may be required before workers can productively exercise the decision-making control that management is willing to give them.

Job-enrichment programs that enhance workers' decision-making responsibilities offer obvious psychological benefits for workers. At the same time, organizations reap invaluable benefits in improved efficiency and effectiveness. By enhancing workers' decision-making responsibilities, management, in effect, can have its cake and eat it, too; management retains control of an essentially autocratic decision-making structure while offering workers the benefits of autonomy.

The problem, however, is that allowing rank-and-file workers a taste of control through limited decision making raises their expectations in three critical ways. First, limited autonomy allows the workers to see that their suggestions can make a difference in the workplace. Good suggestions save the organization money, and the workers come to see themselves as important organizational resources. Workers do not easily forget or surrender this sense of power and accomplishment, and this can prove to be a particularly touchy matter if supervisors are threatened by the successes of their subordinates' suggestions.

Second, workers come to expect the organization to value their opinions. Once management solicits workers' opinions, an expectation is created that their opinions will be solicited in the future. Nothing kills a participation program faster than management's failure to respond to suggestions in a timely fashion—except perhaps failure to solicit workers' opinions when workers expect to be consulted. What would have happened if management at Rowe Furniture had taken 6 months to acknowledge the employees' suggestion about pillow stuffing? Certainly motivation to develop new ideas would have been hampered.

Finally, giving workers limited autonomy raises expectations about compensation. Enriched jobs may be more interesting and more involving for workers, but they also entail more responsibility. Consequently, workers should be (and expect to be) compensated with more pay.

Needless to say, job redesign efforts are not without problems. If management thwarts the expectations that job enrichment engenders in the workforce, enthusiasm for participation will wane. This may be why many attempts by U.S. corporations to become more participative end up being only "gimmicks"—short-lived fads whose time comes and goes.[27] The other choice, of course, is for management to accept and build on workers' expectations that they will take on larger roles in their organizations.

Context Enrichment. Yet another way to increase decision-making responsibility in a job is by giving workers decision-making control over the context of their work, rather than (or in addition to) control over the work itself. Examples of **context enrichment** can include flextime work scheduling and telecommuting.

Flextime Work Scheduling. Organizations that provide **flextime work scheduling** allow workers to decide when to come to work, within company-mandated guidelines. As shown in the example in Figure 11-5, all workers are expected to be at work during certain required hours, but the schedule for the remainder of the workday is flexible and is left up to the individual worker's discretion. Flextime schedules are usually established quarterly or yearly to promote communication and accountability. Flexible work scheduling, which offers workers limited autonomy, can result in job enrichment.

In the flextime schedule shown in Figure 11-5(a), for example, all workers are required to be at work between 10 a.m. and 3 p.m., and everyone takes a standard noon-to-1 p.m. lunch break. However, that accounts for only 4 hours of the 8-hour workday. Which other 4 hours workers will work is left up to each individual employee. Figure 11-5(b) provides a second example of a flextime schedule in which the required work hours are from 9 a.m. to 11 a.m. and from 2 p.m. to 4 p.m., allowing for flexible scheduling around the lunch break as well.

Research by Boris Baltes and associates shows that flextime scheduling does not work well in all settings. In assembly lines and other jobs that depend on worker interaction, production suffers when workers are on different

---

27. Peters, T., Waterman, R. H. (1981). *In search of excellence.* New York: Random House.

| Two Sample Flextime Schedules | ■ **FIGURE 11-5** |

Flextime scheduling enriches a job by giving workers decision-making responsibility over the context in which they work. Workers on flexible work schedules decide when to work and can arrange their work hours around nonwork commitments and interests.

(a) Flex period | Required | Flex period

6 a.m.   10 a.m.   3 p.m.   7 p.m.

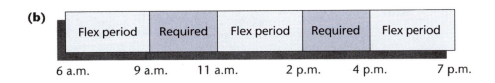

(b) Flex period | Required | Flex period | Required | Flex period

6 a.m.   9 a.m.   11 a.m.   2 p.m.   4 p.m.   7 p.m.

schedules. Likewise, flextime may offer few benefits to managers and professionals who already possess high levels of autonomy in the workplace.[28]

However, flextime does have benefits. First, it allows workers to schedule their work around their personal responsibilities and activities. Workers can accommodate their children's schedules, for example, or attend evening classes. In this way, flextime provides a way for individuals to balance work obligations and personal life obligations. Second, flextime increases workers' satisfaction with their jobs by increasing satisfaction with their work schedules. Finally, flextime may result in higher productivity and lower rates of absenteeism.[29]

Telecommuting. Another popular way companies are increasing context enrichment is through telecommuting. **Telecommuting** permits employees to work at home or near home for all or part of the week. They "commute" by telephone, e-mail, and other means of technology rather than by car or public transportation. Telecommuting is becoming increasingly easier as technology provides alternative means of communication. As mentioned in Chapter 1, estimates on the number of telecommuters in the United States vary, but the range is between three and nine million workers.[30] Individuals may choose to telecommute for a variety of reasons, depending on the needs involved. Figure 11-6 shows how telecommuting contributes to meeting the needs of the individual, the organization, and/or society.

Telecommuting can also give workers control over another aspect of work context—the physical layout of their workstation. "TECHNOLOGY FOCUS ON: Telecommuting" takes a look at some rather unusual examples of the workstations of telecommuters.

28. Baltes, B. B., Briggs, T. E. Huff, J. W., Wright, J. A., & Neuman, G. A. (1999). Flexible and compressed workweek schedules: A meta-analysis of their effects on work-related criteria. *Journal of Applied Psychology, 84,* 496–513.

29. Baltes, et al., Flexible and compressed workweek schedules.

30. Kurland, N. B., & Bailey, D. E. (1999). Telework: The advantages and challenges of working here, there, anywhere, and anytime. *Organizational Dynamics, 28,* 53.

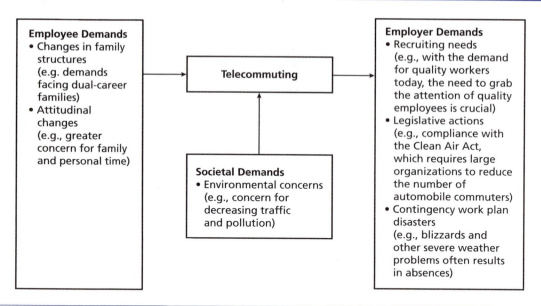

■ FIGURE 11-6 Employee, Organizational, and Societal Demands Contributing to the Growth of Telecommuting

Source: Igbaria, M., & Tan, M. (1998). *The virtual workplace.* Hershey, PA: Idea Group Publishing, p. 339.

TRENDS IN JOB DESIGN

The increasing emergence of job-enlargement and job-enrichment programs parallels the recent emphasis in organizations on employability and the new employment relationship. **Employability** is the notion that employees should be concerned about their own career development, including acquiring the skills needed to keep a job or to obtain a new position.[31] In today's rapidly changing organizations, employees need to be adaptable in order to maintain control over their future.[32] Research by Graeme Martin, Harry Staines, and Judy Pate indicates that today's employees have less job security and work in organizations with leaner structures, and thus they have less chance for advancement, than workers in the recent past.[33] Companies that emphasize workers' need for employability provide channels that assist workers in managing their own careers. Among the options organizations can introduce are programs aimed at developing transferable skills, opportunities for training, and career development discussions—in short, job-enlargement and job-enrichment programs.[34] All these programs enable workers to remain needed and valuable.[35]

Reengineering is another mechanism organizations currently can use to improve effectiveness and make jobs more engaging and satisfying for work-

31. Hendry, C., & Jenkins, R. (1997). Psychological contracts and new deals. *Human Resource Management Journal, 7*(1), 38–44.

32. Nirenberg, J. (1997). *Power tools: A leader's guide to the latest management thinking.* Singapore: Prentice Hall, pp. 336–338.

33. Martin, G., Staines, H., & Pate, J. (1998). Linking job security and career development in a new psychological contract. *Human Resource Management Journal, 8*(3), 20–24.

34. Martin, et al., Linking job security and career development in a new psychological contract.

35. Hendry & Jenkins, Psychological contracts and new deals.

TECHNOLOGY FOCUS ON TELECOMMUTING

HOME OFFICES LOOK WEIRDER ALL THE TIME. For 2 years, companies that called Steven Reinecke for advice on ergonomics had no idea where Reinecke was working. It was probably good that they didn't. Reinecke, then a consultant, was running his business from a sailboat in the Atlantic and Caribbean, where he lived with his wife and infant son. When the baby cried, Reinecke rowed away in a dinghy to call clients. For longer projects, he took to the beach, his laptop hooked to a car battery. Reinecke found that his wild environs helped him to be efficient. Now that technology enables us to work anywhere, people are picking some pretty weird places to work.

When a Dallas consultant held a contest for the most unusual home office, she got more than 50 oddball entries, from old bank vaults and garages to bathrooms. That's where George Kristich does a lot of work for his three-man construction company. While he lathers up in the shower, he says, he also can keep an eye on his computer a few feet away.

Far less oddball but far more dramatic is Phidias Cinaglia's workplace—high atop Utah's Wasatch Mountains. The view from his porch is a sweeping expanse of mountain terrain. The terrain affords "a proportional vastness that expands my own thinking," Cinaglia, a software designer, says. It also makes him highly productive: "While I can't keep that bubble of mental vastness alive for very long, I get a few hours of startling clarity."

Food writer and writing coach Antonia Allegra works from what she calls "a treehouse"—the second floor of a large garage in California's Napa Valley. She watches hawks and squirrels as she works. The setting helps her stay "extremely centered," she says. Friends at dot-com companies have tried to force her into a much faster pace, but she has turned down a couple offers for big-city jobs. She says the suitors are now considering letting her stay in her treehouse.

Regardless of their "weird" working arrangements, these workers claim they are more effective and efficient in their nontraditional workplaces than they would be in more traditional office settings.

Source: Excerpted from Shellenbarger, S. (2000, March 29). Sailboats and showers: Home offices look weirder all the time. *Wall Street Journal*, p. B1.

---

ers. Reengineering is about making fundamental changes in the way work is performed throughout an organization. In particular, improvements are sought in areas of cost, customer service, quality, and speed of production by eliminating activities that do not contribute to the company's value. GTE, a large telecommunications firm, claims that its reengineering efforts resulted in annual savings of $1 billion.[36]

Unfortunately, reengineering efforts often fail because the company fails to link the reengineering to the organization's overall goals and visions. Proper evaluation is needed to determine ways to ensure that the reengineering complements the company's strategic focus.[37] A major bank in the United Kingdom, for example, spent the equivalent of $1 billion replacing branch automation software and hardware. However, within 18 months the bank downsized from 3,300 to 2,500 branches. Clearly, the bank had not needed to invest money in those closed branches.[38] In this instance, by not

---

36. Obeng, E., & Crainer, S. (1994). *Making re-engineering happen.* London: Pitman Publishing, p. xi.

37. Clemons, E. K. (1995). Using scenario analysis to manage the strategic risks of reengineering. *Sloan Management Review, 36*(4), 61–71.

38. Clemons, Using scenario analysis to manage the strategic risks of reengineering.

linking its reengineering efforts to the company's overall goals, the company's job redesign efforts led to a waste of precious company resources.

WORKGROUP PERSPECTIVES

What happens when management takes the successes of job redesign programs seriously? Successes can provide management the refreshing insight that rank-and-file workers are important—if not critical—problem-solving allies. This conclusion inevitably leads to novel approaches in the way the organization functions. Three such approaches are quality circles, self-managed teams, and sociotechnical systems.

QUALITY CIRCLES

Quality circles (QCs) were the "first" trend-setting example of workgroup approaches to job design. Quality circles are small groups of employees who voluntarily meet on a regular basis for the purpose of solving problems involving the organization's products, services, or operations. The agenda of QC meetings is limited to discussing ways to improve quality, reduce costs, or improve productivity in the QC members' immediate jobs. Recommendations then are usually transmitted upward through the organization's hierarchy.[39] QCs can be thought of as a form of job enrichment in that they empower workers to make suggestions and some decisions. Figure 11-7 includes a list of their potential benefits to an organization.

QCs peaked in popularity in the 1980s, when most major companies used them as a way to introduce job enrichment and worker decision-making programs. But today research by Gill and Wong has shown that, although QCs are still used throughout American business (QCs are present in 60% of companies[40]), their popularity decreased during the 1990s.[41]

■ **FIGURE 11-7**   **Benefits of Quality Circles to an Organization**

QCs are a unique way for organizations to increase job enrichment. They can enrich not only individual employees but an organization itself. The following is a list of possible benefits of implementing QCs in an organization:

- Increases communication
- Increases participation
- Reduces resistance to change
- Produces high-quality solutions
- Improves employees' attitudes
- Decreases absenteeism
- Decreases turnover

Source: Benson, J., Bruil, S., Coghill, D., Cleator, R. H., et al. (1994). Self-directed work teams. *Production & Inventory Management Journal, 35*(1), 79–83.

---

39. Gill, R., & Wong, A. (1998). The cross-cultural transfer of management practices: The case of Japanese human resource management practices in Singapore. *International Journal of Human Resource Management, 9,* 116–135.
40. Lawler, E. E., Mohrman, S. A., & Ledford, G. E. (1998). *Strategies for high performance organizations–the CEO report.* San Francisco: Jossey-Bass.
41. Gill & Wong, *The cross-cultural transfer of management practices.*

INTERNATIONAL FOCUS ON
QUALITY CIRCLES

TOYOTA'S LEGENDARY PRODUCTION SYSTEM. Two days each month, more than 50 automotive executives and engineers travel to a sprawling manufacturing complex in Georgetown, Kentucky, to learn how Toyota makes cars. Each tour, which includes an intensive question-and-answer session, last's 5 hours and is booked months in advance. Although the visitors all work for competing automakers, Toyota charges no money for the tours, and no questions are off limits.

Toyota's showing the opposition how it makes cars is a bit like Coke's giving Pepsi a peek at its secret syrup formula. The Toyota Production System (TPS) on display at Georgetown applies not just to manufacturing but to almost everything Toyota does, from product development to supplier relations and distribution. But Toyota officials don't mind. Deep down, they know that the TPS's job designs that visitors observe on their tours—including the infamous QCs—represent the surface of TPS, but not its soul. Toyota isn't worried about giving away important secrets on a plant tour.

That may sound arrogant, but the evidence supports the conviction; despite years of imitation, nobody has succeeded in displacing Toyota as the world's most proficient auto company. Mercedes-Benz may dazzle with its sophisticated engineering, Honda with its engine technology, and Chrysler with its styling. But Toyota sets the standard in efficiency, productivity, and quality. Toyota has doubled its engineering output over the past 4 years while increasing its budget by only 20%—an astounding improvement.

Why has nobody been able to imitate TPS, much less duplicate its results? On the surface, TPS appears simple: Maximize flow, eliminate waste, respect people. But while TPS's concept isn't complicated, its implementation and coordination require blood, sweat, and tears. The company designs (with the help of QCs) the work to flow such that goods arrive in just the right quantity for the customer. These job designs result in a smoother-running plant and keep everybody busy.

The benefits of TPS, including the effective quality circles, enabled Toyota to develop a highly efficient organization where workers work in harmony. Whether Toyota's competitors will start to figure out exactly how the process works is anyone's best guess. Interestingly, however, there are no plans yet to end the plant tours.

Source: Excerpted from Taylor, A. (1997, December 8). How Toyota defies gravity, its secret, is its legendary production system. Though competitors have been trying to copy it for years, nobody makes it work as well as Toyota. *Fortune Magazine, 136*(11), 100+.

However, despite their decrease of popularity in United States organizations, QCs are extremely common in organizations with a Japanese culture and are considered an integral component of the Japanese management style. As shown in "INTERNATIONAL FOCUS ON: Quality Circles," combined with other innovative manufacturing techniques, QCs allowed Toyota to make remarkable strides in manufacturing, product development, and overall organizational effectiveness.

SELF-MANAGED TEAMS

Self-managed work teams take the philosophy behind QCs one step further. Self-managed work teams are groups of employees who make most of their own decisions related to planning their work, determining the pace of work, setting team goals, and redesigning the jobs of team members. In their purest form, self-managed teams are given enough autonomy over resources and decision making so they can produce their product with limited management involvement. Research has shown that self-managed teams have improved the bottom line for many organizations. The benefits are varied; self-managed teams typically eliminate the need for at least one layer of management, significantly raise productivity, and basically change the way work is done in organizations.[42] Self-managed teams are discussed more fully in Chapter 6.

SOCIOTECHNICAL SYSTEMS

Technological advancements in the past decade have resulted in many new developments in the design of group work, mostly in the area of increased automation. Automation typically is incorporated into work design to make jobs more efficient, but often without sufficient attention to its impact on the interest and motivation of workers. **Sociotechnical systems** provides a framework to bridge the concerns and fit of people with the advantages of automation.[43]

Figure 11-8 summarizes the major components of sociotechnical system design: the social system, the technological system, and the moderators. The social system refers to the human elements (including needs and desires) that are part of the work context and that can dramatically influence productivity. The technological system refers to the production technology required, the complexity of the assembly tasks, work interdependence issues, and even the nature of the final product. The social system and the technological system must work together jointly to ensure the future success of the organization. Workers' roles, goals, skills, and abilities all act as moderators. The moderators help define an optimal balance in workers' wants or needs, workers' capabilities, the tasks that need to be done, and the means by which they can be accomplished. In effect, sociotechnical systems address several questions: How can we adapt our technology to meet the needs of our workers, and how can we adapt our workers to optimize our technology potential? How can we strike a balance between what our workers want and what the manu-

---

■ **FIGURE 11-8**   Sociotechnical Systems Model of Job Design

Sociotechnical systems theory is concerned with designing jobs so that there is a fit between the social system of the organization (including meeting such social needs of workers as their need for affiliation) and the technical requirements or limits of the organization's production system.

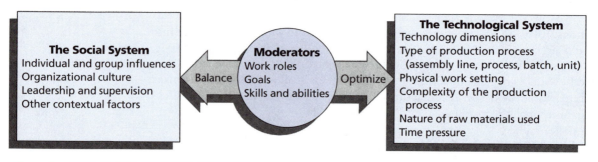

Source: Cummings, T. (1978). Self-regulating work groups: A socio-technical synthesis. *Academy of Management Review, 3,* 625–634; Hellriegel, D., Slocum, J. W., & Woodman, R. W. (1986). *Organizational behavior.* St. Paul, MN: West, p. 382.

---

42. Randolph, W. A. (1995, Spring). Navigating the journey to empowerment. *Organizational Dynamics,* 19–32.
43. System that puts people at forefront. (1996). *People Management, 2*(9), 25.

facturing of our product requires? Successful telecommuting programs offer an example of how a sociotechnical systems approach to job design can help identify an effective balance between technology, worker needs, and organizational objectives.

Critics of sociotechnical systems feel that the model ignores a critical consideration—the environment. As we will discuss in Chapter 15, organizations do not exist in a vacuum; they exist in a complex social environment that they influence and are influenced by. For example, the rapid and widespread adoption of new manufacturing technologies in developing economies (in such places as Eastern Europe, South America, and the Pacific Rim) often far outpaces the development of environmental regulations in those areas. This can lead to severe environmental damage in the form of pollution.[44] Thus, to promote long-term effectiveness, sociotechnical considerations need to strike a balance not only *inside* the organization among the technology, the organization's objectives, and workers needs, but also *externally* between the technology, the organization's objectives, and the environment.

BARRIERS TO JOB REDESIGN SUCCESS

The different approaches to job redesign described in this chapter have the potential to realize tremendous benefits for organizations. Both individual and group approaches to job design seem to be moving in the direction of eliciting greater worker involvement, as a way of doing more to tap the resource represented by the workforce. However, the results of employee-involvement programs are mixed. Many job redesign efforts *have* led to increased job satisfaction, which, in turn, has resulted in lower employee turnover. Research by Edward Lawler, Susan Mohrman, and Gerald Ledford, for example, showed that 81% of Fortune 1000 companies claim that their experiences with employee involvement have been positive or very positive. Benefits included employees' trust in management, organizational processes, decision making, and safety/health of employees.[45] But increased employee involvement does not guarantee positive results. In the same study, 3% of the companies reported having had negative experiences with employee-involvement programs, and 16% reported having had neither negative nor positive experiences.[46] These statistics stand as a sobering testament that choosing a good job design system is not enough. Unless the system is properly managed, increased productivity may not be a result.

Realization of the *full* benefits of job design programs—namely, both workforce satisfaction and enhanced productivity—requires an understanding of the limits of a program. Three limits, or potential barriers, to a successful job design program are addressed in the remainder of this chapter: social information processing, individual differences, and management support.

SOCIAL INFORMATION PROCESSING

Inherent in both the job characteristics model and workgroup approaches to job design is a basic assumption that workers perceive their jobs the way that

---

44. Heller, F. (1997). Sociotechnology and the environment. *Human Relations 50*, 605–624.
45. Lawler, *Strategies for high performance organizations*, pp. 108–109.
46. Lawler, et al., *Strategies for high performance organizations*.

managers intend those jobs to be perceived. As we know from the discussion of perception in Chapter 2, this is unrealistic. Just because a manager decides to give a subordinate some autonomy does not mean that the subordinate will perceive that this is the case. As shown in Figure 2-2 in Chapter 2, subordinates' and supervisors' perceptions often differ dramatically.

The **social information processing** framework of job design emphasizes the importance of perception in understanding how workers react to their jobs.[47] According to this framework, how an employee perceives and reacts to a job depends on social cues provided by coworkers[48] and even on cues provided by the jobholder's supervisor.[49] The roles of perception and social cues in workers' reactions to jobs underscores the importance of conveying positive attitudes, creating a positive atmosphere, and keeping channels of communication open in workgroups.[50] Workers react to perceptions about their jobs rather than to their jobs' objective characteristics. Creating a positive climate that encourages workers to form favorable perceptions about job characteristics may be as important as good job design in achieving positive outcomes.

INDIVIDUAL DIFFERENCES

One of the important points of Chapter 3 is that no two employees are likely to be motivated by quite the same things. This becomes a critical issue in job design. Job design efforts that suit the needs of one employee may be hopelessly inappropriate for another.

The approaches to job design outlined in this chapter differ in what they require of the typical worker. Work simplification requires the least of the worker. Tasks are simple and repetitive; there is very little demand that the employee think on the job or take responsibility. Job rotation and job enlargement assume that employees want at least some variety in their work. Job enrichment and workgroup redesign efforts assume quite a bit more. These approaches assume that the rank-and-file worker is willing to take responsibility for making consequential job-related decisions and that workers do not simply want to be told what to do. This is not always the case. At the highly successful Topeka, Kansas, General Foods' plant, for example, a small minority of workers resisted management's efforts to install self-managing teams. Researchers have found that some workers always prefer highly repetitive, low-skill jobs, even when there are opportunities to take on more interesting tasks.[51] There are a couple ways to handle and minimize the differences among workers. First, increases in worker autonomy should be *voluntary*.[52] Researchers Lin Xie and Gary Johns found that expanding a job's scope or responsibilities may be too stressful for many workers.[53] Therefore,

47. Salancik, G., & Pfeffer, J. (1977). A social information processing approach to job attitudes and task design. *Administrative Science Quarterly, 23,* 224–253.

48. Weiss, H. H., & Shaw, J. B. (1979). Social influences on judgements about tasks. *Organizational Behavior and Human Performance, 24,* 126–140.

49. Griffin, R. W. (1981). *Technological and social processes in task redesign: A field experiment.* Unpublished manuscript, Texas A&M University.

50. Kelly, J., & Kelly, C. (1991). Them and us: Social psychology and the new industrial relations. *British Journal of Industrial Relations, 29*(1), 25–48.

51. Fein, M. (1974, Winter). Job enrichment: A re-evaluation. *Sloan Management Review,* 69–88.

52. Kanter, R. M. (1983). The dilemmas of participation in *The Changemasters.* New York: Simon & Schuster, pp. 241–278.

53. Lin Xie, J., & Johns, G. (1995). Job scope and stress: Can job scope be too high? *Academy of Management Journal, 38,* 1288–1309.

if a worker is uninterested in playing a larger role in the workplace, forcing that worker to do so will result in the worker having less freedom, not more. Further, reluctant participants (e.g., reluctant workers in a QC) are unlikely to make valuable contributions. Sometimes management may simply need to give workers and supervisors time to get comfortable with their new roles.

Second, if management wants to make job enrichment a permanent part of its management approach, employee interest in enriched jobs needs to be assessed before employees are hired. Hackman and Oldham's research on their job characteristics model found that the relationships among job characteristics, psychological states, and outcomes (such as job satisfaction and productivity) are stronger in workers who are high in **growth need strength**—in other words, workers who want to grow and develop in their jobs.[54] Thus, the relationships outlined in Hackman and Oldham's job characteristics model may not apply similarly to all workers. Management can use questionnaires such as the Growth Need Strength (Measure B) to assess the growth needs of prospective employees.

Concerns about the appropriateness of job redesign for some employees should not be used as an excuse not to undertake substantial job redesign efforts. Most managers seriously underestimate the desires of their employees to make positive contributions to the organization and to play larger roles in decision making. Ignoring this untapped resource can be costly.

MANAGEMENT SUPPORT

Many, if not most, job redesign efforts are aimed at rank-and-file workers. Yet the reactions of supervisors and managers above the rank-and-file may be key to job redesign success. Three major concerns must be addressed if a job redesign effort is to succeed: supervisors' and manager's responsiveness, their feelings of being threatened, and how they handle success.

RESPONSIVENESS. A critical issue in ceding limited autonomy to workers is that employees must perceive management to be sincere. Sincerity is often a function of responsiveness—how quickly and completely management responds to workers' suggestions.

Even if an employee-generated suggestion is not a good one—for example, there are practical, budgetary, or political reasons for not implementing it—by responding thoughtfully to the suggestion, management can accomplish two important goals. First, even negative feedback sends the message that management is listening. If employees have the sense that management is just toying with them, they are likely to "dry up" pretty quickly as a source of ideas. Second, in taking the time to explain why an idea was rejected, management provides workers with invaluable input and thereby increases the probability that future suggestions will be offered and adopted.

FEELINGS OF BEING THREATENED. If the lowest-level workers in an organization are given more control through limited-autonomy job redesign

---

54. Hackman, J. R., & Oldham, G. R. (May, 1974). The Job Diagnostic Survey: An Instrument for the Diagnosis of Jobs and the Evaluation of Job Redesign Projects. Tech Report # 4, Department of Administrative Sciences, Yale University.

programs, who is losing that control? From the perspective of most supervisors, the obvious answer seems to be themselves.

Is it any wonder that supervisors may feel threatened? To gain supervisors' support of job redesign programs, their fears must be dealt with. Even if the elimination of supervisory positions is not a legitimate concern, supervisors are likely to worry that increasing the roles of rank-and-file workers will result in a loss of control and potential status. After all, workers at *all* levels of an organization need to feel that they have a sense of control and are making a contribution. Supervisors are unlikely to feel that their authority has been usurped if the scope of their own jobs is similarly enlarged or enriched.

In short, job redesign efforts should not be used as band-aids for productivity, quality, or morale problems. Behind every approach to job design lurks an overall philosophy about the roles of workers at all levels of the organization. The most successful job redesign programs will be ones in which the philosophy is implemented consistently across all levels of the organization, from rank-and-file workers to supervisors to middle managers and up.

HOW MANAGEMENT HANDLES SUCCESS. Interestingly, a final major stumbling block to the success of job redesign programs is what to do when they succeed. Often this turns out to be a problem management is ill equipped to handle.

One serious problem created by successful job redesign efforts is the spiral of rising employee expectations detailed in Figure 11-2. One of the benefits of job redesign initiatives is that employees become more self-respectful and more self-confident and have stronger images of themselves as being capable of making valuable contributions to their organizations. This suggests that successful job redesign efforts must be seen as journeys, not as destinations. Management must continually be prepared to meet the rising expectations of workers to contribute.

Successful job redesign programs can also lead to thorny compensation issues, many of which are discussed in Chapter 12. As workers' jobs are enlarged or enriched, their beliefs in their abilities to contribute to their organizations increases as well. If management does not adjust compensation schemes to reflect the enlarged contributions of its workforce, the reservoir of worker ideas and energy may soon run dry. On the other hand, providing employees with opportunities to take control *and* financial incentives for doing so can pay off in enhanced productivity.[55]

SUMMARY

Traditional approaches to job design focused almost exclusively on work simplification so as to take advantage of efficiency through specialization. But there must be a balance between meeting the needs for work simplification and meeting the personal needs of employees.

Management must face the challenge of providing jobs for workers who have more to offer than ever before and fully expect to have opportunities to

---

55. Posner, B. G. (1990, March). Raising the stakes, *Inc.*, 100–102.

offer what they have to give. Increasingly, organizations are implementing approaches to job design that take into account the needs of workers by making jobs more challenging and involving. Job enlargement and job enrichment are two such approaches. Job enlargement focuses on increasing the range of skills that a job requires. Job enlargement goes even further, by allowing workers to fulfill higher-order needs (such as the need for control) in performing jobs.

The successes of enlargement and enrichment programs have encouraged management to experiment with job design efforts that offer workers even more opportunities for decision making. QCs, in which employees meet to discuss work-related problems, and sociotechnical systems, which combine the benefits of technology with the capabilities of the individual, have gained much attention and in some companies have resulted in significant financial savings and increases in productivity.

In the end, job design efforts are successful only if management supports the philosophy that workers are capable of making valuable contributions to the organization.

KEY TERMS

Context enrichment	**Quality circles (QCs)**
Cross-training	**Reengineering**
Employability	**Self-leadership**
Feedback	**Social information processing**
Flextime work scheduling	**Sociotechnical systems**
Growth need strength	**Task identity**
Job characteristics model	**Task significance**
Job enlargement	**Telecommuting**
Job enrichment	**Work simplification**
Job rotation	

DISCUSSION QUESTIONS

1 Many organizations use an acronym that some feel is the key to successful management. The acronym, KISS, stands for "Keep it simple, Stupid." Is KISS a good rule of thumb in designing jobs?

2 How do enrichment approaches to job design differ from job-enlargement approaches? What are the dangers for management in moving from job enlargement to job enrichment?

3 What are some of the challenges or problems associated with job redesign efforts? What steps do these challenges suggest that management should take?

4 When would enriching the context of a job be a more effective or appropriate approach to job redesign than enriching the content of the job?

5 When might a group approach to job design be more appropriate than an individual approach?

6 Why should feedback be an important part of any job enrichment program?

7 Who is likely to benefit when a company institutes quality circles? Why do quality circle programs fail?

ON YOUR OWN

Job Characteristics Instrument   Think about a job you have held recently, perhaps last summer. With this job in mind, answer the following questions. The scoring instructions follow the questions. In what design areas was your job deficient? How do you think these deficiencies could be corrected?

The following questions are concerned with the characteristics of your job. Each of the questions should be evaluated according to the following responses:

Very Little	Little	A Moderate Amount	Much	A Great Deal
1	2	3	4	5

Two separate responses are required. In column 1, mark your response according to how you evaluate the *actual* characteristic of your job. In column 2, mark your response according to how you would have liked, or *desired*, your job to be.

Question	Column 1	Column 2
1 To what extent does your job provide the opportunity to do a number of different duties each day?	_____	_____
2 How much are you left on your own to do your work?	_____	_____
3 To what extent can you tell how well you are doing on your job without being told by others?	_____	_____
4 To what extent do you feel like your job is just a small cog in a big machine?	_____	_____
5 To what extent do you start a job that is finished by another employee?	_____	_____
6 Does your job require a great deal of skill to perform it effectively?	_____	_____
7 How much of your job depends on your ability to work with others?	_____	_____
8 To what extent does your job limit your opportunity to get to know other employees?	_____	_____
9 How much variety of tasks is there in your job?	_____	_____
10 To what extent are you able to act independently of supervisors in doing your work?	_____	_____
11 Does seeing the results of your work give you a good idea how well you are performing?	_____	_____
12 How significant is your work to the overall organization?	_____	_____
13 To what extent do you see projects or jobs through to completion?	_____	_____
14 To what extent is your job challenging?	_____	_____
15 To what extent do you work pretty much by yourself?	_____	_____
16 How much opportunity is there in your job to develop professional friendships?	_____	_____
17 To what extent does your job require you to do the same thing over and over again each day?	_____	_____
18 To what extent do you have the freedom to decide how to do your work?	_____	_____
19 To what extent does doing the job itself provide you with feedback about how well you are performing?	_____	_____
20 To what extent do you feel like you are contributing something significant to your organization?	_____	_____
21 To what extent do you complete work that has been started by another employee?	_____	_____
22 To what extent is your job so simple that virtually anyone could handle it, with little or no training?	_____	_____
23 To what extent is dealing with other people a part of your job?	_____	_____
24 To what extent can you talk informally with other employees while at work?	_____	_____

Scoring Instructions   For each of the eight job characteristics (A through H), compute a total score by summing the responses to the appropriate questions. Note that some questions are reversed (e.g., #17), and that the response to these should be subtracted from 6 to get a response value. Transfer the scores to the final scores, where column 1 is actual scores, column 2 is desired scores, and column 3 is comparative scores to be provided by your instructor.

Variable	Column 1 Actual		Column 2 Desired		Final Scores 1	2	3
	Question	*Response*	*Question*	*Response*			
	(#1) $=$	$+$ _____	(#1) $=$	$+$ _____			
A	(#9) $=$	$+$ _____	(#9) $=$	$+$ _____			
	$(6 - \#17) =$	$+$ _____	$(6 - \#17) =$	$+$ _____			
	$(\text{Total} \div 3) = A_1 = + \underline{\quad}$		$(\text{Total} \div 3) = A_2 = + \underline{\quad}$		( )	( )	( )
					A_1	A_2	A_3
	Question	*Response*	*Question*	*Response*			
	(#2) $=$	$+$ _____	(#2) $=$	$+$ _____			
B	(#10) $=$	$+$ _____	(#10) $=$	$+$ _____			
	(#18) $=$	$+$ _____	(#18) $=$	$+$ _____			
	$(\text{Total} \div 3) = B_1 = + \underline{\quad}$		$(\text{Total} \div 3) = B_2 = + \underline{\quad}$		( )	( )	( )
					B_1	B_2	B_3
	Question	*Response*	*Question*	*Response*			
	(#3) $=$	$+$ _____	(#3) $=$	$+$ _____			
C	(#11) $=$	$+$ _____	(#11) $=$	$+$ _____			
	(#19) $=$	$+$ _____	(#19) $=$	$+$ _____			
	$(\text{Total} \div 3) = C_1 = + \underline{\quad}$		$(\text{Total} \div 3) = C_2 = + \underline{\quad}$		( )	( )	( )
					C_1	C_2	C_3
	Question	*Response*	*Question*	*Response*			
	$(6 - \#4) =$	$+$ _____	$(6 - \#4) =$	$+$ _____			
D	(#12) $=$	$+$ _____	(#12) $=$	$+$ _____			
	(#20) $=$	$+$ _____	(#20) $=$	$+$ _____			
	$(\text{Total} \div 3) = D_1 = + \underline{\quad}$		$(\text{Total} \div 3) = D_2 = + \underline{\quad}$		( )	( )	( )
					D_1	D_2	D_3
	Question	*Response*	*Question*	*Response*			
	$(6 - \#5) =$	$+$ _____	$(6 - \#5) =$	$+$ _____			
E	(#13) $=$	$+$ _____	(#13) $=$	$+$ _____			
	$(6 - \#21) =$	$+$ _____	$(6 - \#21) =$	$+$ _____			
	$(\text{Total} \div 3) = E_1 = + \underline{\quad}$		$(\text{Total} \div 3) = E_2 = + \underline{\quad}$		( )	( )	( )
					E_1	E_2	E_3
	Question	*Response*	*Question*	*Response*			
	(#6) $=$	$+$ _____	(#6) $=$	$+$ _____			
F	(#14) $=$	$+$ _____	(#14) $=$	$+$ _____			
	$(6 - \#22) =$	$+$ _____	$(6 - \#22) =$	$+$ _____			
	$(\text{Total} \div 3) = F_1 = + \underline{\quad}$		$(\text{Total} \div 3) = F_2 = + \underline{\quad}$		( )	( )	( )
					F_1	F_2	F_3

	Question		Response	Question		Response			
	(#7)	=	+ _____	*(#7)*	=	+ _____			
G	*(6 − #15)*	=	+ _____	*(6 − #15)*	=	+ _____			
	(#23)	=	+ _____	*(#23)*	=	+ _____			
	_____			_____					
	(Total ÷ 3) = G_1 =		+ _____	(Total ÷ 3) = G_2 =		+ _____	( )	( )	( )
							G_1	G_2	G_3

	Question		Response	Question		Response			
	(6 − #8)	=	+ _____	*(6 − #8)*	=	+ _____			
H	*(#16)*	=	+ _____	*(#16)*	=	+ _____			
	(#24)	=	+ _____	*(#24)*	=	+ _____			
	_____			_____					
	(Total ÷ 3) = H_1 =		+ _____	(Total ÷ 3) = H_2 =		+ _____	( )	( )	( )
							H_1	H_2	H_3

Source: Szilagyi, A. D., & Wallace, M. W. (1987). *Organizational behavior and performance*. Glenview, IL: Scott, Foresman.

CLOSING CASE   CHAPTER 11

THE MANAGER'S MEMO

FROM: W. Johnson, Office Manager
TO: D. Washington, Internet Billing Supervisor
RE: Performance of Internet Billing Representatives

I have given serious thought to our conversation about the increase in performance errors, absenteeism, and low morale among our Internet billing representatives. The problem may well lie, at least in part, in the design of their jobs. In reviewing the procedures you sent me, I see that their tasks are quite specialized, routine, and mostly automated—processing bills for Internet orders. In addition, due to the design of their jobs, most of the Internet billers rarely if ever have any direct contact with other departments, such as sales, customer service, or technical support. Redesigning their jobs could do worlds for their morale and motivation, and it could mean see fewer errors and a reduction in the number of sick days taken.

My suggestion is that you consider ways to expand and enrich the work of the Internet billing staff. If you will outline some general ideas, we can meet to discuss them and how they fit in with the overall needs of the firm.

CASE DISCUSSION QUESTIONS

Assume that you are D. Washington, supervisor of the Internet billing staff, and respond to the office manager's memorandum. Select from the job design programs discussed in this chapter those that you think will be most effective, and outline an overall redesign of your staff's jobs. Be as specific as you can.

CHAPTER 12

Maintaining Performance

COMPANIES EXPERIMENTING WITH CREATIVE STRATEGIES TO MAINTAIN PERFORMANCE

In the past decade, companies have tried several revolutionary strategies aimed at maintaining average or better-than-average performance, including decentralizing authority, flattening organization and department hierarchies, and, more recently, inducing weak employees to leave the organization. One organization implementing this and other major management changes is Ford Motor Company, the second largest U.S. automaker. In addition to a buyout program targeted specifically at under performing employees, Ford is retraining 55,000 of its managers in the basics of business. The company's long-term goals are to improve the speed with which the company responds to consumer needs and to increase company growth.

Ford's buyout program, part of its overall compensation and performance-review process, targets employees who do not warrant termination but are not likely to advance. Since the program went into effect in 1998, Ford has reduced its workforce by nearly 9,000 employees. As new employees are hired, the performance bar is raised, which translates into even higher overall performance expectations.

Intel and Microsoft are among other corporations that are using strict performance reviews as a way to keep ahead of the competition. At Microsoft, for example, the employee appraisal system has resulted in annual reductions of its workforce by an average of 5%.

In identifying employees who are least likely to succeed, and thus raising the bar on performance, these organizations are creating highly competitive workforces—a sure way to maintain performance.

Sources: Adapted from Management: Ford rolls out new model of corporate culture. (1999, January 13). *Wall Street Journal,* p. B1; and Schellhardt, T. D., & Goo, S. K. (1998, July 22). Management: At Ford, buyout plan has a twist. *Wall Street Journal,* p. B1.

INTRODUCTION

As the examples mentioned in this chapter's opening vignette illustrate, companies are trying a variety of methods aimed at retaining high-performance employees. It should come as no surprise that research shows that companies which recognize and focus on the varying needs of their employees perform better than companies that do not have such a focus.[1] The various approaches organizations use to maintain effective performance is a central topic of this chapter.

One of the most obvious ways organizations try to maintain performance is by instituting compensation systems that are responsive to the specific goals and needs of the organization. As "INTERNATIONAL FOCUS ON: Compensation" highlights, this is a particularly vexing concern for global organizations, since the needs of expatriate employees are often different from, and sometimes more difficult to meet than, those of their counterparts back

INTERNATIONAL FOCUS ON
COMPENSATION

COMPENSATING EXPATRIATES TURNS OUT TO BE ESPECIALLY CHALLENGING. Developing equitable compensation systems is always difficult. But, as global companies are increasingly discovering, designing competitive, equitable, attractive compensation packages for employees being sent on international assignments is especially challenging. Each expatriate has different financial needs, depending on the assignment and on the country to which he or she is assigned. Also, as organizations have employees stationed in more and more countries, administering global compensation packages becomes increasingly difficult.

U.S. companies have taken several approaches to the problem. The most popular is the "balance-sheet approach," which aims to provide international assignees with the same standard of living abroad that they are used to at home. The disadvantage is that, depending on the cost of living of the country to which the employees are sent, their compensation may be lower after they return home than it was while they were expatriates. Although the main objective of the balance-sheet approach is to make sure that expatriates neither lose nor gain financially compared to if they had stayed home,

some organizations add incentives to employees who take such assignments as a way to induce them to go abroad.

Another increasingly popular approach is referred to as the "home country-based balance sheet". As the name suggests, the aim in this case is to maintain compensation rates abroad that are consistent with rates in the home country. One clear advantage of this approach is that employees more easily become reintegrated into the salary structure when they return home.

Calvin Reynolds, senior counselor at Organization Resources Counselors, emphasizes that in developing compensation packages, managers need to keep in mind not only the philosophies of their organizations but also the specific needs of employees. Managers would be smart to take Reynolds's advice to heart, whether they work for a small organization with few employees or a large multinational corporation with employees throughout the world.

Sources: Adapted from Overman, S. (2000, March). Sync: Harmonizing your global compensation plans may be done more "in spirit" than to the letter. *HR Magazine, 45*(3), 87–92; and Black, J. S., Gregersen, H. B., Mendenhall, M. E., & Stroh, L. K. (1999). *Globalizing people through international assignments.* Reading, MA: Addison-Wesley.

---

1. Watson Wyatt Worldwide. Strategic rewards 1999/2000 [On-line]. URL: *www.watsonwyatt.com*

home. And as we shall see, designing and implementing competitive compensation programs is a complicated process that involves both setting performance goals and conducting performance appraisals. Yet, even with all these systems in place, a manager may still have problems with employees' performance.

COMPENSATION SYSTEMS

Compensation systems are the primary mechanism organizations use to influence employees' behavior. Most compensation systems are developed with two broad goals in mind: to produce desired behavior in employees and to accomplish the first goal within the limitations faced by the organization. The first goal includes motivating employees to join the organization, to remain with it, and to perform well for it. The second goal highlights the constraints most organizations face on their ability to pay, and the limitations determined, for example, by minimum wage regulations and circumstances in external labor markets.

Compensation usually includes more than just the dollars employees receive from their employers. It may also include an array of incentive strategies, cost-of-living adjustments, stock options, and benefits, from health insurance to vacation time. Because they are such an important part of the employee–employer relationship, compensation systems are a major way organizations convey their expectations, including what they want their employees to do and how they should behave.

After designing their compensation systems, many organizations unfortunately discover that the behavior they want from their employees and the behavior their employees are offering are very different from one another. In fact, many compensation systems not only do not reinforce behaviors the employer wants, but also reward behaviors that the employer is trying to discourage.[2]

To understand how this happens, one need only examine the incentive system carefully, focusing on what set of behaviors are actually being rewarded rather than simply listening to what the organization, through its managers, says it wants. Management typically hopes its employees will exert effort in the areas of team building, creativity, and interpersonal relations, yet it has no mechanism in its incentive system to reward these activities. In other cases, organizations ask employees to set challenging goals for themselves and then punishes them when they do not meet those goals.[3]

Another problem organizations encounter is that they hope managers will pay attention to long-run costs and opportunities and institute programs that focus on the future; however, many reward systems reward managers for short-run sales and earnings only. Thus, it is often personally advantageous for managers to sacrifice long-term profit and growth for short-term advantages; such a view, unfortunately, is not likely to be in the best interest of the organization.

As these two general examples suggest, compensation systems are often put in place without careful consideration of their impact on employee be-

---

2. Kerr, S. (1975). On the folly of rewarding A while hoping for B. *Academy of Management Journal, 18,* 769–783.

3. Kerr, On the folly of rewarding A while hoping for B.

havior. In developing or revising compensation systems, managers should examine exactly what employee behaviors are desired. Likewise, if a system is in place, organizations should identify exactly what employee behaviors are being rewarded.

In addition to rewarding the wrong behaviors, compensation systems often do not adequately define what the organization considers desirable behavior and typically fail to develop a performance appraisal system for reliably measuring that behavior.[4] In the case of the Ford Motor Company, for example, the company needed to determine not only what distinguished high-performing from low-performing employees but also a way to quantify that difference. This task is increasingly difficult as more jobs are in service industries and fewer jobs are in manufacturing. It is far easier to count the number of widgets an individual produces than to evaluate the quality of service provided by a mental-health counselor. Also, work is becoming increasingly complex and multidimensional. Technological advances and machine-paced performance reduce variability in job performance, so that differences in performance evaluations are based on subjective employee characteristics rather than on objective performance. In organizations such as Ford, for instance, employees are as likely to be assessed on their leadership qualities and ability to work in a team as on their skill in operating a piece of equipment.

Another obstacle to effective performance evaluation is that the managers who are required to evaluate employee performance often have neither the training in how to assess performance nor the desire to evaluate and defend their assessments. Finally, managers have difficulty identifying the rewards their employees value. Some employees may find certain rewards very reinforcing, whereas others may find those same rewards completely irrelevant.

These are only some of the difficulties organizations may face when trying to develop or implement effective compensation systems. As you read the rest of the chapter, consider the impact each of these obstacles could have on employees' motivation to perform in concert with management's desires and expectations. Would each obstacle affect employees at companies such as Ford, Intel, and Microsoft similarly?

TYPES OF COMPENSATION SYSTEMS

Compensation systems can be defined as the financial reward structures organizations use to compensate individuals for the work they perform for the organization. The general notion is that monetary rewards are the primary mechanism for motivating high performance among employees. In addition, monetary rewards are the most salient of the forms of compensation under the control of organizations. However, for monetary rewards to be effective motivators, a number of assumptions based on expectancy theory must be met. (Expectancy theory is discussed in detail in Chapter 3.) In the following list of these assumptions, we have indicated in parentheses which component of expectancy theory is related to that assumption:

1 Employees must be capable of performing at high levels. Unless employees are capable of performing the required tasks, there is no possibility that high-quality task performance will result (E P).

---

4. Podsakoff, P. M., Greene, C. N., & McFillen, J. M. (1987). Obstacles to the effective use of reward systems. In R. Schuler, S. Youngblood, & V. Huber (Eds.), *Readings in personnel and human resource management* (3rd ed., pp. 270–285). New York: West.

2 Employees must believe they can perform at high levels. Even if individuals have the ability to perform a required task, they are unlikely to exert any effort unless they believe they can accomplish that task (E P).

3 Employees must believe that they will be rewarded with more money for exerting more effort. In other words, employees must believe that there is a relationship between performance and their monetary rewards; more to the point, they must realize that the level of reward varies systematically with the level of performance (P O).

4 Employees must value money. While not all employees value money equally, for money to be motivating, they must value money sufficiently (Valence).

5 Money must be valued relative to other rewards. It must be valued over other incentives, such as peer acceptance. If peer acceptance is valued more highly than money, then the possibility of antagonizing peers because of high performance will restrict the level of performance (Valence).

6 Jobs must allow for performance variation. Jobs must be designed so that individuals may perform at different levels. If jobs are machine paced, then levels of performance, because they are based on the machine, are not subject to worker control. In this case, the notion of high performance is irrelevant (P O).

7 Performance must be measurable. Employees must be convinced that the level of their performance can be reliably measured. If, for example, an employee exerts considerable effort during one evaluation period and little effort in a subsequent period, yet there is no difference in the level of reward, then the "incentive" system may have little influence on the individual's performance (P O).

8 The incentive system must be compatible with the nature of the work (individual versus group). Unless management can assess who does the work, an incentive plan that is not compatible with the nature of the work will probably not be effective because the organization will not be able to attribute contributions of an individual or a group (P O).

If these assumptions are met, then an incentive system is likely to foster high performance. However, these assumptions do not inform the manager about the specific structure of the incentive system. That is, all the assumptions can be met in a piece-rate incentive system, a commission system, or a straight salary system. Recent research has found that different systems result in different performance from employees in different types of jobs. For example, a sales employee will probably benefit most from a pay structure that is partly dependent on commission, whereas an employee at an automobile company such as Ford might benefit more from a structure that rewards overall efficiency (e.g., low rates of error, high rates of production). An effective pay structure is one that matches pay strategies with the job in ways that encourage and reward good performance.[5] Consider the incentive systems shown in Figure 12-1. Each can be broken into plans that reward either individual per-

5. Wood, R. E., Atkins, P. W. B., & Bright, J. E. H. (1999). Bonuses, goals, and instrumentality effects. *Journal of Applied Psychology, 84,* 703–720.

Types of Incentive Systems	■ FIGURE 12-1

A company has a variety of choices in how to structure its compensation system. Some systems reward individuals for their performance, and others reward individuals for the performance of the group as a whole.

Incentive Systems

Individual Incentives	Group Incentives
1 Expectation of current and future performance	Scanlon plan
a Salary-based pay	Profit sharing
b Skill-based pay	Gainsharing
c Standard-hour plan	Employee stock-ownership plan (ESOP)
2 Actual current performance	
a Piece-rate pay	

formance or group performance. It is not uncommon for organizations to use a combination of systems, depending on the work being performed.

INDIVIDUAL INCENTIVES. Organizational actors would typically agree that all incentive systems are based on some aspect of performance: past, current, or potential. Thus, there are a variety of pay-for-performance plans, depending on the particular emphasis necessary for fitting the pay system to the demands of the position, the employee, and the organization. Basing pay structure on expectations of current and future performance necessarily entails consideration of past performance. That is, one could be paid a **salary,** a fixed annual rate of pay for performing a particular set of activities. Such plans are typically directed at employees who are managers, whose work is hard to observe, or whose tasks do not easily fall into easily measurable units. Pay structures based on hours worked rather than a fixed fee or salary are usually reserved for employees who are lower in the organizational hierarchy and whose tasks are less complex than those of salaried employees.

Hourly pay structures are different from standard-hour pay systems. With a **standard-hour-rate plan,** rates are determined not by what the employee actually produces but by the amount of time (determined by industrial engineering standards) that it should take to produce each unit based on historical production figures. Thus, the employee is paid a standard rate for a standard amount of output, regardless of the length of time the employee took to produce the unit.

Another form of individual incentive plan, **skill-based pay,** has been gaining in popularity in U.S. organizations. Because they are person based, not job based, skill-based systems are designed to reward employees for their skills, not their performance of the specifics of the job they are doing. That is, employees are rewarded based on the number of skills they have or on the number of jobs they can do.[6]

The emphasis of skill-based systems is on rewarding employees for a range of work-related attributes. Such attributes might include their knowledge,

---

6. Lawler, E. E., Ledford, G. E., Jr., & Chang, L. (1993, March/April). Who uses skill-based pay, and why. *Compensation & Benefits Review, 25*(2), 22–26.

skills, and abilities—behaviors that make them valuable to their organizations. For this reason, employees tend to view skill-based pay programs as generally fair.[7]

There are several advantages to skill-based pay programs for organizations. One of the most obvious advantages is that they encourage employees to be flexible and develop their skills, which, in turn, makes maintaining a lean workforce easier. As pointed out in the opening vignette on Ford, maintaining a leaner workforce is an effective way for an organization to maintain high performance. Other advantages of skill-based pay programs include increased productivity, decreased labor costs, and reduced turnover.[8]

Pay structures may also be based on current performance. For example, under a **piece-rate plan,** employees are paid a given rate for each unit produced. Rates are based on objective performance; thus, with this system, managers hope to encourage increasing levels of current and future productivity.

It is not necessary to select one or another of these individual incentive programs. Combinations of these two forms exist as well. For example, salespeople may be paid a salary plus commission—a combination piece-rate and a standard-hour-rate plan. Such employees are guaranteed both a minimum wage (standard-hour plan) and rewards based on their sales.

Clearly, the goal of individual incentive plans is to reward the best-performing employees with the largest rewards while encouraging employees to greater levels of future productivity. The disadvantage of such systems is that they are focused on individual behavior. For example, employees might be less likely to go "above and beyond the call of duty" under these plans because they do not think they are getting paid to do so.[9] Thus, many organizations do not rely solely on individual-based compensation systems as a way to reward their employees.

GROUP INCENTIVES. Rare is the organization that focuses solely on individually based performance. Thus, it is important when creating compensation systems to include sufficient flexibility to focus employees' attention on more than their own particular performance—to consider, in addition, how the group, division, or organization as a whole is performing. Group-level incentive plans operate under the same set of assumptions as individual incentive plans; they reward employees for productive behavior that is a function of larger organizational units (e.g., team, profit center, or division).

Research suggests that the rewards and benefits of performance should be directed at the unit that is responsible for and able to affect performance. If a project's success depends on the contributions of an entire department, rewarding only certain individuals would probably lead to increased competitiveness rather than to the cooperation required for successful completion of

---

7. Lee, C., Law, K. S., & Bobko, P. (1999). The importance of justic preceptions on pay effectiveness: A two-year study of a skill-based pay plan. *Journal of Management, 25,* 851–873.

8. Lee et al., *Journal of Management,* and Murray, B., & Gerhart, B. (1998). An empirical analysis of a skill-based pay program and plant performance outcomes. *Academy of Management Journal, 41,* 68–78.

9. Deckop, J. R., Mangel, R. and Cirka, C. C. (1999, August). Getting more than you pay for: Organizational citizenship behavior and pay-for-performance plans. *Academy of Management Journal, 42*(4), 420–428.

the project.[10] A variety of group-based incentive plans have been developed. Most focus on rewarding the group for either saving money or realizing gains in productivity.

Group incentive plans can be categorized under the term **variable pay plans;** that is, they reward employees with extra pay for extra organizational achievements.[11] Research has shown that as the use of variable pay plans increases, organizations experience concomitant increases in performance. This is because individual and organizational goals become more consistent with one another.[12]

Under several variable pay plans, an individual's pay depends directly on the organization's performance.[13] The **Scanlon plan,** for example, is a group-level incentive plan aimed at achieving organizationwide cost reductions.[14] Under Scanlon plans, the entire workforce shares the benefits of achieving increases in efficiency.

Under another popular variable pay plan, known as **profit sharing,** employees receive a percentage of the organization's profits on a regular basis.[15] How much employees receive is usually determined by the net income, revenue, or market share of the organization.

Under another arrangement, known as **gainsharing,** employees are rewarded for improvements in the organization's performance above a predetermined baseline. Operational factors, such as quality, productivity, customer satisfaction, and cost reduction, are used to determine percentage improvements.[16] Companies such as Motorola, General Electric, and 3M have used gainsharing to motivate their employees to work harder and better. When properly implemented, gainsharing correlates with enhanced teamwork and performance improvements that eventually lead to greater overall organizational competitiveness.[17] Thinking back to the opening vignette about Ford, would gainsharing have been effective in motivating Ford's workers and in turning around the company?

Employee Stock Ownership Plans. Under another group-based incentive plan, called an **employee stock ownership plan (ESOP),** employees become owners in the firm and, in this way, are able to share in the organization's profits, just as do traditional shareholders (or those who hold stock in a company, for example). Under an ESOP, the company makes tax-deductible

10. Cooke, W. H. (1994). Employee participation programs, group-based incentives, and company performance: A union–nonunion comparison. *Industrial and Labor Relations Review, 47,* 594–609.
11. Wilson, T. B. (1994). *Innovative reward systems for the changing workplace,* p. 114. New York: McGraw-Hill.
12. Stroh, L. K., Brett, J. M., Baumann, J. P., & Reilly, A. H. (1996). Agency theory and variable pay compensation strategies. *Academy of Management Journal, 39,* 751–767.
13. Gross, S. E. (1995). *Compensation for teams: How to design and implement team-based reward programs.* New York: Hay Group.
14. Collins, D. (1998). *Gainsharing and power: Lessons from six Scanlon plans.* Ithaca, NY: ILR Press/Cornell University Press.
15. Szypko, M. (1999, August). Variable pay: Funding design and metrics. *HR Focus—Special Report on Compensation Systems,* S1–S2.
16. Masternak, R. (1997). Gainsharing: What is it? *Compensation and Benefits Review, 29*(5), 44–45.
17. O'Bannon, D. P., & Pearce, C. L. (1999). An exploratory examination of gainsharing in service organizations: Implications of organizational citizenship behavior and pay satisfaction. *Journal of Managerial Issues, 11,* 363–378.

contributions of stock or cash to a trust fund to buy stock. The stock is then allocated to employees based on their seniority or some other important characteristic of the employment relationship. When employees retire or leave the company, they receive their stock and can either sell it on the market or sell it back to the company.[18] Employees often retire with considerable nest eggs based on the accumulation of stock from their ESOPs.

ESOPs serve as another visible symbol that the company views its employees as critical and important resources. They have been shown to lead to increases in employee satisfaction[19] and to be effective in motivating employees to increase productivity. Managers in firms with ESOPs often see employee participation and ownership as central to the organization's culture and mission, leading to further increases in employee influence in decisions affecting the organization, enthusiasm, and commitment to the organization.

A study by Hamid Mehran looked at the financial performance of 382 companies 2 years before and 4 years after the adoption of an ESOP. The study found that the return on assets for the companies with ESOPs was higher than the return for industry peers that did not have ESOPs. Additionally, 82% of the respondents to the survey believed that the ESOPs would have a positive impact on business results.[20]

EMPLOYEE BENEFITS

In addition to the obvious monetary rewards, employees receive a range of indirect economic rewards from organizations. Figure 12-2 includes a list of possible benefits.

With the increase in global competition and the flourishing state of the American economy, employee benefits have become an increasingly important component of employees' compensation packages. As pointed out in "FOCUS ON: Extended Benefits," organizations are realizing more than ever that to attract, recruit, and retain valuable employees, they have to offer more than competitive salaries; they have to offer competitive compensation packages, too. For many companies, their very survival depends on their ability to develop innovative benefits programs.[21]

One of the most significant effects of offering employees more than just monetary benefits is that it makes employees feel valued. According to a recent study called, *America @ Work*, conducted by Aon Consulting, employee benefits are crucial not only in attracting and retaining employees, but also in increasing commitment.[22] Employees in the study said that the biggest driver of employee commitment was recognition that employees

18. Rosen, C., Klein, K. J., & Young, K. M. (1986, January). When employees share the profits. *Psychology Today*, 30–36.
19. Trumble, R. R., & Knight, D. (1999). The benefits of ESOPs. *Journal of Compensation and Benefits*, 15(3), 10–13.
20. Godfrey, J. E. (2000, January). Does employee ownership really make a difference? *CPA Journal*, 70(1), 13.
21. Ermel, L., & Bohl, D. (1997, November/December). Responding to a tight labor market: Using incentives to attract and retain talented workers. *Compensation & Benefits Review*, 29(6), 25–30.
22. Stum, D. (1998, Fall). Re-inventing employee commitment: The 1998 America @ Work Survey. *Leadership Report* 1–6.

Possible Employee Benefits	■ FIGURE 12-2

Employee benefits may include a wide range of indirect economic rewards. These are some of the possibilities:

Optional Benefits

Pension plans
Vacation time
Holiday pay
Sick leave
Jury-duty pay
Maternity/paternity leave
Funeral leave
Military-duty pay
Health insurance
Dental insurance
Life and accident insurance
Disability insurance
Automobile insurance
Liability insurance
Moving expenses
Severance pay
Employee meals
Discounts on goods and services
Travel pay
Insurance coverage for domestic partners
Employee assistance programs
Wellness programs (i.e., health club membership,
  stress-management programs,
  time-management programs)
Flextime
Telecommuting
Job sharing

Legally Required Benefits

Social Security
Workers' compensation
Unemployment compensation

---

have personal and family lives/responsibilities outside the workplace. When combined with more traditional benefits such as medical and pension plans, compensation packages often help employees create a better balance between their work and family needs. Companies have also found that meeting these needs helps them to remain competitive.[23]

Some organizations are taking a *cafeteria* approach to benefits and allowing employees to customize their benefits packages. Typically, employees are given a core set of benefits as well as "benefit dollars" to allocate as they wish. Thus, a member of a dual-income family with no children might take only the minimum health care coverage and larger life insurance plan, whereas an employee with children might opt for more health insurance and for a prepaid child-care option.

---

23. Lineberry, J., & Trumble, S. (2000). The role of employee benefits in enhancing employee commitment. *Compensation & Benefits Management, 16*(1), 9–14.

FOCUS ON
EXTENDED BENEFITS

THE NEW COMPANY TOWN. In today's tight labor market, compensation systems are increasingly becoming recruiting tools in the crusade to retain employees and keep them productive. As the amount of time employees spend at work increases, and as the competition for talented employees gets stiffer, some organizations are offering amenities that, only a few years ago, would have been considered unthinkable.

BMC Software in Houston actually built a "corporate office park" along the lines of a company town. Within the compound's high walls, people can laze on hammocks strung between pine trees, work out in a company gym, practice jump shots on basketball courts, or hang out around the putting green, horseshoe pits, or beach volleyball court. They can also do their banking, drop off dry cleaning, and have their hair and nails done within the company's self-contained community.

Companies are offering such benefits in hopes of making employees more productive and committed to the organization. Yet, to many people's surprise, these perks often do not help create a good work–life balance for employees—and they may actually reinforce the dramatic separation between work and home. Instead of spending more time at work, employees may be more inclined to push for shorter working hours and more flexible schedules.

Source: Excerpted from Sanghera, S. (2000, May 10). Beguiling benefits. *Financial Times* [On-line]. URL: *www.ft.com*; Useem, J. (2000, January 10). Welcome to the new company town. *Fortune, 141*(1), 62–70; and Giarrusso, T. W. (1998). A few good amenities. *Facilities Design & Management, 17*(9), 50–55.

Allowing employees to customize their benefits plans has two major advantages. First, it increases the value of the benefits package to the individual employee while maintaining per-employee costs. Second, it increases employee awareness of the value of the benefits the company is providing. Without such a system, employees tend to seriously underestimate their value.

NONECONOMIC REWARDS

Managers often focus solely on the economic rewards of employment, not realizing that noneconomic rewards can also be strong influences on performance. Noneconomic rewards can take many forms and can include intrinsic job rewards, extrinsic job rewards, and non-job-based rewards.

Intrinsic job rewards provide employees with a sense of autonomy, power and control, and achievement. Flextime is an example of one such reward; it gives employees greater control over the performance of their tasks by allowing them to set their own schedules, on the condition that they work a certain number of hours weekly.

Extrinsic job rewards are a means by which organizations publicly recognize employees for their performance, often in social settings. Many organizations hold annual banquets or conferences, for example, where they honor employees for doing their jobs well.

Finally, non-job-based rewards accrue by virtue of being employed in a particular organization. Status (by virtue of association with the organization) and the opportunity to live in a favorable geographic location are two examples of such rewards.

TYPES OF DISCRIMINATION

Ideally, any organization should reward its similarly performing employees similarly. However, as we know from previous chapters, in reality, compensation systems are not foolproof. Some systems include various forms of discrimination.

Of all the forms of compensation, monetary rewards are the most easily divisible and the easiest to allocate. However, by their very nature, monetary rewards force organizations to discriminate—between good performers and poor performers. Before proceeding, it's very important to clarify that this type of discrimination is vastly different from unfair discrimination based on non-performance-related characteristics. In fact, of the four types of discrimination, two are legal and two are illegal:

- **Legal and fair.** For example, giving some workers larger pay increases when they outperform other workers.
- **Legal and unfair.** For example, giving a friend a higher pay raise than another employee about whom you are indifferent.
- **Illegal and fair.** For example, requiring women to contribute more than men to employee pension plans. It is fair because women as a group live longer than men and are likely to receive more retirement benefits; however, the court has ruled that it is illegal to require women to make higher pension contributions.[24]
- **Illegal and unfair.** For example, granting a pay raise to an employee of one race whose performance is average and not granting a raise to an employee of another race whose performance is above average.

In addition to compensating everyone fairly, the ideal organization would consist of employees who worked at top capacity whether they were told what was expected of them or not. But, as every manager knows, in the real world people need to be given specific guidelines about what they are expected to accomplish and, in many cases, a time frame as well. In other words, they need to have goals for their performance.

GOAL SETTING

Another important factor in the employee performance equation is the setting of performance goals. **Goals** specify a direction for action and a specific amount of work to be accomplished.[25]

Research has shown that employees who are assigned difficult and specific goals perform at higher levels than those who are assigned general and easy goals or are told merely to "do your best."[26] However, a manager's

---

24. *Manhart v. City of Los Angeles, Department of Water and Power*, 552 F. 2d 581, 13 FEP 1625 (9th Cir. 1976); and *Norris v. Arizona, Governing Comm.*, 486 F. Supp. 645, 22 FEP 1059 (D. Ariz. 1980).

25. Martin, B. A., & Manning D. J., Jr. (1995). Combined effects of normative information and task difficulty on the goal commitment–performance relationship. *Journal of Management, 21*(1), 65–71; and Locke, E. A., & Latham, G. P. (1990). *A theory of goal setting and task performance.* Englewood Cliffs, NJ: Prentice Hall.

26. Phillips, J. M., & Gully, S. M. (1997). Role of goal orientation, ability, need for achievement, and locus of control in the self-efficacy and goal-setting process. *Journal of Applied Psychology, 82*, 792–802.

| ■ **FIGURE 12-3** | **Steps in Setting Performance Goals** |

Setting effective performance goals not only leads to increases in an organization's productivity; it also clarifies what is expected of employees. The six-step process shown here helps managers ensure that the goals employees set are attainable:

1 Specify the general objective or task.
2 Specify how performance will be measured.
3 Specify the standard or target to be met.
4 Specify a deadline for performance.
5 Prioritize goals.
6 Determine coordination requirements.

simply setting challenging, specific goals is not enough. Individuals also need to be committed to achieving their goals.[27] In other words, they must have what has been labeled **goal commitment.** Goal commitment is different from goal acceptance, or the acceptance of the worthiness of a goal; goal commitment is the willingness to exert the effort necessary to achieve it.[28] Factors influencing this level of commitment include the individual's ability and self-esteem, the complexity of the task, past successes, how involving the job is, and the level of support of the supervisor.[29]

In addition to raising the productivity of the organization, employees benefit when they are committed to challenging, specific goals. First, specifying a goal that is difficult but attainable adds a measure of challenge to a task, regardless of the job's innate interest level. Second, goal setting provides employees with an effective benchmark by which they, as well as their supervisors, can measure performance. Goal attainment ensures an employee that he or she is performing at expected standards. Thus, goal attainment also increases employees' pride and confidence in their ability to accomplish assigned tasks.

In setting performance goals for employees, a manager should follow the following six steps, summarized in Figure 12-3[30]:

1 **Specify the general objective or task to be accomplished.** One way employees' attention can be focused on what they are to do is through job descriptions. As described in Chapter 10, a job description usually conveys a great deal of information to the employee, including what tasks need to be performed, what outcome is expected, and what deadlines are important.

2 **Specify how the performance in question will be measured.** Performance on some tasks is more easily measured than performance on others. For example, a salesperson's performance is often evaluated on the

27. Martin & Manning, Combined effects of normative information and task difficulty on the goal commitment–performance relationship.

28. Renn, R. W., Danehower, C., Swiercz, P. M., & Icenogle, M. L. (1999). Further examination of the measurement properties of Leifer & McGannon's (1986) goal acceptance and goal commitment scales. *Journal of Occupational and Organizational Psychology*, 72(1), 107–114.

29. Hollenbeck, J. R., & Klein, H. J. (1987). Goal commitment and the goal setting process: Problems, prospects, and proposals for future research. *Journal of Applied Psychology*, 72, 212–220.

30. Locke & Latham, *A theory of goal setting and task performance.*

dollar value of generated sales; the performance of an administrative assistant may be measured by the number of assignments completed daily; and an assembly-line worker at Ford may be measured on the number of parts he or she assembled in a day or the number of cars his or her team completed in a week.

3 **Specify the standard or target to be met.** In addition to identifying what will be evaluated, a manager should specify exactly what level of performance is expected.

4 **Specify a deadline for performance.** Generally, as the level of responsibility increases, so does the time allowed for performance. For example, semiskilled or blue-collar workers, such as auto workers, might be given daily or weekly goals, whereas upper-level managers might be evaluated yearly or even every 3 or 5 years.

5 **Prioritize the goals.** Employees are likely to have many goals to accomplish, especially as the complexity of their positions increases. Thus, setting priorities among their goals directs effort in proportion to a goal's importance.

6 **Determine coordination requirements.** It is important to consider the amount of coordination and cooperation with other individuals that is needed to accomplish the goals. Depending on the amount of interdependence necessary, the manager should be aware of and account for the increased conflict that is likely to occur.[31]

Goal setting has been shown to be an effective mechanism for improving performance. However, managers should be aware of a number of potential pitfalls. First, setting extremely difficult goals may produce greater levels of effort, but it can also increase the level of risk that managers and employees are expected to take. Risk taking is a component of managing in uncertain environments, but excessive risk taking clearly can be counterproductive. If their goals are too difficult, employees may experience unnecessary stress and, as a result, be less willing to accept and commit to meeting goals in the future.

Second, goals should not be perceived as ceilings on performance. Goals are usually intended to identify the minimum acceptable level of performance, not the maximum.

Third, because goals help direct employee effort, areas of performance for which goals are not set may be ignored. Along this line, goals set for short time periods tend to encourage short-term performance.

Fourth, in high-pressure, unsupportive atmospheres, demanding and difficult goals can lead employees to take shortcuts, cheat, or misrepresent their levels of performance to meet performance demands. Figure 12-4 illustrates some ways managers can avoid each of these pitfalls.

Finally, for goal setting to work, feedback is necessary. Feedback that is timely and self-generated is probably the most useful in modifying work behavior, but employees also need formal, regular feedback in the form of performance appraisals.[32] The next section focuses on the importance of performance appraisals in maintaining employee performance.

31. Northcraft, G. B., & Earley, P. C. (1989). Goals setting, conflict, and task interdependence. In M. A. Rahim (Ed.), *Conflict management: An interdisciplinary approach.* New York: Praeger.

32. Northcraft, G. B., & Earley, P. C. (1989). Technology, credibility, and feedback use. *Organizational Behavior and Human Decision Processes, 44,* 83–96.

■ **FIGURE 12-4**   **Goal-Setting Pitfalls and Potential Solutions**

Goal setting can be a very effective mechanism for improving performance in an organization, but only if it is managed well. For goal setting to be effective, a number of pitfalls must be avoided.

Pitfall	Potential Solution
Excessive risk taking	Specify acceptable risk levels for the employee and the organization
Increased stress	Adjust goal difficulty, increase staff as needed, and ensure that employees have the skills necessary to accomplish their goals
View of goals as ceilings rather than floors	Reward those who exceed their goals
Ignoring of nongoal areas	Make sure that goals are comprehensive, that they are developed for all important areas of performance
Encouragement of short-range thinking	Increase the time span of goals
Dishonesty and cheating	Set an example of honesty in actions, give frequent feedback, and be open to negative information to avoid a climate of high pressure and low support

Source: Locke, E. A., & Latham, G. P. (1984). *Goal setting: A motivational technique that really works!* Englewood Cliffs, NJ: Prentice Hall, pp. 171–172.

PERFORMANCE APPRAISAL SYSTEMS

Earlier in this chapter, we identified the two critical obstacles of effective incentive system: rewarding the wrong behavior and failing to develop an effective performance appraisal system. Performance appraisals often serve two primary purposes. First, they aid organizations in making decisions concerning salary increases, bonuses, and assignments, such as transfers and promotions based on employee performance (and thus making explicit exactly what the organization is rewarding). Second, they contribute to employee development by identifying employees' strengths and weaknesses and by providing feedback on performance.[33] After the general strengths and weaknesses of the employee population are evaluated, directions for training can be identified. In addition, information garnered from a performance appraisal can aid in the maintenance or modification of the organization's selection process. However, there are a variety of other uses (and unintended positive consequences for the performance appraisal process), as indicated in "RESEARCH IN ACTION: Beyond the Performance Appraisal."

---

33. Tziner, A., Joanis, C., & Murphy, K. R. (2000, June). A comparison of three methods of performance appraisal with regard to goal properties, goal perception, and ratee satisfaction. *Group and Organization Management*, 175.

RESEARCH IN ACTION
BEYOND THE
PERFORMANCE APPRAISAL

Martin M. Greller, University of Wyoming; *mgreller@uwyo.edu*

Sometimes our clients can help us recognize how much more there is to a subject. I had done a number of presentations on participation in the performance appraisal review. These examined the nature of the interaction between manager and worker in the very special setting of a performance review.

A friend who knew of this work asked for copies of the papers. The company for which she worked was in turmoil. It was committed to the equality and autonomy of its workers, but the absence of a system of performance appraisal and review meant that problems were not being addressed, to the point that the employees were experiencing a sense of inequity. Still, the three owners of the company could not conceive of imposing the authoritarian appraisal systems that they had experienced when working for large companies. (There were elements of Dilbert in their experiences.) The notion of a participative appraisal struck a chord.

They asked for assistance in establishing such an appraisal system. Consistent with good personnel practice, the first step was a job analysis. Just what were the responsibilities of each job? Because the company's business required a high level of interaction across departmental lines, the job analysis required speaking with engineering aides and technician about the project engineer jobs and speaking with fabricators and aides about technicians. It was concluded that it would

be necessary to gather information from each of these sources to come up with a complete appraisal of an individual. The individual's supervisor would review the comments of the people with whom an individual worked and draw conclusions in light of the preponderance of information. Managers received training in how to conduct a forward-looking and participative review.

A little more than a year later an evaluation was conducted of the system, by which time the company had experienced the review process twice. Although there was considerable satisfaction with the results, everyone was concerned about the time spent on each review. They estimated that it was taking 24 hours of work for each employee's review. That is an astounding amount of time! It turned out that the company had decided to do its own "job analysis" of the work being done by each individual each year. The information would be useful, because each job had its unique components. One of the most popular things was that it allowed people to influence the nature of jobs in the organization in the future.

The company had asked for a participative appraisal review. It ended up with a participative form of organization renewal and redesign. This was actually what it wanted. It was consistent with the organization culture and philosophy. But it took the concept of appraisal beyond anything for which I had been prepared.

CONFLICTS AND PROBLEMS IN PERFORMANCE APPRAISALS

As suggested earlier, performance appraisals are often used to provide valuable feedback, distribute rewards fairly throughout the organization, and counsel employees. In undertaking the performance appraisal task, however, conflicts may arise.

Imagine, for example, the obvious conflict employees must experience in trying to respond to both the counseling and the reward-distribution functions of performance appraisals. A supervisor trying to understand the obstacles that prevent an employee from performing her job at top capacity will want to focus on the employee's perceptions of her job-related problems, weaknesses, and failures. Now assume that the employee wants to make her case for a substantial promotion or increase in salary. The last thing she will want to do is focus on her problems, weaknesses, and failures. Thus, she is likely to gloss over difficulties and talk about only her successes.

It may be that expecting employees to be honest about their shortcomings while simultaneously evaluating them for a salary increase or promotion is asking too much. To address their problems honestly usually means that employees have to go against what they see as their best interests.

Another major difficulty with performance appraisals is that most supervisors are unable to convey negative feedback in a constructive manner. Instead, they are often vague and indirect. As a result, a supervisor may believe that he or she has conducted an evaluation, but the employees in his or her department may be unaware that evaluations have even taken place.

Recent research indicates that there may be a performance-related reason that supervisors are so reluctant to offer negative feedback: Although employees may increase their effort when presented with negative information, they may also decrease their goals or reject the feedback altogether.[34]

Compounding the problems, most organizations offer supervisors few if any incentives to conduct high-quality performance appraisals. "TECHNOLOGY FOCUS ON: Performance Appraisals" describes a software program that is helping managers with limited time or resources.

Most organizations probably hope that their supervisors will spend the time necessary to diagnose why someone is performing poorly and, together with the employee, identify and implement solutions. Yet in most organizations supervisors are rewarded for conducting superficial appraisals because they take less time away from "productive" activities, and, in some cases, they are rewarded for not conducting them at all.

Even supervisors who understand the importance of performance appraisals often find themselves in no-win situations. For example, a supervisor's appraisal of an employee's performance may be very different from the employee's self-appraisal. Under such disparate conditions, even a supervisor with good interpersonal skills will find conducting a positive performance review difficult.

Another reason that performance evaluations may be less effective than they should be is that employees often display considerable discomfort during the procedure. Part of this discomfort can be attributed to anxiety about being evaluated. However, some of the discomfort probably stems from the employee's perceived lack of control over the outcome. Wanda Smith, Vernard Harrington, and Jeffery Houghton surveyed more than 100 state and federal employees to determine their reactions to performance appraisals. The study focused specifically on discomfort levels. The researchers found a strong relationship between beliefs about the importance of the appraisal and discomfort with the process.[35] Thus, one might expect employees whose appraisals are associated with important outcomes to experience the greatest discomfort.

On the one hand, performance appraisals provide valuable information on a number of critical factors affecting the overall health of an organization,

---

34. Nease, A. A., Mudgett, B. O., & Quinones, M. A. (1999). Relationships among feedback sign, self-efficacy, and acceptance of performance feedback. *Journal of Applied Psychology, 84,* 806–814.

35. Smith, W. J., Harrington, K. V., & Houghton, J. D. (2000, Spring). Predictors of performance appraisal discomfort: A preliminary examination. *Public Personnel Management, 29*(1), 21–32.

TECHNOLOGY FOCUS ON PERFORMANCE APPRAISALS

NEW SOFTWARE HELPING MANAGERS TRACK EMPLOYEES. In the challenging area of performance appraisals, managers are always eager for assistance. Help is now available in the form of intranet-based human resources software that assists managers, including information technology managers, in tracking employee performance and in writing performance reviews.

Performance Impact, released in 1999 by Knowledge Point Software, provides managers with tools to develop employee career paths, document performance, and promote communication between employees and managers. For example, templates help managers write performance reviews, and a language tracker audits reviews and alerts managers when inappropriate terminology is used. The software also lets managers set and track employee goals and expectations and offers methods to coach employees to maximize their potential.

Performance Impact includes competency sections that let managers evaluate employees based on the business and job-related competencies that managers set for employees. Forty-five such competencies are included in the software.

Among the organizations using the software are the Crotched Mountain Foundation, a physical rehabilitation facility in Greenfield, New Hampshire. Jerry Hunter, chief information officer of the foundation, says the software has helped Crotched Mountain reduce its number of employee-review forms from 120 to 12.

Hunter says he especially likes Performance Impact's rating system. When an employee review is completed, the software calculates a performance number from 1 to 6. At the foundation, an employee's salary increase is based on that number. "The software hopefully has given employees the sense that reviews and salary increases are standardized," Hunter says. "There is much less subjectivity to the process."

Source: Excerpted from Mateyaschuk, J. (1999, June 14). HR manager for the net: Performance Impact will track employees. *InformationWeek, 738,* 125.

including allocation of rewards and assessment of training needs. On the other hand, performance appraisals are a challenge to managers.[36] Further, there is almost universal dissatisfaction, on the part of both supervisors and subordinates, with the process. This includes dissatisfaction with what is being rated, the instruments used to do the appraisals, the basis on which ratings are calculated, and how often appraisals are conducted. The next section considers each of these concerns.

IMPROVING PERFORMANCE APPRAISAL SYSTEMS

If conducting a valuable performance appraisal is challenging, then creating an appraisal system that an organization will be satisfied with seems to be truly daunting. The figures speak for themselves; although 90% of organizations report having a system in place, approximately the same percentage report being dissatisfied with it.[37] Figures for organizations in the United Kingdom are similarly high.[38] Even in the U.S. military services, which traditionally invest considerable resources in developing appraisal systems, new systems have an expected life of just a few years. The search for an accurate, reliable, and

---

36. Taylor, M. S., Tracy, K. B., Renard, M. K., Harrison, J. K., & Carroll, S. J. (1995). Due process in performance appraisal: A quasi-experiment in procedural justice. *Administrative Science Quarterly, 40,* 495–524.

37. HR execs dissatisfied with their performance appraisal systems. (2000, January 1). *HR Focus,* 2.

38. Performance appraisal systems could do better. (1998, April 1). *Management Today,* 12.

■ FIGURE 12-5 | Types of Performance Appraisal Instruments

Eight different performance appraisal instruments are summarized here. Some of them measure employee traits and some measure employee behaviors.

Trait scale: Evaluates the employee on such factors as commitment, creativity, loyalty, and initiative. It requires the employee's performance to be rated along an unbroken continuum (from excellent to unacceptable) or within discrete categories (superior, satisfactory, unsatisfactory).

GRS: This instrument asks the rater to provide general evaluations of ratees' performance in various areas of the job.

Ranking: The simplest of all comparative techniques, this involves ranking employees from the best to the worst on each dimension being considered.

Paired comparison: Each person is rated against another person; the final ranking depends on how many times a particular employee is ranked better than other employees.

Forced distribution: The number of individuals who can be assigned certain performance categories is limited. For example, only 10% of employees may be rated "very good," 20% "good," and so on.

Weighted checklists: A group of statements, each with a weight attached to it, describes types and levels of behavior. Not only is the actual rating considered in this instrument, but so is the value of that behavior to the performance of the job or task.

BOS: This instrument asks raters to report and describe the frequency of specific job-related behaviors.

BARS: This instrument consists of a set of rating scales, each of which is composed of brief descriptions of critical incidents of effective and ineffective job performance.

---

well-received system may be never-ending, but managers could certainly improve the quality of their performance appraisals by focusing on a couple issues that are at the root of much dissatisfaction with the evaluation process.

RATING SCALES.   In assessing an employee's performance, three types of rating scales are generally used: graphic rating scales, behavioral observation scales, and behavioral anchored rating scales.[39] Figure 12-5 provides basic information on these and five other instruments.

The **graphic rating scale (GRS)** asks the rater to provide *general* evaluations of employees' performance in various areas of the job. The GRS is designed to help the rater, who is knowledgeable about the job, evaluate whether employees are performing effectively in their jobs.[40] Typical factors that are measured include dependability, cooperation, and leadership.

The **behavior observation scale (BOS)** asks raters to report and describe the frequency of *specific job-related behaviors*. For example, if one were rating a salesperson on her performance, the rater would be expected to identify the number of sales completed in a given time frame.

---

39. Tzier, et al., A comparison of three methods of performance appraisal with regard to goal properties, goal perceptions, and ratee satisfaction.
40. Orpen, C. (1997). Performance appraisal techniques, task types and effectiveness: A contingency approach. *Journal of Applied Management Studies, 6,* 139–147.

To develop the **behaviorally anchored rating scale (BARS),** an organization must analyze a job to determine behaviors that reflect varying degrees of performance. Descriptions of these behaviors are then used to define, or anchor, the ratings on the scale. For example, in rating an employee's managerial skills, a rater might have to choose from such options as "consistently meets or exceeds performance targets" to "likely to fail in meeting deadlines and performance goals."

Research indicates that using scales that focus on *behaviors*—such as the BOS and the BARS—increases both the raters' and the ratees' comfort with and acceptance of the performance appraisal and feedback process.[41] Employees seem to prefer behavioral rating scales because they require raters to itemize specific, objective behaviors. In contrast, the GRS, for example, relies on more subjective criteria.

360-DEGREE FEEDBACK. One form of feedback, the 360-degree method, is gaining popularity at companies throughout the country. According to one estimate, more than 90% of Fortune 1000 companies have implemented some version of 360-degree feedback.[42] The companies currently using this method include Exxon, General Electric, Amoco, Caterpillar, Levi-Strauss, AT&T, and Shell Oil.[43] Unlike other forms of feedback, 360-degree feedback is derived from multiple sources: supervisors, suppliers, customers, peers, and even the workers themselves. As outlined in Figure 12-6, there are both pros and cons associated with its use.

WHO SHOULD RATE EMPLOYEES? The easy answer to this question is the employees' supervisor. In the vast majority of organizations, supervisors are the ones who evaluate subordinates' performance. Unfortunately, the easy answer is not always the correct answer. Deciding who should evaluate an employee's performance should depend on several criteria, not just the mere fact that someone is the employee's supervisor. The ideal rater should be aware of the objectives of the employee's position, able to determine whether observed behavior is satisfactory, able to observe the employee frequently, and able to ascertain whether the employee performs at a satisfactory level. To assess performance more clearly, a variety of sources should be consulted, including the individual employee, colleagues, customers, and other individuals inside and outside the firm.[44] With this approach, referred to earlier as 360-degree feedback, the employee receives feedback from everyone with whom he or she has work-related interactions. Let's examine this cast of organizational and nonorganizational actors who might serve as raters and why receiving feedback from such a range of sources might be more valuable than receiving feedback from one's supervisor only.

Supervisors. Supervisors are often viewed as the only people in the organization who are familiar with the responsibilities and duties of each job within

41. Tzier, et al., A comparison of three methods of performance appraisal with regard to goal properties, goal perceptions, and ratee satisfaction.

42. Sherman, A., Bohlander, G., & Snell, S. (1998). *Managing human resources.* Cincinnati, OH: South-Western College Publishing, p. 313.

43. Ghorpade, J. (2000, February). Managing five paradoxes of 360-degree feedback. *Academy of Management Executive,* 140–150.

44. Moravec, M. (1996). Bringing performance management out of the Stone Age. *Management Review, 85*(2), 38–43.

| ■ **FIGURE 12-6** | **Pros and Cons of 360-Degree Feedback** |

Pros

- ■ The process is more comprehensive in that responses are gathered from multiple perspectives.
- ■ The quality of the information is better than with traditional feedback methods. (The quality of the respondents is more important than the quantity of responses.)
- ■ It complements total quality management initiatives by emphasizing workers' relationships with both internal and external customers and teams.
- ■ It may lessen bias and prejudice because the feedback is from more people, not just one individual.
- ■ It may increase employee self-development.

Cons

- ■ The system is complex to administer.
- ■ The process can be intimidating and cause resentment if the employee feels the respondents have "ganged up."
- ■ Opinions may conflict, although they may all be accurate from the standpoints of the respective respondents.
- ■ To work effectively, those involved in providing feedback must receive training.
- ■ Employees may collude or "game" the system by giving invalid feedback on one another.

Source: Sherman, et al., *Managing human resources*, p. 314.

their purview. In addition to knowing these jobs, supervisors should have a grasp of the various strengths and weaknesses of the individuals they supervise. Further, they are the obvious conduits between employees and the organization. Finally, as the organization's agents, they are often able to influence the allocation of organizational rewards and punishments.

The problem with deferring to supervisors for performance appraisals is that supervisors do not always have adequate opportunities to observe subordinates' performance. For example, a supervisor is unlikely to be able to rate a traveling salesperson other than by comparing rates of completed sales. How this person actually performs can only be inferred. Similarly, getting back to the Ford workers described in the opening vignette, their supervisor might not work with them day to day and therefore might be less familiar with their output than are other workers.

Researchers have challenged the use of supervisory ratings as the sole source of performance appraisals for several reasons. The main argument is that supervisors have one perspective on employee performance and, as stated previously, they are often unable to observe employee performance directly. Additionally, as the workforce becomes more team based, as might be the case in a company like Ford, measuring individual performance becomes increasingly difficult.[45]

Employees. Self-appraisals are a popular addition to performance reviews. This form of evaluation is consistent with the trend toward increasing em-

---

45. Fedor, D. B., Bettenhausen, K. L., & Davis, W. (1999). Peer reviews: Employees' dual roles as raters and recipients. *Group and Organization Management, 24,* 92–120.

ployee participation in organizational decision making. In addition, having employees evaluate themselves reduces their level of defensiveness when confronting problem areas or weaknesses. Employees rate evaluations based on self-appraisals as being satisfying. Such evaluations can provide the supervisor with new information about how employees perceive their jobs and the associated problems.

The disadvantages of self-appraisals arise primarily when they are done by inexperienced employees. However, even when employees do not have much rating experience, the discrepancy between their self-appraisals and the performance criteria can be reduced.[46]

Another disadvantage of self-appraisals is that if employees do not have clearly established performance standards or goals by which to measure their performance, they are likely to use different yardsticks than their supervisors. In addition, self-ratings tend to be more lenient and less variable than ratings by supervisors and peers.[47] Few employees believe their performance to be only average.

Peers. Probably the best evidence of the usefulness of peer appraisals is that they have been found to be both reliable and valid. In fact, they routinely have higher predictive validity than supervisory ratings. Another advantage is that multiple raters can participate. Additionally, peers usually have a great amount of interaction with coworkers, often on a daily basis.[48]

The disadvantage of using peers as raters is that peers often resist evaluating coworkers, viewing it as a threat to their relationships. In addition, rather than evaluate performance accurately, peers sometimes choose to evaluate peers strategically—to make themselves look better.[49]

Subordinates. Subordinates have the unique ability to appraise the leadership and management potential of their superiors, and superiors can certainly benefit from this feedback. Appraisals by subordinates also let a leader know what his or her subordinates perceive to be the leader's strengths and weaknesses. Accepting such feedback can enhance future cooperation. Based on research by Leanne Atwater, Paul Roush, and Allison Fischthal, it appears that being given subordinates' ratings positively affects a leader's behavior. Specifically, they found that changes were most likely to occur in areas in which there was the most disagreement between the subordinates' ratings and the leader's self-ratings.[50]

The greatest disadvantage of having subordinates rate their superiors is that subordinates are likely to be (understandably) concerned about the impact their evaluations will have on their relationship with their supervisor. Fear of reprisal may be justified. Also, subordinates may be unaware of the

46. Clapham, M. M. (1998). A comparison of assessor and self dimension ratings in an advanced management assessment centre. *Journal of Occupational and Organizational Psychology, 71,* 193–204.
47. Lee, M., & Son, M. (1999). The agreement between self and supervisor ratings: An investigation of leader-member exchange effects. *International Journal of Management, 16*(1), 77–88; and Clapham, A comparison of assessor and self dimension ratings in an advanced management assessment centre.
48. Fedor, et al., Peer reviews.
49. Carroll, S. J., & Schneier, C. E. (1982). *Performance appraisal and review systems.* Glenview, IL: Scott, Foresman.
50. Atwater, L., Roush, P., & Fischthal, A. (1995). The influence of upward feedback on self and follower ratings of leadership. *Personnel Psychology, 48*(1), 35–59.

criteria to use in evaluating a boss and may therefore rate the superior on dimensions that are unrelated to job success.[51]

Outsiders. Outsiders, such as members of the human resources department, external consultants, and clients of the firm, are occasionally called on to evaluate employees' performance. The benefit of enlisting these individuals is that they rarely have vested interests in the outcomes. That is, their own promotions, raises, or evaluations are not likely to depend on or be influenced by the evaluations they perform. Outside appraisers also provide a different perspective from internal evaluators. Clients or customers, for example, may see a very different side of a salesperson than either the supervisor or coworkers observe.

The major problem with outside reviewers is that employees may find fault with a supervisor who "abdicates" responsibility for conducting performance reviews to outside evaluators. Indeed, the greatest advantage of using outsider reviewers—their different perspective—is also their greatest weakness. Because outsiders typically have little opportunity to observe employees in a variety of settings, their evaluations may be based on limited samples of behavior.

RATER TRAINING. Choosing the best evaluators, using the best evaluation tools, and implementing the best methods for rating performance are clearly ways to improve the performance appraisal process. There is some evidence that the overall validity of the performance appraisal process often hinges on the training of managers.[52] In a field experiment of 111 matched pairs of employees and their managers, Susan Taylor and associates found that managers who used a due-process performance evaluation process expressed significantly greater resolution of problems in their work units and greater satisfaction with their evaluation systems than did the employees in the control group.[53] A due-process performance assessment, according to the researchers, is analogous to the due-process right protected under the Fifth and Fourteenth Amendments of the U.S. Constitution and includes adequate notice, a fair hearing, and judgment based on evidence.

Robert Folger, Mary Konovsky, and Russell Cropanzano elaborated on the process set forth by Taylor and her associates and noted that adhering to the due-process amendments means that organizations must (a) give their employees adequate notice of performance standards and how standards are met, and provide timely feedback; (b) conduct a formal review in which the employee is informed of how the assessment was determined and the employee's right to challenge the review; and (c) allow a fair hearing to take place if there is a dispute over an assessment. In short, performance assessments must be given in a setting that is characterized by honesty and fairness.[54] Research also emphasizes the importance of providing training in the

51. Carroll & Schneier, *Performance appraisal and review systems.*

52. Taylor, M. S., Tracy, K. B., Renard, M. K., Harrison, J. K., & Carroll, S. J. (1995). Due process in performance appraisal: A quasi-experiment in procedural justice. *Administrative Science Quarterly, 40,* 409–429; and Korsgaard, M. A., Roberson, L., & Rymph, R. D. (1998). What motivates fairness? The role of subordinate assertive behavior on managers' interactional fairness. *Journal of Applied Psychology, 83,* 731–744.

53. Taylor, et al., Due process in performance appraisal.

54. Folger, R., Konovsky, M. A. & Cropanzano, R. (1992). A due process metaphor for performance appraisal. In B. M. Staw & L. L. Cummings (Eds.), *Research in organizational behavior* (Vol. 13, pp. 129–177). Greenwich, CT: JAI; and Korsgaard et al., What motivates fairness?

performance appraisal process not only for raters but for ratees, in that employees' perceptions of the fairness of the process have been shown to affect motivation to change behavior, the attitudes of employees, and employees' willingness to stay with an organization.

STRATEGIES FOR CHOOSING RATERS. Although there are clearly specific advantages and disadvantages to choosing each type of rater, some generalizations can be made.

1 Use multiple raters if possible. The probability of obtaining a comprehensive picture of an employee's performance increases significantly.

2 Choose evaluators who have considerable opportunities to observe the employee directly.

3 Use a rater consistent with the type of evaluation desired. If a manager is being evaluated for promotion to upper management, then subordinates' evaluations may be critical. If the supervisor has little opportunity to observe the individual directly, then peers, clients, or customers may be the best choice.

Choices about the type and number of raters can have a significant impact on the quality of the overall performance appraisal process.

THE TIMING OF PERFORMANCE APPRAISALS. Most organizations conduct formal performance appraisals annually. As a result, supervisors are expected to remember and evaluate behaviors that occurred over that entire 365-day period. In such cases, the most recent behaviors—especially if they differ significantly from the person's usual behavior—tend to receive the greatest weight. However, bear in mind that it is difficult enough to remember what transpired 30 days ago, much less to accurately recall what happened a year ago.

There are two solutions to this problem. First, a rater could schedule multiple appraisal interviews—say, four—during the year and have each review cover only the period since the last review. One review each year could be used to produce a summary evaluation for salary and promotion decisions. Second, the rater can use memory aids to help remember behavior. Formally, the rater might keep a critical incidence file containing examples or descriptions of employees' outstanding, good, and poor behaviors. Informally, the rater might record brief observations on employees in a "little black book."[55] Ratees might also want to keep such a diary, noting examples of both good and poor performance on the job.

These suggestions represent ways in which any performance appraisal system can be adjusted to improve its acceptance by employees. However, improving the structure of the system addresses only part of the question of how to maintain performance in a workforce. In fact, many of the problems associated with formal performance appraisal systems appear to have less to do with their structure than with how willing or motivated managers are to commit the necessary time required to produce high-quality performance evaluations.[56] Figure 12-7 contains some advice for managers who are motivated to improve the quality of their performance appraisal systems.

---

55. Henderson, R. I. (1984). *Performance appraisal.* Reston, VA: Reston Publishing.

56. Rice, B. (1985, September). Performance review: The job nobody likes. *Psychology Today,* 30–36.

■ FIGURE 12-7 Performance Appraisals: Advice for Managers

Many of the problems encountered with performance appraisal systems may be less the fault of the system than a matter of the motivation and skills of the managers conducting the appraisals. The following recommendations are for managers who want to conduct more effective performance appraisals:

- Start by getting the big picture in mind. What is the single most important message you want to send to your employees?
- Highlight the key issues you want to discuss. It's easier to cover 4 main areas than 20 smaller ones.
- Highlight the best evidence you have. What are the best examples to support your high and low ratings?
- Give specific examples. Employees will have a better understanding of why you evaluated them as you did if the examples you choose are detailed and concrete.
- Use active listening. The goal is not to come to agreement with employees but to increase their understanding of the strengths and weaknesses of their performance.
- Give employees time to prepare. Consider giving them a written appraisal before the face-to-face meeting.
- Start with your best performers. These might be the easiest employees to talk to initially.
- Review the goals and objectives of each employee's job. This will give the employee specific feedback and let the employee know right away whether he or she has been successful in meeting requirements.

Source: Grote, D. (1998, October). Painless performance appraisals focus on results, behaviors. *HRMagazine, 43*(11), 52–55.

MANAGING FOR IMPROVED PERFORMANCE

Until now, this chapter has discussed general techniques for maintaining employee performance. In this section, we will focus on identifying poor performers and poor supervisors and on developing specific prescriptions for addressing the causes of poor performance. As you read this section, consider especially the dilemma Ford management faced as it sought to identify its weakest performers in hopes of offering them incentives to leave the company.

All supervisors hope that all their employees will perform adequately. When this happens, the job of the supervisor is much easier and there are likely to be few interpersonal problems. Unfortunately, this is not always the case. Most managers must, at one time or another, address a poor-performing employee. In addition to identifying such an individual, the supervisor must diagnose the causes of the poor performance and develop strategies to improve it.

DIAGNOSING POOR PERFORMERS

Knowing that a person is performing poorly is vastly different from knowing *why* this is the case. Poor performance can be highlighted by performance appraisal ratings, behavior (e.g., missed deadlines, tardiness, absenteeism, poor work habits, insubordination), or other violations of performance expectations. When poor performance has been observed, the manager must determine its cause to find the appropriate remedy.

Managers usually assign blame for poor performance based on a process of attribution. Recall that in Chapter 2 we identified three principles people use to attribute behavior to internal or external causes: distinctiveness, consistency, and consensus. Internal causes are those associated with the individual performer, including the person's skills, abilities, effort, and personality. External causes are associated with the environment, such as task difficulty, resource availability, interpersonal demands, and information availability.[57] If an employee is consistently absent from work, for example, the manager needs to determine whether the absences are the result of factors the employee can control.

In spite of the three principles for determining whether to attribute the poor performance to the individual or the environment, there is the *fundamental attribution error*. Managers are likely to blame poor performance on a subordinate's internal (or personal) failings, while subordinates are likely to attribute their failures to external (or environmental) factors that are out of their control. Thus, because of the differences in perspectives, supervisors and employees rarely agree on the cause of absenteeism much less an employee's poor performance.

MAXIMIZING A POOR PERFORMER'S ABILITY

As an aid in developing a systematic understanding of the basis for poor performance, managers should start by asking themselves a series of questions (listed in Figure 12-8). These questions assume that the poorly performing individual is capable but for some reason(s) is not performing at expected levels. Given the theoretical expectations derived from the expectancy theory, managers assume that marginal performance can arise from lack of ability, effort, or support, or some combination of these factors.

The manager's primary concern is with ensuring or achieving a match between the skills of the employee and the task that needs to be accomplished. Matches may be created by altering the skills of the employee through training, changing the job so that there is better fit, or switching employees to create better fit. To maximize support, the manager must ensure that the employee has the resources necessary to accomplish the task and must help remove obstacles to high performance.

In short, the manager must create a supportive work environment. The use of clear performance expectations, adaptive job designs, better interpersonal relations, more performance-specific feedback, and the elimination of unnecessary job/performance constraints are likely to be beneficial in this process. To maximize effort, the manager must convey to the marginal employee that his or her performance falls below standards and that this substandard performance has adverse consequences on other employees, groups, and the organization as a whole. Finally, the manager can serve both as a positive role model and as a provider of clear, positive, performance-specific rewards.

One solution organizations have used to both maintain and improve performance has been to use an instrument called a balanced scorecard.[58] Robert

57. Latham, G. P., Cummings, L. L., & Mitchell, T. T. (1981, Winter). Behavioral strategies to improve productivity. *Organizational Dynamics, 9*(3), 5–23.

58. Kaplan, R. S. (1994, September/October). Devising a balanced scorecard matched to business stategy. *Planning Review,* 15–19; and Kaplan, R. S., & Norton, D. P. (1992, January/February). The balanced-scorecard-measures that drive performance. *Harvard Business Review,* 71–79.

■ **FIGURE 12-8**	**Determining the Cause of Poor Performance**

Has the individual performed at a higher level in the past?
Is the performance deficiency total, or is it confined to particular tasks?
How well do the individual's capabilities match the job's selection criteria?
Has the individual been properly trained in how to perform the tasks expected of him or her?

Support

Have clear and challenging task goals been set?
Are other employees having difficulty with the same tasks?
Is the job properly designed to achieve a best fit with the individual's capabilities?
Do any policies and/or procedures inhibit task performance?
Is the manager providing adequate feedback?
Is the individual being fairly compensated?
Is the work environment comfortable?
Is the manager providing sufficient empathy and emotional support?
Are the individual's coworkers providing sufficient emotional support?
Has the manager actually encouraged high performance?

Effort

Does the individual lack enthusiasm for work in general? for the assigned task in particular?
Are individuals with similar abilities performing at higher levels?
Has the individual been properly recognized for past accomplishments?
Are rewards and incentives provided on a performance-contingent basis?
Is the individual aware of possible rewards and incentives?
Does the individual have an appropriate role model?

Source: Schermerhorn, J., Gardner, W., & Martin, T. (1990). Management dialogues turning on the marginal performer. *Organizational Dynamics, 18*(4), 47–59.

Kaplan and David Norton introduced the balanced scorecard as a way for organizations to assess and improve their performance on four dimensions:

1 Customer perspective. How do customers see us?
2 Internal perspective. What must we excel at?
3 Innovation and learning perspective. Can we continue to improve and create value?
4 Financial perspective. How do we look to shareholders?

The balanced scorecard allows organizations to translate their mission statement and strategy into specific goals. When these goals are then communicated to the entire organization, each employee has a blueprint of the contributions he or she is expected to provide to ensure the success of the business. "Focus On: Maintaining Performance" demonstrates how the Georgia Department of Defense used a balanced scorecard to measure and improve its overall organizational performance and efficiency.

After identifying employees' weaknesses and expectations for the future, managers must then motivate poor performers. The following are some recommendations managers should follow:

■ Recognize that even marginal performers are a source of gains in productivity for organizations.

FOCUS ON MAINTAINING PERFORMANCE

BALANCED SCORECARD SCORES POINTS AT GEORGIA DEPARTMENT OF DEFENSE. When it comes to using the balanced scorecard produced by the CorVu Corporation, the Georgia Department of Defense will defend it to the hilt. The agency has been using the performance appraisal instrument to measure and improve its overall organizational performance and efficiency. The department's goal, like that of other state and federal agencies, is to meet strategic long-term objectives and achieve compliance with federal legislation aimed at maintaining performance objectives.

"As a government agency, it is fundamentally important that we do everything we can to best serve the needs of our communities while optimizing the allocation of tax-payer dollars," said Lieutenant Colonel Don Venn, project manager of balanced scorecard, Georgia Department of Defense.

The balanced scorecard application helps users define clear missions and desired customers, measure performance to gauge progress, and utilize performance information as a basis for more effective strategic decision making. CorVu also enables organizations to tie performance results to budgets, gain insight into problem areas, and create a performance report card on targeted areas for improvement. Users can also analyze performance data by using graphs, gauges, and custom-tailored reports to visually compare actual performance results and planned targets and industry benchmarks.

CorVu provides the agency with a streamlined structured methodology for defining, communicating, and evaluating performance metrics, ensuring strategic decision support and unparalleled performance management functionality. The agency is thus better able to educate personnel, from senior staff to part-time volunteers, on the fundamental structure of the organization and the relationship between group functions and personal responsibilities. Expect to see CorVu gain increasing recognition as a performance management solution for agencies looking to streamline operational efficiency.

Source: Excerpted from CorVu Corporation to provide balanced scorecard solution for Georgia Department of Defense (1999, August 10). *Business Wire.*

- ■ Recognize the need to implement positive turnaround strategies for dealing with marginal performers.
- ■ Be ready to accept at least partial responsibility for the subordinate's marginal performance.

Many of the strategies organizations try as they work to transform poor performers into good employees are described in previous sections of this chapter—incentive systems, goal-setting activities, and performance appraisal systems. While these mechanisms are useful with all subordinates, they are uniquely important for poorly performing employees. These are not easy strategies to implement in most organizations. However, given the cost of replacing poorly performing employees or, even worse, the cost in lost productivity if these employees remain, these strategies are worth considering and implementing.

SUMMARY

This chapter examines how managers and other organizational decision makers can maintain employee performance. The first component of this process is the organization's incentive system. Composed of both economic and noneconomic elements, the incentive system is the most visible way in which organizations influence employee behavior. Wages and nonrecurring economic benefits can influence an employee's behavior if the employee is capable of high performance, believes it is beneficial, sees the relationship between high performance and monetary rewards, values economic rewards, and is involved in tasks in which performance can be measured. The incentive structure also must be consistent with the nature of the work being performed (individual or group based). Examples of individual-based incentive structures are piece-rate and standard-hour systems. Group-based incentive structures include the Scanlon plan and ESOPs.

Employee benefits are indirect economic rewards. One recent innovation in this area is the development of cafeteria benefit plans, which allow employees to customize their benefits packages to better meet family and other personal considerations. Noneconomic benefits include the inherent interest of the job, the quality of the work life, the status associated with belonging to the organization, and the amount of power and autonomy associated with the position.

Unfortunately, having a well-developed incentive system is not sufficient to ensure high levels of performance. Employees also need performance goals. Goals specify the direction for action and the quantity of work to be accomplished. For goals to be effective, they must specify the task to be accomplished, indicate how performance will be measured, specify the level of performance to be achieved, specify a deadline for performance, be accepted by the employee, and set priorities for performance and coordination.

Providing employees with feedback is one of the purposes of performance appraisal systems and is crucial if employees are to reach their goals. Performance appraisal systems have three major functions: to provide feedback, distribute rewards, and counsel employees. Unfortunately, if managers use the same performance appraisal review to accomplish all three objectives, employees are likely to experience conflict in their responses. Should they present their accomplishments in the best possible light, or should they identify various problems and weaknesses encountered over the past year? In addition, the anxiety created by the evaluation may be so great that employees are unable to comprehend or even hear the information being provided.

For performance appraisals to be valuable to employees, evaluations should be based on observable behavior, conducted by raters who have opportunities to observe the ratee, conducted several times per year, and conducted with instruments that measure behavior, not traits. Because managers generally consider the performance appraisal process onerous, companies are eager to try new instruments for arriving at the same information. Some companies use a 360-degree approach that solicits performance-related information from a variety of people, including coworkers and customers or clients. Others use a sophisticated instrument called the BARS to measure performance.

Even if all these components are in place, managers are still likely to occasionally have a poor performer. The best approach to dealing with an underperforming worker is to first determine the cause of the poor performance and then develop strategies for improving productivity.

KEY TERMS

Behavioral observation scale (BOS)
Behaviorally anchored rating scale (BARS)
Compensation system
Employee stock ownership plan (ESOP)
Gainsharing
Goal commitment
Goals
Graphic rating scale (GRS)

Piece-rate plan
Profit sharing
Salary
Scanlon plan
Skill-based pay
Standard-hour-rate plan
Variable pay plan

DISCUSSION QUESTIONS

1 Which of the major systems for maintaining performance is likely to be most effective with professional employees? blue-collar employees? white-collar employees? Why?

2 What factors, besides overt and intentional discrimination, might lead to the large difference in wages between the average male and female worker?

3 In early 1989 controversy arose over what was called the "mommy track" in organizations. What are the advantages and disadvantages of having two career tracks in an organization: one for women with children and one for women without children?

4 How might a cafeteria-style benefits plan ensure that employers do not discriminate in favor of employees with families?

5 Even employees who are rated highly believe that performance appraisals are arbitrary and capricious. How might the typical organization respond to this charge? How might the review process be altered to increase its fairness?

6 In evaluating an employee's poor performance, what is likely to be the manager's first impression about the cause of the poor performance? What factors might lead the manager to adjust this evaluation?

7 How might a manager go about structuring an employee's workday to improve his or her performance?

ON YOUR OWN

Developing a Performance Appraisal System for Faculty   How would you go about setting up a performance appraisal system to evaluate faculty at your university or college? Think about your instructor for this course.

First, consider what you as a student think are the important dimensions of an instructor's behavior. You may want to think about the instructor's values and the behavioral indicators of his or her performance. Next, consider what other faculty (your instructor's peers) might identify as important dimensions of behavior. What might the dean of the business school or the president of the university or college say are important dimensions of faculty behavior?

In the figure below, list the major dimensions of behavior that each rater should consider important. The actual number of dimensions on which the instructor would be rated could vary.

Instructor Rating

Rater	Dimension 1	Dimension 2	Dimension 3
Students			
Dean			
President			
Other Faculty			

How do these four constituencies value each of these dimensions? What would be good behavioral indicators of each? How would you choose which dimensions to use in an evaluation of your instructor?

CLOSING CASE   CHAPTER 12

THE MANAGER'S MEMO

FROM: P. Wilcox, President
TO: O. Hansen, Vice President, Human Resource Management
RE: Dissatisfied Former Employees

As you know, within the past 6 months, three of our most capable divisional vice presidents have left the company to take positions with our major competitor. Clearly, pay was not the problem, as these executives received a level of salary plus bonuses that was until then unprecedented in the industry.

From recent conversations with them and some of the remaining executive team, all I have been able to learn is that there is some dissatisfaction with our performance appraisal system. One of the departing executives made a comment about there being no incentive to innovate.

I really don't understand these remarks. We spent a great deal of time trying to develop a performance rating scale that is fair and that rewards results, not personality. I cannot think of a better system than our method of assigning points for each product that exceeds expected performance, deducting points for failed ideas, and paying a generous bonus based on accumulated points. The system penalizes executives for failures, but it also encourages them to think carefully before launching risky ventures. Furthermore, one of the departing executives had never had an idea that failed. Clearly, they benefited from the performance rating system.

I would appreciate your letting me know what you learned from your exit interviews with these former executives. If the performance appraisal system really is the reason they left, how can we modify it to avoid losing key people in the future?

CASE DISCUSSION QUESTIONS

Assume that you are the vice president of the human resource management division and respond to the president's memo. Assume that the executives who left were in fact dissatisfied with the performance appraisal system. From the information given in the president's memo, what types of compensation was the company generous in providing, and what types were lacking? How can the company modify its performance appraisal system to offer the rewards it is not providing?

EXERCISE PART FOUR: The Hovey and Beard Company

The Hovey and Beard Company manufactures a variety of wooden toys, including animals and pull toys. The toys are manufactured by a transformation process that began in the wood room. There, toys are cut, sanded, and partially assembled. Then the toys are dipped into shellac and sent to the painting room.

In years past, the painting was done by hand, with each employee working with a given toy until its painting was completed. The toys were predominately two colors, although a few required more than two colors. Now, in response to increased demand for the toys, the painting operation has been changed so that the painters sit in a line by a long chain of hooks. These hooks move continuously in front of the painters and pass into a long horizontal oven. Each painter sits in a booth designed to carry away fumes and to backstop excess paint. The painters take a toy from a nearby tray, position it in a jig inside the painting cubicle, spray on the color according to a pattern, and then hang the toy on a passing hook. The rate at which the hooks move is calculated by the engineers so that each painter, when fully trained, can hang a painted toy on each hook before it passes beyond reach.

The painters are paid on a group bonus plan. Because the operation is new to them, they receive a learning bonus that decreases by regular amounts each month. The learning bonus is scheduled to vanish in 6 months, by which time it is expected that the painters will be able to meet the production standard and to earn a group bonus when they exceed the standard.

QUESTIONS

1 Assume that the training period for the new job setup has just begun. What change do you predict in the level of output of the painters? Why?

2 What other predictions regarding the behavior of these painters can you make, based on the situation described so far?

Source: Abridged and adapted from Strauss, G., & Bavelas, A. (1955). Group dynamics and intergroup relations. In W. F. Whyte (Ed.), *Money and motivation* (Chapter 10). New York: Harper & Row.

CASE   PART FOUR: Perfect Pizzeria

Perfect Pizzeria in Southville, a town in southern Illinois, is the second-largest franchise of the chain in the United States. The headquarters is locted in Phoenix, Arizona. Although the business is prospering, it has employee and managerial problems.

Each operation has one manager, an assistant manager, and from two to five night managers. The managers of each pizzeria work under an area supervisor. There are no systematic criteria for being a manager or becoming a manager trainee. The franchise has no formalized training period for the manager. No college education is required. The managers for whom the case observer worked during a 4-year period were relatively young (ages 24 to 27), and only one had completed college. They came from the ranks of night managers, assistant managers, or both. The night managers were chosen for their ability to perform the duties of the regular employees. The assistant managers worked a 2-hour shift during the lunch period 5 days per week to gain knowledge about bookkeeping and management. Those becoming managers remained at that level unless they expressed interest in investing in the business.

The employees were mostly college students, with a few high-school students performing the less challenging jobs. Because Perfect Pizzeria was located in an area with few job opportunities, it had a relatively easy task of filling its employee quotas. All the employees, with the exception of the manager, were employed part time. Consequently, they worked for less than the minimum wage.

The Perfect Pizzeria system is devised so that food and beverage costs and profits are set up according to a percentage. If the percentage of food unsold or damaged in any way is very low, the manager gets a bonus. If the percentage is high, the manager does not receive a bonus; rather, he or she receives only his or her normal salary.

There are many ways in which the percentage can fluctuate. Because the manager cannot be in the store 24 hours per day, some employees make up for their paychecks by helping themselves to the food. When a friend comes in to order a pizza, extra ingredients are put on the friend's pizza. Occasional nibbles by 18 to 20 employees throughout the day at the meal table also raise the percentage figure. An occasional bucket of sauce may be spilled or a pizza accidentally burned. Sometimes the wrong size of pizza may be made.

In the event of an employee mistake or a pizza burned by the oven operator, the expense is supposed to come from the individual. Because of peer pressure, the night manager seldom writes up a bill for the erring employee. Instead, the establishment takes the loss and the error goes unnoticed until the end of the month, when the inventory is taken. That's when the manager finds out that the percentage is high and that there will be no bonus.

In the present instance, the manager took retaliatory measures. Previously, each employee had been entitled to a free pizza and salad, and all the soft drinks he or she could drink for every 6 hours of work. The manager raised this figure from 6 to 12 hours of work. However, the employees had

Source: Adapted from a case assignment prepared by Lee Neely for Professor James G. Hunt, Southern Illinois University at Carbondale. The case appears in Dittrich, J. E., & Zawacki, R. A. (Eds.), (1985). *People and organizations: Cases in management and organizational behavior* (pp. 164–167). DesPlaines, IL. Business Publications.

received these 6-hour benefits for a long time. Therefore, they simply took advantage of the situation whenever the manager or the assistant was not in the building. Though the night manager theoretically had complete control of the operation in the evenings, he did not command the respect that the manager or assistant manager did. This was because he received the same pay as the regular employees, he could not reprimand other employees, and he was basically the same age as or younger than the other employees.

Thus, apathy grew within the pizzeria. There seemed to be a further separation between the manager and the workers, who had started out as a closely knit group. The manager made no attempt to alleviate the problem because he felt it would iron itself out. Either the employees who were dissatisfied would quit or they would be content to put up with the new regulations. As it turned out, there was a rash of employee dismissals. The manager had no problem filling the vacancies with new workers, but the loss of key personnel was costly to the business.

With the large turnover, the manager found that he had to spend more time in the building, supervising and sometimes taking the place of inexperienced workers. This was in direct violation of the franchise regulation, which stated that a manager would act as a supervisor and at no time take part in the actual food preparation. Employees could not be strictly supervised if the manager was working alongside them. The operation no longer worked smoothly because of differences between the remaining experienced workers and the manager concerning the way a particular function should be performed.

Within a 2-month period, the manager was again free to go back to his office and leave his subordinates in charge of the entire operation. During this 2-month period, the percentage had returned to the previous low level and the manager had received a bonus each month. The manager felt that his problems had been resolved and that conditions would remain good because the new personnel had been properly trained.

It didn't take long for the new employees to become influenced by the other employees. Immediately after the manager had returned to his supervisory role, the percentage began to rise. This time the manager took a bolder step. He cut out any benefits that the employees had—no free pizzas, salads, or drinks. With the job market at an even lower ebb than usual, most employees were forced to stay. The appointment of a new area supervisor made it impossible for the manager to "work behind the counter," because the supervisor was centrally located in Southville.

The manager tried still another approach to alleviate the rising percentage problem and maintain his bonus. He placed a notice on the bulletin board, stating that if the percentage remained at a high level, a lie-detector test would be given to all employees. All those found guilty of taking or purposefully wasting food or drinks would be immediately terminated. This did not have the desired effect on the employees, because they knew if they were all subjected to the test, all would be found guilty and the manager would have to dismiss all of them. This would leave him in a worse situation than ever.

Even before the following month's percentage was calculated, the manager knew it would be high. He had evidently received information from one of the night managers about the employees' feelings toward the notice. What he did not expect was that the percentage would reach an all-time high. That is the state of affairs at the present time.

QUESTIONS FOR DISCUSSION

1 How would you characterize the compensation plan for managers and student workers at Perfect Pizzeria? Would you want to work there?

2 What kinds of group dynamics are at work at Perfect Pizzeria during the case?

3 What do you think of the manager's attempts to solve the problems at Perfect Pizzeria? What would you suggest he do instead?

CHAPTER 13

The Environment

THE BATTLE OF SEATTLE

When the World Trade Organization (WTO) planned its global conference in Seattle in 1999, the mood was expected to be quiet and serious. Instead, television viewers the world over watched in horror as mobs of protesters took to the city's café-lined streets. What unleashed such a passionate response? The answer, in short, is basic human and environmental concerns.

Whether a trade organization like the WTO or a large corporation, like Coca-Cola, organizations must often help employees, customers, or other constituencies adapt to changes in the global environment. Several companies, notably Canon (Japan), Ericson (Sweden), Acer Computers (Taiwan), and Coca-Cola (U.S.), have taken the lead in this direction. They have learned the importance of educating employees on the benefits of living and working in an evolving global environment.

Creating a globally literate workplace (one that is cognizant of both internal and external resource dependencies and changes) is a long-term, ongoing process.

The reason so many people, from the WTO meeting planners to city officials, were unprepared for the protests in Seattle was that they failed to understand that while organizations may deem external changes such as globalization significant economic advantages, such changes arouse fears and concerns in working people. Unless companies start addressing some of these concerns, they may also end up with battles on their hands.

Source: Adapted from Rosen, R. H. (2000, February). Battle of Seattle shows need for cultural understanding. *HR News, 14,* 20.

INTRODUCTION

Throughout this book we have focused on the challenges organizations face in understanding and managing *internal* resources. We have explored how individuals behave, how groups interact, and how managers can use knowledge of individual behavior and group interaction to manage organizations effectively. We have also noted examples of research that illustrates the importance of having a comprehensive understanding of these behaviors. But the picture is not yet complete. As this chapter makes clear, organizations are products not only of their internal relationships but also of the environments in which they operate—other organizations, groups, and cultures.

The purpose of this chapter is to explore the evolving global environment in which today's organizations function, in the hope that organizations with which you might be associated will not experience battles similar to those surrounding the WTO in Seattle. First, in order to better understand what we mean by global and organizational environments, we will examine some of the myths related to these environments; second, we will explore the nature of the major forces exerting influence on organizations; finally, we will discuss some strategies organizations can use to manage some of the environmental demands of the 21st century.

THE MYTH OF THE CLOSED SYSTEM

Organizations are often discussed as if they were **closed systems:** completely self-contained operations that function apart from and that are unaffected by external forces. Nothing could be further from the truth. Whether an organization deals directly with world trade issues, as in the case of the WTO, or confronts these issues more indirectly, as an auto manufacturer might, it's impossible to remain isolated or insulated from environmental influences and interactions. Every organization is a product of the large external environment of which it is a part. Figure 13-1 illustrates this point.

The impact of technology (e.g., e-mail, computer networks) on the way work is completed is just one example of an external influence. Susanne Kelly, a vice president at Citigroup, summed up the effect of these forces on organizations large and small: "Today, the world is really comprised of

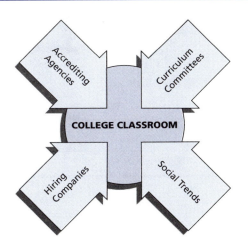

■ FIGURE 13-1

An Example of an Open System

Employees may think organizations are completely self-contained, closed systems, but, in reality, they are influenced by a host of external forces, including government regulations, changes in labor situations, changes in the needs of suppliers, and social trends.

open—rather than closed—systems, and every person is a sensory point, not just the manager. So information flows up, around, and sideways."[1]

An understanding of two concepts—open systems theory and resource dependence—is especially useful in grasping the ways in which the external environment influences the behavior of and within organizations. The importance of these two concepts in turn depends on a third, familiar, concept: perception.

OPEN SYSTEMS THEORY

An **open system** is an organization whose activities are inescapably influenced by its environment. The WTO in Seattle is an extreme example, but most organizations are subject to environmental influence. Open systems share several defining characteristics, as shown in Figure 13-2.

First, all open systems take inputs from the environment. For a manufacturing firm, the input might be raw materials, such as iron ore, leather, or grain. For a service organization, the input might be information and/or requests from clients. Inputs can also include the labor needed for production, the technology used, past learning experiences, and even knowledge.

Second, all open systems transform the inputs they receive. The organization does something to the inputs that adds value beyond the intrinsic value of the inputs themselves. For instance, leather is transformed into shoes, steel into automobiles, and clients' information into proposals. Typically, this process is cyclical. Organizations maintain some consistency over

---

■ **FIGURE 13-2** | **Defining Characteristics of Open Systems**

The environment provides organizations with inputs such as raw materials and labor. Subsequently, organizations add value to these inputs, thereby transforming them. Clients or customers in the environment then consume the outputs of this process of transformation. The process is cyclical: In return for consuming the organization's outputs, the environment provides new inputs for the organization to restart the cycle.

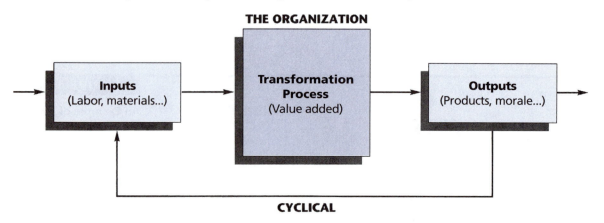

Source: Katz, D., & Kahn, R. L. (1978). *The social psychology of organizations.* New York: Wiley, pp. 23–30.

---

1. Eckhouse, J. (1999, February 2). Get creative with knowledge sharing—In today's culture, businesses must rebuild their processes to take advantage of their knowledge base. *Informative Week*, ER19.

time; they usually repeat the cycle over and over, using the same inputs and processes of transformation.

Third, the process of transformation creates *an output.* An organization's outputs—shoes, automobiles, client satisfaction, profit, or even company morale—are the final products of the transformation process.

An important goal of most organizations is continued survival over time. In fact, some organization theorists suggest that *the* goal of all organizations is transforming inputs into mechanisms for survival.[2]

This idea that organizations exist as a means for survival has an important implication in the context of the open systems model. To ensure its survival, the organization relies on the environment for resources and for the consumption of outputs.[3] Thus, the net value of the transformation process must be positive. If the net value is negative (e.g., if by-products of the process, such as pollutants or worker dissatisfaction, are greater than the value of what is created), the organization will eventually lose its ability to transform inputs from the environment.

THE BOUNDARY-SPANNING ROLE. Research by Aimin Yan and Meryl Reis Louis has taken open systems theory further. They claim that interactions among organizations and elements in the environment (other organizations, customers, etc.) take place in domains they call **boundaries,** where organizations can provide for their long-term survival.[4] However, because organizations do not interact directly with their environments, they must assign individuals to represent them in these interactions. Yan and Louis refer to these individuals as **boundary spanners;** they span the boundary between an organization and forces in the organization's environment.

Because organizations are open systems, *all* members of organizations are boundary spanners to some extent. And certainly all boundary spanners must learn to move freely between their organizations and their organizations' environments. Individuals formally cast in this role may need different skills than other organizational actors; flexibility is particularly valuable.

The role of a boundary spanner is difficult because the individual must work in two worlds without really belonging to both. Take, for example, the job of liaison for a joint venture between two corporations. To be a successful, such a liaison must learn the rules of both corporate cultures and be able to move freely back and forth without forgetting which culture is really "home." In the case of the WTO, the boundary spanner might have functioned as a negotiator between the WTO's officials and the protesters in Seattle's streets.

Boundary spanners perform critical roles in organizations, and organizations are dependent on or have resource dependence on these individuals. Resource dependence is discussed at length in the next section. For now, it is important to bear in mind that this dependence makes the selection and preparation of individuals for this role a critical process.

2. Pfeffer, J., & Salancik, G. (1978). *The External control of organizations.* New York: Harper & Row, pp. 2–3.

3. Cross, R. L., Yan, A., & Louis, M. R. (2000, June 1). Boundary activities in "boundaryless" organizations: A case study of a transformation to a team-based structure. *Human Relations, 53,* 841–868.

4. Yan, A., & Louis, M. R. (1999, January). The migration of organizational functions to the work unit level: Buffering, spanning, and bridging up boundaries. *Human Relations, 52*(1), 25–47.

RESOURCE DEPENDENCE

The open systems model of organizations illustrates the extent to which organizations are susceptible to environmental influences. The reason they are so susceptible is that there is *resource dependence*. As we saw in Chapter 7, resource dependence occurs when one individual needs something (a resource) that another individual possesses. More specifically, the resource dependence described here is an example of a power relationship.

In Figure 13-2, the organization is dependent on the environment for resources or inputs—such as raw materials, labor, and energy—for its survival. Prior transformation systems, their parts or components, and even education are also available in the environment.

Organizations also are dependent on the environment to accept or consume their outputs. A key characteristic of open systems is that there is a net positive flow, which is necessary for an organization to survive. Consumers must be willing to pay more for the organization's outputs than just the cost of transformation. Otherwise, over time, the organization will fail.

Jeffrey Pfeffer and Gerald Salancik emphasized this notion of reliance and interdependence in their **resource dependence theory**.[5] Their theory suggests that firms enter into relationships in search of much-needed resources that are lacking in their operations. The extent that these resources are controlled in the environment is situationally dependent. Figure 13-3 enumerates the conditions that Pfeffer and Salancik claim facilitate resource dependence. One resource that is often in limited supply is highly skilled workers with firsthand experience in a specific industry. As "RESEARCH IN ACTION: Retirement No Longer Means No Work" discusses (page 384), companies are increasingly recruiting older, semiretired workers to fill this need. The relationship seems to work well for both parties: the organization gets a resource (good labor) that it needs to compete effectively, and the

---

| ■ **FIGURE 13-3** | **Conditions That Facilitate Resource Dependence** |

The degree of resource dependence between entities varies. Organizations that need the resource are called *focal organizations*; organizations that have the resources are called *social actors*. According to Pfeffer and Salancik, the following conditions strengthen resource dependence:

1 The possession of a resource by one firm (the social actor)
2 The importance of the resource to the focal organization—its criticality to the organization's activities and survival
3 The inability of the focal organization to obtain the resource elsewhere
4 The visibility of the behavior or activity being controlled
5 The social actor's discretion in allocating, accessing, and using the resource
6 The focal organization's discretion and capability to take the desired action
7 The focal organization's lack of control over the resource that is critical to the social actor
8 The ability of the social actor to make its preferences known to the focal organization

Source: Pfeffer & Salancik, *The external control of organizations*, p. 260.

---

5. Pfeffer & Salancik, *The external control of organizations*, pp. 258–262.

older workers receive ongoing income and derive the satisfaction that often comes with active involvement in an organization.

Research by Somnath Das, Pradyot Sen, and Sanjit Sengupta expanded the theory of resource dependence to include the idea that the nature of the dependence between focal organizations and social actors is not always symmetrical; in other words, organizations don't give and receive resources in equal amounts.[6] In fact, dependency relationships are frequently asymmetrical. Das et al.'s research also suggests that large firms are often more dependent on strategic alliances than are smaller firms, perhaps because larger firms rely heavily on the technological resources in which small firms have specialized. As a result, strategic alliances may enhance the reputations of smaller firms more than those of larger organizations.

Lisa Keister extended the study of resource dependence to the global arena and studied the interactions and dependencies of the 40 largest business groups in China.[7] She found that the more familiar organizations were with each other, the stronger the resource dependence they developed. Keister's research also indicated that resource dependence was strongest when the "supplier" had secure access to the resource and when the firm receiving the resource exhibited high levels of uncertainty about its ability to obtain the resource. Under these conditions, the organization receiving the resource was likely to develop dependence on one supplier, even if that supplier did not offer the lowest rates.

KNOWLEDGE OF THE ENVIRONMENT

According to the open systems theory and resource dependence theory, organizations maintain fluid, changing relationships with other organizations in their environments. However, not all changes in the environment are directly or automatically reflected in commensurate changes in the organization. In other words, organizations and their environments are usually loosely coupled. **Loose coupling** has both advantages and disadvantages. On the one hand, to carry on in an orderly, predictable manner, organizations must be somewhat insensitive to changes in the environment. If an organization reacted to *everything* in its environment, it would spend more time reacting than it would transforming inputs into outputs. On the other hand, an organization that reacts too slowly (or not at all) to significant changes will fail in the struggle to survive.

Chapter 2 describes three processes that determine people's perceptions of what is happening in their environments: attention, construction, and interpretation. How individuals react to changes in their environment depends on whether they realize that a change has occurred, what they decide has occurred, and what importance they attach to what has occurred. Similarly, unless the management of an organization recognizes its dependence on the environment and the need to react to change, changes in the environment are unlikely to cause changes in the organization. In other words, the environment in which an organization operates is a *social construction*—a set of

---

6. Das, S., Sen, P. K., & Sengupta, S. (1998, February). Impact of strategic alliances on firm valuation. *Academy of Management Journal, 41*(1), 27–41.

7. Keister, L. (1999, January). Where do strong ties come from? A dyad analysis of the strength of interfirm exchange relations during China's economic transition. *International Journal of Organizational Analysis, 7*(1), 5–24.

beliefs that individuals in the organization construct based on their interactions with and perceptions of the environment.

Organizational theorist Karl Weick coined the term the **enacted environment** to capture this idea that the environment in which an organization functions is sensitive to the organization's perception of that environment.[8] This process is reminiscent of self-fulfilling prophecy, also discussed in Chapter 2. An organization does not just perceive its environment; an organization *enacts* its environment—it perceives, reacts to, and, *by its reactions*, influences the future perceptions it has of its environment. Thus, organizations take an active role in determining what resources they need (its demands) and in incorporating these demands into the definitions of their environment.[9]

The important point here is that resource dependencies can determine an organization's fate, but the organization's *perceptions* of its dependencies determine the actions it takes. These actions in turn influence the nature of the environment as the organization perceives it.

Research by Todd DeZoort, Alan Lord, and Barney Cargile provides valuable insights into how individuals' perceptions of their environments affect critical decision making.[10] Accounting students and entry-level accountants, for example, exhibit vast differences in their perceptions of the field of accounting. Specifically, after accounting students enter the field, they develop different perceptions from those nurtured by their former professors. Further, as a result of this change in perceptions, entry-level accountants become more likely to feel dissatisfied and quit their jobs. As this example demonstrates, employees' perceptions of their work environments can have a great impact on the turnover and attitudes of employees. How the environment is perceived can also affect whether a company is able to attract high-quality workers, as discussed in Chapter 10.

ENVIRONMENTAL FORCES INFLUENCING ORGANIZATIONS

As shown in the opening vignette, for organizations, and therefore managers, to remain viable in the changing global marketplace, they must become knowledgeable about their environment. This section examines three external influences or sources of external dependence: other organizations, the regulatory environment, and the social environment. These environmental influences are summarized in Figure 13-4.

OTHER ORGANIZATIONS

Other organizations are perhaps the most prominent element of the external environment with which an organization interacts. Our definition of organizations as open systems provides a framework for understanding the kinds of

---

8. Weick, K. E. (1977). Enactment processes in organizations. In B. M. Staw & G. R. Salancik (Eds.), *New directions in organizational behavior* (pp. 267–300). Chicago: St. Clair Press.

9. Marziliano, N. (1998). Managing the corporate image and identity: A borderline between fiction and reality. *International Studies of Management & Organization, 28*(3), 3–11.

10. DeZoort, T. F., Lord, A., & Cargile, B. (1997, October 11). A comparison of accounting professors' and students' perceptions of the public accounting work environment. *Issues in Accounting Education*, 281.

| Sources of External Dependence | ■ FIGURE 13-4 |

Other Organizations

Suppliers: Organizations that provide inputs, including capital, raw materials, and labor
Consumers: Organizations that purchase the organization's outputs
Competitors: Other organizations that produce the same outputs

Regulatory Environment

Laws and court rulings that legislate the behavior of organizations, including what the outputs look like and how transformation processes may create those outputs.

Social Environment

Social adjustment: Societal trends to which the organization must adjust
Social responsibility: The need to make sure corporate actions measure up to the society's moral and ethical standards

---

organizations that exert the greatest impact. As noted in the previous section, an open system takes inputs from the environment, transforms them into outputs, and then offers these outputs back to the environment. This three-stage definition suggests that three types of organizations, corresponding to the three stages of input, output, and transformation, exert the strongest influence on organizations: suppliers, consumers, and competitors.

SUPPLIERS. Suppliers provide organizations with inputs such as raw materials, labor, and capital. Labor (the organization's workforce) is especially important because it provides the energy to transform the organization's inputs into outputs. In service organizations raw materials may not be purchased at all. The service consumer acts as a supplier and provides the input to the service organization.

Research on suppliers has proved illuminating. For example, research by Xavier Martin, Anand Swaminathan, and Will Mitchell found that suppliers are as dependent on other organizations in their environment as are major manufacturers. Thus, they found that the expansion patterns of 547 Japanese automotive suppliers into the United States were influenced by such traditional environmental issues as the number of potential buyers, current buyers, competing suppliers, and noncompeting suppliers.[11]

All organizations need capital to get started—to purchase technology and hire labor. Usually they also need capital to make contact with consumers through marketing efforts. As an organization gets larger, its need for capital grows as well. Large organizations that require lots of capital often need to obtain it from external sources—from banks, by selling shares in the company, or by issuing stock. When an organization sells shares or issues stock, it is selling its potential to make money through the value added during the process that transforms the input into outputs. Thus, shareholders provide organizations with capital in exchange for ownership of a piece of the company.

---

11. Xavier, M., Swaminathan, A., & Mitchell, W. (1998). Organizational evolution in the interorganizational environment: Incentives and constraints on international expansion strategy. *Administrative Science Quarterly, 43,* 566–601.

Shareholders and organizations are mutually dependent; organizations are dependent on the shareholders for financial support, and shareholders depend on organizations to invest their capital in ways that benefit the organization financially. Research by Alan Lewis and Craig Mackenzie sheds interesting light on these relationships. They noted that many investors look for companies that strive to make positive contributions to society and to remain ethically clean, and they often avoid companies that harm society and the environment.[12]

The nature of these relationships is also changing as investment opportunities expand with the increase in globalization. American holdings of international equity increased by a factor of five between 1990 and 1997, from $110 billion to $600 billion.[13] This means that to attract and retain international stockholders, organizations will need to apply effective international management procedures.

But what happens when an organization's financial picture is less than rosy? As investors or part owners in a company, shareholders have the right to voice their views on how the company is being managed. This situation developed in Australia, as discussed in the "INTERNATIONAL FOCUS ON: Shareholders."

Shareholders can influence corporate policy as well. For example, the compensation of executives in organizations with powerful and active shareholders tends to be much more performance based than in organizations with less powerful shareholders.[14] Willingness to respond quickly to shareholders is not always a blessing, however. If their interests tend toward short-term financial gains, top management may find itself selling out in order to look good to its shareholders.[15]

Like capital, the labor supply is a critical concern for organizations. Acquiring labor usually means dealing with individuals rather than organizations, although in some cases organizations in need of short-term assistance may turn to temporary-help organizations or to "headhunters"—companies that specialize in locating workers with the specific talents an organization needs.

By far the most prominent example of a labor organization is a union. **Unions** are groups of workers that have banded together to give themselves more bargaining power with their employers. In years past, management often took advantage of the imbalanced resource dependence that developed between large organizations and individual workers. Unions represent an attempt to ensure more equitable distribution of resources. When workers band together and speak with one voice (that of the union), they can threaten a company with having to replace its entire workforce (for instance, because of a strike or walkout). In this chapter's opening vignette, one of the issues of concern to the demonstrators was that, because of possible changes in trade

12. Lewis, A., & Mackenzie, C. (2000, April). Support for investor activism among UK ethical investors. *Journal of Business Ethics, 24,* 215–222.

13. Useem, M. (1998, November). Corporate leadership in a globalizing equity market. *Academy of Management Executive, 12*(4), 43–59.

14. Gomez, L. R., Tosi, H., & Hinkin, T. (1987). Managerial control, performance, and executive compensation. *Academy of Management Journal, 30,* 51–70.

15. Hill, C. W. L., Hitt, M. A., & Hoskisson, R. E. (1988). Declining U.S. competitiveness: Reflections on a crisis. *Academy of Management Journal, 2,* 51–60.

INTERNATIONAL FOCUS ON SHAREHOLDERS

ACTIVISM IN AUSTRALIA. In an unprecedented development, BHP, Australia's leading copper producer, circulated a statement to its shareholders from the Australian Shareholders' Association (ASA) outlining a number of demands concerning conduct at BHP's annual general meeting. The ASA called for the chairman to instruct individual directors to answer questions about BHP's performance and prospects; for the board to resolve to appoint an independent body to investigate and report to shareholders on BHP's investment evaluation and project-control processes; and for the auditors to attend and answer shareholders' questions.

In Australia at least, activism by both institutional investors and individual shareholders is clearly on the rise. Nearly half that country's population has some form of ownership in a business, and with the Internet and stronger regulatory rules on disclosure, shareholders have better access to corporate information than ever before.

How should corporations in Australia and elsewhere respond? Companies must embrace a new approach to corporate governance and shareholder relations. This approach is characterized by

- More open, transparent, and regular communication with shareholders
- Greater answerability and accountability by directors
- More consultative (and even participatory) involvement of shareholders in corporate governance and corporate strategy

It's only a matter of time before these expectations spill over into legislation and regulations. By adopting such an approach, companies will be better able to manage relations with investors, take into account their expectations, and reduce the market impact of investor disappointment. There aren't many better ways to promote organizational excellence.

Source: Adapted from Bradley, G. (1998, November). Voting with their feet. *Charter*, 34.

laws and practices, union jobs would be "outsourced" to foreign, nonunion workers. The ultimate fear was that union influence on the social environment would be weakened.

Over time, the power of U.S. unions has decreased considerably, in part because businesses have begun to acknowledge the degree to which they are dependent on their workers and in part because workers are already guaranteed safe working environments and decent working conditions under federal legislation. However, as "INTERNATIONAL FOCUS ON: Unions" makes clear, in some parts of the world, such as Hong Kong, injustice persists even when there *are* unions.

CONSUMERS. Just as organizations are dependent for resources on suppliers, organizations are dependent on consumers, in the form of either groups or other organizations. As noted earlier in this chapter, organizations also depend on consumers to consume the organization's goods and, by extension, to compensate the organization for expenses incurred during the transformation process. Some of the profits the organization makes in this exchange are returned to shareholders in the form of dividends, thereby ensuring the shareholders' future support. Some profit becomes working capital for the organization and is used to secure future inputs.

On the one hand, because organizations are so dependent on consumers, organizations often are willing to tailor their outputs to meet consumer

INTERNATIONAL FOCUS ON
UNIONS

UNIONS HAVE LITTLE SAY IN HONG KONG. By the time Tang Sin-hing joined a union, he had driven loaded container trucks an average of 17 hours a day, 6 days a week, for 5 years all over Hong Kong. With 25 deliveries each week, it was hard for Tang to find time to spend with his wife and two daughters. But driving was his passion, and he wanted to stay on—even if relations with his bosses were beginning to chafe.

When the company tried to cut workers' pay by 37%, Tang and about 40 other drivers formed a union. But, as Tang found out, in Hong Kong being in a union can carry a high price, and Tang was soon out of work.

Under the law in Hong Kong, employees can organize into unions, but they have no collective bargaining rights. In other words, unions can operate, but management can choose to ignore them.

Unlike countries such as South Korea and the Philippines, known for their active and influential trade unions, Hong Kong has had a hyperactive economy for decades, and unions have remained docile. The lack of union activism may stem from a corporate culture that traditionally encouraged job switching rather than confrontation with management, said Won Hong, a lecturer on labor issues and social work at the City University of Hong Kong. The attitude changed in the wake of Asia's economic crisis, as companies cut back on salaries to maintain profitability. From 1997 to 1999, more than 23,500 people joined unions, bringing to 22% the proportion of Hong Kong workers who were union members.

Lee Cheuk-yan, legislator and secretary-general of the Hong Kong Confederation of Trade Unions, has repeatedly called for legislation to establish collective bargaining rights and prevent discrimination against union members. It's a common misconception, he said, that union demands for concessions inevitably will deaden Hong Kong's enterprising spirit.

Source: Adapted from Medina, M. (1999, May 12). Unions have little say in Hong Kong. *AP Online* [Online]. URL: *http://ptg.djnr.com/ccroot/asp/publib/story.asp*

demands. On the other hand, if the organization's output is unique or in short supply, the organization may be in a privileged position in the consumer–organization relationship.

We noted earlier that perceptions influence the way individuals view the external environment. Similarly, an organization's understanding of its consumers' perceptions of their environment influences the organization's strategic marketing and planning. A study of Kuwaiti managers demonstrates the implications of this observation in an international context. Abbas Ali, Adbel Aziz Taqi, and Robert Camp analyzed the perceptions of managers in 64 major Kuwaiti firms regarding the business environments of Germany, the United States, and Japan. The managers thought that Japan offered the most effective business environment for global competition and that Japan could surpass the United States both technologically and economically but that the United States was more adaptable to changing global conditions.[16] The message? When targeting consumers in international markets, organizations need to be aware of cultural perceptions.

COMPETITORS. In addition to suppliers and consumers, organizations must account for the effects on their business functioning of competing or-

---

16. Ali, A. J., Taqi, A. A., & Camp, R. C. (1998, January). Kuwaiti managers' perceptions of the national competitiveness of the U.S., Germany, and Japan. *Competitiveness Review, 8*(2), 18–33.

ganizations. Competitors stimulate an organization in two major ways: by exerting financial pressure and by modeling effective behavior.

Financial pressure occurs when an organization is able to transform the same inputs as another organization better, faster, or for less money. Typically, the more efficient organization's outputs become more attractive to consumers and it thereby threatens the competition. An organization that is under financial pressure is usually forced to look for ways to innovate and streamline processes to ensure its survival.

Competitors are also good sources of ideas that can help alleviate financial pressure. For example, many foreign, especially Japanese, organizations put financial pressure on American producers to produce better, faster, and cheaper. In many cases the solutions the American firms adopted were modeled on strategies these competitors had been using.

THE REGULATORY ENVIRONMENT

Regulations are another significant feature of any organization's external environment. **Regulations** include any and all the restrictions on an organization's actions, such as the use of only certain kinds of inputs. Regulations also restrict the behaviors organizations may engage in while transforming inputs into outputs. Examples of regulations that affect the behavior of organizations include the Americans with Disabilities Act (which affects areas such as employee selection, job design, and building construction), the Equal Pay Act and the Fair Labor Standards Act (which regulate compensation of full-time employees in U.S. firms), the Occupational Safety and Health Administration (which regulates working conditions), and the Civil Rights Act of 1991 (which has redefined discrimination in employment practices and established new guidelines for employers' financial liability).

For the most part, government regulations provide important protections. Regulatory agencies police organizations to ensure that they deal fairly with employees and with their environments, including consumers and their immediate neighbors. The WTO provides such services with respect to international trading practices, although, as highlighted in the opening vignette, the agency has had its share of controversy. In most cases, regulations are socially beneficial in the long run. In the short term, as illustrated, again, by the opening vignette, regulations often arouse concerns among employees and consumers that must be managed.

THE SOCIAL ENVIRONMENT

All organizations are part of larger societies, and, consequently, are affected by and must monitor social trends. This section focuses on corporate responsibility and social sensitivity; Chapter 16 discusses many other trends that shape the social environment.

CORPORATE SOCIAL RESPONSIBILITY.   **Corporate social responsibility** has to do with the actions an organization chooses to take (or avoid) and how these actions meet society's expectations related to moral and ethical standards. An organization that fulfills its corporate responsibilities does more than just fulfill the letter of the law. It also exhibits good citizenship and social sensitivity. Such actions do not directly enhance the organization's profits; however, they contribute to the development and well-being of a

RESEARCH IN ACTION
RETIREMENT NO LONGER MEANS NO WORK

Daniel Feldman, University of South Carolina; *dfeldman@darla.badm.sc.edu*

The majority of U.S. and Canadian workers are retiring by the age of 60, but well over half these individuals continue to work in some type of "bridge employment"—part-time, temporary employment workers engage in after retirement from a full-time job but before totally exiting the workforce. In a series of studies, several colleagues and I have been examining why individuals continue to work "in retirement" and the impact of bridge employment on how well people adjust to discontinuing full-time work.

Our research, which used a sample of 924 professionals, suggests that older workers continue to work for three main reasons: (a) a desire to have some structure to their days; (b) continued attachment to the rewarding work of their profession; and (c) a desire to pass on their knowledge and wisdom to the next generation. Moreover, those individuals who worked part time or on a temporary basis in retirement were significantly more satisfied with their lives in gen-eral and adapted more readily to the loss of full-time jobs.

With close to three million people "retiring" from full-time jobs each year in the United States, retirees represent a great resource for organizations faced with acute staffing shortages. In response to this and other research, some companies (such as McDonald's) have recently developed programs targeted specifically at older workers, and other companies (such as Travelers Insurance) are hiring recent retirees over staff from temporary help agencies. In addition, more and more companies (such as IBM) are offering older workers bridge employment opportunities as an incentive to get them to retire "early." Thus, companies can free up full-time jobs for younger workers while still providing older workers with some ongoing income and activity.

This is just one way organizations can better manage their labor resource dependency in a tight labor market.

community, which in turn enhances the organization's likelihood of survival. Examples of actions that demonstrate high levels of corporate responsibility are Ben & Jerry's hiring homeless people to work in its ice cream stores and Scott Paper donating five cents to the Ronald McDonald House for every UPC code mailed in by its customers. Some organizations are even forming social responsibility or public policy committees. And whereas management styles used to be the primary determinant of an organization's reputation, corporate social responsibility has taken over that role.[17]

SOCIAL SENSITIVITY. A corporation demonstrates social sensitivity when it develops a plan to minimize the negative impact of its actions on the surrounding environment. Legislation requires organizations to give workers 60 days' notice before closing a plant; however, it does not require them to help workers find new jobs. Organizations that provide outplacement assistance during tough times will likely find the community more supportive when they resume operations. In some cases demonstrating social sensitivity does not cost an organization anything. In the end, though, corporate responsibility and social sensitivity are bottom-line issues. Organizations are

17. Karake-Shalhoub, Z. A. (1999). *Organizational downsizing, discrimination, and corporate social responsibility*. Westport, CT: Quorum Books, pp. 130–131.

dependent on their environments for resources. Adhering to what is considered acceptable corporate behavior—whether by demonstrating good citizenship or social sensitivity—is an excellent way for an organization to make sure its nest remains feathered.

THE FORMS OF ENVIRONMENTAL FORCES

The previous section described the sources of dependence between an organization and its environment. But what determines the nature of these forces? Why do they need to exist in the first place? This section discusses in greater detail the environmental conditions that lead to dependence. We will focus on four main dimensions: uncertainty, instability, complexity, and beneficence.

UNCERTAINTY

Chapter 1 introduces the idea that uncertainty is a key challenge in managing organizational behavior. Typically, this uncertainty arises because members of the organization lack information; they do not know what is going to happen or when. As suggested in the opening vignette, globalization, leading to a lack of understanding of its impact on individuals as consumers and employees, is one issue that increasingly causes uncertainty. Sometimes, uncertainty leads to problems concerning organizational planning and action. As illustrated in Figure 13-5, environmental uncertainty stems from a lack of clear information; arises because of uncertainty about cause-and-effect relationships, and occurs because of a lack of clarity about the length of feedback cycles.

In general, when conditions are uncertain, an organization is likely to take actions that are wrong. This is because top management is always guessing. Thus, organizations often turn to the environment for assistance.

Three Forms of Environmental Uncertainty ■ FIGURE 13-5

Organizations cannot predict the future; nor can they be completely knowledgeable about their environments. Organizations are therefore often forced to turn to the environment for assistance. The following are three conditions that often give rise to environmental uncertainty:

1 *Lack of clear information about the state of critical variables* in the environment (future price fluctuations, social trends, technological developments, global challenges).
2 *Lack of clear information about cause-and-effect relationships* between organizational actions and environmental responses. For example, if a bank adds a cash station and customer satisfaction increases, is there a causal relationship? Did the cash station cause the satisfaction? Or is it just coincidence?
3 *Length of feedback cycles*, or the time it takes for evidence to indicate that the environment has responded to planning and action by the organization. For example, how long does it take for an organization to understand the effectiveness of its new recruiting strategy? If years pass, short-term problems will never be known.

Source: Lawrence, P. R., & Lorsch, J. W. (1964). *Organization and environment*. Homewood, IL: Irwin.

Organizations functioning in uncertain environments must distribute the risk inherent in uncertain plans and decisions in the hope of gaining an ever-important competitive edge. It appears, for instance, that when uncertainty is high, organizations use more employee-selection testing methods and use them more extensively.[18] Clearly, to protect themselves from the risks associated with uncertainty, organizations sometimes need to take these risks into account as part of their strategic planning.

INSTABILITY

Another issue that organizations are wise to take into account is **environmental instability**—or the rate of change in the environment. If the environment is changing rapidly, remaining flexible and adaptive is critical; otherwise, an organization will not be prepared to change quickly in response to external changes.

Environmental instability can take many forms. The past decade has seen stock markets rise rapidly and fall just as quickly, mergers and acquisitions create mega-giants, European nations merge into one union with its own currency, and a growing feeling that the world is getting smaller as transportation, communication, and technology enable distant cultures to exert increasing influence on our daily lives. Each of these developments (and many others) has dramatically changed the nature of the environment in which organizations operate. Some of these developments represent long-term shifts, and others are only short-term blips on the environmental radar screen. Some instability is apparently ongoing, as suggested in "TECHNOLOGY FOCUS ON: Virtual Organizations," which provides a glimpse at the dramatic impact of technology on office environments. All these developments represent opportunities and dangers for organizations that must be evaluated and (possibly) responded to.

COMPLEXITY

Environmental complexity refers to the number of environmental cues that an organization must monitor because they are critical to its functioning. A complex environment is one in which there is a lot going on that affects the functioning and potential survival of the organization. The WTO was a target of protest in Seattle in large part because the organization is so environmentally complex. From labor issues to discrimination, safety in the workplace, and environmental protection, the WTO deals with hot, controversial environmental issues.

For example, as organizations become more complex as a result of technological developments, they will be forced more than ever to manage complexity in the environment rather than reduce it. Research by Harvey Kolodny and his associates of organizations in France, Sweden, and Canada indicates that this will be true not just in U.S. organizations but in firms worldwide.[19]

18. Ryan, A. M., McFarland, L., Brown, H., & Page, R. (1999). An international look at slection practices: Nation and culture as explanations for variability in practice. *Personnel Psychology, 52,* 359–391.

19. Kolodny, H., Liu, M., Stymne, B., & Denis, H. (1996). New technology and the emerging organizational design. *Human Relations, 49,* 1457–1487.

TECHNOLOGY FOCUS ON
VIRTUAL ORGANIZATIONS

WHAT'S HAPPENING TO OUR OFFICES?
What's happening to the office? The traditional notion of an office as the place where someone goes to work seems to be going the way of the buggy whip, the eight-track tape, and the stenographer. Work is becoming something you do, not someplace where you go.

Technology has made it possible and necessary to redefine the office environment. Technologies, including desktop video conferencing, portable computers, cell phones, collaborative software, and the Internet and Intranet systems, have all converged to forge the foundation of the new office environment. This emerging environment will be unrestrained by geography, time, and organizational boundaries; it will be a virtual workplace, where productivity, flexibility, and collaboration will reach unprecedented new levels.

This exciting new potential comes at a time when increasing global competition and recent advancements in information technologies have forced organizations to reevaluate their structures and work processes. Managers are now challenged to develop strategically flexible organizations in response to the increasing instability in the marketplace. The new resilient virtual environments that have emerged enable organizations to become more flexible by providing an impressive response to the changing world.

Companies such as Procter & Gamble, IBM, Hewlett-Packard, AT&T, and Compaq have learned that you have no choice but to operate in a world shaped by globalization and revolutions in information technology. There are two options: Adapt or die. You need to plan the way a fire department plans; it cannot anticipate fires, so it has to shape a flexible organization that is capable of responding to unpredictable events.

Source: Adapted from Davenport, T. H., & Pearlson, K. (1998). Two cheers for the virtual office. *Sloan Management Review, 39*(4), 51–65; and Townsend, A. M., DeMarie, S. M., & Hendrickson, A. R. (1998). Virtual teams: Technology and the workplace of the future. *Academy of Management Executive, 12*(3), 17–29.

It is important to recognize that organizations incur two costs when they operate in complex environments. First, because there are more inputs, more information collection and evaluation are necessary for planning and decision making to be effective. Second, the more an organization is dependent on external organizations for resources, the more planning and decision making are likely to be constrained. For example, if each environmental factor that a manager considers significantly reduces the likelihood of success in pursuing a possible course of action, the organization may end up with a very small range of realistic alternatives. This could render decision making easy—assuming that the decision maker recognizes the implications of all the constraints.

BENEFICENCE

The final element that shapes an organization's relationship with its environment is the environment's beneficence. **Beneficence** refers to the generosity, leniency, and helpfulness that elements in the environment show an organization. Some organizations are likely to be helped in times of trouble, and some are likely to be attacked.

Why are some organizations helped while others aren't? There are two possibilities. First, the stated goals or values of an organization may be consistent with those of important resource holders in the environment. Second, the outcome of the transformation or production process that takes place at the organization may be a unique and highly desirable product.

MANAGING ENVIRONMENTAL DEPENDENCE

Previous sections of this chapter describe changes in the environment that affect the functioning of today's organizations. The challenge for an organization is to manage its relationship to the external environment efficiently and responsibly. In this section we consider three strategies that organizations use to manage resource dependence: anticipation, negotiation, and control. As shown in Figure 13-6, these approaches differ in the extent to which the organization's efforts are internally or externally focused. With the first strategy—**anticipation**—the focus is on making internal changes in response to external environmental demands. **Control** entails molding the environment to fit the organization's needs. Finally, **negotiation,** as defined in Chapter 5, falls somewhere in between. Many organizations use a combination of these strategies.

ANTICIPATION

Anticipation involves collecting information about actions occurring (or about to occur) in the environment. The organization can then predict and respond appropriately to demands. Two methods are typically used to collect information from the environment: environmental scanning and forecasting.

ENVIRONMENTAL SCANNING. One common approach to **environmental scanning** is surveying. As Richard Hoffman found in a study of firms

---

■ FIGURE 13-6   Strategies for Managing Resource Dependence

Organizations typically manage resource dependence by anticipating actions in the environment or by negotiating or controlling demands of the environment. The strategy a firm chooses to pursue may depend on management's perceptions of the extent of the environmental influence.

Anticipation

> **Scanning**: Collecting information about the environment and its possible actions.
> **Forecasting**: Predicting future actions of the environment, often using statistical models.

Negotiation

> **Lobbying**: Having agents plead the organization's case with regulatory bodies.
> **Interlocking directorates**: Having influential suppliers and consumers on the board of directors to provide policy input.
> **Public relations activities**: Attempting to build up the image of the organization in the environment.

Control

> **Contracts**: Obtaining legally enforceable promises from consumers or suppliers.
> **Buffers**: Stockpiling resources.
> **Joint ventures**: Collaborating with other organizations on joint projects.

in 71 nations, the extent to which organizations use scanning varies across cultures and is most commonly used in organizations characterized as innovative.[20] One frequently used technique for doing scanning is tapping into existing data sources, such as government labor statistics. Productive environmental scanning (for example, searching for information on the Internet) serves to signal to management that changes are needed in the business, including development of new opportunities, new products, and new services.[21] Scanning thus provides a method organizations can use to increase their competitive advantage.

The instability of many environments has made the need to do environmental scanning greater than ever. This is especially true of organizations in rapidly changing fields or markets, where keeping abreast of the latest developments is critical. Research by Reginald Beal shows that both the frequency and scope of environmental scanning (e.g., studying customers, competitors, *and* suppliers) facilitates alignment between an organization's strategies and the demands of its environment, thereby aiding in achieving outstanding performance.[22]

Environmental scanning in the form of **relationship marketing** is an important component of total quality management. Relationship marketing entails more than just collecting information about what customers want. It also involves developing long-term relationships with prospective customers via an intensive exchange of information. At its extreme, relationship marketing involves getting customers to help design products. This not only ensures that the product will be exactly what the customer wants, but it also makes the customer feel a sense of ownership and loyalty to the product.

FORECASTING. **Forecasting** takes scanning to another level by including data analysis using statistical models to predict future environmental demands. Sales departments, customers, the Internet, suppliers, and statistical baselines can all provide helpful and sound forecast information.[23]

One example of an environmental forecast is the social audit.[24] A **social audit** is a mechanism that organizations use to see how well they are responding to the social demands of their consumers, stockholders, and others in their external environment. According to Sandra Waddock and Neil Smith, a social audit enables an organization to score itself on such issues as its core values and ethics policy, as well as the expectations of its key stakeholders. Social audits help organizations develop responsible business practices, which, in turn, help them do well both socially and financially.[25] Social audits are also a means by which organizations can meet challenges to their

20. Hoffman, R. C. (1999, April). Organizational innovation: Management influence across cultures. *Multinational Business Review*, 37–49.
21. Slaughter, R. (1997, December). Developing and applying strategic foresight. *ABN Report*, 5(10), 7–15.
22. Beal, R. (2000, January). Competing effectively: Environmental scanning, competitive strategy, and organizational performance in small manufacturing firms. *Journal of Small Business Management*, 38(1), 27–47.
23. Lapide, L. (2000, Spring). New developments in business forecasting. *Journal of Business Forecasting Methods & Systems*, 19(1), 16–18.
24. Hysom, J. L., & Bolec, W. J. (1983). *Business and its environment*. St. Paul, MN: West.
25. Waddock, S., & Smith, N. (2000). Corporate responsibility audits: Doing well by doing good. *Sloan Management Review*, 41(2), 75–83.

INTERNATIONAL FOCUS ON
SOCIAL AUDITS

THE KPMG UK EXPERIENCE. Social auditing was developed in the 1990s in Britain by The Body Shop, a health and beauty products retailer, and subsequently was adopted by companies ranging from the resources group Royal Dutch Shell to communications giant British Telecom. The process involves verifying the organization's performance with respect to its commitment to workplace conditions, fairness and honesty in dealing with suppliers, customer service standards, involvement in community and charitable activities, and use of nonexploitative business practices in developing countries.

"If you look at what has happened in Britain over the last seven to eight years, you see that at the beginning of the decade environmental auditing and reporting was very much the exception rather than the rule," said David Wheeler, head of the social audit team at KPMG. "Last

financial year, over 70% of the top 100 listed companies included environmental information in their annual reports." It has become a natural thing to do.

"Social auditing can be seen as an active business strategy," Wheeler noted. "It's a way for companies to attract bright graduates, eager consumers, and willing investors."

Clearly, interest in social auditing is growing both inside and outside the business community. Whether the 21st century will see it develop across the globe depends on many variables. Government regulation, as is occurring in Britain, would appear to be a major first step in making organizations aware of their social responsibilities.

Source: Adapted from Watts, T. (1999, September). Social auditing: The KPMG UK experience. *Australian Accountant,* 46–47.

legitimacy and reputations.[26] "INTERNATIONAL FOCUS ON: Social Audits" describes this emerging trend.

Social audits are conducted with three goals in mind. First, the aim is to identify and analyze important trends in the firm's social environment. These might include issues affecting the firm, such as changes in community demographics that could require alterations in recruitment policies, and issues such as plant closings that could have widespread effects on the economy surrounding the company. Second, social audits catalogue the scope of socially responsive programs or actions that the organization is undertaking. Finally, social audits assess the effectiveness of a firm's social actions and programs in addressing identified social issues.

Social audits serve two important functions for organizations. First and foremost, social audits help organizations realize shortcomings they might have in addressing their social responsibilities. An audit is the first step an organization can take to prevent or correct any problems it has in managing the demands from the larger social environment to be socially responsible. In addition, social audits provide important documentation concerning the company's actions. An organization that has conducted a social audit has a paper trail detailing its level of social responsiveness. If the picture the audit paints is attractive, this documentation can be made available as proof that the firm is willing to fulfill its social obligations. Likewise, a firm that conducts periodic social audits—and uses the information appropriately—can

---

26. Raynard, P. (1998). Coming together: A review of contemporary approaches to social accounting, auditing, and reporting in non-profit organizations. *Journal of Business Ethics, 17,* 1471–1479.

be sure that the picture that is presented to the public is of a socially responsive and responsible organization.

NEGOTIATING WITH THE ENVIRONMENT

When practiced by itself, anticipation assumes that the resource dependencies of the environment are a given—something that the organization must face up to and react to. As a strategy for managing environmental demands, negotiation takes a different view—that the environment, in particular the *beneficence* of the environment, is susceptible to influence. An organization can bargain with its environment and negotiate the demands that it places on the organization.

LOBBYING.   One commonly used negotiating or bargaining tactic that organizations use is lobbying. The objective of **lobbying** is to convince representatives of a firm, the government, or another critical player in the environment of the correctness of an organization's worldview. In many cases the stakes are high. For instance, the lobbying party may threaten to withdraw monetary or voting support if the organization it is lobbying, such as Congress, refuses to support the goals of the organization represented by the lobbying party.

INTERLOCKING DIRECTORATES.   Like lobbying, albeit slightly more elegant, creating **interlocking directorates** ensures an organization commitment and support from other organizations. The idea is that by strategically choosing outside members for the organization's board of directors, the company can ensure support from other organizations for its views and objectives. Such support is invaluable when board members return to their own organizations to make decisions that affect the fate of the firm on whose boards of directors they sit.

PUBLIC RELATIONS.   **Public relations** activities, particularly **image advertising,** are another way that organizations foster goodwill and support for their actions and positions. The goal of image advertising is to influence the public's overall perception of the organization. For instance, the organization may want to appear patriotic or community minded. Or it might want to give consumers a good feeling. An organization also can influence its overall image by providing services to communities, as McDonald's does in supporting Ronald McDonald House for critically ill children.

Why should an organization care about maintaining a positive image? The answer is simple: It's good for business. Projecting a good image pays off handsomely in consumers' willingness to use the organization's products. Further, because of the nature of perception, consumers are more likely to have positive perceptions about the quality of a company's actions and products if the company's public image is good. Regulators, for example, are more likely to see a corporation's actions in a favorable light if their overall impression of the corporation is positive.

CONTROL

Some companies have adopted an even more proactive approach to handling resource demands: They actually control them. A variety of strategies are available—including contracts, buffers, and joint ventures—that enable organizations to take control of external resources.

CONTRACTS. A **contract** is one of the simplest and most widespread ways that organizations control their dependence on external resources. Because it is legally binding, a contract can guarantee delivery of a resource, the terms under which this will occur, and the cost of any or all transactions. The point of a contract is to reduce uncertainty about the availability and the timely delivery of resources on which the organization depends.

BUFFERS. Buffers are another way that organizations gain control of their environment and protect themselves from variability and volatility. Stockpiling is one example of a buffer. For instance, if an organization is concerned that its supplies of a certain resource might dry up, it can stockpile when the resource is available in anticipation of the day when it will be hard to come by.

Companies where stockpiling is difficult or impossible may resort to resource redundancy. The idea behind **resource redundancy** is that maintaining relationships with multiple resource suppliers minimizes an organization's dependence on any one resource provider. The assumption is that if one supplier cannot supply a needed resource, the organization can purchase the resource from another supplier.

JOINT VENTURES. Yet another way organizations shield themselves from the effects of operating in a rapidly changing environment is by forming **joint ventures.** Again, the goal is quite simple: Two or more unrelated organizations pool their resources or collaborate on joint projects.

Why would two organizations—even competitors—be willing to take such a drastic move? There are a variety of answers, but they all come down to concerns about resource dependence. Also, in some instances the potential is too great to ignore. Often such a move prevents competitors from gaining an advantage, and typically the benefits of pooling resources are greater and the risks lower than if any one organization took steps to stop the competition on its own.

SUMMARY

The goal of this chapter is to paint a picture of the environment in which today's organizations must function. As the WTO can attest, organizations cannot exist independently of their environments. Organizations are open systems that depend on the environment for resources and are influenced by their interactions with it.

The environmental forces that influence business organizations have both form and content. Environmental forces vary in their uncertainty, stability, complexity, and beneficence. These forces include other organizations, government regulations, and social trends.

The successful management of environmental or resource dependence is key to an organization's survival. Three broad strategies organizations use to manage environmental forces include anticipation, negotiation, and control. Anticipation requires scanning the environment in order to forecast—and therefore be prepared to respond appropriately to—emerging trends and conditions in the environment. Negotiation is the process of influencing resource dependence. Finally, organizations can control resource dependencies through contracting, buffering, and joint ventures.

KEY TERMS

Anticipation
Beneficence
Boundaries
Boundary spanner
Closed system
Contract
Control
Corporate social responsibility
Enacted environment
Environmental complexity
Environmental instability
Environmental scanning
Forecasting
Image advertising

Interlocking directorates
Joint venture
Lobbying
Loose coupling
Negotiation
Open system
Public relations
Regulation
Relationship marketing
Resource dependence theory
Resource redundancy
Social audit
Union

DISCUSSION QUESTIONS

1 What does it mean to say that organizations are open systems? What are the defining characteristics of open systems?

2 In what ways are organizations dependent on their environments? Explain what might be meant by the sentence, "Organizations are a way of turning the environment into survival."

3 On what dimensions of external dependence do the environments of service and manufacturing organizations differ? Does this have implications for how these two types of organizations might manage their environmental interactions?

4 Consider the following prayer: "Grant me the strength to change the things I can change, the patience to endure the things I cannot, and the wisdom to know the differ-

ence." Would this make a good corporate policy for managing resource dependencies? Why or why not?

5 What does it mean to say that an organization and its environment are loosely coupled? Is loose coupling an advantage or disadvantage for an organization?

6 Why is the role of the boundary spanner so important? so difficult? How could an organization prepare one of its employees for this role?

7 What strategies does an organization have for managing its dependence on the environment?

8 How might mergers, takeovers, and acquisitions be seen as a way of managing environmental dependence?

ON YOUR OWN

Exploring Environmental Forces   The following table provides a framework for analyzing the environmental forces that influence the behaviors of an organization. The table asks you to list different sources of environmental influence and to identify strategies for dealing with them. Using a school club or sports team as an example of an open system, fill in the table to complete an audit of the environmental forces influencing the behavior of the club or team. In the first column, list one or two examples of each source of environmental dependence listed on the left. Then fill in examples of each of the strategies available to a club or sports team to successfully manage the influence of these environmental dependencies.

Management Strategies

	Source	Anticipation	Negotiation	Control
Other Organizations				
Regulatory Environment				
Social Environment				

Are any of these boxes harder to fill in than others? Does this suggest anything about what types of strategies might be better for managing different types of environmental forces?

CLOSING CASE   CHAPTER 13

THE MANAGER'S MEMO

FROM: G. Irving, President
TO: P. Rambowski, Vice President
RE: Preparing for Hard Times

These days, the antigun fanatics seem to be shooting their mouths off more and more, and I'm getting concerned about the future of the Top Gun Shops. If the trend keeps up, our chain of gun and ammunition stores could be under siege, maybe from the government, maybe from community activists. And if the market gets any trickier, you can bet that the competition will be stepping up the pressure.

The successful hunter keeps his eyes open at all times. So how can we do the same in our business? We need a plan for keeping an eye on what's going on, for anticipating changes, for taking action where we can.

I'd like your suggestions. Where should we be watching? How should we watch? And what can we do to head off problems?

CASE DISCUSSION QUESTIONS

Assume that you are the vice president, and respond to the president's memorandum. Consider as many aspects of the environment as you can apply to this situation. Besides identifying sources of environmental dependence, describe ways in which the company might be able to manage this dependence.

CHAPTER 14

Organizational Structure and Design

GIANT P&G NEEDS TO CLEAN UP ITS ACT

Procter & Gamble (P&G) is known for products that get out the dirt and leave sinks, clothes, and teeth clean and sparkling. But now, shamed by the competition, the cosmetics and detergents giant itself is having to clean up its act.

P&G experienced the first of several seismic shudders in the mid-1990s as Shout, manufactured by Johnson & Johnson, outsold Tide, P&G's pre-treatment laundry product. The company was equally humiliated a few years later, when Colgate, produced by arch rival Colgate-Palmolive, took a bigger bite out of toothpaste sales than P&G's Crest for the first time in history.

What caused these losses of market share? The answer, the analysts said, was simple: P&G was too big and too slow.

Not one to take defeat easily, P&G announced it was restructuring. The company expects its restructuring program—dubbed Organization 2005—to increase sales by 6% to 8% and to boost earnings-per-share growth from 13% to 15% annually for the next several years. The total cost of the program, after taxes, will be $1.9 billion, but it will yield after-tax savings of about $900 million by fiscal 2004.

"The redesign of our organizational structure, work processes, and culture will pay off in bigger innovation, faster speed to market, and greater growth," says Durk Jager, P&G's president and Chief Executive Officer.

As part of Organization 2005, P&G is reorganizing its business units to focus on products and brands rather than geography. Four regionally based units will be restructured into seven global business units based on product lines: fabric and home care, food and beverages, feminine hygiene, beauty care, tissues and towels, baby care, and health care. A newly created global business services segment will centralize and consolidate administrative functions, such

Source: P&G continues restructuring and streamlines its workforce. (1999, June 14). *Chemical Market Reporter, 255*(24), 47; Bell, S. (1999, June 17). P&G forced by rivals to change old habits. *Marketing,* 15; and Harvilicz, H. (1999, August). P&G takes a substantial charge but performs better than expected. *Chemical Market Reporter, 256*(6), 29.

as human resources, accounting, order management, and information technology. Other elements of the reorganization include simplifying the company's structure and hierarchy to make it more responsive, standardizing its production lines, and aligning manufacturing capacity with its new global business units to cut costs and increase speed to market.

Overall, the program requires 15,000 job cuts worldwide, about 13% of the company's workforce. "These job reductions are principally an outgrowth of changes, such as standardizing global manufacturing platforms, to drive innovation and faster speed to market," says Jager. "Organization 2005 will result in increased motivation and an accelerated rate of sales and earnings growth as the organization becomes more fully aligned behind the global opportunities that are before us." As the leaders involved in the Organization 2005 structure know, captivating the global marketplace will be instrumental to P&G's survival in the 21st century.

INTRODUCTION

An organization's structure is the formal means by which the organization divides the activities of its workforce to accomplish goals and objectives. As suggested in the opening vignette about P&G, sometimes restructuring is critical if a company hopes to remain competitive. In fact, most successful organizations have restructured several times in an effort to improve the coordination of work and employees.

Virtually all complex human activities require two elements of structure. First, the labor must be divided into various component tasks, and second, these component tasks must be coordinated to produce the organization's outputs. As noted in Chapter 1, organizations typically form because complex goals or missions entail a variety of component tasks, more than any one individual could hope to accomplish alone. Thus, different members of the workforce are assigned various component tasks or roles.[1] The different roles and behaviors of the organization's workforce must then be coordinated. This is when a structure emerges. **Organizational structure** is the skeleton that captures the relationships among employees' different roles in the organization. **Organizational design** is the process of creating this structure, grouping roles and activities so that the interdependencies among organizational actors are coordinated effectively and efficiently.

A common way in which an organization's structure is represented to employees and others is through an organizational chart, such as the one shown in Figure 14-1. An organizational chart denotes the formal lines of authority in an organization. Each box on the chart represents a position. Boxes are connected to each other with solid vertical lines (indicating direct reporting relationships). Solid horizontal lines represent communication (but not authority) relationships. Broken lines represent informal or infrequent relationships.

This chapter describes the most common organizational structures and examines the ways they influence the relationships and interactions of the members of an organization. It then identifies the factors that influ-

---

1. Thompson, J. D. (1967). *Organizations in action*. New York: McGraw-Hill.

A Hospital: An Organization Structured by Knowledge and Skills ■ **FIGURE 14-1**

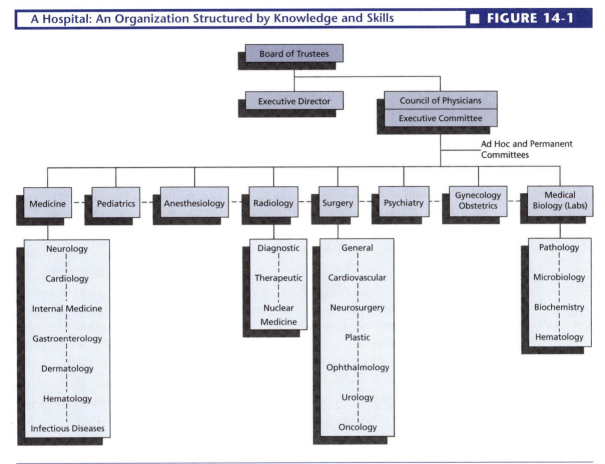

Source: Mintzberg, H. (1979). *The structuring of organizations.* Englewood Cliffs, NJ: Prentice Hall.

ence whether a particular organizational structure is effective. It also examines some of the symptoms that emerge when an organization's structure is inappropriate.

ELEMENTS OF ORGANIZATIONAL STRUCTURE

An organization's structure reflects the way the organization distributes and coordinates work. As shown in the opening vignette about P&G, this structure can be a powerful strategic force. An appropriate structure is essential to the efficient attainment of an organization's goals. In this section, we will consider four design features that organizations use to divide and coordinate work: job specialization, departmentalization, centralization/decentralization, and span of control.

JOB SPECIALIZATION

The overall task of any organization can be divided into various component tasks. Component tasks are those in which the predominant work behaviors are accomplished; in essence, component tasks are what the organization actually does.[2] As an example, at P&G, the overall task is selling household goods. The component tasks include product development, marketing, and sales.

Assigning each member of the workforce a limited number of component tasks—in other words, **job specialization**—enables employees to become very skilled and productive at their assigned tasks. As we saw in Chapter 11, when workers' roles are limited in scope, it is far easier to teach another employee, such as a newcomer, the skills needed to perform well.

DEPARTMENTALIZATION

Departmentalization, or grouping roles based on which jobs fit together, is another feature used to structure organizations. Sometimes related tasks are assigned to the same subunit (a department, for instance) based on the similarities in the required knowledge and skills members bring to their jobs. For example, universities divide faculty into colleges, schools, and departments; the members of each group are more similar as we move down the list of categories or divisions.

In addition to similarity of skills and knowledge, departmentalization can be based on similar levels of skills and abilities. For example, hospitals have distinct departments for doctors, nurses, technical assistants, and volunteers. In this case, employees are grouped based on abilities and skills in caring for patients.

Other organizations group component tasks by their functions. Typical organizational functions include production, marketing, finance, human resources, and accounting. The major advantage of functional departmentalization is that, because employees with similar expertise are grouped together, they can easily share their expertise with one another. At P&G, for example, tasks such as human resources, accounting, order management, and information technology were concentrated in divisions. A disadvantage of this structure is that it tends to create barriers between functions, which can limit communication, decrease the salience of organizational goals, and create unnecessary competition for resources.

Component tasks can also be departmentalized by the types of outputs or products produced. When P&G restructured, for instance, it did so according to product lines: food and beverages, feminine hygiene, beauty care, tissues and towels, and so forth. This often happens as firms grow and coordinating functional areas becomes increasingly difficult. Restructuring based on diversified (product) departmentalization is thus a common response to success. In a diversified organization, all jobs that are required to produce and sell a particular product or group of related products are under the direction of one individual.

Yet another way organizations can be structured is by *the clients they serve* (for example, retail versus wholesale) or *geographic region*. Banks, for example, have different departments for consumer loans, business loans, mortgage loans, and so on. If an organization is geographically dispersed, then it may be necessary to divide groups based on their geographic relationships. It is very difficult to manage an organization over large distances, and diverse social and cultural expectations add to the problems. Examples of product, function, client, and geographic departmentalization are illustrated in Figure 14-2.

---

2. Friedman, L., & Gyr, H. (1998). *The dynamic enterprise: Tools for turning chaos into strategy and strategy into action.* San Francisco: Jossey-Bass, p. 61.

Four Departmental Structures   ■ **FIGURE 14-2**

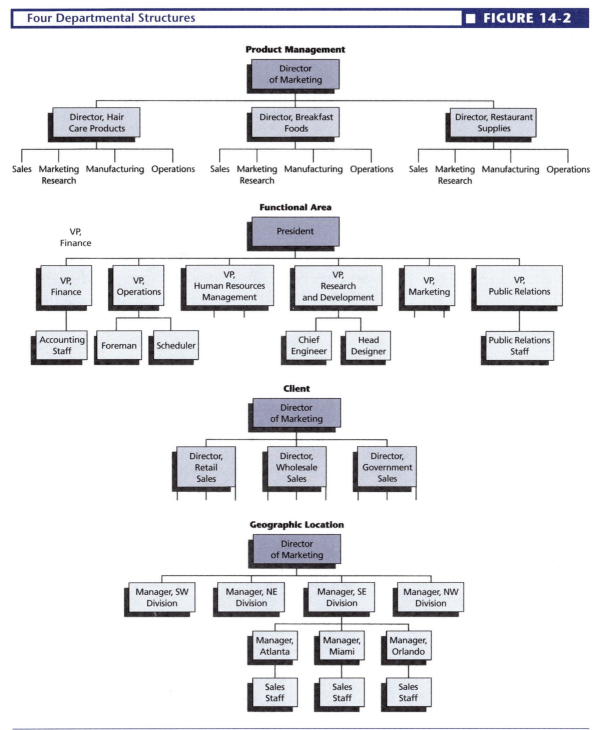

Product Management

Director of Marketing

Director, Hair Care Products

Director, Breakfast Foods

Director, Restaurant Supplies

Sales   Marketing Research   Manufacturing   Operations

Sales   Marketing Research   Manufacturing   Operations

Sales   Marketing Research   Manufacturing   Operations

Functional Area

President

VP, Finance

VP, Finance | VP, Operations | VP, Human Resources Management | VP, Research and Development | VP, Marketing | VP, Public Relations

Accounting Staff

Foreman | Scheduler

Chief Engineer | Head Designer

Public Relations Staff

Client

Director of Marketing

Director, Retail Sales | Director, Wholesale Sales | Director, Government Sales

Geographic Location

Director of Marketing

Manager, SW Division | Manager, NE Division | Manager, SE Division | Manager, NW Division

Manager, Atlanta | Manager, Miami | Manager, Orlando

Sales Staff | Sales Staff | Sales Staff

Source: Gordon, J. R. (1987). *A diagnostic approach to organizational behavior.* Boston: Allyn & Bacon.

One advantage of departmentalization is that it allows organizations to respond quickly to changes in the product, client base, or geographic region. It does so by shortening the lines of communication among individuals whose work is interdependent (e.g., all individuals working on the same product, or all individuals working in the same geographic region). These structures also encourage departmental loyalty by focusing employees' attention on the attainment of a common goal (e.g., the success of a particular product line, satisfying the customer, or serving a specific geographic region). One disadvantage of departmentalization is a tendency toward redundancy. An organization with a product, client, or geographic orientation must assign people in all functional areas (such as sales and personnel) to each product, customer, or geographic area. In addition, because functional area specialists are not focused on their areas of expertise, they may have difficulty keeping pace with changes in their profession.

CENTRALIZATION AND DECENTRALIZATION

Another design feature organizations sometimes opt for is centralization. **Centralization** (also called traditional design) is based on the assumption that meeting the dual needs of division and coordination of labor is equally important. An organization is centralized to the extent that its decision-making power rests with one or a few individuals. In a highly centralized organization, all decisions are made by one person and are implemented through formal channels of authority.

While centralization typically improves coordination of an organization's activities, it can lead to problems. Centralized decision makers often do not have all the information necessary to make good decisions, or they cannot efficiently transmit decisions down to lower ranks. Centralization also appears to be negatively correlated with performance. Research has shown that organizations in which there is easy access to management outperform organizations with traditional structures in which managers maintain central control of the decision making.[3] Research has also shown that centralization hinders entrepreneurial behavior[4] and innovation.[5] Finally, based on a study of 118 large U.S. commercial banks, researchers have concluded that centralization leads to increases in costs.[6]

Because centralized organizations tend to be slow to respond to external pressures, the trend among companies in the United States during the past 40 years has been to decentralize—to push decision-making authority and responsibility lower in the organization, in the spirit of efficiency. Reinhard Mohn, chair of Germany's Bertelsmann Foundation, summed up this orientation: "Centralist leadership structures are no longer capable of meeting requirements in today's competitive environment. We must have the courage

---

3. Rapert, M., & Wren, B. (1998). Reconsidering organizational structure: A dual perspective of frameworks and processes. *Journal of Managerial Issues, 10,* 287–302.

4. Caruana, A., Morris, M. H., & Vella, A. J. (1998). The effect of centralization and formalization on entrepreneurship in export firms. *Journal of Small Business Management, 36*(1), 16–29.

5. Mellor, S., & Mathieu, J. E. (1999). A discriminant validity study of aggregate-level constructs and measures of local union formalization, centralization, and innovation. *Journal of Psychology, 133,* 669–683.

6. Hunter, W. (1995). Internal organization and economic performance: The case of large U.S. commercial banks. *Economic Perspectives, 19*(5), 10–21.

to decentralize responsibility. Creative people need freedom."[7] Durk Jager certainly realized this when he began restructuring P&G.

A major benefit of **decentralization** (spreading decision-making power and authority among a broad group of individuals) is that it enables individuals to concentrate on tasks that add value to the organization (such as product development) by eliminating layers of hierarchy and administrative tasks.[8] In addition, decentralization often lends itself to a more entrepreneurial environment.

Like many management trends, however, decentralization isn't appropriate for every organization. When assessing the need to restructure, organizations should consider several factors before deciding to decentralize[9]:

1 The more change an organization faces and the more quickly decisions must be made, the more likely it is that decentralization will prove beneficial. Decentralization allows a workgroup (for instance, a product division) to respond quickly to changes, rather than having to request instructions through the organization's formal authority channels.

2 As organizations increase in size, centralized decision makers get further and further from the information they need to make high-quality decisions, and it takes longer and longer for information and decisions to travel up and down the organization's formal channels of authority. Thus, growth inevitably leads to decentralization of decision making.

3 Risk often tends to centralize decision making. Where the consequences of making poor decisions are great, top management will be unlikely to relinquish control.

4 Finally, the success of centralization may be a function of the quality of an organization's channels of communication. If the channels of communication are highly efficient, centralized decision makers may be able to gather information and return decisions quickly enough to remain effective.

One way organizations reorganize and decentralize is by introducing self-managed teams. A more complete discussion of these workgroups is found in Chapter 6.

SPAN OF CONTROL

Another important element of organizational structure is **span of control**— the number of people reporting to each manager. Span of control is a major determinant of the size of an organization's workgroups, and it is directly related to the closeness of supervision. Managers who have fewer subordinates can supervise more closely. A narrow span of control is important in an organization or a work unit with a task in which close interpersonal control of subordinates is desired. If the task requires machine-paced, well-learned, or easily monitored behaviors, there is less need for a narrow span of control.[10] In fact, to assess the appropriate span of control, a manager must consider

---

7. Fulmer, W. (2000). *Shaping the adaptive organization: Landscapes, learning and leadership in volatile times.* New York: American Management Association, p. 179.

8. Pfeffer, J. (1998). Seven practices of successful organizations. *California Management Review,* 40(2), 96–124.

9. Dale, E. (1967). *Organization.* New York: American Management Association.

10. Blau, P. M., & Scott, W. R. (1962). *Formal organizations.* San Francisco: Chandler.

■ **FIGURE 14-3**   **Creation of a Flat Organization Structure**

Span of control is a major determinant of the number of hierarchical levels in an organization: The more subordinates each supervisor manages, the flatter the organization's structure. The following diagrams represent an organization before downsizing (a tall organization) and after downsizing (a flat organization).

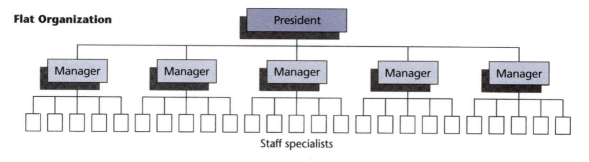

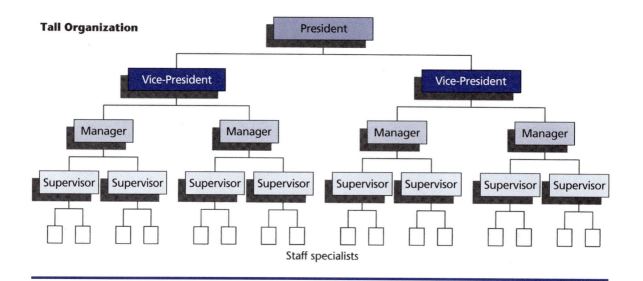

both the routineness of the task and the time required to monitor and coordinate subordinates' activities.[11]

Finally, span of control is directly related to the number of levels in (or depth of) an organization. Typically, the greater the span of control, the fewer hierarchical levels. An organization with few levels appears "flat" in its organizational chart. By contrast, an organization with many levels (and typically a narrow span of control) appears "tall." Figure 14-3 illustrates flat and tall structures.

Are tall organizations or flat organizations more effective? In terms of their overall performance, it seems that flat organizations have an advantage. As Jack Welch, chairman and Chief Executive Officer of General Electric, noted:

> When you take out layers, you change the exposure of the managers who remain. They sit right in the sun. Some of them blotch immediately—they can't stand the exposure of leadership. I firmly believe

---

11. Mackenzie, K. D. (1978). *Organization structures.* Arlington Heights, IL: AHM Publishing.

that an overburdened, overstretched executive is the best executive, because he or she doesn't have time to meddle, to deal in trivia, or to bother people. Remember the theory that a manager should have no more than six or seven direct reports? I say the right number is closer to 10 or 15. This way you have no choice but to let people flex their muscles, to let them grow and mature.[12]

Another advantage of reducing management layers and decentralizing is that these changes tend to result in more rapid decision making.[13]

Flat organizations also provide employees with more direct routes to their customers. When Ford recently shifted to a horizontal structure, productivity in the customer service division increased by 20% and customer satisfaction jumped from 20% to 60%.[14]

Not all the research on restructuring is so positive, however. Management researcher, Warner Burke, for example, found that although an organization's costs may be lower immediately following a reorganization, they may increase in the long run. He found that restructuring could also result in the loss of relationships between employees and customers, an increase in the number of procedures and rules, and the loss of an organizational culture.[15]

So what is an organization to do? The following advice may be of assistance: flattening, removing middle levels, and abandoning formal decision-making procedures may be sensible in an organization that is in trouble, but to grow, organizations need to devote the time, funds, and scope to exploring new ideas and initiatives.[16]

COMMON ORGANIZATIONAL STRUCTURES

The four elements of organizational structure—job specialization, departmentalization, centralization/decentralization, and span of control—represent the ways in which organizations coordinate the component tasks of their employees. Depending on how an organization combines these features, one of three primary organizational structures emerges: the simple structure, the bureaucracy, and the organic structure.[17] Figure 14-4 provides an overview of these three structures and the types of task coordination and control used in each.

SIMPLE STRUCTURE

The **simple structure** is most common in young or small organizations and is typically centralized. Coordination is largely a function of direct supervision, and the top manager has a broad span of control. In fact, in a simple structure it

12. Fulmer, *Shaping the adaptive organization*, p. 185.
13. Durbin, A. J. (1996). *Reengineering survival guide: Managing and succeeding in the changing workplace*. Cincinnati, OH: Thomson Executive Press, p. 15.
14. Boehm, R., & Phipps, C. (1996). Flatness foray (theory of horizontal organization in corporations). *McKinsey Quartely, 3*, 128–143.
15. Burke, W. W. (1997). The new agenda for organizational development. *Organizational Dynamics, 26*, 6–18.
16. Donaldson, L., & Hilmer, F. (1998). Management redeemed: The case against fads that harm management. *Organizational Dynamics, 26*(4), 6–20.
17. Mintzberg, *The structuring of organizations*.

■ FIGURE 14-4 | **Overview of Organizational Structures**

The amount of control needed to coordinate interdependence among employees yields one of three types of organizational structures: the simple structure, the bureaucracy, or the organic structure.

Coordinating and Control Mechanisms

Simple Structure	Direct supervision
Bureaucracy	Standardization of work processes or skills
Organic Structure	Mutual adjustment

Source: Mintzberg, *The structuring of organizations.*

---

is common for all employees to report directly to the top manager, and typically employees have very little discretionary decision-making power. Entrepreneurial firms also have simple structures because inside such firms, everything revolves around the entrepreneur. Its goals are the entrepreneur's goals; its strategy is the entrepreneur's vision. Entrepreneurial firms are often founded by individuals who resist the types of control imposed by bureaucratic organizations and view more formal structures as constraints on their flexibility.

One of the critical problems facing businesses today is how to release and sustain the thrust, initiative, and adaptability of the entrepreneurial spirit in organizations that employ large numbers of people, while at the same time holding individuals accountable for their actions. Bureaucracies, as we shall see, are a primary mechanism for maintaining accountability while unifying hundreds (if not thousands) of employees.

BUREAUCRACY

In their classic study of electronics firms in Scotland, Tom Burns and G. M. Stalker classified all the firms they studied into two types: mechanistic and organic.[18] Mechanistic organizations embody what we now refer to as the bureaucratic form. Bureaucratic organizations are designed to maintain accountability in their structures through predictability. In a bureaucracy, tasks are carefully planned in advance, and both the quantity and the quality of performance are closely monitored. Job specialization is often found in bureaucracies as roles tend to be narrow in scope and responsibilities extremely well defined. A detailed formal authority hierarchy exists to control and coordinate task performance. Rewards are allocated on the basis of following instructions, and compensation and selection are tied to ability to perform within narrow job functions. Consequently, personal achievement is evaluated on the basis of following the rules, not on changing them.[19]

Bureaucracies may be either machine based or professional, depending on whether the organization's transformation technology is machines or people. A **machine bureaucracy** (what most people think of when they think of a bureaucracy) has highly specialized and routine tasks; formalized

---

18. Burns, T., & Stalker, G. M. (1961). *The management of innovation.* London: Tavistock.
19. Rechtin, E. (2000). *Systems architecting of organizations.* Boca Raton, FL: CRC Press, pp. 108–111.

procedures for the transformation process; a proliferation of rules, regulations, and communication channels; a functional departmentalization structure; a large span of control; and an elaborate administrative and technical structure. We explore the negative ramifications of such structures in the "INTERNATIONAL FOCUS ON: Bureaucracies." Even though they have considerable formalization of policies and procedures, machine bureaucracies are also often criticized for their alienated workforces and lack of innovation. Their large size makes them more suited to promoting efficiency than to creativity. Examples of these organizations include the U.S. Postal Service, steel companies, and traditional automobile manufacturing firms.

A **professional bureaucracy** trains its workers to internalize a set of performance and professional standards. Professional bureaucracies differ from machine bureaucracies in that the production technology is composed of professionals who also control most of the organization's power. However, rather than standardize policies and procedures as a machine bureaucracy would, the professional bureaucracy seeks to standardize skills. Professional bureaucracies often provide services rather than products. Examples of professional bureaucracies include hospitals, universities, social work agencies, and consulting firms.

Given the extent of formalization in bureaucracies, what effect do tight structures have on employees? When William Finlay and his associates

INTERNATIONAL FOCUS ON
BUREAUCRACIES

THE RED TIDE. Ocean shipping is tied up in a tangled web of national and international regulation. At its worst, the bureaucratic red tape gets in the way of cargo operations and increases the burden on crews already straining to meet stringent international sailing schedules.

The need for comprehensive regulation covering such vital areas as safety is unquestioned—but not when the bureaucracy duplicates the work involved and needlessly diverts crews from important operational tasks.

It is becoming a hot-button issue at the London-based International Maritime Organization (IMO), the body responsible for much of the regulation that now blankets the international shipping industry. "The feeling now is that we have somehow got to get away from this cycle of disaster followed by reaction followed by regulation," said IMO spokesperson Roger Kohn. "The problem is that marine disasters often stir up emotions and in the aftermath it is all too easy to formulate new regulations based on knee-jerk reaction rather than broad-based analysis," said Kohn. "Everyone is conscious of the fact that every time something goes wrong there is a new

regulation. We are trying to cut back on the amount of regulations and inspections." Regulatory red tape is the inefficient outcome of emotional reactions following marine disasters.

But it is not only inspections that are distracting ships' crews. The industry is also drowning in bureaucratic documentation. Captain Steen Stender Petersen, assistant secretary general of the Baltic and International Maritime Council, pointed to a questionnaire containing more than 300 questions that was sent out by one oil company to its ship masters. "Imagine how long that would take," he said.

Crews are "between a rock and a hard place," said Petersen. "While ships' officers have to be accommodating," he said, "they also are under intense pressure to expedite international cargo operations."

The balance between accomplishing duties within an organization and bureaucratic "red tape" is not always easy, but it must be dealt with to ensure the survival of most organizations.

Source: Excerpted from Cottrill, K. (2000, February 21). Red tide. *Traffic World, 261*(8), 24.

examined this issue, they found that employees who work in less bureaucratic organizations were more satisfied with their work than their counterparts in more bureaucratic companies. Finlay found that organizational openness—allowing frequent information flow and having a low standardization of procedures—was an important determinant of job satisfaction.[20] Bureaucracies work best where profit is not an important objective and where value created is not easily quantifiable (e.g., bureaucracies are often found in education, defense, police protection).[21]

On the positive side, employees in bureaucracies tend to be highly dedicated to these organizations. In addition to having a strong sense of job security, the workers in bureaucratic organizations often have a great sense of belonging (as in the military). Because everyone shares the same values and beliefs, bureaucracies often develop their own cultures.[22] On the whole, though, bureaucracies do not foster the innovation needed to adapt to today's changing markets.

ORGANIC STRUCTURES

The organic organizations that Burns and Stalker identified were far more flexible than bureaucracies, and they were able to adapt more easily when new demands were placed on them. In fact, the defining feature of an organization with an **organic structure** is its ability to respond efficiently and effectively to new demands. Organic organizations also tend to exhibit the following characteristics[23]:

1 **Knowledge and ability, rather than job descriptions or position titles, determine who will participate in solving particular problems.** People are valued for their abilities rather than for their organizational status.
2 **Organizational status and expertise are not assumed to be related.** Decision making is decentralized, and responsibility for decision making is pushed as low as possible to take advantage of the hands-on expertise of even the lowest-level members of the organization.
3 **Communication flows freely in a lateral direction.** The use of project teams and task forces is common (as are liaisons between departments or workgroups), to encourage information sharing across diverse areas of expertise.

Of the varieties of organic structures, three are discussed here. The matrix structure is the most complex and formal. The boundaryless organization and the virtual structure are two new and emerging designs that organizations are using more frequently. Boundaryless organizations and virtual organizations may appear to have less formal structures than matrix organizations.

MATRIX STRUCTURE. The **matrix structure** is particularly useful when an organization wants to focus on developing a particular product or con-

20. Finlay, W., Martin, J. K., Roman, P. M., & Blum, T. C. (1995). Organizational structure and job satisfaction: Do bureaucratic organizations produce more satisfied employees? *Administration & Society, 27,* 427–450.
21. Rechtin, *Systems architecting of organizations,* p. 108.
22. Rechtin, *Systems architecting of organizations,* p. 111.
23. Gullett, C. R. (1975). Mechanistic versus organic organizations: What does the future hold? *Personnel Administration, 20,* 17–19.

centrate on a specific client. Unlike other organizational structures, in which employees usually report to only one supervisor, organizations with a matrix structure have dual reporting structures. Employees report to a long-term manager who manages their professional and technical development, *and* they report to a person who is responsible for the project(s) they are working on.[24] Consulting firms, such as McKinsey, often have matrix structures. This structure enables consultants to devote their attention to particular projects but also provides avenues for their professional and technical development.[25]

As one would expect, matrix organizations are difficult to manage. Because each employee has two supervisors, there is a lot of potential for conflict. An organization should consider using a matrix structure only when the information and geographic and technologic demands are so great that the full-time attention of a subgroup is required.

BOUNDARYLESS ORGANIZATIONS. Boundaryless organizations are another innovative solution to meet changing business needs. General Electric CEO Jack Welch defined companies with this structure as "organizations where the barriers of hierarchy, function, and geography dissolve, and cross-functional teams are empowered to act quickly and in partnership with customers and suppliers."[26]

A basic tenet of boundaryless organizations is that hierarchies and traditional structures put organizations at a disadvantage in reaching corporate goals. One of the first steps many boundaryless organizations take toward removing some of these barriers is to change job titles (e.g., *human resources* to *member relations, subordinates* to *work partners*).[27]

However, just because boundaryless organizations are less formal doesn't mean that the work their members perform is easier than the work of people in formal structures—it's just different. In a study of a commercial lending institution, Robert Cross, Aimin Yan, and Meryl Reis Louis found that in boundaryless organizations work was divided among all levels of the company—everyone was responsible for elements such as goal setting and strategic planning.[28] This is in direct contrast to formal structures, where the majority of work, such as goal setting and strategic planning, is reserved for upper management.

VIRTUAL STRUCTURES. Virtual structures were a logical outgrowth of developments in technology and global expansion in corporate America, and are an outgrowth of the boundaryless organization. A **virtual structure** is an evolving network of organizations or firms joined to share skills, costs, and resources.[29] A challenge to traditional organizations, virtual structures are typically assembled only temporarily and for specific reasons. In addition, in

24. Lawler, E. E. (1996). *From the ground up: Six principles for building the new logic corporation.* San Francisco: Jossey-Bass, pp. 119–120.

25. Lawler, *From the ground up*, p. 119.

26. Nirenberg, J. (1997). *Power tools: A leader's guide to the latest management thinking.* Singapore: Prentice Hall, pp. 158–159.

27. Nirenberg, *Power tools*, p. 205.

28. Cross, R. L., Yan, A., & Louis, M. R. (2000, June). Boundary activities in "boundaryless" organizations: A case study of a transformation to a team-based structure. *Human Relations, 53*(6), 841–868.

29. Dess, G. D., Rasheed, A. M. A., McLaughlin, K. J., & Priem, R. L. (1995). The new corporate architecture. *Academy of Management Executive, 9*(3), 7–20.

■ FIGURE 14-5 | **Characteristics of Bureaucratic and Organic Organizations**

Bureaucratic Organizations	**Organic Organizations**
■ Hierarchical structure, with stable divisions/departments based on functions	■ Flat structure, with temporary work groups/teams based on specific projects
■ Vertical communication dominates	■ Lateral communication dominates
■ Rigid job definitions, set by senior management	■ Flexible job definitions, defined by individuals through interaction with colleagues
■ Power and authority based on seniority in hierarchy	■ Power and authority change with changing circumstances and are based on individual skills and abilities

Source: King, N., & Anderson, N. (1995). *Innovation and change in organizations.* New York: Routledge, p. 100.

RESEARCH IN ACTION
FROM DOWNSIZING TO RESPONSIBLE RESTRUCTURING

Wayne F. Cascio, University of Colorado–Denver; *wcascio@carbon.cudenver.edu.*

When confronted with the need to reduce costs, many of the same executives who tout people as "our greatest assets" see those assets as ripe opportunities for cutting costs. My research, funded by the U.S. Department of Labor, punctured a number of myths about downsizing as a strategy to improve corporate profitability, and it identified an alternative approach, termed "responsible restructuring." Instead of asking "What's the irreducible core number of people we need to run our business?" responsible restructuring asks "How can we change the way we do business, so that we can use the people we currently have most effectively?"

Some of the guidelines for responsible restructuring include the following: Articulate a vision of what you want your organization to achieve; establish a corporate culture that views people as assets to be developed rather than costs to be cut; get the people who have to live with the changes involved in making them; and, by all means, communicate. Share as much information as possible about prospective changes with those who will be affected by them. If cutting costs by cutting people is inevitable, establish a set of priorities for doing so (e.g., outside contractors and temporaries are laid off first) and stick to it. Show by word and deed that full-time,

value-adding employees will be the last to go. Finally, give surviving employees a reason to stay. Explain what new opportunities will be available to them.

Intel, the company that invented the computer microchip and whose average product life cycle is just 2.5 years, has avoided major layoffs through a strong in-house redeployment policy. In fact, the company maintains five career-development centers offering self-assessment tools and career counseling, and it has redefined job skills to encourage employees to find new positions within the company. Opportunities for temporary assignments, in-house training, and funds for re-location help employees find new jobs. Today, the ranks of Intel employees include people who have made successful transitions from shop floor to sales and public relations positions, or from obsolete technology divisions to high-margin technology centers within the company. The entire process is managed through a system that provides centralized tracking and reporting of all redeployment activity. Intel practices responsible restructuring by establishing a corporate culture that regards people as a source of competitive advantage, viewing them as assets to be developed rather than as costs to be cut.

their purest form they have practically no structure at all—no organizational chart, no central office, and no hierarchy.

Apple Computer is an excellent example of a virtual structure. Apple formed an alliance with Sony Corporation—a virtual structure was created—to produce PowerBook notebooks. By combining Apple's software with Sony's production capabilities, Apple was able to get its product to market quickly and, consequently, to gain significant market share.[30]

In determining the feasibility of any structure, management must determine if the structure supports the organization's strategic objectives. Figure 14-5 provides a helpful summary of the characteristics of bureaucratic and organic structures to help determine the best fit.

In the next section we will consider other factors—such as internal and external environments, technology, age, and size—that influence the appropriateness of particular organizational structures.

FACTORS INFLUENCING CHOICE OF ORGANIZATIONAL STRUCTURE

Examples of the common organizational structures—simple, machine and professional bureaucracies, and organic structures—can be observed among both successful and unsuccessful organizations. However, when P&G or another company decides to restructure, what determines whether a particular structure will prove successful? As you read the following sections, consider what issues the managers at P&G needed to take into account before announcing its major restructuring program.

The open systems view of organizations, described in Chapter 13, emphasizes that organizations must manage their dependence on the environment. Thus, the strategies an organization uses to manage and adapt to its environment are reflected in the structure of the organization. As we will see, besides the environment and technology, the organization's life cycle is important in determining its structure.

THE INTERNAL ENVIRONMENT

An organization's internal or task environment has a major impact on the kind of interdependencies it must coordinate. The internal or task environment consists of any factors managers define as relevant to organizational decision making. This environment can be subdivided into three components: the organization's human resources, its functional and staff units, and its organizational levels. Figure 14-6 provides a list of the characteristics of the internal environment. It is unlikely that any one organization would have to address all these issues; however, the list highlights the elements managers should consider.

THE EXTERNAL ENVIRONMENT

After the internal environment has been specified, the external environment must be analyzed. Typically, external environments are categorized into four groups along two dimensions: the simple–complex dimension and the stable–dynamic dimension. The simple–complex dimension focuses on the number of environments in which the organization or its units must function. A

---

30. Dess, et al., The new corporate architecture.

| ■ **FIGURE 14-6** | **Characteristics of an Organization's Internal Environment** |

An organization's internal (or task) environment directly affects the interdependencies that the organization must coordinate. Included in the internal environment are the organization's personnel, its functional and staff units, and its organizational levels.

Human Resources

Educational and technological background and skills of employees
Employees' commitment to the organization's goals and objectives
Previous technological and managerial skills
Level of job-relevant and interpersonal skills
Individual commitment to attaining organizational goals
Interpersonal behavior styles
Availability of labor for the organization
Selection and socialization process of employees

Functional and Staff Units

Technological characteristics of organizational units
Interdependence of units in carrying out their objectives
Amount of conflict and interdependence among employees
Intra-unit conflict

Organizational Levels

Organizational goals and objectives
Process of inspiring individuals and groups to attain organizational goals
Mechanisms the organization uses to direct its employees' efforts
Nature of organization's product or service

Source: Duncan, R. (1979). What is the right organizational structure? *Organizational Dynamics*, 59–80.

lower-level manufacturing group, for example, might be dependent on only its suppliers for raw materials and on the market for sales. By contrast, a strategic planning unit might face a more complex environment. For a product to be successfully produced, the planning unit might have to gather inputs from many different departments in the organization; similarly, many different organizational subunits may consume its output (the strategic plan).

The stable–dynamic dimension reflects the amount of change in environmental factors that the organization must face. A stable environment is one in which there is little uncertainty. Figure 14-7 illustrates the classification of organizational environments based on these two dimensions.

Lisa Friedman and Herman Gyr developed a series of questions that are useful in assessing an organization's internal and external environments[31]:

1 Who are your clients and customers, and what is the nature of your relationship with them? Are customers' or clients' needs and preferences clear?
2 Who are your suppliers, and what is the nature of your relationship with them?
3 How does changing technology affect your enterprise?
4 How do government regulations affect your enterprise?

31. Friedman, L., & Gyr, H. (1998). *The dynamic enterprise: Tools for turning chaos into strategy and strategy into action*. San Francisco: Jossey-Bass, p. 61.

Classification of Organizational Environments ■ FIGURE 14-7

In determining the best structure for an organization, managers need to take into account the stability and complexity of their external environment. Stable environments tend to give rise to bureaucracies, whereas complexity tends to give rise to more decentralized structures.

	Stable	**Dynamic**
Complex	Decentralized Bureaucratic (standardization of skills)	Decentralized Organic (mutual adjustment)
Simple	Centralized Bureaucratic (standardization of work) processes)	Centralized Organic (direct supervision)

Source: Perrow, C. (1970). *Organizational analysis.* New York: Wadsworth.

5 What economic, political, environmental, and social trends are having a significant impact on your enterprise?
6 What new opportunities exist in your environment?
7 What new threats exist in your environment?
8 What is the state of your industry, and how are you positioned within it?

Chapter 13 focuses in greater detail on these environmental issues. The important point here, however, is that before deciding on a structure for an organization, management must do a thorough assessment of the organizational environment. By examining both internal and external environmental influences, an organization can determine where strategic interventions are most needed.[32] Figure 14-8 illustrates the interdependent

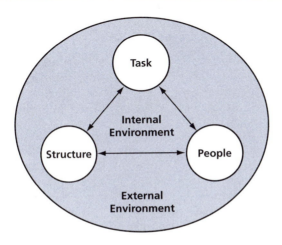

■ FIGURE 14-8

Dynamic Interactions in an Organization

Ideally, an organization's structure should be decided on after assessing both the internal and external environment, as illustrated here.

Source: Friedman & Gyr, *The dynamic enterprise*, p. 37.

32. Friedman & Gyr, *The dynamic enterprise*, p. 38.

relationships between the internal and external environments that exist in most organizations.

TECHNOLOGY

In addition to the environment, management must consider the impact of technology on the functioning and competitiveness of the organization. How demanding are the organization's clients or customers for new products or services? And how quickly do products need to be altered to adapt to changing markets? Organizations with stable structures (e.g., bureaucracies) are often ill suited to coordinate and control the production process when demand is high for new products. An organization with a more adaptive (e.g., organic) structure would be better able to respond efficiently and effectively. Alternatively, if outputs are standardized, customers have few expectations, and product life cycles are long, then more bureaucratic or mechanistic structures will suffice.

Span of control also differs depending on the type of technology the organization depends on. The more complex the technology, the more supervision is needed and thus a smaller span of control is required. However, in organizations that rely on professional employees, the span of control can be larger because professionals who have expert knowledge usually need little close supervision. In addition, as one would expect, the largest span of control can be used in organizations when routine tasks or technologies are in place.

Finally, organizations with routine technologies typically have very clear, standardized performance expectations; their efficiency and output-quantity goals are identifiable and measurable. In firms with nonroutine technologies, the goals are not nearly so obvious. Rather than aim for efficiency and quantity, such firms are more concerned with the reliability and quality of their products.

From this discussion, it's possible to make some predictions about which organizational structures are best suited to businesses with various forms of technology. Machine bureaucracies, for example, are a good fit only for organizations with routine technologies. Likewise, organic structures are most appropriate for companies with innovative technologies.

THE ORGANIZATIONAL LIFE CYCLE

In the previous sections, we focused primarily on organizational structure and its relationship to factors external to the organization: the environment and technology. Now we turn our attention to the relationship between an organization's structure and its life cycle. In the following discussion, we consider the relationship of structure to an organization's age and size.

AGE. As organizations age, they go through predictable life cycles, and their structures are determined in part by the particular stage of development the organization has reached.[33] During each stage in the **organizational life cycle,** the structure, leadership style, and administrative systems follow a predictable pattern of evolution. Friedman and Gyr's research shows that organizations evolve through four phases or cycles.[34]

33. Kimberly, J. R., & Miles, R. H. (1980). *The organizational life cycle.* San Francisco: Jossey-Bass.
34. Friedman & Gyr, *The dynamic enterprise*, pp. 165–183.

- **Exploring stage.** When an organization comes into existence, the primary concern of the founders is to create the product or service and to survive as an organization. There is little formal control in the **exploring stage;** rules change often, and there are few guidelines for handling problems. The structure of the organization is often informal and loose; people create it as they develop. The working hours are long, and the focus is entirely on developing and marketing the product or service.
- **Systematizing stage.** The **systematizing stage** is the adolescence of an organization. Typically, the primary concern at this stage is the need to establish structures, accountabilities, clear roles, and procedures. Employees become increasingly secure as they learn about their responsibilities. Formal relationship roles start to emerge, and the organization begins to maintain efficient routines.
- **Venturing stage.** Organizations that require innovative thinking and creativity to compete in the marketplace eventually need to give their employees greater freedom and responsibility. If this is going to happen, it usually takes place during the **venturing stage.** As employees are given some freedom, the organization redefines itself not by its hierarchies but by its results. Rigid systems gradually are replaced by empowerment. Self-managed and cross-functional teams may be introduced, leading to and reflecting management's acknowledgment that employees are valued for their unique contributions, suggestions, and diversity.
- **Integrating stage.** As the organization matures, it enters the final phase of the cycle. During the **integrating stage** attention is redirected from day-to-day work to sharing corporate visions. The organization offers meaningful work to its employees, and strategic intents and long-term objectives are shared with workers. In turn, employees internalize these goals and apply their skills and creativity to achieve the desired results.

  It is in this stage that organizations typically realize the need to establish connections with their external environments and supporting communities. These relationships may take the company full circle—back to the exploring stage—as it once again defines its purposes and visions.

In general, the older an organization, the more formal its structure is likely to be. Further, as tasks are better understood and complications become more predictable, rules and procedures become more firmly entrenched. As highlighted in the opening vignette, P&G's heavy reliance on traditional approaches to doing business prevented the company from competing effectively.

Not only does the age of an organization seem to be related to its level of formalization, but when the particular industry was founded seems to have a big impact on its structure. In fact, according to one researcher, an inverse relationship appears to exist between the age of an industry and its use of professionals in staff positions and of job specialization.[35]

SIZE.   The size of an organization can be measured in a variety of ways—by its sales figures, its capital investment, its budget, or the number of employees. For the purposes of our discussion, we will use the number of employees as the measure of size.

---

35. Stinchcombe, A. L. (1965). *Handbook of organizations.* Chicago: Rand McNally.

The growth of an organization is often accompanied by an increase in the number of workers. As a result, a manager's span of control is likely to increase with the increase in the need for supervision. Similarly, as the organization becomes larger, it is likely to become more formalized. More tasks need to be broken down for the numerous employees, and over time these tasks become more predictable. The more predictable the task, the more it can be controlled and coordinated through rules, policies, and procedures.

A number of other characteristics are associated with an increase in the size of an organization. In general, they are as follows:

1 More management levels
2 More jobs and departments
3 Increased specialization of skills and functions
4 More formalization
5 More decentralization
6 Smaller percentage of top administrators
7 Larger percentage of technical, professional, clerical, and administrative support staff
8 More written communication and documentation.

There's been a lot of discussion recently about small startup companies and large companies that have downsized, but the truth is that we live in the age of multinational mega-giants. A glance at the headlines provides countless examples: Compaq buys Digital, Wordcom buys MCI, Citibank merges with Travelers, Daimler-Benz acquires Chrysler, and TimeWarner merges with AOL.[36] Obviously, not all companies are lightening their loads.

One of the problems is that, as an organization's structure and complexity increase, so too do the chances for inefficient management and production. This brings us to a critical question: Are large or small corporations more efficient? "TECHNOLOGY FOCUS ON: Organizational Size" explores this issue.

So, how does the management of an organization determine the optimal size for a company? It depends on the nature of the organization.[37] Larger operations do have advantages: capital formation, volume purchasing, funding for research and development, and centralized expertise in engineering, marketing, and accounting. Size is especially important in capital-intensive fields and those that require global operations or brand-name recognition.[38]

But, as we've already seen, more employees can also mean more problems: frequent overextending of capabilities and an inability to adapt to changes. For these reasons, smaller organizations may fare better in evolving environments—especially those undergoing technological changes. As organizations mushroom to more than 1,000 employees, they become very difficult to manage. Often they subdivide into smaller companies as a solution.[39]

36. Malone T. W., & Laubacher, R. J. (1998, September/October). Are big companies becoming obsolete? The dawn of the e-lance economy. *Harvard Business Review*, 145–152.
37. Flamholtz & Randle, *Changing the game*, pp. 181–182.
38. Lawler, *From the ground up*, pp. 90–93.
39. Flamholtz & Randle, *Changing the game*, p. 181.

TECHNOLOGY FOCUS ON ORGANIZATIONAL SIZE

ARE BIG COMPANIES BECOMING OBSOLETE?

In October 1991 Linus Torvalds, a 21-year-old computer science student, made available on the Internet a kernel of a computer operating system he had written. Called Linux, it was a rudimentary version of another operating system called UNIX, which was ubiquitous at the time. Torvalds encouraged other programmers to download his software—for free—and to use it, test it, and modify it as they saw fit. A few took him up on the offer. They fixed bugs, tinkered with the original code, and added new features. Some posted their work on the Internet.

As the Linux kernel grew, it attracted the attention of more and more programmers, who contributed their own ideas and improvements. The Linux community grew steadily, soon coming to encompass thousands of people around the world, all sharing their work freely with one another. Within 3 years, this loose, informal group, working without managers and connected mainly through the Internet, had turned Linux into one of the best versions of UNIX ever created.

Imagine, now, how such a project would have been organized at a company like Microsoft or IBM. Decisions and funds would have been filtered through layers of managers. Formal teams of programmers, quality assurance testers, and technical writers would have been established and assigned tasks. Customer surveys and focus groups would have been conducted, their findings documented in thick reports. There would have been budgets, milestones, deadlines, status meetings, performance reviews, and approvals. There would have been turf wars, burnouts, overruns, and delays. The project would have cost an enormous amount of money, taken longer to complete, and quite possibly produced a less valuable system than Linux.

For many executives, the development of Linux is most easily understood (and most easily dismissed) as an arcane story of hackers and cyberspace that bears little relevance to the serious world of big business. This interpretation, although understandable, is shortsighted. What the Linux story really shows is the power of a new technology—in this case, electronic networks—to fundamentally change the way work is done. The Linux community, a temporary, self-managed gathering of diverse individuals engaged in a common task, is a model for a new kind of business organization that could form the basis for a new kind of economy.

Technological innovation is certainly leading to the devolution of large, permanent corporations into flexible, temporary networks of individuals. No one can yet say exactly how important or widespread this new form of business organization will become, but judging from current signs, it is not inconceivable that it could define work structures in the 21st century. If it does, business and society will be changed forever.

Source: Excerpted from Malone, T., & Laubacher, R. J. (1998). Are big companies becoming obsolete? The dawn of the e-lance economy. *Harvard Business Review, 76*(5), 145–152.

These smaller companies then form alliances and partnerships with still other organizations to obtain valuable resources.

STRATEGY

One cannot conclude a section on the design of organizational structure without examining the impact of corporate strategy. An organization is effective only when it has a well-developed business strategy. Only then can it execute the kinds of behavior necessary to deal effectively with the various components in its business environment. Thus, an organization's structure should reflect the business's strategic plans. "FOCUS ON: Strategy" offers some lessons to help organizations prosper.

FOCUS ON STRATEGY

STRATEGIC IMPERATIVES FOR THE 21ST CENTURY.   With the turn of the century, we are witnessing profound transformations in business organizations. In particular, high-profile mergers and acquisitions have provided a constant flow of front-page news. But beyond the headlines lies a more subtle story, one with greater long-term significance than the acquisitive appetites of auto makers and telecom giants. Heading into the new century, the most important business development is the pursuit of competitive advantage in an uncertain world through new approaches to organizational design.

We believe that four core lessons of organization design will retain their relevance in the 21st century:

1 **The environment drives the strategic architecture of the enterprise.** An organization's capacity to understand its environment and to make the right kinds of strategic changes at the appropriate point in the cycle will determine its competitive strength.

2 **Strategy drives organizational architecture.** The more closely each component of the organization is aligned with the others—and with the strategy—the more effective

the overall performance. Consequently, effective organizations design patterns of formal and informal structures and processes best suited to their strategic objectives.

3 **The relationship between strategy and organization design is reciprocal.** How an enterprise is organized will influence its focus and time horizons, either encouraging or restricting the ability of its people to develop creative strategies.

4 **The basic dilemma of organizational design remains unchanged.** How do we design and manage both differentiation and integration? How do we group people, processes, and operating units in ways appropriate to their unique competitive environments and strategic requirements, while maintaining their link to the larger organization? How do we encourage both divergence and cohesion?

Only through aligning strategy with design can organizations reach their true potential.

Source: Excerpted from Nadler, D. A., & Tushman, M. L. (1999). The organization of the future: Strategic imperatives for the 21st century. *Organizational Dynamics, 28*(1), 45–60.

SYMPTOMS OF DESIGN DEFICIENCIES

Obviously, not all organizations neatly fit the various patterns we've outlined in this chapter. In this section, we examine the organizational conflicts that can arise when there is a mismatch between an organization and its structure.

ORGANIZATIONAL CONFLICTS

Much of what we described in Chapter 5 concerning individual conflict also applies to conflict at the organizational level. In general, organizational conflict occurs because there is poor management of the division and coordination of tasks among interdependent units. Conflicts can arise because of problems in task clarity (the degree to which daily task requirements are known), task complexity (the number of elements to be considered when completing the task), the rapidity of technological change, feedback cycles (how quickly a manager knows the results of a decision), and the goals of the organization.[40] Thus, the more interdependence is required to complete tasks, the greater the potential for organizational conflict.

While interdependence alone may be sufficient to produce some organizational conflict, the way the members of the organization interact can exacerbate its level. In other words, having appropriate organizational structures in place is a way to moderate conflict. As we examine the following prescriptions for managing conflict, we will see a common thread—the need to reduce the interdependencies among organizational units.

BUREAUCRATIC AUTHORITY. Bureaucratic authority is based on the assumption that the members of an organization accept the right of top management to invoke rules, regulations, and procedures to structure how groups and individuals interact. Typically, issues over which there is conflict are passed on to the next higher authority level for adjudication.

LIMITED INTERACTION. When a bureaucracy gets overloaded with demands to resolve conflicts, it is sometimes a good idea to limit the interactions among conflicting groups. Such interactions often involve competition, which can prevent the participants from focusing on common goals. It is sometimes useful to give the groups a superordinate goal that requires them to coordinate their activities. This strategy works best when the rules and procedures necessary to complete the task or meet the goal are well known and understood.

INTEGRATING DEVICES. The strategies mentioned so far focus on conflict that is only temporary. What happens when the interdependence and uncertainty inherent in performing organizational tasks are so great that permanent conflict is unavoidable? In this case, the organization may need to implement more formal conflict-management strategies. Among the options are liaisons, integrators, task forces, and project teams. The goal of such **integrating devices** is to enhance communication across groups while maintaining an appropriate level of interaction.

Liaisons are boundary spanners who facilitate coordination and communication between interdependent organizational units (e.g., production and sales departments). Liaisons typically are located in one department or organizational unit but are responsible for working with other units.

The more different organizational units are in structure, goals, and orientation, the greater the opportunity for conflict. When coordination of organizational units becomes this complex, an organization may choose to have an integrator. An integrator manages (i.e., coordinates and moderates) the relationships among diverse units. To perform this role effectively, the individual needs a wide set of contacts within various units; some understanding of each unit's goals, orientations, and organization; the ability to talk the language of each unit; the ability to trust the members of the units; some expertise that members of the units respect; and skills in conflict management and resolution.[41]

Coordination may also be enhanced by the use of task forces. A task force consists of a group of people brought together to accomplish a specific assignment. Typically, task forces are disbanded when they complete their

40. Brett, J. M. (1984). Managing organizational conflict. *Professional Psychology: Research and Practice, 15,* 664–678.

41. Duncan, *Organizational dynamics,* pp. 59–80.

assignments. Each member of the task force represents the interests of one organizational unit (a department, for instance) and communicates the task force's decisions or recommendations back to that constituency. Task forces are created by upper-level management to solve problems that require horizontal coordination. Thus, they take some of the pressure off the organization's formal structure with respect to conflict management.

When long-term interdepartmental activities demand strong coordination efforts, an organization often forms a project team. A permanent task force, a project team is often composed of midlevel or executive-level members of the organization. Project teams are often referred to as administrative committees or operations review committees.

SUMMARY

This chapter examines the components of an organization that determine its structure, the factors that determine which structure should be put into place, and the problems an organization can face when its structure is not suited to meet the demands placed on it.

Job specialization (how the organization divides its primary task into jobs), departmentalization (how jobs fit together), centralization (the degree to which decision making is delegated), and span of control (how many employees report to a manager) are critical elements of organizational structure. These elements differ depending on how an organization coordinates and controls its employees during the process of creating its product or service.

Typically, organizations are structured in one of three ways. A simple structure is most common in young or small organizations. Employees typically report to one person, usually an entrepreneur who views a formal organizational structure as restrictive. When greater structure is required and tasks are specialized and routine, an organization may become bureaucratic and develop a more elaborate administrative structure.

When an organization must remain flexible, an organic structure is often appropriate. This structure enables the organization to respond quickly to changes in the market, technology, and product mix. Integrating mechanisms such as liaisons, integrators, task forces, project teams, and matrix structures are the hallmarks of an organic structure. Other, newer, organic structures include virtual structures, most commonly used by virtual, technologically driven organizations, and boundaryless organizations, organized around self-managed teams.

Among the factors that affect the structure of an organization are the demands from its internal and external environments, the technology required to produce its product or service, and the organization's life cycle. A machine bureaucracy is more appropriate for an older, larger organization with a routine technology and a predictable, stable environment. An organic structure is best suited for a smaller, younger organization with a turbulent, unpredictable environment and nonroutine technology.

The structure of an organization is not stable; rather, organizations—like people—follow well-ordered life cycles. This life cycle includes an exploring stage, a systematizing stage, a venturing stage, and an integrating stage.

Organizational conflicts are related to deficiencies in organizational design. These problems are likely to occur if there is a poor fit between an organization and its structure—in other words, if the organization cannot meet the environmental demands placed on it or successfully handle the problems associated with its stage in its life cycle.

KEY TERMS

Boundaryless organizations	**Organic structure**
Centralization	**Organizational design**
Decentralization	**Organizational life cycle**
Departmentalization	**Organizational structure**
Exploring stage	**Professional bureaucracy**
Integrating device	**Simple structure**
Integrating stage	**Span of control**
Job specialization	**Systematizing stage**
Machine bureaucracy	**Venturing stage**
Matrix structure	**Virtual structures**

DISCUSSION QUESTIONS

1 How does organizational design differ from organizational structure?

2 If organizations face considerable task interdependence, uncertainty, and a dynamic environment, what structural mechanisms can they use to manage these factors more effectively?

3 In a matrix organization, how does the role of a functional manager differ from that of a project manager?

4 What are the costs and benefits of a machine bureaucracy? an organically structured organization?

5 Why is it important to foster creativity and innovation in older organizations?

6 Why must increased interaction among organizational units be managed?

ON YOUR OWN

Analysis of an Organization's Structure   For this exercise, you should select an organization with which you are familiar. The organization may be your family, church, fraternity or sorority, class, or a firm with which you have been associated throughout a summer job or part-time employment. Answer the following questions about that organization.

Description   Draw the firm's organizational chart, showing lines of authority, influence, and communication.

Diagnosis   Describe and evaluate the organization's departmentalization, span of control, and job specialization.
   Describe and evaluate the coordinating mechanisms.
   Describe and evaluate the internal environment and the technology, age, and size of the organization.
   Is the organizational structure appropriate, given the answers to the questions above?

Prescription   What changes could be made in the organization's structure to enhance its fit *and* its performance?

Source: Gordon, J. R. (1987). *A diagnostic approach to organizational behavior.* Boston: Allyn & Bacon.

CLOSING CASE   CHAPTER 14

THE MANAGER'S MEMO

FROM: Joe E. Gittleman, CEO, Good Foods
TO: Brandy L. Bechina, Senior Vice President,
                 Business Development
RE: E-Commerce Division

With all the technological changes occurring in the retail food business, it has become more and more apparent that Good Foods needs to start an e-commerce division. We're already trailing other companies in this regard. I suspect that our recent loss in market share is a direct result of our not offering this service. Good Foods currently has three operating divisions: dry grocery, refrigerated foods, and frozen foods. Not one of these divisions has a full-time person who's working on e-commerce. Yet our customers and suppliers are demanding this service.

   The new entity that I propose we create will be a business-to-business operating unit. On the one hand, we absolutely need to be able to ensure that we meet the changing needs of our new e-commerce customers. On the other hand, maintaining our more traditional organizational structure, so that we can continue to meet the needs of our long-term, established customers, is as important as ever.

   Brandy, I want you to lead this new e-commerce division. Please send me a business plan that outlines how you will design the organizational structure of this new division. I am particularly concerned about how this division will fit into our current organizational structure. I expect this at your earliest possible convenience.

CASE DISCUSSION QUESTIONS

Assume that you are the Vice President of business development for Good Foods, and respond to the memo from Joe Gittleman, the Chief Executive Officer of Good Foods. How might the company change its structure and design to improve its situation? How should the company transition so as to accommodate e-commerce customers while maintaining its traditional business base (90% will operate in this traditional manner)?

CHAPTER 15

Managing Change

PEACE POPS AND RAINFOREST CRUNCH

The scenario is familiar. A small company becomes astonishingly success-ful. The success leads to growth, and the growth forces the company to change. Soon, what made the company great when it was young and small threatens to disappear.

The company could be any in America or elsewhere. In this case, it's Ben & Jerry's Homemade, Inc., Vermont's super-premium ice-cream maker. Throughout the illustrious history of Ben & Jerry's, the company culture has been described as fun, charitable, and socially responsible. As one example, the Ben & Jerry's Foundation, established in 1985, spends 7.5% of the com-pany's pretax income on a broad spectrum of social issues. The company strives to hire disabled employees, provides free therapy and counseling for employees, takes workers on company outings, and even brings in massage therapists during high-stress production periods. More to the point, the company's emphasis on meeting the needs of families and strong commit-ment to social causes are not just add-ons; they are at the core of the Ben & Jerry's corporate mission.

Yet these core characteristics of the Ben & Jerry's culture regularly come under attack. When the company was small, everyone knew everyone, everyone bought into the mission, and Ben & Jerry's really did feel like fam-ily. With rapid growth in the early 1990s, challenges in the form of newly created departments, companywide memos, and even MBAs in suits and ties threatened the company's strong culture. Amid such turbulent changes, Ben & Jerry's fought hard to maintain the characteristics for which it had gained so much attention, leading to wide acclaim for human resources programs instituted to support the growing organization.

Source: Adapted from Branch, S., & Beck, E. (2000, April 13). For Unilever, it's sweetness and light. *Wall Street Journal,* p. B1; and 1992 Optimas Awards (1992, January). *Personnel Journal, 71,* 51–61.

Not surprisingly, given its strong market presence and profitability, Ben & Jerry's has often been courted as a target for acquisition. Finally, in April 2000, Unilever, maker of Lipton tea, Wishbone salad dressing, and Ragu pasta sauce, succeeded in acquiring the famous ice-cream maker. Facing another cycle of change, founders Ben Cohen and Jerry Greenfield have insisted that the "heart and soul" of the company will be preserved. Summing up his philosophy, Jerry said, "The idea, I think, is to maintain the values of your culture, and yet bring it along with you." To this end, despite the fact that Ben & Jerry's has undergone significant change, you can count on the company to fight to protect its "social mission and brand integrity."

INTRODUCTION

Even when an organization gets off to a good, even spectacular, start, no one can guarantee that it will remain successful. Management techniques that have worked in the past may not work in the future. Organizations exist in changing, uncertain business and social environments that constantly challenge managers. As the story of Ben & Jerry's demonstrates, being able to adapt to both internal and external changes is not only critical to an organization's success but often necessary for its very survival. Success in business is a journey—a continuing battle to adapt—not a destination. This is true both of companies that are relatively small, like Ben & Jerry's, and of large multinational organizations, like Unilever.

This chapter examines ways organizations meet the demands for change. It begins with a discussion of the forces that clash in organizations—forces for change and sources of resistance. It then describes the characteristics of an organization that is ready for change. Next, a four-stage model of change is presented, followed by a discussion of organizational development as an alternative approach to managing the change process. The chapter concludes with a discussion of an important example of a change occurring in many American businesses—corporate reorganization.

THE DYNAMICS OF CHANGE

Organizations, like people, are creatures of **habit;** they do things the same way, over and over again, in large part because these ways are familiar and make people feel comfortable. As discussed in Chapter 6, habits in the form of group rules or norms for behavior often represent accumulated organizational experience and learning. It should not be surprising, then, that not everyone embraces change with equal enthusiasm.

In physical terms, the equivalent of habit is inertia. **Inertia** is the tendency of an object to continue in the same direction with the same velocity or intensity unless some force for change influences its behavior. A billiard ball on a pool table, for instance, will continue in the same direction until it encounters another object—another ball, a side rail, a human hand. According to the laws of physics, the object will always alter its direction when it encounters a force for change. This is an important difference between people and physical objects: People are not passive objects. When people encounter a force for change, they do not have to alter their direction; they can choose whether to do so. An acquisition, such as Unilever's acquisition of Ben &

Jerry's, is an example of a momentous change that forces everyone in the new company to decide whether to embrace the culture and decisions of the acquiring company or to wait for changes to be forced through the organization. The overarching challenge for top executives is how to manage the delicate tension between the forces for change and the sources of resistance. When these tensions are managed correctly, the outcome should be not only a financially profitable organization but one whose organizational behavior is healthy.

FORCES FOR CHANGE

The first step in managing change is recognizing the forces for change—both internal and external.

INTERNAL FORCES. Internal forces for change are signals from inside an organization that change is necessary. Sometimes the signals are direct, such as a strike, which sends a clear message that employees are dissatisfied. The strike leads to negotiations that remedy major problems concerning compensation arrangements or working conditions. At other times, the signals may be more subtle. High levels of absenteeism or turnover may indicate smoldering dissatisfaction among the workforce. In this case, the challenge for management is to anticipate when the numbers are spiraling out of control so that more serious—even catastrophic—problems (such as a walkout, a work slowdown, or wholesale workforce desertion) can be avoided.

Internal problems may also be reflected indirectly. Tasks that don't get done on time, messages that do not get received or returned, workers who don't seem to understand their roles, meetings that go on and on and on without resolution—all of these are indirect indications that an organization's management habits are not working and need to be overhauled.

Internal forces for change often reflect an organization's failure to accomplish its mission. For all organizations, survival is the primary objective. Problems such as excessive turnover and dwindling market share threaten an organization's survival, forcing it to respond. For many organizations, however, monetary survival is only one aspect of the corporate mission. At Ben & Jerry's, for example, the company's effectiveness is also measured by how well it fulfills its social responsibilities. Whatever an organization's goals, success will be measured by attainment of those goals—or their abandonment in the face of external pressures.

EXTERNAL FORCES. A myriad of forces in our environment can lead to change. This section focuses on what are currently, and to a great extent historically, have been the major catalysts for change in organizations.

Social Forces. We have discussed in previous chapters many of the social forces exerting pressure for change on organizations. These include the changing demographics of America's workers (e.g., aging workers, Generation Xers and Ys), and the change in the actual nature of work (e.g., telecommuting, flexible work arrangements). Further changes are reflected in recent statistics which suggest that in the next 3 years, organizations will lose 50% of their intellectual capital as workers retire[1] and that the average tenure of

---

1. Garcia, R. (2000, June 15). *Developing a high performance work force.* Paper presented at the annual meeting of the Human Resource Management Association of Chicago (HRMAC).

the managerial workforce has shifted from 15 years to 30 months.[2] What do these social changes mean for U.S. corporations? As discussed earlier, they mean that managers will need to rethink recruiting strategies, selection criteria, and even the way managers design jobs.

Political Forces. Political forces also exert tremendous effects on the behavior of organizations. For example, the affirmative action policies of the 1970s and the comparable worth debates of the 1980s influenced organizations' internal management habits. Comparable worth in particular led many organizations to reexamine their compensation schemes, giving rise to an entire generation of merit-based compensation plans. Other political trends, such as movements to encourage or discourage mergers and acquisitions or the recent antitrust decisions involving Microsoft, more directly affect the climate in which organizations exist by regulating their behavior. Beyond the United States, the sweeping political changes in Eastern Europe and the shift toward privatization are having profound effects on multinational organizations as they make global business decisions.[3]

Technology. Rapid advances in technology constitute yet another external force for major change in organizations. The Industrial Revolution forever changed the face of manufacturing. Following the Industrial Revolution were a variety of smaller revolts, including the inventions of the concept of interchangeable parts and of the modern assembly line. More recently, advances in technology such as wireless communications and computer networks have made communication and transportation faster and better.[4] Increasingly, information networks are connecting people around the world, leading to increased collaboration and information sharing and, ultimately, increased productivity and efficiency. Advanced technologies, such as the Internet, are affecting all organizations—regardless of their size or the nature of their business—as illustrated in the "TECHNOLOGY FOCUS ON: External Forces."

Market Factors. Market factors—both local and global—also lead to change in organizations. A decreasing market share should be a signal to a company that changes are needed. Pressure from new competitors may mean that a company has to slash its prices or institute internal cost-savings programs to maintain profit margins. Although the estimates vary, it's suggested that 70% to 85% of the U.S. economy is affected by international competition. Businesses now work and interact with more consumers and suppliers who have access to global markets and infinite amounts of information via the Internet. The introduction of new products and changes in the tastes and preferences of consumers demands a response from companies, as do changes in and influences on the behaviors of suppliers. All these changes affect such decisions as how businesses reach their customers and sell their products.

SOURCES OF RESISTANCE TO CHANGE

Even with all these forces pushing organizations to shift direction, some individuals and organizations resist the need to change, as illustrated in

---

2. Fergusen, C. (2000, April). *The next generation of HR capabilities.* Paper presented at the meeting of the International Personnel Association, St. Petersburg, FL.

3. Kotter, J. P. (1996). *Leading change.* Boston: Harvard Business School Press, p. 19.

4. Kotter, *Leading change,* p. 19.

TECHNOLOGY FOCUS ON
EXTERNAL FORCES

THE IMPACT OF TECHNOLOGY ON EDUCATION.   The gothic spires of Virginia Tech tower over the expansive drill fields in the heart of campus, a remnant of the university's military-school past. Indeed in just about every respect, Virginia Tech's picturesque campus embodies the solemn, timeless look of academia, imbuing all who visit with a powerful sense of place—that is, until they get to math class.

In an old department store building in a strip mall near campus, Virginia Tech teaches large portions of its undergraduate math curriculum electronically, via CD-ROM and Web browser. Hundreds of networked computers fill the former retail space, which is open to students 24 hours per day, 7 days per week, allowing them to work at their own pace. Some courses simply offer supplementary materials online; in others, lectures, quizzes, and everything else is done electronically.

As the Virginia Tech experience shows, from community colleges to the elite schools of the Ivy League, changes in technology and society are forcing a deep, fundamental reevaluation of nearly every aspect of higher education.

Change is accelerated by a new generation of private companies aiming to cash in. In the past 2 years, prestigious universities such as Johns Hopkins, Columbia, and Georgetown have teamed up with Caliber Learning Networks of Baltimore, Chicago's Unext.com, and other companies to offer online courses. The for-profit University of Phoenix system currently enrolls 61,000 adult students in a mix of distance courses and traditional classes held in office buildings and other rented spaces across the country.

The changes taking place in America's Ivory Towers are forcing the academic world to confront vexing questions. If students can work at their own pace and direction, what constitutes a course? When students can take a course anywhere in the world online or using a CD-ROM, what happens to the idea of a campus? And how many elements of traditional campus life—social interaction, classroom dynamics, relationships between students and teachers—can be stripped away without diminishing the value of the learning?

At the very least, technological and social change are inspiring educators to consider multiple definitions of higher education. "Is higher education simply a matter of acquiring a narrow skill set? If so, distance learning might work just as well as traditional methods," said Steven Bossert, dean of Syracuse University's School of Education. "But if you see it as a broader process of social participation and emotional maturation, those who attend traditional residential colleges will have a distinct advantage."

At bottom, some educators say, the most important technology-related question here is a fairly simple one: Does the use of technology help educators to teach and students to learn? "The only thing that matters about technology is how well it does the job of bringing teaching and learning together," says Mr. Christopher Lucas, Professor of Higher Education at the University of Arkansas. "After all, it's just a tool."

Source: Excerpted from Dreazen, Y. J. (1999, December 31). Student, teach thyself: The classroom of the future won't have much in common with today's version; For one thing, there probably won't be a classroom. *Wall Street Journal Millennium (A Special Report): Politics & Society,* p. R46.

Figure 15-1. For these individuals and organizations, the signals to change are never translated into appropriate responses or actions. Sometimes the signals are simply ignored. Sometimes top management heeds the signals and plans appropriate actions, but the actions are never implemented—at least not in the way they were planned. Habits, resource limitations, threats to power and influence, fear of the unknown, and defensive perceptions are all examples of sources of resistance.

HABIT.   Despite the proliferation of dot-com enterprises, many people still do not shop for either services or products online. Are they unaware of the advantages—the efficiency—of shopping via the Internet? Possibly, but more likely they are simply more comfortable making familiar trips to the grocery

■ **FIGURE 15-1**

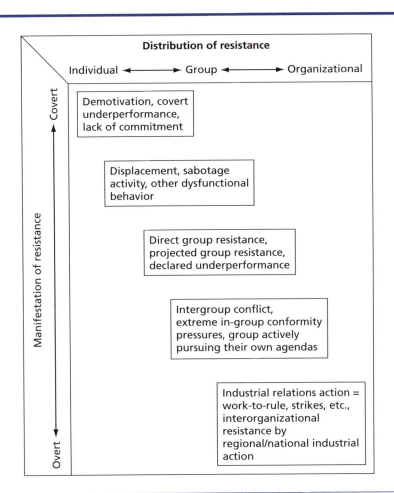

Manifestations of
Resistance to Change

Source: King, N., & Anderson, N. (1995). *Innovation and change in organizations.* London: Routledge, p. 171.

store, shopping mall, and drugstore. They have in fact developed a habit of
doing so—in other words, they've developed inertia. This tendency for objects
to maintain their current trajectory is a primary cause of resistance to change.

In many cases, inertial resistance to change stems from an individual's
realization that changing will entail short-term costs. Figure 15-2 shows
three typical patterns of performance when a change occurs. Pattern A is
what top management hopes for. The change occurs at Time 0. There is no
immediate decrease in performance, and, over time, performance gradually
increases until it reaches a stable higher level.

Patterns B and C illustrate what usually happens. Pattern B, a classic bell
curve, represents the notion that purely economic views of motivation may not
take into account the complexities that drive workers' behavior. Top managers
hear or read about something that they think is a great idea—self-managed
teams, for instance; the idea is implemented, and workforce performance improves immediately. Unfortunately, the improvement occurs not because the
idea is a good one but rather because the idea is a new one and people are enthusiastic about trying something new. When the enthusiasm disappears, so
do the improvements in performance.

■ **FIGURE 15-2** | **Three Patterns of Change**

Changes in organizations can affect their performance in many ways. Most managers hope that the changes (A) will immediately and permanently improve the organization's functioning. In some cases, changes (B) cause immediate improvements that unfortunately do not last. Most of the time, though, changes (C) result in short-term losses that are eventually recouped when the changes are fully institutionalized.

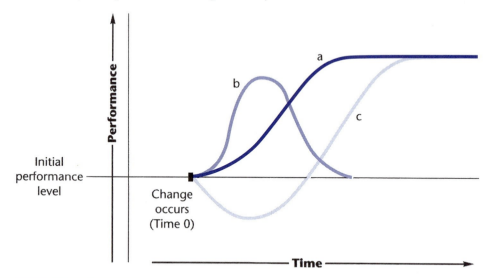

Source: Gibson, J. R., Ivancevich, J. M., & Donnelly, J. H., Jr. (1988). *Organizations* (6th ed.). Plano, TX: Business Publications.

Pattern C illustrates a short-term loss from a change that has long-term value. For example, after installing a new computer system, an organization often needs to shut down its older system for some period of time. As dependent as many organizations have become on technology, this shutdown can mean loss of sales, delayed services, and much more—all potentially leading to lost revenue. In such cases, some short-term costs have to be absorbed to derive the long-term benefits. Knowing ahead of time that many of these costs are unavoidable can create a substantial psychological barrier to change. Any lost revenues and lost goodwill likely to occur as a result of the change should be recouped eventually. But those short-term costs can be painful because old habits are probably familiar, comfortable, and workable, even if not spectacularly efficient and up-to-date.

RESOURCE LIMITATIONS. Sometimes organizations avoid making changes because the costs are prohibitively high. From a manager's perspective, probable short-term losses (Pattern C change) may represent more than just a psychological roadblock. Going back to a previous example, let's say that the manager responsible for the computer system upgrade had no one to answer to for that short-term loss. What if instead, that loss were going to show up as red ink on a chief executive officer's (CEO's) annual report to the shareholders, or as a quarterly loss on a division manager's performance appraisal? The short-term bad news could cost the CEO or division manager opportunities in the long term—especially if the company or division was successful without the benefit of the changes. In these cases, the inertia can be traced to the manager's short-term need to ensure his survival.

THREATS TO POWER AND INFLUENCE. Changes in organizations often result in the rearrangement of power relationships. In particular, power arising from expertise may be undermined. Consider, for example, the merger of Citicorp and Travelers Property Casualty, the largest corporate merger to that time. Sanford Weill and John Reed, the CEOs of the two companies, were a powerful duet. Both men were giants in their fields, with egos to match, and many observers predicted that their power-sharing agreement was destined to collapse.[5] During the two years they shared the reins, there was extensive turnover in the executive team and obvious discord between the co-CEOs.[6] Finally, the board of directors voted out John Reed; the power struggle in the executive suite had been divisive and had cost the company too much valuable time, money, and human resources.[7]

FEAR OF THE UNKNOWN. The sources of resistance that we have discussed so far all arise from an understanding of the probable consequences of a change in management habits. Some consequences, of course, cannot be foreseen, and the uncertainty that is part of any organizational change presents another source of resistance.

Employment opportunities provide a classic example of an event that often leads to resistance arising from uncertainty. If you are offered a transfer to another part of your company, should you go? Your salary and job assignments, even the housing costs and climate, are all known variables, or can be, before you make your decision. But what about the personalities of your new coworkers? What about the quality of your lifestyle? These are all questions that need to be answered. If your current situation is good or even just okay, is a transfer worth the risk of losing the nice parts of your life? In the terms of Figure 15-2, what if you never recoup those short-term losses?

In the case of organizationwide changes, similar uncertainties arise. Will I still be able to perform well under the new management? Will my ideas still be appreciated even though I'm from the acquired organization? Similar questions were on the minds of many former employees of Ben & Jerry's as they imagined their lives after the company's takeover by Unilever.

DEFENSIVE PERCEPTION. Managers who understand their own resistance to change may correctly perceive when change is necessary and act on that need despite their reservations or trepidations. The fear is that because a manager has a personal bias, he or she will be unable to perceive that change is necessary.

In Chapter 2 we noted that perception is a constructive process, albeit one that can be biased. Managers who sense trouble on the horizon if a particular change occurs may be less likely to perceive that a change is necessary. The signals may be there; however, the managers may be unwilling to see them or interpret them for what they are. A supervisor who fears a short-term loss in productivity may fight tooth and nail against the introduction of new machinery, if for no other reason than to be absolved of personal responsibility for the outcome.

---

5. Gasparino, C., & Beckett, P. (2000, April 14). Alone at the top: How John Reed lost the reins of Citigroup to his co-chairman. *Wall Street Journal*, p. A1.

6. Loomis, C. (2000). First: The Citigroup saga—down with duets—Weill goes solo. *Fortune Magazine, 141*(10), 52.

7. Sellers, P. (2000). First: CEO deathmatch! Behind the shootout at Citigroup. *Fortune Magazine, 141*(6), 27–28, 32.

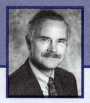

RESEARCH IN ACTION
INTERNATIONAL JOINT VENTURES

Randall Schuler, Rutgers University; *Schuler@rci.rutgers.edu*

In their efforts to better serve a major customer, U.S.-based Davidson Instrument Panel sought to locate a plant near the newly built Ford plant in Genk, Belgium. Knowing the costs and benefits of doing this alone, Davidson's management decided to join forces with England's Marley Corporation. Together, they created an international joint venture to be located in Born, The Netherlands, near Genk. Our international study was of this joint venture and the two companies, Davidson and Marley, that created the joint venture, aptly named Davidson-Marley BV. Our study was done in four parts.

In the first two parts, we interviewed all the key stakeholders in the joint venture. We interviewed the managers about their perceptions of the entire joint venture, including asking questions about such things as their goals and objectives and their perceptions of the other company. Managers in England and in the United States were interviewed separately. We then wrote up reports so that each manager could read what the others said. In effect, our writing and reporting revealed to each of the companies what the other one was thinking. This helped each set of managers develop trust and under-

standing of the other. It also alerted them to what they needed to be aware of as they formed the joint venture, Davidson-Marley BV, and as they made such important decisions as *who* should be selected as the managing director and the human resource director and *how* these decisions should be made.

In the second part of our study, we investigated the joint venture itself. We interviewed the managing directors on two different occasions. During this time we learned that via our previous research both parents of the joint venture (Davidson and Marley) had learned important lessons from each other that affected the success of Davidson-Marley BV. The directors indicated that Davidson and Marley had learned to respect the importance of the local customs and traditions of the area in Born. This resulted in many changes, but central was the recruitment and selection of directors who were intimately familiar with the language, customs, politics, and regulations of the Born area. To us, this highlighted the importance of "thinking globally and acting locally." In addition, we learned how sound research can positively influence the outcome of a joint venture.

Another way in which individuals and organizations react to change is by developing a defensive posture—a reflection of their wish to maintain the status quo. When managers exhibit defensiveness, opportunities to change are likely to be missed.

Resistance can also surface *after* the wheels of change have been put in motion. An organization's workforce may voice resistance by sabotaging the implementation of new plans, perhaps in the hope of changing a management decision. The craftsmen who wrecked the textile mills in the early days of the Industrial Revolution were acting on their fears about the possible consequences of a technological revolution and were hoping to reverse the trend. Managers need to be able to recognize and face the opposition, and then balance their arguments against the need for change.

A MODEL FOR CHANGE IN ORGANIZATIONS

While there are many ways of conceptualizing the process of change in organizations, the model devised by psychologist Kurt Lewin is the best known and provides the simplest framework for understanding the process. Lewin's approach, known as the *force field model*, says that organizations are held in

■ **FIGURE 15-3**

**Four Phases
of Change**

There are four distinct phases to organizational change efforts. During the diagnosis phase, the organization identifies what needs to be changed; unfreezing prepares the organization for the change; during movement, the change actually occurs; and refreezing ensures that the change had its intended effects and no unintended ones.

equilibrium by equal and opposing, driving and resisting, forces. Driving forces might include competitive pressures, new technology, environmental concerns, and innovation from within the organization. Resisting forces could include established customs and practices, union agreements, and the organization's culture.[8] In equilibrium, each set of forces balances the other.

Lewin believed that any organizational change process designed to achieve equilibrium must move through three phases of change: unfreezing, movement, and refreezing.[9] Over the years, researchers have revised Lewin's model in a variety of ways and have identified other phases of the change process.[10] In our discussion, we will consider one additional phase: diagnosis. The relationships among these four phases are depicted in Figure 15-3.

DIAGNOSIS

Realizing that change is needed, or even having systems for meeting the demands of change, is not equivalent to knowing what change is necessary. The forces for change signal the need to alter management habits. The next challenge for management is figuring out what actions to take in response to those signals. **Diagnosis** involves three separate tasks:

1 Identify the problem.
2 Isolate its primary causes.
3 Develop an appropriate and effective solution.

8. King & Anderson, *Innovation and change in organizations*, p. 137.
9. Lewin, K. (1951). *Field theory in social science*. New York: Harper & Row.
10. Lippitt, R., Watson, J., & Westley, B. (1958). *Dynamics of planned change*. New York: Harcourt Brace.

**A Framework
for Diagnosis**

Weisbord's "six-box" organizational model provides a road map for identifying problem areas in an organization. Each box represents one aspect of the organization that may be inhibiting its effective response to environmental forces for change.

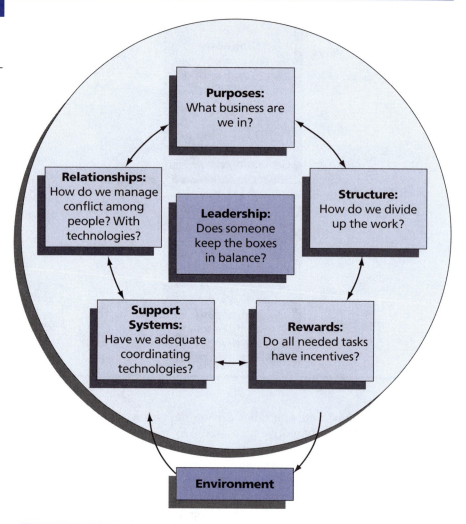

Source: Weisbord, M. R. (1976). Organizational diagnosis: Six places to look for trouble with or without a theory. *Group and Organization Studies, 1,* 430–447; and Burke, W. W. (1987). *Organizational development: A normative view.* Reading, MA: Addison-Wesley.

Figure 15-4 shows one framework for thinking about these tasks and the appropriate responses to the need for change. The framework includes six places to search for problems, their causes, and solutions when a change is needed[11]:

■ **Purpose.** An organization's purpose is what it is supposed to be doing—its charge or mission. Enlarging this mission through vertical or horizontal integration, for instance, is a common way to respond to the need for change.

■ **Structure.** An organization's structure consists of its reporting relationships, which are usually reflected in the organizational chart. These relationships in turn reflect how work is divided up in the organization.

---

11. Weisbord, M. R. (1978). *Organization diagnosis: A workbook of theory and practice.* Reading, MA: Addison-Wesley.

- **Relationships.** Relationships have to do with the ways in which people in an organization get along—the group dynamics. Are there obvious conflicts, and, if so, what are their origins? Are communication channels in place to ensure that workgroups or individuals who need to share information have a way to do so? Are role expectations clear? Are there role conflicts?

- **Rewards.** As noted in Chapter 3, the law of effect suggests that only behaviors that occur can be rewarded. If an organization wants quality, it needs to reward quality; if it wants quantity, it needs to reward quantity. Too often compensation schemes reward one set of behaviors (say, individual achievement) when an altogether different set of behaviors (such as cooperative collaboration) is really desired.

    As suggested in Chapter 3, it's important to remember that the term *rewards* refers to more than just money. Nonmonetary rewards include job satisfaction and feelings of belonging or accomplishment on the job.

- **Support systems.** The elements in an organization that assist personnel in accomplishing their work tasks effectively are called **support systems.** Examples include the Internet, intranets, videoconferencing, and e-mail. Each of these support systems can dramatically help or hinder the efforts of a workforce.

- **Leadership.** Leadership entails coordinating and initiating action. Someone must monitor signals, decide when change is required, and move the organization forward to accomplish the change process effectively. Without adequate leadership, important signals may be missed, poor diagnoses may be made, inappropriate actions may be planned, and appropriate actions may never be implemented.

These six components hardly comprise an exhaustive list of ways to identify where problems are likely to arise or to find solutions to problems in organizations. However, they provide a framework for formulating plans for possible organizational change. There are also several ways to approach the *collection* of information about the organization during the diagnosis phase. These data-collection efforts assist in isolating the causes of problems and developing appropriate and effective solutions.

The strengths and weaknesses of several common information-collection procedures are summarized in Figure 15-5. Interviewing, for instance, provides opportunities to collect rich, probing information. Its value, however, is highly dependent on the interviewer's skills and the awareness and forthrightness of the interviewee. Trustworthy diagnosis generally comes at the cost of combining multiple collection techniques. Once a problem has been diagnosed and a potential solution identified, unfreezing, the real business of change, begins.

UNFREEZING

Unfreezing is the process of getting an organization ready for change. As shown in the model of organizations presented in Chapter 1, uncertainty, complexity, and conflict all present barriers to change efforts. The unfreezing stage is the time when resistance can be broken down and therefore when barriers can be lowered.

Once management has chosen a course of action, it's time for management to share its insights about the problem, its probable causes, and the identified solution with the other members of the organization. This process

■ **FIGURE 15-5**	**A Comparison of Methods of Data Collection**

Each of these four methods of data collection has strengths and weaknesses. Questionnaires, for example, are easy to administer to large numbers of employees, but their predetermined format can bias the information that respondents supply. The best way to collect information is to use some combination of these techniques.

Method	Major Advantages	Potential Problems
Interviews	■ Adaptive—data can be collected on a range of subjects ■ Source of "rich" data ■ Empathic ■ Possible to build rapport	■ Cost ■ Interviewer bias ■ Coding and interpretation difficulties ■ Self-report bias
Questionnaires	■ Responses can be quantified and easily summarized ■ Easy to use with large samples ■ Relatively inexpensive ■ Elicits large volume of data	■ Non-empathic ■ Predetermined questions miss issues ■ Overinterpretation of data ■ Response bias
Observations	■ Data are reported on observed rather than reported behvaior ■ Real time, not retrospective ■ Adaptive	■ Coding and interpretation difficulties ■ Sampling inconsistencies ■ Observer bias and questionable reliability ■ Expense
Unobtrusive measures	■ Nonreactive—no response bias ■ High face validity ■ Easily quantified	■ Access and retrieval difficulties ■ Validity concerns ■ Coding and interpretation difficulties

Source: Nadler, D. A. (1977). *Feedback and organization development: Using data-based methods.* Reading, MA: Addison-Wesley, Table 7.1.

helps employees understand the need for the change and promotes ownership of the problem by the entire workforce. Generating ownership even at the level of rank-and-file workers is critical if the change effort is to go smoothly, without hostility, resentment, or sabotage. Imagine for a moment how the rank-and-file workers at Ben & Jerry's would feel and react to the merger with Unilever if they were adequately prepared by their management for this change. Now imagine how they would react if they were unprepared for the merger.

MOVEMENT

If the foundation for change has been laid effectively during unfreezing, the actual **movement**—implementation of the change plan—should be trivial. In fact, the ease of implementation is generally a good gauge of how well the unfreezing process has broken down potential pockets of resistance. If the process of unfreezing has been handled well, all employees should understand why the change is necessary and their individual roles in the process. However, as is true during other phases of the change process, keeping channels of communication open and active is critical. If implementation of the change plan creates confusion or unforeseen problems, early detection may be critical to the prevention of a groundswell of workforce resistance.

An important decision for management during the movement phase is whether to use **external change agents.** Brought in from outside the organization, these expert consultants are hired specifically to execute a change. Their value lies in their experience and objectivity. Because they have supervised similar changes in other organizations, these specialists have the experience necessary to identify subtle sources of resistance and know the best strategies for dealing with them. Further, because they are not part of the social fabric of the organization, external change agents are more able to respond objectively to forces of resistance.

REFREEZING

After a change has been fully implemented, **refreezing** occurs. This is the process of institutionalization, of making the change into an organizational habit. New systems are monitored to track the consequences of implementing the change, and lots of questions are raised and, one hopes, answered: Have any unforeseen problems developed? Have any members of the organization become disenfranchised or lost power or status? If so, how should these problems be handled? Did the change solve the problem it was intended to address? If not, should something different be tried? The refreezing stage gives management time to reflect on what has occurred and to get the workforce settled into new routines.

AN ALTERNATIVE APPROACH TO CHANGE

The four-phase model of change we have been discussing is a traditional problem-focused approach to managing change in organizations. In contrast, several other, less traditional, approaches aim to make the organization more *behaviorally healthy*. One such approach is organizational development. **Organizational development (OD)** is a planned process of organizationwide change, including implementation of new strategies and structures, aimed at improving the organization's overall effectiveness.[12]

OD differs from traditional approaches to organizational change in several important ways. First, as mentioned above, traditional change efforts are *problem focused*; organizational development efforts are *process focused*. The aim is to teach the employees behaviors that will improve their ability to cope with problems as they arise. Sometimes the goal is to develop individuals' potential. More typically, it's to develop the potential of a group or the organization as a whole. Activities often involve elements of group dynamics, such as interaction patterns that are causing or sustaining problems. The assumption is that in organizations or groups that are behaviorally healthy, problems are anticipated and therefore prevented or quickly resolved.

12. Cummings, T. G., & Worley, C. G. (1997). *Organization development and change* (6th ed.). Cincinnati: South-Western College Publishing, p. 2.

BEHAVIORAL HEALTH

A **behaviorally healthy organization** is sound financially; however, it's also an organization in which patterns of interaction have been established that enable the organization to *remain* sound. Typically, its financial soundness reflects, at least in part, on four other characteristics: the organization has open avenues of communication, is highly adaptable, is innovative, and has established arrangements for succession.

COMMUNICATION. Andy Pearson, the former president of corporate mega-conglomerate Pepsico, noted, "We have 120,000 employees stashed in various places around the world, and I frankly have no idea what the hell they're doing."[13] If you held stock in Pepsico, would you find his comment encouraging? Probably not. Certainly the complexity and uncertainty of organizational life make it difficult for any executive to stay in touch with all levels of a major organization. However, for an organization to remain healthy, people *must* know what's going on. This means that managers have to do a lot more than create the potential for communication. They also have to ensure that communication actually occurs. Subordinates must report to supervisors, supervisors must report to managers, and so on, so that communication is always possible.

Management should never find itself in the position of not knowing what is going on below him. If things are fine, then management needs to be hearing this from subordinates. If things are not fine, then this information should be conveyed through established communication channels. Without active channels of communication, it's impossible for anyone to know what's working and what isn't, or whether there are forces for change in the organization. Research by John Ford and Laurie Ford shows that for intentional change to occur, an organization must have active channels of communication; specifically, managers must engage in conversations with their subordinates and their superiors.[14] By practicing the right types of conversations, managers can create, sustain, and complete the changes that their organizations need.

ADAPTATION. Activating communication channels is a futile exercise if an organization is not prepared to change when the need arises. Organizations must be able to adapt, to alter their plans to fit new constraints, as well as to weather storms on the business horizon. The job-rotation and cross-training arrangements mentioned in Chapter 11 are examples of business schemes that provide management flexibility.

Flexibility can also be achieved by devising multiple ways to accomplish tasks. Many large Japanese firms, for example, hire temporary employees at the first sign that demand for a product is increasing. They therefore avoid having to terminate or lay off employees if the increase proves to be only temporary, as happened in the case discussed in "INTERNATIONAL FOCUS ON: Adaptation."

Finally, problem-solving groups are often an effective means by which companies promote the need for adaptability. Quality circles, for example, meet on a regular basis to address operational issues. When a problem arises, a system to identify solutions is already in place.

13. Waterman, R. H., Jr. (1987). *The renewal factor.* New York: Bantam, p. 71.
14. Ford, J. D., & Ford L. W. (1995). The role of conversations in producing intentional change in organizations. *Academy of Management Review, 20*(3), 541–570.

INTERNATIONAL FOCUS ON ADAPTATION

CHANGING THE RULES. In the years since it opened its doors, the South Africa–based Freeplay Group, which makes self-powered radios and lanterns, has been recognized repeatedly for its commitment to both economic growth and social justice. In 1999 the company logged revenues of $50 million, far higher than the expectations of its business plan, but it also donated 50,000 radios to refugee camps in Kosovo. In addition, Freeplay employs hundreds of South Africans who desperately needed decent jobs or a second chance, including people with disabilities and ex-convicts.

In January 1999 demand for Freeplay's products exploded. To keep up with demand, the company increased its capacity in South Africa and started assembling some of its products in China. But, just as the company was catching up with all the demand, growth slowed—leaving Freeplay with excess inventory. Given that it cost Freeplay $6 more per unit to produce in South Africa than in China, the company opted to cut back in South Africa and to lay off 197 employees.

Freeplay hopes to hire back all the people it let go. But in adapting to one short-term problem, the increase in demand, it failed to anticipate another more serious challenge—preserving the jobs of the South African workers Freeplay had claimed to support.

Source: Dahle, C. (2000, May). The Freeplay Group—Changing the rules? *Fast Company, 34,* 42.

INNOVATION. A healthy organization is one that is constantly changing, preventing crises by instituting new habits before old habits have a chance to become obsolete. Tom Peters, in his book *The Circle of Innovation*, noted that in today's world, where "global competition [is] heating up by the picosecond," organizations have no choice but to be innovative.[15] Recent research by Henrich Greve and Alva Taylor suggests that innovation leads to changes ranging from strategic to operational.[16] Thus, innovations can actually influence organizations to look for other, more innovative ways to compete and maintain healthy positions in the global arena.

Healthy companies have active systems in place for generating new ideas. In some companies, employee-involvement programs (such as those discussed in Chapter 11) are sources of both product and management innovations. In other companies, innovations are evident in such management practices as the incentive system or work-sharing system and in the arrangement of production equipment. Research by Michael Hitt and associates shows that in many industries innovation is critical in determining an organization's value.[17] Other research supports this claim by noting that the market values companies that exhibit rapid technological change.[18] As exemplified by the recent boom in the dot-com industries, shareholders do seem to value companies that have shown that they are innovative. Dot-coms that have been able to anticipate technological innovations have received tremendous support on the stock exchange. One could argue that success may now be

15. Peters, T. (1999). *The circle of innovation.* New York: Vintage, p. xiv.
16. Greve, H. R., & Taylor, A. (2000). Innovations as catalysts for organizational change: Shifts in organizational cognition and search. *Administrative Science Quarterly, 45*(1), 54–80.
17. Hitt, M. A., Hoskisson, R. E., Johnson, R. A., & Moesel, D. D. (1996). The market for corporate control and firm innovation. *Academy of Management Journal, 39,* 1084–1119.
18. Bettis, R. A., & Hitt, M. A. (1995). The new competitive landscape. *Strategic Management Journal, 16* (special issue), 7–19.

much more determined by what an organization can do in the future than by what it has done in the past. While recent drops in the Nasdaq have made some investors cautious, most still agree we now live in the age of knowledge. A behaviorally healthy organization is best able to stimulate innovation and respond effectively to internal and external changes.

SUCCESSION. Just as organizations must plan for the fact that their management habits will eventually be obsolete, so too they must anticipate and plan for **succession** (turnover, retirement, even promotion) among members of the workforce. Unless they are anticipated, personnel changes can bring even the best-laid plans to a screeching halt.

A healthy organization is constantly cultivating replacements for key personnel to ensure that it is never left in the lurch. In some companies, this process is facilitated by means of the kinds of mentor–apprentice arrangements mentioned in Chapter 10 or the task cross-training discussed in Chapter 11. These arrangements accomplish two important components of any succession plan: They expose subordinates to the duties and responsibilities of their supervisors, and they allow supervisors to evaluate subordinates' potential to handle additional responsibilities.

In-house training programs are another means by which companies simultaneously enhance and evaluate employee potential. Arthur Andersen, for example, maintains a training site in St. Charles, Illinois, where it renews and reviews management potential. Other companies, such as IBM, have tuition-sharing and release-time programs to help employees further their education at local colleges and universities. Finally, in response to the changing demographics of the workforce, organizations are increasingly rehiring retirees. Honda Motor Company announced that it will begin such a program in 2003 in an effort to cope with the anticipated decline in the labor force.[19] The state of Maryland introduced a similar program as it struggled to fill 11,000 jobs in its public school system. Those who are rehired will not even lose retirement benefits.[20] Finally, Wells Fargo hires its retirees, nicknamed the "Silver Bullets," for part-time and temporary assignments.[21] If managed successfully, these programs may dramatically increase the flexibility of the workforce by retaining the expertise of the "old hands" while unblocking promotion opportunities for ambitious younger workers.

As you can see, a behaviorally healthy organization can correctly identify the need for change because it has an effective and active communication system and a way to implement change when the need arises. The assumption is that if a problem—anything from a deteriorating market share to an increase in the number of employee grievances—does occur, some aspect of the organization is not functioning effectively. In essence, all problems are seen as process problems. Not surprisingly, then, organizational development interventions are designed specifically to improve one or more aspects of the behavioral health of an organization.

In addition to its focus on behavioral health, organizational development efforts frame change more dynamically than do traditional change efforts. Proponents of the former see an organization as constantly evolving; any

19. Honda to rehire retirees up to age 65. (1999, November 8). *Japan Transportation Scan.*

20. Ferrechio, S. (1999, September 22). State permits schools to rehire retirees without risking pensions. *Washington Times*, p. C2.

21. Blackwood, N. (2000, April 7). Retired give way to rehired. *San Francisco Business Times*, p. 3.

change management undertakes is one small step in a continuous loop. This runs counter to traditional view of change in an organization as a static process in which management identifies a problem and the time horizon for change extends only as far as the resolution of the problem. In the terms of the four-phase model of change, the refreezing phase does not occur in a company pursuing organizational development. The feedback phase is simply the beginning of a new phase of diagnosis.

Finally, in organizations with traditional approaches to change, diagnosis (identification of the problem, probable causes, and potential solutions) is a management activity. In other words, the process favors **"top-down" problem solving.** The rest of the workforce is informed about a change only when unfreezing begins. In strong contrast, organizational development efforts proceed on the assumption that involvement by the entire workforce is essential throughout the change process, especially during diagnosis. The emphasis here is on **"bottom-up" problem solving**—an approach that may be a drastic departure from tradition for some managers but that is clearly in sync with the job design needs and desires of U.S. workers, as discussed in Chapter 11.

Several organizational development techniques are discussed in this book, including team building (Chapter 6) and quality circles (Chapter 11). Both are process-focused efforts. The object of these activities is not to solve particular problems but to create an organization that is behaviorally healthy over the long haul. Both activities address organizational problem solving naturally, by making the organization more communicative, adaptive, and innovative. Similarly, both activities are long term and dynamic. Finally, both team building and quality circles are bottom-up problem-solving processes that foster participation by the entire workforce.

The particular orientation of organizational development will become clearer as we examine two other intervention techniques: survey-guided development and quality-of-work-life programs.

SURVEY-GUIDED DEVELOPMENT

Survey-guided development (or survey feedback) is one of the most widely used organizational development techniques. It has been used in businesses, schools, hospitals, government operations, and the military. The results, however, have been mixed. Nonetheless, evidence suggests that if an organization is going to use only one OD technique, survey-guided development is the technique most likely to produce both process and outcome benefits. This is because the ideas for change come from those who will be living and working with the changes.[22]

Survey-guided development involves the use of questionnaires to construct a picture of an organization's internal functioning and problems. What distinguishes survey-guided development from traditional survey efforts is the amount of involvement it requires from rank-and-file workers. When an organization undertakes a traditional survey effort, rank-and-file workers participate only by filling out the questionnaire. By contrast, with survey-guided development, not only do employees at all levels fill out the survey but they also interpret the results. In some cases, employees even

---

22. Porras, J., & Berg, P. O. (1978). The impact of organizational development. *Academy of Management Review, 3,* 249–266.

participate in identifying the issues that the questionnaire will address. The rationale behind encouraging employee participation is simple: It gives top management three opportunities to solicit employee input—by participating in the design of the survey, by completing the survey, and by interpreting the results.

In its ideal form, survey-guided development is not a one-shot technique but is used regularly (such as annually or semiannually). Used in this way, it offers top management an effective method for tracking the development of organizational processes and problems both regularly and systematically.

Because the intended output is a picture of the workings of the organization, survey-guided development is used primarily as an aid in diagnosis. It's no wonder, then, that research has found that the technique works best when it is combined with other techniques in a broader-scope OD program.[23] However, when the idea for change comes from within the organization (as with survey feedback), unfreezing and promotion of the change are more effective.

QUALITY-OF-WORK-LIFE PROGRAMS

A **quality-of-work-life (QWL) program** is an example of a broader-scope organizational development effort. QWL programs create the foundation for management to be receptive to change and structures that help management recognize the need for change based on workers' demands. Thus, QWL programs are best characterized as systemwide attempts to simultaneously enhance organizational effectiveness (usually defined in terms of productivity) and employee well-being through a commitment to participative organizational decision making. Unlike survey-guided development, QWL does not refer to one particular technique. Rather, QWL programs provide organizations with frameworks for pursuing their organizational development goals through the use of any number of specific OD techniques.

Two OD techniques that are highly recognized are team building and employee wellness programs. The aim of team-building programs is to help workgroups become more effective in accomplishing tasks. In contrast, wellness programs often include employee assistance programs (EAPs) and stress-management programs.

Research shows that having balance in their work and personal lives is the number-one reason employees give for feeling happy on the job, which, again, fosters a behaviorally healthy organization.[24] Recent research also indicates that links exist not only between QWL programs and overall employee satisfaction but between QWL programs and an organization's financial performance—the bottom line.[25] Thus, organizations have numerous incentives to implement QWL programs, which aim to enhance the overall work experience.

Ernst & Young (E&Y) is one organization implementing QWL programs. In the past, E&Y consistently demanded that its employees sacrifice

---

23. Porras & Berg, The impact of organizational development; and Nicholas, J. (1982). The comparative impact of organizational development interventions on hard criteria measures. *Academy of Management Review, 7,* 531–542.

24. Students place high value on work/life issues. (2000, March). *HR Magazine,* 30.

25. Lau, R. S. M., & May, B. E. (1998, October). A win–win paradigm for quality of work life and business performance. *Human Resource Development Quarterly,* 211.

FOCUS ON QUALITY OF WORK LIFE

CHANGING PRIORITIES. The U.S. workforce has changed its priorities. College students and recent graduates now rank balancing work and personal life issues higher than compensation, according to a survey conducted by Jobtrak.com. This is a drastic switch from the 1980s, when job seekers and students consistently listed compensation as the number-one motivator that kept them on a job and happy.

For the survey, more than 2,000 college students and recent graduates responded to this question: Which do you value most in your career decision? Their answers ranked as follows:

■ 42% said balancing work and personal life.
■ 26% said compensation.

■ 23% said advancement potential.
■ 9% said location.

"Balancing work and personal life is the most important value as it takes into consideration all the plus and minus points in all respects," said one researcher for Jobtrak.com. "Having time to spend with your family and friends makes working worthwhile."

Given these changes in workers' demands, managers should no longer assume that increasing workers' compensation will solve organization problems. Instead, fostering a behaviorally healthy organization requires a more complex, comprehensive, and dynamic policy.

Source: Adapted from Students place high value on work/life issues. (2000, March). *HRMagazine,* 30.

family commitments for work. However, E&Y is now fighting the effects of having cultivated such a culture—namely, high turnover. In a move to reverse this trend, E&Y is working hard to help employees balance work–life equations. Partners and staff from across the country are evaluating how E&Y does business. Based on this evaluation, E&Y has implemented QWL programs that include telecommuting, mentoring, and an effective feedback process.[26] This is clearly an attempt to make E&Y a more behaviorally healthy organization.

QWL programs typically emphasize the importance of worker rights and industrial democracy. Program objectives often include increasing job security, instituting reward systems, and expanding the opportunities for growth and workplace participation.[27] Several of these objectives are targeted in "FOCUS ON: Quality of Work Life."

In keeping with the overall philosophy of organizational development, the immediate focus of a QWL intervention is on improving organizational processes, such as communication, coordination, motivation, and personal development. The implicit assumption is that improving these processes will enhance attainment of the individual objectives mentioned previously. It's important to bear in mind that the success of a QWL effort depends in large part on various organizational factors, including top management's commitment to the program and the effectiveness of labor-management steering committees. However, when executed well, QWL programs have been shown to be an effective OD effort that leads to enhanced behavioral health.[28]

26. Kruger, P. (2000). Jobs for life. *Fast Company, 34,* 236–252.
27. Lau & May, A win–win paradigm for quality of work life and business performance, p. 211.
28. Lawler, E. E. (1986). *High-involvement management.* San Francisco: Jossey-Bass, p. 136.

CHANGE IN CORPORATE AMERICA

As illustrated in the opening vignette on Ben & Jerry's, the business climate of the 1990s was, to put it charitably, turbulent. In addition to heightened global competition, rapid technological growth, and massive regulatory changes, major mergers and acquisitions made huge marks. Approximately 30,000 mergers and acquisitions were completed in the United States alone during the decade.[29] And although experience shows that mergers and acquisitions often fail to realize their anticipated payoffs, organizations continue to see them as answers to their problems.[30] Why do so many reorganizations fail to achieve their goals? In the final few pages of this chapter, we will attempt to answer this question, using the framework for change we have been discussing.

MERGERS AND ACQUISITIONS

Mergers and acquisitions highlight the spectrum of complex problems that major corporate change creates. As discussed in Chapter 10, on paper mergers and acquisitions often look like good ways for organizations to combine resources and compete more effectively in the global marketplace. Unfortunately, in real mergers and acquisitions resources are not just combined on paper but involve people and dynamic organizations. The success of the Unilever acquisition of Ben and Jerry's discussed in the opening vignette is yet to be determined.

One problem that almost always arises is that merging leads to redundant functions. For example, each company may have a payroll office that is almost large enough to handle this function for the entire new entity. This could necessitate cutbacks or transfers of staff to areas that are short on personnel. **Downsizing**—reducing the size of the workforce—may also occur as a reaction to a downturn in demand for the product. Finally, some mergers and acquisitions are quickly followed by general "housecleaning"—replacement of key employees with newcomers not wedded to the old management habits of either company or against the idea of selling off or closing down less profitable or outdated operations and facilities.

Such turmoil can prove extremely damaging to workers' morale. Downsizings, for example, often cause disruptions in communication channels that are integral to perceptions of organizational justice, leading to job insecurity and uncertainty.[31] Workers may become less productive because of uncertainty about their job responsibilities and their relationships with supervisors and coworkers. They may be concerned about their job security and even experience feelings of betrayal if management is not communicative about impending possibilities. Unplanned turnover among key employees is also likely to occur if they think that the new entity is unstable or that their influ-

29. Marks, M. L., & Mirvis, P. H. (1998). *Joining forces: Making one plus one equal three in mergers, acquisitions, and alliances.* San Francisco: Jossey-Bass.

30. Tetenbaum, T. J. (1999). Beating the odds of merger and acquisition failure: Seven key practices that improve the chance for expected integration and synergies. *Organizational Dynamics, 28*(2), 22–36.

31. Shah, P. P. (2000). Network destruction: The structural implications of downsizing. *Academy of Management Journal, 43*(1), 101–112.

ence or power has been eroded. Is it not surprising, then, that mergers and acquisitions have a success rate (as measured by their ability to outperform the stock market or deliver profit increases) of only 20% to 40%?[32] What can top management do to make sure its company is in that very small successful percentage?

In the process of unfreezing for a merger or an acquisition, organizations must keep their channels of communication open and active. Naturally, workers will want to know what is going on—who is buying whom, what the company's new name will be, who will be in charge, and so on—even if there will be little change in their jobs. In the face of little or no information, employees are likely to imagine the worst and to act accordingly. Meetings and memoranda can help diffuse a lot of hostility or concern that takes hold in uncertainty. Employees also should be given opportunities to ask questions. Strategic concerns on the minds of top management may have no relation to what is on the minds of employees (their benefits package, for instance). It is critical that their questions and concerns are addressed.

An important element of a major corporate reorganization involving downsizing is an **outplacement program** to help displaced employees find new jobs. Many programs also offer services for workers who choose not to stay on. Good outplacement programs can do a lot more than just soothe a guilty corporate conscience. They also send a strong psychological message to the remaining members of the workforce that the organization is not going to abandon them.

Employees should also be educated about "survivor guilt," common among workers who remain after a reorganization. Even though survivors are, in some sense, the winners in reorganizations, they often feel that they have lost control.[33] Imagine, for example, how demoralized a worker feels after discovering that she will be reporting to a manager who has just been demoted three grades.

Survivors are likely to have two overriding concerns: Why was I allowed to remain? and Will I be the next to go? (Of the four factors often identified as concerns by survivors, job security and related items, such as pay and benefit issues and performance feedback, are often uppermost in their minds.) Although management may never be able to answer the first question to the survivors' satisfaction, it can address the issue of job security. If the remaining employees feel secure that successful outplacement programs are in place, this may help them turn their attention to the new work at hand, rather than become obsessed about their future in the company. Teresa Amabile and Regina Conti examined a large high-technology firm before, during, and after a major downsizing. Their research showed that following the downsizing both productivity and the work environment improved.[34] This was due in part to the firm's successful handling of those who were laid off, as well as those who were left behind.

---

32. Tetenbaum, Beating the odds of merger and acquisition failure; and Harrington, H. J., Conner, D. R., Horney, N. L. (2000). *Project change management: Applying change management to improvement projects.* New York: McGraw-Hill, p. 10.

33. de Vries, M. F. R., Kets & Balazs, K. (1997). The downside of downsizing. *Human Relations*, *50*(1), 11–50.

34. Amabile, T. M., & Conti, R. (1999). Changes in the work environment for creativity during downsizing. *Academy of Management Journal*, *42*(6), 630–640.

ORGANIZATIONAL DECLINE

Yet another major change in corporate America has been organizational decline. The term **organizational decline** has at least two meanings. The first definition is used to describe a cutback in the size of an organization's workforce, budget, resources, clients, and so on. The second refers to the view that mature organizations become stagnant, bureaucratic, and passive. These conditions may herald an organization's increasing inability to stay in touch with changing markets, technologies, and client preferences.

Researchers in this area have identified four causes or sources of organizational decline: organizational atrophy, vulnerability, loss of legitimacy, and reduced environmental support.[35] **Organizational atrophy** occurs when an organization continues to respond to a situation in a certain way, although the situation has actually changed and therefore calls for different responses. Organizations experiencing this form of perseverance sometimes behave in ways that were once successful and, as a result, become increasingly vulnerable to failure.

Vulnerability is the second source of organizational decline. At some point in an organization's life, it is more susceptible to decline. For example, most organizations experience a "liability of newness."[36] The organization may have problems with inefficiency or in establishing a stable set of suppliers and customers. Frequent interpersonal conflicts may also occur.

Loss of legitimacy is the third source of decline. This occurs when an organization focuses its energy on economic gains and does not cultivate political acceptance. This issue is probably more salient in public than in private organizations. The test of legitimacy commonly revolves around the development of a powerful constituency that resists the efforts of other groups to dismantle the organization. Of the four sources of decline, organizations seem most capable of combating a loss of legitimacy.

Loss of environmental support is the fourth source of decline. This occurs when there is no longer support in the external environment for the organization. Organizations faced with this situation can either find another niche, product, or service, or they can downsize. Managing the form of organizational change is a difficult process for most organizations.

MANAGING DECLINE. After managers have figured out the source of a decline in performance, the next step is to develop a response to the problem.

Four general categories of responses to declines in performance, can be placed on a continuum as illustrated in Figure 15-6.

Large, bureaucratic organizations are most likely to respond defensively. For example, adhering to organization rules and policies may become more important than addressing the goals behind them.

Another reactive way that organizations respond to decline is with retrenchment, specifically cutbacks. Thus, layoffs may occur based on seniority or performance, or there may be across-the-board cuts in funding and resources. Either way, the focus is on solving the "problem." Unfortunately, management may attach the wrong solution to the right problem (e.g., as responding to a lack of innovation by cutting the research and development budget) or use the right solution but in response to the wrong problem (e.g., laying off production workers when the problem is with research and devel-

35. Whetten, D. A. (1980). *The organizational life cycle.* San Francisco: Jossey-Bass.
36. Stinchcombe, *Handbook of organizations.*

| Management Responses to Organizational Decline | ■ **FIGURE 15-6** |

There are four categories of organizational responses to decline. Defending and responding are reactive responses; generating and preventing are proactive responses.

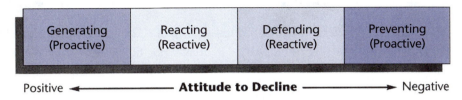

| Generating (Proactive) | Reacting (Reactive) | Defending (Reactive) | Preventing (Proactive) |

Positive ◄——————— **Attitude to Decline** ———————► Negative

Source: Whetten, *The organizational life cycle.*

opment). In either case, implementing a solution will alleviate management's concerns.

The next two responses to organizational decline, preventing and generating, differ from responding and defending in that they are proactive—that is, they remove hazards that could cause the organization to decline in the future. An organization uses a preventing tactic when it needs to increase its competitive advantage and remove potential threats. P&G responded in this way when it was threatened by Johnson & Johnson and Colgate-Palmolive. "FOCUS ON: Responses to Organizational Decline" examines the preventing tactic. Preventing tactics can include participating in mergers and acquisitions, changing public opinion and influencing consumer preferences, and shaping economic and social policy. These actions are based on the notion that organizations must act to reduce uncertainty by circumventing the need to respond reactively to the environment.

The intent of the fourth response to organizational decline—generating—is to develop self-designing organizations. Such organizations are characterized by informal lines of communication, loose criteria for performance evaluation, slack resources, experimentation, tolerance of occasional failure, frequent movement of personnel within the organization, and a high regard for innovation.

However management responds to the symptoms of organizational decline, the decline affects an organization and its employees. The following are some of the affects organizational decline can produce:

■ Increasing levels of stress among organizational actors as the importance of making good decisions and the penalties for bad decisions increase.
■ Increasing levels of interpersonal conflict as the organization's resource base dwindles.
■ Layoffs and cutbacks directed at the most vulnerable members of the organization—low-skilled, low-income, and minority employees—coupled with attrition among the most mobile and best qualified employees, resulting in a reduction in the variability of employees and the ability of the organization to respond creatively to the decline.
■ Death of the organization, either through management's failure to adapt to changes in the environment, political vulnerability, decision demands, or a transformation (such as a merger or an acquisition).

Clearly, management must handle organizational decline appropriately to ensure the survival of the organization.

FOCUS ON
RESPONSES TO ORGANIZATIONAL DECLINE

MAKING A COMEBACK. "Toys 'R' Us is hideous!" my mother announced to me after a recent visit to the giant toy retailer. She and a friend had spent hours rambling through the unkempt aisles, unable to find anything they were looking for. The saleswoman wasn't much help either. "She refused to stand up and show us where to go," my mother huffed. "I'm never going back to that place."

Complaints like those must make chief executive officer John Eyler cringe. Since taking the helm, Eyler has been trying to reinvigorate the company's slack sales growth by dreaming up ways to make Toys 'R' Us stores as appealing as the set of *Babes in Toyland*. The chain is showing some early signs of improvement, including a 43% earnings jump during the first quarter of 2000.

There's even more promising news from the e-commerce front. Many forecasters and consumers presumed that Toysrus.com would suffer a quick death after it failed to deliver all its orders by Christmas Day 1999. But, surprisingly, Toysrus.com has come alive, and it has announced a strategic alliance with online giant Amazon.com.

That's not to say things are perfect. As my mother will tell you, Toys 'R' Us still needs to improve the atmosphere in its stores. That's why Eyler has transformed 16 locations into "lab stores." The new layouts will include shopping gimmicks such as Animal Alley, a section overflowing with easy-to-grab stuffed animals.

There's a similar service-oriented strategy under way at Toysrus.com. As early as summer 1999, Toysrus.com was strengthening its operations in preparation for the onslaught of holiday shoppers. The subsidiary redesigned its Web site to handle more orders, opened two additional distribution warehouses, and brought new blood to management—including David Braxton, a former American Express executive who will run customer services. Toysrus.com even persuaded Softbank Venture Capital to throw in $60 million of capital. As Toysrus.com chief operating officer Jonathan Foster puts it, "We feel we've learned a lot from our mistakes."

That may be, but the company still hasn't passed the toughest test—my mom.

Source: Excerpted from Kover, A. (2000, July). After an unmerry Christmas, Toys 'R' Us is on the mend. *Fortune, 142*(2), 41.

SUMMARY

To respond effectively to the ever-changing demands around them, organizations must constantly be prepared to change. A key challenge for managers is to maintain the delicate balance between external forces that encourage or demand change and forces within organizations that resist it. To strike this delicate balance, managers must be able to recognize the need for change and identify and manage sources of resistance to it.

The change process entails four stages: diagnosis, unfreezing, movement, and refreezing. During diagnosis, problems are identified and their causes are isolated. Unfreezing lays the foundation for change. The movement stage is when changes are executed. Finally, during refreezing the changes are institutionalized and management in the organization checks to make sure the identified problem has been solved and no new problems have arisen.

Organizational development is a less traditional approach to managing change in organizations. It assumes is that problems occur in organizations because they are not behaviorally healthy. Organizational development change efforts are therefore aimed at improving organizational health—communication, adaptation, innovation, and succession—in an attempt to preempt the need for a one-time turbulent change. In the case of one OD technique, survey-guided development, workers participate in the process of developing, completing, and interpreting questionnaires that construct a picture of the organization's internal processes and problems. Worker participation is also critical to QWL programs. These systemwide efforts to improve workforce effectiveness and morale are grounded on a foundation of commitment to formal workforce participation in organizational decision making.

During the 1990s American businesses were forced to confront a wide range of large-scale internal and external changes, from bankruptcies to hostile takeovers, mergers, and major reorganizations. Upheavals of this magnitude play havoc with an organization's ability to remain efficient and effective. Managing these changes has become a key management challenge.

KEY TERMS

Behaviorally healthy organization
Bottom-up problem solving
Diagnosis
Downsizing
External change agent
Habit
Inertia
Movement
Organizational atrophy
Organizational decline

Organizational development (OD)
Outplacement program
Quality-of-work-life (QWL) program
Refreezing
Succession
Support systems
Survey-guided development
Top-down problem solving
Unfreezing

DISCUSSION QUESTIONS

1 Considering what you have learned about participative approaches to decision making, in what if any circumstances might top-down change efforts be more appropriate than organizational development activities?

2 What are the differences between the steps involved in traditional change efforts and the process of organizational development?

3 Why would instituting a survey-guided development activity probably be a useful first step in an organizational change or development program?

4 Refreezing is often a forgotten and neglected phase of organizational change efforts. Does this help explain why apparently successful change efforts often do not have lasting effects? Why is refreezing so important? What are some of the likely repercussions if it is not done?

5 What skills are likely to be required of a manager in a turbulent industry or during turbulent times?

6 Why is change usually easier to manage in a behaviorally healthy organization than in an unhealthy one? Do you think change would be easy or difficult to manage in a company like Ben & Jerry's that is committed to its employees' welfare?

7 Are some sources of resistance to change more "rational" (that is, more justifiable) than others? When might a little inertia (or even a lot) be a good thing?

8 Organizational development is a vehicle for change in organizations. In many organizations, however, organizational development itself represents a change. What kind of unfreezing might be needed to ensure success when organizational development techniques are instituted?

9 What two primary factors might cause a decline in an organization? What are some possible ways that management could respond to the decline?

> ## ON YOUR OWN

Likert's Profile of Organizational Characteristics   Are you in a workgroup that is ready for change? Keeping that group in mind, fill out the questionnaire below. For each question on the left-hand page, circle the phrase on the righthand page that best describes your workgroup. Your instructor will give you scoring instructions that will tell you where your group stands and if it might be ready for some changes.

Leadership

  1 How much confidence is shown in subordinates?
  2 How free do subordinates feel to talk about their jobs to superiors?
  3 Are subordinates' ideas sought and, when worthy, used?

Motivation

  1 Is predominant use made of (a) fear, (b) threats, (c) punishment, (d) rewards, or (e) involvement?
  2 Who or what division/department is responsible for achieving the organization's goals?

Communication

  1 How much communication is aimed at achieving the organization's objectives?
  2 What is the direction of the information flow?
  3 How is downward communication accepted?
  4 How well do superiors know the problems faced by subordinates?

Decisions

  1 At what level are decisions formally made?
  2 What is the origin of the technical and professional knowledge used in decision making?
  3 Are subordinates involved in decisions related to their work?
  4 What if any relationship exists between the decision-making process and motivation?

Goals

  1 How are organizational goals established?
  2 How much covert resistance to goals is there?

Control

  1 How concentrated are review and control functions?
  2 Is there an informal organization resisting the formal one?
  3 What are cost, productivity, and other control data used for?

System 1	System 2	System 3	System 4
None	Condescending	Substantial	Complete
Not at all	Not very	Rather free	Fully free
Seldom	Sometimes	Usually	Always
1, 2, 3 occasionally	4, some 3	4, some 3 and 5	5, 4, based on group-set goals
Mostly at top	Top and middle	Fairly general	At all levels
Very little	Little	Quite a bit	A great deal
Downward	Mostly downward	Down and up	Down, up, and sideways
With suspicion	Possibly with suspicion	With caution	With an open mind
Know little	Some knowledge	Quite well	Very well
Mostly at top	Policy at top	Broad policy at top, more delegation	Throughout but well integrated
Top Management	Upper and middle	To a certain extent, throughout	To a great extent throughout
Not at all	Occasionally consulted	Generally consulted	Fully involved
Nothing, often weakens it	Relatively little	Some contribution	Substantial contribution
Orders issued	Orders, some comment invited	After discussion, by order	By group action (except in crisis)
Strong resistance	Moderate resistance	Some resistance at times	Little or none
Highly at top	Relatively high at top	Moderate delegation to lower levels	Quite widely shared
Yes	Usually	Sometimes	No—same goals as formal
Policing, punishment	Reward and punishment	Reward—some self-guidance	Self-guidance problem solving

Source: Likert, R. (1975). *The human organization.* New York: McGraw-Hill.

CLOSING CASE   CHAPTER 15

THE MANAGER'S MEMO

FROM: Brad Stroh, Chief Technical Officer
TO: Anngenette Gittleman, Procurement Manager
              Steve Tomez, Production Manager
CC: Bob Kahuna, CEO
              Dave Woner, CFO
RE: New Technology

As you know, all our competitors have shifted to purchasing supplies and equipment via online services. This has resulted in some very impressive gains in efficiency. BIGCO Corporation has already slashed its prices, to which we must respond. However, as Bob and Dave have determined, because of our technological deficiencies, if we cut our prices in line with BIGCO's, we are certain to fall short of our financial projections.

To allow us to compete more effectively, several new software packages are being installed. Revised cost projections are based on everyone in purchasing getting up to speed on use of this software over the next 6 months. Introducing this software will result in reductions in two critical areas of production: direct material costs and overhead expenses. In addition, we will be able to reduce our workforce by 17%.

The first software package we are installing was created for us by Ariba and will streamline our procurement process for indirect MRO (maintenance, repair, and other) goods. This will eliminate rogue purchases, give us buying power as an organization, and subsequently reduce the number of procurement staff.

Starting next week, we are also using Free Markets to set up an e-exchange so that we will be able to purchase direct production materials online. This will optimize our production efficiencies, lower direct costs, increase collaboration with our suppliers, and reduce headcount.

Steve, the Free Markets package will interface with our SAP enterprise resource planning system. It appears that most of your organization has yet to integrate SAP into your management systems; implementing the new initiatives as quickly as possible is critical. The overall health of our company depends on it.

Thanks, and good luck. Please begin informing your teams about the new systems and changes.

CASE DISCUSSION QUESTIONS

Assume that you are the production manager and respond to the vice president's memorandum. What sources of resistance must you prepare for? What actions can the company take to make the change to more technologically driven systems as beneficial as possible? What, if anything, should the company do for the workers whose positions will be eliminated?

CHAPTER 16

Inclusion: Managing Diversity in the Workplace

ADVANTICA: A MODEL OF INCLUSION FOR THE REST OF AMERICA

In its 2000 listing of "America's Best Companies for Minorities," *Fortune* magazine honored the Advantica Restaurant Group, the parent company of the Denny's, Coco's, and Carrows restaurant chains, as the very best in the nation. Of the 1,200 companies *Fortune* compared, Advantica ranked highest in 15 categories, including minority representation on boards of directors; number of minority corporate officers, officials, and managers; number of minorities among the 50 highest-salaried employees; number of minorities in the total workforce; new minority employees hired in the past year; retention of minority employees; and diversity training.

"We are extremely proud to be recognized as the top company in America for embracing inclusion," said James B. Adamson, president and chief executive officer (CEO) of Advantica and Denny's. "Inclusion and diversity are integral to the way we do business, something we focus on each day throughout our organization. We have come a long way and are committed to continuing our efforts in being a truly inclusive company."

Things certainly have changed at Advantica. When Adamson joined the company in 1995, Advantica had just settled two class-action lawsuits involving race discrimination at Denny's. Today three African Americans and a Hispanic American serve on Advantica's 11-member board of directors. Forty-seven percent of Advantica's more than 45,000 employees are minorities: 31% of Advantica's employees are Hispanic American; 11% are African American; and 6% are Asian-Pacific American. Thirty-five percent of Denny's franchise restaurants are minority owned, and Advantica's annualized minority purchasing contracts for 1999 reached $110 million, or 17% of the total annual food and nonfood purchases.

Source: Adapted from, Advantica, Denny's parent company, cited as best place in the nation for minorities. (2000, June 26). *Business Wire*.

The company has received several other awards, in addition to the award from *Fortune*, for its efforts to promote inclusion. The Council of Economic Priorities awarded Denny's its 2000 Corporate Conscience Diversity Award for outstanding achievement in corporate social responsibility, and *Working Woman* magazine ranked Advantica eighth in its 2000 survey, "Top 25 Companies for Women Executives."

Advantica is certainly on the right track when it comes to managing—and demonstrating the benefits of—an inclusive workforce. The company has now become a model for the rest of corporate America.

INTRODUCTION

At some point in Advantica's history, management must have come to a profound realization: To attract a loyal, creative workforce and be more competitive, it had to change its programs and policies concerning employee recruitment and development. First, Advantica had to become more inclusive. Second, Advantica needed to manage its new diverse workforce effectively to ensure that the workers would be productive and eager to remain with the company. Considering the challenges Advantica faced in reaching its objective to become more inclusive, its success as well as the success of other large corporations in creating inclusive workforces is truly remarkable. Such transformations in a company's culture do not happen without great effort.

Organizations like Advantica have several reasons to become more inclusive: (a) Diversity leads to a wellspring of creativity, innovation, and successful long-term adaptation; (b) the demographics of the labor force are changing quickly and dramatically, exerting strong forces for change on organizations; and (c) becoming more diverse is often the socially right thing to do—and it is often legally required. Yet, as we have seen in other situations, managers often get caught in a knowing–doing gap; they often know how and why they should do something, such as make their organization more inclusive, but they don't know how to manage such a major transformation in their organization, which is much more easily said than done. Thus, they succeed in reaching their goal of making their organizations more inclusive, but have difficulty managing the attendant changes that occur.

This chapter focuses on the challenges of creating and managing a workforce composed of a mix of women and men, White and minority employees, young and old employees, and straight and gay employees. Unless organizations learn to embrace people of different races, ages, and sexual orientation and educate their employees accordingly, businesses could be seriously at risk.

This chapter opens by examining the first step management needs to take in managing diversity efforts—recognizing that the composition of the U.S. workforce has changed and that discriminating against groups and individuals is not only socially irresponsible but carries stiff penalties. Without a foundation in "the basics," managers will be unable to build and effectively manage a diversity program. As Advantica illustrates, management needs to take action—to develop goals and programs aimed at making their organizations more inclusive. Thus, also included in the chapter are ideas about how organizations can close the knowing–doing gap.

THE CHANGING DEMOGRAPHICS OF THE WORKFORCE

A great deal of media and organizational attention has been focused in recent years on the topic of diversity in the workforce—in other words, differences in the workforce defined by race, ethnicity, gender, sexual orientation, disabilities, and age. There is some evidence that organizations are aiming less for diversity and more for **inclusion,** suggesting a shift in emphasis from employees' differences to their similarities. Figure 16-1 provides a historical perspective on how management has dealt with this challenge.

Most of the discussions surrounding efforts to make the workplace more diverse or to foster inclusion have focused on people's innate differences—in age, race, gender, ethnicity, and sexual orientation. Yet other differences or individual characteristics—such as educational background, marital and family status, work experience, and socioeconomic status—also have significant repercussions in the workplace. The most effective workgroups, for instance, have high levels of information diversity (differences in perspectives stemming from differences in experience, expertise, and education) and low levels of value diversity (differences in defining a group's mission, goal, task, or target). Further, research has shown that group problems and decreases in performance and morale are more likely to stem from differences in values than from social diversity.[1] This finding is in direct conflict with current business management thinking, which says that social diversity, not differences in values, creates conflict and decreases productivity.

The recent move toward globalization in corporations and the dramatic change in the composition of the workforce have been major catalysts for organizations like Advantica to develop new approaches to recruitment, hiring, and other management practices. Among some of the most overt changes, the workforce is getting significantly older, and over the next 10 to 20 years it will include ever-increasing percentages of women and minority group members. Some more progressive organizations have taken advantage of their employees' different experiences, perspectives, and orientations to influence their organizations. As part of this process, management also needs to become more cognizant of its clients' diverse needs. Only through such inclusion can businesses truly begin to understand their customers, anticipate their needs, and fulfill their expectations.[2]

One of the major social challenges affecting all organizations is that the demographic base of American consumers is changing. Further, more than ever, if customers do not feel respected and valued, they will take their business elsewhere. Understanding customers' needs is crucial to gaining their respect and ultimately to gaining that all-important competitive edge.

Paralleling the influx of women into the workforce, women are becoming more influential consumers. In fact, women spend 85% of all consumer dollars. Equally dramatic, African Americans, Hispanics, and Asian Americans are expected to spend $600 billion annually on goods and services in this decade.[3] Older Americans also control a large proportion of consumer dollars—more than 50% of all discretionary income.

---

1. Jehn, K. A., Northcraft, G. B., & Neale, M. A. (1999). Why differences make a difference: A field study of diversity, conflict, and performance in workgroups. *Administrative Science Quarterly, 44,* 741–763.
2. Casico, W. F. (1995). *Managing human resources.* Boston: McGraw-Hill.
3. Wheeler, M. L. (1995). *Diversity: Business rationale and strategies.* New York: Conference Board.

The diversity continuum shows how organizations have responded over the past decades to changes in the social environment of the workplace.

Affirmative Action **1960–1975**	**Valuing Differences** **1975–1985**	**Managing Inclusion (Diversity)** **1985–Present**
Quantitative. Emphasis is on achieving equality of opportunity in the work environment through the changing of organizational demographics. Progress is monitored by statistical reports and analyses.	**Qualitative.** Emphasis is on the appreciation of differences and the creation of an environment in which everyone feels valued and accepted. Progress is monitored by organizational surveys focused on attitudes and perceptions.	**Behavioral.** Emphasis is on building specific skills and creating policies that get the best from every employee. Efforts are monitored by progress toward reaching goals and objectives.
Legally Driven. Written plans and statistical goals for specific groups are utilized. Reports are mandated by EEO laws and consent decrees	**Ethically Driven.** Moral and ethical imperatives drive this culture change	**Strategically Driven.** Behaviors and policies are seen as contributing to organizational goals and objectives such as profit and productivity, and are tied to rewards and results.
Remedial. Specific target groups benefit as past wrongs are remedied. Previously excluded groups have an advantage.	**Idealistic.** Everyone benefits. Everyone feels valued and accepted.	**Pragmatic.** The organizational benefits; morale, profits, and productivity increase.
Assimilation Model. Model assumes that groups brought into the system will adapt to existing organizational norms.	**Diversity Model.** Model assumes that groups will retain their own characteristics and shape the organization as well as be shaped by it, creating a common set of values.	**Synergy Model.** Model assumes that diverse groups will create new ways of working together effectively in a pluralistic environment.
Open doors. Efforts affect hiring and promotion decisions in the organization.	**Open attitudes, minds and the culture.** Efforts affect attitudes of employees.	**Opens the system.** Efforts affect managerial practices and policies.
Resistance. Resistance is due to perceived limits to autonomy in decision making and perceived fears of reverse discrimination.	**Resistance.** Resistance is due to a fear of change, discomfort with differences, and a desire to return to the "good old days."	**Resistance.** Resistance is due to denial of demographic realities, of the need for alternative approaches, and of the benefits of change. It also arises from the difficulty of learning new skills, altering existing systems, and finding the time to work toward synergistic solutions.

Source: Adapted from Gardenswartz, Lee & Rowe, Anita (1993). *Managing Diversity: A Complete Desk Reference and Planning Guide.* Business One Irwin.

Demographic trends indicate that the workforce of the future will be a complex mix of male and female individuals of different ages and ethnicities. Managers will be increasingly challenged to find ways to motivate this diverse group to perform.

The quest to understand why some managers have resisted the idea of inclusion, and why other managers have responded more favorably to the idea, has revealed some surprising and some not-so-surprising findings. First, people are still more comfortable with and seek out people whom they consider similar to themselves. This is not surprising given that research shows that people who are similar demographically (in age, race, and sex, for instance) are more likely to have had common experiences, to share similar values, and to understand one another better.[4] Likewise, employees with same-sex mentors report receiving greater social support than those with opposite-sex mentors.[5] Arup Varma and Linda Stroh obtained similar findings in their research on same-sex work relationships and performance evaluations. Their research shows that both female and male supervisors tended to respond more favorably toward subordinates of their same sex, and a preference to interact with those "like me" is often present at the unconscious level. While most employees would not intentionally favor men over women or vice versa. Varma and Stroh's research shows that the unconcious behaviors are equally as damaging as concious behaviors.[6]

Yet, employees and organizations clearly benefit from diversity. For example, research shows that diverse groups are often more creative and better at problem solving than more homogenous units.[7] Teams composed of diverse members are also better at brainstorming innovative solutions to problems in the global environment. Perhaps not surprisingly, the benefits of demographic diversity and inclusion efforts are more obvious when an organization values group performance more than it values individualism.[8]

4. Byrne, D. (1971). Attitudes and attraction. *Advances in Experimental and Social Psychology, 4.*

5. Koberg, C. S., Boss, R. W., & Goodman, E. A. (1998). Factors and outcomes associated with mentoring among health-care professionals. *Journal of Vocational Behavior, 53*(1), 58–72.

6. Varma, A., & Stroh, L. K. (In Press). The impact of same-sex LMX dyads on performance evaluations. *Human Resource Management Journal.*

7. Wheeler, *Diversity.*

8. Chatman, J. A., Polzer, J. T., & Barsade, S. G. (1998). Being different yet feeling similar: The influence of demographic composition and organizational culture on work processes and outcomes. *Administrative Science Quarterly, 43,* 749–780.

Research by Sherry Schneider and Gregory Northcraft highlights another interesting perspective. They suggest that organizations benefit first from diversity, as evident in increases in innovation, creativity, and adaptation. Employees *then* start to internalize the benefits of inclusion. This is because employees often think of themselves as bearing the initial costs (such as additional time spent organizing diverse groups) and do not recognize the short-term benefits (such as increased productivity).[9]

RACIAL DEMOGRAPHICS

After all is said and done, are efforts at fostering inclusion really working? Combined, African American and Hispanics still hold fewer than 2% of U.S. executive positions. Clearly, Advantica is atypical. The gap between the races also shows up in the unemployment rolls. According to the Bureau of Labor and Statistics, African Americans were twice as likely as Whites to be unemployed in 1999—a ratio that has remained unchanged since the 1970s. Also in 1999, African American teens were 2.5 times more likely to be unemployed than White teens; again, the ratio is comparable to what it was in the 1970s.[10]

Similarly, African American employees have advanced in professions more slowly than White employees. Thus, although African Americans consistently made up about 11% of the total U.S. workforce between 1983 and 1999, as recently as 1999 they accounted for only 5% of the engineers and 5% of the attorneys.[11]

Earnings data are no less depressing. According to data from the U.S. Bureau of Labor Statistics, for every dollar a White man earned in 1979 (the first year for which figures are available), an African American man, on average, earned 76 cents. Two decades later, the figures were identical. One conclusion we can draw from these statistics is that the workplace has responded very slowly to the changing demographics of the workforce.

But are inclusion programs doing anything to remedy the situation? With the millions of dollars invested in inclusion efforts, are companies getting their money's worth? Catalyst, a nonprofit research organization, examined this question.[12] Of the African American women who responded, only 36% said that the diversity programs in their organizations were effective in challenging racism. On the whole, the study found that the number of African American women who benefited profoundly from inclusion programs was a mere 12%. Clearly, management has not learned how to foster inclusion in organizations, even in organizations that have made an effort to hire African American employees. In other words, management is not managing its inclusion programs effectively.

THE INFLUENCE OF GENERATION XERS

In addition to the shift in racial demographics, the ages and educational levels of American workers have been changing. From 1986 to 1996, for instance, educational levels increased by 19%, concomitant with increased demand for technological proficiency.[13] Another change is the growing influence of

9. Schneider, S. K., & Northcraft, G. B. (1999). Three social dilemmas of workforce diversity in organizations: A social identity perspective. *Human Relations, 52,* 1445–1467.
10. Grossman, R. J. (2000). Race in the workplace. *HR Magazine, 45*(3), 40–45.
11. Grossman, Race in the workplace.
12. Grossman, Race in the workplace.
13. Bureau of Labor and Statistics. (1999). *Report of the American workforce,* 49.

FOCUS ON
THE NEW WORKFORCE

MANAGING AND MOTIVATING GENXERS.
What are the values of GenXers? Are they really that different than those of older coworkers? A landmark study has begun to address these questions by delving deeply into the values of GenXers.

The research, which was commissioned by Deloitte & Touche and the Corporate State, profiled 104 senior executives aged 35 and older and 52 GenXers ages 21 to 34 working in business. Among the key findings are the following:

■ Having parents who have been casualties of downsizing, restructuring, and so on has led GenXers to strike out on their own and develop themselves as a brand.

■ GenXers are entrepreneurial by nature and act like independent contractors rather than company "lifers."

■ Although hard working and committed to the growth and success of the companies they work for, GenXers are less loyal than older executives. Ninety percent say they could easily find a new job right now if they wanted to.

■ Perhaps as a result of the unstable world they grew up in, GenXers crave stability and structure: 95% describe an ideal work environment as one that is "stable," and 77% describe it as "clearly structured."

From the research it's clear that GenXers have a strong sense of individual control, initiative, and confidence. What, then, should corporations do to attract, manage, motivate, and retain them? The research provides several important adaptive strategies.

First, give GenXers the opportunity to learn, take responsibility, and sharpen their professional skills on a regular basis. Findings suggest they will respond well to the challenge. Second, give GenXers short-term rewards and recognition to remind them they are valued by the organization. Being a central part of the organization is important to GenXers. Third, GenXers need to understand how the work they do fits into company objectives. Communicate company goals and elaborate on how the GenXer's work fits into those goals. GenXers also respond best to a clear set of expectations. Last but not least, support and encourage mentoring relationships and programs. GenXer's who are protégés need to know they're being mentored. With the help of these suggestions, organizations can effectively tap into the value of the GenXers.

Source: Adapted from Anon. New strategic research on Generation X: Invaluable to the future of corporate leadership; Research launches second annual summit on corporate issues for women CEOs. (1999, September 30). *Business Wire.*

Generation Xers (GenXers), those born between 1960 and 1980. Their nontraditional views have forced managers to develop innovative ways to manage this cohort and groom them for leadership positions. "FOCUS ON: The New Workforce" is a brief glimpse at this generation's perspective.

GRAY POWER

As GenXers assert a stronger influence, the proportion of the workforce made up of older workers is increasing, and many of these people are likely to impede the progress of their younger coworkers. As older workers become a larger and more politically powerful group, it is likely that they will demand more job security, employee rights, and programs designed to meet their specific needs. Simultaneously, with the increase in life expectancy and the removal of mandatory retirement laws, there will be fewer workers to support the increasingly large population receiving Social Security benefits. The discussion that follows elaborates on the importance of including older workers in the mainstream of corporate America.

FOCUS ON OLDER WORKERS

GETTING BACK IN THE FAST LANE. Robert Lutz tried to enjoy retirement. He really did. The 68-year-old former president of Chrysler Corporation gave speeches, promoted a management book he had written, and served on the boards of several big companies. He tried living life to the fullest, too, riding his motorcycles and flying his jet fighter plane. He did that for 4 months. Then he gave up and took a job as CEO of a failing car-battery company in Reading, Pennsylvania. What a relief.

"Those of us who enjoy our jobs do not sense them as being work," said Lutz. "If you enjoy it and you are in great physical and mental health, you ask, why should I stop? Why waste this resource?"

Many executives have a hard time giving up the perks and power that come with their jobs, and some try to hang on well past the age of 70.

But few have the nerve to do what Lutz did and risk their reputations by starting over at a floundering company.

Once released into retirement, Lutz missed the sense of purpose that came with his old job. Also, his 91-year-old banker father, still went to work every day at Credit Suisse in Zurich. Most of all, Lutz missed the feeling of being in charge.

Lutz's current contract calls for him to stay on the job for 2 more years, by which time he will be 70. After that, he says, "we'll see," but he's enjoying himself now. "If you hate work, or if you want to play golf, and all you can do is count the days to retirement, then taking another job makes no sense," says Lutz. "But if you enjoy it, you say, why should I stop?"

Source: Adapted from Taylor, A. (2000). Getting back in the fast lane. *Fortune, 141,* 417–418.

There are already more than 34.4 million people 65 or older in the United States. That's around one in every eight Americans. And those who made it to 65 years in 1997 can expect to live for another 17.6 years.[14] This means that nearly 1.7 million workers aged 55 to 64 are in the labor force.[15] Couple this trend with the lifting of legally mandated retirement ages, and it's easy to see that organizations will have to rethink traditional ideas about older workers.

Contrary to some incorrect stereotypes, older workers are more reliable, are absent less, have high levels of commitment, and have better work habits than their younger counterparts.[16] Older workers even make significant investments in career development. Research indicates, for example, that older workers are more likely than their younger peers to participate in career training. They are also more accommodating to the expectations of others.[17] Developing programs to encourage older workers to actively contribute to their organizations is a challenge organizations should consider worth the investment.

Whether for economic, social, or other personal reasons, some older U.S. workers are returning or attempting to return to work even after retirement. This is the topic of "FOCUS ON: Older Workers." This phenomenon is quite common in Japan as well. For instance, Japan's leading machine-tool maker,

---

14. Gerbman, R. (2000). Elder care takes America by storm. *HR Magazine, 45*(5), 54.

15. Rix, S. (2000, April). Update on the older worker: 1999 gains continue; Officials project some increases in participation. *AARP,* 48–51.

16. Brotherton, Phaedra. (2000). Tapping into an older workforce. *Mosaics, 6*(2), 4.

17. Greller, M. M., Simpson, P. A., & Stroh, L. K. (2000). *A human capital approach to worklife vitality.* The Hague, Netherlands: ICOH Scientific Committee.

■ **FIGURE 16-2**

Factors Shaping the Career Motivation of Workers from Mid-Life On

Numerous factors influence the career behavior of older workers. The following graphic represents some of the issues management must be prepared to deal with when an organization employs older workers.

Source: Greller & Stroh, Careers in midlife and beyond, p. 244.

Okuma Corporation, is implementing a program to rehire older workers as instructors for younger employees. And Yokogawa Electric Corporation is developing an engineering subsidiary to invest in the skills of older workers.[18] These examples illustrate that it's possible for organizations to both adapt to changing societal trends and make better use of their human resources.

Research suggests that organizations should make the best use of older workers's talents by approaching these people as individuals with unique career planning and promotional opportunities.[19] And, as noted previously, managers need to educate themselves about the special contributions older employees can make.

Managers are also advised to recognize that the circumstances and needs of older workers are different from those of younger workers.[20] In particular, tremendous forces, as illustrated in Figure 16-2, influence and shape older employees' career motivations. Individuals' and society's beliefs and attitudes about age and aging—social aging—also have a tremendous effect on older workers' expectations about what they can and cannot do, and on what others expect that older workers can and cannot do.

Likewise, with the graying of America, more younger workers have partial or total responsibility for the care of their parents. For example, 70% of the 3,900 employees at Fannie Mae, a Washington, D.C.–based home finance company, will face dilemmas about elder care in the next few years.[21] This change is also putting pressure on work organizations, as employees require additional time off, insurance options, and other programs to assist them in evaluating their elder-care options. To manage its situation, Fannie Mae hired an on-site elder-care manager. Fannie Mae claims that "for every dollar [it] spend[s] on eldercare benefits, we estimate a return of $1.50 through higher productivity, retention, reduced absenteeism, and turnover."[22]

18. Analysis—Japanese firms move to rehire retirees [Online]. (1998, February 25). *Asia Pulse.* URL: *http://www.asiapulse.com*

19. Sterns, H. L., & Milklos, S. (1995). The aging worker in a changing environment: Organizational and individual issues. *Journal of Vocational Behavior, 47,* 248–268.

20. Greller, M., & Stroh, L. (1995). Careers in midlife and beyond: A fallow field in need of sustenance. *Journal of Vocational Behavior, 47,* 232–247.

21. Wells, S. (2000). The elder care gap. *HR Magazine 45*(5), 38–46.

22. Wells, The elder care gap.

RESEARCH IN ACTION
FORMAL MENTORING AT MILLER: COMPUTER DATING OR THE REAL THING?

Belle Rose Ragins, University of Wisconsin–Milwaukee; *ragins@uwm.edu*

Mentors make a difference. Employees with informal mentors advance faster in organizations, receive greater compensation, and have more positive job and career attitudes than those who lack mentors. Many organizations recognize the importance of informal mentoring and have attempted to replicate these relationships by assigning formal mentors to employees. In fact, it's estimated that one third of the nation's major companies have formal mentoring programs. But are mentor–protégé relationships effective? Some critics argue that formal mentoring is like computer dating—it's too artificial and lacks the "chemistry" of informal relationships. *Is* formal mentoring like computer dating, or can these relationships develop into true love? If formal mentoring is effective, how should a formal program be structured to make the most of these relationships?

John Cotton, professor of management at Marquette University, Janice Miller, assistant professor of management at the University of Wisconsin–Milwaukee, and I investigated these questions in a national study of 1,162 employees. We compared employees with formal mentors, informal mentors, and those who lacked mentors. We found that the type of mentor didn't matter as much as the quality of the relationship. Employees who had high-quality mentors, whether formal or informal, had more positive work and career attitudes than those who lacked mentors. However, individuals with low-quality relationships did not fare better than those who lacked mentors, and in some cases they fared worse. While the average informal mentor was better than the average formal mentor, high-quality formal mentors were better than low-quality informal mentors.

From our research, it was clear that while formal mentors are no substitute for informal mentors, not all mentors are created equal, and all formal mentors are not worse than all informal mentors. We also found that even the best-designed program could not compensate for a pool of poor-quality mentors. We concluded that a formal mentoring program is only as good as the mentor it produces and that the key to a good mentoring program is to recruit and train motivated and talented mentors.

Miller Brewing Company applied our research in developing its mentoring program for employees in Milwaukee, Wisconsin. The objectives were to increase the number of employees in the succession planning pool, the career satisfaction and commitment of Miller employees, and the overall pool of mentors in the organization. From our research, Miller recognized that selecting and training high-quality mentors were critical components for program effectiveness. The organization used a careful screening process in which mentors who volunteered for the program were not automatically allowed to serve but were carefully selected based on their mentoring and coaching skills, job performance, commitment to the relationship, interests, and time availability. Both mentors and protégés had to have the support of their managers, who were also included in the orientation process. The program was voluntary for both mentors and protégés, but participants were required to make a year-long commitment to the relationship and to meet for at least an hour once a month. To try to build chemistry in the relationship, protégés were asked to select their top three choices of mentors from a list of candidates, and, where possible, matches were made based on those preferences.

A critical component of the Miller program was training. Both mentors and protégés underwent intensive, 2-day skills-building workshops that developed and honed the coaching and interpersonal skills necessary for the development of effective mentoring relationships. Follow-up and evaluation are always important, and Miller used ongoing evaluations and bimonthly supportive workshops to tweak the program and ensure the success of these relationships.

After evaluating the program, Miller plans to develop additional formal mentoring programs for use with other employee groups in the organization. Miller hopes that with careful planning, selection, and training, formal mentoring relationships can move beyond "computer dating" and become the "real thing."

DISCRIMINATION

One might expect that overt discrimination in corporate settings is a thing of the past. But, unfortunately, that's not the case, as Advantica learned only too well when it was hit with two major class-action suits. A survey of residents of Bloomington, Illinois, drives home this point: 83% felt that Blacks were frequent victims of discrimination, 76% felt that Hispanics often encountered racism, and 67% felt that women and American Indians were discriminated against as well.[23] With the emergence of the Internet and other advanced technologies, discrimination is also appearing in novel forms, such as in offensive e-mails.[24]

U.S. legislation, including the 1963 Equal Pay Act and the 1964 Civil Rights Act, makes it illegal to discriminate against workers based on color, race, religion, sex, or national origin, or to pay men and women different amounts if they have equal skills, exert equal effort, have equal responsibilities, and are working under similar conditions. However, given that 25,000 cases involving sex discrimination were brought before the Equal Employment Opportunity Commission in 1997 alone, organizations are obviously slow to adapt to these legal changes in their social environment.[25]

Another group for whom inclusion is still a concern is Americans with disabilities. Enacted in 1992, the Americans with Disabilities Act requires reasonable accommodations in existing structures (and all new structures) for job applicants with disabilities who request them. The goal is to ensure that a disability is not a barrier to effective job performance.

Although positive changes have occurred as a result of these laws, including in organizations like Advantica, the changes have focused primarily on helping to ensure that organizations hire women, people of color, people with disabilities, and other people who traditionally face discrimination. But even with these efforts, considerable challenges remain, especially for women and gays.

WOMEN IN THE WORKFORCE

Without a doubt, women have made monumental strides in the business world; as just one example, women-owned companies now represent a whopping 40% of U.S. businesses and account for annual revenues of more than $3.6 trillion.[26] At the same time, as others argue, a **glass ceiling** still exists that keeps women from advancing simply because they are women.[27] In many cases, women are making it into middle levels of management, but few make it beyond.

Further, women are discriminated against in many organizational settings. Women still hold only 10% of senior management positions in Fortune 500 companies and only 4% of CEO, president, and vice president po-

23. Survery: Blacks most discriminated against. (2000, May 16) *The Pantagraph Associated Press*, p. A5.
24. Discrimination takes on subtle forms. (2000). *HR Magazine, 45*(5), 29.
25. Davison, H. K., & Burke, M. J. (2000). Sex discrimination in simulated employment contracts: A meta-analytic investigation. *Journal of Vocational Behavior, 56*, 225–248.
26. Freeman, L. (2000, June). The top 500 women-owned businesses. *Working Woman*, 52.
27. Morrison, A. M., White, R. P., Van Velsor, E., and the Center for Creative Leadership. (1987). *Breaking the glass ceiling: Can women reach the top of America's largest corporations?* Reading, MA: Addison-Wesley.

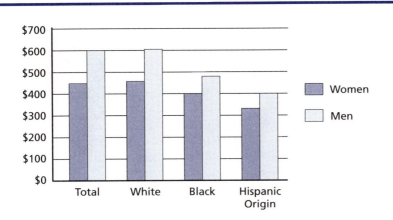

Source: Bowler, Women's earnings.

sitions.[28] Research by Karen Lyness and Donna Thompson focuses on some dramatic male–female differences and similarities. They found, for instance, that although women receive comparable compensation and have comparable attitudes toward work, they have positions with less authority, receive fewer stock options, and are given fewer international assignments than male executives. The women in Lyness and Thompson's study also ranked lower on job satisfaction than the men.[29]

Other data are equally significant. Although women's earnings have increased since 1979 by 14% and men's have decreased by 7% on average, women still earn significantly less than men (only 76% of men's earnings).[30] And, as shown in Figure 16-3, these numbers are seen across ethnic groups. Such disparities undoubtedly fuel animosity and tension between workers.

In addition to fueling animosity and tension, discrimination can cost a company millions of dollars in lawsuits. For example, as part of the settlement of one noteworthy comparable worth case involving nurses, word-processing operators, library technicians, and clerk typists, the employers were forced to pay out $482 million over 6 years. The finding was based on the fact that these employees were paid about 20% less than employees in comparable male-dominated jobs.

This isn't to say that women haven't made great strides in recent years. They have—especially true in information technology (IT) fields. According to research by *Information Week*, the median salary for women IT staff members in 1999 was $50,000—only 9% lower than the salary for men in IT.[31] This promising trend is also seen in managerial positions in IT. The median salary for women IT managers in 1999 was $68,000, versus $72,000 for men—only a 6% difference.[32]

28. Meyerson, D. M., & Fletcher, J. K. (2000). A modest manifesto for shattering the glass ceiling. *Harvard Business Review, 78*(1), 127–136.

29. Lyness, K. S., & Thompson, D. E. (1997). Above the glass ceiling? A comparison of matched samples of female and male executives. *Journal of Applied Psychology, 82,* 359–375.

30. Bowler, M. (1999, December). Women's earnings: An overview. *Monthly Labor Review,*13.

31. Mateyaschuk, J. (1999, April 26). Gender gap is smaller in technology. *Information Week,* 258.

32. Mateyaschuk, Gender gap is smaller in technology.

There are several popular ideas about why women generally earn less than men. Among them are that women (a) have to leave the workforce intermittently for family reasons; (b) have preferred styles of interacting (or leading) that are suited to lower levels of management; (c) select careers in lower-paying industries; and (d) are less committed to their positions and their companies. In one sample consisting of male and female managers in 20 Fortune 500 companies, all of whom had similar levels of education, worked in similar industries, and earned similar percentages of their family incomes (80%), the women earned an average of 11% less than the men, despite having done "all the right stuff."[33] A follow-up study several years later showed that the women still earned significantly less than the men, even when the women took jobs with companies that appeared to have higher glass ceilings.[34] Obviously, not all organizations have embraced inclusion as it relates to gender issues.

Succeeding in the business world also appears to take a greater personal toll on women. Although there are certainly exceptions, most very successful women in corporations are single or married, without children. Thus, for many, the choice for many women appears to be to pursue a career or have a family.

DISCRIMINATION BASED ON SEXUAL ORIENTATION

Discrimination on the basis of sexual orientation is rampant—at least toward openly gay men, whose salaries average 28% less than those of male heterosexuals. Interestingly, this does not appear to be true for openly lesbian women.[35] Nor does sexual disclosure significantly appear to influence lesbian women's work satisfaction or occupational stress levels.[36]

In addition to working to ensure that gay men and women are not discriminated against in hiring and promotion decisions, companies are increasingly having to tackle another hot-button issue: whether to provide health and other benefits to the partners of gay and lesbian employees. "FOCUS ON: Discrimination Based on Sexual Orientation" examines this question. Although research has shown the United States becoming increasingly accepting of gay lifestyles[37] organizations are still slow to adapt in the area of benefits.

Organizations that develop programs and strategies to better ensure acceptance of gays and lesbians in their workforces are likely to discover that there are benefits in doing so. As stated earlier, only through including all groups in the workforce can an organization truly understand its diverse clients. Given that homosexual men and women represent about 10% of the population, typically have few or no children, and have relatively large amounts of disposable income, they are clearly a potentially lucrative market

33. Stroh, L. K., Brett, J. M., & Reilly, A. H. (1992). All the right stuff: A comparison of female and male career patterns. *Journal of Applied Psychology, 77,* 251–260.

34. Brett, J., & Stroh, L. (1998). Jumping ship: Who benefits from an external labor market career strategy? *Journal of Applied Psychology, 82,* 331–341.

35. Black, D., Gates, G., Sanders, S., & Taylor, L. (2000, May). Demographics of the gay and lesbian population in the United States: evidence from available systematic data. *Demography,* 139–154.

36. Driscoll, J., Kelley, F., & Fassinger, R. E. (1996). Lesbian identity and disclosure in the workplace: Relation to occupational stress and satisfaction. *Journal of Vocational Behavior, 48,* 229–242.

37. Gays/lesbians gain acceptance in some areas. (2000, April 7). *Research Alert,* p. 9.

FOCUS ON
DISCRIMINATION BASED ON SEXUAL ORIENTATION

BIG THREE OFFERING SAME-SEX PARTNER BENEFITS. Ford Motor Company's thousands of gay, lesbian, and bisexual employees welcomed the recent announcement from the U.S. big three automotive companies that they will finally provide partial same-sex domestic partner benefits for their U.S. employees. Gay, Lesbian or Bisexual Employees (GLOBE), which has active chapters in the United States, Great Britain, and Germany, is one of seven company-sanctioned employee resource groups at Ford. One of GLOBE's top priorities since forming in 1994 has been to ensure domestic partners benefits.

Aware of the adverse public reaction its announcements could generate, GLOBE is extremely proud that Ford is taking the lead among auto makers in the area of benefits for domestic partners. Gay and lesbian employees of Ford, General Motors, and DaimlerChrysler are now one giant step closer to being on equal footing with their married coworkers in the area of overall compensation. Cindy Clardy, GLOBE's external communications officer, noted, "Full domestic partnership benefits are simply equal pay for equal work and are the price of admission for any company which seeks to successfully market to gay and lesbian consumers."

More than 3,000 U.S. companies currently provide benefits to same-sex domestic partners. Combined with such recent marketing efforts as corporate sponsorship of the 2000 Sydney Gay and Lesbian Mardi Gras, Ford's benefits are helping to attract brand loyalty within the $514 billion gay and lesbian market.

Ford GLOBE and Ford Motor Company have worked in partnership over the past 6 years. Ford was the first and only U.S. auto company listed on the 1999 Gay and Lesbian Values Index of top 100 companies working on gay issues. Ford was also recognized on a 1999 list of top 25 companies for gay employees. Domestic partner benefits, coupled with a Ford recruiting presence at such events as the annual Midwest Bisexual Lesbian Gay Transgender College Conference, and corporate sponsorship of April's National Lesbian and Gay MBA Conference will help ensure that Ford remains an employer of choice for the best and brightest talent available, regardless of sexual orientation.

Source: Announcement of same-sex domestic partner benefits applauded by Ford's gay, lesbian, and bisexual employees [Online]. (2000, June 8). *PR Newswire.* URL: http://www.prnewswire.com/

for services and products. What better way to become knowledgeable about this potential market than by hiring gay and lesbian employees?

INCLUSION AS A MANAGEMENT CHALLENGE

To reap the benefits of inclusion, employers need to understand its potential benefits and trade-offs. On the one hand, now that more women and older people are in the workforce, organizations are discovering that employees consider family priorities just as important as work obligations. Men and women are still ardently committed to their jobs, and both groups are increasingly more willing to trade long hours of overtime for quiet evenings with family and friends. "INTERNATIONAL FOCUS ON: Changing Expectations" explores this hot topic. On the other hand, as fathers become increasingly committed to childrearing, women should have more freedom to focus on their careers. One thing is certain, however: As discussed in the following section, for both men and women balancing work and family responsibilities is difficult.

INTERNATIONAL FOCUS ON
CHANGING EXPECTATIONS

FROM HERE TO PATERNITY. Tim Fischer and "sensitive New Age guy" are not terms that automatically sit comfortably together. But in resigning his leadership of the Australian National Party and as deputy prime minister for "family reasons," Fischer has shown that he is as sensitive and New Age as the best of them. His actions represent a movement that, while not exactly sweeping the Australian workplace, is gathering lots of support: People want a job and a life.

They especially want balanced work and family commitments. However, what people want and what they get are still widely divergent. For, although some companies offer a new mother paid leave after the birth of a baby, paid leaves for new fathers are rare. And, even if organizations offered it, would men feel they could take it?

Taking time off from work to look after the kids is often called the "mommy track," and it is not considered a good career decision. Nevertheless, a growing band of men are on the "daddy track" and are fortunate enough to work for or-ganizations that accommodate them. What's more, they're discovering that their decision is not negatively affecting their job prospects.

One such father is John Sears, a senior investment strategy analyst in AMP's investment strategy and economics department. He has made the most of AMP's paid paternity leave and flexible workplace provisions on two occasions. Employees at AMP are offered 6 weeks' paid leave if they are a child's primary caregiver. This forms part of their total entitlement of 52 weeks' leave, the remainder of which is unpaid.

Corporate Australia has come a long way in the past 20—or even 10—years. In the 1980s, men didn't take time out for their kids. It just wasn't done, and there simply weren't provisions for it. Clearly, corporations are now much more interested in helping employees balance work life and family issues.

Source: Adapted from Bland, L. (1999, July 24). Employment from here to paternity. *Sydney Morning Journal*, p. 1.

With all these changes in work environments, organizations will have to adapt by making employees' work responsibilities more routine and predictable or by providing alternatives such as on-site child and elder daycare, offering greater flexibility in work hours, or instituting job sharing or similar structural changes. Equally critical, organizations will need to increase the ability of employees to communicate within and between diverse groups.

As part of their efforts in this direction, many companies are investing in training designed to improve employees' sensitivity to and understanding of the diverse individuals with whom they work. Many companies are also supporting the creation of affinity groups such as Women in Management and People of Color as ways to encourage workers to develop networks where they can discuss career and other personal and professional issues.

One such group at Dean Foods, DF*WINS (Dean Foods Women Innovating Solutions), has been shown to be extremely useful to women in that organization. The group was charged by the senior management at Dean Foods with creating a network to assist women in management with unique career development issues. A small group of management women at Dean Foods represents the steering committee. This committee surveys the women in management at Dean to determine their unique career needs and then holds quarterly meetings that feature topics drawn from the survey results. The key to the success of this group is that Howard Dean, CEO of Dean Foods, and Dick Bailey, chief operating officer, are true champions of this effort.

Similar groups have been formed at other large organizations. They have been shown to have a significant impact on group members (e.g.,

The past decade has brought a change in employees' levels of commitment to their organizations. More executives are spending more time with their families, in part because of the introduction of such organizational and technological changes as flextime and telecommuting.

FOCUS ON COMMUNICATION IN DIVERSE GROUPS

THE EFFECTS OF MEDIA. As recently as 10 years ago, only "techies" used e-mail, there was no Internet as we know it today, and videoconferencing technology was way beyond the budgets of most organizations. As a result, the use of distributed groups as a common building block for reaping the benefits of organizational diversity was mostly a twinkle in someone's corporate eye. What a difference a decade makes. Today, technology not only makes all these options possible, it also presents potentially difficult and significant choices about how distributed groups should meet.

Michael Pratt, Mark Fuller, and Gregory Northcraft have studied the interactions of distributed groups and the impact technology can have on a distributed group's effectiveness. Their work highlights the importance of choosing an appropriate communication medium when distributed groups meet. The richness of a communication medium is its capacity to convey social context clues such as eye contact, facial expressions, posture, voice tone, inflection, and volume. Researchers have found that media richness greatly influences communication effectiveness. The richer the medium, the greater the potential for synergistic group interactions. Media richness also directly influences psychological closeness within groups. Richer media, such as face-to-face communication, promote stronger group identification by fostering more personal interactions,

which in turn promotes bonding within the group. Finally, media richness also directly influences felt similarity—another important determinant of identification with other group members.

Pratt, Fuller, and Northcraft suggested a few ways managers can foster stronger group identification in distributed groups that have diverse group membership. First, new groups should start with a somewhat lean communication medium, since very rich media may foster identification with social categories (such as race or gender) rather than with the group itself. Second, new groups should attempt to include members with high levels of experience with the selected communication medium. Experience with a communication medium enables rich communication to take place even with lean communication media. Third, to facilitate the speed with which individuals develop a sense of group identity, distributed groups need to make the group's identity distinctive and self-enhancing (e. g., remind members of shared goals and values). In short, it's important to remember that careful management of communication media offers diverse groups ways to expand their opportunities to do what groups are for—work together effectively.

Source: Adapted from Pratt, M. G., Fuller, M. A., & Northcraft, G. B. (2000). Media selection and identification in distributed groups: The potential costs of "rich" media. *Research on Managing Groups and Teams, 3,* 231–255.

women, minorities), and, equally important, on the upper levels of management. These groups seem to be catalysts for change and increased awareness of the unique challenges faced by women and the members of other minority groups in organizations. With this understanding, organizations have been able to take appropriate actions that have benefited not only their domestic and global performance but also their sensitivity to and understanding of their customers and employees.

SUMMARY

This chapter examines workforce inclusion from a variety of perspectives. The changing demographics of the workforce and the reactions of managers and organizations to these changes are major determinants of performance both individually and organizationally. The aging of the workforce, the increasing participation of GenXers, and other demographic changes demand a radical rethinking of benefits, recruiting strategies, and incentive structures.

Discrimination will continue to be a challenge to management, even in the face of government legislation against it. Employees have the right to cooperative acceptance—the right to expect that they will be treated with respect, regardless of their race, sex, age, religion, or other demographic characteristics.

Among the issues emphasized in this chapter is the value and importance of effectively managing an inclusive workforce. This aspect of management will become increasingly critical in the 21st century in determining the competitiveness of U.S. corporations. But this is just one challenge that the next generation of managers will face. Other challenges lie ahead, including how to foster creativity and innovation among employees, meet the needs of the changing workforce, and establish organizations in which the rights of employees and employers are maintained. Closing the knowing–doing gap has never been more important.

KEY TERMS

Generation Xers   **Glass ceiling**   **Inclusion**

DISCUSSION QUESTIONS

1 What is inclusion, and how does it differ from diversity in the workplace?

2 What recent changes in the workforce have challenged organizations to rethink their management strategies?

3 Why is having a heterogeneous workforce critical to maintaining high levels of organizational creativity and innovation? What problems are likely to result when there is great variety (both males and females, people of various races and cultures, and so on) in the workforce?

4 What management challenges do GenXers present to organizations?

5 Numerous popular press articles suggest that corporations are making few adjustments in response to the changes in the educational levels, ages, and racial and ethnic mixes of the workforce. What are some of the reasons for this apparent nonresponsiveness?

6 What are some of the influences and issues that managers should be aware of when dealing with older workers?

7 What groups are still discriminated against in the workplace, and what tactics are managers using to try to include groups that have traditionally been discriminated against?

ON YOUR OWN

Balancing Roles: Managing Multiple Perspectives   On a sheet of paper, draw a large circle. Reflect on how you have spent your time in the preceding week, and divide the circle as if it were a pie, into sections representing the different roles you played in that week, such as roles that relate to work, family, home, and all other parts of your life. The size of each section should be proportionate to the amount of time and energy you invested in that particular activity. Labels for these sections might include student, employee, friend, spouse, and so on.

Now consider what roles are most important to your sense of identity. Number the sections from most important (1) to least important (this number will be determined by how many sections you have in your pie). Note that the numbers frequently do not correspond to the size of the sections. Consider which of the sections in your pie tend to contribute to role overload—that is, what activities and roles infringe on other important activities and roles? Identify those sections of your pie.

In light of the conflict and issues you have identified, complete the following role management inventory. When you have answered all the questions, score the inventory according to the instructions that follow the questionnaire. Which is the most important coping style(s)? Is this optimal for you?

Role Management Inventory   How do you deal with these conflicts or issues? How do you do each of the following?

	Nearly All the Time (5)	Often (4)	Sometimes (3)	Rarely (2)	Never (1)
1 Decide not to do certain activities that conflict with other activities.	_____	_____	_____	_____	_____
2 Get help from someone outside the family (e.g., home maintenance help, child help).	_____	_____	_____	_____	_____
3 Get help from a member of the family.	_____	_____	_____	_____	_____
4 Get help from someone at work.	_____	_____	_____	_____	_____
5 Engage in problem solving with family members to resolve problems.	_____	_____	_____	_____	_____
6 Engage in problem solving with someone at work.	_____	_____	_____	_____	_____
7 Get moral support from a member of the family.	_____	_____	_____	_____	_____
8 Get moral support from someone at work.	_____	_____	_____	_____	_____
9 Integrate or combine roles (e.g., involve family members in work activity, combine work and family in some way).	_____	_____	_____	_____	_____
10 Attempt to change societal definition of sex roles, work roles, or family roles.	_____	_____	_____	_____	_____
11 Negotiate or plan with someone at work, so their expectations of you are more in line with your own needs or requirements.	_____	_____	_____	_____	_____

	Nearly All the Time (5)	Often (4)	Sometimes (3)	Rarely (2)	Never (1)
12 Negotiate or plan with members of your family, so their expectations of you are more in line with your own needs or requirements.	_____	_____	_____	_____	_____
13 Establish priorities among your different roles, so that you are sure the most important activities are done.	_____	_____	_____	_____	_____
14 Partition and separate your roles. Devote full attention to each role and when you are in it.	_____	_____	_____	_____	_____
15 Overlook or relax certain standards for how you do certain activities (e.g., let less important things slide a bit sometimes, such as dusting and lawn care).	_____	_____	_____	_____	_____
16 Modify your attitudes toward certain roles or activities (e.g., coming to the conclusion that the *quality* of time spent with spouse or children is more important than the *quantity* of time spent).	_____	_____	_____	_____	_____
17 Eliminate certain roles (e.g., decide to stop working).	_____	_____	_____	_____	_____
18 Rotate attention from one role to another. Handle each role in turn as it comes up.	_____	_____	_____	_____	_____
19 Develop self and own interests (e.g., spend time on leisure or self-development).	_____	_____	_____	_____	_____
20 Plan, schedule, and organize carefully.	_____	_____	_____	_____	_____
21 Work hard to meet all role demands. Devote time and energy so you can do everything that is expected of you.	_____	_____	_____	_____	_____
22 Do not attempt to cope with the role demands and conflicts. Let role conflicts take care of themselves.	_____	_____	_____	_____	_____

Scoring

■ Add up the values you entered for items 1 to 12. Divide by 12. This is your *role-definition score*:

_____

■ Add up the values you entered for items 13 to 17. Divide by 5. This is your *personal-reorientation score*: _____

■ Add up the values you entered for items 18 to 22. Divide by 5. This is your *reactive coping score*: _____

Interpreting Your Scores   These three scores give you some indication of the extent to which you use each of the three strategies. The scores can range from a *high* of 5 to a *low* of 1. If you score *over 3* on a scale, you score relatively high, meaning that you make frequent use of this strategy. A score of *less than 3* indicates relatively infrequent use of this strategy. Here are some problems that may be indicated by your scores on the three scales:

Low Role-Redefinition Scores   You often let others place unrealistic demands on you. You need to negotiate with these people, your role senders, to make certain that the roles they impose on you are compatible with other responsibilities and interests. Some ways of doing this include the following:

■ Simply agree with role senders that you will not be able to engage in certain activities (e.g., accept specific one-shot volunteer jobs, but do not accept continuing positioning).
■ Enlist assistance in role activities from other family members or from people outside the family (e.g., cleaning or babysitting help).
■ Sit down with the role senders (boss, spouse, children) and discuss the problem. Together, work out an acceptable solution.
■ Integrate conflicting careers by working with your spouse or in related fields (so that the two careers become more like one). This method of coping has been described as "linking up."

If you can successfully reduce conflicts by practicing some of these proactive coping strategies, you will be stopping the conflicts at the source, and chances are that you'll be very happy with the results—*you* will be managing the situation.

Low Personal-Reorientation Scores   Your problem is that you don't distinguish between the roles assigned to you; you lack a clear vision of what roles are truly important. You need to reevaluate your attitudes about various roles and take on only those heading the list. The following are some hints to help you achieve this:

■ Establish priorities ("A child with a high fever takes precedence over school obligations. A child with sniffles does not. A very important social engagement—especially one that is business related—precedes tennis.")
■ Divide and separate roles. Devote full attention to a given role when in it, and don't think about other roles. ("I leave my work at the office. Home is for the family and their needs.")
■ Try to ignore or overlook less important role expectations. ("The dusting can wait.")
■ Rotate attention from one role to another as demands arise. Let one role slide a bit if another needs more attention at the time. ("Susan needs help now. I'll pay those bills later.")
■ Remember that self-fulfillment and personal interests are a valid source of role demands. ("Piano and organ playing are a release for me while the children are small and need me at home.")

This style of coping means changing yourself rather than the family or work environment, although personal reorientation may be a necessary step to take before you can accomplish real role redefinition. Before you can change other people's expectations of you, you have to be clear about what you expect of yourself. Personal reorientation alone is not significantly related to satisfaction and happiness.

High Reactive Coping Scores   You try to take on every role that happens your way. You cope with conflict by working harder and sleeping less. Your style of coping includes:

- Planning, scheduling, and organizing harder.
- Working harder to meet all role demands. (As one expert on women's roles and role conflict said in frustration, "After years of research, I've concluded that the only answer to a career and a family is to learn to get by on less sleep!")
- Using no conscious strategy. Let problems take care of themselves. This reactive behavior, in contrast to role redefinition, is a passive response to role conflict. Not surprisingly, people who use this style report very low levels of satisfaction and happiness (passive coping).

Reactive coping is not a very effective way of dealing with multiple roles. Rather than managing them, you are letting them manage you. If your goal is to eliminate conflict, then you need to reorient your perceptions as a first step toward negotiating with others to restructure the roles in your life.

Source: Developed by Francine S. Hall. "Role pie " based on activity originally developed in Forisha, B. L. (1978). *Sex roles and personal awareness.* Morristown, NJ: General Learning Press, pp. 198–199; and adapted by Donald D. Bowen. Parts of this exercise were adapted from Hall F. S., & Hall, D. T. (1979). *The two-career couple.* Reading, MA: Addison-Wesley, pp. 75–79, 104–106.

CLOSING CASE   CHAPTER 16

THE MANAGER'S MEMO

TO:	Dr. Molly Freeman, Consultant to River Falls Women in Management Group
FROM:	D. L. Brown, CEO, River Falls Paper Company
CC:	Christine Langlands, Senior Vice President, Operations
RE:	Exclusion of Administrative Assistants in Women's Group

It has come to my attention that RF's women in management group refuses to allow RF administrative assistants to attend meetings or become members. In particular, I've recently learned that Christine's administrative assistant is seriously concerned about the exclusivity of this group, especially since RF is currently putting so much emphasis on fostering inclusion. Christine has insisted that admins should attend the group's meetings and is requesting my support. Christine notes that many secretaries have college degrees and are very interested in furthering their careers at RF. Christine further claims that the past three meetings have covered topics that are of special concern to our admins (mentoring, performance review, and inclusion) and that these women would benefit greatly from this networking experience. Christine has a strong argument to support this claim.

I would very much like to be supportive of your charter, which apparently excludes administrative assistants from group membership; however, I find myself in a major dilemma. How can I profess to be the champion of our inclusion efforts, on the one hand, yet support an exclusive women's group that ignores the needs of administrative assistants, on the other?

Unless you provide a sound argument for why the administrative assistants should not be part of your group, I suggest you consider changing your charter. In addition, I would like you to provide an alternative solution to this dilemma, if one exists. Please respond ASAP, as I think this problem could intensify rather quickly.

CASE DISCUSSION QUESTIONS

Assume that you are the consultant to this women's group. Would you recommend including the administrative assistants in your group? How would you respond to the CEO? the administrative assistant? Christine Lang-

lands? Is there an alternative to this problem (other than admitting the admins to this group)? Is it possible to justify an exclusive group in an "inclusive" environment?

EXERCISE   PART FIVE: Sears versus Kmart

This is a field exercise you can do the next time you go shopping. It is designed to help you explore the significance of various aspects of organization structure on effectiveness and goal accomplishments.

You will be asked to analyze two different establishments in the same line of business. You will compare these firms as carefully as you can to see what makes them really work. Since you've probably visited one or both of these stores, you already know something about them. But try to imagine that you are seeing them for the first time. Then try to integrate what you have learned in this chapter and from other experiences in this book about how firms are managed.

Form groups of about four and read your assignment. As a group, visit each store (preferably in the same general area). You might want to evaluate service, quality, price, and so on.

Your Assignment

Your group, Fastalk Consultants, is known as the shrewdest, most insightful, and most overpaid management consultant firm in the country. You have been hired by the president of Sears to make recommendations for improving the motivation and performance of personnel in their operations. Assume that the key job activity in store operations is dealing with customers.

Recently, the president of Sears has begun to suspect that his company's competitor, Kmart, is making heavy inroads into Sears's market. He has also hired a market research firm to investigate and compare the relative merits of products and prices in the two establishments, and he has asked the market research firm to assess the advertising campaigns of the two organizations. Hence, you will not need to be concerned with marketing issues, except as they may have an impact on employee behavior. The president wants you to look into the organization of the two stores to determine the strengths and weaknesses of each.

Source: Jauch, L. R., Coltrin, S. A., Bedeian, A. G., & Glueck, W. F. (1989). *The managerial experience: Cases, exercises, and readings* (5th ed., pp. 165–166). Hinsdale, IL: Dryden.

The president has established an unusual contract with you. He wants you to make recommendations based on your observations *as a customer*. He does not want you to do a complete diagnosis with interviews, surveys, and behind-the-scenes observations. He wants your report to be in two parts:

1 Given his organization's goals of profitability, sales volume, and fast and courteous service, he wants an analysis that will compare Sears and Kmart in terms of the following concepts:

- Organizational Goals
  Conflict?
  Clarity?
- Environment
  Stable/changing?
  Simple/complex?
  Certain/uncertain?
- Size
  Large?
  Medium?
  Small?
- Personnel
  Knowledgeable?
  Well trained?
- Horizontal Division of Labor
  Formalized policies?
  Departmentalization?
  Standardization of rules?
- Vertical Division of Labor
  Number of levels?
  Span of control?
  Centralization?

- Communication
  Directness?
  Openness?
- Leadership Style
  Task oriented?
  People oriented?
- Jobs
  Variety?
  Wholeness?
  Interaction?
  Freedom?
  Time of work?
  Location of work?
- Employee Motivation
  Type?
  Intrinsic/extrinsic?
  Rewards?
  Support?
  Coordination?
  Decision making?

How do Sears and Kmart differ in these aspects? Which company has a better approach?

2 Given the corporate goals listed in Part 1, what specific actions might Sears's management take in the following areas to achieve these goals (profitability, sales volume, and fast and courteous service):

- Job design and work flow?
- Organization structure (at the individual store level)?
- Employee incentives?
- Leadership?
- Employee selection?

After completing your contract with the president of Sears, prepare a report for presentation to the class. This should include:

- Specific recommendations you have considered in Part 2.
- Reasons for these suggestions, based on your knowledge of leadership, motivation, job design, organization, and so on.

CASE   PART FIVE: The Dashman Company

The Dashman Company was a large company that made many types of equipment for the U.S. armed forces. It had more than 20 plants, located in the central part of the United States, whose purchasing procedures had never been completely coordinated. In fact, in most matters, the head office of the company had encouraged each of the plant managers to operate with their staffs as separate independent units. Late in 1940, when it began to appear that the company would face increasing difficulty in securing certain essential raw materials, Mr. Manson, the company's president, appointed an experienced purchasing executive, Mr. Post, as vice president in charge of purchasing, a position especially created for him. Mr. Manson gave Mr. Post wide latitude in organizing his job, and he assigned Mr. Larson as Mr. Post's assistant. Mr. Larson had served the company in a variety of capacities for many years, and he knew most of the plant executives personally. Mr. Post's appointment was announced through the formal channels usual in the company, including a notice in the house newsletter published by the company.

One of Mr. Post's first decisions was to immediately begin to centralize the company's purchasing procedure. As a first step he decided that he would require each of the executives who handled purchasing in the individual plants to clear with the head office all purchase contracts they made that were in excess of $10,000. He felt that if the head office was to coordinate in a way that would be helpful to each plant and to the company as a whole, he must be notified that the contracts were being prepared at least a week before they were to be signed. He talked over his proposal with Mr. Manson, who presented it to his board of directors. They approved the plan.

Although the company made purchases throughout the year, the beginning of its peak buying season was only 3 weeks away at the time this new plan was adopted. Mr. Post prepared the following letter to be sent to the 20 purchasing executives of the company:

> Dear _____,
>
> The board of directors of our company has recently authorized a change in our purchasing procedures. Hereafter, each of the purchasing executives in the several plants of the company will notify the vice president in charge of purchasing of all contracts they are negotiating that are in excess of $10,000, at least a week before the date on which they are to be signed.
>
> I am sure you will understand that this step is necessary to coordinate the purchasing requirements of the company in these times, when we are facing increasing difficulty in securing essential supplies. This procedure should give us in the central office the information we need to see that each plant secures the optimum supply of material. In this way the interests of each plant and of the company as a whole will best be served.
>
> Yours very truly,

Mr. Post showed the letter to Mr. Larson and invited his comments. Mr. Larson thought the letter was excellent, but he suggested that because

Source: This case was prepared by George F. F. Lombard, Richard S. Meriam, Franklin E. Folts & Edmund P. Learned as the basis for class discussion rather than to illustrate either effective or ineffective handling of an administrative situation.

Mr. Post had not met more than a few of the purchasing executives, he might like to visit them all and take up the matter with each of them personally. Mr. Post dismissed the idea at once because, as he said, he had so many things to do at the head office that he could not get away for a trip. Consequently, he had the letters sent out over his signature.

During the following 2 weeks, replies came in from all except a few plants. Although a few executives wrote at great length, the following reply was typical:

> *Dear Mr. Post,*
>
> *Your recent communication in regard to notifying the head office a week in advance of our intention to sign contracts has been received. This suggestion seems a most practical one. We want to assure you that you can count on our cooperation.*

During the next 6 weeks the head office received no notices from any plant that contracts were being negotiated. Executives in other departments who made frequent trips to the plants reported that the plants were busy and that the usual routines for that time of year were being followed.

QUESTIONS FOR DISCUSSION

1 Was the centralization of purchasing at Dashman necessary?

2 Was the letter from Mr. Post sufficient to implement the new procedure?

3 Why did the head office not receive any notices of contracts being negotiated?

GLOSSARY

accommodating   A strategy for interpersonal conflict that maximizes the other party's concerns or outcomes. (5)

accommodation   The process of selecting among a number of available sensory inputs. (2)

active listening   A form of communication in which the receiver accepts responsibility for ensuring the proper transmission of the intended meaning. (6)

adjourning   The stage of group development in which a group disbands. (6)

affect   A favorable or an unfavorable evaluation of an individual's beliefs. (2)

Alderfer's ERG theory   A theory of motivation which states that there are three broad categories of needs: existence, relatedness, and growth. (3)

alternative source   Another way to fulfill a resource dependency, thereby reducing an individual's dependence on any one source; a form of slack. (7)

anchoring-and-adjustment effect   The tendency of individual perceptions or judgments to be similar to a reference point, even when the reference point is arbitrary or irrelevant. (2)

anticipation   Making internal changes in the organization to respond to the environment's demands. (13)

approach–approach conflict   A type of conflict that occurs when an individual must choose between two equally attractive options, both with positive outcomes. (5)

approach–avoidance conflict   A type of conflict that occurs when an individual must choose among options with both positive and negative outcomes. (5)

arbitration   The resolution of a conflict by a neutral third party who, after hearing both sides of a dispute, determines a final, binding outcome. (5)

attention   An individual's choice of where to direct and how to ration his or her limited sensory input system. (2)

attitude   Beliefs and feelings that lead an individual to respond consistently to people, ideas, and situations. (2)

attribution   The process of perceiving the causes of actions and outcomes; provides models of how other people function, what their motives are, and what determines their behaviors. (2)

attribution model of leadership   A model of leadership that deals specifically with perceptions and subsequent behaviors of organizational actors. The model has two facets: leader attributions for and reactions to poor performance by subordinates, and observer attributions for and reactions to poor performance by the leader. (9)

availability bias   An assessment of the frequency or likelihood of an event's occurrence based on how easily it is remembered, even though memory recall is influenced by factors unrelated to the frequency of an event. (4)

avoidance–avoidance conflict   A type of conflict that occurs when an individual must choose between two equally unattractive options, both with negative outcomes. (5)

avoiding   A strategy for interpersonal conflict that is suitable when one has little concern for his or her position or little concern for the position and desires of the other party. (5)

balanced scorecard   A tool used by managers as a substitute for leadership that is a comprehensive snapshot of the organization, incorporating four main perspectives: the financial perspective, the internal business perspective, the innovation perspective, and the learning perspective. (9)

behavioral observation scale   A scale that is used to assess employees' performance by asking raters to report and describe the frequency of specific job-related behaviors. (12)

behaviorally anchored rating scale (BARS)   An employee evaluation format in which the organization analyzes a particular job to determine what types of behavior reflect varying degrees of performance, using actual descriptions of behavior to define the ratings. (12)

behaviorally healthy organization   An organization whose internal interaction patterns—including successful communication, adaptation, innovation, and succession—put it in a position to become and remain financially sound. (15)

belief system   A stored set of theories and expectations about how and why the world works. (2)

beneficence   Generosity, leniency, and helpfulness of the environment concerning needed resources. (13)

bottom-up problem solving   A type of problem solving that involves workers in all phases of the change process, beginning with diagnosis. (15)

boundaries   Domains where interactions among organizations and elements in the environment (other organizations, customers, etc.) take place. (13)

boundary spanner   An individual such as a liaison who represents an organization in interactions with the forces in its environment. (13)

boundaryless organizations   Organizations without barriers of hierarchy, function, and geography, where cross-functional teams are empowered to act quickly and in partnership with customers and suppliers. (14)

bounded rationality   A model of individual decision making that diverges from the rational ideal in that it is based on a limited perspective, the sequential evaluation of alternatives, satisficing, and the use of judgmental heuristics. (4)

brainstorming   A group creativity technique that facilitates free discussion and exchange of ideas by withholding criticism of ideas, encouraging unusual ideas, generating as many ideas as possible, and piggybacking ideas. (8)

buffer   A mechanism that reduces the environmental shocks or interdepartmental conflict to allow an organizational unit to complete its task more smoothly. (5)

bystander apathy   Failure of observers to lend assistance in emergency situations; an example of the results of social anchoring effects on judgment. (7)

career ladder   A specific series of jobs or experiences necessary to advance in an organization. (10)

career path   A job-progression routes along which employees advance through an organization. (10)

cautious shift   The tendency of a group as a whole and each group member to be less willing to accept risk after a group discussion than prior to it. (8)

centralization   Resting decision-making power with one or a few individuals, based on the competing needs or coordination and division of labor. (14)

charisma   Persuasiveness derived from personal characteristics desired or admired by a reference group. (7)

charismatic leadership   A technique used by transformational leaders to develop a common vision of what could be, discover or create opportunities, and strengthen organizational members' control of their own destinies. (9)

closed system   A completely self-contained organization that functions apart from and is unaffected by what goes on around it. (13)

coalition   A collection of individuals who band together to combine their individual sources of power. (7)

coercion   The threat of punishment for not engaging in appropriate behaviors. (7)

collaborating   A strategy for interpersonal conflict that is suitable when both parties concerns are equally important, when the issue is too important to compromise, when trying to engender commitment among the parties, or when trying to gain insight. (5)

commanding   A management function of directing and motivating the workforce, often by generating direction and enthusiasm of work through leadership. (1)

communication   The transmission of information and understanding through the use of symbols. (6)

compensation system   A major way an organization conveys to its employees what it wants done and how they should behave, consisting of wages or salaries, benefits, nonrecurring financial rewards, and noneconomic rewards. (12)

competing   A strategy for interpersonal conflict that is suitable when the individual is concerned about his or her own needs, issues, or outcomes, such as in an emergency or critical situation, when the other party is untrustworthy, or when the individual or group is sure of the correct solution. (5)

complex learning   A form of learning that requires acquisition of new behaviors not yet available in a worker's behavioral repertoire. (3)

complexity   An overabundance of inputs that managers must keep track of, consider, and manage. (1)

compromise coalition   A coalition in which all members are interested in the same issues but each is flexible enough about specifics to make sure the coalition gets its way. (7)

compromising   A strategy for interpersonal conflict that is suitable when both parties' goals are important but not worth the potential disruption of more aggressive strategies. (5)

conditioning   The use of reinforcement and punishment to create habits. (3)

conflict   Differences among the perceptions, beliefs, and goals of organization members. (1)

conformity   A form of social inhibition in which a group member engages in a behavior and professes to be part of a group even though the member believes it is incorrect or inappropriate. (7)

consequences   The good or bad result following from a behavior. Consequence is a central concept of the law of effect. (3)

construction   The process of the perceiver organizing and editing sensory inputs in a way that makes them potentially meaningful; subject to both input source and perceiver influences. (2)

content theories of motivation   Theories that focus on the factors within people that motivate them to perform (e.g., the theories of Maslow, Herzberg, and McClelland). (3)

context enrichment   A way to increase decision-making responsibility in a job by giving workers decision-making control over the context of their work, rather than control over the work itself. Examples of context enrichment include flextime work scheduling and telecommuting. (11)

contingency   The relationship between actions and their outcomes. Contingency is a central concept of the law of effect. (3)

contingency model of leadership   A theory which suggests that leadership effectiveness is determined both by the characteristics of the leader and by the level of situational favorableness that exists. (9)

contract   A legally binding document that guarantees an organization delivery of and terms for a particular resource. A contract may be used as part of a control strategy to manage environmental demands. (13)

contrast effect   The tendency of individual perceptions of judgments to be seen as very different from an extreme reference point. (2)

control   Strategies organizations use to control their environments such as contracts, buffers, and joint ventures. (13)

coordinating   A management function of creating a structure through which members can produce the organization's central goods or services. (1)

controlling   Monitoring and correcting the progress of an organization toward its goals. (1)

corporate social responsibility   The actions an organization chooses to take (or avoid) and how these actions meet society's expectations related to moral and ethical standards. (13)

covariation   A central principle of attribution theory, stating that behaviors are attributed to causes that are present when the behaviors are present and absent when the behaviors are absent; covariation is judged by distinctiveness, consensus, and consistency. (2)

creativity   An individualistic, novel, idea-generating process. (4)

cross-training   Encouraging workers to learn their coworkers' jobs; provides challenges for workers and flexibility for management. (11)

custodial leadership   A process used by transactional leaders to improve working conditions, compensation, and fringe benefits. (9)

decentralization   The act of spreading decision-making power and authority among a broad group of individuals. (14)

decoding   The process by which receivers extract meaning from a message. (6)

deindividuation   Submersion of personal identities and personal responsibility of group members in the identity group. (7)

delegator   One who returns responsibility for dispute resolution to the involved parties or passes that responsibility to someone else. (5)

Delphi technique   A group decision-making technique that minimizes interaction among members in which members complete mailed questionnaires and a coordinator summarizes results. (8)

departmentalization   Grouping tasks into organizational units according to the knowledge and skills required or based on similar levels of skills and abilities. (14)

diagnosis   The first stage in the process of change, which involves figuring out what actions to take in response to signals that change is needed and includes identifying the problem, causes, and an appropriate and effective solution. (15)

diffusion of responsibility   Sharing the credit or blame for the outcomes of a group's actions over the entire group. (7)

distributive justice   Fair treatment of employees in awarding organizational rewards or in administering organizational punishment. (3)

distributive negotiation   A common negotiation strategy in which parties decide only how to allocate a fixed amount of resources. (5)

diversity   The heterogeneity of a group with respect to the members' personalities, genders, attitudes, backgrounds, and experience levels. (8)

downsizing   Reducing the size of an organization's workforce. (15)

effectiveness   The ability of an organization to accomplish an important goal, purpose, or mission. (1)

efficiency   The amount of effort required to deliver a promised good or service; it can be increased through specialization and economies of scale. (1)

emotional intelligence   One's ability to effectively deal with ambiguity and use sound judgement in performing their job. (9)

empathy   The ability of an individual to appreciate another's perspective. (6)

employability   The notion that employees should be concerned about their own career development, including acquiring the skills needed to keep a job or obtain a new position. (11)

employee (socioemotional)-oriented leadership   A technique used by a leader that emphasizes the individual worker's needs in managing group performance; also called initiating consideration. (10)

employee stock ownership plan (ESOP)   A group-based incentive plan in which an organization contributes to a trust fund to buy stock, which is allocated to employees based on seniority. (12)

enacted environment   The idea that the environment in which an organization functions is sensitive to the organization's perception of that environment. (13)

encoding   A process of creating a message for a receiver. (6)

enhancement   An attempt to augment the positive consequences of one's behavior to increase the perception of fairness among employees; the opposite of justification. (4)

entitling tactic   An attempt to gain responsibility for positive events and their consequences in order to increase the perception of fairness among employees; the opposite of excuse. (4)

environmental complexity   The number of environmental cues that an organization must monitor because they are critical to its functioning. (13)

environmental instability   The rate of change in the environment. (13)

environmental scanning   The process in which the organization collects information from the environment. (13)

equity theory   The theory that workers exchange appropriate work behaviors for desired consequences; a basis of distributive justice. (3)

escalation   The committing of additional resources to failing causes based on the slim hope that there will be a dramatic change. (4)

expectancy   Workers' cognitions concerning the likely consequence of their actions. (3)

expectancy theory   The theory that worker behaviors are a function of workers' beliefs about consequences and contingencies. (3)

expected value   The value of an option, determined by summing the values assigned to each possible consequence of an action, multiplied by the probabilities that each of these possible consequences will occur. (4)

expert power   Individual power based on the possession of special information, knowledge, or ability. (7)

explicitness   The extent to which an individual cannot deny that a behavior occurred; serves to commit individuals to their actions. (10)

exploring stage   The second stage in the organizational life cycle, characterized by few guidelines, changing rules, and informal and loose organizational structures. At this stage, people create the organization as they develop, focusing primarily on developing and marketing the product or service. (14)

exposure   The extent to which an individual openly and candidly divulges feelings and information when communicating. (6)

external change agent   An expert consultant from outside an organization whom management brings in specifically to facilitate a change. (15)

externality   A cause of workers' behaviors or the consequences of those behaviors that are beyond the worker's control. (3)

factfinding   A form of third-party intervention in which a neutral third party determines a reasonable solution based on evidence presented by the parties, who are not bound to follow the recommendation. (5)

feedback   The receiver's reaction to a sender's message. (6)

five-stages perspective   A theory of group development which proposes that all groups pass through a predetermined sequence of developmental phases. (6)

flextime work scheduling   A method of context enrichment in which management gives workers limited discretion in arranging tier work hours. (11)

forecasting   A process of environmental anticipation in which the organization uses mathematical models to predict future environmental demands. (13)

forming   A stage of group development in which group members decide whether to join the group, learn the traits and strengths of other members, and identify a leader. (6)

framing   A judgmental heuristic that decision makers use to deal with risk in which they become increasingly likely to take risks when confronting potential losses and increasingly likely to avoid risks when confronting possible gains. (4)

free rider   A person who accepts the benefits of being a member of a group but is unwilling to contribute to the good of the group. (4)

fundamental attribution error   The tendency of individuals to perceive others' behaviors as being caused primarily by stable, internal characteristics (such as personality) and to perceive their own behavior as primarily a response to environmental characteristics. (2)

gainsharing   A group incentive plan in which employees are rewarded for improvements in the organization's performance above a predetermined baseline. (12)

Generation Xers (GenXers)   Individuals born between 1960 and 1980. (16)

glass ceiling   A barrier that keeps women as a group from advancing to executive management simply because they are women and not because of their individual abilities. (16)

goals   Specific directions for action and a specific quantity of work to be accomplished. (12)

goal commitment   The extension of effort, over time, toward the accomplishment of a goal and an unwillingness to give up or lower the goal. (12)

graphic rating scale   A scale that assesses employees' performance that asks the rater to provide general evaluations of employees' performance in various areas of the job. (12)

group   An organized system of two or more individuals who are interrelated so that the system performs some function, has a standard set of role relationships among its members, and has a set of norms that regulate the function of the group and each of its members. (6)

group development   The process of identifying and resolving present and future group interaction problems. (6)

group objectives   The goals, purposes, and functions that a group is trying to achieve. (6)

groupthink   The tendency in highly cohesive groups for members to seek consensus so strongly that they lose the willingness and ability to critically evaluate one another's ideas. (8)

growth need strength (GNS)   The interest of a worker in growing and developing on the job. (11)

habit   The tendency of a person or an organization to do things the same way, over and over again. (15)

halo effect   The tendency for an individual's perception of an input on one dimension to influence his or her perceptions of that input on other dimensions. (2)

Herzberg's two-factor theory   A theory of motivation developed by Frederick Herzberg that focuses on two categories: hygiene factors and motivators. (3)

horizontal conflict   Conflict between people at similar organizational levels. (5)

hygiene factors   In two-factor theory, workers' basic needs or pay, safety on the job, quality of supervision, a social environment; fulfillment of these needs prevents dissatisfaction. (3)

idiosyncrasy credits   Leeway given to group members to violate group rules and norms because of consistent past adherence to those rules and norms. (6)

image advertising   Attempts to influence the environment's overall perception of an organization. (13)

inclusion   A modern view of diversity that shifts the emphasis from employees' differences to their similarities. (16)

inertia   The tendency of an object to continue in the same direction with the same velocity or intensity unless impacted by some force of change. (15)

information overload   The state of perceivers when their sensory input systems are overwhelmed with new, unusual, attention-grabbing inputs. (2)

information richness   The information-carrying capacity of an item of data. (6)

input source influence   A characteristic of a source object or event that affect perceivers' attempts to direct their attention, including motion, distinctiveness, novelty, vividness, contrast effect, anchoring-and-adjustment effect, and halo effect. (2)

instrumentality   Workers' belief that attaining the required levels of performance will produce desired personal outcomes. (3)

integrating device   A strategy of conflict management aimed at enhancing communication across groups and maintaining appropriate levels of interaction. (14)

integrating stage   The fourth and final stage of the organizational life cycle, characterized by a shift in attention from day-to-day work to sharing corporate visions. (14)

integrative bargaining   A cooperative negotiation strategy which assumes that there can be an expanding amount of resources for the parties to divide. (5)

interactional justice   A form of justice in which employees determine whether the quality of the interpersonal treatment they receive is fair. (4)

interlocking directorates   A negotiation strategy for managing environmental demands in which a corporation appoints to its board of directors representatives from a variety of organizations on which it is dependent. (13)

interpretation   The process of assigning meaning to a constructed representation of an object or event. (2)

irreversibility   The extent to which behavior cannot easily be revoked or undone, serving to commit individuals to their actions. (10)

jargon   Special words or common words used with special meaning that summarize a group's common experiences and history and allow simple communication of complex meanings. (6)

job analysis   The gathering of information about a job in an organization, including a description of tasks and activities, results (of products or services), and the equipment, materials, and working conditions that characterize the job. (10)

job characteristics model   A theory of job enrichment in which the presence of five job characteristics (skill variety, task identity, task significance, autonomy, and feedback) leads to critical psychological states (meaningfulness of work, responsibility for work outcomes, and knowledge of work activity results) that in turn result in positive work-related outcomes such as productivity and worker satisfaction. (11)

job description   A written document that specifies an individual's role in the organization. (6)

job enlargement   A redesign of work tasks that increases the number of tasks in a job to make it more interesting and involving. (11)

job enrichment   A redesign of work tasks that makes a job more interesting and involving by allowing workers to fulfill higher-order needs such as achievement and control. (11)

job rotation   A method of increasing workers' skill variety by allowing them to switch jobs occasionally. (11)

job specialization   The division of the overall mission of an organization into various smaller tasks. (14)

Johari window   A device for assessing and categorizing managers' communication styles along the dimensions of exposure and feedback. (6)

joint venture   A collaboration in which two or more unrelated organizations pool their resources to work together on projects. (13)

judgmental heuristics   Rules of thumb, or shortcuts, that reduce the information-processing demands on decision makers. (4)

knowledge management   The ability to retrieve, capture, combine, create, distribute, and secure knowledge. (3)

law of effect   The primary principle managers defer to as they attempt to build good work habits. (3)

leader–member exchange (LMX) model   A model based on exchange theory that stresses the importance of individual relationships between the leader and subordinates. Each relationship is termed a vertical dyad. (9)

leadership   An increment of influence over and above an employee's mechanical compliance with routine directives of the organization. (9)

learned needs theory   A content theory of motivation which proposes that three categories of needs— affiliation, power, and achievement—are learned, not innate, desires. (3)

learning organization   An organization that continually strives to expand its storehouse of knowledge. (3)

least-preferred coworker (LPC) scale A questionnaire that measures how respondents characterize their feelings about a person with whom they work least effectively. A high LPC score (favoring the least preferred coworker) suggests that the leader derives satisfaction and a sense of accomplishment from relationships with others; a low LPC score suggests that the leader emphasizes completing tasks, even at the expense of interpersonal relationships. (9)

legitimate power A type of power that is based on individuals' authority to control the behavior of others for their own good and for the good of a social system. (7)

line–staff conflict A conflict between employees who are involved directly in some aspect of producing the organization's product and employees who provide technical and advisory assistance to the line. (5)

lobbying A negotiation strategy for managing environmental demands in which a representative of an organization convinces source of resource dependence in the environment of the correctness of the organization's perspective. (13)

locus of control The extent to which people think they can control the consequential events in their lives. (2)

logrolling A form of coalition in which participants lend each other power so that each can pursue interests not shared by other coalition members. (7)

loose coupling The relationship of an organization and its environment in which what happens in the environment may or may not be reflected by immediate changes in the organization. (13)

machine bureaucracy An organizational structure that uses highly specialized and routine tasks, formalized procedures for the transformation process, a proliferation of rules and communication channels, a functional departmentalization structure, a large span of control, and an elaborate administrative and technical structure. (14)

managerial function An activity that must be performed for an organization to outperform individuals, including planning, organizing, staffing, and controlling. (1)

managerial grid A leadership training program conducted by Robert Blake and Jane Mouton that reflects two dimensions of leader behavior: concern for production (task-oriented leadership) and concern for people (socioemotional leadership). (9)

managerial leadership The second stage of leadership, according to David Berlew, which emphasizes providing subordinates with work that is less routine and more challenging, building cohesive work teams, and giving employees more say in decisions that affect them directly. (9)

Maslow's needs-hierarchy theory The prototype among several hierarchical theories of human motivation, which divides human wants into five distinct categories that are pursued in hierarchical order: basic physiological needs, safety needs, belonging/affiliation needs, and self-actualization needs. (3)

matrix structure An organizational structure characterized by dual reporting. Employees report to both a long-term manager, who manages their professional and technical development, and to a separate project manager. (14)

mediation Resolution of a conflict by a neutral third party who can control the interaction between the disputants but has no authority to force a solution on them. (5)

mentor A senior employee whose primary role is to instruct a less experienced protégé. (10)

moderating variable A variable that influences the effects of another variable on behavior. (2)

motivators In two-factor theory, factors that provide worker satisfaction, such as the opportunity for achievement, responsibility, and recognition through work. (3)

movement The third stage in the process of change; implementation of the change plan. (15)

naïve realism A person's thinking that his or her own perceptions represent objective reality. (5)

negotiation A process whereby two or more parties decide what each will give and take in an exchange between them; a class of strategies for managing environmental resource dependence. (5, 13)

neutralizers of leadership Factors that paralyze, destroy, or counteract the effectiveness of leader behaviors, making it difficult for them to have an impact. (9)

noise A characteristic in the immediate context of communicating individuals that interferes with communication. (6)

nominal group technique (NGT) A group decision-making technique that focuses on generating alternatives and selecting among them by asking group members to independently write down ideas, present them in turn, clarify them for the group, and rank them by voting privately. (8)

nonverbal communication Interpersonal communication that occurs through any channel other than formal verbal communication. (6)

norm An informal, unstated rule that governs and regulates group behavior. (6)

norming A stage of group development in which group members define a set of rules and roles to coordinate group interaction and make pursuit of the goals effective. (6)

objective self-awareness An individual's perception of his or her own role in causing behaviors and their consequences. (2)

organizational ombudsman An individual who interprets policy, counsels disputing parties, resolves disputes, provides feedback, and identifies potential problem areas for senior management. (5)

open system An organization whose activities are inescapably influenced by its environment. (13)

organic structure A flexible organizational structure that can respond efficiently and effectively to new demands. (14)

organization A form of human association for the attainment of a common purpose that combines the talents and efforts of its members. (1)

organizational atrophy An organization's use of a particular response to a situation long after the situation has changed. (15)

organizational behavior The description and explanation of how people behave in organizations. (1)

organizational behavior modification (OB-Mod) The systematic application of simple conditioning and reinforcement theory principles to the management of organizational behavior. (3)

organizational commitment The relative strength of an individual's identification with and involvement in a particular organization. (10)

organizational culture The expectations and practices of an organization, including shared philosophy; attitude toward employees, leaders, heroes, rituals, and ceremonies; and belief about the direction of the organization. (10)

organizational decline A decrease in the size of an organization's workforce, budget, resources, clients, and so on; a mature organization's inability to stay in touch with changing markets, technologies, and client preferences, leading to stagnation, bureaucracy, and passivity. (15)

organizational design The creation of organizational structure, involving grouping roles and activities so that the interdependencies among organizational actors are coordinated effectively and efficiently. (14)

organizational development (OD) Systemwide application of behavioral science knowledge and reinforcement of organizational strategies, structures, and processes for improving an organization's effectiveness. (15)

organizational life cycle A predictable pattern of evolution of an organization's structure, leadership style, and administrative systems. (14)

organizational socialization A process of conveying the organization's goals, norms, and preferred ways of doing things to new employees. (10)

organizational structure The skeleton of an organization based on the relationship among its positions or roles. (14)

organizing In Fayol's management functions, arranging for an organization's material and personnel resources. (1)

outplacement program A program that focuses on finding new jobs for displaced employees or those who choose not to stay on after a major corporate reorganization. (15)

path–goal model A model of leadership which suggests that if leaders are able to link effort, performance, and desired outcomes, subordinates will experience high job satisfaction because the path to job performance and subsequent rewards is more direct. (9)

perception The process by which individuals receive and interpret sensations from the environment so they may act on them. (2)

perceptual set The expectations that a perceiver brings to a task, based on suggestions, beliefs, and previous experiences. (2)

performing The stage of group development in which group members work within the group's structure to pursue the group's and members' goals. (6)

personality The characteristics that lead an individual to behave in consistent ways over time. (2)

person–organization fit The compatibility between an individual and the organization for which he or she works. (10)

piece-rate plan An incentive plan in which employees are paid a given rate for each unit produced. (12)

planning Management thought processes that precede action in an organization. (1)

political conflict A problem that occurs when different members of an organization pursue different personal (rather than organizational) agendas. (7)

political system A collection of individuals or groups that must work together and speak with one voice, even though each has a private agenda to pursue. (1)

procedural justice Equitable treatment of employees in the processes by which organizational rewards are allocated and punishments are administered. (3, 4)

procedural justice theory A theory which suggests that workers are most satisfied with the outcomes they receive at work when they believe that the processes used to determine those outcomes are fair. (3)

process theories of motivation Theories that focus on the process by which rewards direct behavior, such as the expectancy, equity, and reinforcement theories. (3)

professional bureaucracy A bureaucracy that trains its workers to internalize a set of performance and professional standards. (14)

profit sharing A group incentive plan in which employees receive a percentage of the organization's profits on a regular basis. (12)

providing-impetus tactic Delegating conflict back to the involved parties, with the implied threat that if they don't resolve it, someone else will, and the resolution will not be to either party's liking. (5)

psychological contract A set of unwritten, reciprocal expectations between an employee and an organization. (10)

public relations Negotiations strategies for managing environmental demands in which an organization actively controls its interactions with the environment using activities such as image advertising. (13)

punctuated equilibrium A theory that a project team's development is triggered by the project's deadline. (6)

punishment The administration of an unpleasant consequence (e.g., docking a worker's pay) in response to inappropriate work behaviors. (3)

quality circles (QC) Voluntary groups of workers that meet periodically to discuss and develop solutions to problems related to quality, productivity, or product cost. (11)

quality-of-work-life (QWL) program A system-wide attempt to simultaneously enhance organizational effectiveness (usually defined in terms of productivity) and employee well-being through a commitment to participative organizational decision making. (15)

rationality The basing of a decision on careful and calculated action alternatives and their consequences. (4)

realistic job preview A mechanism used by an organization to present both the desirable and undesirable aspects of the job and the organization, to provide the potential employee with more complete and accurate information about the position. (10)

reengineering Making fundamental changes in the way work is performed throughout the organization, focusing on improvements in cost, customer service, quality, and speed of production. (11)

referent power Individual power based on a high level of identification with, admiration of, or respect for the powerholder. (7)

refreezing The final stage in the process of change, which consists of institutionalizing the change and monitoring the systems that have been put in place to track the consequences of implementing the change. (15)

regulation The legal restriction of behaviors in or by organizations. (13)

reinforcement A reward for a behavior that increases the probability that the behavior will be repeated. (3)

relationship marketing A form of marketing that involves the development of a long-term relationship with prospective customers via intensive information exchange. (13)

representativeness An outcome's resemblance of its cause. (4)

resource dependence theory A theory which suggests that firms enter into relationships in search of much-needed resources that are lacking in their operations. (13)

resource dependency An individual's need for resources, which exposes the individual to influence. (7)

resource pooling Combining the perspectives, ideas, suggestions, and information of all members of a group. (8)

resource redundancy A means of preventing the lack of a particular resource by maintaining relationships with several suppliers. (13)

resource scarcity The lack of a particular commodity (e.g., food, love, attention, cars, clothes, opportunities) for all to accomplish their goals. (5)

reward power Individual power based on the control of resources valued by another; the opposite of coercive power. (7)

risk The uncertainty associated with a particular decision alternative of choice. (4)

risk averse A quality in a decision maker that makes him or her willing to pay a premium to avoid risk by ignoring the expected-value solution. (4)

risk neutral A quality in a decision maker that gives him or her the same attraction to risky and certain outcomes if they have the same expected value. (4)

risk seeking A quality in a decision maker that makes him or her willing to pay a premium to experience risk. (4)

risky shift The tendency of a group as a whole and each member individually to be more willing to accept greater levels of risk after a group discussion than prior to it. (8)

role The set of behaviors appropriate to a particular position occupied by individuals in a group or an organization. (6)

role conflict A type of conflict that occurs when two or more role-specific activities, or expectations of other organizational members, are incompatible. (5)

role differentiation Establishment of clear concepts for group members of how their specific duties and responsibilities contribute to the realization of the group's goals. (6)

role therapy A training technique in which someone from outside the group comes in temporarily to act as a catalyst to improve the effectiveness of group interaction by ensuring that role differentiation has been accomplished appropriately. (6)

satisficing Forgoing the optimal solution in favor of one that is acceptable or reasonable in order to save the time and effort needed to make extended comparisons. (4)

Scanlon plan A group-level incentive plan aimed at achieving organizationwide cost reductions. (12)

selection The process of collecting and evaluating information about an individual in order to extend an offer of employment. (10)

self-efficacy A worker's beliefs that he or she can produce required levels of performance by engaging in appropriate work behaviors. (3)

self-esteem   An individual's self-respect. (2)

self-fulfilling prophecy   An expectation about how someone is likely to act that actually causes the person to meet the expectation. (2)

self-leadership   An individual-level approach to job redesign aimed at developing workers' self-direction and self-motivation and ultimately, their effectiveness in the workplace. (11)

self-managed team   A team that assumes the tasks of the former supervisor. (6)

self-perception   A person's examination of his or her own actions that decides his or her attitudes. (2)

self-reinforcement   A person's punishment or reward of himself or herself in the hopes of acquiring desired actions. (3)

self-serving bias   The tendency of perceivers to attribute the causes of actions or their outcomes in a way that reflects well on the perceivers or absolves the perceivers from responsibility for poor outcomes. (2)

simple structure   An organizational structure common in young or small organizations in which coordination is largely a function of direct supervision, the top manger or entrepreneur has significant control, employees have very little discretionary decision-making power, and there is little formal policy or procedure. (14)

situated expertise   A group's transactive memory system and an understanding of group members' external ties. (8)

situational leadership model   A model of leadership which states that leaders are effective when they use the most appropriate leadership style for the situation. (9)

skill-based pay   An individual incentive system in which employees are rewarded based on the number of skills they have or on the number of jobs they can do. (12)

slack   Excess resources that can minimize conflict because they reduce the amount of necessary interaction. (5)

social anchoring   Forming perceptions or judgments in an extremely uncertain situation by relying on the opinions of others. (7)

social audit   A mechanism an organization uses to see where it stands with respect to corporate-responsibility demands by identifying important issues in the social environment, cataloging the actions presently being taken, and assessing the effectiveness of these actions. (13)

social comparison theory   A theory of perception in which individuals construct a perception, judgment, or belief about the world, and then check its accuracy by comparing it to the perceptions and judgments constructed by others. (7)

social context   The influential context for all behavior that is created by the individuals in groups and organizations. (7)

social facilitation   The tendency for the presence of others to enhance an individual's energy level. (7)

social identity theory   A theory of perception in which individuals classify themselves and others into various categories, such as race, age, gender, religious affiliation, professional membership, and other groups. (2)

social information processing   A framework of job design that emphasizes the importance of perception and social cues from coworkers and supervisors in understanding how workers react to their jobs. (11)

social learning theory   A learning theory proposed by Albert Bandura which states that people learn from watching others and that the likelihood that the learned behavior will be repeated is determined by modeling (i.e., people display behaviors that they have observed as being good and avoid behaviors that are seen as producing negative outcomes). (3)

social loafing   An individual's decreasing the amount of effort he or she puts into a task because he or she is working on that task with other people. (7)

sociotechnical systems   Frameworks to bridge the concerns and fit of people with the advantages of automation. (11)

span of control   The number of people reporting to a manager. (14)

standard hour rate plan   An hourly payment rate based on the amount of time, determined by industrial engineering standards, that it should take to produce each unit. (12)

status   A position or role in the social hierarchy. (6)

stereotype   A complex set of expectations ad beliefs associated with specific personal characteristics, such as gender, race, or occupation. (2)

stockpile   A store of resources set aside for future use, such as money put into savings for a "rainy day"; a form of slack. (7)

storming   The stage of group development in which the group decides what its goals and priories will be. (6)

strong situation   A situation in which contextual demands are likely to cause everyone to behave the same. (2)

substitute for leadership   An individual, organizational, and task characteristic that has the capacity to serve the same purposes as leader behaviors. (9)

succession   Turnover, retirement, or promotion of personnel. (15)

successive approximation   Reinforcement of increasingly better attempts at a final desired behavior; it may include shaping or chaining. (3)

support systems   Elements in an organization that assist personnel in accomplishing their work tasks effectively, such as production technology. (15)

survey-guided development   The use of questionnaires to construct a picture of an organization's internal process and problems; also called survey feedback. (15)

synergy A mutual influence process of stimulation and encouragement among members of a group. (8)

systematizing stage The second stage of the organizational life cycle, typically called the adolescence of an organization. At this stage, the primary concern is the need to establish structures, accountabilities, clear roles, and procedures. (14)

task identity The sense of completion and achievement that occurs when the set of assigned tasks allows the worker to see a process through from start to finish. (11)

task interdependence Power accruing to a particular job or group of jobs in an organization when two or more employees must depend on each other to complete assigned tasks. (7)

task significance A worker's sense that a good or poor performance on the job makes a difference to someone. (11)

team development A team's inward look at its own performance, behavior, and culture for the purposes of correcting dysfunctional behaviors and strengthening functional ones. (6)

telecommuting A type of job design that permits employees to work at home or near home for all or part of the week. (11)

theory of social exchange The theory which states that social behavior is an exchange of material and nonmaterial goods (such as approval and prestige), and that in relationships people continually monitor the rewards and costs of working out balanced exchanges. (7)

third-party intervention An involvement in a conflict of someone not directly concerned, as in arbitration, mediation, or factfinding. (5)

top-down problem solving The diagnosis of a problem by management, with the rest of the workforce being informed only during unfreezing. (15)

trait A characteristic, usually expressed as a dimension in which every person can be measured. (2)

transactional leader A leader who motivates followers by exchanging rewards for services. (9)

transactive memory The combination of knowledge related to each individual within a team and the team's awareness of who knows what. (8)

transformational leader A leader who arouses intense feeling and generates turbulent one-to-one relationships with followers and is inspirational and concerned with ideas rather than processes. (9)

two-way communication Communication in which receivers can return messages to senders. (6)

uncertainty Not knowing for sure; may include future actions or events, or relationships between actions and consequences. Also, the consequences of an action that can be known only in terms of a perceived likelihood of occurrence. (1, 4)

unfreezing The second stage in the process of change, which involves lowering barriers to change by selling the diagnosis, understanding the implementation, and preparing for the consequences. (15)

union A group of workers who have banded together to give themselves more bargaining power with their employer. (13)

valence The perceived value of a behavior's consequences. (3)

values An individual's core understanding of what is important to him or her. (2)

variable pay plan A compensation plan that rewards employees with extra pay for extra organizational achievements. (12)

venturing stage The third stage in the organizational life cycle, in which employees are given greater freedom and responsibility in order to promote innovative thinking and creativity to compete in the marketplace. The organization defines itself by its results, and empowerment of employees is critical. (14)

vertical conflict A conflict between people at different levels in an organization. (5)

vicarious learning The acquisition of desirable behaviors through observation of the behaviors of other people; also called social learning. (3)

virtual structures An evolving network of organizations or firms joined together to share skills, costs, and resources. (14)

visibility The observability of behavior, serving to commit individuals to organizations by making their association with them public knowledge. (10)

vision A view of what the organization wishes to become, often used as a substitute for leadership. (9)

volition The extent to which individuals believe they have a choice in their behaviors, serving to commit them to their actions. (10)

weak situation A situation in which the appropriate behavior is not at all obvious and in which people therefore are fairly free to decide for themselves what to do. (2)

work simplification The design of work tasks to make them simple and easily mastered so that each worker can become expert at some small number of tasks and learn to do them repeatedly with lightning speed and no mistakes. (11)

work standards Specific instructions for doing a task, including expected time for completion and expected volume of output. (2)

PHOTO CREDITS

NAME INDEX

SUBJECT INDEX